Cyclic and Collective -

Further Art and Science of Flying Helicopters

Shawn Coyle
Chief Helicopter Instructor
National Test Pilot School, Mojave, CA, USA

Helobooks, a Division of
Mojave Books Limited

Library of Congress Card Number -

ISBN - 0-9726368-0-3

Manufactured in the United States.

Published by

Helobooks, a Division of Mojave Books Limited

PO Box 787

Mojave, California, 93501

ph (661) 823 8068

fax (661) 823 8413

email - info@mojavebooks.com

Web - www.helobooks.com - www.mojavebooks.com

Printed and bound by Consolidated Reprographics, Costa Mesa, CA

Publishers Cataloging in Publication Data

Coyle, Shawn C

Cyclic and Collective: Further Art and Science of Flying Helicopters

First Edition

Bibliography: p.

Includes index.

1. Books - United States - Aviation 1. Coyle, Shawn, 1950 -

II Title - Cyclic and Collective, 2003

III Title - Cyclic and Collective

PREFACE

The helicopter has evolved to a wonderful tool for a wide variety of daily tasks, ranging from news reporting to dramatic rescues and airborne ambulances. Yet how it works is often a mystery to those watching, and sometimes even to those piloting the machines.

This book may remove some of the mystery. Aside from those who are starting to learn to fly helicopters, it may also be useful to those who are interested in the basics of how these machines operate.

Nothing will replace the helicopter for many missions. Tilt rotor aircraft will eventually take their rightful place in the hierarchy of aviation, and fixed wing airplanes will retain their roles, but some things can be performed most economically by rotors fixed above the fuselage.

WHY TWO "BOOKS"?

There are two 'books' for several reasons.

Beginners need more simple explanations sufficient for initial understanding, while experienced pilots will be looking for a more in depth coverage of the same subjects. Secondly it is more natural to cover the basics in one section, so the neophyte helicopter pilot could learn a lot in one place about what are very complex machines. To cover everything about performance, for example, would overload the beginner, while to cover only what the beginner needed would leave out important items for the professional.

This first 'book' concentrates on the basic aerodynamics of the helicopter, a bit of performance, weight and balance, effects of controls, some of the important primary flight exercises, basic emergency procedures and a number of miscellaneous things I thought important. To keep in step with most students, this book will cover a piston engined helicopter typical of those found in basic training. Since it is difficult to know each reader's knowledge of aerodynamics, physics and mechanics, it is assumed to be low. If you wish a review of physics relevant to helicopters, a short chapter at the beginning should refresh those parts that need refreshing.

The second 'book' goes into significantly more detail to explain complex phenomena. It builds on the basic theory and practice earlier, and is based around turbine helicopters with hydraulically boosted flight controls, such as are commonly found in commercial operations.

In general, the books will progress, (in a more or less orderly fashion) from the basics to the more complex. The helicopter is a machine, and as such must obey physical laws. There are (gratefully for both reader and author) few formulae in this book - they will be used only when they help with understanding the fundamentals and physical laws.

Those wishing more theoretical knowledge are invited to look at the series of books by Ray Prouty, or Simon Newman's 'Fundamentals of Helicopter Flight'. Aspects related to flying and what the pilot is likely to see in the cockpit are covered in more detail here, as that is my background.

Obviously there will be sections which fall in between, and they are apt to spring up nearly anywhere- look for subjects which may be of particular interest to you.

Neither book will cover every aspect of aviation as it relates to helicopters. To achieve a sense of comfort in aviation, it is necessary to know and understand many subjects such as weather, radios, navigation, flight computers, airspace, maps and charts. (Get used to learning if you're interested in aviation.) Many of these subjects are better covered in fixed–wing–related books listed at the end.

Why Did I Write This Book?

The answer eluded me for a while. Initially I thought it was because there was a gap in the helicopter book market. Then the reason changed to sharing some of my experience. Now the real reason, at last, appears to be coming through. I have enjoyed flying helicopters, and doing a myriad of things that can only be done with helicopters, and wish that others can continue to do those same type of things with increased knowledge and greater safety.

Keeping Things in Perspective

Helicopter flying is not inherently dangerous. When flown by properly trained, reasonable people, helicopters are safe and invaluable. I have had my share of adventures* when flying, but that is the nature of anything out of the ordinary. The experiences related here only to illustrate the peculiarities of helicopter flying. By explaining some of the mysteries, perhaps a bit of the glamor may disappear, but at least someone may understand.

The less well understood aspects of helicopters have contributed to accidents. We should be prepared to learn the proper lessons from the misfortunes of others, as they are worthwhile learning points for us all. Incidents and accidents will be analyzed to show specific lessons.

There are many chicken–and–egg situations which arise in trying to explain complex phenomena. Readers will find it may be necessary to accept an early explanation that becomes clear later.

Standard Disclaimers

The view expressed here are purely personal and definitely unofficial. They do not represent the views of National Test Pilot School (my employer in the day job) nor any professional organizations with which I may be affiliated.

There are many techniques and methods in these books. These are the result of observations and experimentation while flying in a wide variety of helicopters. These techniques may not be appropriate to all types of helicopters, nor for all skill levels of pilots or ambient conditions. For this reason conditions are given only approximately. In some cases, specific advice is given to avoid what turned out to be close calls for me. This advice is meant to prevent others from re-inventing the wheel, or being embarrassed. I can make no claim for these maneuvers working at all times for all helicopters - the reader is reminded to take care and be responsible for their own actions and remaining within the limitations in the Flight Manual. Good judgment of what is safe and unsafe must be left to the properly trained individual.

Obviously nothing in this manual should be taken as superseding any procedures mandated by various State rules and regulations, aircraft or equipment manufacturers limitations or company operating manuals.

While the author and publishers have exhaustively researched the subject to ensure the accuracy and completeness of the information contained in this book, we assume no responsibility for errors inaccuracies, omissions or any inconsistency herein. Any slights of people or organizations are unintentional.

I would recommend that, if at all possible, once you obtain your license, you take the opportunity to attend the factory school for the type(s) of helicopter you are going to fly. This will ensure you get the word straight from the horse's mouth about the idiosyncrasies of a specific type you will spend a lot of time in, and learn the techniques from the professionals.

Political Correctness

There is no intention to demean members of either (any?) sex by the use of gender–related pronouns. Men can fly helicopters just as well as women†.

* But so far, (knock on wood), no accidents...

† and I didn't put this in to gain sales from the Whirley Girls either...

Aim of every flight

The aim of every helicopter flight I make is to walk back into the office - anything else is gravy. There are days when the aim can be accomplished without even getting into the helicopter - one look at the weather and say - "Not today."

Every so often, I have had to ask myself "What is this flight for?" to help keep things in perspective.

This philosophy is only one way to look at flying, and rather than try to convince you of about the correctness of my way of thinking, I would prefer that you develop your own philosophy of what is the aim of every flight you make.

God bless, and safe, enjoyable flying.

Terms Used

Many terms are loosely used in the aviation world. This causes problems within the community that speaks English as a first language, and creates even bigger problems when working across languages. In an attempt to be scholarly, correct and make life easier for those trying to learn this subject, terms will be used in a disciplined sense.

> '*Hover*' is an example of such a term. Whenever it is used in these books, it will be (boringly) specified as zero–airspeed or zero–groundspeed hover. The difference is important.
>
> '*Height*' is distance Above Ground Level (AGL) or obstacle, while '*altitude*' refers to distance Above Mean Sea Level (MSL). Where necessary, altitude is prefixed by either 'pressure' or 'density' altitude.
>
> *Airspeed* will be given in Knots Indicated AirSpeed (KIAS).
>
> *Flight Manual* (FM) is meant to refer to Pilot Operating Handbook, Rotorcraft Flight Manual or the various military names these books are known by*.

A more complete set of terms is given in the Definitions section at the back.

Readers will often be asked to use their imagination. For example, even though we are talking about a three bladed helicopter, many of the side views of the rotor system will show a two–bladed hub - it is still an articulated hub, it's just easier to show two blades than three.

Dedication

This book is dedicated to designers who turned concepts into designs, engineers who turned designs into useful bits of machinery, the skilled workmen who turned those bits of metal into living objects, all the dedicated mechanics who kept those machines breathing. I would like also to thank all those who passed on their ideas and knowledge, both instructors and students that I have learned so much from. Finally, I would like to thank the Grand Aeronautical Engineer, from whom all ideas and concepts flow.

Mom and Dad- thanks for all the support over the years.

To my family- now you know what kept me locked in the dungeon for so long. Thanks for your patience, regular food and water.

To Al Stewart and Al Radecki- the only two men brave enough to read the whole thing with an editorial pen in hand- thank you very much.

To Ray Prouty- thank you for all you've done to help me understand how helicopters fly. I only wish your books had been in print when I went through Empire Test Pilot School!

Introduction to the Second Edition

While writing the first edition of this book, a conscious effort had to be made to stop, and get this thing into print. Aside from leaving something for a second edition, I realized that if I didn't stop, the first edition would never get published.

* In other words, the book with the limitations, procedures, etc.

The subtleties of the piston engine as it is used in the helicopter needed to be covered, and some fundamentals of flying could be improved upon.

The sharp reader may also notice that sometimes a phenomenon is explained several different ways. Aside from more pages, it is an attempt to ensure that if one explanation didn't satisfy or seem clear, the second explanation may provide the missing key to understanding.

And just before I put this book to bed, I had the ingnomius misfortune to not listen (twice) to the still small voice that told me I should switch fuel tanks, and ran a helicopter out of gas... No-one was injured, and the damage was relatively minor, but it was particularly humiliating for a guy who wrote some tough words on the subject (see "Fuel Systems" on page 259 to more fully understand why I am embarrassed). I join yet another club that I hope won't have to admit you as a member.

Corrections and Additions

I welcome corrections and suggestions for future editions. Please send them to:

e-mail: shawn.coyle@mojavebooks.com
mail: PO Box 787, Mojave, CA, 93501, USA

FOREWARD

Shawn Coyle is a noted test pilot who has flown more different helicopters than most people can identify. His Pilot Reports in *Rotor and Wing* magazine on Russian and other European helicopters are classics of this genre. This book is a 'new and improved' edition of his '*The Art and Science of Flying Helicopters*'.

Since 1996 when the first edition came out, Shawn has moved from England to Canada and now to California. During that time he has picked up new information and re-thought some old ideas. His years with Transport Canada as a certification flight test pilot brought new insight into the civil and legal implications of items in the flight manual.

This edition contains major additions and revised discussions of many subjects. As a whole, it clearly explains not only how the helicopter flies, but also what the pilot needs to know to make his time in the cockpit productive and safe.

Ray Prouty
Westlake Village, California
January 2003

1 Some Fundamentals

2 Introduction to Helicopter Aerodynamics

3 The Rotor Blade

4 More Basics of the Helicopter

5 Air, Wind and Weather

15 'Twixt Heaven and Earth,

16 Lift-off and Touchdown

17 Introducing Emergencies

18 Engine Failures for Beginners

19 Peculiarities of the Helicopter

20 Flight Manuals, Rules and Regulations

21 Miscellaneous

22 For the Professional Helicopter Pilot / Instructor

23 Advanced Helicopter Aerodynamics

24 Flight Controls and Rotor Heads

25 Advanced Performance

26 Other Components

27 Advanced Helicopter Flying

28 More Instruments

29 The Turbine Engine

30 Advanced Engine Failures

31 Advanced Emergencies

35 Other Helicopter Types

36 Night and Instrument Flying

37 Automatic Flight Control Systems

38 Miscellaneous Musings

1 Some Fundamentals

MATH AND PHYSICS REVISITED

In order to understand how a helicopter operates, it is necessary to have an understanding of the principles controlling physical objects, as well as the mathematical basis for some of the calculations that are needed.

Not everyone is an engineer, and fewer have studied advanced mathematics or physics. I've made an attempt to simplify the explanations and minimize the equations*, however, some are unavoidable. This chapter should explain the fundamentals of the physical laws important to helicopters.

Vectors

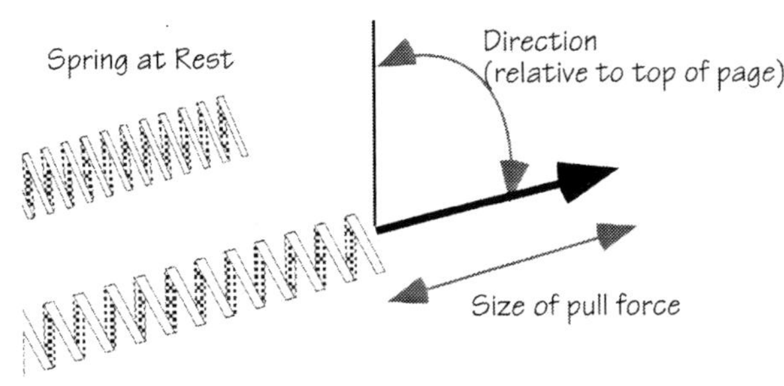

Figure 1-1 Vector Defined

One of the things that isn't easy to immediately grasp is the concept of a *vector*. Since vectors are used a lot in this book, take the time to understand what they mean.

A vector is a way to represent graphically, something with both size and direction. Take a spring for example. It's not possible to pull on a spring without a direction of pull. This gives a force (size) and direction of pull. This can be represented by a vector. Normally the direction of pull is of no importance but it is for us.

NEWTON'S LAWS

If you don't remember much from high school physics, you should remember Sir Isaac Newton's three laws†. Helicopters may not have studied physics or law, but they do obey these three.

Newton's First Law

A body tends to stay at rest or in motion in a straight line unless disturbed by some external force.

In simple terms, if you want to change the uniform (steady) motion in a straight line of an object, you need to apply an external force to it. If you want to turn a corner in a car, you have to apply an external force to the car, (the friction of the tires on the road is such a force - try turning a car on ice to show how this is true). If you want to turn a helicopter, or move a helicopter that is hovering, you need to apply an external force to the body of the helicopter.

In steady motion, all the forces are in balance. Throw the forces out of balance or add an external force and the forces attempt to re-balance themselves while the motion is changed to stay in a (new) uniform motion.

Newton's Second Law

Force is proportional to Mass times Acceleration.

What does this mean? In simple terms it means, with identical acceleration (i.e. the same gravity) a large mass will exert a greater force than a smaller one. Sounds so simple, but remember gravity is an acceleration, so we often confuse mass and weight (weight is a force).

* Evidently each equation in a book reduces the number of readers by 50%, and I want to keep both of you.
† What happened before Newton came along is anybody's guess. Things must have been pretty chaotic.

Newton's Third Law

For every action there is an equal and opposite reaction.

Sounds simple enough- if two people are standing on a perfectly smooth, frictionless surface, and one pushes against the other, both will move apart. Since a helicopter in a zero airspeed hover has very little friction acting against it, the action of turning the main rotor tends to want to rotate the fuselage the opposite way. More about this important fact later.

OTHER PHYSICS AND MATHS TERMS

Momentum and Inertia

Momentum is the mass of a body multiplied by its velocity. *Inertia* is the resistance to change (stay at rest, or in uniform motion in a straight line). A body at rest has zero momentum, but it does have inertia. It is still necessary to apply a force to a resting body to make it move (i.e. overcome inertia). Momentum and inertia are important concepts for flying helicopters because a heavy helicopter has a higher inertia than a light one, and requires greater forces to change its flight path.

Speed

Speed is the rate of change of distance per unit of time. For example, a helicopter that travelled 100 nautical miles over the ground in one hour has a ground speed of 100Knots (nautical miles per hour).

Velocity

Velocity is speed *and* direction. Our helicopter with a ground speed of 100Knots must be going somewhere, so we need to say where - for example, a speed of 100Knots on a track of North. Since it's pretty hard to have speed without direction, we often confuse these two terms. When we use velocity (instead of speed) we are using a vector.

Acceleration

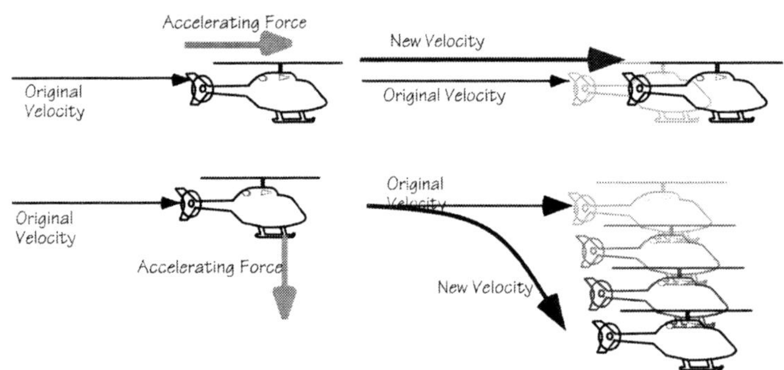

Figure 1-2 Accelerations

Acceleration is not just an increase in speed, as we often think. It is *rate of change of velocity*. Since velocity has speed and direction, acceleration can be either the rate of change of speed or rate of change of direction. Slowing down is an acceleration (typically called negative acceleration). Turning in forward flight is acceleration. Turning in a zero-groundspeed hover is not acceleration of velocity (since you're going nowhere...).

Figure 1-2 shows two accelerations - one pushing to change the direction of velocity, and in the other case to change the speed. Thus, acceleration has both magnitude and direction, it too is a vector.

Equilibrium

Derived from the Greek word meaning equal amounts of librium*, it means everything in balance. This implies zero acceleration.

* possibly an early Greek tranquilizer?

Vectors, Resultants and Resolving

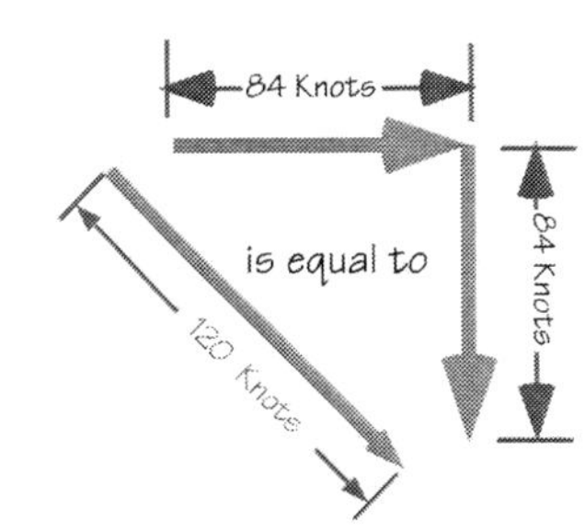

Figure 1-3 Resolving Vectors

Something with both magnitude and direction (such as a velocity) can be considered as a vector. The velocity has both magnitude (speed) and direction. Vectors can be added, multiplied or split apart if appropriate units are used.

For example, a helicopter heading southeast (135°) at an airspeed of 120Knots has a velocity to the east of 84Knots and to the south of 84Knots, as shown below. This is relatively easy to see, and is called *resolving* the airspeed to two different axes.

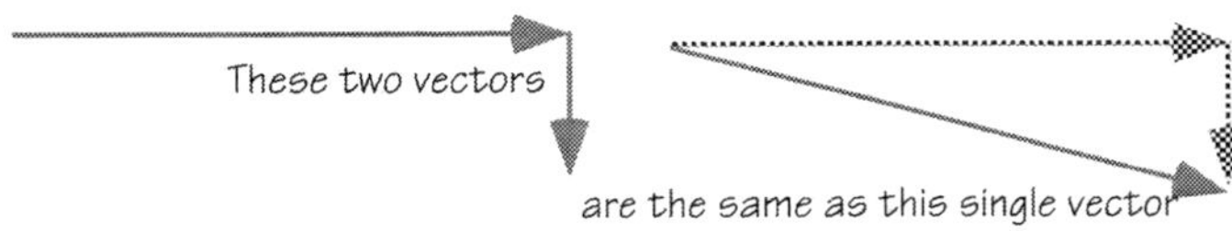

Figure 1-4 Adding Vectors

The opposite of resolving an existing velocity is combining two or more velocities. If two velocities are combined, for example air with both horizontal and vertical velocity, then the resultant is as shown Figure 1-4. Here's a more complex example.

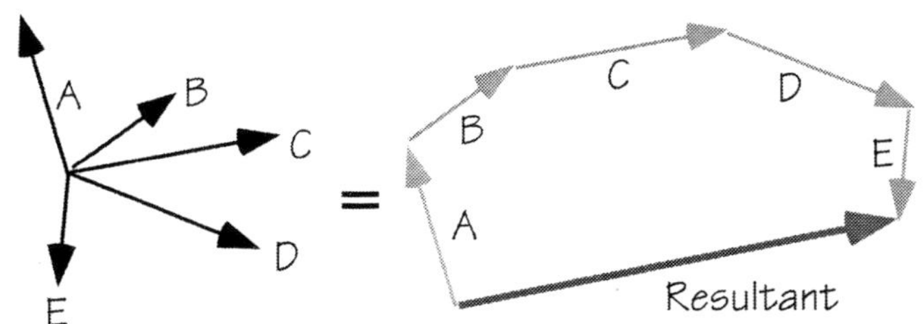

Figure 1-5 Adding More than Two Vector

In the helicopter world, the vectors we most often want to resolve are force vectors.

For example, a thrust vector from a rotor blade will have components that are relevant in both the vertical and horizontal axes.

Moments and Couples

Moments

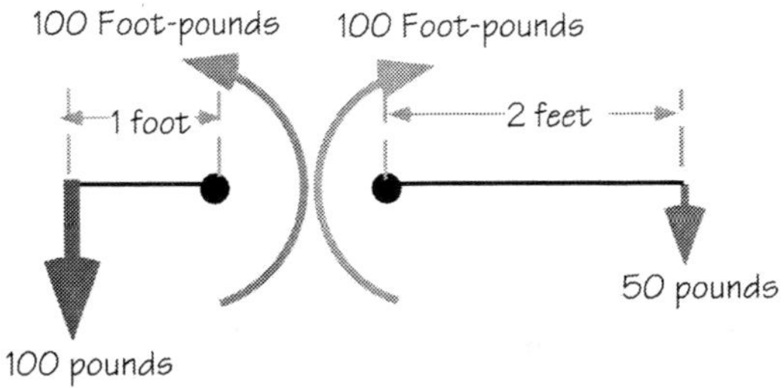

Figure 1-6 Moments Defined

There will be mention later of *moments* and *moment-arms*, and this is as good a time* as any to clarify them. For those who have not encountered a moment before, it is the reaction at a pivot point of a force (e.g. 50 pounds) multiplied by the distance (e.g. 2 feet) from the pivot point that the force acts about, giving units of foot–pounds.

A small force acting at a long distance may have the same moment as a large force acting at a small distance, shown in Figure 1-6. Moments are important in many descriptions of how helicopters work. The symbol for a moment is an circular arrow, as shown below.

* Sorry about the pun. This is the first of a great many. You've been warned.

A playground teeter-totter is a good example of the use of moments. If you're an adult trying to balance a small child on the other end, you know you'll have to sit close to the center when the child sits at the very end. Your weight multiplied by the distance to the pivot point must equal the weight of the child on the other end multiplied by their distance to the pivot point in order for you to balance each other.

Torque is another word for a moment.

Couple

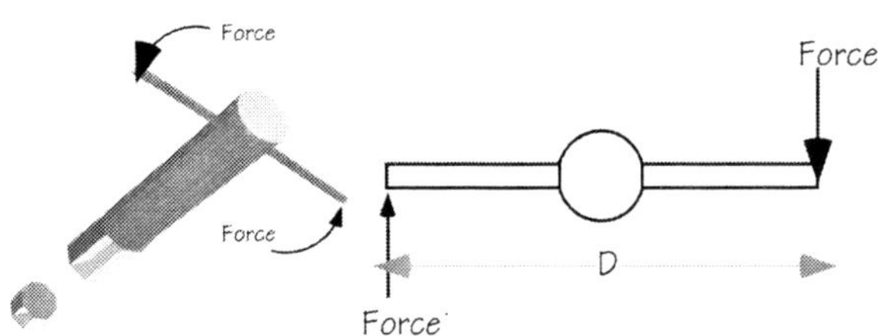

Figure 1-7 Couple Defined

A *Couple* is similar to a moment, except there are two forces acting in equal and opposite parallel directions. The main difference between a moment and a couple is that the couple normally is considered to have two equal forces. Figure 1-7 shows a couple. There is no lateral reaction at the pivot for a couple.

Balance of Forces

It is important to understand how forces balance (or don't balance). Consider the following two examples. In Figure 1-8 a), the forces and moments are in balance- there is no turning moment and no net reaction at the pivot point. In Figure 1-8 b) however, the moments may be in balance, but the forces are not. There is a net sideways reaction at the pivot point of 30 lb.

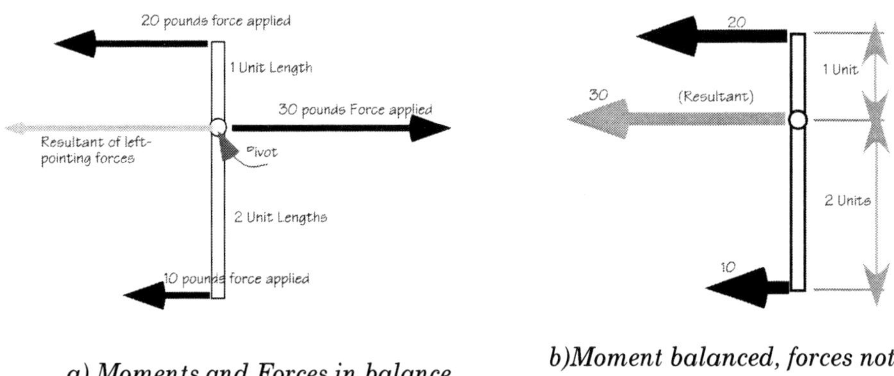

a) Moments and Forces in balance

b)Moment balanced, forces not in balance

Figure 1-8 Forces and Moments

Dimensional Correctness*

In the world of physics, one of the ways to check to make sure your formulae are correct is to ensure the units work out correctly. This is easy to do when you use consistent units.

Distance and Time

We use units of distance and time quite a bit in aviation. The units we will use in this book for the purposes of talking about physics are L for distance, and T for time.

Mass, Force, Energy and Work

Mass

Mass is not a force. We mortals who spend nearly all our time standing or sitting in an environment with a constant one gravity (1G) environment suffer great confusion over the difference between mass and weight.

* No, not some new version of political correctness, this has existed for years. And it works.

Mass has units in the Imperial units system of *slugs*, but we commonly (and incorrectly) use pounds instead. Since most of the time we're only concerned about the effects of mass in a 1G environment* we'll perpetuate the confusion by adopting the simple common term pound (lb.) to describe mass.

In the metric system, mass is in units of Kilograms (kg).

Weight is a force. It has units of pound-force (lbf.) or Newtons (N).

Some books use pounds-force (lbf) or pounds-mass (lbm) to distinguish between mass and weight.The difference between mass and weight may be more clear if you think of two lumps of the same material, one on a weigh scale, and the other on a balance bar, as shown in Figure 1-9 a) below. In a 1G situation (i.e. sitting still on the earth) both methods of measuring will show the same value. Put them both in a whirling centrifuge, or an airplane doing a tight turn at 60° of bank, (pulling two times the force of gravity or 2G), and the mass on the weigh scale will show it 'weighs' twice as much, but the balance will be the same as it was sitting still on the ground. Figure 1-9 b) shows this. The mass hasn't changed, although the weight has doubled.

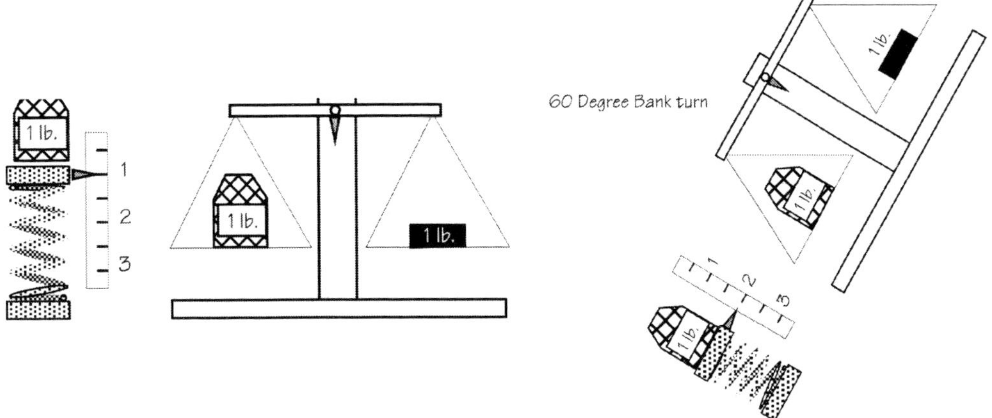

1G Sitting on the Ground, no momvement

2G - a steep turn, for example.

Figure 1-9 Weigh Scale vs. Balance

Force

Force is the ability to cause motion or change the direction of motion. It must act against something. The dimensions of force are (Mass x Acceleration) or ((Mass x Distance) / Time ^{2})

$$F = \frac{M \times L}{T^2} \quad \text{(EQ 1.)}$$

Units of force are pounds (lb.)

Energy

Energy is the ability to do work. Energy can be in many forms, however the ones that interest us in helicopters are typically only three: namely potential, kinetic and energy of rotation.

Energy cannot be created or destroyed in the level of physics we're interested in†.

The dimensions of energy are ((Mass x Distance^2)/(Time^2) or:

$$\text{Energy} = \frac{M \times L^2}{T^2} \quad \text{(EQ 2.)}$$

Units of energy are foot-pounds.

* helicopters don't do a lot of maneuvering that would increase the G level significantly, and all the performance things we're concerned with happen in a 1G environment, so it's not going to screw things up too much.

† There are other energies like chemical energy in the fuel and the heat energy in the air left by the passing of the helicopter, but we'll ignore these.

Potential Energy

Potential energy is the energy 'stored' in a body with respect to a surface due to a height difference between a body and a frame of reference (or surface). Since most of our flying is with respect to the earth, the potential energy of most concern is our height difference above a particular spot on the earth. The formula for potential energy is:

$$\text{Potential Energy} = M \times g \times h \qquad \text{(EQ 3.)}$$

where:

M = Mass
g = Acceleration due to gravity
h = Height above a reference, typically the ground.

Kinetic Energy

Kinetic energy, or the energy due to motion, is motion with respect to some reference. For most of our work, this reference will be motion with respect to the air, but sometimes we have to consider it with respect to the earth. Kinetic energy is a little understood type of energy as there is a squared effect for the velocity term. The formula is:

$$\text{Kinetic Energy} = \frac{M \times V^2}{2} \qquad \text{(EQ 4.)}$$

where:

M = Mass
V = velocity (note the squared term - important in later discussions)

Energy of Rotation

The third type of energy we are concerned with in helicopters is *energy of rotation*. This is quite similar to kinetic energy, at least in the formula. The formula for kinetic energy is:

$$\text{Rotational Energy} = \frac{\Omega^2 \times I}{2} \qquad \text{(EQ 5.)}$$

where:

Ω = Greek symbol for speed of rotation. (note the squared term)
I = mass moment of inertia about the axis of rotation.

Work

Work is the result of a mass moved through a distance. Not much of our discussion will worry about work. Work is also another word for energy. Same units, though.

Power

Power is the rate of doing work or of using energy. In other words, how fast is one unit of mass being moved (one pound being moved one foot per second). We are worried about power, as it takes power to do nearly anything, and in the helicopter world, we never seem to have enough of it.

The dimensions of power are ((Mass times Distance^2)/(Time^3) or

$$\text{Power} = \frac{L^2 \times M}{T^3} \qquad \text{(EQ 6.)}$$

Even though the helicopter is stationary when it's hovering, its got parts that are moving, like the rotor blades. That takes power.

Typical units of power are horsepower (550 foot pounds per second, which doesn't look like the correct units, but remember that pounds in this case are mass (slugs) times acceleration (feet per second^2)); or kilowatts.

GRAPHS AND SUCH

Graphs* and other diagrammatic ways of showing data are a part of life in aviation. They are just another way to show how two pieces of information relate to one another.

* It's difficult for an engineer who uses graphs as an everyday tool to have to explain graphs, but then again, if it helps the other reader to understand the rest of the book, it's worthwhile.

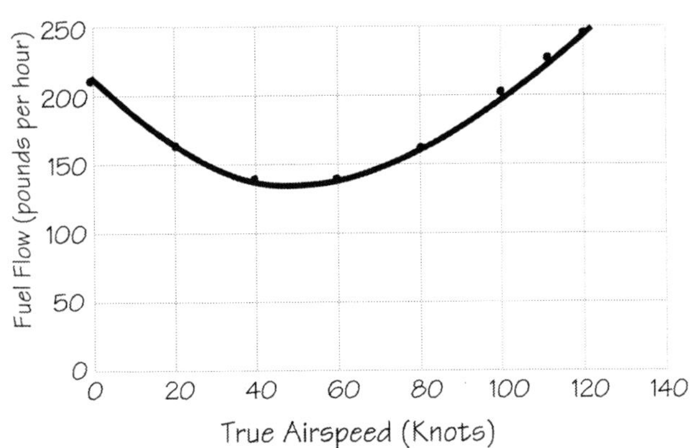

Figure 1-10 Graph of Fuel Flow vs. Airspeed

Most graphs have the intersection of the horizontal and vertical lines at the zero point, however some do not, in order to present data more clearly. While graphs are often constructed from measuring one unknown quantity (say fuel flow) against another known quantity (say True Airspeed), once the graph has been made, the measurements can be made in either direction.

An additional point about graphs is they permit a small number of data points to be used to develop a more general view of the situation. For example, we don't need to take data at every possible combination of airspeed and fuel flow, if we can understand the general shape a line drawn through the data points would make. Then, if we need to know the fuel flow at an airspeed we didn't measure, for example, we can *interpolate* between the two points we did measure.

If we want to know the fuel flow beyond the area we did measure, we can *extrapolate*, but that is often inaccurate. We don't do much extrapolating in this book.

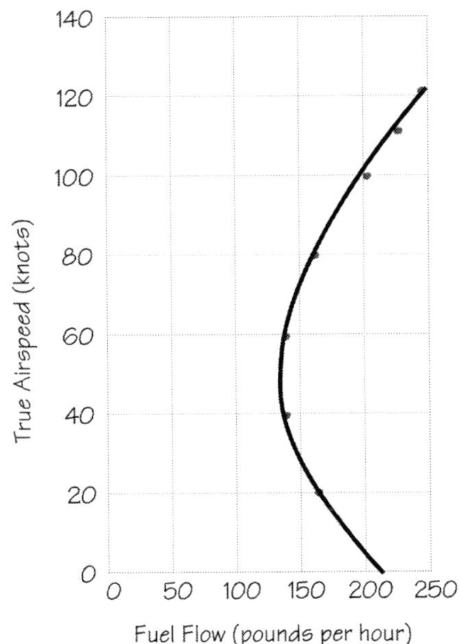

Figure 1-11 Graph of Airspeed vs. Fuel Flow

Some examples of graphs follow, along with notes on how to look at them.

The axes (plural of axis) of the graph should be set up in such a way to make it easy to read, and typically has the fixed item (the thing you can control) on the horizontal or x axis, and the variable item (the thing you want to measure) on the vertical axis. For someone interested in the fuel consumption of the helicopter, it's likely they would want to know what the fuel flow is at a particular airspeed, hence the graph in Figure 1-11 is oriented so by looking at a particular airspeed, the relevant fuel flow is easy to find. (It is unlikely that you would want to know the airspeed for a particular fuel flow, since this could occur at two different airspeeds, as shown in Figure 1-10.)

Nearly all the graphs used in helicopter flying, as well as in this book, will be oriented so an easily measurable item is on the bottom, and the variable quantity is on the vertical axis.

Putting Together Some of the Basics

A practical example of these fundamentals is in order. We'll combine the description of forces and moments with graphing some results from a small experiment that's relevant to aviation.

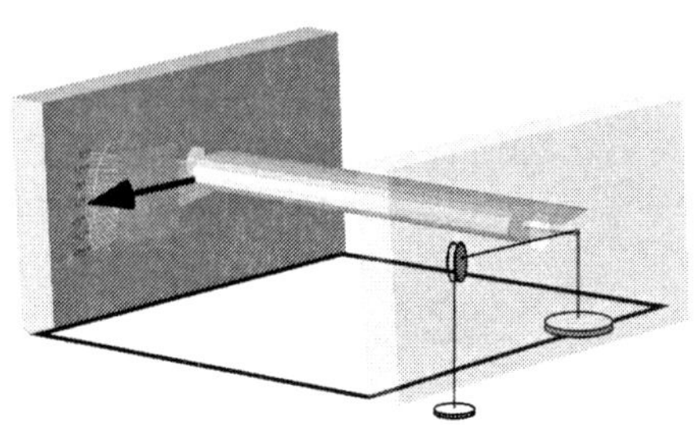

Figure 1-12 Wing Segment in Wind Tunnel

Consider a small section of a wing with air passing over it. Since we're trying to be scientific about looking at this, we want to change the angle this wing meets the air, as well as the speed of the air, so we can measure what happens. To do this, we'll put the wing segment in a wind tunnel, with a pivot for the wing to tilt around. See Figure 1-13 for a view of the basic arrangement.

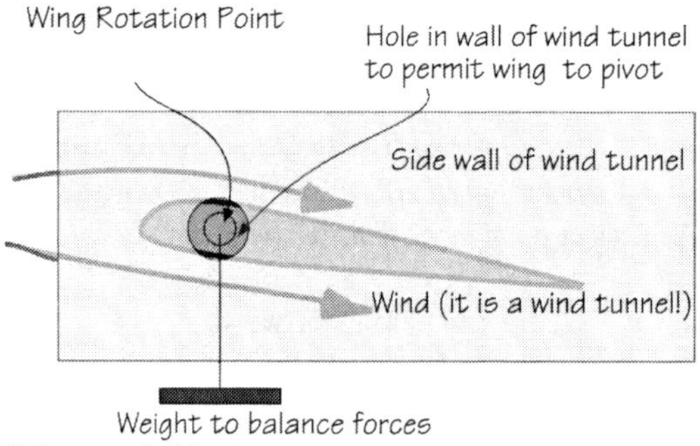

Wing Rotation Point
Hole in wall of wind tunnel to permit wing to pivot
Side wall of wind tunnel
Wind (it is a wind tunnel!)
Weight to balance forces

Figure 1-13 Wing With Weights

We can guess that when the air is flowing, the wing will be generating a force of some sort, so we'll start by just trying to balance the wing in the tunnel, using just one angle of wind and changing the speed of wind to begin. Since we can weigh the wing and supporting bits, we would know how much force is being generated when the wing is 'floating' in the pivot.

As the force generated by the wing increases however, we need to add some weights to keep the wing pivot floating in the middle again. When we have balanced the aerodynamic lift of the wing with weights, we know the lift force (at 1G weight is the same as mass (mass times acceleration). This is shown in Figure 1-13.

Unfortunately, this doesn't tell us very much. There are lots of combinations of angle of wind and wind speed that can balance the weight of the wing. Every time we change the speed of the wind in the wind tunnel, we have to fiddle with the angle to balance the whole arrangement. There are also lots of combinations that do not exactly balance the wing, which is frustrating. We also notice the wing is also always pressing against the back of the slot, so the wind is producing both a lifting force and some other resisting force.

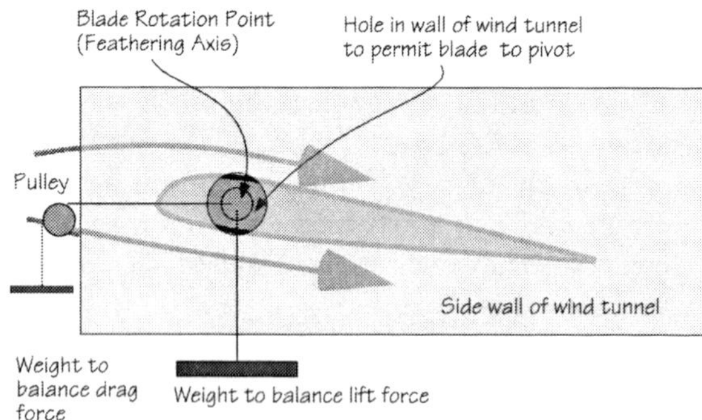

Figure 1-14 Wing with Lift and Drag Balanced Weights

Pretty soon, someone clever comes up with the idea of using a variety of weights and changing them to measure both the forces. Figure 1-14 shows this new arrangement. Pretty soon we're measuring up a storm., but it's still not quite correct.

Weights are cumbersome and require lots of fiddling, so someone else clever suggests we use a spring balance.

We want to measure the lift force the wing is making with respect to some fixed reference. We'll use the angle of the wind, and make the spring balance so it's always perpendicular to the wind. We'll call this force *lift*.

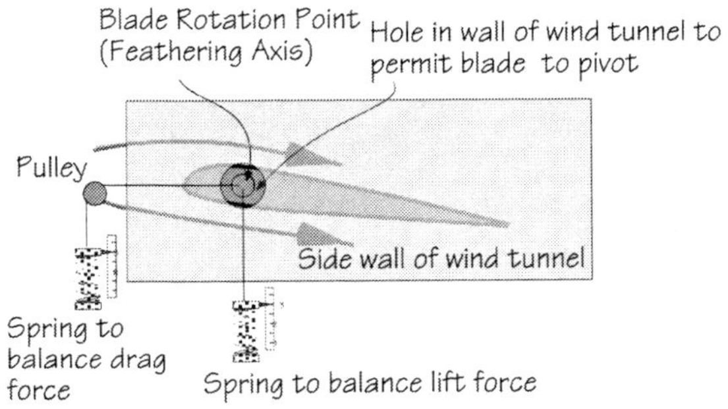

Blade Rotation Point (Feathering Axis)
Hole in wall of wind tunnel to permit blade to pivot
Pulley
Side wall of wind tunnel
Spring to balance drag force
Spring to balance lift force

Figure 1-15 Wing With Horizontal and Vertical Springs

Remember the wing is pushing against the back of the pivot hole? We attach a spring to the carrier to measure the horizontal force as well. We'll call this force *drag*. See Figure 1-15.

Eventually, we get a satisfactory arrangement of spring balances and pivots, and we're able to take some more useful measurements.

You won't see this sort of set up used in wind tunnels now, as more advanced methods have been developed, but this example helps to illustrate the points needed.

We'll use some of the concepts developed here later in the book, but for now, they'll illustrate vectors and forces.

Table 1 shows the results of our measurements for lift and drag vs. angle of wing.

AoA (degrees)	Lift Force (grams)	Drag force (gram)
0	0.0	10
1	1.0	10
2	2.1	10
3	2.9	10
4	4.1	10
5	5.0	11
6	6.1	12
7	6.9	13
8	8.1	15
9	8.9	17
10	10.2	20
11	11.1	23
12	12.1	26
13	13	34
14	14.1	40
15	15.2	50
16	15.9	65
17	17.1	80
18	18.0	95
19	18.0	off scale
20	16.0	off scale!

TABLE 1. Measurements of Lift and Drag vs. Angle of wind

The first thing we're going to do is graph the results. The results of measuring the amount of lift force as the angle of wind changes are shown in Figure 1-16. Notice how the wing was producing zero lift when it had 0° angle with the wind, and as we increased the angle, the amount of lift increased until we had quite a steep angle (at about15°).

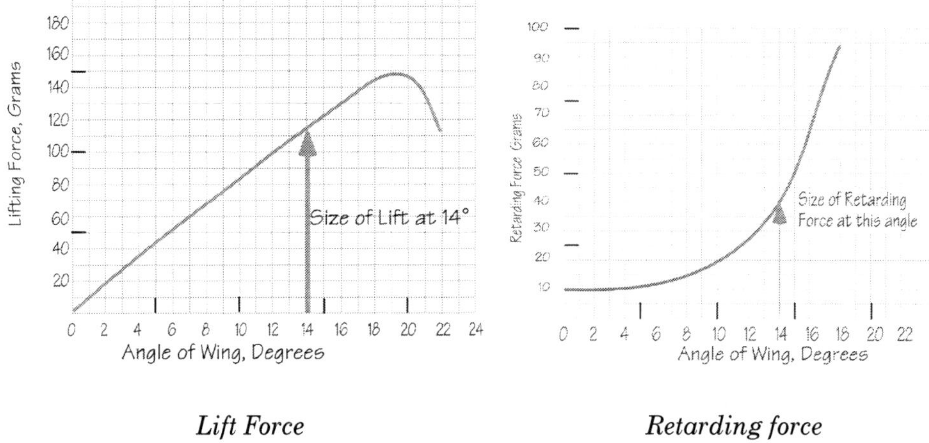

Lift Force *Retarding force*

Figure 1-16 Force vs. Angle

Also note that on the previous graphs we plotted the individual points separately, and then joined them together so we could accurately interpolate what the lift would be at an angle we didn't directly measure.

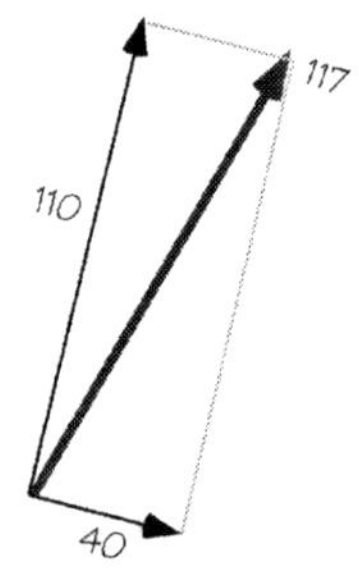

Figure 1-17 Total Vector acting on Wing

Notice how we can draw a line up from the horizontal axis to the lift force. This is the size part of the lift vector. The direction part of the vector comes from the angle the wind is hitting the wing.

We also measured the retarding force on the wing as the angle changed, and graphed it in a similar manner to the lift force.

The size of the vector we give to the retarding force is the amount of force, and as the drag force acts parallel to the wind, always pushing the wing back, so the direction of the vector will always be parallel to the wind.

We're going to plot the total vector for one angle, in this case 14° of wind. From these two vectors, we can develop a total vector acting on the wing, and this is shown in Figure 1-17. One last thing before we leave this subject.

If we think of this wing as being rigidly attached to a fixed wing airplane*, this will give us a practical example of resolving a force into two axes. We want to know what the useful lift force is at any one time, as well as the less–than–useful retarding force. The wing is attached to the airframe at an angle, and in order to know these two forces with respect to the airframe, we must resolve them from the overall reaction on the wing, to a frame of reference of the airframe. This is shown in Figure 1-18.

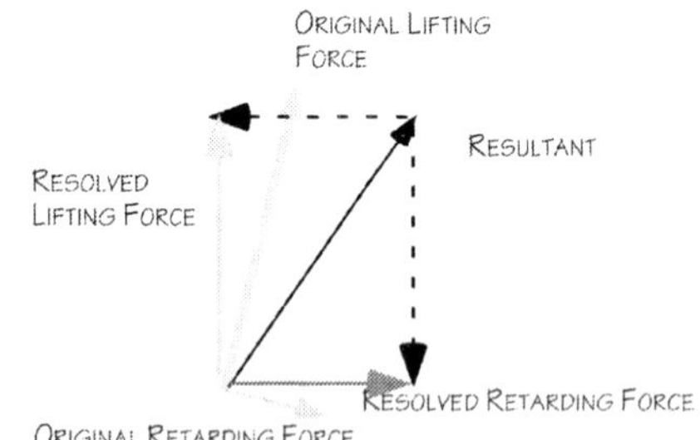

Figure 1-18 Resolving the Vector to the Airframe

If you didn't have a great background in math and physics, at least now you know enough to follow the rest of the discussions in this book.

Summary of Chapter 1

This chapter has introduced the basic concepts of the physics behind the helicopter and spelled out some important terms. The reader is armed to begin the journey into understanding helicopters!

* Yes I know this book is about helicopters, but it will help to illustrate a point.

2 Introduction to Helicopter Aerodynamics

Terms Used

Zero Airspeed vs. Zero Groundspeed Hover

The word *hover* is confusing. We think of a hover as being stationary with respect to the ground, yet the airframe and rotors only react to airspeed. If there's no wind, the term 'hover' means both a zero groundspeed and a zero airspeed hover. Whenever there is wind, things become less clear. To explain the aerodynamic terms in this book, we'll be using a zero airspeed hover (and will say so). In the hands-on flying, we'll talk about a zero groundspeed hover (and make that clear also).

Center of Gravity (CG)

The *center of gravity (CG)* is defined as the point of balance of all the weight forces of the body. There will be equal weight moments ahead of and behind the CG, above and below it and left and right of it. The CG of any object, be it a whole helicopter or an individual rotor blade will be shown by its common symbol, in Figure 2-1 below.

Figure 2-1 Center of Gravity symbol

Aerodynamic Terms

Before discussing how the helicopter flies, let alone its performance or flying characteristics, it is first necessary to understand basic aerodynamic terms. These basics include how lift and drag are created and the effect of certain factors on lift and drag. We will progress from a small segment of an airfoil, then expand this segment into a blade and discuss some of the peculiarities of blades, and then put several blades into a rotor disk.

Airfoils

An *airfoil* is any surface producing more lift than drag when passing through the air at a suitable angle*. The airfoil's shape is designed to bend the air flowing around it, with minimum interference to the smooth passage of air. The main and tail rotor blades of the helicopter are airfoils, and air is forced to pass around the blades by mechanically powered rotation. In some conditions, parts of the fuselage like the vertical and horizontal stabilizers, can become airfoils.

Airfoil Section

The *airfoil section* is the cross sectional shape (or profile) of the blade. Characteristics of an airfoil shape are:

- rounded leading edge to ensure smooth flow,
- a sharp trailing edge (to keep the wake behind the airfoil small), and
- specific shaping to reduce turbulence and separation of the layer of air immediately around the surface of the wing. (This layer is called the boundary layer, as it forms the boundary between the airfoil and the smooth air away from the wing.)

Helicopter rotor blade airfoils may have *symmetric* or *non-symmetric* sections. A symmetric airfoil has the same curvature on the upper and lower surfaces, while a non-symmetric airfoil has different upper and lower surface curves. Blades found on training helicopters and early helicopters are symmetric.

* anything that produces more drag than lift should be called an airbrake.

Most modern helicopters use non-symmetric airfoils. More details of non-symmetric shapes are in Chapter 23,"Advanced Helicopter Aerodynamics". Figure 2-2 shows the symmetric types of airfoil and Figure 2-3 shows the non-symmetric type.

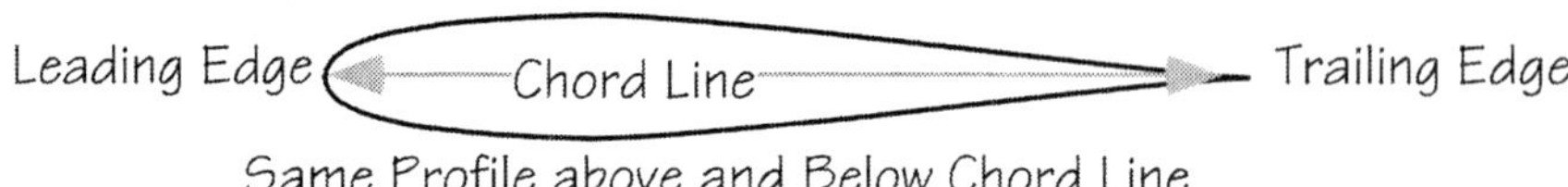

Figure 2-2 Symmetric Airfoil

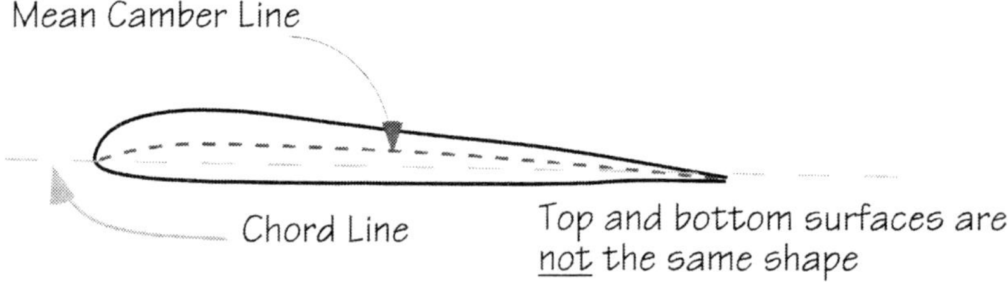

Figure 2-3 Non-symmetric Airfoil Sections

Chord and Mean Camber Lines

The *chord* line of an airfoil is a straight line from the leading edge to the trailing edge of the airfoil. It is used as a reference to determine two different angles. The first is the mechanical angle the blade has with respect to the hub, and second is the aerodynamic angle the blade has with respect to the airflow (they are different, as you will see). *Mean camber line* is a line drawn halfway between the upper and lower surfaces of the airfoil. In a symmetric airfoil the mean camber line and the chord line would be the same - in a non-symmetric blade the mean camber line is curved. Figure 2-2 and Figure 2-3 show these details for both types of blades.

Blade Pitch Angle

The *blade pitch angle* is the angle between the blade chord and the rotor hub. The main rotor hub is used for this reference, as the blades are attached to it. Blade pitch angle is controlled by the pilot through the flight controls, and may be considered as an easily measured, mechanical angle. Figure 2-4 shows the blade pitch angle* with respect to the main rotor hub.

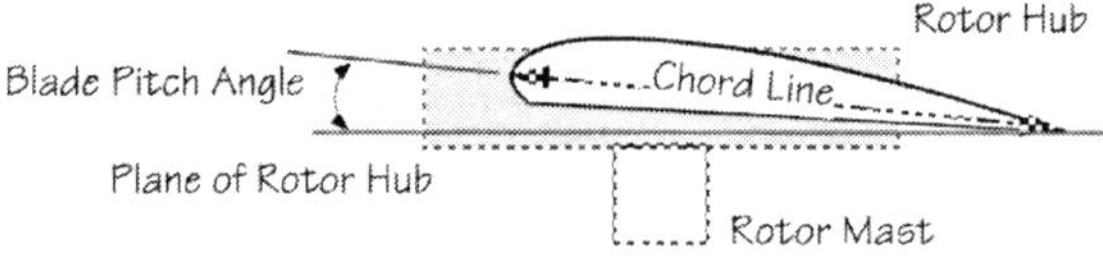

Figure 2-4 Blade pitch angles

Typically the range of blade pitch angle is from 4 to 15° of pitch at the root of the blade†.

* This is shown for the part closest to the hub. The blade is actually twisted, and this is discussed on Figure 23-11 on page 215

† Some manufacturers put markings on the root end fitting of the blade for maintenance adjustments of the blade pitch angle with the collective lever and cyclic stick in a fixed or rigging position.

Blade Segments

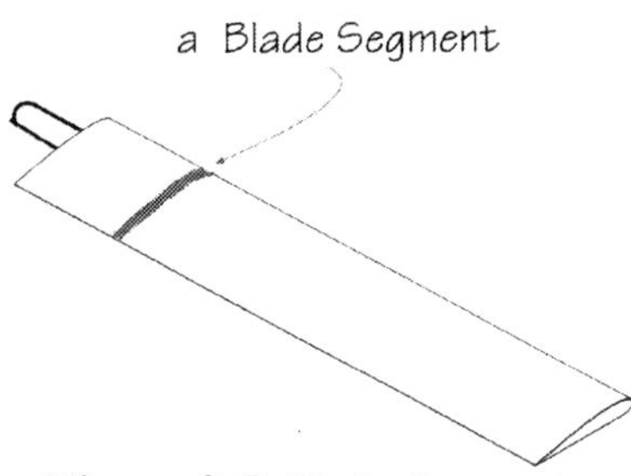

Figure 2-5 Blade Segment

As a helicopter rotor blade rotates many changes occur in airspeed, blade pitch angle, and so on. To more simply understand the effect these changes have, it is necessary to start with a small section of the blade, called a *segment*, as shown in Figure 2-5.

Resultant Air Flow.

Airspeed creates both lift and drag. Fixed wing people have things easy, as air typically only comes from one direction, but we rotary wing folk have a broader view of life and let the air come at us from nearly any direction, including from the side, behind, above and below. To keep things simple initially we'll consider the wind speed to be zero, and that only the blades are moving.

Since we're talking only about the rotor blade individual segment we will first concern ourselves with *Resultant airFlow* (*RaF*). Resultants, as you will remember from the introduction, are two vectors combined.

Airflow on a Blade Segment

Air can be made to flow past a surface in two ways, by moving an object through the air, or by moving the air past the object. It matters little which way it happens. This is resultant airflow, and in the helicopter we achieve this resultant airflow by rotating the blades. The resultant airflow has two parts to it - horizontal and vertical. How they are made needs some explanation.

Relative Angle on the Rotor

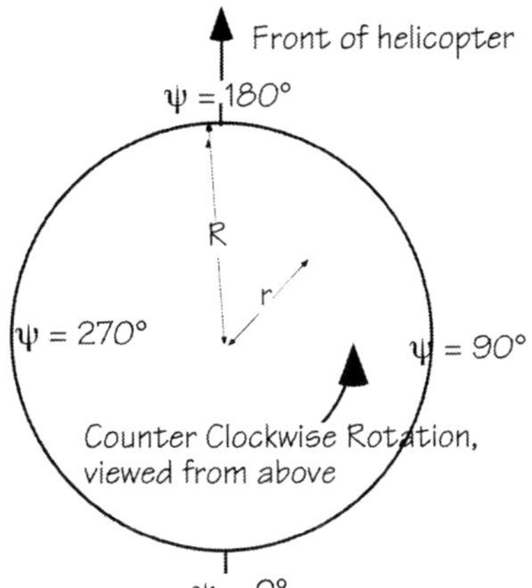

Figure 2-6 Blade Azimuth Position

It doesn't much matter where the blade is around the circle of its rotation in a zero airspeed hover- the speeds will all be the same. This isn't the case if we add wind, so we start to worry about the blade angle with respect to some reference. The blade at the back of the helicopter is at $\psi = 0°$, while the blade at the right side is at a ψ of 90°.

Just to make things confusing, the reference normally used is different from the relative wind reference*, and is shown later in Figure 4-5 on page 32.

Horizontal Component of Airflow

When the helicopter has zero airspeed, the size of the horizontal airflow component depends only on the position of the segment on the blade. A blade segment

* Don't blame me, I didn't make it up. Evidently, it came from the autogyro folks, long ago.

close to the hub will have a lower speed of horizontal airflow than a segment near the tip. This is shown in Figure 2-7. For the most part the horizontal airflow is due to the rotation of the blades and is in the plane of rotation of the blades.

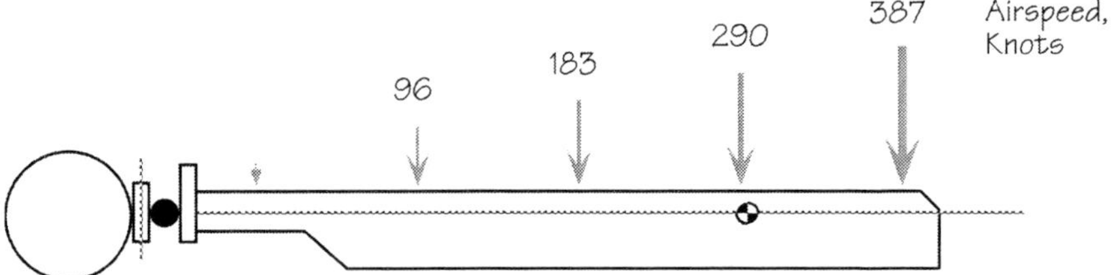

Figure 2-7 Size of Horizontal Airflow vs. Position on the blade

When the whole helicopter is moving with respect to the air, the horizontal airflow on a segment is the sum of the airflow due to rotation and the relative airspeed of the airframe. This is shown in Figure 2-8.

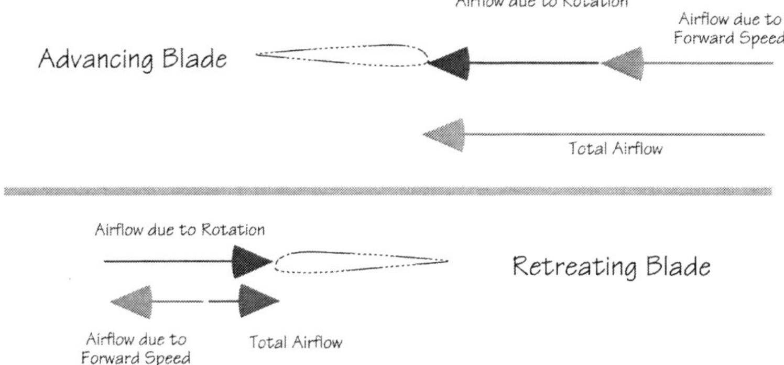

Figure 2-8 Horizontal Airflow due to Rotation and Relative Airspeed

Vertical Component of Airflow

Even in a zero–airspeed hover, there is a vertical component of airflow, as the blades are pushing air down to support the helicopter. This is called the *induced velocity*.

Induced Velocity

Induced velocity is the speed of the air being pushed down by the rotor. If the rotor is thought of as a pump, it must accelerate a mass of air downward to keep the helicopter aloft. The acceleration of air in the hover is from zero speed (a long way above the rotor) to a final velocity. For simplicity we'll consider this downward velocity to be equal along the length of the blade, and we'll ignore the influence of the ground for now.

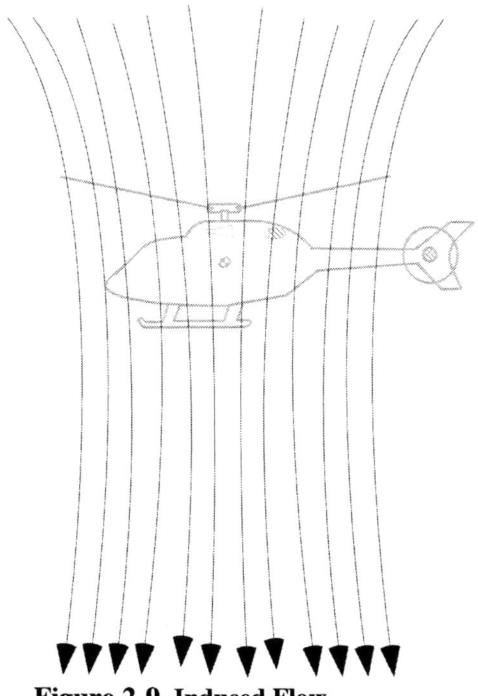

Figure 2-9 Induced Flow

The induced flow is the mass of air accelerated downwards by the rotor. Figure 2-9 shows how the air being pulled down by the rotor also affects the air close by, but that's of no real consequence for us. The name 'induced' comes from the fact that the rotor forces this velocity onto the air*. Don't confuse induced flow with inflow.

The induced velocity changes when the helicopter weight changes or when it climbs or descends. It is very important to understand how those changes affect the RaF. For example, if the helicopter climbs in the hover, it is pushing more air down through the rotor system, the velocity of the air from the top of the rotor is increased, and the inflow velocity increases, but the induced velocity decreases.

Similarly, if the helicopter descends in the hover, then the inflow velocity decreases, but the induced velocity increases. The helicopter isn't pushing as much air down and the induced velocity is more than in the hover at a steady height.

Combining the Two Components

The two velocities we have just talked about separately, the horizontal component (due to blade rotation) and the induced velocity (or vertical component) now are put together to form the Resultant airFlow, which we'll call by its shorthand form of RaF.

Angle of Attack

The *Angle of Attack (AoA)* is the angle between the RaF and the chord line of the airfoil. This is an aerodynamic angle, and is different than the blade pitch angle. AoA is invisible to the naked eye, and needs special instruments to measure. To minimize confusion, the Greek symbol α (alpha) and/or the abbreviation AoA is used to denote angle of attack. The AoA on a blade segment is shown in Figure 2-10. The larger the angle between the chord line and the Resultant airFlow, the greater the AoA.

Several examples of RaF are shown below. In the first three examples the helicopter is in a zero airspeed hover.

Figure 2-10 shows the RaF at a blade segment about mid-way between the hub and the tip. In subsequent diagrams this 'baseline' will be shown in light grey for reference.

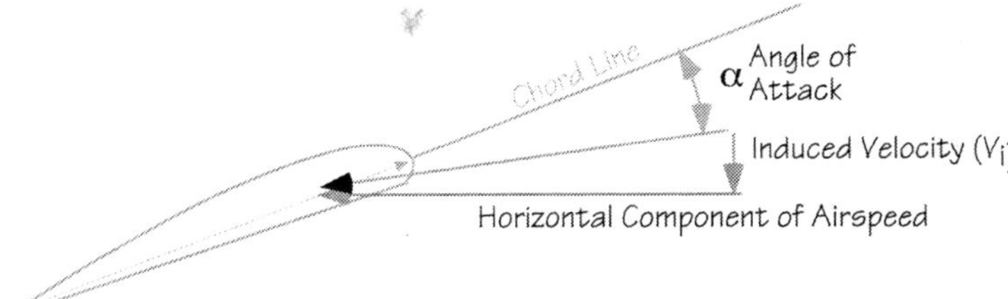

Figure 2-10 Resultant airFlow, halfway along the blade

* Not that the air has much choice about the matter...

Figure 2-11 below shows a segment closer to the hub. Notice how the induced velocity (vertical component) is the same size, but the airspeed due to rotational velocity is smaller making the overall angle that the air hits the blade smaller.

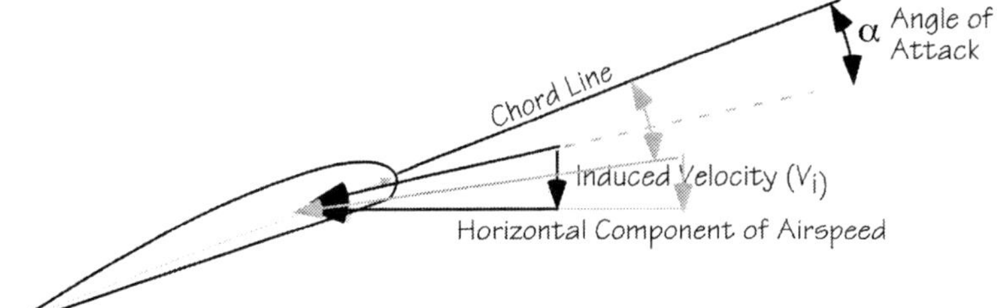

Figure 2-11 Resultant airFlow, root of blade

Figure 2-12 shows a segment close to the tip. Notice how the higher airspeed has increased the length of the horizontal component, while the vertical component of induced velocity stays the same length as the previous two examples. The AoA is now much larger.

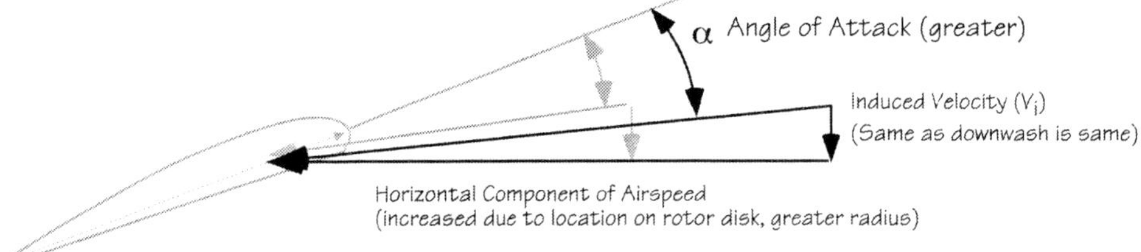

Figure 2-12 Resultant airFlow tip of blade

We'll stick with the blade segment used in Figure 2-12, (near the tip of the blade, no forward airspeed) but this time we'll start climbing vertically in the hover. Notice in Figure 2-13 how the induced velocity (vertical component) changes, affecting the AoA.

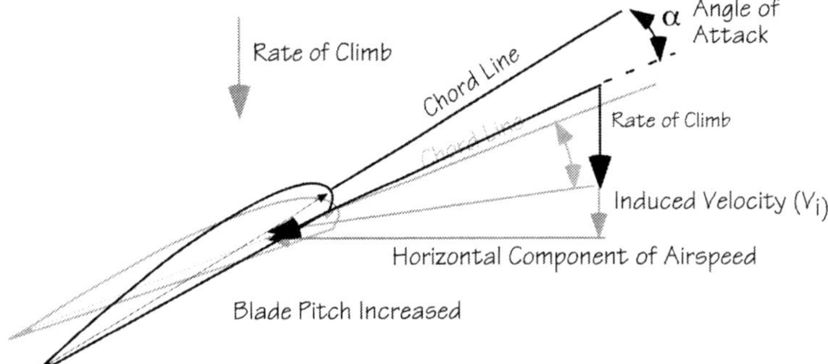

Figure 2-13 Resultant airFlow with helicopter climbing vertically in the hover

Figure 2-14 shows the same as Figure 2-12, but this time, the helicopter is descending vertically in the hover. The inflow velocity is reduced, and the induced velocity increases, increasing the AoA.

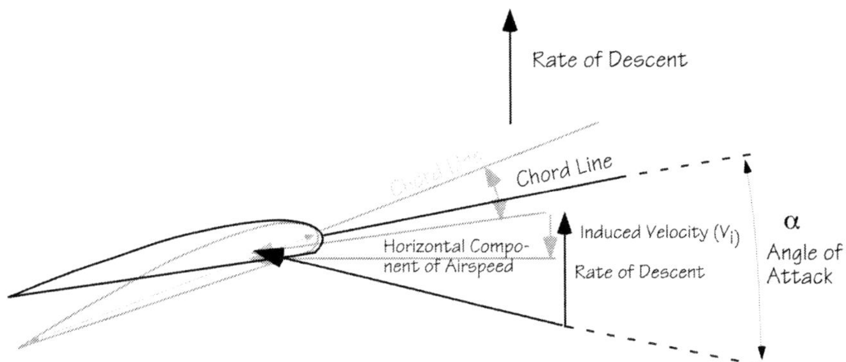

Figure 2-14 Resultant airFlow with helicopter descending in the hover

Now, we're ready for a completely different situation by adding some airspeed caused by the helicopter moving. Figure 2-15 is the blade segment in Figure 2-12 above, but with some forward airspeed added. Notice how the induced velocity is the same, and the longer horizontal component makes the angle of the RaF larger.

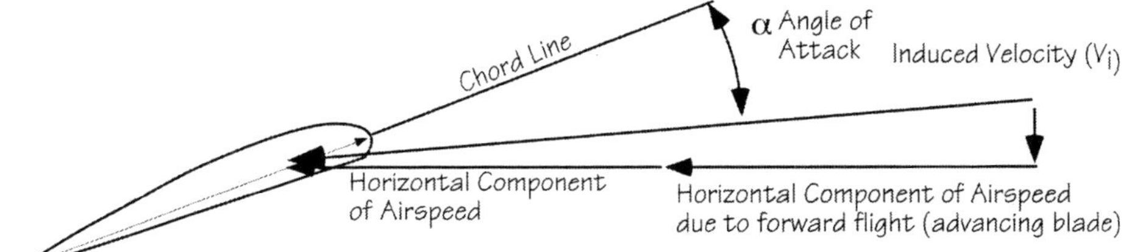

Figure 2-15 Resultant airFlow tip of Blade with Helicopter with Forward Airspeed

Resultant Airflow at a Blade Segment

Blade segments react only to Resultant airFlow (RaF)– that is, the combination of horizontal and vertical airflow. We will only look at the side view of RaF to keep things simple.

It should be obvious there are two things that can change about the RaF- the size of the vector, and the angle at which it strikes the airfoil segment. We've already talked about how the size can change.

Remember that in these last few diagrams we haven't changed rotor RPM (N_R) or blade pitch. We could go on with more diagrams showing how these new items affect AoA, but only at the risk of driving us blind or insane, or both. We'll only briefly touch resultants again, don't worry.

It should be obvious that AoA at a blade segment is only partly controlled by the pilot. It is affected by airspeed, blade pitch angle, rotor RPM (N_R) and other factors.

Even in the hover, as the blade rotates around the disk each segment sees different horizontal and induced velocity, and hence different size RaFs and AoA. In the hover, these changes will be easy to show. The situation is completely different in forward flight, both the size of the RaF and the AoA will change a lot around the disk.

Changing Blade Pitch Angle

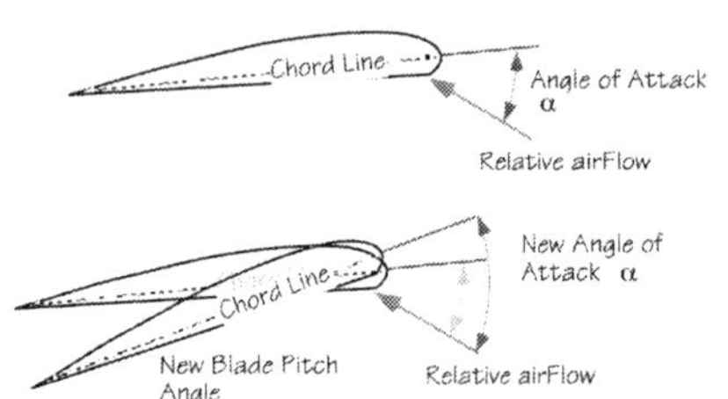

Figure 2-16 Changing Blade Pitch to Change AoA

Obviously if we change the pitch of the blade we will change the AoA. This is shown in Figure 2-16 for just one segment of blade.

Explaining Vector Diagrams

Remember the springs we put on the wing in the first chapter? They're going to be used for more than just explaining graphs!

In order to explain many of the peculiar ways that a rotor blade operates, it's necessary to use lift vector diagrams. These are ways to show how the lift and drag interact to produce different effects. My experience with lift vector diagrams when learning helicopter aerodynamics was not a positive one. In fact, I still dislike lift vector diagrams - a profusion of arrows that seem to appear from out of knowwhere*, which should somehow be self explanatory (and mostly aren't), and only confuse things. Before my attempt to make this more clear and simple, we have to explain one more item with respect to airspeed, lift and drag.

Lift

Lift is the useful force developed by the airfoil, caused by a reaction to air passing around it. Some textbooks would have you believe it is due solely to Bernoulli's principle†, and others would have you believe it's due only to Newton's Third Law.

Bernoulli's Explanation‡

Bernoulli found that as a liquid was forced to move through a narrow space, it increased velocity and decreased pressure. This is shown in Figure 2-17 below. Air is liquid at the sort of speeds we worry about, and so it shares this property.

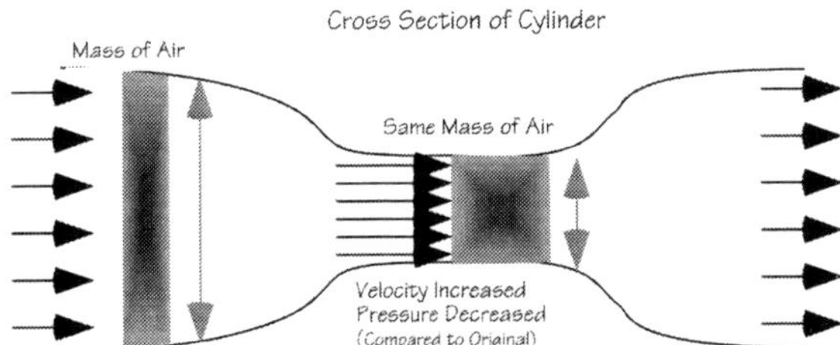

Figure 2-17 Velocity and pressure in a venturi.

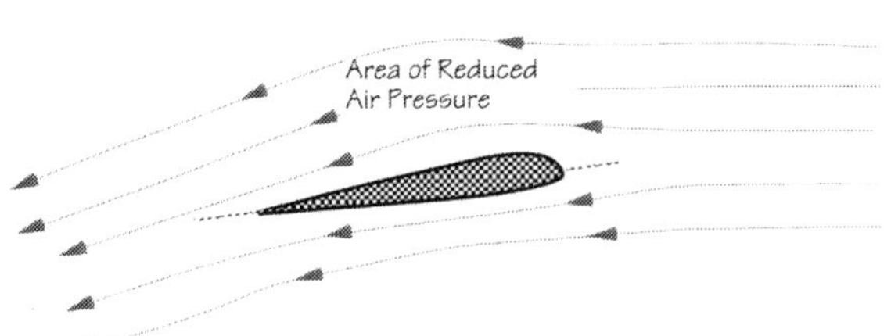

Figure 2-18 Lift According to Bernoulli

At first, it's difficult to understand how this affects us. The simple answers is that the upper surface of an airfoil resembles the lower half of a venturi tube, (the upper half of the venturi tube is replaced by layers of undisturbed air that have pressure). The curvature of the airfoil causes the air to speed up and reduces the pressure of the air. The difference between the decreased pressure above the blade and the 'normal' pressure below results in a upward force on the blade, called *lift*.

If we were able to measure the air velocity all over the surface of an airfoil, (outside the boundary layer), we would clearly see an acceleration effect on the upper surface like that seen in the venturi. Then if we were able to cover the airfoil with a lot of pressure sensors we could also see the distribution of the

* Yes, it's spelled incorrectly, but I couldn't pass up the opportunity to make new word.

† What follows will probably be treated as heresy in some schools of aeronautics, but if it helps your understanding, keep your own counsel.

‡ I'm sure he didn't apply this to airplanes as they didn't exist when he lived, but he developed the basic theory.

pressure. The relationship between the local air velocity and the static pressure is predicted by the Bernoulli equation, so we don't need to measure both- one or the other will be enough. Experiments like this are done routinely by aerodynamics students to demonstrate and prove these concepts.

Figure 2-19 Lift According to Newton

Newton's Explanation*

Another explanation for lift is Newton's Third Law - *For every action there is an equal and opposite reaction.* This explanation would have you believe that the true source of lift is the wing, acting at an angle to the wind, pushing the air down and forcing the wing up. This explanation is also often called the inclined plane method, so called because a sheet of plywood inclined to the wind will deflect air and produce lift.

This concept is also called the momentum theory.

The Real Source of Lift

Either concept is valid for predicting the amount of lift. The two methods are presented to let the reader understand there are (at least) two major ways of looking at this. I'd like to add a third that combines the two and addresses the concept of mass of air, whose importance will become clear.

The best answer is both Bernoulli's Theorem and Newton's Third Law work together to produce the lift force.

A mass of air is deflected down, in two ways - the bottom surface helps to push the air down, and the curved top surface pulls the air above the wing down as well. The increased pressure on the bottom and the decreased pressure on the top work in conjunction to help push the wing up. The important concept to remember is a mass of air is deflected down. Since the air has changed direction, its been accelerated.

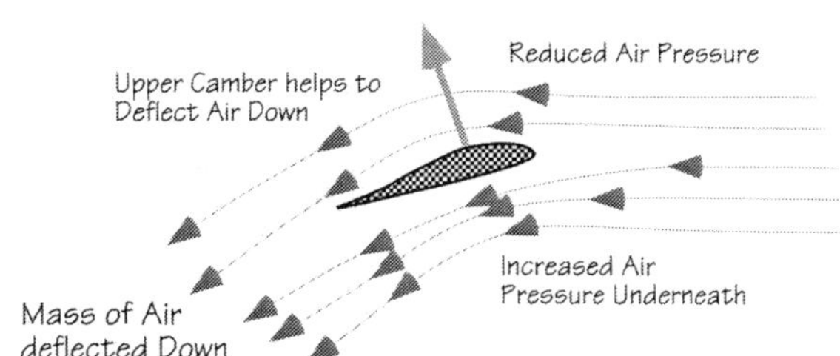

Figure 2-20 Real Source of Lift

The bottom of the blade acts as an inclined plane, deflecting the air downward. Curving the upper surface of the airfoil also helps in deflecting the airflow - in fact, it produces the main part of the lift. The deflection of air by the bottom part of the wing helps to increase the pressure reduction on the top of the wing, and increases the mass of air deflected.

In fixed–wing airplanes, there is an option on how to produce the necessary amount of lift to maintain flight - either a lot of air is given a small amount of deflection (a small angle of attack for high airspeed) or a small amount of air is given a large amount of deflection (a large angle of attack for low airspeed). In a helicopter, the blade pitch changes to control the amount of air deflected (and its direction), and thus control the amount of thrust or lift produced. The reason for emphasizing a mass of air being deflected will become clear later.

What's Wrong with The Bernoulli and Newton Explanations?

As individual explanations, they leave a lot to be desired and appear to be in opposition.

One or two things make Bernoulli's explanation suspect as the only source of lift. First, there appears to be nothing that says the air particles must meet up at the trailing edge of the airfoil, so why should they go faster over the top? The other part of the story about the air speeding up needs to come from our normal view of airfoils producing lift.

* Like Bernoulli, Newton made this up without ever seeing an airplane

We normally think of airfoils in wind tunnels, where the wing is still, and the air is moving. In real life, its the other way around, with the air being still and the wing moving. Think of the air as a body of water. When you move your hand through the water, you are displacing the molecules, which want to return to their original position when your hand has passed. Air is similar. When the wing or airfoil has passed through the air, the molecules want to be back in their original position, unless they have been moved by something. That something is lift.

The relatively sharp trailing edge of the wing prevents air from the bottom moving around to the top, which explains part of the story as to why the air on the top must move more quickly in its path than the air underneath.

Newton's explanation doesn't explain why an airfoil needs to have a specific shape - according to this way of thinking, a flat board would work all the time. In fact, the air will help to make its own shape, and there have been several clever demonstrations where non-aerodynamic shapes produced surprising amounts of lift. The 'Newton' method also doesn't explain stalling of the blade very well. So neither answer by itself is sufficient and a combination of the two provides a more complete explanation.

More Discussion of Lift

How much lift is produced depends on the characteristics of the airfoil shape, the AoA and the Resultant airFlow at the segment (if we assume the blade segment doesn't change size and the air density stays the same - reasonable assumptions I'm sure you'll agree).

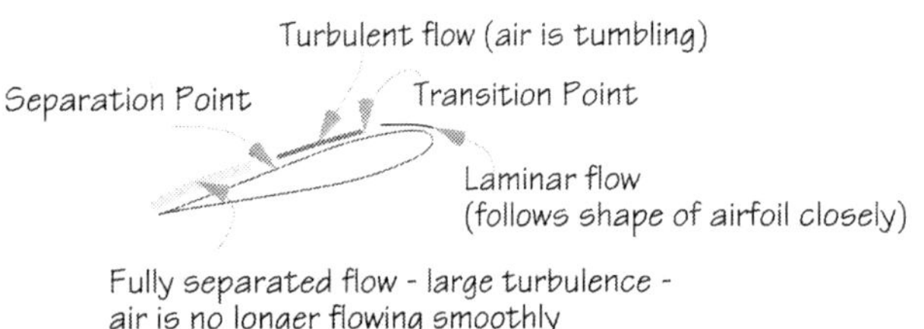

Figure 2-21 Separation of Airflow

Increasing the AoA will increase the lift, up to a point. When the AoA becomes too high, about 14 to 15° for most airfoils, the wing produces less useful lift because the airflow has separated from flowing smoothly over the top surface of the airfoil, and is said to be *stalled*. Stalling occurs when the lift does not increase as the angle of attack increases. and the airflow on the top surface starts to separate away from the skin of the wing.

The airflow will separate at some point during its passage over the top of the wing, and exactly where this will occur depends on the angle of attack and the shape of the airfoil. At a low AoA, the separation point will be a long way back on the airfoil. It will move forward as the AoA increases, until, at the stall AoA, it will be quite close to the point of maximum thickness of the airfoil. This is shown in Figure 2-21.

We will be discussing how much lift the segment produces shortly. First, the concept of the *Coefficient of Lift (CL)* must be introduced. C_L is a measure, without dimension, of the amount of lift a particular airfoil shape will produce. Put another way, it is a relative measure of the ability of an airfoil shape to deflect the airflow and produce lift*. (Those who are interested may find out more than they may want to know about C_L from any aerodynamics textbook.) The C_L of a symmetrical airfoil shape with a changing AoA is shown in the left side of Figure 2-22 below. Since there is no lift produced at 0° AoA, this curve represents a symmetrical airfoil. The right side of Figure 2-22 shows the C_L curve for a non-symmetrical wing.

Different shaped airfoil sections will have different shapes to the C_L curve.

As the airflow meets the segment at steeper and steeper angles, the blade segment produces more and more lift, up to a certain point where the airflow over the blade starts to break away. This is called the stall AoA, noted below. Above the stall AoA, a great deal of turbulence occurs as the airflow above the airfoil is unable to flow smoothly over the wing. If the angle of attack is permitted to increase further, the amount of lift produced decreases rapidly. Beyond the stall AoA, the segment isn't producing much of value to holding the helicopter up in the air.

* Different airfoil shapes have different C_L curves.

The turbulence obviously does not help to deflect the mass of air smoothly down, and it also contributes a greatly increased drag. Stalling is not a good thing for this reason alone, but there are other reasons why it is to be avoided.

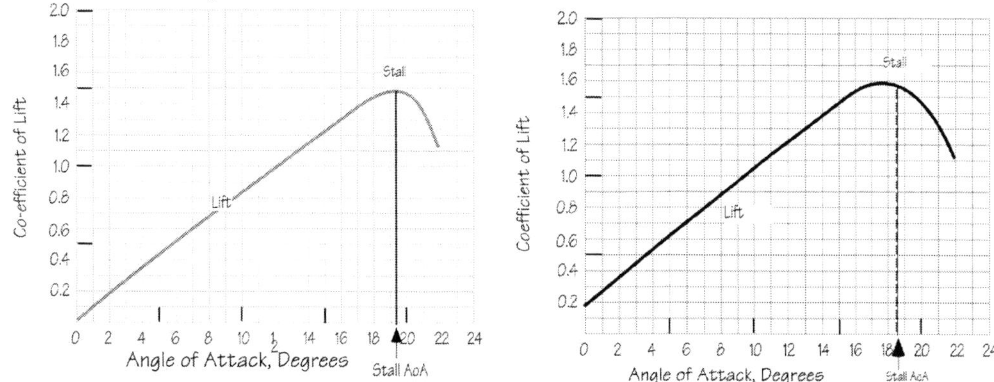

Figure 2-22 Lift vs. Angle of attack - (left) Symmetrical Wing (right) Non-Symmetrical Wing

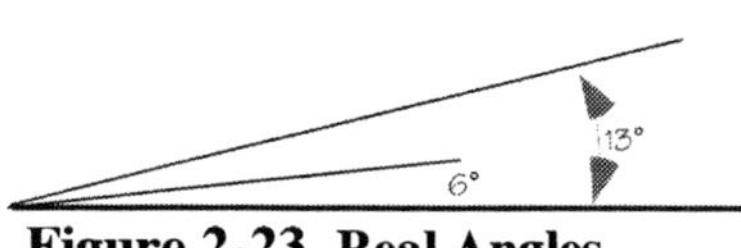

Figure 2-23 Real Angles

There is one other thing to be brought up that is relevant in Figure 2-22 above. Notice how small the angles are. Since we are trying to demonstrate concepts rather than absolute data, the angles used from now on will be exaggerated for clarity. Figure 2-23 shows the real size of the angles.

Formula for Lift

The basic formula for lift for a helicopter rotor blade airfoil is the same as for a fixed–wing airplane.

$$L = \frac{1}{2} \times \rho \times V^2 \times S \times C_L \qquad \text{(EQ 7.)}$$

where:

- L = Lift force Units = (F)
- ρ = Greek symbol for rho (shorthand for air density). Units = (M/L^3)
- V = Velocity of the air at the section. Note the airspeed needs to be True Airspeed. Helicopter people use RaF velocity. In some cases, we can also substitute rotor RPM for RaF velocity. Units = (L^2/T^2)
- S = Surface area of the blade segment. Units = (L^2)
- C_L = Coefficient of Lift (from Figure 2-22, C_L vs. Angle of Attack).

~~Three~~ ~~Four~~ Five* things about this formula need to be pointed out.

- First, ρ, the Greek symbol for air density tells us the amount of lift will change as the density of the air is changed. In other words, if the air is thinner, less lift will result at the same AoA. This becomes important in Chapter 6,"Basic Helicopter Performance".
- The second part to be considered is the 'V' term (airspeed over the airfoil). In a zero–airspeed hover, the rotation of the rotor blades provides all the airspeed, so in this case only, the V can be replaced by rotor RPM.
- The third part is that the 'V' term is more than just a straightforward V, it's V squared. This means that at the same conditions of AoA, density and wing area, doubling the speed will mean four times the lift instead of just twice the lift.
- Fourth, the astute reader may wonder why the one-half at the beginning. The answer is that $\frac{1}{2} \times \rho \times V^2$ is measurable all by itself and is used in many other areas. It's called dynamic pressure and is what pitot tube measures.
- Fifth, the units all work out, so the equation is dimensionally correct.

* People kept telling me more neat things about this equation.

$$F = \frac{M}{L^3} \times L^2 \times C_L \times \frac{L^2}{T^2} \text{ (lb.)} \qquad \text{(EQ 8.)}$$

$$F = \frac{M \times L}{T^2} = M \times A \text{ (lb.)} \qquad \text{(EQ 9.)}$$

Aerodynamicists use calculus to estimate the total lift on a single blade and then the whole rotor disk. We won't be doing that - the reader will probably be delighted to find we will hardly touch the lift formula again.

Drag

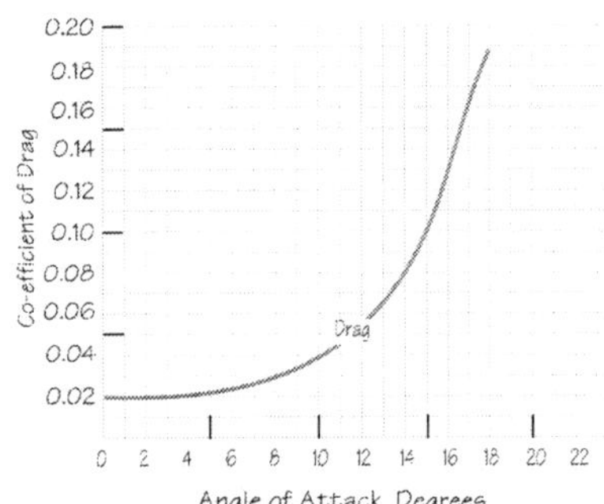

Figure 2-24 Drag vs. Angle of Attack

The inescapable part of moving an airfoil through the air is that it produces *drag*. Drag can be thought of as the horizontal equivalent of lift, acting to slow down the rotor. Like lift, the amount of drag produced will vary according to the AoA, (all other things being equal) and the dimensionless way of measuring it is shown in Figure 2-24 below. For this airfoil and airspeed, note the drag is increasing steeply prior to the stall. The formula for drag is the same as for lift, except C_D is used instead of C_L. The units are a force, same as lift.

Another way to look at C_D is that it is a measure of the ability of the shape to interfere with the flow of the air.

There are several sources of drag on the blade, namely induced and profile drag.

Previously we saw that Bernoulli and Newton can be used to measure the lift force quite accurately. Strangely, they all fail completely when trying to measure drag. This is because they all ignore viscosity and turbulence, the fundamental causes of drag.

Induced Drag

Induced drag is due primarily to the change in angle of the airflow as it goes by the airfoil. Induced drag always acts parallel to the RaF. Since the change in AoA is directly tied to the amount of lift produced, induced drag is generally considered to be the result of producing lift.

Explaining induced drag is difficult and the adventurous student may wish to examine other books. Suffice to know that producing more lift will also produce more drag.

Profile Drag

The *profile drag* of an airfoil is the drag caused by the air flowing around it, for example, the skin friction. It is nearly constant until the blade approaches the stall AoA, at which point it increases significantly, due to the flow becoming turbulent as it separates from the surface. The sources of this profile drag can be seen in Figure 2-21 on page 20. They include:

- Roughness of the surface, or skin friction
- Airfoil shape (or section), or the drag due to the form of the shape, called form drag.
- Airspeed at the Blade section.

In graphical terms, the airflow over the blade will, at some point, become turbulent. How turbulent the airflow becomes and what effect that has on profile drag depends on the angle of attack and the speed of the air.

On to Vector Diagrams

So we've had a look at a more direct physical explanation of what air does. Now, we'll replace spring forces with lines, where the length of the line represents the force measured on the spring balance used in "Putting Together Some of the Basics" on page 7. These lines are vectors, as they have both magnitude (size) and direction. The size of the vectors we can get from two graphs, the lift vector from Figure 2-22 on page 21, Coefficient of Lift, and the second, drag vector from Figure 2-24 on page 22. That leaves the problem of the direction of the two vectors. Because we didn't want to get too complex with measuring forces, we set up the spring balances so they always measured the lift force perpendicular (or 90°, or a right angle) to the RaF, and the drag force was always measured parallel to (or in line with) the RaF. Now we come to the first of the problems with regard to names. In order to develop this discussion, we're going to have to resort to the use of upper and lower case letters, as well as subscripted letters. Nothing to be alarmed about.

We'll call the basic lift and drag from the RaF little l and d, since we're dealing with a small part of the big picture.

The airfoil (or blade) segment is acted on by Resultant airFlow (RaF). Lift (l) acts perpendicular to the RaF, and in turn when added to the Drag (d) produces a resultant vector or Total Reaction (TR). This is shown in Figure 2-25 below.

There are two distinct steps in this process-

- From the lift (l) and drag (d) Vectors find the Total Resultant (TR)
- Resolve the Total Resultant (TR) to get Useful Force (UF) and Retarding Force (RF) as they affect the rotor hub.

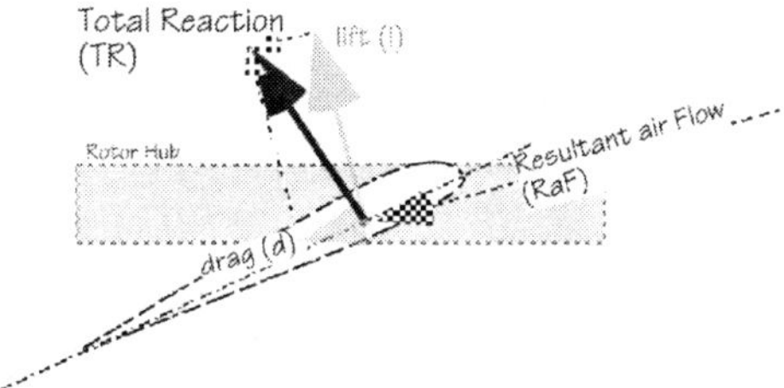

Figure 2-25 Lift Vectors Basic

Zero Angle of Attack

If the RaF is parallel to the chord of a symmetrical airfoil, then the AoA is zero, no air is going to be deflected and no lift produced. Drag will be produced. This is shown in Figure 2-26.

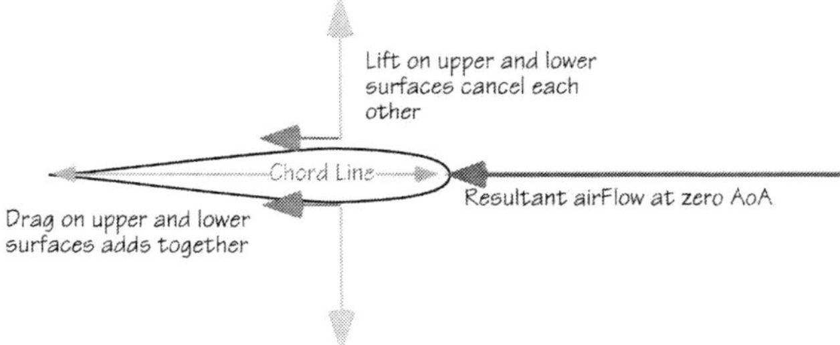

Figure 2-26 Symmetrical Blade with Zero AoA

We are interested in how the TR will affect the helicopter - i.e., the amount of TR available to support the helicopter, and how much power will it take to drive the rotor blades around.

It is necessary to resolve (or rotate) the TR vector into vectors that are parallel to the rotor hub, or Useful Force (UF) and perpendicular to it - the Retarding Force (RF). Hopefully, this is all very clearly shown in Figure 2-27. All we are doing is measuring the lift and drag as they would have been measured if we could do it directly on the rotor hub.

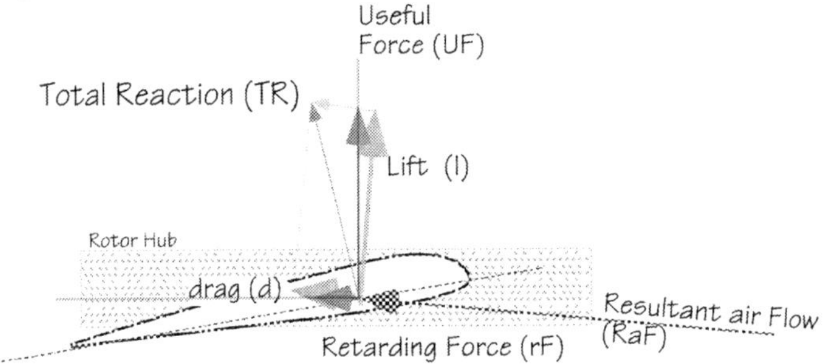

Figure 2-27 Lift Vectors Resolved

It is worth spending some time with this diagram, as variations of it appear in other sections.

As the speed of the horizontal airflow and the size and direction of the vertical component of airspeed change, they will change the AoA and the RaF speed. In turn, the size and angle of the lift and drag vectors will change dramatically.

The study of lift vectors can become really quite tedious and tiresome, so is best taken in small doses. We'll leave lift vectors for now, and will revisit them later in Chapter 8,"The Aerodynamics of Autorotation".

Summary of Chapter 2

This chapter has tried to break a complex subject into some manageable parts that can be digested (after suitable chewing, of course) in an attempt to understand some of the rather complex things that go on when the blades are turning.

3 The Rotor Blade

GENERAL

The blade is merely a series of airfoil segments joined together. To describe the position of a segment along the rotor blade, the convention used is to say it is at a fraction, $\frac{r}{R}$ of the rotor radius R, with 0 being the hub and 1.0 being the tip. Thus a segment at 0.75r is three quarters of the way to the tip from the hub.

A rotor blade may have more than one type of section, in order to make best use of the lift, drag and other properties of each type of airfoil section. An example is shown in Figure 3-1. The large 'paddle' on the end of the blade is deliberate, and is known as the BERP tip (British Experimental Rotor Program). The letters 'RAE' in this case mean Royal Aeronautical Establishment - the British organization that developed these blade profiles.

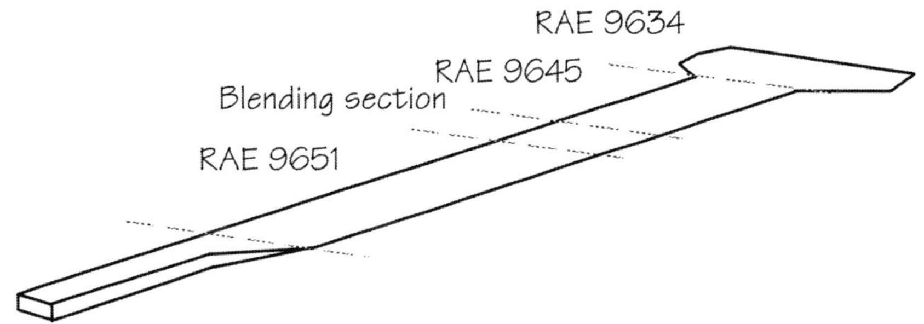

Figure 3-1 Different Airfoil Sections on a Rotor Blade (From the Westland EH-101)

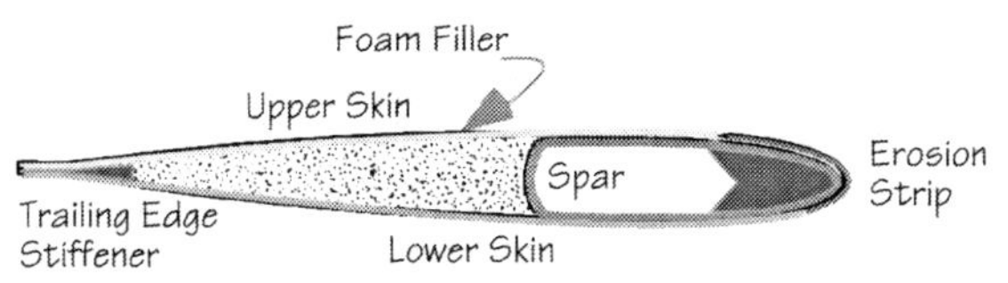

Figure 3-2 Typical Blade Cross Section

In terms of construction, the rotor blade typically has a spar and upper and lower surface skins. The interior is filled with a foam or honeycomb core for rigidity. See Figure 3-2 for a typical blade cross section.

Axes of the Blades

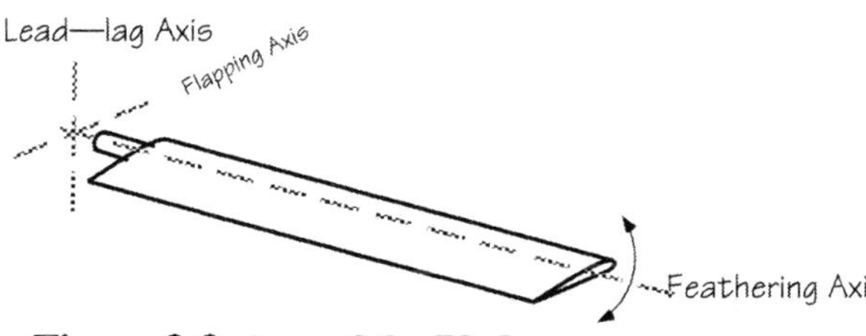

Figure 3-3 Axes of the Blade

Just as we have reference lines for the blade segment (chord), so too do we have reference lines for the blade, but in this case we refer to a blade axis. An *axis* is merely a line drawn for reference. The rotor blade has 3 axes, namely: the *feathering*, *flapping* and *lead-lag* axes, as shown in Figure 3-3.

The feathering axis is the axis about which the blade changes pitch (and AoA); the flapping axis is the axis the blade flaps up and down about; and it leads and lags around the lead–lag axis. In our example helicopter's rotor head, each of these axes have a hinge in the hub to permit these actions. There is a good reason for these hinges.

Tip Losses

It is worth mentioning that airflow gets really complicated at the very tip of the blade, just as at the end of a fixed wing airplane wings. This causes some slight losses in overall efficiency, but not enough to worry the beginner helicopter pilot, especially as we can do nothing about it.

Lift on a Whole Blade

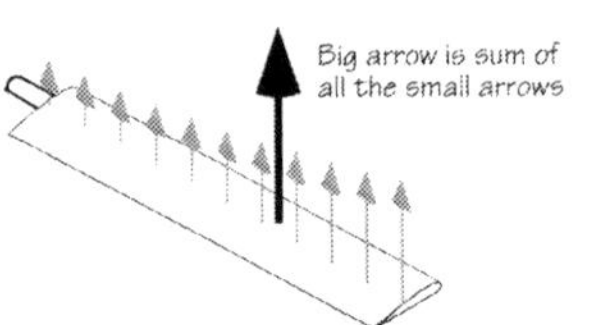

Figure 3-4 Total Lift on the Blade

For simplicity, assume the thrust produced by all the segments on a blade act from a single position, namely the center of gravity (CG) of the blade. We are only interested in the part of Useful Force that is of use to us, namely the part acting perpendicular to the rotor hub. This is shown in Figure 3-4.

Coning Angle

In side view, the rotor blades are angled up slightly from the hub when they are producing lift. The first point to make here is the *coning angle* will only happen in helicopters with flapping hinges - a more detailed explanation of rotor hubs is in Chapter 25,"Advanced Performance". Hubs without a flapping hinge will have only a small coning angle due to blade bending. In most helicopters, the coning angle is small, 2 to 5°.

The coning angle results from the combination of centrifugal and lift forces acting on the blade.

Rotation produces centrifugal force and tries to keep the blades flat, while lift tries to raise the blade. The two forces produce an angle between the rotor hub and the tip of the blades. The coning angle of most helicopters is quite small, indicating the centrifugal force acting on the blades must be much larger than the lift force. (If the two forces were equal, for example, the coning angle would be 45° and much less lift would be available to support the helicopter.) Coning angle is shown in Figure 3-5.

The maximum coning angle attainable before the rotor stalls is about 10° for most modern helicopters. Note that coning angle itself doesn't cause the stall, it's merely one visible symptom.

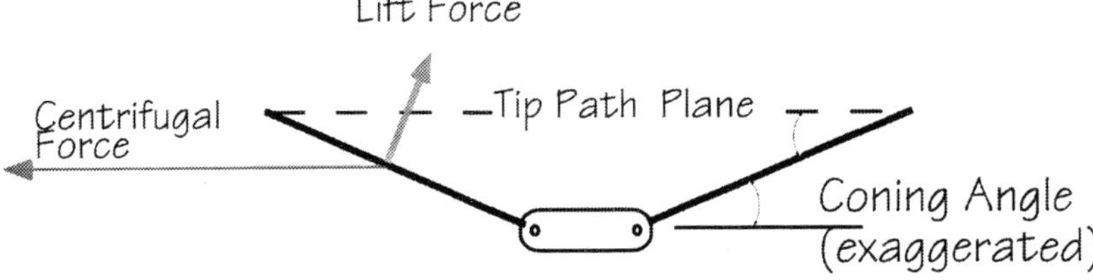

Figure 3-5 Coning Angle (Exaggerated)

Pre-Coning

Many helicopters' rotor blades are attached to the hub at a small positive angle. This is called *pre-coning* and it is built into the rotor hub to reduce stresses on the blades, and the hub. An example of pre-coning is shown in Figure 3-6.

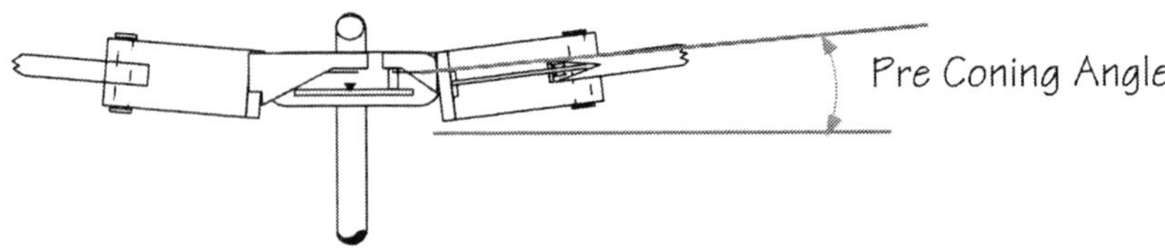

Figure 3-6 Pre-coning

How Lift Gets to the Hub

Wait a minute, you say. If lift developed by the blade acts at the CG of the blade, this will produce a moment (distance from the blade CG to the flapping hinge multiplied by the lift force). But the blade is hinged at the flapping hinge, and it's not possible to transmit a moment across a hinge. (All of these are true). So how do we get all that lift transmitted to the rotor hub to do some good for us?

Astute question. The answer lies in the centrifugal force produced by rotation of the blade and the coning angle.

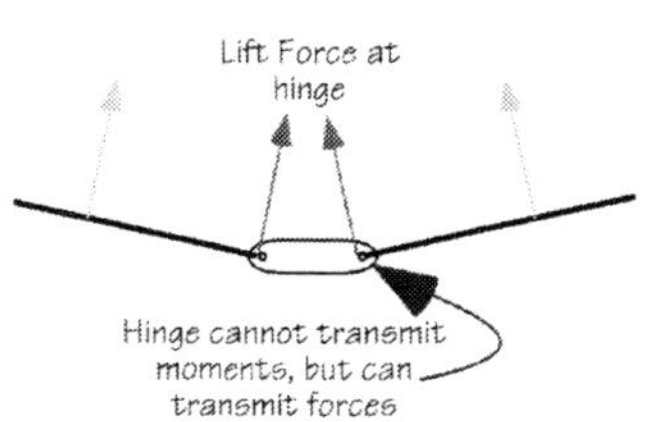

Figure 3-7 How Lift Gets to the Hub

At the flapping hinge the centrifugal force is the larger of the two forces. This resultant must be resolved into the useful lift force and the force the hub has to restrain to stop the blade from flying off. Designers worry about both of these, we will only concern ourselves with the lift force. See Figure 3-7. So we have a lift force at the hub thanks to the coning angle.

Drag on the Whole Blade

Just as lift on a whole blade acts from one source, so it is necessary to think of the drag acting from one place. Like the lift, it is assumed to act at the center of gravity, as shown in Figure 3-8 below.

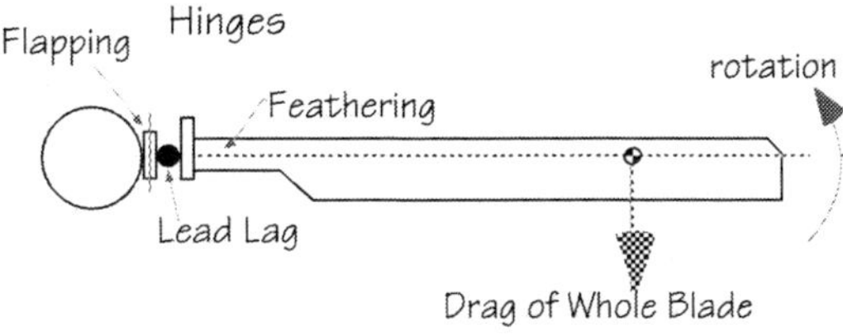

Figure 3-8 Drag on the Whole Blade

Blade Dragging*

This is the equivalent of coning angle in the lead–lag axis of the blade. Just as the blade is coned due to lift, in our articulated rotor head the blade is going to be *dragging* behind the ideal position. This is shown in Figure 3-9 below. Obviously, as the AoA and drag change, the angle behind the ideal position will also change. This has some major implications to be explained later.

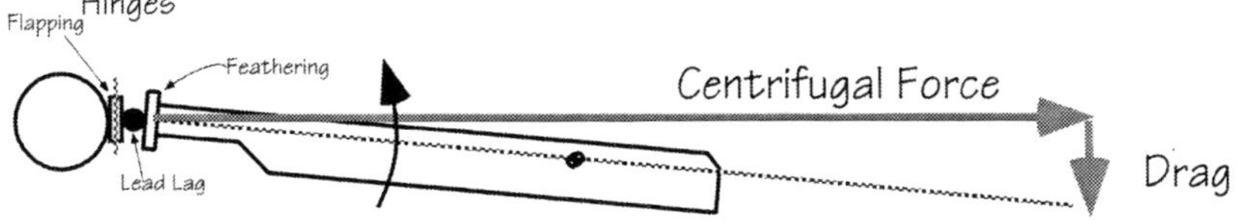

Figure 3-9 Blade Dragging

Blade Flapping

The blade is free† to change pitch, to lead and lag (back and forth), and to flap (up and down). The blades are constantly changing pitch angle as they travel around the disk.

It works this way - in forward flight the rotor disk is tilted to produce a forward–angled Useful Force (accept this explanation for now). The lowest part of the disk is forward, and highest part is aft. The blade on the advancing side (90° position) has the minimum blade pitch angle and AoA. It is descending towards the lowest position at the front - falling down through the air if you like. The blade on the retreating side (270°) is at a very high blade pitch angle and AoA and is climbing towards the highest position at the back of the disk.

* No, this isn't a male blade dressed in women's clothing.
† Well, sort of free - blade pitch is actually under the control of the pilot, but may be considered to be free.

The rotor blade experiences this rising and falling with respect to the rotor hub as it rotates. It makes calculation of the AoA at any blade segment more difficult than looking at coning angle, azimuth position and RaF of the airframe or rotor disk.

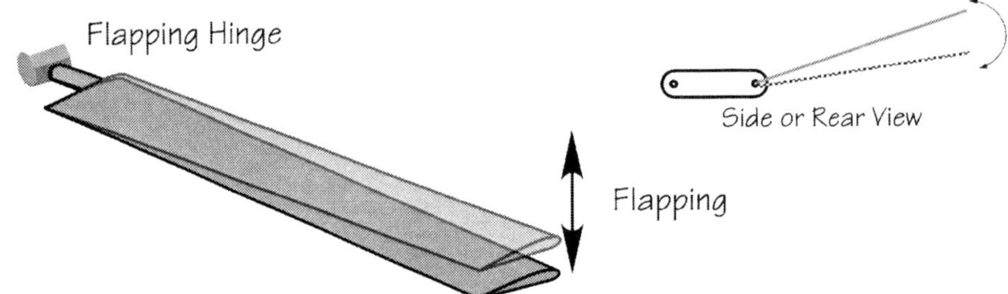

Figure 3-10 Flapping Motion

Reasons for Lead–Lag motion

The blade changes pitch, lift and flapping angle as it makes its merry way around the circle of its existence. Why the requirement for leading and lagging?

Change in Drag

Remember the blade produces lift, and with lift comes induced drag (or drag due to lift). Drag acts horizontal to (that is, in the same plane as) the rotation of the blade. For example, our generic helicopter would have the blades 120° apart in a vacuum, or in a zero airspeed hover. In a zero-airspeed hover, the blade would be dragging at a constant angle behind the ideal position (the drag being constant at all blade azimuths in this condition). However, helicopters never operate in a vacuum, and only rarely operate in a zero-airspeed hover, so in all other cases, the change in drag as the blade rotates (due to changes in lift) are quite large.

As lift increases, drag increases, and the larger drag force tries to slow down the blade. When the drag decreases as lift decreases, the blade tries to speed up. So far, so good. This slowing down and speeding up would produce very large changes in the forces in the blade, if the blades were rigidly attached to the hub. These changes would quickly fatigue the blade and it would break. These large forces need to be removed, and one way to do that is to put in a hinge. See Figure 3-11. We have one reason for a lead–lag hinge. Now comes another.

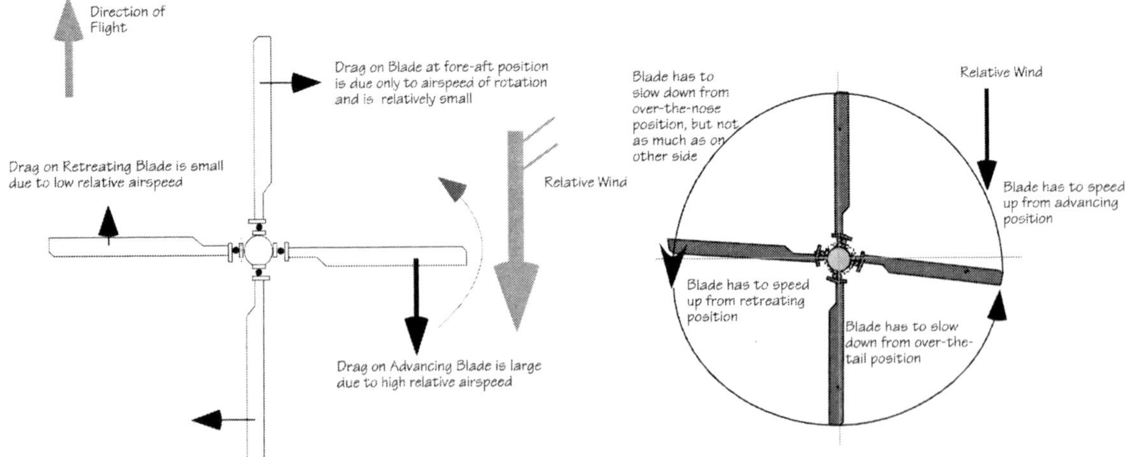

Figure 3-11 Drag Change with Airspeed

Center of Gravity Movement

As the blade flaps up and down (for a whole host of reasons such as changes in the lift force), the blade CG moves closer to and farther away from the center of the hub. If there was no coning angle already imposed on the blades, this flapping up and down would be confusing enough. It is necessary to remember the blades are also coned, and the flapping happens in addition to the coning. The Law of Conservation of Angular Momentum* requires the blade to speed up (as the CG moves toward the center of the hub) and slow down (as it moves out). We'll take a moment to explain this law.

A Brief Moment to Study Law

Conservation of Angular Momentum

All bodies in motion have momentum, that is mass times velocity. A body spinning around has a certain amount of momentum due to the mass spinning at some distance from the center. Most bodies have no way to change the distance between the mass and the center of the body, but for those bodies that do have the ability to change the distance, some surprising effects take place. If no external force is added to speed up or slow down the rotation, then the total momentum stays the same. This is the application of two principles studied earlier (Newton's First Law, and rotational energy).

Perhaps the most common example is in figure skating. A skater twirling on the toes of the skates has a certain amount of momentum, and no way to change that momentum. (We'll ignore the friction of the skates on the ice). When the twirling skater's arms move closer to the body, the distance of the arms from the center reduces, and since the momentum doesn't change, the only effect possible is for the skater to rotate more quickly.

A similar effect can be seen on a playground merry-go-round. Put some people on the outside edge and start it spinning. Without pushing, have the people move into the center. The speed of rotation increases. Move the people back to the outside, and it slows down again - the angular momentum is constant - the mass times the velocity times the inertia stays the same.

The total moment (momentum) can't change, so the velocity has to change to compensate for the change in location of the mass.The same thing happens to a helicopter blade- as the mass moves closer to or farther away from the center, the blade will increase or decrease speed with respect to the hub. Figure 3-12 shows the CG movement as the blade flaps up and down. In this diagram, the normal position of the blade and the position of the CG is considered to be the zero-airspeed hover position. Even when operating with a constant N_R, the blades change velocity as they go around the disk.

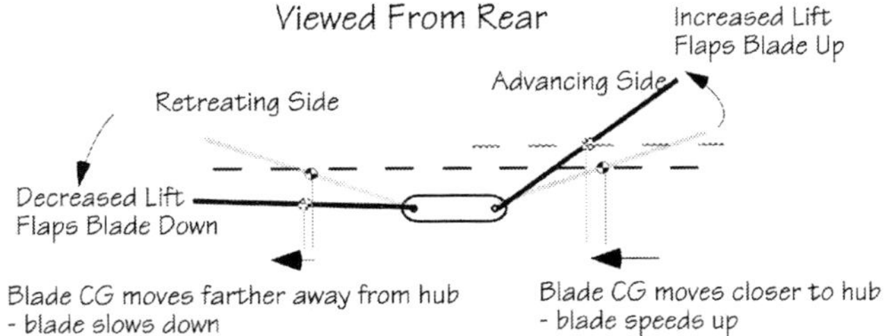

Figure 3-12 CG Movement Due to Blade Flapping

* Some call it Coriolis Effect, and it's just a variation of Newton's Laws

If the blade were rigidly attached to the hub, these two effects (changes of drag and movement of the blade CG) would introduce very high stresses to the root of the blade. Most metal rotor hubs and blades could not handle these stresses for very long. A lead–lag hinge, which permits the blade to move back and forth solves the problem.

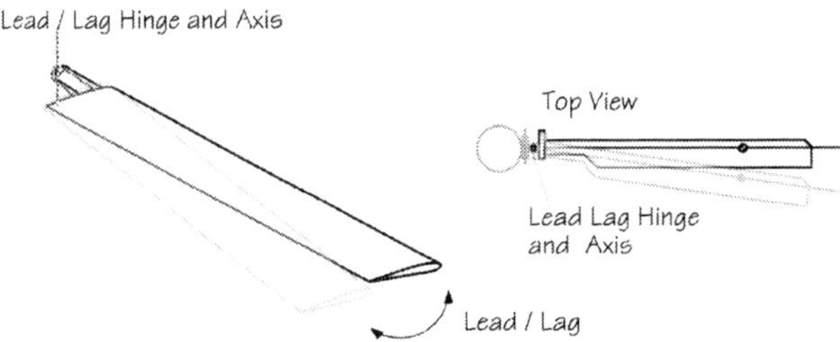

Figure 3-13 Lead–Lag Motion

Feathering of the Blade

Needless to say, there are some who would say this whole discussion has been approached the wrong away around. The flapping and lead–lag are results of many factors, and the only part of the whole process under the control of the pilot is blade feathering. This is shown in Figure 3-14 below.

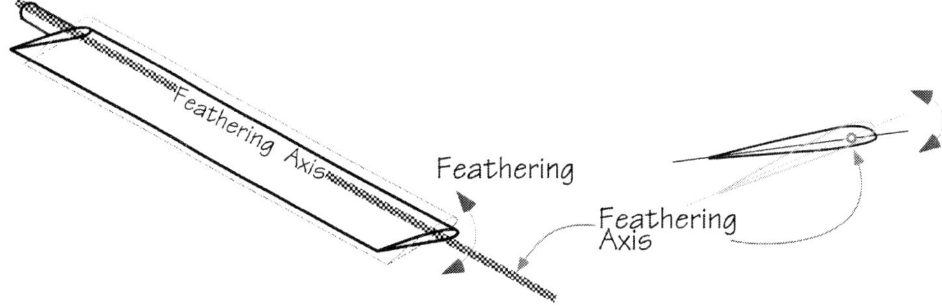

Figure 3-14 Blade Feathering

Summary of Chapter 3

This chapter has introduced the building blocks of understanding helicopter aerodynamics, starting with blade segments and putting them together into individual rotor blades. The next chapter will talk about these blades forming a disk, and some of the aerodynamics of said disk and how it is controlled.

4 More Basics of the Helicopter

In this chapter we take the individual blades and put them together to form the main rotor, and then discuss its features. Tail rotors are also covered. Up to now, everything we've discussed applies to all helicopters and rotors. Now we start to become more specific...

Generic Helicopter

The helicopter used in the beginner's part of this book is a combination of many different makes and models. This is for simplification and also lets us cover a lot points at once.

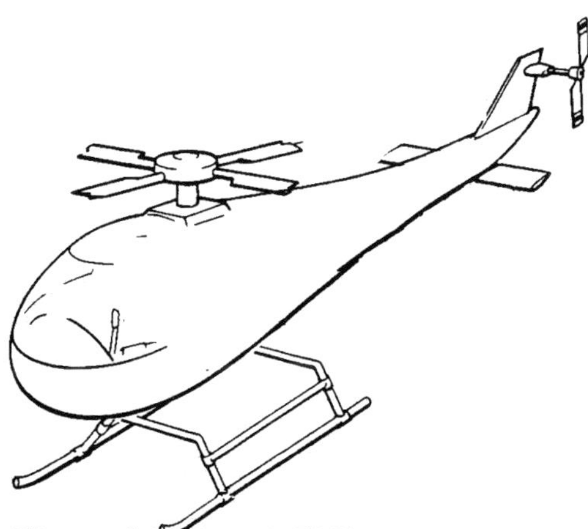

Figure 4-1 Generic Helicopter

The generic helicopter, shown in Figure 4-1, is a piston engined machine, with a four-bladed fully articulated rotor, a tail rotor and seating for two people. It has skid undercarriage, and no governor on the engine*.

The Whole Rotor

The rotor disk is merely several rotor blades together. Each of the blades makes its own individual contribution to the total lift and drag. In forward flight, the size and nature of these contributions depends upon the relative location of the blade on the disk (or azimuth) at any moment.

Telling the Blades Apart

Normally, the pilot doesn't need to worry about which blade is which - they should all appear and act the same. From time to time, such as on a pre-flight inspection or when carrying out blade tracking, it may be necessary to tell the blades apart.

Since there is more than one blade† on a helicopter - how exactly do you tell them apart? The method adopted by most manufacturers is to color–code them and their associated components - red, green, etc. It is thus normal to talk about the 'green' blade, the 'red' pitch change rod, the 'white' tail rotor blade and so on. Look for small colored dots or stripes of tape on the blades, pitch change rods, and so on.

Gyroscopic Precession

It is intended only to introduce the subject of *gyroscopic precession* at this point - the way it affects the control of the rotor will be dealt with later in this chapter. As this phenomena has a major effect, understanding is important.

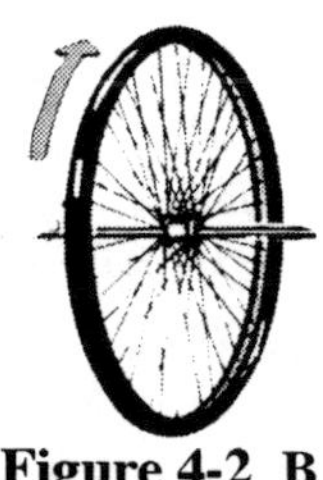

Figure 4-2 B icycle Wheel Spinning

The rotor system of the helicopter is a fairly heavy set of components, rotating at high speed. This makes it like a gyroscope, which has several important implications. If you have ever held a spinning bicycle wheel by the axle‡, and tried to change the angle of the wheel's rotation relative to the earth (or, more correctly stated technically, the plane the wheel is rotating in), you have experienced some of the properties of a gyroscope. If you stood on a swiveling table while you held the wheel, you would've seen the phenomena more clearly - when you tried to change the plane of rotation of the wheel, you would've rotated.

* Don't worry if you don't understand all the terms now. By the time you finish this book, you'll be able to throw these words around with confidence.

† There have been several helicopters made with only one blade- but obviously they weren't commercially successful, or they would still be around...

‡ If you haven't, it's worth trying. Take the wheel off the bike first, though.

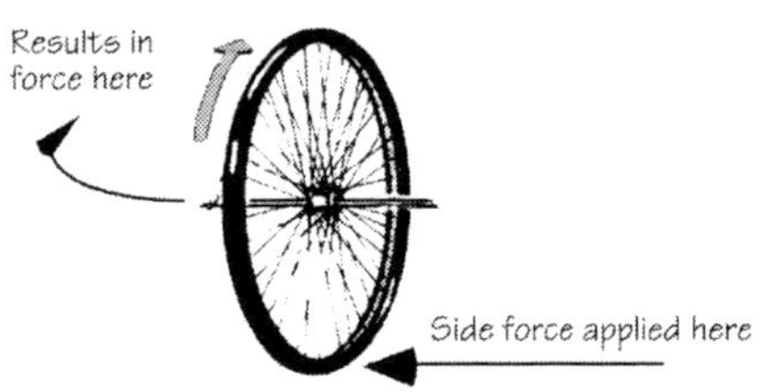

Figure 4-3 Gyrocscopic Forces

One of the properties of the gyroscope is *precession*. Simply stated, when a force is applied to deflect the gyroscope, the effect is seen 90° later in the direction of rotation. For example, if an 'up' force is applied to the edge of the gyroscope, the effect takes place 90° further around the direction of rotation. If you take a gyroscope (or bicycle wheel) spinning clockwise when viewed from the right side, and try to push to the left at the bottom (i.e 6 o'clock position) down, it will rotate left about the vertical axis. This is shown in Figure 4-2 and Figure 4-3.

For a rotor system, the effect is that whatever happens to the blade in terms of changing pitch (and hence AoA and lift and drag) will show up in the position of the blade 90° later. If we increase the pitch angle at the 0° position (back of the disk), the lift force at that point will increase and the effect will be felt 90° later. This is where the blade position will be at its highest (in other words, at the right hand side of the disk for our convention of rotation).

Airframe Relative Airspeed

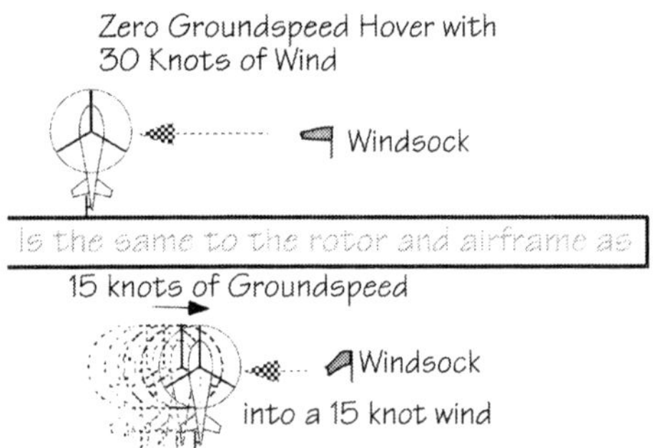

Figure 4-4 Airframe Relative Airspeed

Airframe relative airspeed is the direction and speed of air relative to the airframe of the helicopter. For example, a helicopter maintaining a stationary ground position in a 30knot wind from the right hand side is experiencing a 30knot relative airspeed from the right. Similarly a helicopter moving to the right at 15knots of ground speed with a wind of 15knots from the right is experiencing a 30knot relative airspeed from the right side. This is shown in Figure 4-4.

Remember that the airframe and rotor only react to airspeed*. They know nothing about groundspeed. We also know that we can have the wind coming from any direction in a helicopter, so we need a convention to say where it is with respect to some reference. We choose the front of the helicopter as the starting point.

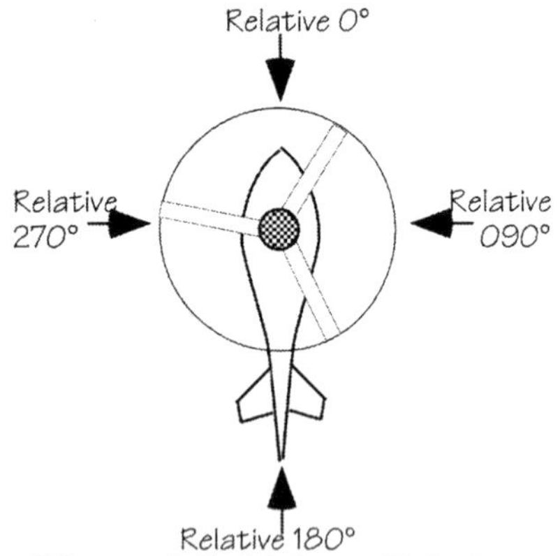

Figure 4-5 Airframe Relative Wind Convention

There is an angle convention for relative wind direction with respect to the airframe. 000° is over the nose of the helicopter, and proceeds clockwise so 090° is on the right hand side, and 180° is over the tail boom. This is shown in Figure 4-5. You may not use this much, but if you're trying to be precise, it's nice to know how talk proper.

The combination of wind and aircraft motion relative to the ground is often confusingly called 'sideward flight'. I have had many helicopter pilots ask why anyone would ever want to move sideways across the ground at relatively high speed (as opposed to facing the direction of travel). This is how many understand the term 'sideward flight'. When asked if they had to hover (zero–groundspeed hover) with a wind from the side, they would respond, "All the time". When it was explained this was what 'sideward flight' meant, they agreed the term was confusing. A more clear and precise expression is *side wind* or *rear wind* and that's what will be used in this book.

Relative Airflow and Disk

Earlier there was discussion of relative airflow for blade segments - this can now be expanded for the disk as a whole.

* Except when the airframe is sitting on the ground or water

Compare the airspeeds seen at the same parts of the disk in a hover (Figure 4-6a) to those seen at a high forward speed. What is the airspeed on the helicopter in Figure 4-6b?*

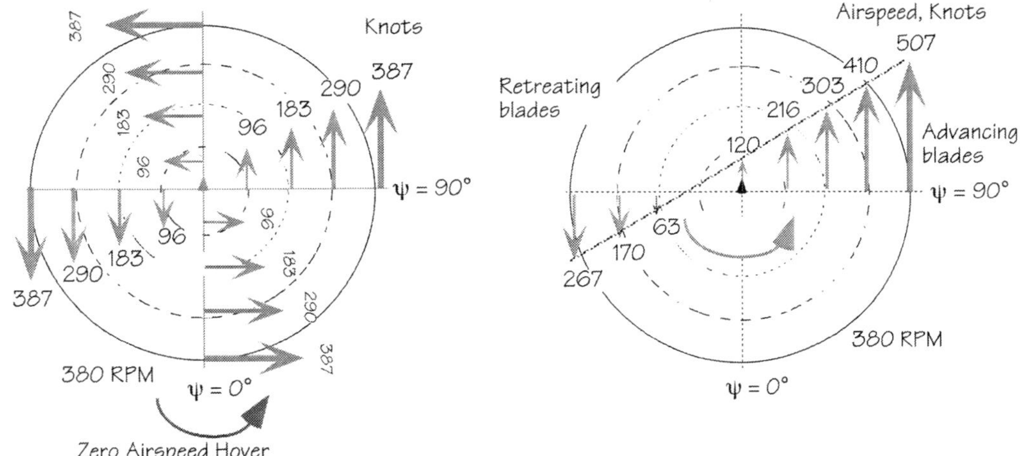

Figure 4-6 a) Zero–Airspeed Hover(b) High Forward Airspeed

Forward Flight and Dissymmetry of Lift

Early helicopters (before 1920) did not have the control mechanisms or performance necessary to achieve forward flight. That turned out to be a good thing, as they would have encountered the problems which were solved only when the autogiro came along (early 1920's). The autogiro has similar characteristics to the helicopter with regard to blade stresses and lift. At even modest forward speeds the first autogiro would roll to one side, (the retreating side of the disk) due to what has become known as *dissymmetry of lift*. The solution is discussed in the section on rotor hubs, but for now we will concentrate on the cause of the problem.

The terms '*advancing*' and '*retreating*' blade are used in helicopter aerodynamics. The retreating blade is moving away from the direction of flight, and the advancing blade is moving towards it. The advancing blade is at μ = 90° and the retreating blade is at μ = 270°. In more conventional terms, for our example helicopter, the advancing blade is on the right side and the retreating blade is on the left†. When the airspeed of forward flight is combined with the rotational airspeed of the blades, one side (the advancing side) of the disk sees a higher airspeed, and the other side (the retreating side) sees a much lower overall airspeed. This was shown graphically in Figure 4-6. In this figure, there is a 240 knot difference between the airspeed at the tip of advancing and retreating blades.

What effect will this have on the lift produced by the blades? For the largest difference, we'll compare segments close to the tips of the blades. We will only compare the lift on the left hand (or retreating) tip with the lift for the tip on the advancing (or right hand) side. For simplicity, let's start by saying the AoA is 7°, the same‡ as a similar segment on the advancing side. Everything else (ρ (air density), S (area of the blade segment), and C_L (Coefficient of Lift)) being the same, the lift on the tips of the two sides looks like this:

$$L = \frac{1}{2} \times \rho \times S \times C_L \times V^2 \quad \text{(EQ 10.)}$$

(C_L, S, ρ are equal on both sides of the disk in this example, so the difference in lift between the two segments depends only on the V or airspeed at the segment)

Left (or retreating blade) Lift	Right (or advancing blade) Lift
267^2= 71,289 lb.	507^2 = 257,049 lb.

* 120 Knots - either by doing the maths (dividing the difference between the two tip speeds by two), or looking at the airspeed at the center of the hub.

† In forward flight. For helicopters whose rotors turn in the 'other' direction, it's the opposite side.

‡ This can't happen, of course, but this is example is trying to show why it can't happen.

The result is:

$$\frac{(257,049)}{71,289} = 360\%$$

It's easy to see how having 360% (or 3 times) more lift on one side than on the other would cause the helicopter to roll. It's like having a fixed wing aircraft with one wing that grows larger and one that grows smaller as the airspeed increases.

The result is a very large difference in lift between the advancing and retreating side, which would roll the helicopter over. We have used an example of 120 knots as an extreme case, but even at quite slow airspeeds, (around 20 knots) the difference in lift from the advancing to the retreating side can be enough to cause problems.

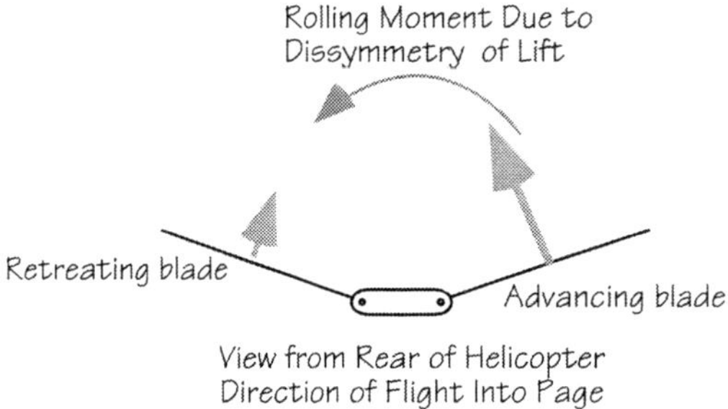

Figure 4-7 Dissymmetry of Lift

Fortunately, something has been done about it - in fact two things have been done about it. The first is the cyclical changing of blade pitch, and the second is the natural flapping of the blades caused by the cyclical changing of pitch.

Cyclical Change of Pitch

So how can we equalize the lift? Several options spring to mind- increase the retreating blade lift, or decrease the advancing side, or a bit of both. What do we have to work with?

The 'V' term is fixed, as is the density (ρ), the blade area (S), so the only term that can be changed is the C_L. The only way to change the C_L is by changing the angle of attack (AoA), and the only way to change the AoA is by changing the blade pitch angle. Remember AoA is indirectly controlled by blade pitch angle.

In our example, the C_L would have to change a tremendous amount (reduce over 300% on the advancing side) to equalize the lift.

By giving the blade on the advancing side a lower pitch angle (and hence AoA and C_L) than the blade on the retreating side, we can start to equalize the lift between the two sides. If we can increase the AoA on the retreating side at the same time, we'll get closer to equal lift on both sides.

Since the dissymmetry of lift gets worse as airspeed increases, we need to have the difference between the AoA on the advancing and retreating sides increasing as the helicopter goes forward.

If the mechanics are worked out correctly, the blade on the 'retreating' side will have an increase in blade pitch, (as well as AoA and C_L), and thus lift.

If we use our example blade and its diagram of C_L and C_D (Figure 2-22 on page 21), by using an AoA of 4° on the advancing side (with an C_L of 0.35), we make the total lift at the tip 92,675 units. If we work backward from this lift, for the retreating blade to have equal lift with the advancing blade, we need a C_L about 1.3, which equates to an AoA of about 16°.

The mechanics of how these changes in AoA occur will be covered in more detail in Chapter 23,"Advanced Helicopter Aerodynamics". For now we can say that by setting up the rotor head so the blade pitch angle at the advancing side is minimum, and the blade pitch angle at the retreating side is maximum, we can solve our problem of dissymmetry of lift.

$$L = \frac{1}{2} \times \rho \times S \times C_L \times V^2 \qquad \text{(EQ 11.)}$$

(S, ρ are equal in this example, C_L and V are varied)

	Left (or retreating) Side	Right (or advancing) Side
AoA	15°	3°
C_L (from Figure 2-22)	1.3	0.2
Lift	1.3 × 2672 = 51, 400	0.2 × 5072 = 51, 400

This method of equalizing lift also has the advantage of tilting the whole rotor disk forward, (which is what we want, as we should be moving forward).

The reduction of pitch on the advancing side means the blade at the 090° blade azimuth position (on the right hand or advancing side) is at a lower pitch angle relative to the blade on the opposite side of the disk. It also means gyroscopic precession then puts this same blade at its lowest position on the disk at the front. Since this is the way the disk should be tilted in forward flight, everything works well! (Don't worry, the mechanics of controlling blade pitch will be discussed shortly - more chicken and egg!)

Flapping to Equality

Another way of overcoming dissymmetry of lift is flapping of the blades. This method was used in autogiros before the invention of cyclic pitch, and still applies to tail rotors today. This was touched on briefly in Chapter 2 in the discussion about AoA changes due to flapping.

In forward flight, starting at the rear of the disk, (0° azimuth position) the rotor blade is experiencing an increase in relative airspeed (and hence lift) as it starts to advance towards the 090° position. This increase in lift makes the blade want to move up (and the flapping hinge lets it move up), but the act of moving up decreases the vertical component of velocity seen at the blade and decreases the angle of attack, slightly reducing the lift.

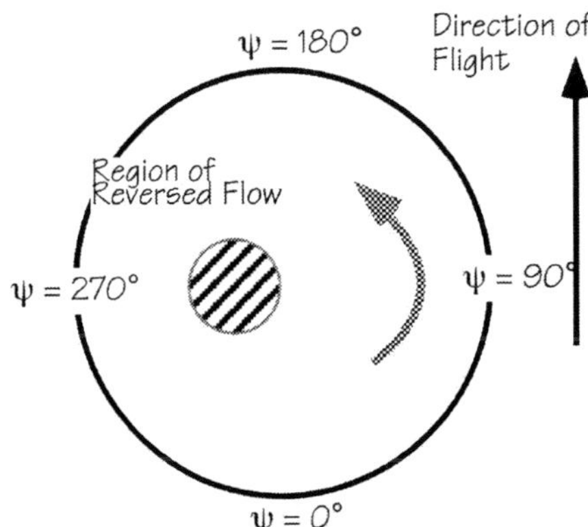

Figure 4-8 Reversed Flow Region

This velocity increase continues all the way to the front of the disk, with the airspeed gradually decreasing until, at the 12 o'clock (180° azimuth) position, it's back to essentially only rotational airspeed again.

An opposite effect takes place on the blade moving from the 'over the nose' (180° azimuth position): it sees a reduction in relative airspeed and hence lift, and it wants to fall. As it falls, it experiences an increase in AoA, which has a slight increase in lift. The two effects help to equalize the lift between the two halves.

Helicopters use both flapping and cyclic changes of pitch to equalize the lift.

In forward flight, there will be an area of the disk where the air is actually flowing backwards across the blades. This is called the area of *reversed flow*, and obviously it contributes a great deal to drag relative to airflow (not to blade rotation which it actually helps), and very little to lift. It is shown in Figure 4-8, and changes size with forward airspeed. It is actually a mixed blessing, as the drag in this reverse flow region helps to turn the rotor!

TOTAL LIFT FROM THE DISK

Tip Path Plane

The *tip path plane* (TPP) is the plane described by the tips of the rotor blades as they rotate. For simplicity, it is flat as shown in Figure 4-9 below. Having solved the problem of dissymmetry of lift, we can move on to other things.

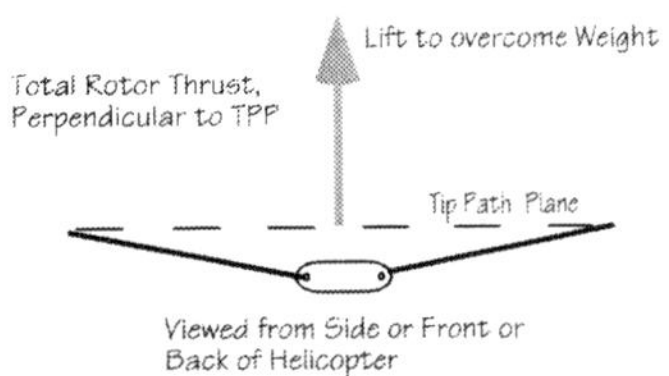

Figure 4-9 Tip Path Plane and Total Thrust - Zero–Airspeed Hover

The sum of the Useful Force of all the blades is the total rotor thrust, and it can be assumed to act from the hub, perpendicular to the plane made by the tips of the blades. This is shown in Figure 4-9 for a helicopter in a zero–airspeed hover. (Note there are only two blades shown here - this is for simplicity only.)

If we tilt the disk, (in order to move into forward flight), the total reaction will have both horizontal and vertical components. These components are called Thrust (or horizontal component) and Lift (or vertical component)*. In Figure 4-10 below the tilt of the tip path plane is greatly exaggerated. The reasons for this tilt lie in the requirements for the helicopter to be in trim, which is discussed in Chapter 5, Balance and Weight.

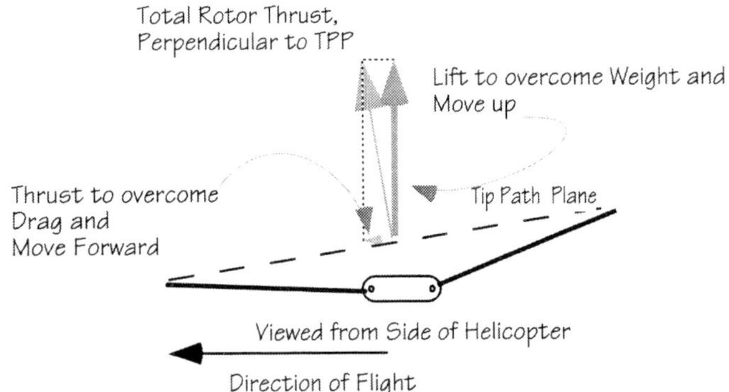

Figure 4-10 Tilted Tip Path Plane in Forward Flight

DRAG AT DIFFERENT PARTS OF THE DISK

Just as we could calculate the lift at different parts of the disk, we can compare the drag. Remember the two formulas for lift and drag are nearly the same, with only the coefficient being different.

We'll compare the drag on the advancing blade and the retreating blade for the same conditions of moderate airspeed.

Just as there is dissymmetry of lift, there is dissymmetry of drag. Unlike lift, drag can be unequal on the two sides of the disk, without the adverse effect of unequal lift. But drag becomes something that must be catered for on each blade because it changes so much with rotation. Figure 3-11 on page 28 shows the drag for the advancing side, retreating side and the fore-aft positions

Total Drag on the Disk

The total drag on the disk is the sum of the drag of each blade. It is possible to use drag as a way to measure the lift being produced. Since the drag acts from the aerodynamic center of the blades, which are at some distance from the hub, it is shown as a moment - i.e. some foot pounds of moment (or torque)†.

It takes engine power to turn the rotor, and the amount of power it takes to turn the rotor at constant RPM depends upon the drag from the rotor. This is shown in Figure 4-11 below.

* Sorry about all the changing of terms, and repeated use of the same words, but there is a scarcity of suitable simple words to explain these phenomenon.

† Unfortunately, no one has found a really good way to do this.

In a steady hover, the lift produced is equal to the weight of the helicopter, so indirectly, we can measure lift by knowing how much power it takes to hover.

The drag needed to just turn the blades when the helicopter is on the ground is a good indication of this. At *Minimum Pitch on Ground* (MPOG)*, it normally takes between 20% and 30% of the rated power to turn the rotor blades at normal N_R before we get any usefulness out of them.

Another way to look at this is that the engine is needed primarily for overcoming drag created by the rotor blades producing lift. Or if, you like, lift is a useful secondary effect of turning the blades!

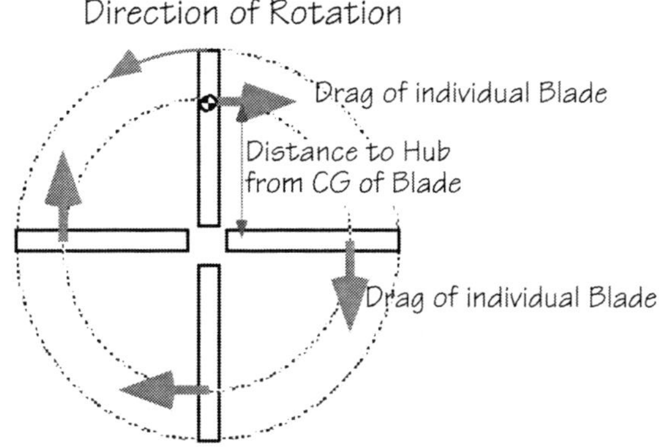

Figure 4-11 Drag Moment on the Hub in a zero airspeed hover

Keeping the Blades Clean

If you think about this for a moment, one of the sources of drag is friction on the blades. Fixed–wing aircraft obtain performance improvements by waxing the wings and fuselage, yet you hardly ever see anyone waxing and cleaning off the accumulation of small bugs and dirt on helicopter blades. There are some fuel savings to be made, but mostly performance improvements to be seen if you keep the blades clean! Tail rotors too!

This is one of the reasons why ice build-up on the blades is a bad thing. The drag is increased at the same time as the lift reduces. A double whammy!

Flapback or Blowback

Let us take a rotor turning at a steady speed, sitting on the ground, with the controls neutral, and no wind. Suddenly, a wind gust of 10 knots hits the rotor disk from the front. This changes the relative airspeed on the blades. One is now advancing into the wind, and one retreating. Since the horizontal component of relative airflow across each of its segments has increased, the lift of the advancing blade increases. This means the advancing blade (at μ of 90°) will start to flap up, and the effect will be at a maximum 90° later, so the blade at the front of the helicopter will be higher than it was to prior to this gust. The blades on the retreating side will similarly see a reduction in lift and thus the back of the disk will be lower than before the gust. The pilot has not moved the controls, but the rotor disk has moved and tilted the tip path plane backwards slightly. This phenomena is called *flapback* or *blowback*, and is shown in Figure 4-12 below. This is one of the reasons for the earlier statement that the tip path plane may be at an angle to the mast.

The rotor will always flap away from the relative wind.

* also known as *Flat Pitch*

The rotor will flap back in forward flight, however the effect is hidden from the pilot. The only time it becomes apparent is during a transition to forward flight, when an additional cyclic stick input is needed to overcome the flapback due the change in airspeed.

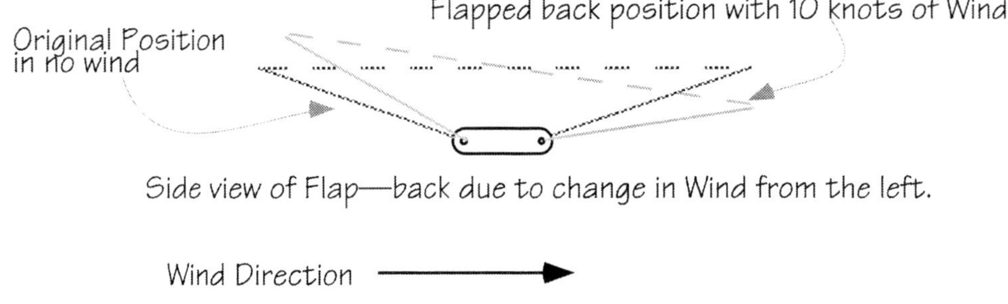

Figure 4-12 Flapback or Blowback of the Main Rotor.

Rotor Heads and Components

The rotor head of any helicopter is a fascinating study of mechanical system design, and represents the culmination of lots of design, as well as trial and error. What appears to be very simple is in reality very complex, and truly a thing of beauty. Given there are so many different designs of rotor heads, this part of book can only touch on some of the major themes. Again, the aim is to proceed from the simple to the complex. This is covered in more detail in Chapter 24,"Flight Controls and Rotor Heads".

Fully Articulated Rotor Hub

The most common rotor head type (in terms of number of different models and types using the concept) is the *fully articulated* head. In the section on blades, and for our example helicopter, we are using a fully articulated system. This system uses hinges to reduce the stresses the blades produce which would otherwise be transmitted to the hub. Different helicopters have different order of the hinges from the hub outboard - some put the flapping hinge first, others the lead lag hinge first, etc. Figure 4-13 shows a typical fully articulated rotor head. It's called fully articulated because it can move in all the possible axis.

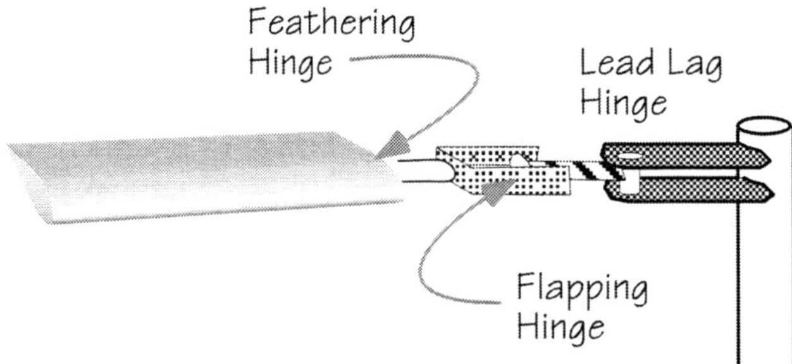

Figure 4-13 Fully Articulated Rotor Head

It's easy to see why we need a feathering hinge, and we discussed 2 reasons for a lead- lag hinge. But why do we need a flapping hinge?

Without the flapping hinge, we would not be flying helicopters today. The credit for the flapping hinge goes to Juan de Cierva, whose initial experiments with autogiros were unsuccessful. At a fairly slow speed in the takeoff run, they would all roll over to the left, and no amount of control input would stop the roll. He analyzed the problem as a dissymmetry of lift between the advancing and retreating side, but the solution was evasive. Eventually he came up with the flapping hinge as a way to let the two sides of the disk achieve their own equilibrium of lift, and this solution has been used in many helicopter rotor heads since in one way, shape or form.

The principles of rotor systems covered here are applicable also to the two–bladed teetering head, with some exceptions as covered in "The Teetering Rotor Head" on page 233.

Control of the Rotor

The Swashplate

There is a problem trying to transmit the commands of the pilot to the rotating mass of metal overhead. The way this is most frequently accomplished is through the *swashplate* system, although other systems do exist. The swashplate has two main parts - the fixed part that is firmly attached to the non–rotating part of the airframe, and the rotating part, which is attached to the rotor. The driveshaft (or main rotor mast) passes up between the two swashplates to drive the hub, as is shown in Figure 4-14 below.

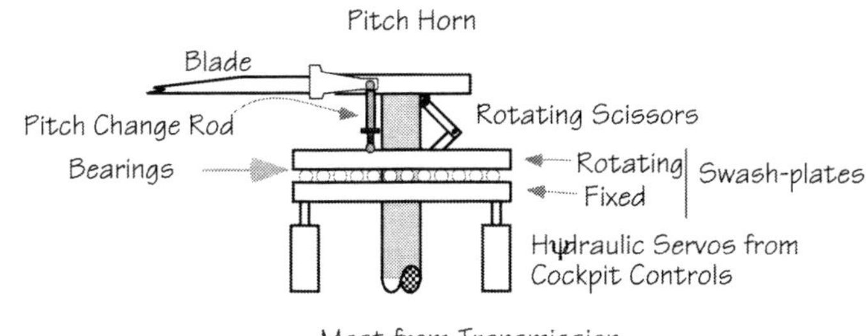

Figure 4-14 Swashplate

Other mechanisms for transmitting the pilots inputs to the rotor blades are discussed in Chapter 24,"Flight Controls and Rotor Heads".

Phasing of Control Inputs

The ideal helicopter will have the pilot directly controlling the tilt of the tip path plane. The first problem of how to transmit these commands from a stationary part of the airframe to the rotating rotor blades so they behave correctly, is solved by the swashplate.

The second problem is that to move the blade against the aerodynamic forces acting on it, some moment arm will be needed. (This is the reason the pitch change rods are relatively far away from the pitching axis of the blade - they need some leverage.) We now add the pitch change rod system to the swashplate, as shown in Figure 4-15 below. Tilt the swashplate, and the pitch change rods transmit this movement to the blades and eventually the rotor blades follow the swashplate position. This still hasn't solved one of the problems, namely the gyroscopic properties of the rotor disk*.

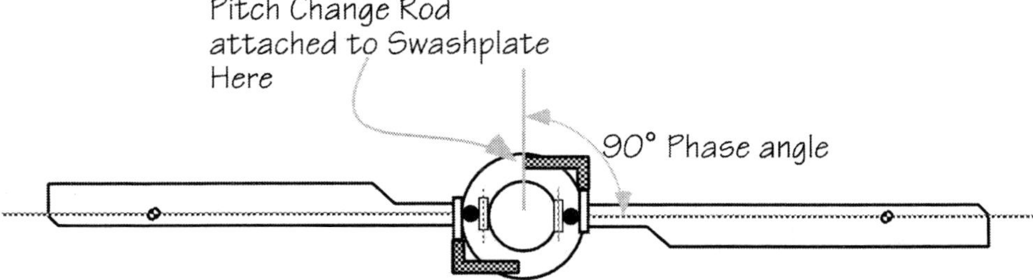

Figure 4-15 Top View 90° Control Phasing

* Rumor has it that Igor Sikorsky didn't believe in this gyroscopic effect for quite a while, but finally came around.

Control of the direction of main rotor thrust must take this gyroscopic characteristic into account. For example, if it is desired to tilt the tip path plane forward, the input to the rotor disk must be made 90° prior to the place of desired action. This is called *control phasing* and is shown in and Figure 4-15 above and Figure 4-16 below.

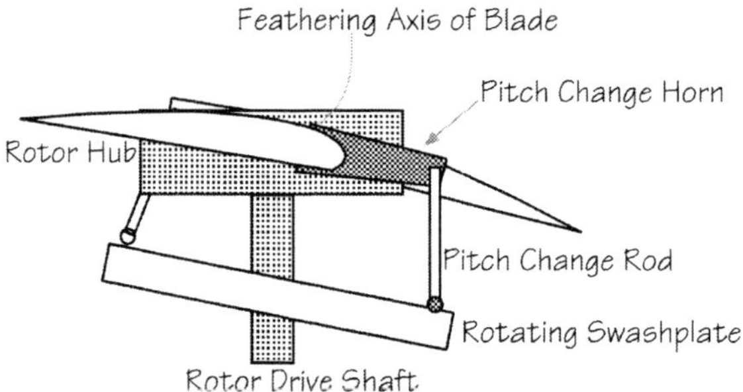

Figure 4-16 Side View of 90° Phasing

In this case, the pitch of the rotor blade must be decreased 90° before the lowest point desired in the tip path plane, and increased 90° before the highest point desired. Phasing of the control inputs means where the pitch change rods meet the swashplate must be 90° before the radial position of the blade.

Another way to look at this phenomena is to consider what happens in a zero–airspeed hover when the pitch on a blade is changed. For example, the blade over the tail boom is given an increase in blade pitch. This increases the angle of attack and the lift force on the blade. The blade wants to move up, however the gyroscopic effect results in the blade reaching its maximum position 90° later. The blade will be at its highest point when it is at the right hand (090° azimuth) side of the helicopter.

If the opposite were to happen to the blade over the nose of the helicopter, (i.e. a reduction in blade pitch) the effect would be for the blade on the left hand side to be at the low point, and the tip path plane to tilt to the left. Eventually, the helicopter would move to the left.

In two–bladed helicopters, the control rods are attached to the blades in such a way to ensure they get their input from the rotating swashplate 90° early. This is relatively simple on a two–bladed head, but is an engineering challenge with more than two blades. Figure 4-17 shows a side view of a typical swashplate, when moved by the cockpit controls.

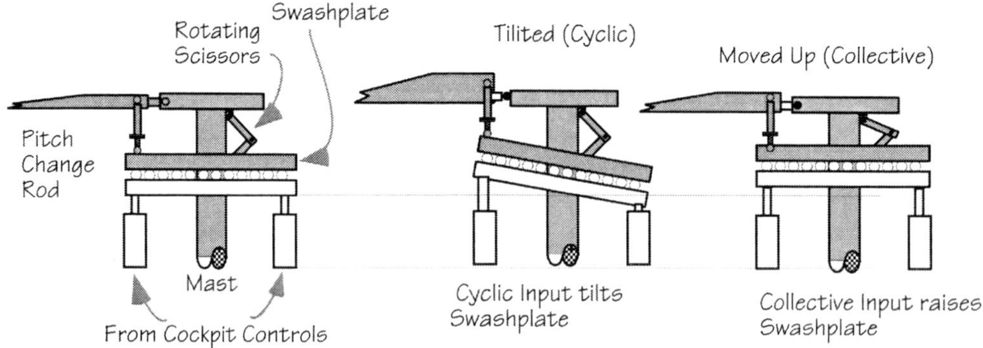

Figure 4-17 Swashplate Positions

Rotating Scissors Assembly

An interesting element of the control mechanism is the *rotating scissors** - why is it there? The answer is to make sure the rotating swashplate stays in the same angular position with respect to the rotor mast and hub. It wouldn't do to have the swashplate moving around the shaft, changing position relative to the shaft, changing the phase angle of the inputs.

* Is this plural or singular? I can' t figure it out. I have never seen a scissor by itself.

So What?

A lot of material here for the beginning helicopter to pilot to absorb. Don't expect to remember all of it (thank God, I can hear you say). There is no requirement for you to be able to design a rotor head, but you should remember that someone has gone to a lot of trouble to make sure you have a suitable set of controls so that the helicopter will respond in a natural manner.

TAIL ROTORS

Something has to be added to stop the fuselage turning in the opposite direction to the main rotor's direction of rotation. (Remember Newton's third law - for every action, there is an equal and opposite reaction?) The engine is attached to the fuselage, and when the engine tries to turn the rotor, the fuselage will want to turn the opposite direction to the rotor. In the hover, there is no airflow over the fuselage to stop the rotation, so something must be added.

The reaction between the rotor and the fuselage is called *torque*. The amount of torque depends upon the power applied to the main rotor, and is more fully explained in "Top View Balance of Forces - Torque Reaction" on page 69. Obviously something must stop the fuselage rotating, or we'd never have a successful helicopter*!

Anti-Torque Control

In the hover, there is no aerodynamic pressure acting on the vertical stabilizer to stop the rotation, and the most common way to prevent the fuselage rotating is the tail rotor†. It is typically located at the end of the tail boom and is mechanically coupled to the main rotor. It produces thrust to oppose the rotation of the fuselage.

Since the amount of power given to the main rotor is changeable, this changes the torque reaction on the fuselage, and the thrust of the tail rotor must be increased or decreased to neutralize the torque effect.

The tail rotor is the most common way of accomplishing this. It is simple and direct, and for small helicopters, the lightest way of controlling the yaw axis of the helicopter.

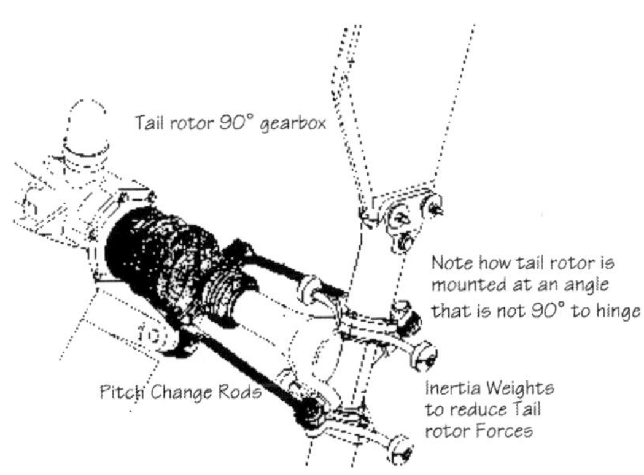

Figure 4-18 Typical Tail Rotor

The pitch of the blade is controlled by the pedals, which change collective pitch only‡. The pitch range needed by the tail rotor to provide thrust in both directions is quite large, in fact, much larger than the main rotor. Total travel is typically about 40° of blade angle.

The tail rotor has an unenviable task - working in incredibly confused airflow, at very high rotational speeds, and with the ever–present danger of people walking into it, or of being used as a bush-clearing tool. The very job it is trying to do is often made more difficult by obstacles (such as vertical stabilizers) placed in the path of its airflow. Figure 4-18 shows a typical tail rotor.

In a typical light helicopter, the tail rotor can take between 5 and 15% of the total power installed.

Where and why the tail rotor is placed is obvious, however it is not without its own special problems - covered in more detail in Chapter 7,"Balance and Weight".

* But we would have very interesting spinning top.
† Other types of anti-torque control will be covered later.
‡ The tail rotor of the Super Puma (SA-332) incorporates some cyclic feathering to reduce stresses. There are no lead–lag hinges. Several other helicopters have similar tail rotor control systems.

Summary of Chapter 4

This chapter has built on the basic aerodynamics presented in the previous chapters by integrating the blades into a disk and talking about features of the rotor disk. Many of the effects discussed here may be hidden from the pilot, as they have been overcome by design. That does not mean they don't happen, or that the pilot should ignore them.

The next chapter will make a break from aerodynamics, and explain some things about the atmosphere, in general terms as a preparation for understanding performance. Be prepared for some of the concepts here to be raised again.

5 Air, Wind and Weather

Introduction

This chapter is placed close to the beginning of the book so you can begin to understand the fundamental properties of the air. There are two distinct parts to this understanding- one a scientific one, with some numbers (but not too many), and another that is definitely more 'touchy-feely'. The scientific one, describing the atmosphere, will be used in explaining lots of the performance aspects of helicopter flying, while the part about the wind will hopefully awaken and develop an intuitive feel for watching all the things that show us where the wind is. After all, we cannot see the air or wind to measure it and must rely on other indications, whether from instruments or external signs such as smoke or dust.

What Temperature is That?

Most of the world uses the metric system, except, it seems, aviation. We not only use feet, but nautical miles. The one place where aviation does seem to be pretty standard is in the use of the Celsius (°C) temperature scale instead of Farenheit (°F). Since nearly all items related to temperature are available (if not given only) in °C, - *Outside Air Temperature* (OAT) on the aircraft air temperature indicator, and temperatures provided by the weather services are nearly always in °C, that's how we'll talk for this book.

Where do we Measure Vertical Distance From?

To really confuse neophytes, we worry about two different vertical measurements. One is for measuring distance above the ground, which is correctly known as *height*, and is taken from Above Ground Level, abbreviated (AGL). The other reference is relative to distance above Mean Sea Level (MSL), and is called *altitude*. Try to be precise when using these terms, as they mean two different things.

You can be at a height of 100' AGL while at an altitude of 5,000' MSL.

International Standard Atmosphere

Not all air is the same - some days are hot, some cold, some windy, some calm*. Some are hot and muggy, while others are dry and cold. How can we measure (much less predict) performance of the helicopter if the air is different from one day to the next? How can we compare the performance of different types if they are tested in different conditions? Many years ago, it was decided to develop a standard model of the atmosphere called the *International Standard Atmosphere (ISA)*, which describes the air in a precise way.

Standard Day

The ISA 'standard day' is at sea level, (0' altitude) at an air temperature of 15°C (59°F), with an air pressure to support a column of mercury 29.92" high in an evacuated cylinder†. Away from sea level, the air is assumed to cool at a standard lapse rate of 1.98°C per 1000' ‡. At all times, there is assumed to be no wind and no water vapor in the air in the Standard Atmosphere.

Pressure Altitude

Pressure altitude (PA) is altitude measured against a standard barometric condition of 29.92" (or 1013.2 millibars (mb)) of mercury. In other words to obtain the pressure altitude, set 29.92 in the altimeter window. The resulting altitude can be compared to the ambient barometric pressure (i.e. the altimeter setting air traffic control provides (or the reading in the setting window when the altimeter is set to read the altitude AMSL)) for interest's sake. In most parts of the world, helicopter flying is with reference to an altimeter setting giving the height above sea level. Performance measurements always use pressure altitude. The reader may ask why

* As they say here in Southern California, don't trust air you can't see...
† For those who use the millibar scale, it's 1013.2 millibars.
‡ Up to the sort of altitudes that helicopters work at - it gets different at really high altitudes

this is so - we equate the performance on any given day to a known standard. If you like, it is a way of ensuring that all performance values can be equated to the conditions that exist when you are flying. More on this as the chapter goes on.

A rule of thumb is:

- every inch of barometric pressure at sea level that the ambient pressure differs from standard equals 1,000' pressure altitude difference*.

For example, a barometric pressure of 30.42" at sea level gives a pressure altitude of -500' (the pressure is higher than standard, so the pressure altitude is lower). At 5,000' AMSL, (taken from a map elevation and set on the altimeter) the pressure is found to be 29.52", so the pressure altitude would be 5,400' if 29.92" were set on the sub-scale of the altimeter.

Standard Temperature for an Altitude (or Lapse Rate)

This results in a formula for determining the 'standard temperature' at Pressure Altitude (PA) measured in feet Above Mean Sea Level (AMSL):

$$\text{Standard Temperature at Pressure Altitude} = 15°C - \left(\left(\frac{\text{Pressure Altitude}}{1,000'}\right) \times 1.98°C\right) \qquad \text{(EQ 12.)}$$

At 5,000' pressure altitude, the standard temperature should be

$$15°C - \left(\left(\frac{5,000'}{1,000'}\right) \times 1.98°C\right) = 5.5°C \qquad \text{(EQ 13.)}$$

For those who don't want to remember it's exactly 1.98°C per 1,000', a rough approximation of 2°C per 1,000' is pretty darn close. For our example, this gives

$$15 - (2 \times 5) = 5°C \qquad \text{(EQ 14.)}$$

Non-Standard Day

The standard day is mighty rare - I've seen something close to it twice in my life, (only in pressure altitude and temperature, there was always a wind and humidity) so it is necessary to be able to describe other conditions with respect to this elusive creature. So we're left with a lot of non-standard days. We describe how much of a difference from standard by comparing it to the normal temperature for that pressure altitude.

If the term 'ISA +15 °C' is used, it means 15°C warmer than standard at all altitudes. At sea level, this is 30°C; and at 5,000'PA, +20°C (+5°C being the 'standard' temperature at 5,000'PA). This is another way to say 30°C at sea level is warm, (ISA +15), but relatively speaking, 30°C at 5,000'PA is really warm, (ISA +25) at least as far as performance is concerned. So air temperature is more than just temperature - it must be considered against the 'standard' air temperature for that pressure altitude.

In Figure 5-1, there is a line labeled ISA - this shows the 'standard' OAT at that pressure altitude.

Density Altitude

The density of an object is the mass per unit volume. Remember the lift formulae? The "ρ" term in the lift equation is Greek letter rho, for the density of the air. This section will show how it is determined.

Density altitude is a measure of the density of air corrected for ambient temperature. Another way of saying this is

- it is the equivalent pressure altitude with standard temperature.

* Sorry, but there is no easy–to–calculate rule of thumb for those who use millibar altimeters. One mb equals about 30 feet. Which leads to another question - why don't all altimeters have both types of windows on them?

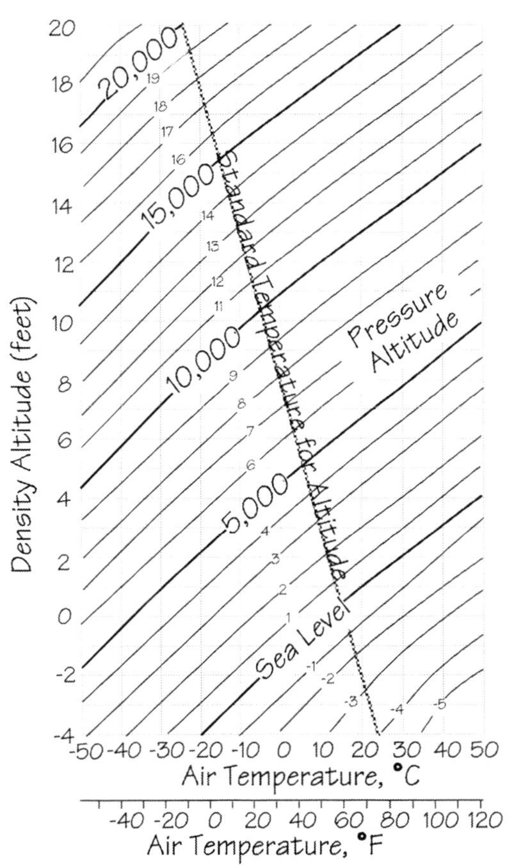

Figure 5-1 Standard Density Altitude Chart

For example, on a hot day, the density of the air is less than standard for that altitude. This affects power *required* by the airframe, sometimes significantly. For this reason, density altitude is used - it is a combination of the pressure altitude (obtained by setting the altimeter scale to standard pressure (29.92" or 1013.2 mb) and correcting it for the air temperature. For example, 1,800' pressure altitude and +40°C gives a density altitude of 5,000'. Conversely, at 9,000' pressure altitude and -36°C, the density altitude is also 5,000'. The air is the same density as air at 5,000', +5°C. The chart at Figure 5-1 shows how to calculate density altitude. Note the line that says "Standard Temperature for Altitude". This is the ISA standard temperature for that altitude.

Such charts are normally found in FMs, and are often used to refer to the rest of the performance charts.

Sometimes, FM charts will incorporate a density altitude calculation. If part of the chart required pressure altitude and OAT be used prior to extracting more data, this is just a way of ensuring the density altitude calculation is made. An example of this is shown in Figure 5-2.

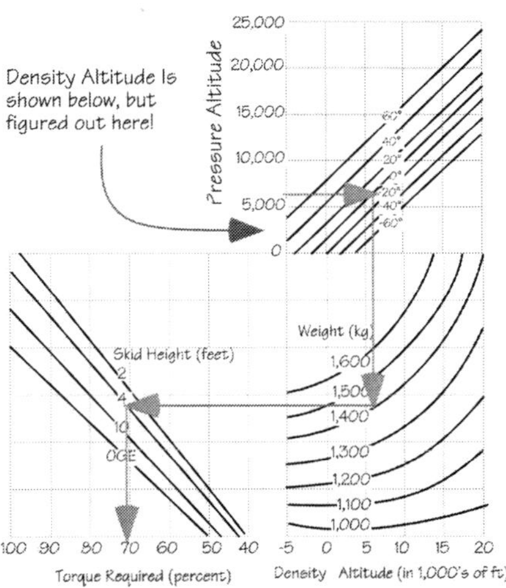

Figure 5-2 Performance Chart with DA Calculation on the Top

Importance of Understanding Density Altitude

Helicopter pilots need to understand density altitude for two reasons. It affects:

- the power required by any airframe in nearly every situation, and
- the power available from a piston engine (but not a turbine engine... see Chapter 29,"The Turbine Engine" for more details)

Avoiding Confusion

An easy way to confuse things is by talking about conditions as being 'better' than ISA. Does this mean warmer than ISA or colder than ISA? Be precise and say ISA+ x° or ISA- x°.

Other confusing terms are high or low *density* as opposed to high or low *density altitude*. High density (lots of molecules of air per cubic foot) is a low density altitude (i.e. -2,000 feet- Death Valley on a cold day) whereas low density (few molecules per cubic foot) is high density altitude (i.e. 8,000 feet). Be precise (and different) and say high density altitude or low density altitude. If you have to use just 'density' say 'low air density' or 'high air density' to avoid confusing people. Perhaps using 'thinner air' or 'more dense air' would also help keep things clear.

The How and Why of Density Altitude

All this engineering explanation may have confused you. A simple way to understand this very important point about aerodynamics is that the thinner the air (the higher the density altitude), the less lift the blades will produce with everything else being equal. Now, if you've ever tried jogging in the mountains, you'll know the air is definitely thinner, but if the air is hotter, it is also thinner (which is how hot air balloons can work*). Now, we have no direct way of measuring the thinness or thickness of the air, so a convenient way is to use an equivalent of altitude. Unfortunately, some folks have not understood the importance of density and have been embarrassed (or worse) when they asked their aircraft to perform beyond its capabilities in air that was much thinner than anticipated.

Relative Humidity

Relative humidity is the measure of how close a body of air is to the maximum amount of water vapor it is capable of holding. Confused? The explanation is relatively simple.

How much water in the form of vapor that a volume of air can hold depends on the air temperature. The warmer the air, the more water vapor it can hold. When a volume of air has all the water vapor it can handle at that particular temperature, it is said to be *saturated* and the relative humidity is 100%. At this point, clouds will form, and adding any further water vapor will cause the excess to fall out of the air, as rain or snow (depending upon the temperature). Cooling the air that is saturated will result in the air not being able to hold all the water vapor, and the result will also be precipitation. This is shown in Figure 5-3 below.

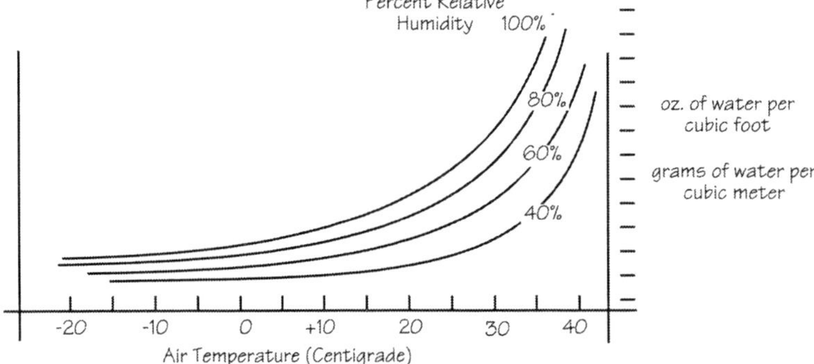

Figure 5-3 Relative Humidity vs. Air Temperature

Humidity decreases the density of a volume of air because the mass of a molecule of water vapor is less than the average mass of the gases that make up air. Less mass means that in a given volume of air, adding water vapor displaces other gases and the overall weight per unit volume goes down, and the effect is the same as increasing density altitude.

Hot air can hold quite a bit of water without becoming saturated, and when air close to saturation is cooled, the water vapor will start to show up as clouds, mist, fog or rain. Air cools as it ascends, so at some point the relative humidity will also rise until at some height, the relative humidity will be 100% and clouds will form.

Relatively speaking, warm air (which normally occurs closer to the surface of the earth than at great altitudes) will be able to hold a great deal more water than really cold air.

The normal humidity for the ISA is none, nil, zip, nada, zero percent. Typically, this doesn't happen anywhere in the world, but a standard had to be set. Normally, humidity is ignored in the density altitude charts, as it requires a hygrometer†. A good rule of thumb is in high humidity and hot temperatures, add 1,000' to the density altitude.

* But this book isn't titled Burner and Gasbag - the Art and Science of Hot Air Balloons.

† Or a set of wet and dry bulb thermometers, and I don't know too many people who carry these in their helicopter...

If you are lucky enough to have aviation grade weather information available, then the difference in degrees between the air temperature and the *dew point* can also indicate the amount of humidity. Not much difference between these two temperatures means high humidity, lots of degrees between the two means a dry day.

Dew Point is the temperature where that body of air will be saturated and water vapor will start to fall out of the air- clouds will form, or if there is a suitable piece of material available, drops of dew will be deposited.

If you're in fog or rain, the humidity is 100%, isn't it? Not necessarily. Fog will be 100% humidity, but rain can be falling from above into drier air, which may not have 100% humidity. In some cases, rain will fall and evaporate in the drier air, long before it hits the ground. This is called *virga* - rain falling but not hitting the ground.

Wrong Information

The barometric altimeter isn't accurate in all conditions. For example, if you don't have the correct pressure set in the window, don't expect the information you read on the dial to be correct. If you are a great height above the source of the barometric pressure setting and the temperature between you and the source is not conforming to the ISA model, don't expect the altimeter to be correct either[*]. "Corrections to the Altimeter in Cold Weather" on page 290 shows how cold weather affects these errors.

We won't try to confuse things by using words like 'True Altitude', as this isn't a recognized term, but we'll compare actual altitude[†] to indicated altitude.

The barometric altimeter is calibrated for ISA conditions of lapse rate and temperature. Simply stated, if you are warmer or colder than ISA, or you know the lapse rate is not 1.98°C per 1,000 feet, you can expect there to be a difference between what your altimeter says (indicated altitude) and where you actually are (actual altitude above mean sea level). Look in books on weather[‡] to find out more about this phenomena.

More Wrong Information

The altimeter is not the only instrument that isn't always telling the truth. The airspeed indicator also only indicates the truth close to the surface of the earth and at relatively low airspeeds.

The fundamental function of the airspeed indicating system is to show the difference between the static air pressure and the total air pressure or the dynamic air pressure. If you remember that concept, the indications and corrections to the airspeed indicator become easier to understand.

There are several different ways to look at airspeed - the value that is shown on the airspeed indicator (called the *Indicated Air Speed (IAS)*), and the airspeed after the IAS is corrected for errors due to the position of the pitot and static ports, called the *Calibrated Airspeed (CAS)*. *True Air Speed (TAS)* is CAS corrected for non-standard temperature and pressure. At high speeds (greater than 200 Knots) and high altitudes (above 10,000 feet AMSL) there is a large enough difference between IAS and TAS to worry about. Since the helicopter seldom ventures above 10,000' and never above 200 Knots, these differences are often ignored[**].

If we start with the IAS, i.e. the airspeed we see on the instrument, we should realize that this is merely the measure of the difference between the static air pressure and the total pressure of the air entering the pitot tube, which is then registered on the face of the instrument.

* Ah! How will you know? The answer is 'you won't'. Don't worry about it too much.

† The only reason for mentioning this at all, is that during the expected lifespan of this book GPS will be able to provide incredibly accurate information (is it height or altitude?), and you may wish to know why you are reading something different on your pressure altimeter.

‡ Listed in the Bibliography

**If you want accurate navigation however, you need to pay attention to calculating TAS.

Being a mechanical instrument, the airspeed indicator is going to have errors in displaying information. Added to those are the errors found in flight testing, (errors of measuring airspeed and altitude, given in correction charts in fixed wing aircraft*) and the result is Calibrated Air Speed.

Unfortunately, we know that air is not uniformly dense or the same temperature. This give rise to the need to make a correction to the CAS in order to determine the real speed through the air.

Density altitude is also used indirectly when you compute True Airspeed (TAS). True Airspeed is the real airspeed, not what's shown on the airspeed indicator. For most helicopter operations, low to the ground, and a slow speeds (i.e. less than 150 knots), the difference between Indicated Airspeed (IAS) and TAS is small. If, on the other hand, you want to go long distances and need to know your real airspeed, TAS is the only correct answer. TAS is covered in a lot more detail in Chapter 25,"Advanced Performance", but for now, you should understand that the airspeed indicator shows indicated airspeed, which ain't necessarily the true airspeed value.

Nearly everything you'll be asked to do in the early stages of learning to fly helicopters will be by reference to Indicated Airspeed, so that should ease your mind a bit as well.

There, that wasn't so bad, was it? Now you know quite a bit more about something you thought was simple.

Wind!

In my experience, us helicopter pilots are much more conscious of both wind speed and direction than our fixed–wing compatriots†. The reasons for this are many and varied, but perhaps it is due to helicopter operations being carried out close to the ground, where the wind is of greater influence. The only time fixed–wing aircraft have to really worry about the wind is when they takeoff and land - otherwise it is merely a minor navigation problem.

In training, most establishments and flight schools have wind socks or other direction indicators to show where the wind is, and often air traffic control will be available to tell you the wind strength. Away from the apron strings of an airport‡, we are left to our own devices.

It seems all helicopter pilots eventually pick up wind sense, but are never really taught it. Here is my two cents worth to help improve the situation.

Knowing The Wind from Natural Sources

Prior to landing in a remote area, when there is no one to tell you the wind direction, and there is a scarcity of wind socks, it is prudent to learn to use all the signs ~~mother~~** nature (or man) has provided.

- Windsocks come in a variety of types, and will show a relative strength of wind, depending upon how rigidly they stick out. Some will be fully out with 15 knots of wind, and others will be fully out with 10 knots of wind. I don't know of any way to find out which is which except by asking the airport owner (who may not know either).
- Flags or banners are nearly as good as windsocks, except they aren't calibrated.
- Trees are a good indication of wind - at least in the summer when they have leaves. Most deciduous trees turn their leaves in a strong wind so the silvery–colored underside shows: if you can see this, you are probably heading downwind; if the leaves look normally green, then you are probably flying into wind. The tops of tress may be bent with the wind, but be careful, prevailing wind could have given a permanent bend.
- Grass (if it long enough) can show waves, like water. The wind needs to be about 12-15 knots for this to happen with fields of grass.
- Water may show shadows (smooth, unruffled surface) on the upwind (lee) side of lakes and some smooth rivers; waves will be hitting the shore at the downwind side. Whitecaps on water means the wind is probably at least 15 knots, but nautical books are better for explaining this using the Beaufort Scale.
- Moored boats and seaplanes normally point into the wind (unless anchored at both ends).

* But not for helicopters - why not?

† ...nearly said brothers, another sexist habit. Sorry.

‡ Someone else had to tell me how subtle this pun was by pointing out that the British term for the parking area of airports was called an apron...

**nearly fell into another sexist trap there...

- Smoke and dust clouds are useful for direction and strength - if the smoke is nearly horizontal the wind is quite strong! A 45° angle of smoke rising from a small to moderate wood fire shows about 10 to 15 knots of wind. Large fires produce quite strong updrafts and can confuse the picture with regard to wind strength and direction.
- The downwash pattern of the helicopter can be used. If visible, (such as when hovering over grass) it will be shortened on the upwind end, and stretch out a long way behind on the downwind side.
- Clothing drying on a line can help, if you are over an ecologically-aware neighborhood with clotheslines instead of clothes dryers.
- Shadows of clouds will show the direction of the wind at altitude, which may be different than at the surface. (but be careful...)
- Clouds of dust or snow blown up by other helicopters or vehicles on the ground can be useful.
- If you do a very precise turn at a constant bank angle airspeed and altitude, through 360°, the difference between your start point and your end point will show you the wind direction, and if you measured the distance between the two points and know the time it took to do the turn, you could figure out the wind speed as well... The way to do this is to fly a 2 minute turn accurately (marked on most turn and slip indicators), at a constant airspeed and altitude noting the point where the turn is started and where it ends (Navy pilots used to drop smoke floats if over the ocean). See Figure 5-4. Student pilots are not expected to be able to do this, but you never know when it might be worthwhile remembering.

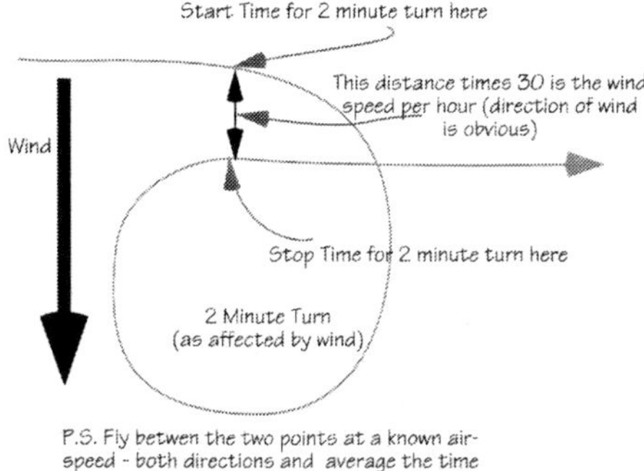

Figure 5-4 Determining Wind Direction From a Turn

Wind Speed Change with Height

Interesting things happen to the wind speed and direction as height above ground changes. Anyone who has flown a kite* can testify to this - the friction of passing over the various small items like grass, trees, buildings and so on, slow the wind down in the boundary layer next to the earth. As you increase height above ground and the friction effects decrease, the wind will normally increase in strength. Over an open field, this change in wind strength can be quite marked within as little as 30 feet.

A typical profile of wind speed vs. height above ground is shown in Figure 5-5. Notice the different effect shown in Figure 5-6, which is for a city. The city example doesn't show the wind speed and direction down inside the concrete canyons, which can be remarkably different from the top of buildings.

The important point about this diagram is when approaching to land, expect the wind speed close to the ground to be less than at 100' AGL. Many a helicopter pilot has been tricked by a sudden drop-off of wind speed close to the ground.

* ...and I'm not referring to any light helicopter or fixed–wing aircraft here - I mean a real kite. With a string.

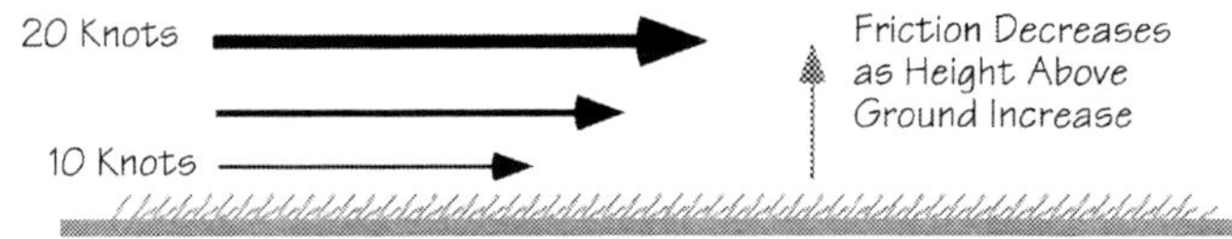

Figure 5-5 Wind Speed with height

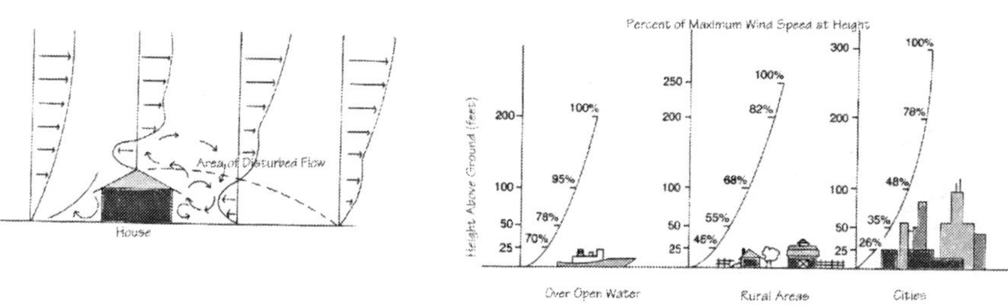

Around Houses *Different Environments*

Figure 5-6 Wind Speed vs. Height for Different Environments

Wind Direction Change with Height

If you were ever to find a group of aviators more attuned to wind than helicopter pilots, they would be sky divers. Because they hate walking long distances from their touchdown point to the jump plane, they become amazingly attuned to the wind.

Their experience is that winds above 500' AGL are rotated about 30° clockwise from the surface wind*, as well as being generally stronger. If you determined the wind from the method described above, don't count on the same wind on the ground.

Wind Shift and Turbulence

The subject of wind strength and direction is a nice lead–in to wind shifts and turbulence. Because of the vast number of places where helicopters operate, it is impossible to discuss all the possible areas where turbulence and wind shifts could occur. Two will be mentioned for your consideration.

The first is found when operating near a line of high trees. The trees do two things - first, they shelter the area downwind from the wind, and secondly, they induce down–drafts in their immediate lee. The helicopter pilot approaching to land downwind of a line of trees without due regard to this could be severely embarrassed.

A second, and perhaps more extreme example is to be found on oil rigs and ships. The wind blowing around the superstructure creates very strong turbulence laterally, longitudinally and vertically. The approach direction in these situations is not always at the discretion of the pilot, due to decks, flare stacks and other obstacles. An indication of wind speed and direction is necessary, and, particularly for military ships, a wind over deck limitation may be made that depends upon relative wind speed and direction, weight, roll angle of the ship, day or night operation, and so on.

Since most skid–equipped helicopters will land nearer buildings than wheel equipped helicopters, it pays to beware of the turbulence from buildings. Don't let down drafts catch you!

A Lesson from the Birds

Watch some birds for a while. Notice they always takeoff and land into wind. Without fail. Must be a reason for it.

How do they know where the wind is from when there are no visible signs- does the Great Air Traffic Controller in the sky give them a wind check on short final?

* Northern Hemisphere only. Opposite where the Southern Cross is visible.

WEATHER

During your training as a helicopter pilot you will have to study weather (or meteorology). What you won't be taught is about how weather affects helicopters in a direct sense, nor how to look at the micro-climate in your area and how it affects helicopters. The following section might spark some interest in becoming a weather watcher and junior forecaster.

Doesn't the Weather Office Tell Me Everything I Need to Know?

Fixed wing airplane pilots worry about the weather because most of their flights take them to airports that are a long way away. They need to know if the weather is going to be good, bad or ugly when they should get there. This is what the aviation weather system is set up for. It doesn't help helicopter pilots as much, because our flights are shorter in range (mostly) and duration. There is one more reason, and that has to do with the sort of places where helicopters are used most often.

Most of our work is in remote areas, without access to weather reporting or prediction services, and as a result, helicopter pilots often have to become local experts in weather.

So What do We Need to Worry About?

Local Conditions

If the weather office isn't close by, you still need to worry about the weather, and from more than just a legal point of view. Some of the local weather effects that should concern you are:

- Upslope flow (if you live in an area with some overall tilt, when the wind is from one direction, the cloud bases may be lower than with other wind directions)
- Fog can often form quickly if the conditions are suitable. You need to know what local conditions can produce fog without much prior warning. What time of day, what cloud conditions, wind and so on are things to ask about.
- Wind shear can happen when the winds are strong, but depending on the direction of the wind and local obstacles, can be more pronounced in one direction over another.
- Mountains can have a big effect on the weather- high winds can make some routes unflyable due to turbulence. Upslope and downslope winds often occur at a repeatable time every day and generate their own weather.
- Hot air can be produced by fires or volcanoes and have significant effects on performance (just when you need everything going for you...)

The list could go on for a long while. Ask the locals, and pay attention yourself.

An Example

When I was flying in Cold Lake, Alberta, many of our trips took us west to Edmonton. There was only one patch of slightly high ground between the two places. The Canadian Prairies slope up towards the west, so when the wind was from the east, and as air was pushed up the slope, it would cool and the moisture would condense out in clouds at this high ground, giving lower ceilings there than elsewhere. We learned to expect bad weather near this higher ground, and would make a decision to continue or turn back based on the ceiling there.

The weather around the Canadian province of Newfoundland and Labrador has such profound local effects that a book has been published to try to help sailors (and aviators) to cope with the effects of winds from different directions. An example of how this has been done is shown in Figure 5-7 below.

ETAGAULET BAY
This area is known for very strong east to southeasterly winds. "Mountain waves" off the Mealy Mountains can cause instant storm conditions. The effect of these winds is felt from the mouth of the bay to well out in the lake. (EC P.31)

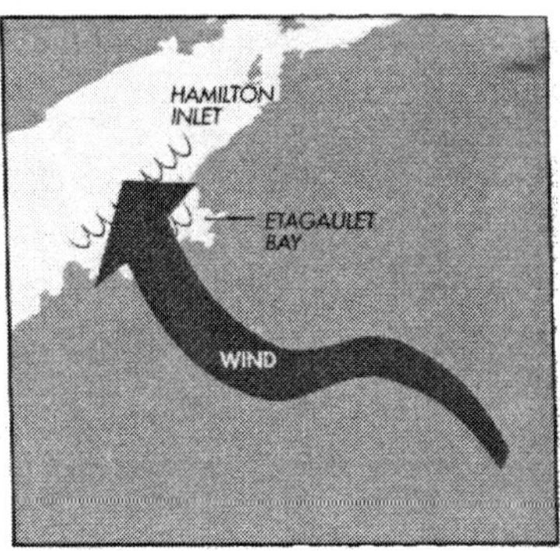

Figure 5-7 Weather in Labrador

The moral is to learn how wind and weather will work where you are.

What Should I Do With This Knowledge?

The student helicopter pilot is probably not going to be put in the position of having to make a decision about going flying based on the weather. This is a shame, because it enables experience to be gained in a very controlled and safe manner.

If all you are doing is practicing hovering, then you can probably do this with a very low ceiling and poor general visibility. On the other hand, cross country flying will need reasonable weather, both for visibility and cloud base. Winds are another matter altogether, and your proficiency and experience will dictate whether trying to hover with winds of 25 knots is OK, or whether 10 knots would stretch you.

Hopefully the first time you have to decide the weather isn't good enough is not when you are by yourself and have other pressing reasons to press on.

Summary of Chapter 5

This chapter covers three of the important things every helicopter pilot needs to understand intuitively- the properties of the air and the wind, and the local weather effects.

6 Basic Helicopter Performance

Introduction

Only enough performance to understand the basics of helicopter flying will be covered here. Items of more interest to the experienced helicopter pilot will be found in Chapter 25,"Advanced Performance". This chapter will present more information than you'll see in the Flight Manual (FM) for any light helicopter, but present it in a different format. This information is necessary to understand what you'll see in the FM.

Airframe Performance Defined

For academic clarity, airframe performance is independent of the engine. Airframe performance basically deals with the power (or fuel) required by the airframe, whether in the hover, forward flight, climbing or descending.

To simplify:

- airframe = power required
- engine = power available

The reason for the split in performance between engine and airframe is simple: the airframe doesn't care if it is being powered by a steam engine or the latest gas turbine. Similarly, the engine doesn't care if it's powering a helicopter or a water pump. Power required and power available are two separate items.

For example, the engine power must be used to propel the ancillary devices (electrical equipment, hydraulic pumps, and so on) as well as the rotor. We will talk about piston engines in Chapter 10,"The Piston Engine", and turbine engines in Chapter 29,"The Turbine Engine".

The first item to be understood is the air itself, and for that reason, the previous chapter discussed the atmosphere. The very air we and our engines breathe and our blades beat into submission is a subtle substance. Because it has so many variables, air is often different from what we think.

Measuring Performance

We measure the performance of the helicopter in a variety of indirect ways. Typically in a light piston engine helicopter, the only gauges related to performance are engine RPM and manifold pressure.

These are not of much help to us in measuring the performance, as a great many things can happen in between the manifold pressure gauge and the power being put out. In more advanced helicopters we have torquemeters, but with a piston engine, determining how much power is being used is really quite difficult. So if the graphs you see in the next part merely say a percentage of power used, please excuse the simplification. It should make the transition to turbine helicopters a bit simpler. Chapter 10 shows how power is determined.

Hover Performance

The term 'hover' for this section will mean zero–airspeed. From a performance point of view, a zero–groundspeed hover in a 20 knot wind is the same to the helicopter as flight at 20 knots airspeed. Zero–airspeed hover performance is the power required by the helicopter to remain in a stationary position with respect to the air.

There are two basic types of zero–airspeed hovers - one where the power required to hover is affected by the presence of the ground, and the other where the presence of the ground does not affect the power required to hover. Since it is easier to explain out of ground effect first, this will be dealt with before explaining how being close to the ground affects the helicopter.

Out of Ground Effect (OGE)

OGE implies the ground is not affecting the power required to maintain a constant height. It doesn't mean the rotor wash is not hitting the ground, merely the proximity of the ground does not affect the power required. Literally, the helicopter is only sitting on the column of air it is pushing down.

To make a height change when hovering OGE will require the power be changed, and then when the new height (still OGE) is obtained, the power will need to be adjusted back to the first power setting again. Looking at Figure 6-1, if we want to change height from point C to point D, it will be necessary to increase the power slightly to start a rate of climb, and then when height D is approached, decrease the power to stop the rate of climb, back to the original power setting (assuming the wind doesn't change in between the two points). As a beginning helicopter pilot, you shouldn't be doing too much hovering out of ground effect, however it's worth knowing the technique.

In Ground Effect (IGE)

Hovering *IGE* is when the height above ground affects the power needed to lift the helicopter. This happens at skid heights between fractions of an inch off the ground until about 0.75 to 1 rotor diameter above the ground[*]. The effect of the downwash of the air gradually dissipates as we increase the height above ground. The power required to hover vs. height above ground in a zero–airspeed hover is shown in Figure 6-1. (There are no numbers given in the horizontal axis deliberately.)

If you are hovering at height A with power of 55%, to climb to height B will require a smidgen more power (58%). If you can set that power exactly, you will still overshoot the height slightly, as you have a small rate of climb and some vertical inertia. Eventually you will settle at height B. Looking at this the other way around, if you are at height B and want to descend to height A, even if you accurately set the power to the correct level, you will descend through it and then slowly bounce back up to the correct height.

If you are trying to see this phenomenon by hovering at different heights and using slightly different power settings, it will only work well with very light winds (less than about three knots). The reason is that even a light wind will change strength quite markedly from the surface to 30' AGL.

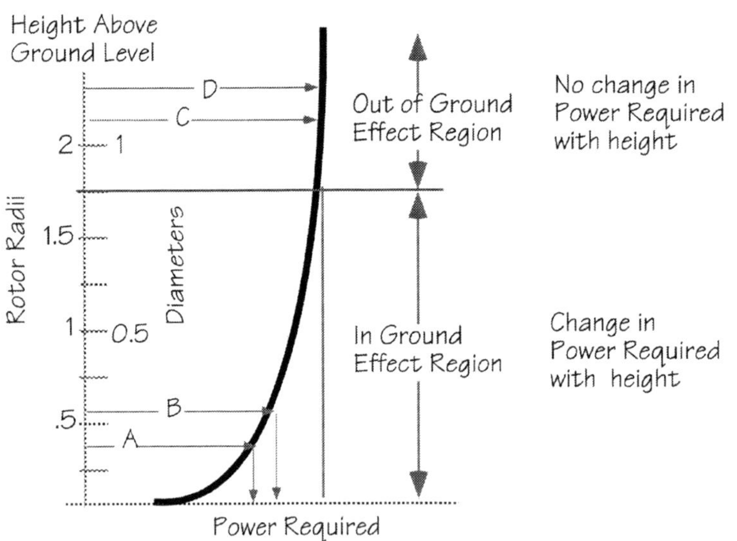

Figure 6-1 Change in Power Required vs. Height above Ground

Normally, the power required to hover OGE is 8 to 10% more than hovering at about 3 to 5' IGE. This difference assumes no wind. A useful exercise is to see if adding 10% power above that required to hover at 3 - 5' IGE on a calm day will let you climb vertically above obstacles.

How Does Ground Effect Happen?

Ground effect affects[†] helicopters a lot. How does it do this? There are several ways to explain it, and we'll try most of them.

First of all, consider a can of thick Vermont ~~Canadian~~ maple syrup[‡] being poured onto a stack of pancakes. If you change the height of the can above the pancakes while trying to maintain a steady pour rate, you will notice when the height of the can above the pancakes is low, the flow pattern of the syrup where it comes out of the can is affected by the syrup hitting the pancakes. This is similar to ground effect and the air being pushed down by the helicopter. The flow in front a rock in a river also shows how objects affect things upstream.

Another way to understand ground effect is the air hitting the ground is forced to move sideways, affecting the air above it. The effect is to slow down the air above, and this slows the induced flow. Slowing the induced flow means the angle of attack of the air onto the rotor blade decreases, decreasing the drag and the lift. Since we are operating in an area of the C_L and C_D curves where there is larger

* Whether this distance relates to skid height or rotor height from the ground is of little importance - the distance is approximate and variable, depending on the wind, disk loading of the helicopter, surface etc.

† This is another of those puns that just happened. I didn't plan it- honest.

‡ Nothing wrong with being patriotic - (now that I've made the USA my home, I'd better change this too.

change in drag than lift for the same change in AoA, the power required to turn the rotor goes down more than the lift produced by the rotor, and the result is the pilot sees a reduction in the power required to hover in ground effect.

Interestingly, if you move the helicopter hovering in ground effect over a different type of surface, you may see a change in the power required to hover at the same height. Long grass absorbs power (it takes energy to make it wave around, and there is more friction involved) more than smooth pavement, and the helicopter will need more power to hover over tall grass than smooth pavement.

Still another way to think of ground effect is to consider the helicopter hovering over a large water or oil tank just about the diameter of the rotor. (See Figure 6-2.) When the helicopter is hovering high above the tank, there is very little resistance to the air driven into the tank, and as well, the air can spill out the top. As the helicopter gets lower to the top of the tank, the air has a more difficult time getting out, and the pressure inside the tank will start to increase. As the helicopter gets lower and lower, the pressure inside the tank will continue to increase and will stabilize when the rotor is at the level of the top of the tank. No more air can be stuffed inside. The rotor would have an easy time to stay on top of this can of air. You can see an effect like this with the exhaust fan in a kitchen or bathroom. When there is a wind blowing against the outside opening, the fan will work only until it has pumped as much air into the duct as it can, or when the pressure is as much as it can maintain- then the fan just spins doing very little real work.

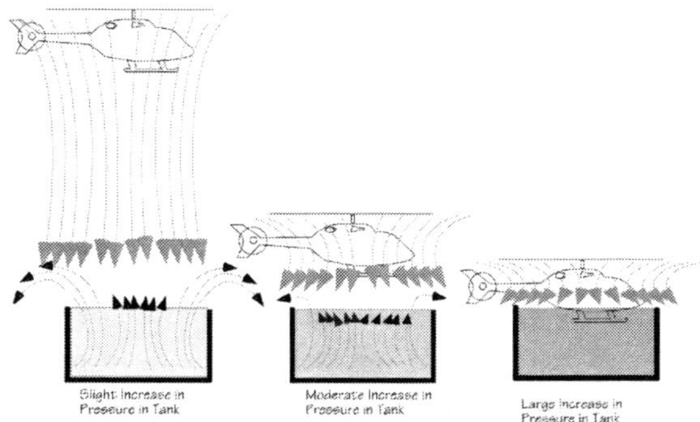

Figure 6-2 Hovering Over Large Open Tank

An interesting possibility, and only remotely related to what happens in real life with ground effect, but it might help someone to understand the fundamentals of how ground effect works.

Using a Crane to Lift Instead of an Engine

If we were to replace the rotor of the helicopter with a crane, and wanted to hold the helicopter at 3 feet above the ground, it shouldn't come as a surprise to most people that it takes the same force to lift the helicopter as the lift force the rotor must produce*. Notice the word 'force', not power.

It doesn't take a rocket scientist† to realize it should take a crane the same amount of force to hold the helicopter at 30 feet or 300 feet above the ground, or for that matter at a 10,000' above the ground, assuming we could get such a crane.

When we talk about hover performance, we talk about the power required to hover, maintain altitude, etc. There is a lot of difference between force and power- how do we make this apparent leap in terminology? We also know it takes considerably different amounts of power to hover a helicopter in the same conditions. Why?

* Ignoring for the moment the effect of the downwash on the top of the fuselage
† Or even a helicopter scientist

The simple answer is a lift *force* has to be produced, and the only way we have to produce the lift force is by turning the rotor. Remember that force equals mass times acceleration (F=m x a, or the mass of air must be accelerated (i.e. have its velocity changed) by the rotor). It takes power to overcome the drag of the rotors, therefore we are correct in both ways. The lift force is produced by power. We can only measure power in the helicopter, so that is why we use the terms we do.

The amount of power to hover changes as the height AGL due to the induced flow being affected by the ground. This means the drag of the rotor blades is reduced closer to the ground to produce the same lift force.

POWER REQUIRED VS. DENSITY ALTITUDE

If we try a zero airspeed hover at 3' AGL at sea level and then 3' AGL at the top of a high mountain, we'd quickly notice a big difference in the power required to hover. Why is this?

The rotor has to produce the same amount of lift force to hold the helicopter up. Remember the Lift Formulae? As air density decreases, at the same N_R, the lift force produced will decrease. The only way to obtain the same lift at the same N_R is to increase the Coefficient of Lift (C_L) and the only way to do this is to increase AoA on the blades. This is accomplished simply by raising the collective lever. The unwanted side effect of increasing AoA is the Coefficient of Drag (C_D) increases at the same time. Increased drag requires more power from the engine, and the power required to produce the same amount of lift increases.

Hover Ceilings*

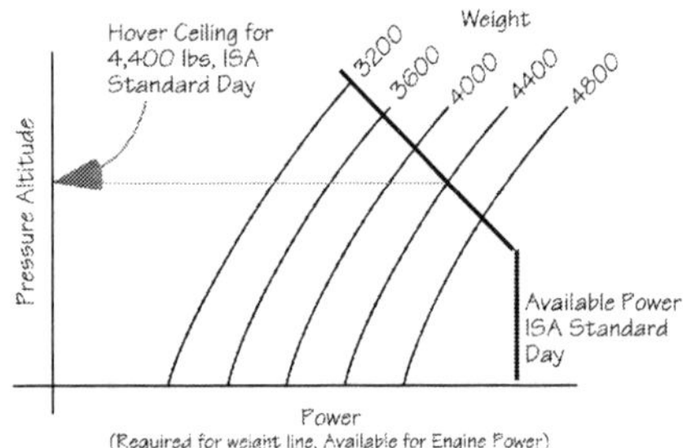

Figure 6-3 Hover Ceiling

Looking at the performance charts for a typical light piston engine training helicopter, at a certain weight, there will be a ceiling (altitude above mean sea level, and air temperature) above which it cannot hover in ground effect. This are shown in Figure 6-3.

Not shown is the lower ceiling (altitude and temperature) where it cannot hover out of ground effect

The reason for this limitation is that the power demanded (or required) by the helicopter is more than the power available from the engine. Power available will be discussed in the chapters on engines.

FORWARD FLIGHT PERFORMANCE

This section covers airspeeds greater than 40 KIAS. Airspeeds below this are dealt with later.

An often confusing term is 'level flight'. The curve in Figure 6-4 below was developed by flying at a constant altitude and a steady airspeed and measuring the power required to maintain that condition, and repeating this for a variety of airspeeds. We don't expect beginning helicopter pilots to be able to fly accurately enough to get data to produce this type of curve, but merely to understand what the curve means.

You certainly won't see a chart like this in a flight manual, however its effects show up in several places, so pay attention.

Power Required vs. Airspeed

The power required to maintain level flight changes dramatically with airspeed. A typical example for one weight and density altitude is shown in Figure 6-4. There are several things to note with this figure - first of all, the vertical scale is power required. This figure can be used to determine the airspeed where minimum power required (V_Y†) and maximum power margin (or surplus power available) occurs. For our example helicopter, the power available at the continuous rating determines the maximum level flight airspeed (V_H‡) of the helicopter. On Figure 6-4, points of interest are:

* No, not a new type of interior decoration...

† This is the first of the 'V' speeds that you will come to know. Its a shorthand for minimum power speed.

‡ The 'H' is for horizontal speed - this is maximum speed that the helicopter can maintain in level flight using maximum continuous power.

- the relatively small change in the power required between 40 and 80 KIAS, (marked (A))
- the steep rise in power required as airspeed increases beyond 80 KIAS (marked (B)).
- To maintain level flight below about 60 KIAS, it actually takes more power to go slower and maintain a constant altitude (marked (C)). This is often called 'the backside of the power curve'.

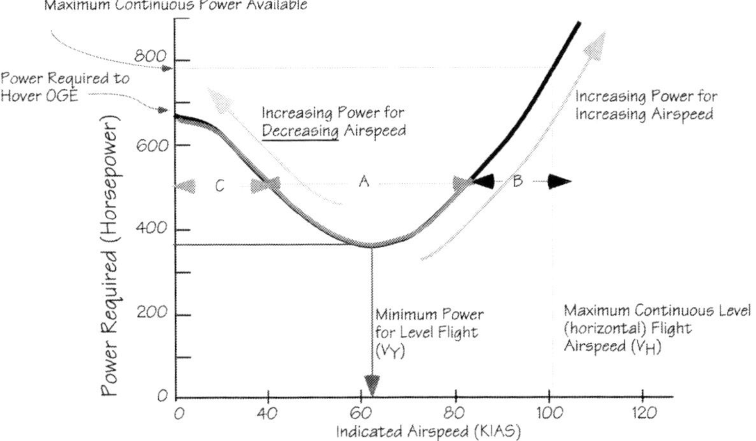

Figure 6-4 Power Required vs. Airspeed

Some other ways to look at this chart are:

- for speeds above V_Y:
  - ➤increasing power would result in a climb, or if you were to try to maintain a constant altitude, result in an increase in airspeed
  - ➤decreasing power would result in a descent, or if you were to try to maintain a constant altitude, require a decrease in airspeed
  - ➤if you were to increase airspeed but not increase the power used, the helicopter would descend
  - ➤if you were to decrease airspeed, but not decrease the power used, the helicopter would climb
- for speeds slower than V_Y:
  - ➤if you were to increase airspeed but not decrease the power used, the helicopter would climb
  - ➤if you were to decrease airspeed, but not increase the power used, the helicopter would descend

What You Can't Do with This Chart

This chart cannot be used to determine the airspeed for maximum range, nor strictly speaking, maximum endurance. These airspeeds depend on engine fuel flow characteristics, and are covered later. Another way to understand the reason for needing a different chart (fuel flow vs. airspeed) to determine best range and maximum endurance is that the helicopter has fuel in the tanks, instead of power. The chart is useful for autorotation airspeeds such as minimum rate of descent and maximum range (no wind) in autorotation.

The 'Backside' of the Power Curve

In the fixed wing world, a lot of emphasis is placed on flying in the *backside* of the power curve. This is partly because fixed wing airplanes stall if they go too slowly, and also because the only time fixed wing airplanes use the back side is when they are approaching to land, so you don't want to get things wrong close to the ground.

Helicopter pilots typically don't spend too much time thinking about the backside of the power curve, but we should. We use it on every approach and landing, and sometimes forget the principles concerned. Exercises in flying at airspeeds below V_Y are useful to develop the pilot's knowledge of this area.

Perhaps the reason we don't concentrate on this area is that by the time we get to a point where we are on the backside of the power curve, we are flying by reference to the ground, and not paying much attention to the instruments.

To emphasize the back side of the power curve, remember-

- pulling the nose up, without increasing power results in a descent in the long term
- pushing the nose down without decreasing power results in a climb in the long term

The reason for the 'in the long term' is that there is an initial movement the opposite way.

If you look at things another way, there are two airspeeds for any power setting except minimum power speed.

For the reasons just outlined, the region of airspeed slower than V_Y is called the "region of reversed command" or "backside of the power curve".

Low Airspeed Power Required

Figure 6-5 shows the power required vs. airspeed for the low speed region. The same criteria used in level flight (constant airspeed, altitude, etc.) were used to develop this curve.

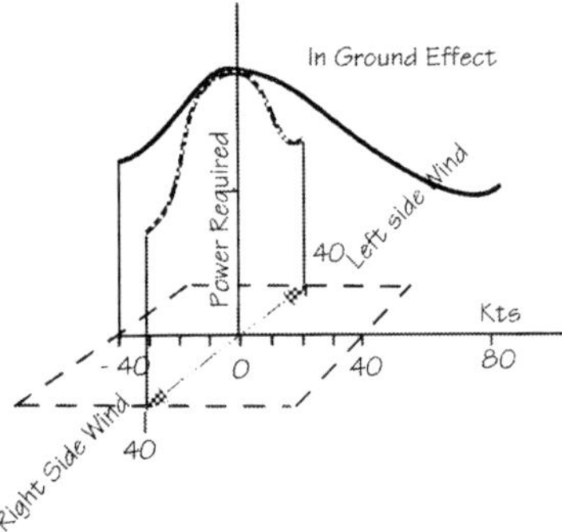

Figure 6-5 Power Required vs. Airspeed, <40 KIAS

Some artistic license has been taken to show the maximum power required occurs away from zero–airspeed. For very complex reasons explained in "Peculiarities of Low Airspeed IGE" on page 243, the maximum power to maintain height does not happen at zero airspeed, but for IGE, it happens at a about 8 to 10 knots of airspeed. Out of ground effect, the maximum power required is at zero airspeed. The same general shape as the power required vs. forward airspeed curve is seen with side and rear airspeeds, namely the power required for level flight decreases rapidly from the zero-airspeed condition. This can cause problems.

Say you're hovering at 3' AGL and don't notice that there's about 20 knots of wind. You do note that you have lots of power available before you would reach a limit. This is called a power margin (and it's a good thing normally). You fly away to your arrival point, which is not quite as windy, in fact, the wind is calm. You think you have plenty of power available to hover, but as you come into the hover, you're unpleasantly surprised to see you are out of power.

A less common, but similar problem is if you are hovering with your tail into the wind and again have a large power margin. You need to transition into forward flight by going through zero airspeed. No problem, you think. I have lots of power in hand. Not so fast, moose-breath. You have to pass through an area where the power required is considerably greater than where you are. You may not have enough!

Climb and Descent Performance - Simplified

The helicopter needs to climb, and the information on rates of climb in the FM uses V_Y airspeed, not hovering. There is more detail on climb and descent performance in Chapter 25.

What is probably missing in the FM is any discussion of the service and absolute ceilings of the helicopter. The *service ceiling* is the maximum altitude the helicopter can attain while sustaining a 100 foot per minute rate of climb. The *absolute ceiling* is the maximum altitude AMSL the helicopter can attain while in level flight. These two important altitudes probably will not be featured in the FM*. These two altitudes will be well above the hover ceilings of the helicopter.

For this stage of your training, you should be aware that if you want to get the maximum rate of climb, you should use the V_Y airspeed, shown as the lowest power required on Figure 6-4.

Flight Manual Charts

The flight manual charts for hover performance for light helicopters combine airframe performance with engine performance to tell the pilot what his helicopter will be able to accomplish. Engine performance is explained in more detail in the chapters on Piston Engines (Chapter 10) and Turbine Engines (Chapter 29).

An example of a Hover In–Ground–Effect capability was shown earlier in Figure 6-3 on page 56. Notice how this only shows the pilot what maximum weight the helicopter can be hovered at, and without showing if there is any performance margin remaining for winds, maneuvering in the hover, transitioning to forward flight or stopping a rate of descent while landing vertically.

There are some misconceptions about Flight Manual charts that should be cleared up. The charts in most manuals are if anything, slightly pessimistic about what the helicopter should be capable of attaining. The airframe manufacturer knows what sort of performance the helicopter under test is actually producing, compared to what the minimum performance helicopter should be able to attain in the field. The manufacturer also knows what is typically attainable by the average pilot.

As if that isn't enough, the certifying authorities† will ensure the testing is adjusted for a minimum specification engine, and suitably worn rotor blades, etc. To make sure performance figures are conservative, the certifying authority will normally spot check the performance in field tests.

V Airspeeds

You'll see quite a lot of airspeeds written in a shorthand called V speeds. The V is shorthand for Velocity. Just about every airspeed you'll use regularly has been identified by this technique. A list of those speeds used in light training helicopters is given below, along with the appropriate definition.

Name	*Definition*
V_{NE}	Velocity Never Exceed. The red line on the airspeed indicator (which may be modified by density altitude). A "limitation"[a].
V_Y	Velocity for minimum power required for level flight. This is bottom of the curve for power required in level flight vs. airspeed. An advisory airspeed, not a limitation. Also known as minimum power airspeed.
$V_{NE\ autorotation}$	Velocity Never Exceed in Autorotation or power off flight. A "limitation".
V_H	Maximum Horizontal Airspeed - the airspeed attainable with continuous power in level flight. An advisory airspeed, normally not a limitation.
V_{NO}	Velocity Normal Operating. Depending on the country, may be a limitation. Normally 10% less than V_{NE}

a. See Chapter 20

* ...and as a student pilot you probably wouldn't want to go to either of them anyway.
† ...people like me in my previous daytime job with Transport Canada.

Load Factors

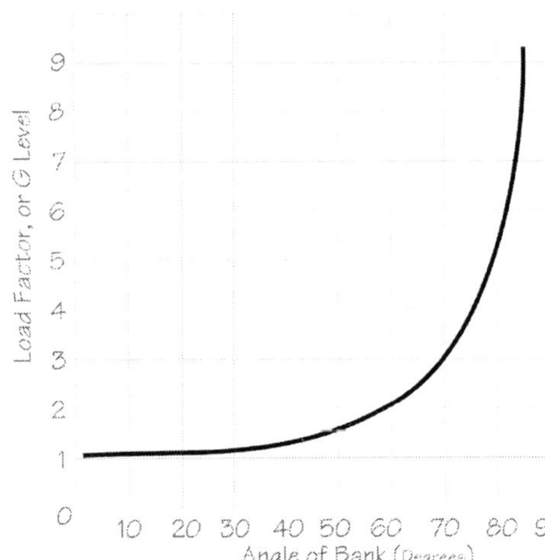

Figure 6-6 Load Factor vs. Bank Angle, Level Turn

The helicopter doesn't always fly straight and level. Whenever it is turned in forward flight, or pulls up from a dive, it experiences an increase in *load factor* or G loading. For most of the turns you will be doing as a student helicopter pilot, you won't have to worry too much about load factors, however you should understand the principles.

Load factors can affect performance, and is seen by the airframe as an increase in weight. The amount of the weight increase varies with the bank angle. For example, from Figure 6-6 below, the load factor in a 60° angle of bank (AOB) turn in level flight is 2. The pilot experiences this as a sensation of increased weight. From a performance point of view, the aircraft also experiences a doubling of weight. To maintain level flight in this condition will require a large increase in power - equivalent to doubling the weight of the machine*.

Load factors have another important place in helicopter aerodynamics. By changing the apparent weight of the helicopter (increasing it in a pullout, and decreasing it in a pushover), the load factor plays an important effect on N_R.

Fixed wing pilots may be surprised to learn that many helicopters do not have maximum positive G limit defined†. This is because the rotor reaches its limit of ability to produce lift long before any significant G is reached. It takes a lot of G to do structural damage to the airframe in normal flying.

Summary of Chapter 6

This chapter has covered the very fundamentals of hover and forward flight performance. It was stated at the beginning of the chapter that it assumed there would be sufficient power from the engine in all cases. This obviously isn't true, and as this is one of the many other aspects to performance essential to safe flight, it will be covered later. This chapter should have provided enough detail to let us get onto the more interesting parts of how to actually fly a helicopter.

* But not a doubling of the power required

† see "Mast Bumping" on page 393 for low G limits

7 Balance and Weight

The title of this chapter is correctly sequenced. One of the foremost problem of flying helicopters is maintaining balance of the various forces, and one of the factors affecting balance is how heavy the load is, as well as its position in the aircraft.

Understanding of the balance of forces is important to the understanding of how we control the helicopter.

The Importance of Center of Gravity

Aside from legal limitations in the FM*, there are practical considerations for understanding the location of the Center of Gravity (CG), and its effects. The CG position must be described in three different axes - longitudinal, lateral and vertical. Figure 7-1 shows these axes.

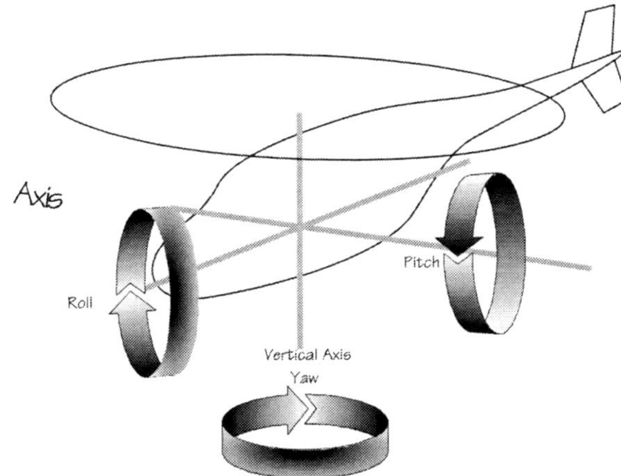

Figure 7-1 Axis of Helicopters.

Since there are three axis (longitudinal, lateral and vertical), then there are also three different reference planes for the CG - cunningly these positions are also called longitudinal, lateral and vertical. The CG must be measured for relative position in each of these planes - in other words there is forward/aft CG, a left-right CG and a vertical CG position. These meet at one point on the airframe that can be defined by physical measurements, although you can't really see it except in diagrams.

All the forces acting on the helicopter must act through the CG, and the moment arm from the source of those forces (such as rotor or fuselage) to the CG has a very large effect - move the CG closer to the tail rotor for example, and the tail rotor must work harder to produce the same moment to turn the helicopter. While that may sound strange, it works like this:

- A certain moment is needed to yaw the helicopter:
  - ➤If the CG were a long way away from the tail rotor, (i.e. had a long moment arm) a small amount of force from the tail rotor would be needed to produce this moment.
  - ➤If the CG were closer to the tail rotor (i.e. had a small moment arm) a large amount of force from the tail rotor would needed to produce the same moment.

* You may not know it, but in many countries, operating overweight will invalidate your certificate of airworthiness and your insurance as well.

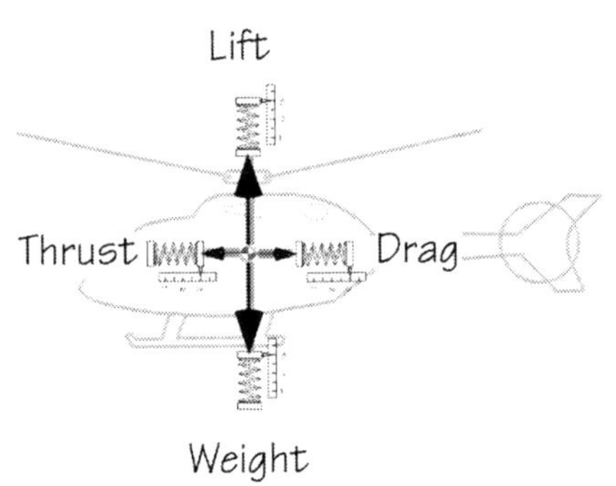

Figure 7-2 Spring Balances attached to CG

If we want to continue our analogy of a spring balance as a way to represent forces, the CG is the place where the spring balances would connect. We would need three sets of spring balances- one for vertical forces (weight), one for lateral forces, (lateral drag) and one to take care of fore-aft forces (longitudinal drag). Two sets of springs are shown in Figure 7-2.

Calculating Weight and Balance

Weight

It should be self-evident that the overall weight of the helicopter is important for performance considerations. It's also important for legal reasons*. If the helicopter is too heavy, it will not be possible to get the hover or vertical climb performance indicated in the flight manual, or elements of the structure may be overloaded. If you think the helicopter is at 1,800 lbs., when it really weighs 2,100 lbs., you might be surprised, very surprised! Just try to lift those 300 pounds yourself, and consider what the engine has to do...

The weight consists of three basic elements - the empty weight of the helicopter, the useful load (or payload) and the total or *gross weight* (the sum of the previous two). The total weight cannot (legally) exceed the maximum gross weight permitted for the helicopter. If you deliberately overload a helicopter, on the other hand, you probably deserve what can happen to you. Be aware that many helicopters will not always be capable of lifting the 'maximum gross weight' because of power available from the engine.

Depending upon the atmospheric conditions at the time, the total weight that can be lifted into the hover may be less than the maximum permitted gross weight. Consult the FM for the weight capability under different conditions of pressure altitude and temperature.

The useful load is thus the disposable weights such as pilot, passengers, baggage, cargo and fuel. Useful load must be adjusted according to the mission† - if maximum passengers are to be carried, it may be necessary to have less than full fuel tanks!

Real Weights, Please

There is a tendency in the aviation community to simplify everything. This happens with weights of passengers. The various rules say you can estimate the weight of male passengers at 170 pounds and females at some lower figure‡. I don't know about most male passengers, but I last saw 170 pounds too many years ago. The payloads of most light helicopters are small enough anyway, and we are fooling ourselves if we continue to use estimated weights.

Several of the major helicopter operators on the US Gulf Coast have put scales beside their helicopters for passengers to be weighed prior to flight, so they use actual weights. Given the consequences of overloading, shouldn't we all do the same? No more estimated weights, please.

Balance

Balance is more difficult to understand than weight, as it relates to the location of the center of gravity. If it is too far forward, or off to one side, there may not be sufficient tilt of the rotor disk remaining to control the helicopter in all conditions. How can the point of balance be calculated?

There are a great variety of ways of determining the location of the CG, and each manufacturer has a preferred method. All are basically the same - a datum location** is used as the point to measure the distance to the various disposable weights, and the moment arm each of these disposable weights is added to a basic weight and balance for the empty helicopter. Two datums that are commonly used are the one placed ahead of the nose of the helicopter, and one placed at the rotor mast. Both examples will be shown.

* See "Limitations" on page 185 for more details.
† Which raises the interesting question - at what point does the payload essential for the mission mean that the pilot has to be left behind?
‡ Now if that isn't blatant sexism, I don't know what is.
**Interestingly, it doesn't really matter where you put the datum, the answer will come out the same.

All manufacturers provide charts for calculating CG (it's required for certification). I've found that if a manual (i.e. paper and pencil) approach is understood, it will make the use of charts easier. This manual method is also called the weight–moment–CG method*.

The first items that must be determined in either case is the 'basic weight and CG location'. These numbers are found in a section of the FM (or the helicopter technical log), and must be current to reflect any changes in the non-removable equipment (such as radios, heaters, etc.). It has two parts-the basic (or empty) weight and the location of the basic (or empty) CG.

This, by the way, is the reason for a 'personalized' copy of the FM for each helicopter- the basic weight will be different, depending on the radio equipment, interior, and so on. The empty weight CG position will also be different from machine to machine.†

Datum Forward of the Nose.

In this case, all the weights and moments are added, and the final CG determined by dividing the total moment by the weight. An example of such a method is shown in Figure 7-3.

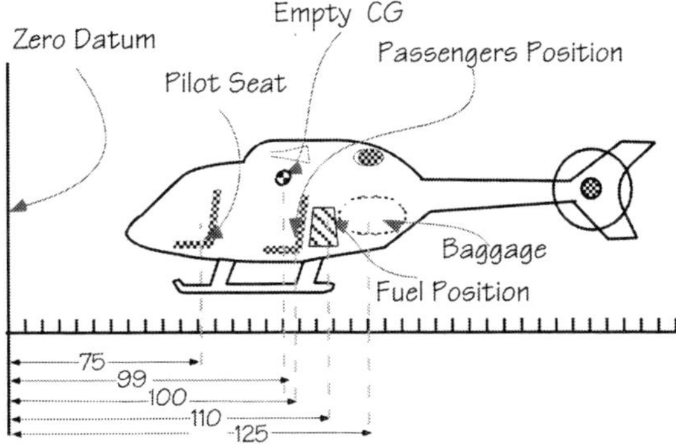

Figure 7-3 Datum Forward of the Nose

For this example, the helicopter has an empty weight of 1,200 lbs., and a CG position of 99.3" aft of datum. The passengers, fuel, pilot and baggage weights were determined by weighing and the positions of their location determined from the loading charts. The calculations look like this:

Item	Weight (pounds)	Arm (Inches from Datum)	Moment (inch-pounds)
Empty Weight	1,200	99.3	119,160 (1,200 x 99.3)
Pilot	180	75.0	13,500
Baggage	100	125.0	12,500
Passengers	360	100.0	36,000
Fuel	250	110.0	27,500
Total	2,090		208,660

$$\text{CG Location} = \frac{\text{Total Moment}}{\text{Total Weight}}$$

$$= \left(\frac{208,660}{2,090}\right) = 99.83 \text{ inches aft of datum}$$

* Most electronic navigation computers also use the weight–moment–CG method.

† Evidently accumulated dirt under the floorboards can also change the empty weight significantly. Keep clean!

In this case, the CG has shifted towards the rotor mast (i.e., aft) by 0.53" when the load is added.

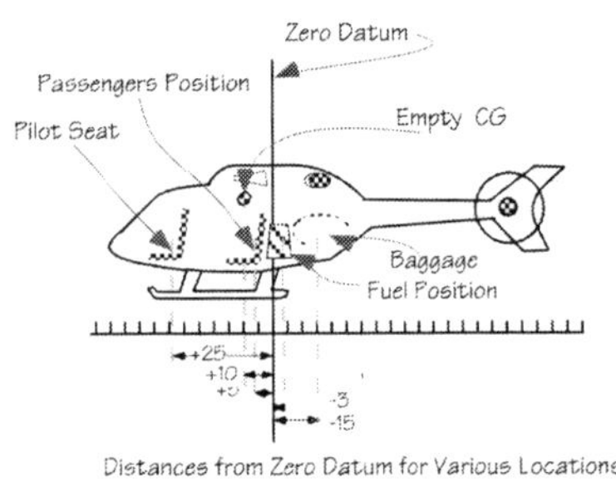

Figure 7-4 Datum at Rotor Mast

Datum At Rotor Mast

The calculations for the datum line being at the rotor mast are as easy as for the datum well forward of the nose. An example of such a calculation on a different helicopter is shown below.

Item	Weight (pounds)	Arm (" from datum) + =ahead of datum - = behind datum	Moment (inch-pounds) (positive)	(negative)
Basic	6,700	+5	33,500	
Pilot	180	+15	2,700	
Baggage	200	-48		-9600
Fuel	900	-2		-1,800
Passengers Row 1	0			
Row 2	540	0	0	
Row 3	540	+36	19,400	
			55,600	-11,400
Total	9,060		**+44,200**	

$$\text{CG Location} = \frac{\text{Total Moment}}{\text{Total Weight}}$$

$$= \left(\frac{44,200}{9,060}\right) = 4.88 \text{ inches aft of datum} \quad \text{(EQ 15.)}$$

In this case, the CG has moved forward slightly from the empty case.

WEIGHT AND CG DIAGRAM

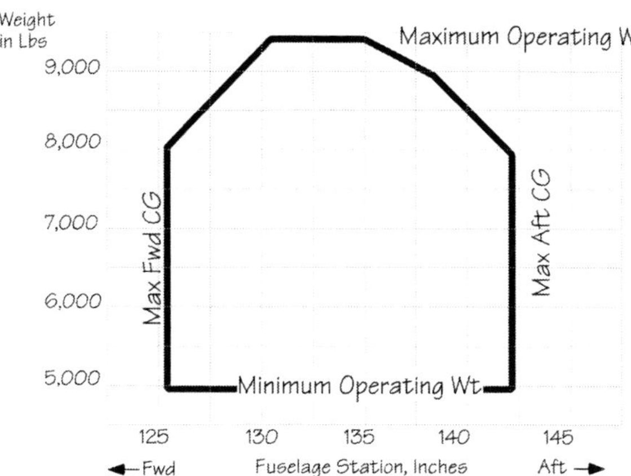

Figure 7-5 Sample Weight and CG Limits Diagram

The FM will show the limitations of CG and weight for the helicopter. An example is shown in Figure 7-5 below. It is common to have the allowable range of CG change with weight.

The diagram shows that the CG range permitted at high weights is less than that at lower weight. The reasons for this can be complicated, but are typically due to stresses on the rotating components at high weights. The manufacturer wants you to have as large a CG range as is safe.

Weight vs. Loaded Moment Method

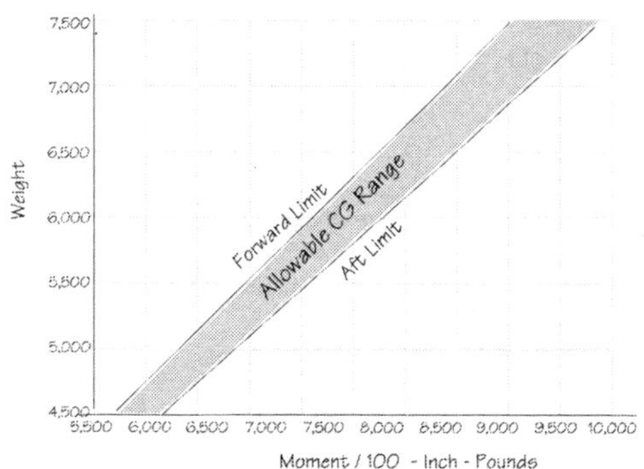

Figure 7-6 Weight vs. Loaded Moment Graph

Another method of calculating whether you are within the limitations is available from a diagram of empty weight vs. loaded moment, as shown in Figure 7-6. If your empty weight is within the limitations prescribed, then you can use this simpler method to calculate what has to be loaded where to respect the limitations.

Yet Another Way to Measure CG

Another way to measure CG is to pre-calculate the moments and only require the pilot to move along the necessary lines a set number of squares. An example of this is shown in Figure 7-7 below. Note how the small arrow-shaped squares are different sizes depending on their location with respect to the datum.

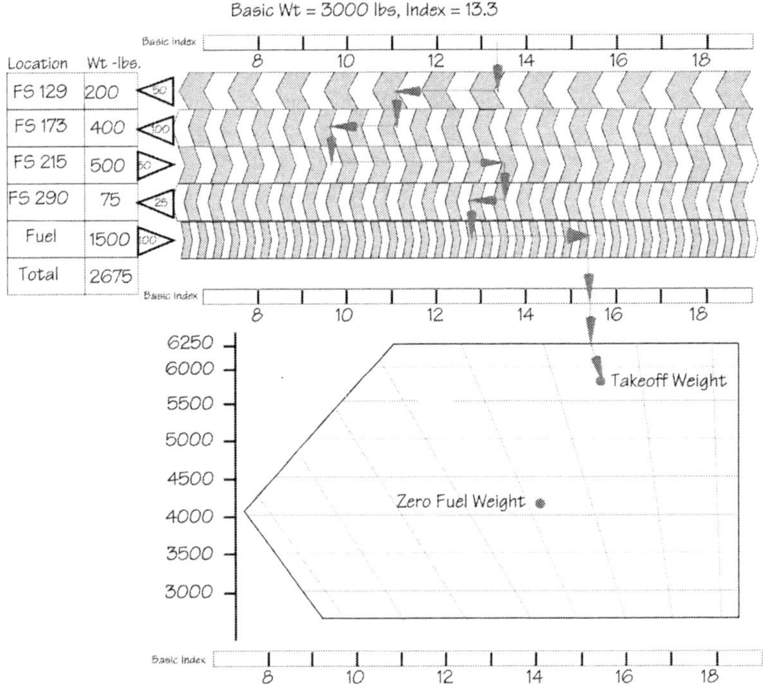

Figure 7-7 Arrow- type Weight and CG Diagram

Longitudinal CG

The longitudinal center of gravity is the most commonly changed CG in helicopter operations, and it is also the one with the most immediately noticeable effect. Forward CG, for example, requires a more aft cyclic stick position with respect to the airframe to keep the rotor disk level in the zero-airspeed hover.

If this sounds slightly strange, consider the rotor disk must be parallel with the ground in a zero–airspeed hover. The fuselage merely takes up a natural attitude hanging below it. The cockpit controls are taken with reference to the fuselage, so with a forward CG and the helicopter fuselage hanging nose–down under the rotor, the pilot will see the longitudinal cyclic is more aft that with a neutral CG.

Since longitudinal CG position is an important factor in fixed wing flying, it has received a lot of emphasis in helicopters as well*.

Typically the more weight that is added, the more forward the CG will be, so the 'minimum light weight, aft CG' case is often only possible in a stripped down version of most helicopters.

More than one light helicopter has a minimum pilot weight limitation in the FM. However, if a detailed calculation of weight and balance is made once the helicopter is equipped with radios and interior, it may be impossible to be out of CG limits with a pilot who is lighter than the limitation. Look at the weight and balance carefully!

The manual should really state a minimum weight in the front seat- a lot of pilots weigh way less than 170 lbs.†.

Lateral CG

The lateral CG position is also important and, for many helicopters must be considered carefully. Since the cockpit and cabin of most helicopters are generally symmetrical about the longitudinal axis, it is relatively easy to calculate the lateral CG position. The method of calculation is similar to the 'datum near the mast' example. Unfortunately, often limitations are missing for the allowable lateral CG.

* Most helicopter certification requirements have a historical basis in fixed–wing flying.

† Yes I know this is a pun, and I almost said a lot of female pilots are less than 170 lbs., but as one of my lighter male friends said, that would be sexist.

The lateral CG envelope is the reason why some helicopters can't handle someone hanging from the skids, when others can. Regardless of what the movies show you, only some helicopters can do that sort of thing, and several have ended up rolling over because of it.

Don't think that only a static weight is all you need to know. A recent accident involving a police helicopter shows the perils of not considering everything. Seems that two policemen were to practice getting into the helicopter while it was in the hover. Both were to get in on the same side. Whether the pilot even considered the lateral CG of two men standing still isn't known, but he certainly didn't consider the effective weight when two large men both jumped up onto the same side at the same time. The helicopter promptly fell on its side and beat itself to pieces. Even full lateral cyclic didn't stop the rolling motion. The problem? Try jumping on your bathroom scales and see how high the weight goes... That is how much real weight was being applied to the skid, not the static weight of the two men

Figure 7-8 shows a lateral CG position, viewed from the rear. The importance of lateral CG will be shown later.

.

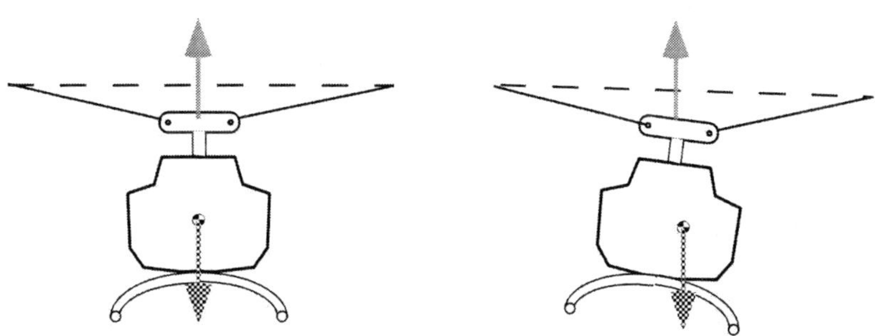

Figure 7-8 Lateral CG Position

Vertical CG

The vertical CG position generally moves very little on light training helicopters, and the only interest is in knowing it exists. In normal operations, there is no need to try to measure the position of the vertical CG*. More detailed discussion about vertical CG is in the Chapter 23,"Advanced Helicopter Aerodynamics", as it has a large effect in some conditions.

* ...and difficult to measure (impossible without a very specialized laboratory) ...if you were interested.

Balance of Forces

General

The rotor system produces an overall thrust vector, (from Chapter 2) that is resolved into a longitudinal component (thrust) and a vertical component (lift). The fuselage reacts to moving through the air by producing a variety of horizontal forces called drag, and it weighs something (weight), and these both act through the CG. This is shown in Figure 7-9.

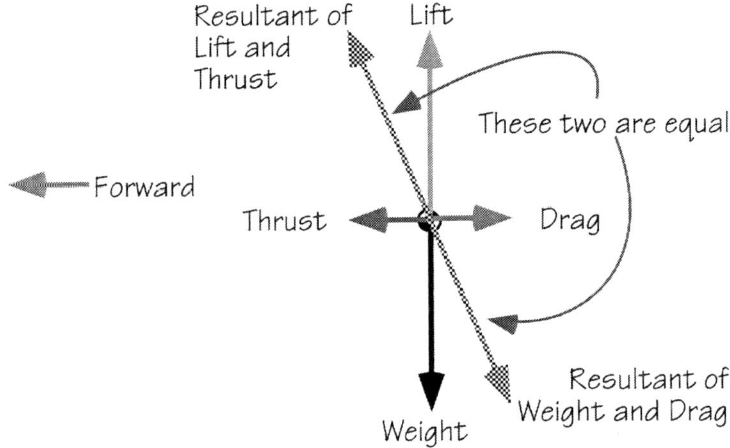

Figure 7-9 Outline of Balance of Forces

For a steady condition, the resultant of lift plus thrust must be in line with the resultant of weight plus drag. They must also be equal in size. If they are out of balance, then the helicopter will accelerate to try to put the forces in line and in balance.

Newton's Second Law of Motion states "A body stays in its state of rest or uniform motion unless disturbed by some external force acting upon it."

In simple terms, when everything is in balance, things stay the same. This can be a steady airspeed, a steady hover or whatever. When the pilot wants to change things, he must change the balance of forces. The only way the helicopter pilot can change the balance of forces is by changing the size and angle of the thrust vector, which will change the thrust and lift components.

When Nature adds a gust of wind, this is an external way to change the balance of forces.

The helicopter has freedom to move in all three axes, so it is necessary to look at all of these axes for an understanding of the balance of forces. Since we can only show 2 axes at one time on flat paper, it will be necessary to show three different views to get the whole picture. (It also makes it easier to explain).

When the helicopter is in a stable condition, be it hovering, steady level flight or a steady climb or descent, the sum of the forces about the CG is zero, and the forces are said to be in balance. The moments are likewise all balanced. When something upsets the balance, either a gust or a control input, the helicopter accelerates until the forces are again balanced.

Figure 7-10 shows the side view of the balance of forces for a helicopter in a zero–airspeed hover. Note the drag or horizontal thrust forces are zero. In this case, if the lift were increased, the helicopter would accelerate upwards, (i.e. a slight increase in positive G would be felt) until the lift decreased to a value equal to the weight in a steady climb*.

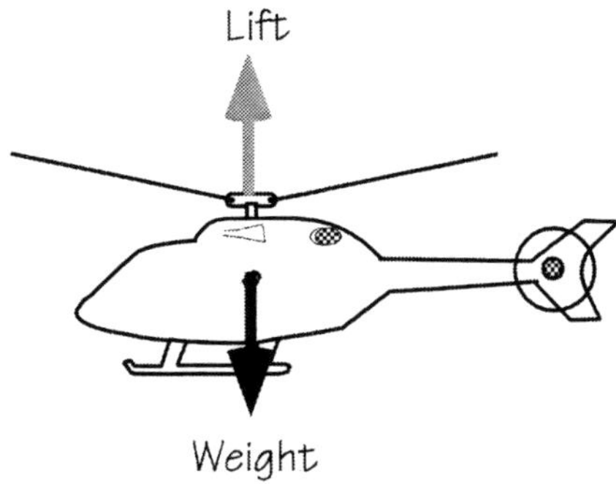

Figure 7-10 Balance of Forces in a Zero–Airspeed Hover

Balance of Forces in the Hover

Side View Four Basic Forces

In this zero–airspeed hover case, the lateral CG position is of no consequence (for the time being). There are four forces acting on the helicopter, namely:

Lift	The vertical force required to support the weight of the helicopter. Normally the vertical component of total lift. Acts from the rotor hub.
Drag	The horizontal force generated by the passage of the helicopter through the air. Normally acts in a horizontal manner from the CG. (There is no horizontal drag in a zero–airspeed hover and we normally ignore downwash on the fuselage in the hover)
Thrust	The horizontal force required to overcome the drag of the helicopter. Normally the horizontal component of the total lift (or thrust) and acts from the rotor hub. Forward is positive. (note there is no thrust in a zero–airspeed hover)
Weight	The vertical force due to the effects of gravity on the mass of the helicopter. More correctly called load factor. Down is positive. Acts from the CG. Vertical drag due to downwash from the rotor can add from 2 to 10% to the overall weight.

These forces line up, as shown in Figure 7-10 above.

Top View Balance of Forces - Torque Reaction

In this view, the vertical position of the CG is of no consequence. The rear and top views of balance of forces are nearly impossible to separate due to the tail rotor effects.

Rear View of Balance of Forces

The rear view of the balance of forces adds another dimension to the understanding of the helicopter. In this plane, the vertical and lateral positions of the CG become important, as they determine the balance of forces with the tail rotor. For the ease of understanding, longitudinal CG position is ignored, and the lateral CG position is on the Centerline.

* This is for an out-of-ground effect hover.

The use of the tail rotor to counter-act the torque effect of the main rotor has an unwanted side effect*. This is called *translating tendency*, or *tail rotor drift* because of the tendency of the tail rotor to push the helicopter sideways (In some circles, this is known as translating the helicopter across the ground. Since the term is clear and only applicable to this phenomenon, it is the best one to use).

The main rotor creates a torque reaction (or moment) with the fuselage. This can be represented as two forces acting at either end of the fuselage, as shown in Figure 7-11a below. To stop this torque reaction, an equal and opposite set of forces (or a couple) could be added as shown in Figure 7-11b, however, this would be difficult to implement mechanically, would look awful and be downright dangerous†.

The same effect is possible if a single reaction were placed at one end, as shown in Figure 7-11c. This is a representation of the way a tail rotor works. Notice how two of the arrows cancel each other out immediately, and what remains are two arrows pointing in the same direction at opposite ends of the fuselage (Figure 7-11d). If the main rotor-fuselage reaction were able to be prevented by a couple (an equal and opposite set of forces) instead of a moment, there would be no translating tendency. Still another way of looking at this is to consider the tail rotor is acting at the CG of the fuselage, pushing it sideways.

Main Rotor reaction on Fuselage (black arrows)	*Could be stopped by two forces at opposite ends of fuselage (Grey arrows)*	*Instead is stopped by larger force at one end (striped arrows)*	*The overall effect is of two arrows pushing at one side*
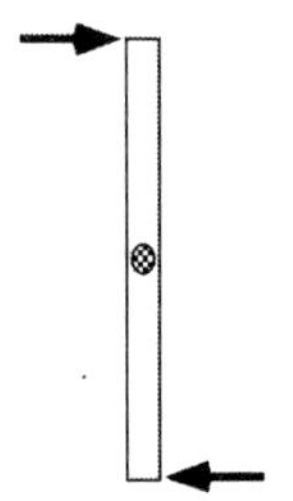	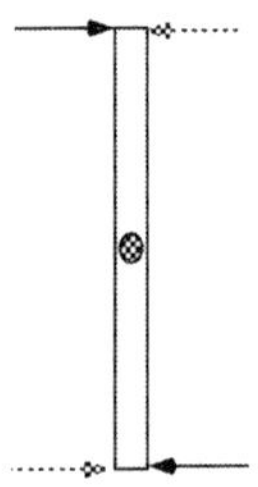	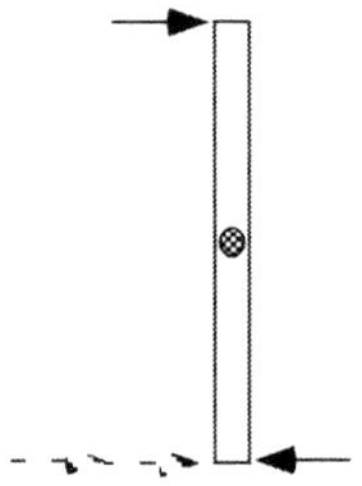	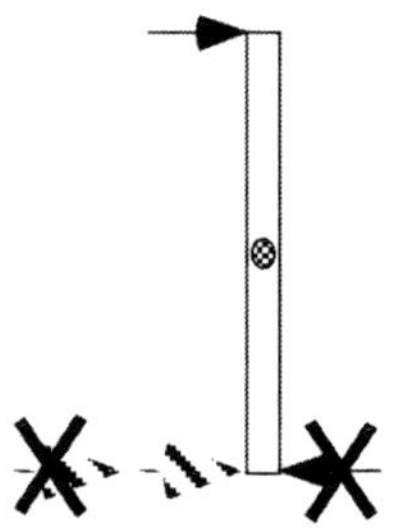
The rotor exerts a couple on the fuselage	But this would be impractical		Cancelling out the forces, we are left with two pushing the same way

Figure 7-11 Translating Tendency

Translating tendency can be corrected in several ways - for main–rotor/tail-rotor helicopters, the principal method is to tilt the thrust vector of the main rotor, as shown in Figure 7-12. In turn, this can be accomplished by some or all of the following:

- the pilot, who must adjust the controls to tilt the main rotor disk
- the flight control system, which puts in a bias to tilt the main rotor disk to the left when the stick is in the middle, or
- mounting the main rotor transmission so the drive shaft is tilted to the left permanently.

* The pun is deliberate
† It's bad enough to have to drag on behind you. Can you imagine having one in front?

Of the three, the first two will result in a pronounced lateral tilt to the fuselage - this is the reason why many helicopters hang one skid low in the hover (for our generic helicopter, it will be left skid low) and land on one skid first instead of both together. It also makes touchdowns on slopes easier in one direction than another!

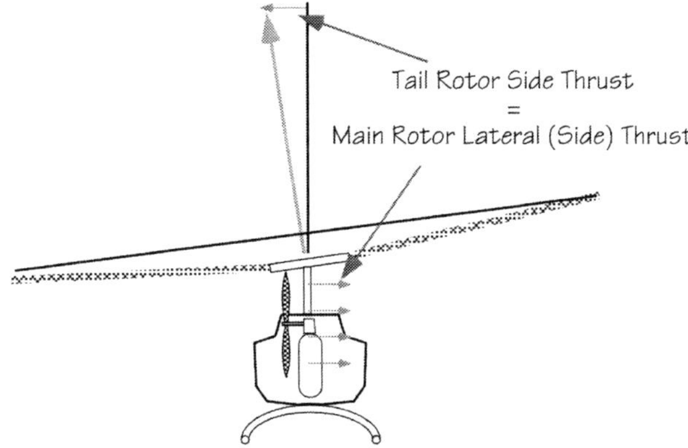

Figure 7-12 Balance of Forces - Rear View

The tail rotor can use a small amount of thrust to balance the main rotor reaction on the fuselage - it uses the long distance from the CG to the tail rotor to generate a moment (force times distance).

The amount of translating tendency depends upon the vertical location of the CG and the position of the tail rotor with respect to both the CG and the main rotor hub. To a lesser extent, lateral and longitudinal CG position also come into play.

Translating tendency is mostly well hidden from the pilot - it's there, and it doesn't normally affect things. The two places where it does have an affect are in the initial stages of a engine failure in the hover and when sitting on the water in a float equipped helicopter*. Both are discussed in more detail later.

Trim

The concept of trim is essential to an understanding of balance of forces in forward flight. The size and angle of the thrust of the main rotor is the primary consideration. The horizontal component of thrust (due to tilting of the disc) must be enough to overcome the drag of the fuselage, while the vertical component must be enough to support the weight of the helicopter. Thus the total thrust of the rotor and the angle of the tip path plane (essentially perpendicular to the rotor thrust) are fixed by the flight condition- more speed, equals more tilt.

There is another balance consideration that must also be met for the helicopter to be in trim†, namely the moments about the CG of the fuselage must be balanced. Several things can generate moments about the CG beside the rotor, namely the thrust vector not going through the CG, or pitching moments generated by the horizontal stabilizer or the fuselage. If these moments don't balance themselves, the rotor must do the balancing by moving (technically called flapping) with respect to the mast.

Rotor tilt is normally controlled by the pilot and the fuselage attitude is a by-product of tilting. On the other hand, if the pilot does not move the controls, and an imbalance occurs, the rotor will move (flap) and the fuselage will follow the rotor to keep the whole system in balance, or trim.

Balance of Forces - Forward Flight

The same concepts and principles used in the previous section for understanding the balance of forces apply when the helicopter is in forward flight. There are one or two minor items that make things slightly more difficult to explain - namely:

* see"Fixed Floats Effect on Stability and Control" on page 366

† And in this instance we are not talking about the slip ball in the middle

- the helicopter is not symmetrical when viewed from above, that is, if we draw a line down the center of the helicopter it is different from right to left side (mostly due to the tail rotor), and the rotor itself is not behaving symmetrically due to advancing and retreating blades.
- there is a pronounced forward tilt to the overall Lift vector

Side View of Balance of Forces

When viewed from the side, the balance of forces in forward flight has two additional items missing from the hover case, namely Thrust and Drag. Thrust is produced by the tilting of the Lift vector and acts at the rotor hub, and Drag is produced by the passage of the helicopter through the air and acts at the CG. In simple terms, the sum of the forces produce resultants that act from the rotor hub and CG respectively. They must align to be in balance. This is shown in Figure 7-13 below.

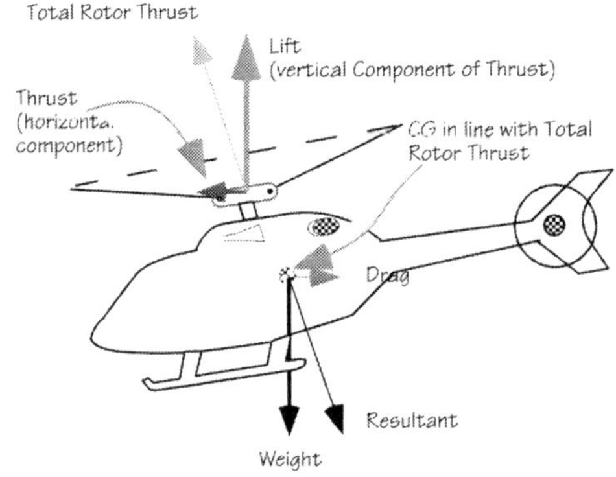

Figure 7-13 Side View of Balance of Forces, Forward Flight

When these forces are out of balance (not in equilibrium) then the helicopter will accelerate until the forces balance out and equilibrium is achieved.

Let's say the helicopter is in the cruise as shown in Figure 7-14a. Everything is in balance, when the pilot suddenly reduces collective lever, (simultaneously reducing the size of the Thrust and Lift vectors) and changes the cyclic stick (and hence changes the tilt of the two vectors). This is shown in Figure 7-14b. The resulting imbalance of forces will produce a moment about the CG that will try to align the Weight + Drag resultant under the new Thrust + Lift resultant, and the helicopter will nose up until the two vectors align, causing our machine to decelerate and descend. Figure 7-14c shows the final result.

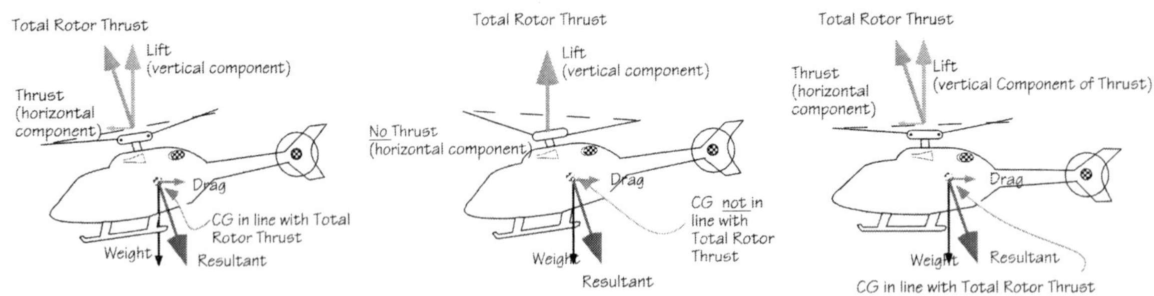

Figure 7-14 Reduction of Thrust + Lift Alignment of Vectors

Top View of Balance of Forces Forward Flight

The top view of the balance of forces in forward flight is nearly the same as in the hover, only this time the tail rotor will be pushing the helicopter sideways through the air. The pilot (who is keeping the ball in the middle* see Figure 9-1 on page 81) will have some inherent sideslip, as the rotor disk will need to be kept quite near to level in order to keep the airframe level. Pushing the helicopter sideways will result in some side wind all the time, called *inherent sideslip*.

Inherent Sideslip

Inherent sideslip is the sideslip the single rotor helicopter has all the time, but doesn't like to talk about. The tail rotor and vertical stabilizer(s) are always pushing to the side, and the rotor is also tilted to the side. The nose may not be pointed exactly at the track of the helicopter. More discussion on inherent sideslip is found in "Inherent Sideslip" on page 365.

Rear View of Balance of Forces - Forward Flight

- is missing. Since the Thrust and Drag vectors act mostly in the vertical sense, they make little difference to the balance of forces when viewed from the rear. This is valid only if the CG is kept in the middle, however that is an advanced case and we'll leave it alone…

Summary of Chapter 7

This chapter has covered the basics of balance of forces and weight and balance. Later chapters will show how it is necessary to control the forces generated by the rotor to change the balance and control the helicopter.

* This description is based on a helicopter using a slip ball and not a slip string. The difference between the two will be discussed in "Sideslip and Side Force" on page 81.

8 The Aerodynamics of Autorotation

Introduction

Many people wonder how the helicopter blade can produce lift in autorotation. In fact one of the questions most asked of helicopter pilots is

- "How do you glide down if the engine stops?"

The helicopter takes advantage of the ability of an airfoil to produce lift when air is forced to move past it, even if the engine is not providing power. In this aspect, it is the same as a windmill, or even an autogiro. The main difference is the driving force is provided by air passing up through the rotor from underneath as opposed to wind passing through - although in all cases the air is flowing more or less perpendicular to the blades.

Both the windmill and the autogiro are always and only operating in a mode call *autorotation*. This chapter will explain how a helicopter rotor can maintain rotational speed (N_R), and support the helicopter like a parachute when the source of engine power is removed.

To be very technically precise, the term autorotation means zero torque. A windmill that is pumping water or grinding grain is extracting energy from the air and working in a 'negative torque' mode. This is defined as 'windmill brake state'. The helicopter rotor is also in this mode, as it has to produce torque to drive the tail rotor and overcome transmission losses. To keep things simple, we'll use the term autorotation.

Much of what is explained in this chapter is quite detailed, and may quickly be forgotten. We certainly don't want you thinking about the theory on the way down to the ground when the engine has failed... The reasons why there are limitations on N_R, airspeed and so on in an autorotation should be easier to understand.

It is interesting to note the rate of descent in autorotation for most helicopters is just about the same as if the rotor were replaced by a parachute of the same diameter.

Autorotation Defined

Autorotation is a condition where the rotor blades are driven solely by the airflow coming up from beneath the rotor. There is no contribution from the engine. Note this condition may be possible with the throttle open and without a needle split (but the engine will not be contributing to driving the rotor). Your instructor should be able to show you this condition, if it occurs on your type of helicopter.

If we didn't have autorotation, we wouldn't have helicopters, at least not single engine helicopters, as we couldn't handle the consequences of an engine failure.

Autorotation is also one of the reasons why we have such a large range of blade pitch angles controllable by the pilot. If you look at Figure 25-6 on page 243, you'll see how little the collective actually moves in powered flight from the hover to maximum speed. Aside from an obvious need to descend, the reason for the rest of the range of movement of blade pitch is for autorotation.

Conditions Necessary for Autorotation

The first condition for autorotation is the rotor blades must already be turning. Most windmills and autogiros can start from a stopped condition, helicopter rotors are designed differently.

In powered flight, the helicopter rotor will be at some positive angle of attack, and have quite a lot of drag. The engine is producing the power to overcome that drag.

If the engine fails, the drag must be reduced quickly, so the pilot reduces the collective pitch to a very low value. Now what?

Lets say we were hovering (zero airspeed hovering) a long way above the ground. This will simplify the discussion to begin with, but is definitely not a recommended maneuver.

The engine fails -

We have lowered the collective and the helicopter is now descending vertically (don't worry about how we got to this situation...). Air is flowing up from underneath, and to understand exactly what is going on, we must revisit the previous discussions about angle of attack, lift vectors and so on.

Lift Vectors Again

Remember how lift acts perpendicular to the relative airflow and drag acts parallel to it (same as our earlier discussions).

Figure 8-1 shows how the horizontal component of RaF is affected by the position of the segment, and how this will affect the angle of attack. For simplicity, we'll assume an untwisted blade (constant pitch along its length).

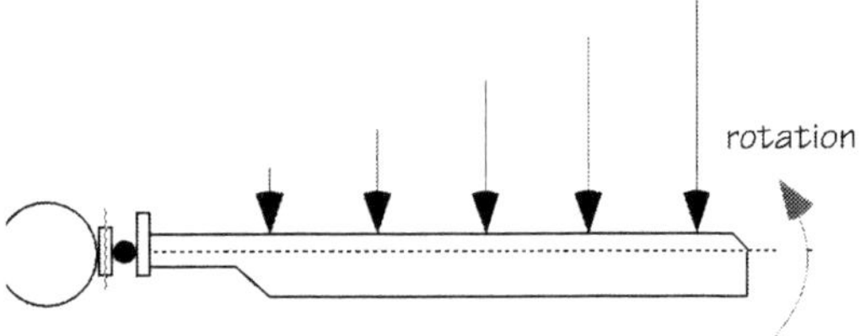

Figure 8-1 Rotor Blade with Different Horizontal Airflow, Zero Airspeed Autorotation Descent

We'll split the blade into different areas, and look at a segment from each. Starting from the hub, we'll number them 1 to 5. We'll make a safe assumption that the vertical velocity of the air is uniform. As the helicopter is descending, it would be difficult to have a different rate of descent at different parts of the blade!*

Before we get further into lift vectors, we need to look at the other component, Relative airflow (RaF). The size of the horizontal component will change. As it is in the hover, the horizontal component is related directly to the distance away from the hub.

The main thing to watch in the following processes is the direction of tilt of the total reaction (or TR), especially whether it is pointing ahead of or behind the direction of rotation of the blade.

We'll start at the root of the blade, where the horizontal component of airspeed is lowest. Notice how this makes a very large angle of attack, which actually puts the blade segment into a stalled condition. Stalled airfoils are not normally considered healthy things, as there is a large amount of drag for the lift produced. In this area, the TR is tilted behind the vertical and is trying to slow the rotor down. Blade segments in this area are said to be stalled, hence the name of 'stalled region'. We'll call this 'area 1'. A high AoA, you will remember is close to, if not above the stall angle.

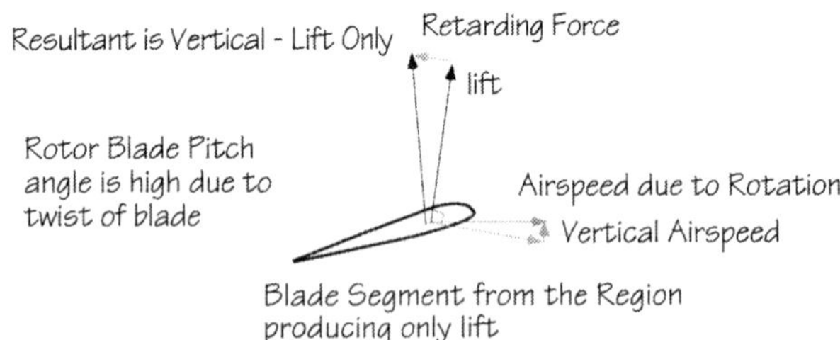

8-2 Lift Vectors in Area producing only Lift

As we move out farther on the blade the rotational velocity increases the horizontal component of airspeed, and the angle of attack decreases. The blade moves away from the stall, and the most the TR can be said to do is not slow things down. The overall reaction of the thrust vector is vertical, so this small section only produces lift, as shown in Figure 8-2. We'll call this area 2.

* There is some controversy about the exact distribution of the different areas that are about to be described - everyone is in agreement that there are sections that drive the rotor around and other sections that are tending to slow it down. The disagreement lies in which section is placed where on the blade.

As we move farther out on the blade (area 3), the increase in horizontal airflow component starts to have a more positive effect. When the lift vectors are resolved, it is easy to see how it is leaning forward of the vertical, as shown in Figure 8-3. The leaning forward part is helping to turn the blade, and it is easy to see why this part of the rotor disk is called the driving area of the disk. We'll label this area 3.

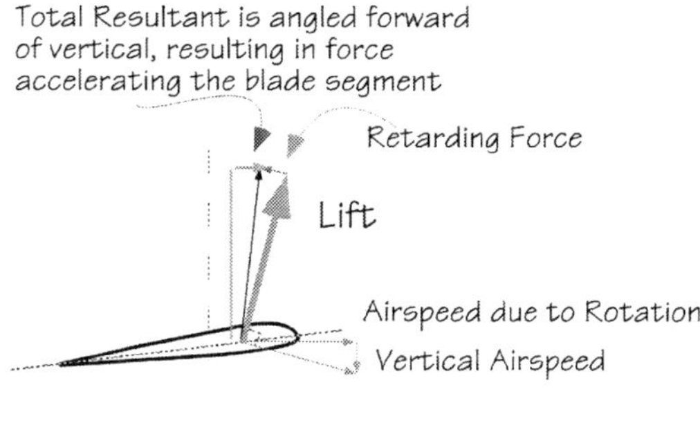

Figure 8-3 Lift Vectors in Driving Area

As we proceed farther out toward the tip the obvious assumption is that things should just get better and better - the horizontal airflow component is getting bigger and bigger isn't it? Unfortunately, several things spoil this illusion.

The first is the higher horizontal airspeed component increases the profile drag of the blade significantly. The drag is thus much larger and this tilts the overall thrust vector aft, behind the vertical. This is shown in Figure 8-4. We'll call this area 5 for reasons that will become obvious shortly.

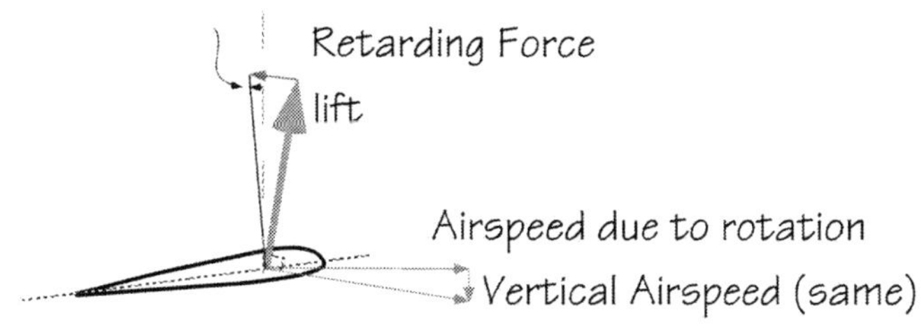

Figure 8-4 Lift Vectors in Driven Section of Rotor Blade

The second effect is the tip vortices (which are always present), increase the induced drag (drag due to lift), and further tilt the overall thrust vector aft, even more behind the vertical.

It should be obvious if one section is producing a thrust vector that drives the rotor blade forward (area 3), and one section produces a thrust vector that is slowing the blade down (area 5), somewhere between the two there will be a small area doing neither. This is area 4, and area 5 is called the driven area.

So, overall, our rotor disk now looks like Figure 8-5. There are three distinct areas- one is stalled, one is driving the rotor around, and one is trying to slow the rotor down. It is important that the total effect of all of these areas be kept in balance. Too large a driving area, and the rotor will speed up. Too large a driven area and the rotor will slow down. How we control the rotor speed then simply depends upon controlling the overall pitch of the blades.

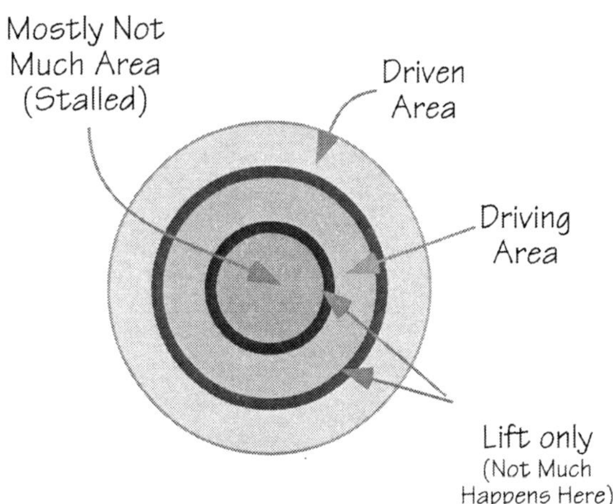

Figure 8-5 Areas of Disk in Vertical Autorotation

If the rotor is speeding up, a small increase in collective will increase the blade pitch, and hence angle of attack, all along the blade. This will change the balance of driving to driven areas (increasing the driving and decreasing the driven) and slow the rotor down. It may be necessary to maintain some collective pitch to keep the rotor speed from increasing.

If the rotor is too slow, then it should be obvious that reducing the blade pitch will be necessary. If the collective is all the way down, everything at the pilot's disposal has been accomplished.

The explanation so far has been for a straight, untwisted blade. Since most rotor blades incorporate some twist, Figure 8-5 would look somewhat different, but would still have driven and driving sections in balance.

It's important to remember that up to now, we've been talking only about a vertical autorotation. In other words, we've been descending straight down at zero forward airspeed. While this helps to introduce the complex aerodynamics of autorotation, we don't fly like this very often, for reasons that will become clear. So what changes when we introduce forward flight?

EFFECT OF FORWARD FLIGHT

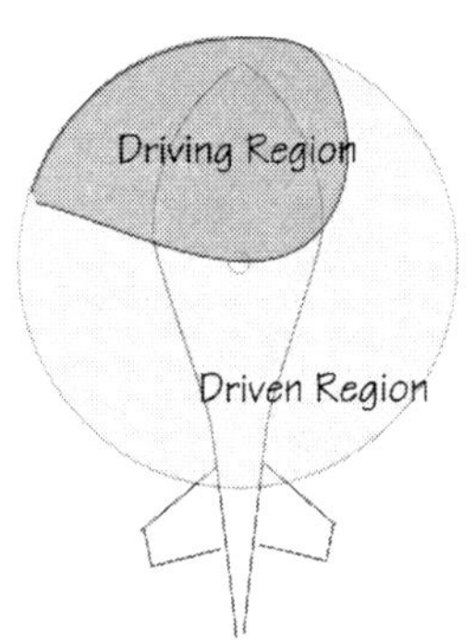

Figure 8-6 Effect of Airspeed on Autorotation Areas of the Disk

Forward airspeed will change the pattern of the driving and driven areas, not the overall balance. For example, adding forward speed will require the rotor disk to be tilted with respect to the airflow. This forward speed will also have an effect on the size and location of the driving and driven areas. This is shown in Figure 8-6. If the airspeed increases too much, it is possible that the driving area will become too small with respect to the driven area, and the N_R will decay. For this reason there is often a V_{NE} in autorotation.

We have already seen that there will be a dissymmetry of lift between the advancing and retreating sides of the disk

How the Blade Works in Autorotation

In strictly technical terms the rotor disk can work in one of three conditions - (1) the power–absorbing i.e. engine driven, lift producing (or normal) state, (2) the vortex ring or turbulent wake state (sort of halfway being driven by an engine and being driven by the air flowing up from beneath it) and (3)the autorotation state (where the rotor is extracting energy from the air flowing up from below it). For these reasons the rotor can work well in either the 'normal' or 'autorotative' states, not in-between. In some more advanced textbooks the term used for autorotation is 'windmill brake state', but you don't need to worry about that here.

N_R in Autorotation Descent

Many helicopters FMs have a chart of N_R vs. weight and density altitude for setting the blade pitch in autorotation. An example is shown in Figure 8-7. The reason for setting this blade pitch angle is to prevent too little or too much blade pitch as the baseline angle.

Too little blade pitch with the collective full down (*flat pitch* or *Minimum Pitch on the Ground* (MPOG) may result in unwanted vibration when sitting on the ground. It may also show up as too low a torque value at MPOG. It is also shown by the N_R being too high in an autorotation.

Too high a blade pitch setting causes the N_R to be too low in autorotation, resulting in less than desired autorotative performance and too high a torque at MPOG.

Another way to read this graph is that increased weight for the same disk area gives a higher N_R in autorotation with the collective full down. To maintain the same N_R at this higher weight requires the collective to be raised, increasing the blade pitch angle and drag, and making the driving region slightly smaller. Same approach for increased density altitudes - to maintain N_R at the nominal value, the collective must be raised.

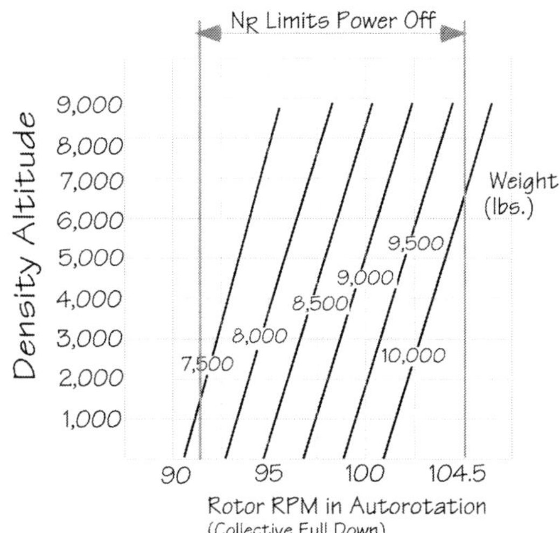

Figure 8-7 Rotor RPM in autorotation Chart

From this comes an observation about high–disk–loading helicopters - namely, they will not take kindly to the collective being lowered all the way in autorotation. One helicopter type that had grown in weight by over 40% from its conception without an increase in rotor diameter has to have the collective about one quarter of the way up at the best of times to keep the N_R in the green. One day it was necessary to go to 18,000 feet in this machine and then autorotate down - the collective was at least halfway up until we got below 10,000'!

Another Use for the Autorotation RPM Chart

The autorotational N_R chart shows several things. First, at the same density altitude, the N_R will go up for an increase in weight. Secondly, at the same weight, the N_R will go up as density altitude increases (or air density decreases). We can learn several things from these observations.

Effect of Density

The effect of a change in air density is to change the N_R for the same weight. Thinner air (i.e. higher density altitude) and the N_R will increase. So what?

The effect is often seen if a helicopter is operated at high density altitudes, when the N_R had been set at a lower density altitude. In order to keep the N_R within limits, it may be necessary to hold the collective up slightly. While nearly all training helicopters have the collective full down in a stabilized autorotational descent, not all helicopter types are like this- don't become too rigid in your flying*.

Effect of Weight

As the weight of the helicopter increases, the N_R will increase for the same density altitude. We don't have much opportunity to change the weight by adding or subtracting things from the helicopter while descending, aside from turning the helicopter and increasing the load factor. We can also flare the helicopter at the bottom of the descent. Both the turn and the flare are going to increase the effective weight of the helicopter, and this will increase the N_R. This effect is probably secondary to the effect of an increased airflow due to the turn, both will help to increase the N_R.

If there is a need to push over (i.e. drop the nose quickly) the helicopter in an autorotation (see Chapter 30,"Advanced Engine Failures" for types of maneuvers that might require a push over), the effective weight will go down. This will cause the N_R to decrease as the effective weight of the helicopter is decreased. The change in inflow to the rotor disk (for a short while it will be coming from the 'wrong' direction) will also cause the N_R to decrease.

* More than one pilot transitioning from a two-bladed helicopter to a multi-bladed one has oversped the rotor by instinctively putting the collective full down.

Summary of Chapter 8

We had a good reason for looking at lift vectors, and how they keep us under control in an autorotation. This might help to understand how the rotor works in various stages of Chapter 18,"Engine Failures for Beginners", which is the fundamentals of how to fly an autorotation.

9 Instruments and Warning Systems

Airframe Instruments

Other books cover the instruments common to both aircraft and helicopters such as magnetic compasses, radios and navigation instruments. Not wishing to re-invent the wheel, let alone re–calibrate its roundness, the interested reader is asked to refer to these. This chapter will deal only with the helicopter–specific instruments, or aspects of these otherwise standard instruments might impinge on rotary wing aviation. Airframe instruments are those instruments that aren't related to the engine.

Sideslip and Side Force

An important but misunderstood instrument in the helicopter is the *slip ball*. A typical slip ball in straight and level flight is shown in Figure 9-1.

It measures side force or lateral balance, nothing more or less. The slip ball is of little use in the hover and low airspeed environment, when it is more important to keep the helicopter aligned with the direction of travel than to keep the side force zero. Typically, the slip ball is only used above 40 to 60 KIAS.

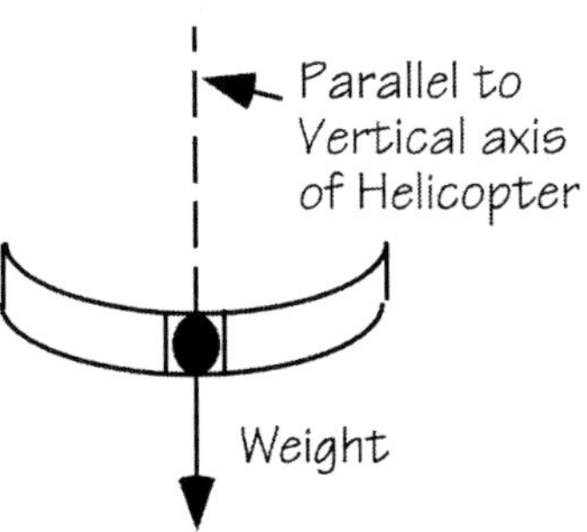

Figure 9-1 Straight and Level Flight or sitting on level ground

The slip ball might also be more correctly called the *inclinometer*.

What the Slip Ball Measures

To begin with, it doesn't measure sideslip, and it doesn't measure lateral acceleration. The slip ball measures the difference between the vertical axis of the aircraft and the centrifugal force*. When they are lined up, the slip ball is in the middle (assuming its that way with the helicopter resting on a flat level surface). When the slip ball is out of the center, a force is acting to one side or the other. If you like, you can consider the slip ball as a lateral inclinometer, useful in the hover for measuring the lateral CG, if conditions are suitable†. The following diagrams show the problem

:

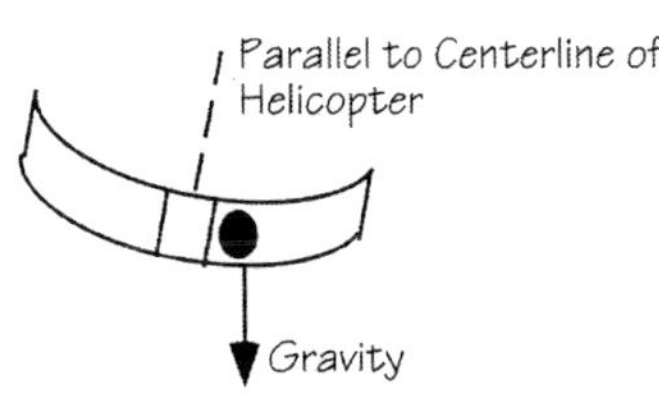

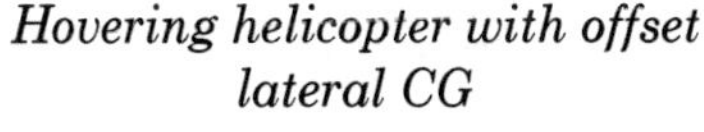

Hovering helicopter with offset lateral CG

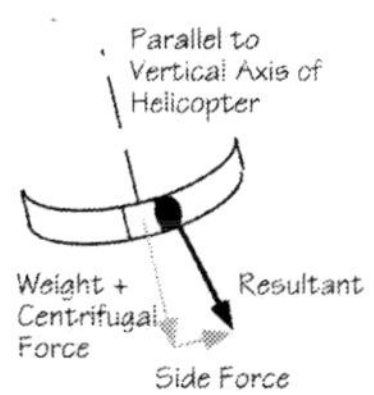

Helicopter in uncoordinated turn (forward flight)

Figure 9-2 Slip Ball Positions

The slip ball measures the line of the resultant between centrifugal force and gravity in comparison to the centerline of the helicopter. The slip ball can be off–center with no turn rate - it means the vertical axis of the aircraft is aligned to something different than where the

* Evidently there really is no such thing as centrifugal force in physics. It is an illusion created by centripetal force and inertia. Lets us keep our illusions.

† Which raises the question of why we don't have a similar device in the longitudinal axis to measure longitudinal CG.

combined 'centrifugal force plus gravity' vector is pointing. In the hover, with an offset lateral CG, the ball may be well off to one side - there is no turn rate, so the gravity vector is not in-line with the vertical axis of the helicopter. Figure 9-2 shows this.

What is Side Force?

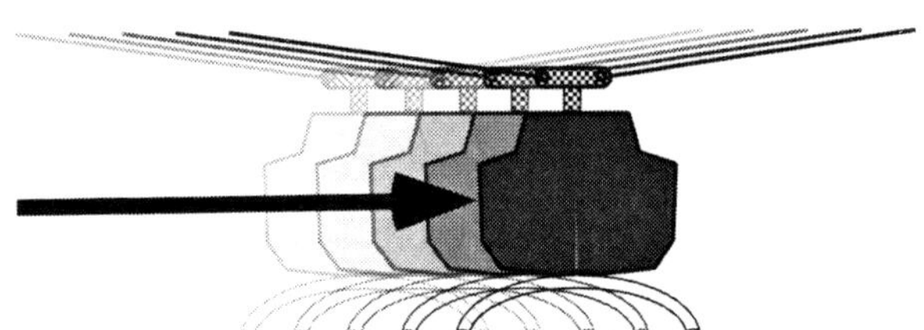

Figure 9-3 Side Force

Wait a minute - what's *side force*? It's the force pushing the helicopter to the side. Sources for side force are the tail rotor and fuselage effects as well as the main rotor. Figure 9-3 shows side forces. It's sort of measured by the slip ball - when the ball is stationary, the side acceleration is zero. There may still be a side force, but it is balanced by other forces and is not producing an acceleration. The sum of the side forces are in balance.

At speeds between 40 and 60 KIAS, small side forces (or out of balance conditions) can create large changes in heading without causing the ball to move. This is another explanation for instrument flying being difficult below 60 KIAS in most helicopters.

At less than 60 KIAS, there is very little airspeed across the vertical stabilizer, so there is very little in the way of force to help keep the nose pointed forward.

What is Sideslip?

Side force is different than *sideslip*. Sideslip is lateral airspeed or side wind. The helicopter has some inherent sideslip (see "Inherent Sideslip" on page 73) when in the cruise with wings level* and the slip ball centered. Confused? I'm not surprised. Inherent sideslip is similar to translating tendency, and is caused by the tail rotor. It is always pushing to the side, and in forward flight, with no indication to the pilot the helicopter is moving sideways that he can correct, it will drift sideways. This is called inherent sideslip, as it's always there.

A simple explanation for this part though. On the ground, on a level surface with the rotor stopped the airframe should be level, and the slip ball should be in the middle†. Depending upon the lateral CG and relative wind, there may or may not be some angle of bank and slip ball displacement when the helicopter lifts into the hover.

There is normally no suitable instrument to quantify sideslip unless a low airspeed system or yaw vane is fitted.

I recall one incident in a formation of Bell UH-1N's where an unusual situation arose. Two helicopters were in line astern (one behind the other). I was leading and enjoying the navigation and flying when the other pilot called on the radio

- "Is your slip ball in the middle?" he asked.
- "Of course - it's always in the middle - you're dealing with a professional pilot" I replied.
- "What's your heading, and is your compass aligned?" came the next question.
- "225° and yes, the compass is aligned, and it's the same as the standby compass." (I thought I'd show him how on the ball‡ I was.)
- "OK - I'll take the lead" As he outranked me, I let him.

We switched lead helicopters and I could more clearly understand his concern. I asked him the same questions -

- "Is the ball in the middle?"
- "Yes, I'm also a professional," was the reply.
- "What's your heading?"

* OK so helicopters don't have 'wings' to level - this means no bank angle.

† There are several helicopters where this is not the case- on the ground, the attitude indicator will not show level, and the slip ball will not be in the middle- the designer built them this way. Don't worry.

‡ You'll have to believe me this pun wasn't deliberate.

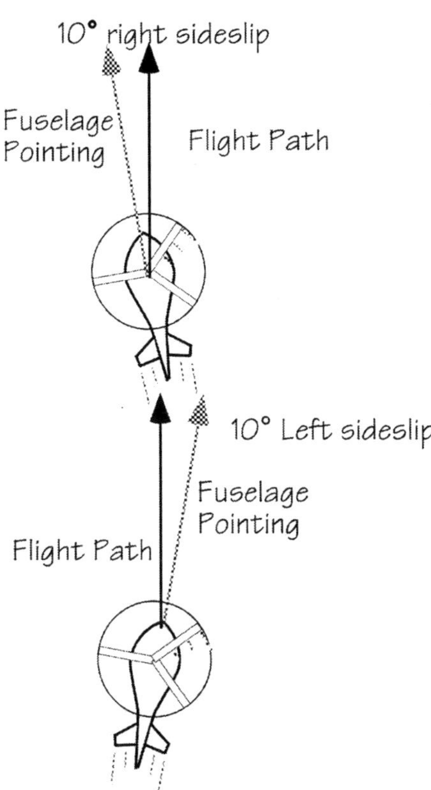

Figure 9-4 Two Helicopters Both with the Slip Ball in the Middle

It was about 10° different from mine, and yes, his compass was aligned and agreed with the heading on the standby compass. Since we were both in formation, and going the same place how could we have two different headings? Figure 9-4 shows what was happening.

What was the cause of the problem?

The answer was we had opposite lateral CGs. I had an internal auxiliary fuel tank on the left side, and three passengers sitting on that same side. My boss also had an auxiliary fuel tank and three passengers on the same side as his fuel tank, but his was on the right side. We were both flying with the ball in the middle, and naturally had very different inherent sideslips. I won't try to draw the weight and balance vector diagrams, don't worry.

Were we wrong*? I don't know. I suppose the purist would insist on flying with the ball in the same place it was when we lifted into the hover.†

Slip Strings

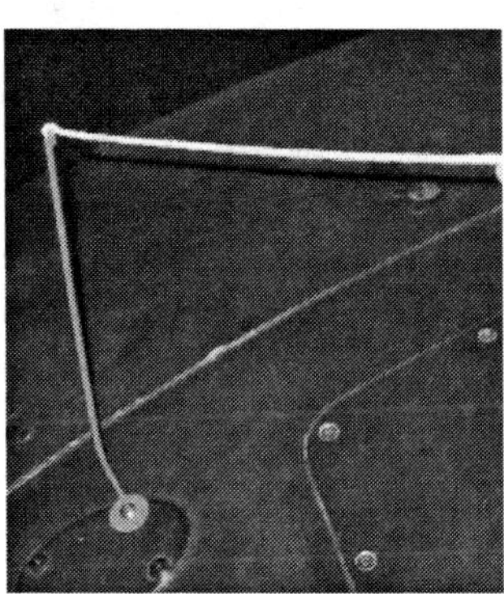

Figure 9-5 Slip String

Several helicopter types have no slip ball. While this may seem strange, in the early days of helicopter flying, when these types were certified, the importance of sideforce was not as well understood. Certainly flying in clouds wasn't considered. Several new types also forsake the slip ball for a slip string. How these are supposed to be used at night or in cloud is a mystery to me, but they exist, so one must learn to use them. If the helicopter has neither, the slip string is by far the easiest to fit, and can be used to reduce the sideslip in cruise flight and reduce the drag. The simple way to learn to use the slip string is it is the opposite from the slip ball - step on the fixed end of the string to keep it in the middle. Never seen a slip string? See Figure 9-5 .

The slip string also has some merit in vertical climbs – the Gazelle and the Alouette, featuring both a slip ball and slip string, had a very shallow curvature to the slip ball track. In the Alouette, fully loaded in the Alps with maximum power and the ball in the middle, we were lucky to get 300 feet per minute rate of climb at minimum power speed. The slip string was all over the place, because the slip ball was happy to be in the middle with nearly any amount of sideslip. When the safety pilot suggested (tactfully, but forcefully) I should use the slip string, and keep it in the middle, we got 1,000 feet per minute rate of climb, and the

* The boss is always correct, so I guess the question should be 'was I wrong?'

† Flight tests have shown how flying with the slip ball in the same place it is in a hover into wind results in less drag and increased range.

slip ball was still in the middle. Other times in the Gazelle, it was not possible to get good flight test data of any sort around 40 to 60 KIAS if the slip ball was used, but very easy if the slip string was the 'instrument' for balance. There is a place for both slip string and slip ball.

So why aren't slip strings fitted to all helicopters? Someone suggested that at least one company's marketing department won't let them be put on the aircraft because a competitor's machine had them, but that's so petty as to be unbelievable*. Aside from the obvious requirement to make them glow in the dark for night flying, the real answer evades me.

Engine Transmission and Rotor Instruments

The engine instruments fitted to most helicopters are quite straightforward and show the power or performance being demanded of the engine. For piston engine helicopters, the engine RPM and Manifold Pressure (boost) gauges are nearly the same as those in fixed–wing aircraft.

Turbine engines in helicopters have some slight differences from fixed–wing aircraft and are covered in Chapter 29,"The Turbine Engine". This chapter will deal with the instruments on the piston engined helicopter.

N_R Warnings

The low N_R warning is installed for a variety of reasons, but the main one is to warn the pilot the N_R is below the minimum established for continued safe flight after the engine has failed. The rotor continues to function and provide lift below the rotational speed where the warning sounds but not too far below that speed- it just won't be as efficient. The N_R warning is also there to make sure the pilot who didn't notice the engine had failed would lower the collective lever when he hears the horn.

It helps the pilot to stay out of more trouble.

If the low N_R warnings do appear (sound, flash or whatever) there is no need for undue alarm - lower the collective lever smartly until these pesky things go away. You'll be trained until this reaction is instinctive, so get used to it, and learn. If the warnings are on, and the collective lever is fully down already, there is not much more the pilot can do to get the rotor to turn faster.

High N_R warning signals are almost always warning lights - and you need to be looking inside to see them, so it is better to listen to the N_R and make corrections accordingly.

At least one helicopter accident has been caused by the pilots misinterpreting a high N_R signal for a low one, and lowering the collective lever. This of course unloaded the rotor even more, and the engine overspeed protection shut down the engine completely, making a real mess of everyone's day. High N_R warnings are less likely to occur first in emergency situations and are (normally) less life threatening than low N_R warnings, and it pays to know which is which. High N_R warnings may show up when turning in autorotation or the flare, but otherwise would normally not be present unless something is wrong. Some helicopters have a rapidly fluctuating tone in the audio system for high N_R. Many light training helicopters do not have a high N_R warning system at all, so learn to depend on your ears.

Transmissions and Gearboxes

The transmission system in a helicopter is used to change the direction and speed of rotation of the engine output. Since most piston engines have a power output that is parallel to the horizon, it needs to be changed in direction to turn the rotors blades attached to the mast (which should stay pretty close to perpendicular to the horizon). Since the piston engine turns at about 2,500 RPM, and the rotor needs to be between 350 and 500 RPM for most light helicopters, a speed reduction is also necessary. This is all carried out efficiently by the transmission.

Transmission Oil Temperature and Pressure

We rotary wing people worry a lot about transmissions - they keep us airborne and if they fail, we are in deep trouble. So we worry about the health of the transmission and its oil. Seems simple enough.

There are still many helicopters with sensors in the transmission that can be slightly misleading. Get a copy of the maintenance manuals, or if there is a ground school training package, a cutaway drawing of the transmission. Does the transmission oil temperature sensor sit where it will always get oil past

* or entirely believable, depending on how cynical you are.

it, even if the oil level is low? If not, what happens when the oil level starts to fall - a leak in the system somewhere - will the high oil temperature light work before the transmission casing starts to melt?

Are there at least two sensors for oil pressure - one for a caution light, and one for a pressure gauge in the cockpit? If there are not at least two separate systems (both sensors, wires and indicators) for indicating oil pressure, how will you know if you have only a sensor failure or a real oil pressure failure when the warning light comes on, or the cockpit pressure gauge drops?

Chip Detectors

Since the helicopter relies on things rotating to stay aloft, there is naturally a healthy interest in seeing all the whirling parts stay whirling. Small particles of metal in the lubrication systems of engines and transmissions are harmful to continued whirling, so when they appear, it is wise to let the pilot know about it as soon as possible. Hence the advent of the chip detector.

Chip detectors are placed strategically so all the oil in a component, be it transmission or engine flows past a detector at one time or another. Most of the chip detector systems are magnetic, as the worst metal to be breaking up is iron–based. The chip detector works on the principle that anything metal which is breaking up will produce small chips of metal that will eventually fall across the small gap between two parts of the circuit*, and let an electrical current pass, lighting up a light in the cockpit. This tells the pilot something is in the transmission or oil system that shouldn't be, and appropriate measures can be carried out.

Unfortunately, in the compromise between sensitivity of the detector and size of typically untroublesome bits of metal, someone sided with finding things that are not really dangerous. Chip detector lights got a bad reputation for crying wolf.

Figure 9-6 Chip Detector

A better solution has been to apply a current to the chip detector to burn off the offending piece of metal (normally called fuzz - hence the name for the device Fuzz-Buster†), and if it can't be burnt off by a particular amount of current, then it's a pretty serious sized piece of metal and needs to be acknowledged. If the current burns off the bit of fuzz and another one appears immediately, it's also probably fairly serious and should be investigated - on the ground. A typical Chip Detector is shown in Figure 9-6.

Of course, there are even more modern systems that detect a gear about to lose a tooth‡, but that's really advanced stuff (see "HUMS" on page 263).

Summary of Chapter 9

This chapter has covered the basics of helicopter instruments and sensors used in a light training helicopter. While it may seem like there is a lot to learn here, the fundamentals will pay dividends in any helicopter or fixed wing aircraft.

* Much the same as a bug zapper - the magnet on the detector attracts metal like the light attracts moths and when drawn in the complete a circuit across two contact.

† It has nothing to do with the Police...

‡ the helicopter equivalent of a tooth fairy perhaps?

10 The Piston Engine

INTRODUCTION

The piston engine used in most light training helicopters is similar to most car engines*. This may surprise some student pilots. Both are 4 stroke engines and many parts, such as starters, alternators and so on are same accessories found on a car. The modern car has a sophisticated engine control system of electronic ignition and fuel injection, where the helicopter engine uses technology that is much older, simpler and less efficient. In this chapter many problems inherent to the piston engine will be discussed and you'll probably wonder why you've never heard of these in your jalopy. In cars, the solutions have been made transparent to the driver, however helicopter pilots still have to put up with (and compensate for) these problems.

We'll run through basic principles of operation, then go from starting up the engine, operating it and finally shutting it down.

PRINCIPLES OF OPERATION

The *four stroke* engine is named because it has four parts to its operation. The four distinct strokes are:

- Intake - the fuel and air are drawn into the cylinder
- Compression the fuel and air mixture is compressed
- Power a spark ignites the mixture causing it to burn and expand
- Exhaust the burned mixture is forced out of the cylinder.

This sequence is shown in Figure 10-1.

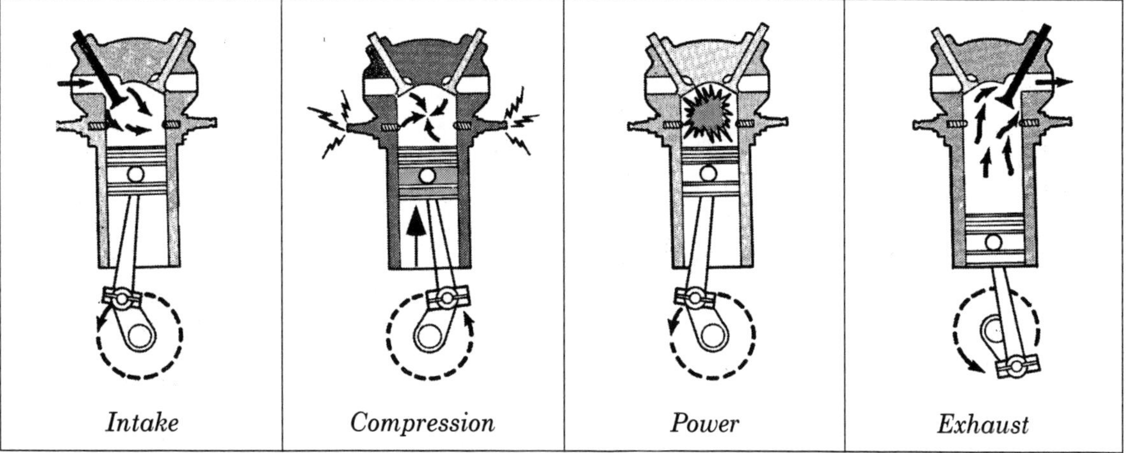

Figure 10-1 Four strokes of engine

Components

The piston engine in most helicopters has many of the same components as car engines, so they won't be discussed in detail. Some of the important differences are aircraft piston engines have a dual ignition source and are air cooled, as opposed to car engines having a single ignition source and liquid cooling with a radiator. Most of the engines you'll come across in training use carburetors, whereas most cars are now fuel injected. With the carburetor comes a mixture control and a carburetor heat control. There are necessarily, a few more engine instruments in the helicopter cockpit than you'll find in the family mini-van.

* Although not much more sophisticated than an air-cooled Volkswagen engine.

Dual Ignition

The ignition system in most helicopter piston engines will be a *magneto* system. This type of system does not require a battery voltage to operate, so the engine can continue to operate in the event of a total electrical failure. To ensure spark gets to the engine, two magnetos and two spark plugs are used.

Cooling

Burning fuel produces a lot of heat, and heat has to be taken away from the engine. In a car, the water pump and radiator take care of that, but this type of engine has been found to be too heavy for most aviation uses, so air cooled engines are used. These have a lot of fins on the cylinders, and requires air moving across the fins to draw away the heat. Unfortunately for the helicopter engine, most of the time when a lot of power is needed (and heat generated) is in the hover, when there isn't much air flowing past the engine. For this reason, most helicopter engines have an fan attached to them to push lots of air past the cylinders.

One of my A&P friends reminded me of the importance of oil for cooling. In fact, one of the four uses of oil is to cool*, so it is important to make sure that your oil coolers are clear and cleaned frequently if operating in dusty or grassy environments.

RPM Ranges vs. Auto Engines

Helicopter piston engines have invariably been of seized–wing parentage, designed to be attached to a propeller. A propeller on a light airplane typically turns at 2,200 - 2,600 RPM, so the engine has probably been designed to work well at that RPM. Car engines are different and normally designed to provide most of their power at near 6,000 RPM. No aircraft piston engine would survive at that high RPM.

An aircraft engine may spend 10% of its life at 100% power and 10% at idle, and the remaining at 80-90% power in the cruise. A helicopter engine has a similar spectrum of use. On the other hand, a car engine spends most of its time at less than 30% power, and very little at maximum power. It's no wonder that car engines last so long, and are so reliable. Fuel efficiency is also easier to design and build into an engine that is going to be used in this manner. Our flying machines are still well behind the automobile piston engine, but catching up! I hope it comes sooner than later.

Basics of Carburation

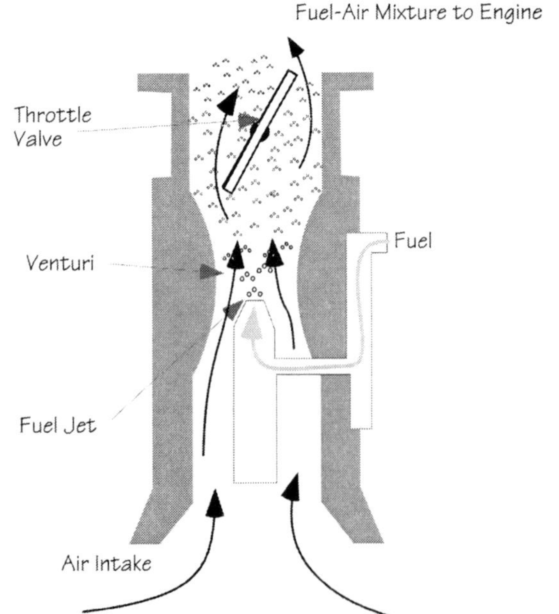

Figure 10-2 Basics of Carburation

The important part of the engine for the beginning helicopter pilot comes down to the carburetor, and some of its features.

The carburetor works by atomizing fuel into the air, creating a fuel-air mixture suitable for combustion. This mixture is drawn into the cylinders to be ignited and burned to produce power.

The important point for the pilot to understand is that the carburetor mixes fuel mechanically. Air rushes past a restriction in the throat of the carburetor, shown in Figure 10-2, which speeds up the air. Speeding up the air will reduce the air pressure (Bernoulli again), and the difference between the air pressure in the throat of the carburetor and the air pressure in the fuel chamber causes the fuel to flow into the throat (or venturi) of the carburetor and mix with the air passing. This atomizes the fuel, mixing it completely prior to be being drawn into the cylinder.

* The other three are seal between metal surfaces, clean dirt out between things like bearings, and lubricate

If you've ever held a wet finger[*] up in the breeze to see which way the wind is blowing, you'll know a breeze will cool the skin on the upwind side more quickly than on the downwind side.

If you've ever spilled some gasoline on your exposed skin, you will also notice the fuel cools your skin as it vaporizes.

Both of these (cooling due to increased velocity and vaporizing) are occurring in the throat of the carburetor as the fuel is mixed with the air. These contribute to carburetor icing, discussed later.

The amount of air entering the carburetor is controlled by the throttle (or butterfly) valve, which in turn is controlled by the pilot. Like a car, opening the throttle on most aircraft piston engines puts a small amount of additional fuel into the system in anticipation of an increased engine power output (this is accomplished by the accelerator pump on car engines using a carburetor, and some aircraft engines also have this device).

Vaporization

The carburetor works by vaporizing the fuel into a predictable fuel-air mixture by weight. The ideal mixture depends on whether the engine is accelerating, decelerating or at a constant power setting. We normally think of air and liquids in terms of volume, but this ideal mixture must be a ratio by weight. However to get the same ratio of fuel to air by weight when the volume of air flowing through the carburetor changes so much from idle to maximum power is difficult. Also don't forget that the density of air changes dramatically with altitude and temperature.

A carburetor is far more complex than the diagrams here show. In fact, given the problems faced, it's amazing they are not much more complex.

Because the carburetor works with air pressure to move fuel, it does not adequately compensate for air density, and some way to make adjustments for this must be found. Two basic ways exist to do this- automatic or manual. We don't need to concern ourselves with automatics except to know that they involve a great number of inter-related ports, orifices, valves, needles, bellows and other widgets working behind the scenes to keep the mixture right. The manual method is the cockpit mixture control., discussed "Mixture Control" on page 98.

Normally, this works fine, but at really cold temperatures, the fuel may not want to vaporize well. Cars have solved this problem by incorporating temperature sensors in the carburetor air intake. If the air is too cold, the air is taken from a shroud around the exhaust manifold that heats the air to a suitable temperature. This helps in vaporization.

In a helicopter, in cold weather the carburetor air inlet temperature should be around +30 to +35°C (100°F). If you have a carburetor air temperature gage, use of some carburetor heat may help vaporization, but may make the problem of carburetor icing slightly worse. Refer to the FM or the engine manufacturers procedures.

Humidity also has an effect on vaporization. Water vapor particles take up more space than air particles. This has a two-fold effect on performance. First of all, less weight of air is available to enter the fixed volume of the cylinder, and secondly less volume is available for fuel to vaporize. Moist air also does not permit the fuel / air mixture to burn as evenly. High humidity can cause up to 7% less power available from the piston engine.

* Hopefully, it's your wet finger you're holding...

Piston Engine Helicopter Instruments

Figure 10-3 Engine and Rotor RPM Gage

Despite what you may think, there are surprisingly few instruments in a piston engine helicopter, and relatively few limitations to remember, particularly compared to a turbine engine. The two main gages are shown in Figure 10-3 and Figure 10-4.The engine and rotor RPM gage is relatively easy to understand, but the workings of the *manifold pressure gage* requires some explanation. It is worth noting that in many piston engine helicopters, the engine RPM needle is the largest needle, not the rotor RPM needle - the reasons for this are not clear, especially when the two are joined (in single gage applications) when the engine is running, and when the engine stops running, you really care only about the rotor RPM and it is the smallest!

Manifold Pressure

If you look at the typical piston engine intake system on a helicopter, you'll see it contains a throttle and, somewhere in the intake manifold, a pressure sensor. It should be downstream of the throttle valve.

The manifold pressure gage measures the air pressure in the intake manifold of the engine. Sounds simple enough. In many ways, it's like the altimeter, but instead of measuring pressure and converting it into an equivalent altitude, it is measuring and displaying the pressure directly, with less accuracy than an altimeter.

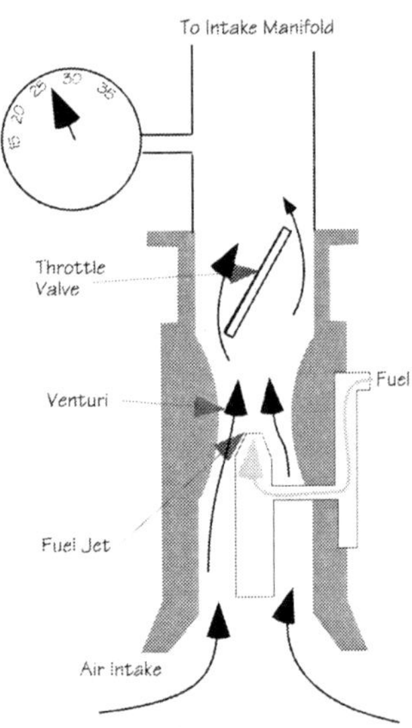

Figure 10-4 Measuring Manifold Pressure

If you've flown any fixed-wing aircraft, you will notice airplanes with fixed pitch propellers do not have a manifold pressure gage, while those with variable pitch propellers have them. The reason is that in a fixed pitch propeller, the pilot can only control the speed of the engine, not how hard the engine has to work to turn the propeller.

To start from the simplest part, with the engine off, the manifold pressure should equal the barometric pressure. If you are at sea level on a standard day, the barometric pressure will be 29.92" of mercury, and with the engine stopped, the manifold pressure gage should read pretty close to that value. If you are 5,000' above sea level, on a standard day, then the manifold pressure should read 24" (approximately 1" of mercury for every 1,000' of altitude). Theoretically, this is the maximum pressure the engine can produce, but, as will be seen, is optimistic by some amount. We will only talk about non-supercharged or non-turbocharged engines here.

Figure 10-5 Manifold Pressure Gage

Air is being drawn into the cylinder by the action of the piston going down, creating a vacuum. The restriction to the flow of air at idle is due to the throttle, which is only partly open, (this means the butterfly or throttle valve is nearly closed). The pressure in the intake at idle is low. If you see zero on the manifold pressure gage, it's broken- a piston engine couldn't run without drawing air into it.

With the engine driving the rotors, the throttle is more open, and at high power, the throttle will be fully open, with the minimum restriction to air flowing into the intake manifold. The manifold pressure will be high.

Because of the restricting nature of the carburetor, the intake manifold must always have less pressure than the outside air, (at least for an un–supercharged or non-turbocharged engine).

The limitations on manifold pressure are developed from practical tests on a dynamometer that measures the power output of the engine at different RPM and manifold pressures.

Thus to accurately measure engine performance in a piston engine helicopter, it is necessary to know both engine RPM and manifold pressure. The mathematics of actually measuring power from a piston engine are pretty tough, so we'll avoid them.

What Use is the Manifold Pressure Gage?

One other note about the manifold pressure gage. I'll make the very bold statement that

"By itself, the manifold pressure gage doesn't tell you much worthwhile."

The reason for this statement is that what you as the pilot are most interested in is how much margin remains before you can't get any more power out of the engine. This gage does precious little to help in that regard. What you are required to do, is look up on a table what the maximum manifold pressure you can get for the conditions you are flying in. So, if you took off from sea level, and are trying to land at your friend's cabin at 4,000' above sea level, you have to fly by the cabin, note the conditions of pressure altitude and temperature (4,300' PA, +30°C), then use your chart to figure out how much manifold pressure you will have available. Not a nice thing to have to do if it's turbulent, and windy with the doors open, etc.

What we need is a manifold pressure gage with a barometric capsule in it, with some suitable margin built in for the inherent losses in that helicopter type's engine. Either that, or a small moveable bug on the manifold pressure gage to be set by the pilot.

While all helicopters will have a maximum manifold pressure listed in the FM limitations section, I'm not sure you can ever get to that value with normal operating RPM unless you have turbo- or super-charging.

Starting

A problem with any piston engine is kicking it into life. The aviation piston engine is no different, but there is a difference with a helicopter. The starting system is normally 'sized' so it can turn over the engine, but not the combination of the engine and rotor. If the starter were made big enough to turn both, it would be significantly heavier, and take a much larger battery. The combined weight would cut into the useful load of the helicopter.

A clutch is used to disconnect the engine from the rotor during the start. When the engine is running, the clutch permits the engine to drive the rotor system. There are two distinct ways of doing this.

Clutches

Since the rotor must be gradually accelerated from rest, a means to gradually introduce the power from the engine to the rotor is needed. Once the two parts are running together (or engaged), they need to stay engaged. This is all accomplished by the *clutch*.

The clutch in a helicopter is like those used in cars. For those of you who panic at the thought of driving a 'standard' transmission car, relax. You don't have to shift gears, start from a stop on hills or anything tricky like that*.

Once the engine is at the proper conditions for engaging the rotor (temperatures and oil pressures in the correct range), the clutch is engaged.

There are two types of clutches used in piston engine helicopters, those automatically engaged and those controlled by the pilot.

Centrifugal (or Automatic) Clutch

Automatically engaged clutches typically operate with engine RPM and use a principle of centrifugal forces. As the engine speed increases past a certain RPM, springs in the clutch shoes are overcome and the shoes contact the drum of the clutch. The rotor will start to turn, slowly at first, and as engine speed increases, the shoes become more solidly attached until the drum is turning at the same speed as the engine. Not that common on new helicopters.

* Like its not hard enough to hover...

Idler or Manual Clutch

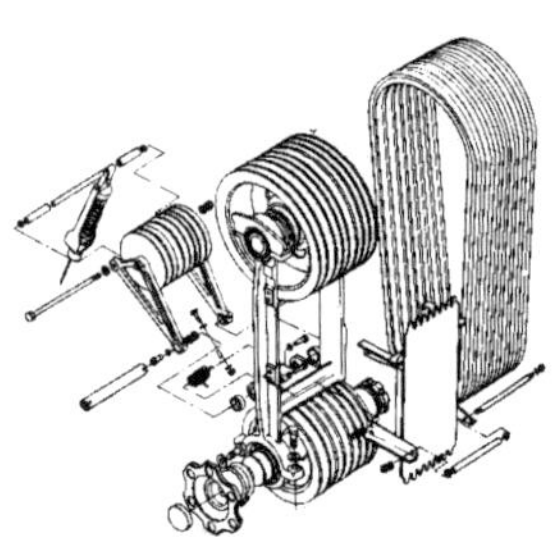

Figure 10-6 Manual Clutch

These types of clutches are usually powered by an electric motor controlled by a switch in the cockpit. They are used in helicopters using drive belts to connect the engine to the transmission- the idler holds the belts away from driving the transmission. The cockpit switch moves a small electric motor to engage the belts, and once engaged, the belts will stay engaged until the helicopter is shutdown. In some machines, the clutch appears to be nearly automatic, but the pilot has to move a switch to engage it, so it really is a manual clutch. In Figure 10-6, the small set of pulleys on the left hand side is the clutch mechanism, and it is driven into place by a small motor and held in place by the springs slightly farther to the left.

Free–Wheel Units

This is as good a time as any to introduce something not found on cars. In a helicopter, the consequences of engine failure are more severe than in a car, so it's necessary to let the rotor turn without the engine driving it around.

The results would be pretty drastic if the rotor system in autorotation had also to turn over the engine (it would be impossible if the engine were seized...). No matter what type or size of helicopter you will fly, all of them have *free-wheel units*. The typical way the rotor is split from the engine is through a free-wheeling unit - an example of which is shown in Figure 10-7.

Inner and Outer Parts turning at same RPM

Outer Turning Much Faster than Inner

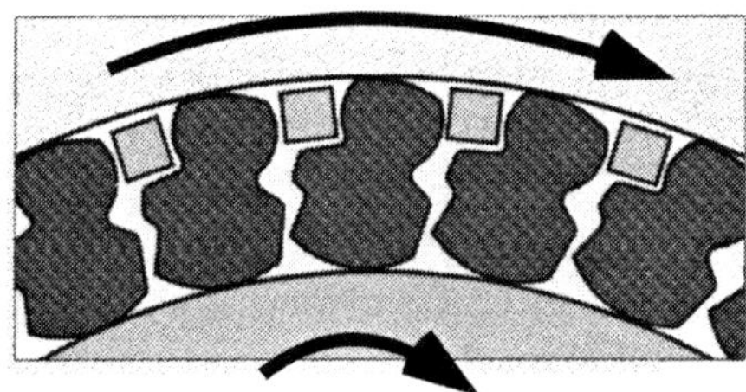

Figure 10-7 Free-wheeling Unit in Normal Drive Position, and in Free-wheeling Position.

The free-wheel unit is just another piece of the drive train, and is seldom cause for concern. It comes into play most noticeably when the rotor transitions from a practice autorotative condition to being driven by the engine again. Free-wheel engagement should be smooth, with a gentle re-application of power as the rotor and power turbine speeds match.

Piston–Engine Helicopter Power Control

Power in a piston–engined helicopter is a function of rotor speed (N_R) and manifold pressure. The two instruments used for displaying power are naturally enough, rotor speed (or N_R) and manifold pressure. The throttle of the piston engine can be thought of as an RPM controller, and the collective as the way of controlling manifold pressure. Nothing in helicopters is ever easy, and it is simplistic to separate the two items too rigidly - the two intermix.

Once you become proficient at hovering, a good way to demonstrate the interrelationships of power and N_R is to change the N_R in the hover (at the same height AGL) to the minimum N_R permitted, and note the manifold pressure. Then, hover at the maximum N_R permitted and note the manifold pressure. This should show the inter-relationship of the two, as well as being a good proficiency exercise. As you increase N_R you'll need a lower collective position, and as you decrease N_R you'll need a higher collective position to maintain the same height above the ground. This also demonstrates the 'squared' term in the lift formula*.

Rotor RPM

Since the rotor and the engine are directly coupled when operating normally, engine RPM and N_R are often displayed together on the same gage. Engine RPM is controlled by the throttle directly, and indirectly by the collective. If the power demanded by the rotor is not high enough, the N_R will be high - there is too much power, which could be absorbed by turning the rotor faster. Raising the collective increases the blade pitch and thus drag on the rotor blades and reduces the N_R (and engine RPM as well).

POWER OUTPUT

The power a piston engine is capable of delivering is difficult to measure, as it depends on the atmosphere the engine is operating in, and the torque that is being demanded of the engine. The torque is the amount of resistance the engine can put up with. For example, a engine with a lot of '*torque*', can overcome resistance more easily than one with little torque. In a car, the ability of an engine to produce torque for different road conditions is overcome by the use of a transmission. Different gears are used in different conditions. If you have ever tried to start from a stopped condition in a standard transmission in 3rd or 4th gear, you will have an appreciation of torque.

In aircraft a variable gear transmission cannot be used for reasons of weight, reliability and so on*. Hence we are given a narrow range of engine RPM to work in, as this is the most effective range from a power and torque point of view.

A chart of typical torque vs. engine RPM and power vs. engine RPM are shown in Figure 10-8. Notice the shape of the curve, particularly below the optimum RPM.

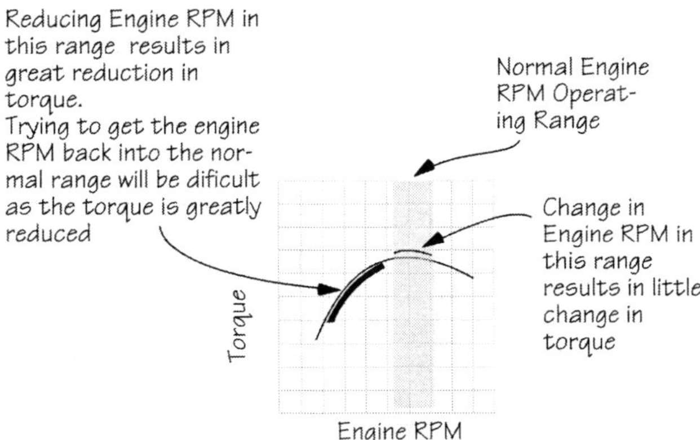

Figure 10-8 Typical Torque vs. Engine RPM

MEASURING PISTON ENGINE HELICOPTER POWER

The theoretical maximum manifold pressure is the barometric pressure outside, however this is impossible to obtain except for very brief periods. The normal steady state manifold pressure is going to be slightly less than the ambient pressure because the intake manifold itself has restrictions and creates losses. When the engine is running at maximum power, it is typical to see 1-2" less pressure on the MP gage than the pressure setting on the altimeter (assuming you're at sea level) because of these losses.

Same Engine in a Seized Wing Airplane

Often the same basic engine model is used in both fixed and rotary wing aircraft. Since we don't typically publish power setting tables for helicopters, we need to visit the same engine in a fixed wing airplane to shed some further light on things.

* Lift varies as N_R squared.

* Do you fancy changing gears as you come in to land, or takeoff? How would we work the clutch with both feet needed to work the pedals?

The maximum manifold pressure for this engine is 28", at sea level, standard day. This is nearly 2" less than the ambient pressure of 29.92". Therefore we should never be able to get this pressure difference (2") at 5,000', should we? Looking at the table for our fixed wing engine, we can see the maximum manifold pressure at 5,000' altitude is not much less than at sea level. How can this be?

First of all, we mentioned earlier that at high altitudes, the maximum air pressure would be lower. At 5,000' (ISA standard day), the barometric pressure is 24.92", so we should expect the maximum MP at 5,000' to be about 23", but it's higher. The reason for this is the engine has to expend energy to get rid of the exhaust gases. At altitude, there is less resistance to these gases being passed due to reduced air pressure.

It should also be noted this engine can only put out 75% of its maximum power at the noted RPM up to 5,000'. Above that altitude, it is not capable of putting out more power than that.

Strange, isn't it, that a chart from a fixed wing aircraft which is so useful should be missing from a helicopter with the same engine?

Carburetor Icing

Nearly every light piston engine helicopter has a carburetor, and nearly every aviation device with a carburetor has a problem with icing.

Why do Carburetors Ice Up?

The carburetor works on the principle of drawing air through a venturi or restriction. This reduces the air pressure as the air speeds up. Reducing the air pressure also reduces the temperature of the air, by as much as 10°C. If the air temperature was only 10°C to begin with, it's easy to see how this can put the air temperature in parts of the carburetor at or close to freezing.

If that air contains a lot of water vapor, even the most casual observer will figure out what will happen to the water... The result is that carburetor icing can happen at air temperatures well above freezing, and often when least expected.

Cars have the same sort of problem, but preheat the air by directing it around the exhaust manifold before going to the carburetor

The amount of air temperature drop is going to depend upon the change in air speed in various parts of the carburetor. With the throttle fully open, the reduction in area of opening is almost nil and the airspeed is (relatively) low at the throttle. When the throttle valve is partly closed, the air is constricted and has to flow more quickly past that part of the carburetor. More speed equals less air pressure and lower temperatures, which is why you may not see carburetor icing at high power settings but you will at low or reduced power. Partial power has the largest drop in carburetor temperature, and is the time most prone to iced carburetors. When do partial power settings occur in helicopters? During a descent, which is reason for adding carburetor heat just prior to descending.

Remember as the fuel evaporates it cools, so adding fuel will remove heat from the area.

More Carburetor Icing Explanation

For those of you who want to know more about why carburetor icing can happen with air temperatures well above freezing, and less than 100% humidity, here's the explanation.

Figure 10-9 shows a graph of the amount of water a given air temperature can hold for different amounts of relative humidity. The numbers on the right are the weight of water each unit weight of dry air can hold. For example, at 100% humidity, air at 15°C (59°F) can hold only 0.012 pounds of water for every pound of air. If there is more water than that in the air, it will fall out as rain or clouds. The same graph has more lines to show the amount of water different percentages of relative humidity represent. For example, 50% humid air at 15°C (59°F) is, as expected, about 0.006 pounds of water for every pound of dry air. So what?

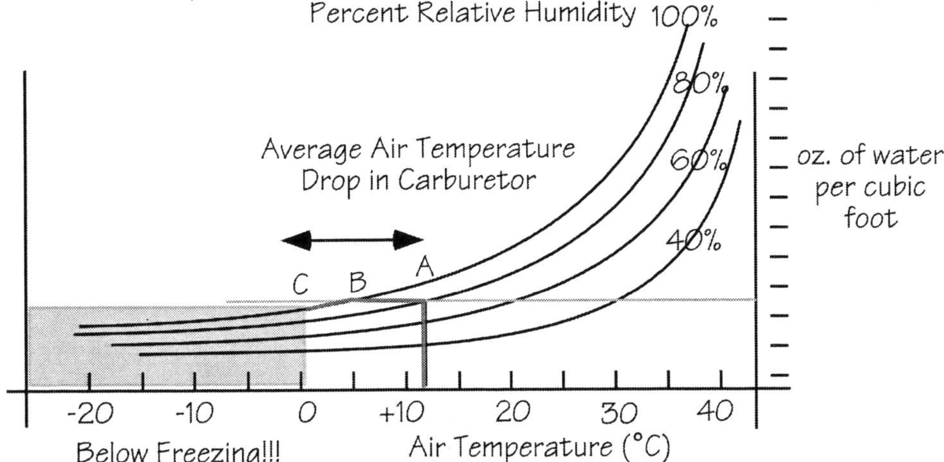

Figure 10-9 Water Vapor vs. Temperature

Remember earlier it was stated that in general terms, hot air can hold more moisture than cold air? Here's where this becomes significant. Notice how 100% relative humidity at 0°C (32°F) is only 0.004 pounds of water per pound of dry air. That's all the water vapor the air can hold at that temperature.

There is another temperature that is important, and that is the dew point temperature. This is the temperature at which the humidity is 100%, and the excess water vapor will 'fall out' of the air onto any other surface (hence the 'dew'). This is shown in Figure 10-10 as the 'wet bulb' temperature - this is temperature bulb that is kept wet and will give a different temperature due to the cooling effects of the air. The less water vapor in the air, the more the dry air can cool the wet bulb by evaporation. The greater the difference between the wet and dry bulb temperature, the lower the relative humidity.

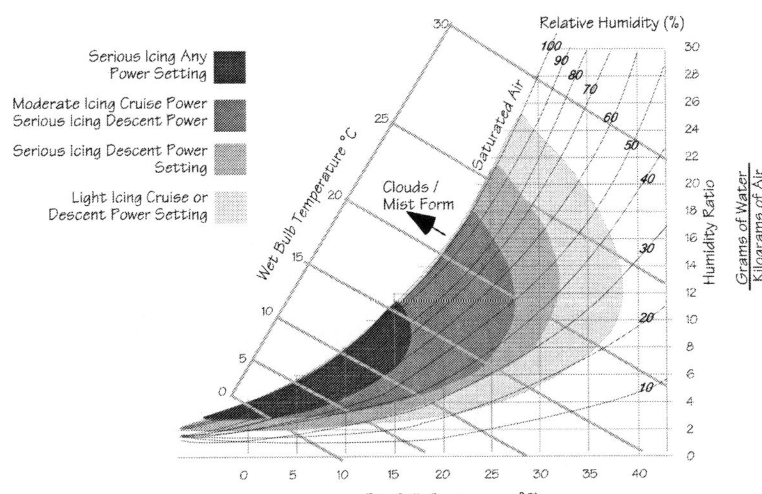

Figure 10-10 Wet Bulb Temperature and Carburator Icing

To understand the rest of the story we have to go back to the physics of the carburetor.

Remember how air is sped up in the venturi, (and this is reflected by the less than full open carburetor throttle valve having a very low manifold pressure), and the vaporizing of fuel in the carburetor caused things to cool down? Part of the problem of speeding up the flow of air is that it causes the temperature to drop*. Combine the temperature drop due to faster air in a partly open throttle and the temperature drop due to fuel vaporization, and you get quite a temperature drop.

Lets say the drop from the outside air, to the coolest spot in the carburetor is about 10°C (about 25°F), from 10°C (approximately 50°F) and the air was only about 75% relative humidity to begin with. 75% relative humidity at 10°C equals about 0.006 pounds of water per pound of dry air.

We don't have any way to remove that amount of water from the air prior to it getting to the carburetor, so it must remain in the volume of air. Cooling the air moves us down to the air temperature in the carburetor, which is 0°C (32°F). At 0°C, the freezing point of water (or the formation point of ice, whichever way you want to look at it), the maximum amount of water a pound of air can hold in suspension at 100% relative humidity is 0.004 pounds. So where does the other 0.002 pound go? It falls out of the air as water, or at that temperature, as ice. Voila, as they say in France, ice forms in the carburetor, even on a warm day with less than 100% humidity.

Effects of Icing

So what's so bad about ice in the carburetor?

The first thing ice does is restrict the amount of air that can be drawn through the intake, so less power can be developed. If you need maximum power and the intake is partly restricted, you aren't going to have maximum power.

The second thing ice does is affect the airflow around the venturi and prevent proper mixing of the fuel and air.

If the throttle is opened when ice is present, not much will happen, as the increase in airflow will decrease the temperature even father.

Symptoms of Carburetor Icing

Symptoms of carburetor icing are:

- a decrease in manifold pressure at the same power setting. Since we don't often leave the power setting constant for long periods of time in helicopters, this symptom may be difficult to detect.
- the engine runs rough. The fuel-air mixture is too rich. Unfortunately, helicopters vibrate and it is difficult for the inexperienced pilot to differentiate between a rough engine and normal vibrations.
- a loss of power. Since we are often changing the power demand in helicopter flying, this may not be easily apparent.

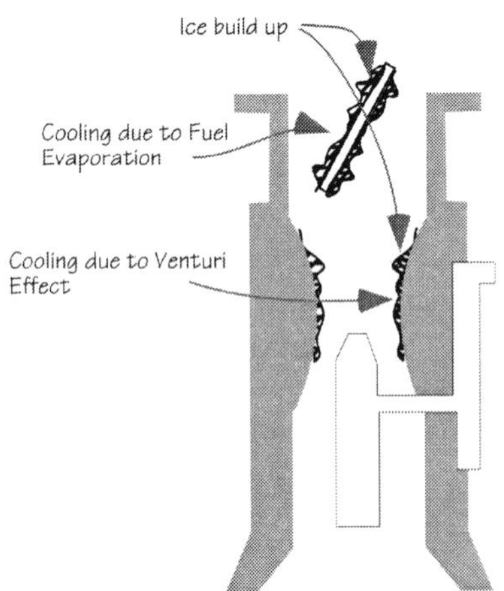

Figure 10-11 Carburetor Icing

So it's not hard to see symptoms that are normally easy to spot in fixed wing airplanes may be difficult to spot quickly in the a helicopter. Hence the suggestion (if not requirement) to fit a carburetor air temperature gage.

With Carburetor Air Temperature gage

A carburetor air temperature gage will obviously be of use to tell you when the air in the carburetor intake is getting close to freezing. It can be useful, but remember carburetor icing can occur at air temperatures above freezing, and some carburetor temperature gages can be misleading.

Without a Carburetor Air Temperature Gage

Without a carburetor air temperature gage, life is slightly more difficult - you as the pilot have to know the symptoms of carburetor icing from the list above. Your helicopter may have different symptoms altogether.

* If you have experienced a Canadian winter you know the meaning of wind chill and understand this very well.

Carburetor Heat

Since this problem appears to be pretty common, and we've had piston engines in one form or another for about 100 years, it's a pretty safe bet someone has done something about this state of affairs. That something is called *carburetor heat*, and it's controlled by the carburetor heat knob in the cockpit.

When this knob is pulled out, the intake path of the air is changed so the air gets heated (normally by passing it by the exhaust manifold, which is always warm). This air should be warmer and more importantly drier than the normal intake air, and solve the problem. A typical carburetor heat system is shown in Figure 10-12.

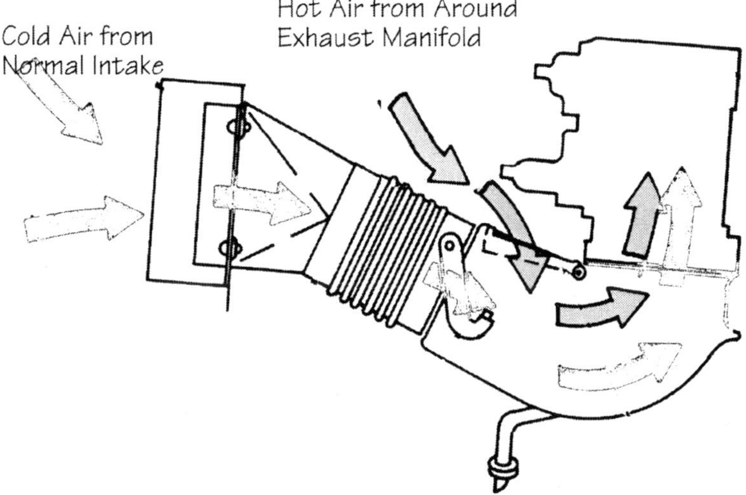

Figure 10-12 Typical Carburetor Heat system

It is interesting to note that recent models of Robinson helicopters have incorporated automatic carburetor heat when the collective lever is below a certain setting, and more recently yet, have said to consider leaving it on for the whole flight.

In most aircraft (both fixed and rotary wing), the carburetor heat bypasses the air filter, so if operating in dusty air, the engine is exposed to dirty air.

Prevention of Carburetor Ice

The best defense is a good offense. So aside from fitting a carburetor air temperature gage and paying attention to it, remember anytime the air has moisture, and the air temperature is less than 20°C, carburetor icing can happen.

When it does happen- apply and leave the carburetor heat on full until you are absolutely positively sure certain the ice is gone.

I've read too many accident reports where the pilot had a hard landing and no obvious cause could be found, as the engine ran perfectly following the accident. Carburetor icing was suspected as a cause.

A note of caution for those without carburetor air temperature gages. If you think you're getting iced up, either use full carburetor heat or none. Partial heat may set up the exact conditions for icing without you knowing it. In temperatures below freezing, partial carburetor heat can warm the air enough to let the water vapor (in crystal form) melt and then re-freeze on the throttle valve.

Also expect when carburetor heat is first added the power will decrease slightly. This is due to the warmer, less dense air being added. Remember the power available from a piston engine will depend upon density altitude, and when you add carburetor heat, and change nothing else, the density altitude at the engine intake has just gone up.

If the engine is running rough and you apply carburetor heat, remember it may take a while to melt any ice already formed. Apply the heat early and be prepared to stick it out.

If you have a governor on your piston engine, it may mask the symptoms of carburetor heat- the governor maintains the N_R without your direct control.

Mixture Control

Another control you won't have come across in the family jalopy is a *mixture control*. This is a way to adjust the ratio of the fuel–air mixture. For most helicopter flights, the only time this control is used is to shut off the engine at the end of the flight.

You have already seen air is not what we think it is, and density of air (or density altitude) is the important factor for many helicopter performance considerations.

The fuel-air mixture burned in the piston engine will be a mixture by weight, instead of volume of fuel and air. A given volume of air can be light or heavy, depending upon the density of the air.

Note the mixture should be based on weight, but many carburetors aren't smart and attempt to mix on the volume of air. The problem is that as altitude is increased, the air becomes less dense, and unless the fuel mixture is adjusted for this change in density, the fuel-air mixture may become too rich. This problem isn't peculiar to aviation engines. Cars with carburetors that have been properly tuned at sea level often have difficulty at higher altitudes unless the carburetors are re-set*.

For most of the heights and altitudes helicopters operate at, if the mixture is set correctly on the ground, it should be correct during the flight.

If you notice the engine starts to run rough during a climb, then, after you've checked the carburetor heat, by all means consider leaning out the mixture, but do it slowly. Many carburetors fitted to helicopters have an altitude compensating device so the pilot doesn't have to worry about this, but for those that require mixture adjustment, pay attention. The unfortunate part for those who don't have the altitude compensating device is that you have to use the mixture control. Why is this bad? Leaning the mixture is the way the engine is shutdown at the end of the flight, so beware of leaning too much, as you can shut down the engine without really wanting to†. Cylinder head temperature gages (if they have been installed) can help in determining proper mixture in the cruise.

Caution

Read the engine manufacturers manual carefully. One manufacturer recommends leaning the mixture only above 5,000' AGL during the climb, and any time when cruising. Since most helicopter cruising is of short duration (except long cross country flights), it is debatable whether there is any practical benefit to be gained by leaning the mixture. Especially when you have to remember to make the mixture rich again for approach and landing...

Throttle Handling

The response of a piston engine to throttle movements is generally quite rapid but how this translates to the rotor depends on the helicopter type‡. A helicopter with a low inertia rotor will respond more quickly to throttle than a helicopter with a high inertia rotor. For those with some fixed wing piston engine experience, the response will seem very long and the reason is the fixed wing propeller is a thing of little weight compared to any rotor system.

There is a lot of discussion about which of the two power controls (throttle and collective) in the helicopter controls which parameter (manifold pressure and RPM). Lets look at the problem from a larger perspective.

The rotor blades are driven by the engine, which is overcoming the drag. If the engine is putting out the correct amount of power, this will relate to both a torque (which you can't see in a piston engine helicopter) and engine / rotor RPM. Change the drag on the blades by moving the collective lever and the RPM will change. If you want to keep the N_R constant, you will have to change the torque (power) the engine is providing, by moving the throttle.

* Operating a high altitudes can also require a more lean mixture than at sea level- don't automatically use full rich mixture.

† It's happened lots of times, and will happen lots more times...

‡ I've heard the British 'Skeeter' used by the UK Army Air Corps seemed to have the rotor RPM needle tied directly to the throttle. It had blades with a wooden spar and fabric covering that weighed almost nothing...

Since the engine is mechanically coupled to the rotor, the engine and rotor RPM will eventually be the same, but the torque (and MP) will be different. We have no way of measuring torque in a piston engine*, but we can measure manifold pressure, so we see a change in how hard the engine has to work to maintain the RPM.

Changing the power will also change the torque the engine is producing. Normally, this is not a major problem, unless you let the engine RPM get too low.

OVER-PITCHING

Over-pitching the rotor blades of piston engine helicopter happens all too frequently, and so it appears to be little understood or appreciated in theory or practice.

Over-pitching is a phenomena that can happen to a piston engine helicopter when the pilot does not control engine RPM and rotor pitch correctly. Since the condition is characterized by the N_R and engine RPM being too low and the blade pitch being too high - the name, over-pitching is both descriptive and appropriate. It appears this is a problem only on piston–engined helicopters without governors, but as there are quite a few of them around, it's a point worth mentioning.

The problem starts with the N_R being lower than it should be. Either the pilot isn't paying attention, or the throttle correlation with the collective is poorly set up, or you're out of power - in any case, the N_R is too low. The N_R being lower than it should be requires the blade pitch angle to be higher than normal to maintain the hover or other flight condition, which also means the drag on the blades is higher than normal (remember the C_L and C_D curves from Chapter 2,"Introduction to Helicopter Aerodynamics"?)

A piston engine will have characteristics of torque vs. RPM as shown in Figure 10-8.

There are two parts to the curve- the front side, shown in part A, and the back side of the curve, shown as part B. On the front side of the curve, the engine produces less torque as the engine increases speed. This may be a good thing, as if the engine slows down, it will produce more torque until it reaches the top of the curve.

For example, our pilot is hovering with the engine operating at 2,500 RPM. He is using x foot–pounds of torque. He raises the collective without changing the throttle, which increases rotor drag. This slows the engine to 2,400 RPM. He now has more torque than he had before, which is the same total power. This will mean the engine will not slow down any further.

This is fine, as long as the pilot keeps the engine RPM on the correct side of the curve. What happens when the pilot is on the wrong side?

Wrong Side of Torque Curve

The pilot is hovering at a much lower engine RPM, lets say 2,200 RPM. It's still within the green arc of engine and N_R, but close to the bottom of the green. The engine is putting out 150 SHP. He raises the collective to overcome a gust, same as before, which slows the engine to 2,100 RPM, however the torque goes down, and the power put out by the engine goes down. Since the pilot needs total power to hover, the helicopter settles. The natural reaction of the pilot is to raise the collective to stop the descent, which increases the drag on the rotor, and further slows the engine rotor combination - this is a vicious cycle that can only be broken by reducing the power demand on the engine. The pilot has to increase the engine RPM. Opening the throttle is the obvious first step, but what if the throttle is already open? Then the only way to do get out of the situation is by lowering the collective. Not an easy thing to do when the ground is rising up already!

Only on Some Piston Engine Helicopters

This situation used to be the case on all piston engine helicopters, and then, someone started putting governing systems onto them. I believe it was first used by Robinson Helicopters, and this dramatically changed things. All their recent production machines have governors, and so only those flying other machines need to worry about over-pitching.

* Although I've heard rumors of such a device being made...

A simple analogy to over-pitching is trying to accelerate from a stop in a manual transmission car on a hill. If you don't keep the engine RPM up, you will stall the engine.

Coning Angle and Over-pitching

Whatever the cause of over-pitching, the situation is that the rotor pitch is too high and engine RPM is too low. With a helicopter with a flapping hinge, this also creates another problem relating to coning angle. When the N_R is low and the lift is high, the coning angle is greater than at optimum RPM, that is, the blades aren't as straight out as before. If we were able to take two different helicopters with identical rotor systems, except one had a flapping hinge and the other did not, and make the same reduction in N_R at the same lift condition, we would have two slightly different results. The helicopter with the flapping hinge would have a higher rate of descent than the other machine, due to the change in coning angle, and its effect on total lift.

This works as follows - at a set coning angle the area of the rotor disk is x $ft.^2$. Even a small decrease in N_R will significantly increase the coning angle, causing a reduction in the overall area of the rotor. Put another way, the effective length of the blade used to produce useful lift has been reduced, and this results in a larger–than–normal reduction in overall lift than might have been expected from just the decrease in RPM. This is shown in Figure 10-13 below. The changes have been amplified to show the effect - the real change in area is extremely small, but in a situation where every little bit counts, it is worth mentioning.

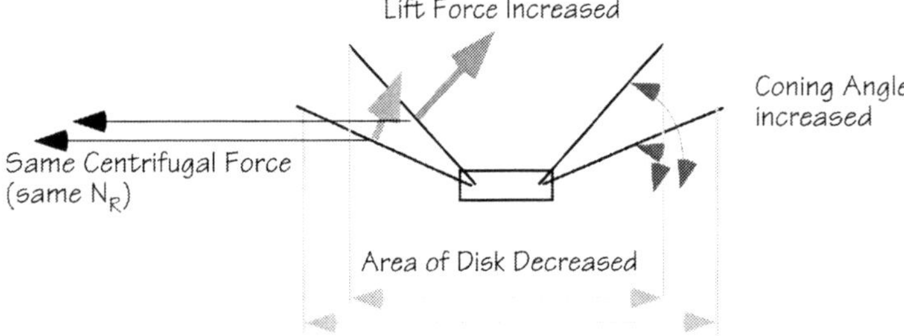

Figure 10-13 Reduction in Rotor Area with Reduced N_R

Figure 10-13 shows the effect of increasing the blade pitch angle. Increasing the blade pitch increases the AoA and thus the thrust. The greater the lift, the greater the coning angle, since the centrifugal force remains constant at a fixed N_R. (Most helicopter rotors turn at more or less constant N_R.) Note also increasing the coning angle decreases the area of the disc. Also note that the slower the N_R the less the centrifugal force and the greater the coning angle.

Even if the overall lift produced by the blade is the same, increasing the coning angle also has an effect at the hub by tilting the lift vector away from the vertical more. (Remember how lift gets to the hub in the articulated rotor (See "How Lift Gets to the Hub" on page 26.).

Since the pilot is busy trying to do other things than worry about coning angle at this time, the reaction to the things that are happening is of concern - if the reaction is to pull up on the collective to stop the rate of descent, the result is an ever–tightening circle of events - even further reduced N_R, higher coning angle, less lift and so on. If the reaction is the correct one - get the N_R and engine RPM back, then things will be better - you may have no option but to hit the ground, but at least you'll hit the ground under control, and in a manner more to your choosing. This is an example of having to learn to overcome some deeply ingrained instincts in order to survive.

If the engine power available is already at its maximum, there is only one solution - lower the collective to reduce the drag on the blades, so the N_R will recover to its normal setting. If the engine power available isn't at a maximum, then the pilot may be able to recover the situation by increasing power by opening the throttle, but this is much slower and less certain solution - the engine has to work very hard to get the rotor RPM back if it can. (Do you have the time and airspace to be wrong?). The problem is how does the pilot know if the engine is at its maximum power available, (the N_R is already low, so that's no help in diagnosing the situation) and the engine is already doing all it can? The answer is to reduce collective pitch first.

Turbine Engines and Over-Pitching

The mechanisms by which a turbine engine produces power are completely different, and will be explained in more detail in Chapter 29,"The Turbine Engine". The reaction of the engine to an over–pitching is very different. The reader should be aware this is another difference between the two types of engines.

THROTTLE CO–RELATORS

These are also sometimes called collective pitch - throttle *synchronization* units, *synchronizers*, or *co–relators* or *anticipators*.

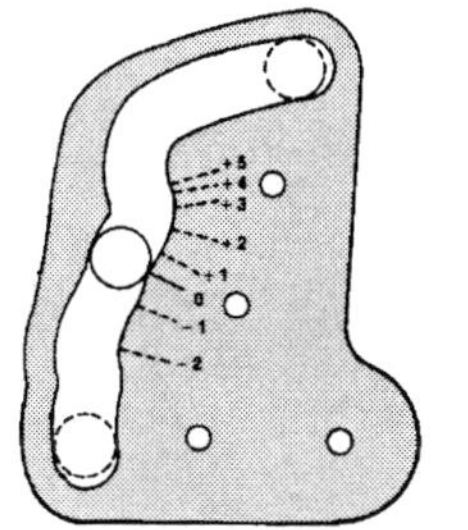

Figure 10-14 Throttle Co-Relator

Since the engine power must be changed every time the collective position is changed, and it is in a normally predictable manner, many piston–engined helicopters incorporate a co–relater between the throttle and the collective. An example is shown in Figure 10-14. A cam in the throttle linkage 'reads' the collective position and adds a certain amount of throttle automatically when the collective is raised, and reduces it when the collective is lowered. These systems work well when adjusted properly, but they do wear, and may have the opposite effect desired.

In one piston–engined helicopter I flew, throttle had to be rolled off when the collective was raised, and rolled on when it was lowered. On this particular helicopter, the co-relator became known as an 'analog randomizer'.

FUEL INJECTION

Some helicopter piston engines use fuel injection instead of carburetors. The main differences are the fuel is injected directly into the intake manifold which means there is less danger of carburetor icing.

Unfortunately, fuel injected engines have developed a bad reputation for being hard to start, especially when warm. On the other hand, they offer more precise fuel metering and are a requirement to take advantage of electronic fuel controls, such as fitted to all modern cars. The amount of space the section on fuel injection compared to the space taken for carburetors should give you some indication of the things the pilot has to worry about.

PISTON ENGINE GOVERNORS

So with all these problems of trying to maintain N_R constant, is it any wonder a *governor* for the piston engine came along? I'm just surprised it took as long as it did. Governors have been around since the steam engine, and the technology to control a piston engine has certainly been used before.

How Does the Governor Work?

The governor is told by the pilot (or pre-set control rigging) to maintain a value of N_R. It can adjust either collective position or throttle position, (or possibly both) to maintain a value of N_R. If it senses a low N_R, it can either reduce the collective or increase the throttle, or both, depending on the logic and set-up of the governor.

Pedal Movement and Power Demand

In the piston engine helicopter, without an engine governor, the effect of changing pedal position is seen as a change in overall power demand. Adding left pedal demands more power and an adjustment to the throttle should be made to maintain height. If you are already at maximum power, then adding left pedal will cause the helicopter to descend. You may be better off using right pedal if you are close to maximum power. This is mentioned because for turbine engine helicopters or those piston engine machines with a governor, things are very different!*

* This 'very different' aspect is explained in Chapter 29,"The Turbine Engine"

PERFORMANCE RULES OF THUMB FOR PISTON ENGINES

Since the FM's for most piston engine helicopters are pretty thin on performance information, a few rules of thumb for determining what can be lifted or carried have been developed. They are most useful when we don't have easy reference to the FM (like, in-flight). One rule of thumb for a particular model of the Bell 47 was that each 1" of manifold pressure was worth about 175 lbs of weight. So if you had 2" of manifold pressure between what you were hovering with (in ground effect) and the maximum you could pull at that altitude and OAT, then you could lift another 350 pounds.

If you don't know what those rules of thumb are, you should be able to make your own by careful observation.

TURBOCHARGERS

Not many light piston engine helicopters used in training have *turbochargers*, but enough do to warrant some discussion. The turbocharger used to be an exotic beast, but is now quite common on even family cars.

The turbocharger works by directing exhaust gases around a small turbine, which is directly connected to a small compressor. The compressor stuffs air into the pistons, literally cramming more air in than would be found due to normal aspiration. You almost get something for nothing, as the exhaust gases were going out anyway.

The turbocharger will only work above a certain engine RPM, as this much speed is needed for developing the exhaust gas pressure to turn the turbine. Below this RPM, the turbine won't be providing enough power to work the compressor efficiently. When the engine runs at really high speed, too much exhaust gas is developed and some must be dumped overboard using what is known as the waste gate. The waste gate also regulates the pressure output of the turbocharger to the intake manifold and automatically compensates for changes in air density as altitude changes.

Since most aircraft piston engines are required to produce power over a fairly narrow range of RPM, the turbocharger can be sized for that range, and can be a very efficient system for most aircraft engines.

The benefit of a turbocharger is it provides is more power output for the same size of engine. By cramming more air into the same volume, more fuel can also be crammed in and burned efficiently. This produces more power. You will notice that with a turbocharger, you can have more than atmospheric pressure on the manifold pressure gage.

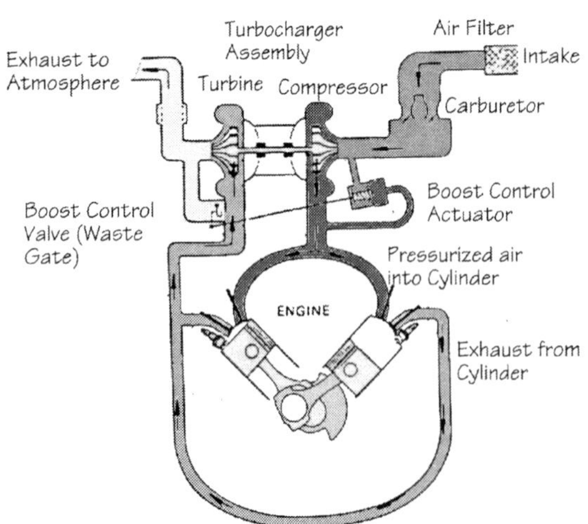

Figure 10-15 Typical Turbocharger

The downside is the turbocharger runs at very high speeds, and at high temperatures, and this is hard on metal. As if that weren't enough, the bearings the compressor and turbine spin on are lubricated with oil, and if the engine is shut down from a 'hot, running at high power' situation, the bearings are likely to be very warm. This can cause the oil to literally bake itself into a solid, and we all know that solids don't lubricate well.

The solution is to let the engine run at a slow speed for several minutes prior to shutting it down, as would be required by the FM.

OTHER COMPONENTS OF THE ENGINE

Oil and Oil Pumps

The engine requires oil to operate. Most of us think oil is only there to lubricate, but it actually has 4 functions:

- cool- by moving heat away from bearings
- clean- by moving dirt and metal particles away from between metal surfaces

- seal- by sealing between metal surfaces to prevent air getting between the two
- lubricates - making it easy for the two surfaces to slide over or by one another.

From these functions, it's easy to see why you need to make sure the oil quantity is correct, as too little oil will not provide enough volume to cool properly, will get dirtier faster and will heat up a great deal.

Oil also degrades with heat, and it is for this reason, more than because oil is dirty that it is changed very frequently. As the oil heats up, parts of it are driven off as vapors, and this changes the viscosity of the oil. Too much heating, and the oil becomes too thick as much of the oil is 'boiled away', and it doesn't flow properly.

Lose the oil pump, and none of the neat things oil carries out will be done. Since the engine relies on the oil, it's important to know if you loose oil pressure- because you'll be without an engine pretty soon.

Cold oil doesn't flow very well, and thus won't be able to lubricate. For those of us fortunate enough to live in a really cold climate, it's educational to turn an open can of oil upside down at -40°C and watch it not move out of the can. That's one of the main reasons for pre-heating the engine in cold temperatures.

Generators

Most helicopters have an alternator to provide electrical power for instruments, lights, radios and so on. The alternator is not much different than the type fitted to most automobiles, however we normally have an ammeter fitted to helicopters to monitor the functioning of the alternator- all you get in most cars is an idiot light.

Fans

Most helicopter engines are air-cooled, for weight–saving reasons. These type of engines are common on fixed wing airplanes and rely on the airflow of forward flight to ensure cooling. Since helicopter engines have to put out their greatest power in the hover, when airflow is at a minimum, we can't depend on that to keep the engine cool. The solution is a large fan bolted directly to the crankshaft- when the engine is turning, the fan is cooling. Still, it pays to have something in the cockpit to make sure the fan hasn't become plugged up, and a cylinder head temperature gage is normally part of the cockpit instruments.

Fuel Systems

The fuel system of most piston engine training helicopters is pretty simple. Just a single tank with a pump and a drain. Some machines, notably, the Bell 47 and Hiller family have the fuel tanks above the engine, so gravity acts as the fuel pump, but for those with the tank lower than the engine, a pump is necessary. Some hidden things necessary are vents, filters and sumps.

Vents are needed in the fuel tank system to make sure the tank doesn't collapse as fuel is drawn out of it by the pump or engine. Without a proper vent, the tank would be developing a vacuum as the fuel level drops. This is the reason for checking the vent is clear in the pre-flight inspection. Be aware of a vent tube that may have been rotated to face in the wrong direction*. Since most helicopter fuel vents face aft, facing forward means the vent would be pressurizing the fuel tank, something just as bad as not venting!

Filters are necessary to make sure the fuel getting to the engine is clean. Not much else needs to be said about the goodness of that.

Sumps in the fuel tank are necessary to make sure any water finds its way to the lowest point in the tank so it won't get taken into the engine. This is why the fuel drains are placed in the sump of the tank so any water would be found in the pre-flight inspection.

Operation of the Piston Engine

Pre-Start

It may be necessary to pre-heat the engine† to warm up the oil.

* By all means determine what the correct direction is for you helicopter type. A lot of fixed wing airplane vents face forward, but I don't know of any helicopter ones that do.

† At least, where I used live in Canada in the winter it sure was necessary. Others may not be so lucky to have these character–building climates.

Fuel Draining

Like all aircraft, draining fuel during the walkaround pre-flight inspection is a necessity. Water can collect in the fuel tanks, and really make a mess of your flight if it decides to go into the carburetor at the wrong time*.

Starting

Follow the instructions for your engine. Know how to start a cold engine and a warm engine (on the ground and in-flight).

Check to make sure the manifold pressure gage shows something pretty close to the altimeter setting, or if you're at a high altitude, an appropriate value.

If the engine is not fuel injected, it may be necessary to use the fuel primer to help kick the machine into life. Follow the procedures in the FM (or taught by your instructor). If it is fuel injected, then the procedure may be different for warm and cold engines. Know your engine!

Post Start Checks

Check that the oil pressure is within limits. During cold weather, it may be necessary to wait until the oil warms up and the pressure drops to within limits prior to advancing the throttle beyond idle.

Magneto Check

Check that the engine continues to run smoothly on each magneto system. There will be a small drop in engine RPM when only one magneto is working, and you want to make sure both are working properly.

Carburetor Heat Check

Make sure the carburetor heat is functioning correctly. You're particularly interested in seeing it's off for takeoff. Don't assume that just because the lever is in, that the carb heat is off.

Lift-Off

When the helicopter is lifted to the hover, and the N_R is in the proper range, note the manifold pressure and other information such as oil pressure and temperature. See "Rules of Thumb" on page 257. on what options you may have for techniques to transition to forward flight depending on the margin between the manifold pressure you are using and the maximum possible.

In-Flight

Monitor the engine instruments from time to time. Piston engines depend upon oil to stay turning, and falling oil pressure or rising oil temperature are hazardous to long engine life. Depending upon the type of flying, it may be possible to use the mixture control to adjust the fuel/air mixture.

Descent

Be on the lookout for carburetor icing prior to and during the descent. If you're operating in an area of high humidity, be particularly vigilant for carburetor icing. Re-set the mixture to full rich, if you've leaned it during the cruise and it is appropriate to do so for the conditions.

Shut Down

On some engines, it's normal to carry out a dead magneto check to make sure when you shut the magnetos off, the engine will stop. This is a good habit from our seized wing brethren we should retain.

Derated Engines

To improve the safety margins in helicopters, derated engines are often used. This mean simply that the engine was capable of putting out more power than allowed on that helicopter. The airframe manufacturer has decided that it is better to have an engine capable of putting out 200 shp limited to 150 shp all the time and with a minimum of stress on the engine, than having one straining to put 150 shp. There is very good logic to this- helicopters use maximum allowed power a lot more frequently than fixed wing airplanes do, and it the consequences of engine failure are much more immediate in helicopters than airplanes.

---

* Which raises the question – is there ever a 'right time'?

Engine power output decreases with density altitude. If the engine were rated at 100 hp. at sea level, it would not be able to produce that power at 5,000' density altitude. If the maximum power of the engine was 150 hp, but it was artificially limited to 100 hp at sea level, then at 5,000 feet it would probably still be able to put out 100 hp.

Summary of Chapter 10

This chapter has covered the piston engine as used in most light training helicopters. When operated within the limitations and procedures outlined by the manufacturer, there should be few problems, the background information given here may help to keep pilots out of trouble.

11 Dear Student

You are about to take up flying a machine that will surely challenge you in many ways. Among these challenges are a tremendous amount to learn academically and new skills in coordination, judgment and discipline.

Don't worry.

It is possible to fly helicopters. Many others have succeeded, and you should be able to as well*.

It has been said one of the main differences between doctors and the rest of the population is knowing and understanding about 2,000 special words. I can't vouch for the number of words for doctors, nor for the exact number for aviation in general or helicopters specifically, but I can vouch there are a lot of different words and TLA's (Three Letter Acronyms) you must learn to use. To be more precise, you must learn to use them correctly. A lot of these words are listed in the definitions at the back, and need to be understood clearly by the time you get your license.

The Chinese have a good saying for learning new concepts and ideas-

- "Memorize now, understanding will come later."

Students need to be aware of the problems facing their instructors, and instructors need to be reminded of some of the things the student is going through. Notes for instructors are in Chapter 22,"For the Professional Helicopter Pilot / Instructor".

Instructors - What They Know and Don't Know

To quote Carl Lewis in one of his books (*Sagittarius Rising*)-

> *"A good instructor was (and still is) a pretty rare bird. It needs some guts to turn a machine over to a half-fledged pupil and let him get into difficulty and find his way out. Instruction demands besides an ability to communicate oneself to another person (the secret of all good teaching) and is not as simple as it seems. Add to this the great patience, the quality of inspiring confidence and an extremely steady flying ability in the man himself†, and it will be obvious that nobody look down his nose at an instructor."*

Instructors start from a distinct advantage over you. They know how to fly helicopters. Pay attention to what they say, but realize there will be a communication barrier between you and the instructor whether either of you want it or not. If you don't understand what the instructor wants or says, ask.

I don't want to start a revolt among helicopter students, far from it. What I do want is that you learn in the best way possible.

Not all instructors are perfect. They are not there to show you how well they can fly the helicopter. They are there to teach you.

No instructor knows everything, and distrust those who say they do.

Personality Differences

These happen. Don't worry about it. I've been good friends for many years with someone who I just couldn't communicate with in the cockpit initially. A change of instructor was good for both of us.

Flying Training Briefings

Helicopters are much more expensive to operate than fixed–wing aircraft and for most students, it seems like they are spending money at an incredible rate. The first thing you should remember is flight time is a lot more expensive than ground instructional time, and you're paying for it!

---

* On the other hand, if your instructor recommends you not pursue a career in aviation, the advice may be worth listening to.

† Since this was written in the 1920s, we'll excuse any sexist pronouns.

It is worthwhile to insist on a thorough briefing prior to each lesson, and a thorough debriefing after it. Even if this costs extra in terms of money for instructor time, it is cheaper than not understanding what you are to be shown, or what you actually saw. The briefing should be complete and cover the points to be learned from each lesson. It's your money.

The Essential Pre-Flight Briefing

Obviously, the aim of the trip should be explained, as well as the detailed exercises to be carried out, and so on. Some items may be considered as standard, if it's laid out that way by the instructor and school - for example -

- how to change who has control of the helicopter
- all other air traffic will be called out by the clock angle, and as 'high', 'same altitude' or 'low' depending on its height relative to you.
- who will handle the radios
- details of the weather for the trip
- what particular points will be emphasized during the trip

Checklists

Why do we use checklists? Basically, because we don't want to forget anything important. Memory requires training and constant practice to keep sharp, and some of us don't get to fly all that often.

It's worthwhile to make up your own checklists when learning to fly any machine - it helps you memorize the necessary actions to start and shutdown the machine. You may want to memorize these actions before starting, but they soon become second nature, and you should learn them the full, correct way.

Having said that, most light civilian helicopters lack officially published pocket sized checklists. If you are going to make up your own, ensure it follows the sequence laid out in the FM. Think about what you need to start any helicopter - fuel, electrics and probably a few other minor things. It's not appropriate to use the whole FM as the checklist while you're flying - it's too large and not laid out for use in the air.

For the various emergency procedures, memorize those requiring immediate action. This advice, is of course, very little help for civilian helicopters, as the FM doesn't say which ones are critical. For starters, consider those emergencies to be critical where you wouldn't have time or capability to get out the checklist. I would recommend engine failures, fires, transmission failures and tail rotor failures as items that would fall into the critical category. The main thing is to be familiar with the checklist and the appropriate items in it you will use in-flight.

Military operators have a slightly easier time - most of their FM's and checklists have color–coded sections, with red for critical emergencies, yellow for non-critical and so on. There often isn't a choice - memorize the red section emergencies or else!

If you have a chance, cross check the original equipment manufacturer's manuals for related equipment.

See "Flight Manuals, Rules and Regulations" on page 185. for even better reasons for making up your own checklists.

For Those Who Make Checklists

Don't make the checklist too long and complex. It won't be used, despite any wording in operations manuals. Expect your pilots to memorize quite a few things, and make them learn to double check their work. How is a single pilot supposed to use a checklist and fly at the same time, if both hands have to be on the controls all the time?

All Those Gages and Clocks!

The first time you sit in the cockpit of a helicopter is a bit overwhelming. There are a lot of things to pay attention to- the problem is how do you learn all this. The following section should help a bit.

Blindfold Cockpit Checks

Blindfold cockpit checks used to be very popular in military flying organizations, but for some reason have fallen out of favor, perhaps because some people used to go overboard and make you know every single circuit breaker (a totally unnecessary operation). I don't understand why blindfold cockpit checks have died away, as they instill a great deal of confidence in the ability to find things quickly. Can you find the fuel shutoff without looking at it? A few moments in the cockpit prior to flying any helicopter will help with this. Pick the major items such as fuel and battery switches with your eyes closed: can you identify them by feel alone?

The way to do blindfold cockpit checks is first, to make up a blindfold (helmet bags or headset bags seem to be about the correct size), and then put it on once you're inside the cockpit*. Have someone else call out items for you to identify, and help you if you can't find them immediately. Switch around and help your friend do the same thing - you will both learn from it. Concentrate on the major things, but if you cover everything, it will instill a great deal of knowledge as well as confidence.

Besides, this is free training.

For Both Instructor and Student

Transfer of Control

Before you start committing aviation with any instructor, it's necessary to know who is going to be doing what, to whom and where.

There will be times when it is necessary for the instructor to demonstrate a maneuver and then for the student to repeat it. There will be moments when it's not clear who is doing the aviating and who is merely along for the ride. This is true even in a side–by–side cockpit. In my experience, I have only seen one surefire, never-fail method of changing who is in control, so there is never any doubt.

When control is to be transferred, the person at the controls says "You have control". The other person takes control of the helicopter and says "I have control". The person relinquishing control confirms "You have control." The transfer is not complete until then.

I have seen lots of other attempts to change control while attempting to appear casual and cool. Frankly, none of them work. Insist on only this method, and you should never go wrong.

Following Through on the Controls

There are lots of times when it is nice to follow what the instructor is doing more closely - this is called 'Following Through'. It consists of putting hands and feet lightly on the controls and following the movements without putting any pressure or movement of your own into the equation. When the instructor says, "Follow me through", now you'll know what he means.

While you are following him through is an excellent time to learn to anticipate what he is going to do, and see if your judgment is the same as his - you'll get there in good time.

Where to Look

If there is one problem at the root of many attempts to fly helicopters, it's where to look. I have transitioned many experienced helicopter pilots to new types, and consistently found where they were looking played a major part in their overall ability to control the aircraft. So, before you get into the air, take a moment to consider where you should be looking when you are flying the helicopter.

Outside, Mostly

The first place you should be spending most of your time looking is outside, not inside at the instruments. Develop the ability to scan quickly at an item of interest, and then look outside again. This can be developed by sitting in the cockpit with a companion, without the engine on, and as they call out (at random) the names of various engine and airframe instruments, you touch the named instrument quickly while blindfolded. When you need to glance at them in-flight, you know where they are, and can do the following, almost by instinct:

- immediately locate the relevant instrument
- see what it reads
- look back outside and say out loud what the instrument reads
- mentally compare the reading to what it should be

* I'm assuming you'll make sure you can breathe with this thing over your head...

- make a suitably–sized adjustment to the necessary control while looking outside (for example N_R may be low, so make a small adjustment to the throttle or collective as appropriate)
- glance at the necessary instrument again
- see what it reads
- look back outside and say out loud what the reading is

and so on. The actual place on the ground you should be looking at is also important, and will be covered in the next chapter.

Look Around

Once the trick of learning to glance at instruments is learned, the next thing to do is to put your head on a swivel and keep it there. This is particularly true when in forward flight. Look around for other traffic, obstacles, birds, and so on.

Look into every turn and call out it is clear in that direction. This is not just to impress your instructor you have looked into the turn, but so you will remember to look every time you change the direction of flight. Don't worry if you say it out loud when you're alone. You won't feel like a fool, and if anyone else is there who isn't a pilot, they'll a) be impressed and b) pick up the habit themselves...

Pay attention to blind spots in your helicopter, and be aware of the blind spots of other aircraft. Call out other traffic to the instructor and to yourself.

Collision Course

We owe a lot of things in aviation to nautical traditions. One of these is how to tell if you're going to collide with something. Simply stated, if you spot something in the windshield, and it stays in the same place on the windshield and gets bigger, you're probably going to run into it*.

Post-flight

Walkaround

A quick walkaround the aircraft after you land is worthwhile. Oil leaks are easier to spot, as well as lots of other things people would be upset at finding on the next pre-flight inspection.

What the Post-Flight Debriefing Should Cover

The debriefing should happen, quick as it may be. The student and instructor should discuss the main learning points and arrive at an agreement about how the trip went, and what's next.

While it may seem an unusual thing, the post flight debriefing is almost as important as the pre-flight briefing. In my experience, it may be better if the student leads this debriefing to cover what he remembers of the trip, as it will help to improve his ability to observe and remember. The instructor will probably need to correct the student from time to time, and this may become annoying. It is worth remembering when the student graduates, he probably won't have anyone else, let alone an instructor looking over his shoulder all the time. A self–critical student is well on the way to maturity.

Summary of Chapter 11

As a student, you should have learned something from this chapter- what your instructor should be doing, why it's being done, some of the problems you may be facing, and how perhaps you need to think about how best to communicate them. Hopefully, it gives some deeper insight in to the sort of things you need to consider as you go about the task of accepting and gaining knowledge.

* For God's sake, don't go out and try this just to prove me correct.

12 Before You Strap In...

This chapter will cover some of the fundamental changes in thinking you must make as a helicopter pilot, and will prepare you for the knowledge your instructor is about to impart.

INTRODUCTION

Helicopters are difficult to understand*, and initially appear difficult to fly. Let no-one convince you it is easy to learn to fly a rotary wing aircraft - yet it is possible, as many have proven†. What makes learning to fly difficult is that some aspects of controlling this machine are contrary to deeply–ingrained instincts, especially if you've flown fixed wing airplanes. These instincts must be changed to handle this new method of movement, in the same way any other new skill needs to have new habits. Steering a car in a skid is an example of an instinct that must be learned.

In adapting to rotary wing aviation, many fixed–wing pilots must throw away old ideas. The largest change in thinking that must be made is that only very small movements of the flight controls are needed in most helicopter maneuvers.

At somewhere around 10 hours of experience, 'something' clicks, and the whole picture starts to come together. I wish I knew what the 'something' was, because maybe it could be bottled...

Because of the difficulty of acquiring new habits, it is necessary to have a good, experienced instructor. The novice helicopter pilot must learn not to give in to his early, incorrect instincts for self preservation, and explaining and demonstrating will be needed to convince the student of the need for certain actions. Expect a lot of time to be spent in briefing and debriefing - in fact, be *very suspicious* if you don't get a lot of time in front of a chalkboard.

Entering and Exiting The Helicopter (rotors turning)

While this may sound silly to put this in a book on helicopters, as a student you should learn how to get in and out of the helicopter with some grace‡ and safety. I'm not talking about when the machine is stopped and getting into a passenger seat. I'm concerned with doing it with the rotors turning and with flight controls in place. Better to practice with the engines stopped on the ground, than to have to try to figure it out in a rushed situation.

Learn how to maneuver your legs and feet around the various angles and corners, what to avoid, and what you as the pilot may need to particularly guard against happening.

If you know how to do it, you are much better placed to brief passengers or others on how to do it as well.

PRIOR TO LIFT-OFF

There are a whole host of things you will have learned prior to getting close to the helicopter and starting to actually fly. This chapter attempts to tie some of those things more closely related to the hardware and mechanics of what you need to do.

TERMS USED

To avoid confusion, the act of leaving the ground (or water) and attaining an airborne condition will be called *lift-off*. We'll try to avoid the term takeoff, as it means too many different things in a helicopter. I've not found a clear definition of the word takeoff that doesn't confuse things - is a takeoff lifting to the hover, or moving from a hover to forward flight?

The only time the words 'takeoff' will be used is for the takeoff power rating, and for running takeoffs.

Similarly, the words 'landing' won't be used commonly in this book. It can have too many meanings. The only time it will be used is for running landings or other very specific maneuvers. We'll use the term *touchdown* to describe the act of, well, touching down on the ground or water.

---

* Even with the help of this book...
† It should be noted that helicopter pilots can be the product of unskilled labor...
‡ Ladies- wear slacks or trousers!

Pre-Flight Actions

The pre-flight check starts long before you get anywhere close to the helicopter. The first thing to do with every flight is to determine what is the aim of the flight, (besides walking back into the office). Aside from the self-checking of mental preparation and attitude for the flight, there are the weather checks, the pre-flight planning of weight and CG, range, fuel and so on that are legally required (as well as a good idea in the first place). There will also probably be paperwork from the mechanic to say the machine is in proper order.

Pre-Flight checks

The pre-flight check itself starts when you first lay eyes on the machine. What is close to the helicopter that could affect it? What could we affect when the rotor starts and we lift to the hover?

Are there are any items close by on the ground that might not be noticeable from the cockpit? Ropes lying over the skids, skids sunk in the mud, ground handling wheels still attached, and so on.

Common sense is needed. I was told of a helicopter that had been parked for a long and snowy winter. It was literally dug out of a snowbank to prepare it for flight. Everything seemed normal until the runup, when a very high frequency vibration started at the back of the machine. Before it could be shut down, the whole tail rotor gearbox and tail rotor departed the aircraft.

Seems like snow had melted and run into the drain holes of the tail rotor blade and re-froze. The drain hole appeared clear during the walkaround, but the weight of the ice was enough to cause the failure.

Walk-Around checks

A pre-flight inspection of the helicopter is in order, and the exact requirements for this will depend upon the make and model of machine. It is also always wise to have this pre-flight check verified by someone else every once in a while, as we all forget things.

A detailed walk-around of the helicopter prior to getting strapped in is not just something to waste your time on. It's essential. The only time I wouldn't bother about a walk-around is if I've just exited the helicopter in the last 5 minutes, nothing has been done to it (like refueling), no-one has gone near it, there are no signs of anything leaking or dripping from it and it was working fine before it was shut down. Even then, I feel guilty. Otherwise, check everything over.

The walkaround listed in the FM is likely to be pretty vague and long-winded. It may not help you very much in understanding what you should be looking for and at. It's written that way for a lot of legal reasons, and not a lot of technical reasons.

A written checklist may help for the first two or three times you do the walk-around, but you really should become familiar enough with the machine you can do it from memory.

Remove all the necessary covers, plugs and tie-downs. Do this before you start the rest of the pre-flight inspection. Then make sure you've got everything removed as you do the normal inspection.

Every once in a while, it's nice to check to make sure all the necessary paperwork is with the helicopter. I've been caught once in a most embarrassing way...

I remember one such instance, when I casually asked the flight engineer when a particular feature had been changed on a helicopter - (a rivet was purposefully left out of a piece of tail boom attachment for inspection purposes). I must have logged more than a thousand pre-flights of this type of helicopter, and I asked, in all innocence, when this had been changed. The look of shock which crossed the man's face was quite remarkable, and he shuffled and looked at the ground and said quietly, "It's always been like that, sir." I think my face turned every one of the shades of embarrassed red in the color spectrum.

Drain the fuel if it's the first flight of the day. Make sure the helicopter is on a level surface prior to draining the fuel, to make sure the sump has had a chance to catch any nastiness that might have been lurking in the tank.

I can't give more specific instructions for any types of helicopters in this book. There are too many variables. Take the time to get an experienced mechanic or pilot to show you the walkaround, and possibly learn it from two or three different people. Have them watch you as you do a walkaround and let them correct your errors.

Start–Up checks

There are not too many things needed to start most helicopters. Electrics, fuel and the controls (including the throttle) in the proper place. Electrics generally is just the battery, although you should know how to start with an external power source as well. Fuel means fuel getting to the engine, so know where the switches are for the various pumps and valves. Controls includes the throttle, so make sure you won't be surprised if you hit the starter...

For most light training helicopters, it is possible to move the flight controls with the rotor stopped, and this is normally checked every flight to ensure everything is still connected, and that the linkages aren't binding.

Before you turn on the battery make sure everything is in order, and that things that shouldn't be on are off.

Some organizations insist on the radio being on prior to start, and some airfields even require authorization before starting the rotor. Having the radio on is a good idea, as if anything goes wrong during the start, you can call for help pretty quickly.

Last chance to make sure the rotor blades (main and tail) are untied![*]

Starting the engine should be simple enough, but beware the cold or damp weather can make starting some piston engines a bit tricky. Hot engines can have some peculiar habits for starting as well.

Most piston engine helicopters incorporate a clutch between the engine and the rotor system. Some engage automatically, others need to be selected. In nearly all cases the engine has to be running at the correct RPM and temperature before you engage the rotor.

So you've got the rotor system started. Feels like the helicopter is alive, doesn't it? Now's the time to start being really careful.

Energy and the Rotor System

With the rotors turning, the helicopter is literally a living, breathing animal, and must be treated with a great deal of respect. Unlike a fixed–wing aircraft which needs relatively little attention to the controls until the start of the takeoff run, the helicopter controls require constant attention whenever the rotors are turning. While this is obvious in flight, it is perhaps more critical when the helicopter is sitting on the ground, and you think you can forget about the controls. Every movement of the controls will affect the tip path plane - they certainly will apply forces to the fuselage. The pedals can rotate the helicopter even while the skids appears to be welded to the ground.

Pre-Lift-off Checks

Engine and Systems Checks

These will vary from helicopter type to type. Some will require that the freewheel unit be checked for correct operation, others that a hydraulic system be verified to be normal.

One that is common is to make sure that all the oil temperatures and pressures are in the correct operating range. This is to ensure that oil that is too cold is not going to be forced to work in the engine or transmission under high power settings, possibly damaging seals and internal components. It also means that there is a good chance that everything is warmed up nicely and evenly and no undue stresses will be generated by cold temperatures.

Piston engines need to have checks of the magnetos and carburetor heat prior to every flight.

It's always a good idea to move the flight controls around to make sure the rotor disk is going to respond. Don't move the controls too quickly or too far, but make sure you give them a wiggle to make sure they are operating smoothly. Some helicopters require the controls to be moved in specific directions to check hydraulic actuators.

Make sure the electrics are working properly, and that associated systems like navigation equipment is on and working as it ought to.

* There are those of us who have started with the blades tied down, and those who will... and to those who say it won't happen to me, remember these words when it does.

Last Chance Check

Immediately prior to adding collective pitch, the controls should be centralized (unless you're on a slope). As the collective lever is raised, you should be noticing the movement of the helicopter, until just prior to leaving the ground, you should be able to pause and determine that the CG is within limits and that you're not going to get dynamic rollover*.

Holding the Controls

Light Training Helicopters

In helicopters without hydraulic systems, the rotor blades feed back forces to the cockpit controls, and the pilot must be positive in efforts to control the machine. Trim systems are often fitted that use a small motor to re–datum a spring system to a new 'neutral' force point. The end result is the pilot must apply some force to make sure the controls move the rotor disk in the desired direction, but don't hold too tightly.

Control Pressure, Not Control Movement

The controls of most helicopters are surprisingly effective, that is, they can generate large moments with very little actual movement of the cockpit controls or the rotor disk. This large moment will have a big effect on the airframe.

For this reason, rather than talk about physically moving the controls of most helicopters, it is better to talk about applying pressure to them. For example, rather than saying, move the cyclic stick to the 2 o'clock position, it is more precise to say, apply pressure to the 2 o'clock position. The tip path plane will move there in a goodly fashion, without over–controlling. When making corrections, a slight pressure may be more effective than an actual movement†.

Since an overly tense hand can't sense small changes in pressure, this is all the more reason to adapt a relaxed and light grip on the flight controls. This is rather more difficult with the pedals, for reasons that will become clear later. The effect here is the feet should be resting lightly on the pedals and be ready to apply a slight pressure rather than a movement, unless a rapid heading change is needed.

The collective lever is the final control to be addressed. Because of the sensitivity of the helicopter to small changes in power, particularly in the hover, it is necessary to keep the power changes to a minimum - again, slight pressures are preferred to actual movements.

Another way to learn how to understand pressures is to try to balance something (broom handle, wooden chair on two legs) with one end on the floor, just using one finger on either side of the object. Once the point of balance is close, it only takes small pressures from the fingers to keep the object balanced. That's what pressures are.

Function of Controls

The flight controls of the helicopter are the means the pilot has to both stabilize and control the helicopter. They are the means of changing the balance of forces about the CG. The two main controls, the cyclic stick and collective lever, are used to control the tilt and amount of main rotor thrust respectively, and the pedals are used to control the thrust of the tail rotor.

* See "Rollover" on page 179
† And you can only apply a slight pressure if you are holding the controls lightly.

Figure 12-1 Cockpit Controls

For the purposes of this chapter, the rotor will be assumed to be operating at a constant RPM. Figure 12-1 shows how the controls are laid out in a typical light training helicopter.

Collective Lever

The collective lever is located on the left side of the pilots seat and operates in an up and down manner, pivoting about the rear of the lever. Through a series of suitable mechanical linkages*, it changes the pitch on all the rotor blades by an equal amount (or collectively, hence the name). Raising the collective lever increases the pitch on all the blades, and lowering the collective lever decreases the pitch.

Changing the pitch angle of the blades indirectly alters the angle of attack. The lift and the drag forces on each blade and on the rotor as a whole change as well.

Throttle

The change in lift is the desired effect, and the change in drag is an undesired effect. The change in drag tries to change the N_R. To maintain the N_R at a constant value following a change in collective, the engine power must be changed, normally by the pilot in a piston–engined helicopter, but sometimes by the governor if one is fitted†. Changing collective pitch results in a change in torque between the main rotor and fuselage which must be corrected by use of the tail rotor pedals.

Cyclic Stick

Earlier, in Chapter 2, the means of changing the blade pitch angle to equalize lift in forward flight was mentioned, and the blades were said to change pitch cyclically (every cycle). This gives rise to the name of the control for changing the tilt of the tip path plane- namely the cyclic stick.‡

The cyclic stick is the means to control the direction of the thrust by changing the tilt of the tip path plane. This tilt does not significantly change the magnitude of the thrust vector. If the cyclic stick is moved forward, the tip path plane tilts forward. If the cyclic stick is moved to the left, the tip path plane tilts to the left, and so on. This is accomplished by a series of suitable mechanical linkages between the cockpit and the swashplate. Figure 12-2 shows a typical flight control circuit of push rods and bell cranks.

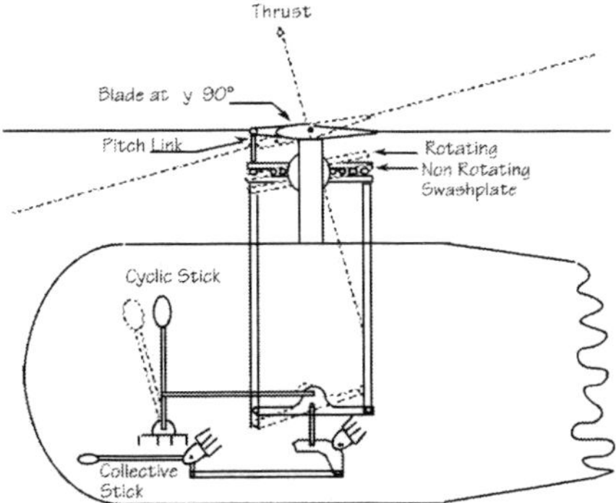

Figure 12-2 Simple Flight Control Run

* It's well worth spending a bit of time looking at the swashplate and rotor blades on a helicopter that is new to you while someone else moves the cockpit controls, using a hydraulic ground test stand, if needed.
† Governors are covered in "Governing systems" on page 306.
‡ I wonder if it would make any difference if it had been called the 'tilter'.

Tail Rotor Controls or Pedals

The last major flight control in the helicopter are the set of pedals used to change the pitch on the tail rotor. These are normally quite straightforward and work through a series of (easily understood) mechanical linkages from the cockpit to the tail rotor.

The pedals control the thrust of the tail rotor, and compensate for the torque of the main rotor. They are also used to overcome the lateral force generated by side winds either in the low airspeed or forward flight. *They are not used to turn the helicopter in forward flight!*

In the hover and low speed environment, the pedals control the heading of the helicopter, and must be adjusted to maintain the desired heading when either the power or the relative wind is changed.

Effects of Controls

One of the first things you will discover is it seems nearly impossible to learn how to control a helicopter. At least, that's how it feels to nearly everyone I've ever seen. The reasons why this is difficult, if you're interested, are covered in "Why are Helicopters Difficult to Fly?" on page 280. At the moment though, you're busy trying to figure out what is going on.

The effects of the controls in the different flight regimes of the helicopter will be covered in the offending chapters, as there are subtle differences.

Downwash

Look around the helicopter. You are about to generate quite a bit of wind with the rotor system. Is there anything that might be adversely affected by that wind?

Hand Signals

While it's unlikely that as a private pilot you will have to be following many ground signals. They are normally used for marshalling over underslung loads and the like. But you never know when someone might start waving at you in a purposeful way. Best to learn the signals normally given to helicopters. They are included below.

Better advice yet is to practice using these signals. Have another helicopter pilot give you the signals (in a safe and controlled manner), so that you can learn what they will look like before a stranger gives them to you. The next good learning experience is to give the signals to someone hovering a helicopter so you can get an idea of what the problems facing the ground guide are. It will make a better pilot of you.

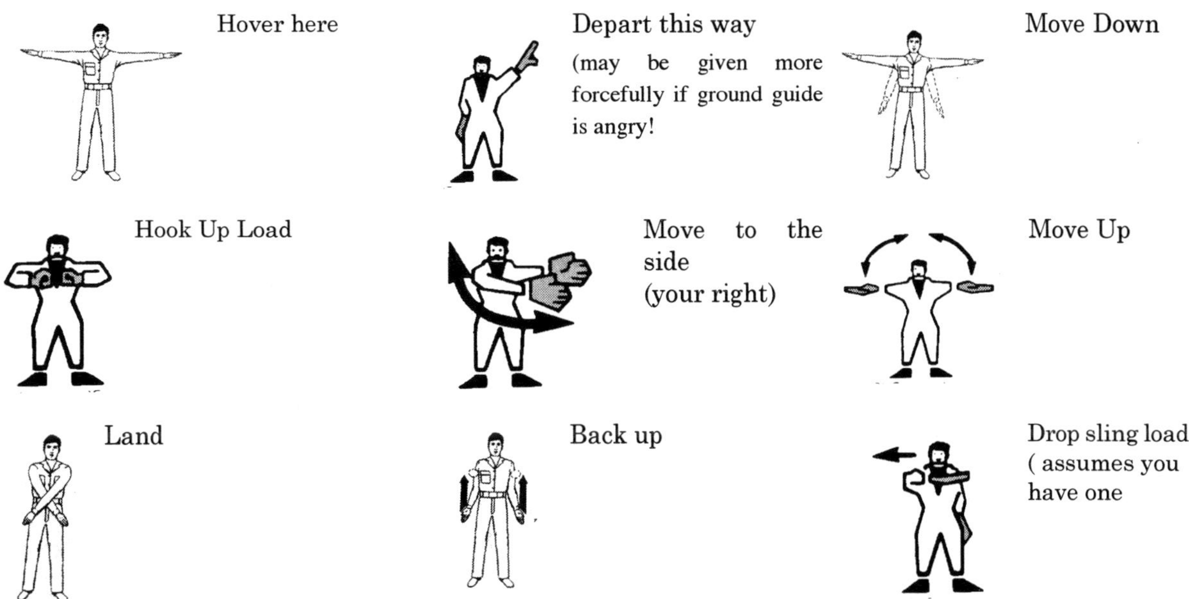

Figure 12-3 Ground Marshallers Signals

Some Other Things

There are places where it is obviously not a good idea to land. Figure 12-4 shows some of those.

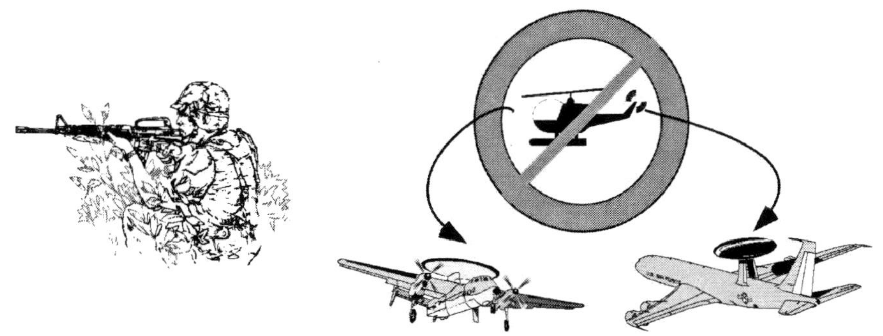

Places Where People Point Guns at you

Do Not Try to Land Here, even when the aircraft are on the ground

Figure 12-4 Good places to avoid Landing

Summary of Chapter 12

This chapter has covered some of the things that will happen between walking out to the aircraft and commiting aviation. These are important to the task of flying a helicopter, and should be stressed prior to starting flying. If mastered early, learning is much easier and more fun for all.

13 Helicopter Flying – The Basics

General Introduction

Helicopter flying, and in particular hovering, is about as close as one can ever get to perfect flying - in other words, when you have mastered the art - you can literally be where you want to be without realizing exactly how you got there. Visualization is a large part of the trick here, and for guidance on what visualization is, I recommend Richard Bach's wonderful book - Johnathan Livingstone Seagull.*

Hovering, however, is challenge to learn, and so it is not taught first in most schools. For that reason, we'll begin with the easier task of forward flight and taper on to the tougher stuff in due course.

First will come the 'science' bit, so you'll learn the correct information, then the 'art' stuff so you'll know when to use the correct knowledge.

Forward Flight

In contrast to hovering, forward flight is a piece of cake to learn, so that's where we'll begin our adventure†. Airspeed makes the helicopter feel more stable and solid. The helicopter appears to respond quickly to any control inputs, particularly in pitch and roll. Maintaining heading and balance (ball in the middle) is easy as airspeed over the vertical stabilizer helps keep the correct end forward.

Effects of Controls in Forward Flight

Cyclic stick

The cyclic stick always controls the direction of rotor tilt, and thus the direction of rotor thrust. Tilt the disk forward, and the helicopter accelerates forward. When the forces of thrust and drag are in balance, the acceleration stops and the helicopter is at a steady airspeed.

To turn the helicopter in forward flight, it is necessary to tilt the thrust vector to one side. Moving the cyclic stick to one side will tilt the thrust vector, and causes the helicopter to roll. As long as the thrust vector is tilted with respect to the fuselage, the helicopter will continue to change its angle of bank. When the angle of bank is what you want, (or if you like, thrust vector is where it is desired to be with the earth), the roll rate needs to be stopped. To stop the roll rate, put the cyclic stick back in the middle with respect to the helicopter (A more complicated way of saying this is to put the rotor back in line with the vertical axis of the helicopter or stop tilting the thrust vector with respect to the fuselage and the helicopter stops at a roll attitude (or bank angle and stays there.) In other words, put the stick back in the middle!)

Bank angle alone will not turn the helicopter in forward flight. Aft cyclic stick is needed to change the bank angle into a change of heading.

In simple terms, a turn in forward flight needs to have the nose moving across the horizon, and that needs some aft cyclic stick.

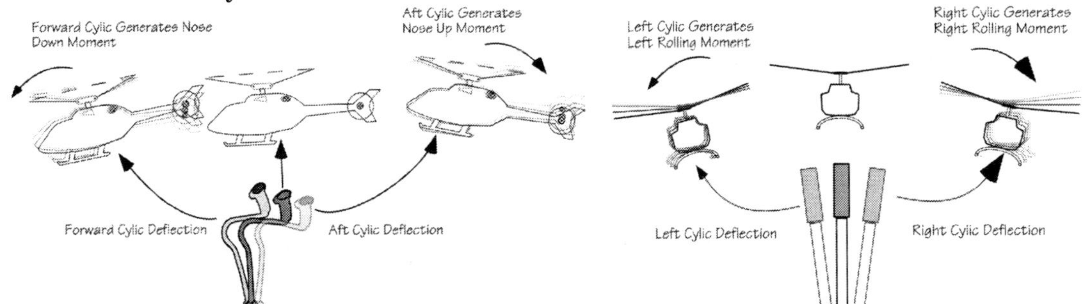

Figure 13-1 Effect of Cyclic stick

---

* Read the book- it takes less time than watching the movie.

† If you want to start somewhere else, go ahead, it's just most instructors will teach the forward flight stuff first.

Collective lever

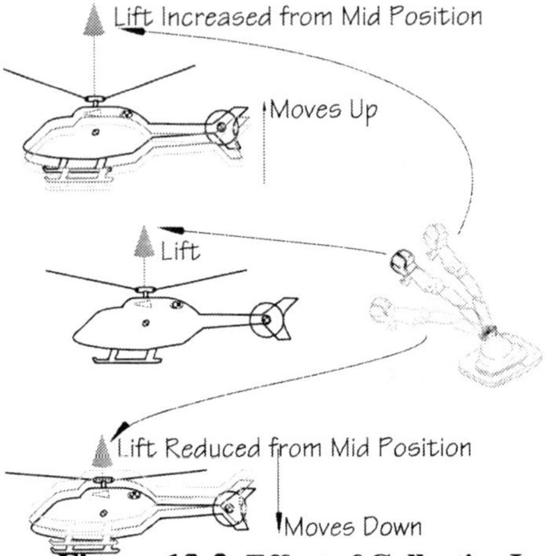

Figure 13-2 Effect of Collective Lever

The collective lever controls the amount of thrust, or the size of the thrust vector. This changes the overall balance of forces, mostly in the vertical axis, so it is reasonable to expect the main effect is to control rate of climb and descent. It is easy to think the collective lever controls other things such as airspeed, but it really only influences them.

Pedals

Hover

In the hover, the pedals are used to change the heading of the helicopter, or to keep it straight with changing side winds. In a perfect, no wind day, the pedals actually control yaw rate, but this happens seldom, so as a beginner, you need to know that in the hover, the pedals are used to stop and start turns to change heading, and to correct for changes in side wind.

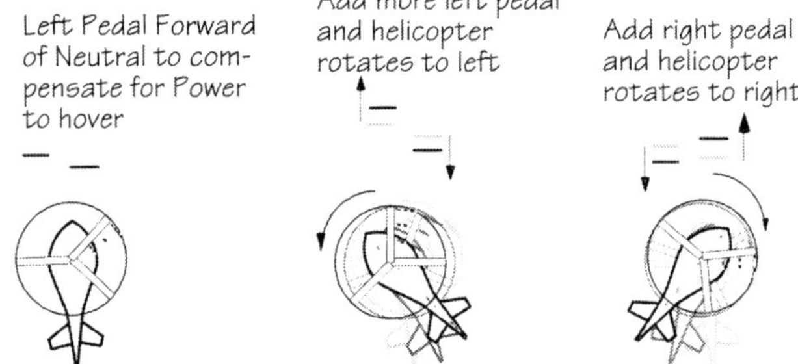

Figure 13-3 Pedals in the Hover

Forward Flight

Pedals are not used to turn the helicopter in forward flight*.

In forward flight, the pedals are used to control side force, or in terms visible in the cockpit, slip ball or slip string position†. They are used to maintain balance. In a steady cruise, small changes in pedal position may be needed for slight adjustments in ball position when power or airspeed changes are made, or when turning, but these should be minor changes only.

If the collective lever setting is kept constant, and the airspeed is changed, the change in airspeed over the vertical stabilizer may affect the amount of tail rotor needed to keep the ball in the middle.

* Sorry to have state this, but I've seen a lot of neophyte helicopter pilots try to turn with the pedals in forward flight.
† The subtle, but important difference between slip strings and slip balls was be discussed in "Slip Strings" on page 83.

Several people have commented to me that there is a large difference between the sensitivity of the pedals in forward flight (where only small pressures are needed) and in the hover, where bootfuls are necessary. This is because in forward flight, the vertical fin provides a lot of force that the tail rotor needs to overcome to change the balance of forces, and this is absent in the hover.

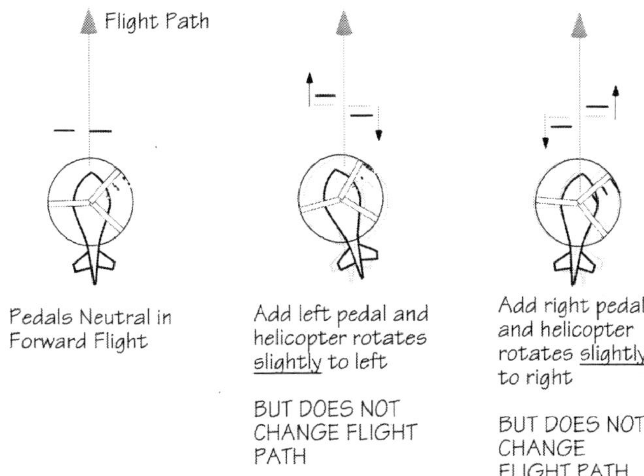

Figure 13-4 Effect of Pedals in forward flight

Summary of Effects of Controls

Longitudinal cyclic stick controls tip path plane tilt, and hence pitch attitude and thus airspeed; collective lever still controls the amount of total rotor thrust and hence altitude and rate of climb at a constant airspeed; and lateral cyclic stick controls roll rate and hence angle of bank. Pedals control the thrust of the tail rotor, and hence the balance of the helicopter – it all sounds so simple.

An idea that is probably new to non-aviators is most easily introduced in forward flight, is the concept of 'Attitude Flying'.

Attitude Flying

There is a distinct relationship between fuselage pitch attitude and airspeed, and the beginning pilot would be wise to learn and apply this concept. A typical example of this relationship of pitch attitude and airspeed is shown in Figure 13-5 below. Note absolute values of pitch attitude (for example +5° or -3.5° nose down) are missing, as many helicopters lack an attitude indicator with accurate markings, and the pitch attitude will change with different CGs. The concept is the fuselage requires more nose down pitch as airspeed increases. Also note that not much change in fuselage pitch is needed for a large change in airspeed.

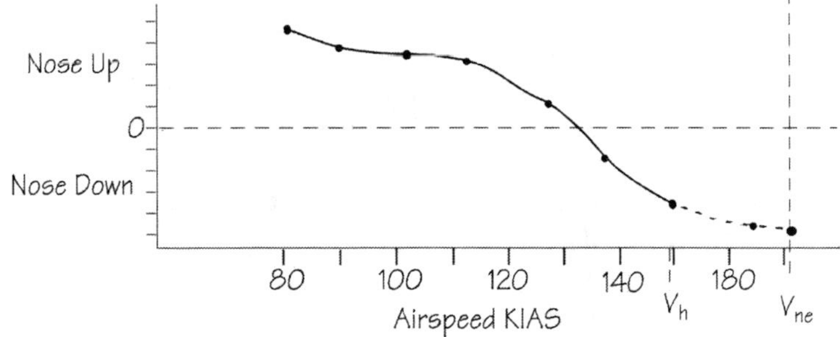

Figure 13-5 Change in Pitch Attitude with Forward Speed

The way to use this airspeed vs. pitch attitude relationship is to note the place where the horizon crosses the vertical pillar of the windshield, and then use that position as the way to maintain level flight. Occasionally glance inside to see if the airspeed or altitude have changed. If they have, then make small adjustments to the pitch attitude (i.e. where the horizon crosses the vertical pillar in the windshield) and see what happens. To make sure the student learns how to do this, the instructor should cover up the flight instruments, while making the student change airspeed and maintain height, or turn and climb and descend while maintaining airspeed. Every so often, uncover the instruments to let the student see what has changed (or not changed).

When a change in airspeed or altitude is required, the pilot should be using external references, as opposed to the aircraft instruments, especially the airspeed indicator and pressure altimeter. The aircraft instruments are there to refer to, rather than fly by*.

Cruise

In the cruise, the power setting is constant (that is N_R and collective lever position) are unchanged- the engine instruments of manifold pressure, engine and N_R should be pretty much the same.

That having been said, the helicopter is still unstable, and will wander away from where it's put by the pilot. You will have to make small (that is, barely perceptible) corrections to keep the machine from wandering away from the pitch and roll attitudes you want.

Don't worry, it will be come second nature in a short while.

What cannot be stressed enough is the need to look outside and recognize the attitude the helicopter is flying at. Sounds simple, and it will become second nature, but for now, you'll have difficulty visualizing the whole thing. See Figure 13-6 for an example of how it might look.

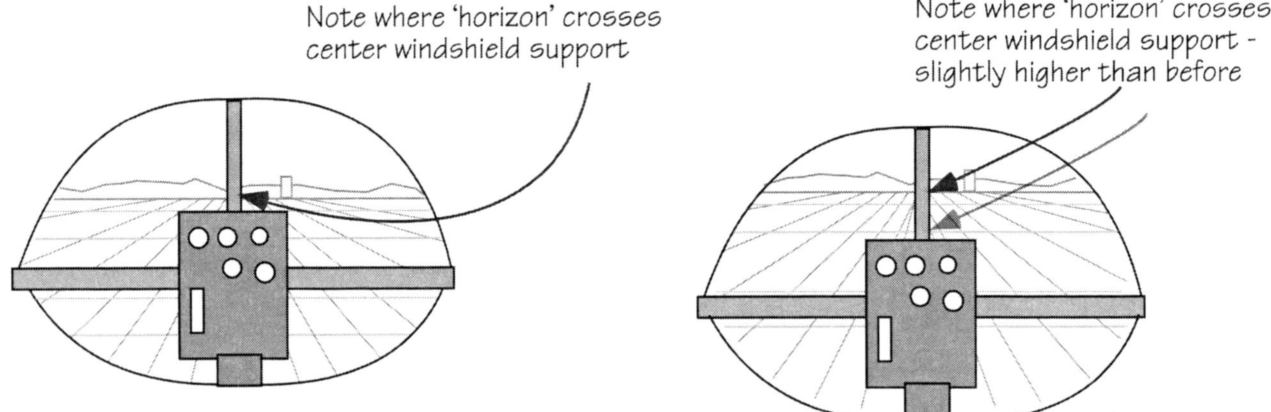

Figure 13-6 Attitude Flying a) Moderate Airspeed b) Faster Airspeed

So you start at a moderate airspeed, lets say 70 KIAS and 1,500' height above the ground. For this part, it's important to be at a moderate distance from the ground. Note the altitude from the altimeter- that's what we'll be using for a constant height.

If you don't move the cyclic stick, the helicopter will start to wander in one direction or another. For the sake of somewhere to start, lets say it starts to move up. The movement will be slow and at first, imperceptible. You will notice it is happening because the helicopter will start to climb and the airspeed will decrease. Your instructor is charming, but pitiless about small errors, he wants you to be back at 1,500' and 70 KIAS.

How do you get back there? Just putting the nose back to the same place on the horizon won't help, as the airspeed is now down to, say, 60 KIAS.

There are actually two steps to the process. The first step is to stop the deviation from getting any worse (i.e. don't let the attitude get larger) and the second step is to get back to the original condition. You will have to put the nose a bit lower than it was before and wait until you have the 70 KIAS nearly regained, then adopt close to the same attitude as before. A power correction may be needed to regain the correct altitude.

* Obviously, if the helicopter is to be flown IFR, looking outside won't work, but that's beyond the scope of this section.

With a little time, you'll learn to feel the small changes that signal the deviation from the desired condition and make the corrections to the cyclic stick immediately and correctly.

Changing Airspeed in Level Flight

A useful (no, make that necessary) exercise is to change airspeed while maintaining level flight. This will show the effects of controls, as well as bring home some of the points raised earlier in performance about power required vs. airspeed.

Start with some good external line features, like a straight road, power line or railroad, or some other distinct feature several minutes flying time away. This will help you keep straight during the rest of the changes you'll be going through.

The first thing to notice is each control will definitely affect one part of the equation*. In helicopters, the fore-aft cyclic stick controls pitch attitude which controls airspeed, and the collective lever controls power which controls rate of climb or descent. Since 'cyclic stick-controls-pitch-attitude-which-controls-airspeed' is cumbersome, it's easier to say cyclic stick controls airspeed. Since we want to maintain level flight, that is, rate of climb or descent zero, the collective lever can still be thought of to maintain climb or descent.

The same advice as before holds true- where the horizon cuts across the nose is an approximate place to hold. See what effect a small change pitch attitude has before making a more drastic change.

Start by reducing airspeed by smoothly coordinating the two movements of controls, that is, easing the cyclic stick slightly aft, while reducing the collective lever a small amount. Easy to say, but difficult to do in the real world the first time.

A bit of eyes-closed simulation may help†. You are flying level at 70 KIAS and you want to reduce the airspeed to say, 40 KIAS. Visualize what could happen - either you get things perfectly coordinated or you don't. Chances are pretty good you won't get it exactly - no problem. So what has happened if you have following symptoms: - airspeed is reducing at a satisfactory rate, but you are climbing? Since cyclic stick controls airspeed, that control is OK. Collective lever controls rate of climb/descent, and that's what needs correcting - you're climbing too much. What are you going to do? Reduce the collective lever a small amount to see if that reduces the rate of climb. It won't happen immediately, but give it 5 or so seconds. Don't believe the vertical speed indicator, look outside and feel in the seat of your pants.

Of course, having changed the collective lever will affect the pitch attitude of the helicopter, and the yaw balance, so you'll have to make an adjustment to the longitudinal cyclic stick and the pedals. The whole process gets repeated until it becomes second nature.

So, now it's time to get a bit smarter. You notice that at this N_R, the manifold pressure for 40 KIAS is 25" (for example). So from 70 KIAS, you reduce collective lever to give you 25" of manifold pressure and bring the cyclic stick back to what you think is about the correct spot. But now the airspeed is too high and you're descending. What happened? Same logic- cyclic stick controls airspeed, which is too high, so you haven't brought the cyclic stick far enough back. Collective lever controls rate of climb, so maybe it's too far down for the amount of cyclic stick you've using. Don't change the collective lever immediately until you see what the airspeed and rate of climb are doing.

It's also a lot easier to do this in the cockpit than it is to describe it- it will become intuitive.

Smooth Airspeed Changes

Practice until you can make a smooth change from one airspeed to the next without climbing or descending. Anticipate as you increase airspeed from the minimum power speed, you'll need to increase collective lever, and as you reduce airspeed from high speed to minimum power speed, you'll need to reduce collective lever.

When you start to change airspeed behind the power curve, things work backward, if you remember the power required vs. airspeed curve.

* Also be advised there are several schools of thought about which control affects which part. This technique has worked for every helicopter (and most fixed wing airplanes) I 've flown.

† Obviously on the ground only

The point is not to become a slave to exact, or even approximate numbers. Do what you have to do to make the change smoothly and with anticipation.

Oh yes, don't forget to keep the nose pointed straight while you make the power changes. This too will take anticipation, but will become second nature. (That's the reason for the long straight road, power line, or railroad, by the way).

Back Side of The Power Curve

It's worth spending some time flying on the back side of the power curve, just to get to understand what happens here. It'll pay huge dividends later on.

The *back side of the power curve* is those airspeeds less than the airspeed where minimum power is needed to maintain flight. Lets say our minimum power airspeed (or V_Y) is 60 KIAS. What happens when we want to slow down to an airspeed below this? You'll need fairly calm air to demonstrate this effect.

Set the airspeed at 60 KIAS and adjust the power to maintain level flight, and then without changing power slow down slightly, to try to maintain 45 KIAS and the original heading. Strange, you notice, I'm descending. To stop descending, you'll need to add some power, since collective lever controls rate of climb. When you're stable and level at 45 KIAS, try slowing down to a slower speed, if one is marked on your airspeed indicator. Lets say 30 KIAS is the slowest mark, so we'll go for that, without changing the power.

Same problem as before- when you're stable at 30 KIAS, the helicopter will be descending. Without changing the power, accelerate to 60 KIAS and notice what happens to the rate of climb.

Two Airspeeds for the Same Power!

What a deal! You can have two airspeeds for the same power setting! Here's how to prove it. Set the helicopter in level flight at an airspeed above the V_Y. Once you're stabilized there, without changing power, reduce airspeed to below V_Y and see try to maintain level flight, without trying to use a particular airspeed. You'll be climbing for a short while, but once you're below V_Y, you'll find the second level flight airspeed for the same power setting.

There's no real use for this exercise, except to reinforce the concept of power required and the front and back sides of the power required curve.

Climbs and Descents

You won't want to (and can't) cruise at one altitude and airspeed all your life, so you must learn to climb and descend. In a helicopter, it is necessary to do several things at once when a change is made from level flight to a climb or descent.

First all, it should be made clear which cockpit control will control what outside parameter. Since the two parameters we want to control most closely in a climb or descent are airspeed and rate of climb, it follows the same logic should be used as before- cyclic stick controls airspeed, collective lever controls rate of climb and descent.

Just like stopping at a STOP sign, you have to anticipate how much to lead the climb or descent in order to arrive smoothly at the correct altitude. About 10% of your rate of climb or descent is a good figure to start with. So if you're climbing at 500 feet per minute (FPM), then start leveling 50' prior to the assigned altitude.

As with airspeed changes, practice going from high speed climbs to low speed descents to low speed climbs to high speed descents. Remember to keep the ball in the middle!

Anticipate what you are going to need to do if given a change in both airspeed and altitude.

There are also a variety of ways the climbs/descents can be conducted - by changing airspeed to that for best rate of climb or minimum rate of descent, maintaining the same airspeed, or some other figure. In any case, the pilot should have a clear idea of the parameters to be maintained or obtained. One of the best ways to demonstrate this is to attempt to maintain an airspeed and heading while climbing at a set rate (say 500 fpm), and when this is mastered, enter a climb or descent with one airspeed, stabilize in the climb (or descent) at another airspeed and then change to another airspeed at the end of the climb or descent. Do this so the transition from level flight to the climb is smooth and seamless. For example, from the cruise at 80 KIAS, enter a climb at 500 fpm at 60 KIAS and then level at the new altitude using 40 KIAS.

Make no mistake, this is not easy to do the first several times you attempt it, but it helps to develop your ability to anticipate and co-ordinate the controls.

Use attitude flying to make these big changes- don't chase the needles.

TURNS

Turns are necessary, as we don't live in a linear world. Generally speaking, turns can be split into three groups - small angle of bank turns, medium and steep turns.

A Note

Always look into the turn before you start to make sure you're not going to run into another aircraft or bird or other obstacle to continued aviation. The 'Big Sky' theory only is a theory...

Gentle Turns (up to 20°Angle of Bank)

In forward flight, turns are made by banking the helicopter. This means tilting the disk. There are going to be two parts to this tilting the disk- the first part is tilting the disk with respect to the helicopter, and the second part is the tilting the disk with respect to the earth.

Tilting the disk with respect to the helicopter is made by moving the cyclic stick laterally a small amount. This generates a rate of rolling, and since the helicopter has very little inertia in roll (compared to pitch), the roll rate might appear at first to be quite high for a very small amount of lateral cyclic stick. For this reason don't use a lot of movement or force when starting the turns. When you tilt the disk with respect to the helicopter, it will generate a roll rate- that is, it will continue to roll while you hold the cyclic stick displaced from the center of the helicopter. When you want to stop rolling, the cyclic stick will be have to be returned to the center (laterally). In technical terms, lateral cyclic stick commands roll rate.

So when the bank angle is what you want it to be, the cyclic stick will be placed back in the middle (with respect to the cockpit)*.

Nose Drop

Another thing will be happening as well though- the nose of the helicopter will want to drop. The reason the nose will start to drop is tilting the total thrust vector of the rotor will reduce the amount of lift acting vertically. A slight amount of aft cyclic stick pressure (and a very small movement if you were measuring) will be all that is needed to maintain the airspeed and altitude for most gentle turns.

Since you probably want to maintain a constant altitude and airspeed when you turn, it will be necessary to add some aft cyclic stick to keep the nose in the same relative position with respect to the air as in level flight. Since you're turning, it's useless to try to maintain the horizon cutting across that spot on the windshield you used in level flight.

Increased Power

You'll also notice the helicopter will either slow down if you try to maintain constant altitude, or descend if you try to maintain constant airspeed. The reason is related to the dropping of the nose- the thrust vector has less vertical component. To maintain airspeed and altitude, you'll need to increase power slightly. For the sort of bank angles we're talking about in gentle turns, the increase in power will be small.

Don't forget to decrease power when you roll out of the turn!

A Changed Sight Picture

In fact, one of the problems of turns in a helicopter is the sight picture will be different for turns to the left and to the right. The horizon will be cutting across the canopy or windshield in a different way if you are turning to the left (I'm assuming you're sitting on the right hand side as a student)- the horizon will be slightly below the level flight position. If you're turning to the

* For those flying the Robinson, you'll get the drift of what I mean - neutral lateral cyclic position.

right, the horizon will be above the level flight position. The reason is you are controlling the roll around the center of the helicopter, and you're not sitting in the center. This is shown in Figure 13-7. The left hand picture shows the real world, and the right hand picture shows what you see.

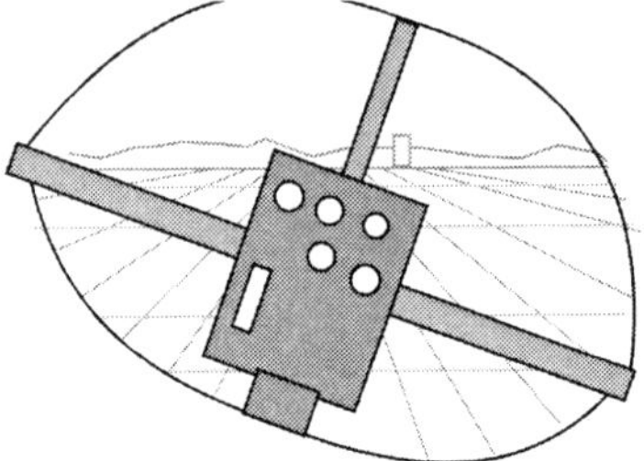

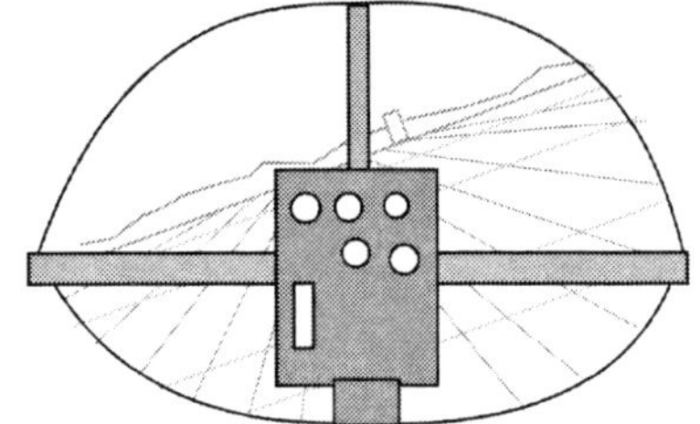

Figure 13-7 Sight Picture in Level Turn

Slip Ball

It may be necessary to correct the slip ball position in the turn. The balance of forces has been upset from level flight, and the slip ball will probably be displaced to one side or another. A small amount of pressure on the pedal towards which the ball is displaced (or if you prefer, step on the ball) will put everything into trim again. This is also one of those things you will learn in the seat of your pants- how to keep the slip ball in the middle without having to pay too much attention to the darn thing. Don't worry, you will learn it.

Practice

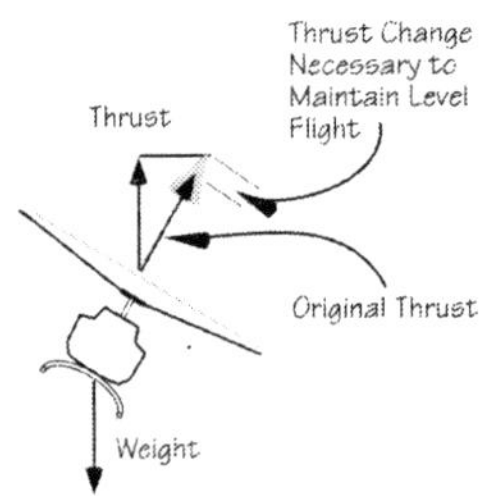

Figure 13-8 Change in Thrust Vector in Turns

Just like climbs and descents, turns need to be anticipated. A faster turn will need more anticipation. To begin with, practice turning roll out on specific landmarks. When you can do that smoothly and easily, try using the heading gyro and aim for a specific heading. When you're really practiced, try it on the standby magnetic compass!

A mark of a perfect 360° turn (constant altitude, anyway) is the small bump you'll feel when you fly through your own rotorwash!

Medium Turns (20 to 45° Angle of Bank)

The medium turn is not much different from the gentle turn, just a bit more of everything. The angle of bank will be steeper, so you'll need more aft cyclic stick and a larger change in power. Slip ball will need more attention. Same as before, try turning to specific outside landmarks first. Keep the rotor tip path cutting the horizon at the same place, and occasionally check inside to see how things are going.

Steep Turns (Greater than 45° Angle of Bank)

Steep turns are different. Things are more exaggerated than even medium turns, and happen much more quickly. Rolling into and out of steep turns will be more rapid than the previous turns, and the amount of aft cyclic stick will be quite large, as will the amount of excess power needed. There is one other major difference, and that's the G you'll feel. At 60° of bank in a level turn at constant airspeed and altitude, you'll be pulling 2G, or twice your normal weight. In this turn you'll need a lot of head movement to make sure you don't run into others sharing the airspace - you're turning pretty quickly.

Developing a 'Seat of the Pants' Sense

After some time, you'll start to develop a sense of where you're going and what's happening that is best described as 'flying by the seat of your pants'. It's an important sense, but only one of many senses. In fact, there are times later in life when you have to learn to treat it with suspicion, but for now, it's worth developing. I only wish I could describe what it is more clearly, so more people would develop it.

Summary of Chapter 13

This chapter has covered the easiest part of learning to fly the helicopter, that is forward flight, up and away. Next, we're on to the more difficult bits...

14 The Divine Art of Hovering

Introduction

Having learned the fundamentals of controlling the helicopter in forward flight, the next step is hovering.

To the Hover!

In many schools, hovering is one of the last items to be taught, as it is perhaps the most difficult skill to master*.

Since it's the most difficult, it is covered after you've learned the fundamentals.

Hovering More Easily

Do you remember the first time you tried to hover? It was probably in a large, open field. (If you haven't tried hovering a helicopter yet, you probably will be put in such a place – wait for it...) It is obstacle-free, and everything is uniformly green (or brown or white - depending upon the season).

What is the typical result for the student? A lot of wandering around the field, with little real learning and lots of frustration. Why? What sort of information is there to give visual cues about movement? Not a lot. Everything is the same color and texture, so there is very little real information about what the helicopter is doing. Everywhere the student looks, there is a very small amount feedback about how he is doing with regard to trying to hover. Also, there is no real incentive to be accurate - one part of the field is as good as another. More detailed reasons as to why this makes things difficult will be given in Chapter 27,"Advanced Helicopter Flying", but for now, here is a possible solution to the problem.

The situation is much better if there is something for the pilot to look at - for hovering at 3 to 5 feet above the ground, the cues should be somewhere about 30 to 50 feet in front of the helicopter. Any further away, and the feedback of cues is too little, and the hover cannot be maintained accurately. If references closer in are used, this may give too high a feedback and overcontrolling will result. It is also necessary to have two references - one in front for lateral movement, and one slightly to the side (about the 2 o'clock or 10 o'clock position) for fore–aft movement.

I have used runway signs, marks on the runway, etc. as cues, and had good success in having non-pilots hovering reasonably (within 10 feet of the spot) within 45 minutes. The incentive of something that could be run into immediately in front, staring you in the face helped to concentrate the student on where to look. The student has an immediate cue about movements, (backwards, forward and side to side) and can make corrections very easily.

Vertical References

Vertical references are most worthwhile. What is meant by this? It is difficult to obtain information about lateral or fore–aft drift or height when hovering over a uniform surface. Some of this information can come from the horizon or distant objects, but we need to see things close by to get good overall cues. Vertical cues are subtly different - we need to have something to measure height by - and looking at an object sticking up in comparison to its background, lots of good cues can be gained. Figure 14-1 shows how this works. Note the relative distance vertically between the top and bottom edges of the sign and the things behind it, or the vertical distance between the sign and the edge of the runway. As you move up and down or back and forth, these relative distances all change, and that is how you judge perspective. When hovering OGE for example, use the sides of buildings or the tops of trees with respect to more distant objects, and so on for vertical cues.

* Other things learned later are more difficult to master, but the concept of hovering is initially not easy.

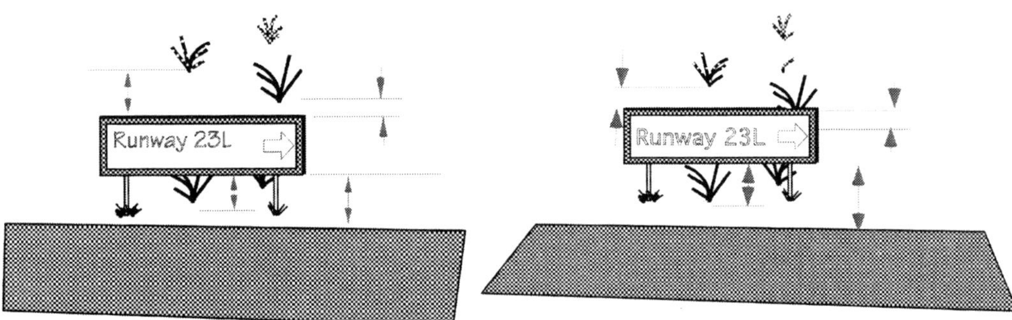

Figure 14-1 Vertical Cues

Aim of Hovering

The aim of hovering is to maintain a steady position over the ground. This means the pilot must know how accurately the hover is to be maintained, and there are sufficient visual references to be able to know you're hovering this accurately. It is nearly impossible to hover accurately over the ocean, for example, without other references to tell you if you are moving. Waves and the foam on the surface won't do, by the way, they move too. If the rotor downwash is visible, it can be used as a rough guide, but conditions need to be ideal for this.

Anytime except calm conditions the wind is going to push the helicopter around. Your task is to keep the helicopter in one place. Accept this as a fact of life. The change in wind is a change in relative airspeed, which causes a change in pitch attitude, and a movement across the ground, and a change in power required to maintain height, and a change in the torque balance, and a change in the transverse flow effect - Hey if it was easy, anybody could do it!

Correcting back to the desired position is straightforward, and consists of making adjustments in the controls to correct the attitude and stop the movement, and then further control inputs to return to the desired position.

It should be remembered that in ground effect (IGE), the collective lever is a height controller, so only very small changes in collective lever should be necessary. Changes in airspeed affect the power required to maintain height as well, further emphasizing the need to make only small changes in speed (ground and/or air speed). This is another way of saying if a large change in groundspeed is made near the hover and the collective lever isn't moved, expect the helicopter to climb or descend quite markedly.

Concepts of Hovering

A few exercises may help to get the concepts of hovering straight, but first a pesky difference in wording must be sorted out.

Hover - Zero Groundspeed vs. Zero Airspeed

Earlier we talked about the zero airspeed hover in order to simplify the aerodynamic explanations. We know full well pilots want to hover with respect to the ground, so in this part, we're going to talk about the stationary with respect to the ground hover. This means anytime there's a wind, the helicopter is affected by it.

Most of the time when you're flying, you'll be blessed with a wind, however, from time to time, the wind will be calm*, and you may notice some differences in the way the helicopter reacts. In a calm wind, you're in a zero-airspeed hover at the same time as you're in a zero-groundspeed hover.

Effects of Controls - Hover and Low Airspeed

Having described all the problems of flying the helicopter, it is time to stop making excuses and get down to making the machine do our bidding. First, we should examine the effect of the various controls. You will notice the title of this section is introduces the term 'low airspeed', so before we examine the effects of controls, we need to understand what we are talking about.

* Those of you into Zen would try to figure out if the wind is coming from everywhere all at once, or going to everywhere all at once...

In the previous chapter, we were in forward flight, up and away from the ground. All the controlling was with respect to airspeed, heading, and altitude. Now, we're closer to the ground, and we are using different references, such as groundspeed, track across the ground and height above ground. To make a clear distinction between the two, because the controls are used in slightly different ways in the two areas, we'll call one 'forward flight' and the other area 'low airspeed'.

Forward Flight and 'Low Airspeed'

Forward Flight will be defined in this book as airspeeds above 40 KIAS, with the direction of flight roughly the same as the direction of the nose of the helicopter*, leaving 'Low Airspeed' to be anything slower, including side and rear airspeeds. The reasons for this arbitrary division are many: the pitot system doesn't function well below 40 KIAS†; flight at speeds slower than 40 KIAS is with reference to the ground whereas flight above this speed is with reference to airspeed and the air mass. Besides, a line had to be drawn somewhere...

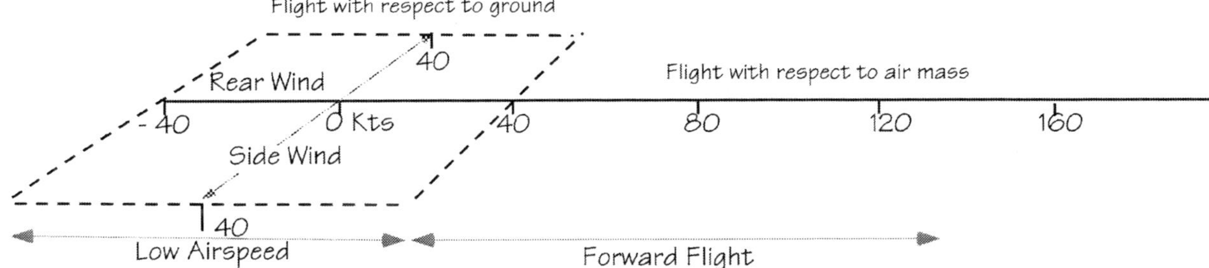

Figure 14-2 Forward Flight vs. Low Airspeed Division

Back to the effects of controls.

In simple terms, the easy way to understand how to fly the helicopter is to consider the cyclic stick as the way to control the tilt of the rotor disk (or the thrust vector), and the collective lever as the controller of the size of the thrust vector. Because it is difficult to split out axes and controls in a helicopter (there are no ailerons or elevators), the terms longitudinal and lateral cyclic stick will be used. Longitudinal cyclic stick is fore/aft cyclic, and lateral cyclic stick is left/ right cyclic. The pedals are used to point the fuselage with respect to the wind or chosen heading.

Hover / Low Airspeed

It helps to consider the cyclic stick as the controller of position and ground speed. In a zero–airspeed hover, the rotor disk is parallel, and the thrust vector perpendicular, to the ground. If a wind is present, the rotor disk and thrust vector must be tilted into the wind to stop the helicopter moving. The collective lever controls the height above the ground.

Cyclic stick

In the hover, think of the cyclic stick as independent of the direction the fuselage is pointing. Where the cyclic stick is pointed is where the helicopter will go, regardless of the heading of the fuselage (within reason). To move to a new position, visualize a line between the top of the cyclic stick and where you want to go. The thrust vector needs to be tilted in that direction. For example, the point desired is slightly to the left front, about the 10 o'clock position. From a steady hover, apply slight pressure to the cyclic stick in that direction, and the helicopter will start moving across the ground. With zero wind, the fuselage stays pointing close to its original heading. The helicopter may slow down again, or do something that appears strange, but keep applying the slight pressure to the cyclic stick in the direction of the desired position, and you will move towards the target.

* ...and hopefully the nose of the pilot as well.
† as will be shown in a later chapter.

This method presupposes a good idea of where you want to be - visualization of the objective, and a good set of references to tell you when you are there all make a large difference. (Remember if you want to hover over a spot, you won't be able to see the spot when it's underneath you, so you need to pick some surrounding features to tell you when you're over it - another reason why large flat fields aren't of much help.) This may sound like an overly simplistic approach, but it works.

When nearly over the desired spot, it is natural to slow down to stop. The disk and thrust vector must be tilted slightly away from the direction of travel position in order to slow down. At the zero–groundspeed hover, the cyclic stick should be back at the same position as at the start of the maneuver. The pressure on the cyclic stick is thus initially in the direction to start (and keep) moving, a slight pressure opposite the direction of motion to slow down and a final correction to stabilize in the hover. Figure 14-3 shows the sequence of moves from start to finish of moving slowly to a new hover position.

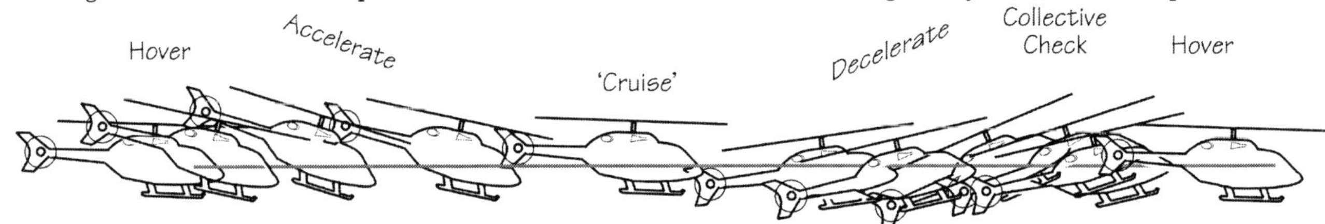

Figure 14-3 Sequence of attitudes from hover to hover

Overcontrolling in the Hover

I know you're supposed to concentrate on the positive, and not tell people the mistakes they're going to make, but learning to hover is a classical example of a problem every helicopter pilot has experienced. I'll describe the problem, as students will immediately identify with it because they've seen it, and then describe the solution.

The Problem

There is a lag between the time a cyclic stick input is make and when the machine is seen to respond to the input. While is lag is whiling away the hours, the student pilot is uncertain about what has happened - nothing seems to be going on. This is especially true in the pitch axis, which has a large inertia compared to roll.

The problem is something is going to happen, but the student doesn't know when that will be. The typical response to having put a control input in with no immediately apparent result - (nothing happened!) is to put in another input. The total input will then be so large that an opposite input will be required to correct for the first one. Unfortunately, the second input has the same lag as the first. The result is a lot of very large control inputs and increasingly large and alarming attitude changes until the instructor takes control.

You're hovering over a spot and the instructor gives you control. You start to drift forward. Here, in step-by-step fashion is what happens when you overcontrol:

- A small aft cyclic stick input is made
- Nothing seems to happen
- Since you want to stop the forward motion, a larger aft input is made
- The nose starts to pitch up, then it *really* pitches up
- Helicopter starts to accelerate backward (all too rapidly for your liking)
- You put in a healthy forward cyclic input
- Nothing seems to happen to the pitch rate or the rate of travel across the ground
- More forward cyclic stick input at about the same time as the nose starts to drop
- Helicopter starts to accelerate forward

'You have control' you yell at the instructor as you wonder if you'll ever get the hang of this game.

Sound familiar?

Now lets look at how to correct this. It's called anticipation.

- A small aft cyclic stick input is made and the stick returned to about the same place it started from.

- Nothing seems to happen, but you're cool, you know it will in just a second or so.
- Nose begins to pitch up, but not too rapidly
- The helicopter stops drifting forward
- The nose settles to the correct position

...and so on.

Much easier wasn't it.

The real question is how to learn about the anticipation. This is another of those skills only experience can teach you. If I could put this in a bottle, I'd be rich.

Cyclic Stick as a Position Controller

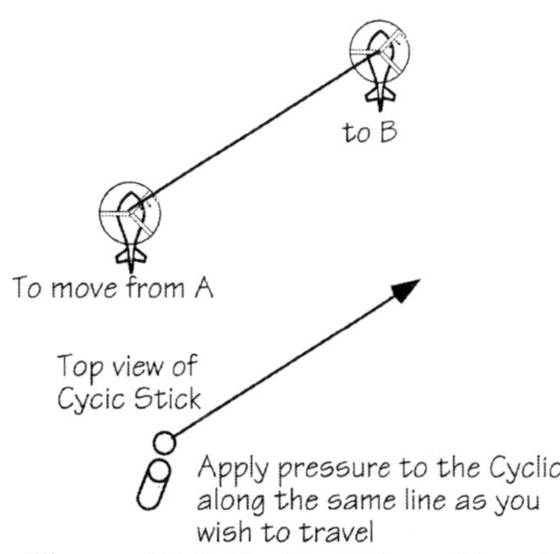

Figure 14-4 Cyclic stick vs. Direction of Travel in Low Airspeed.

The other way to look at the cyclic stick is as a controller of lateral and longitudinal position, and to a lesser extent, ground speed. When hovering along a line, lateral cyclic stick controls lateral position with respect of the line. Too far to the left? Add a bit of right cyclic stick until you are where you want to be. Similarly, longitudinal cyclic stick controls forward speed along the line. In total, the cyclic stick controls tilt of the rotor disk and thrust vector. Figure 14-4 shows this in a different sense.

Collective Lever

Collective lever control has two distinct parts in the low speed environment. The first is in the in-ground-effect (IGE) hover with zero wind; the second is the out-of-ground effect (OGE) hover, or the IGE hover with wind. Reasons for this distinction are given in more detail in Chapter 6,"Basic Helicopter Performance". Remember, the collective lever controls the amount of thrust.

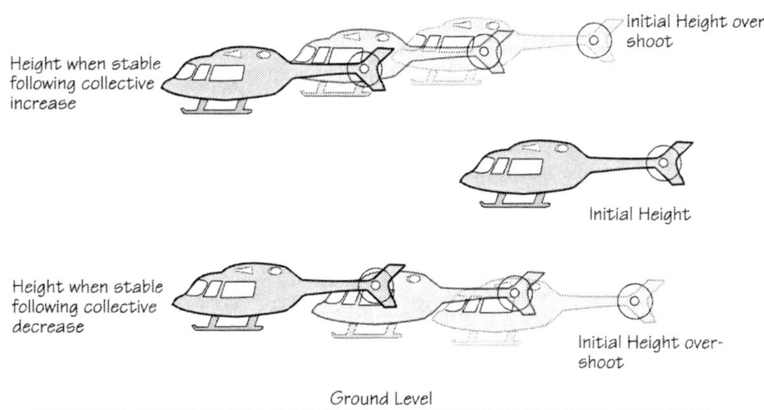

Figure 14-5 Height Change Following Collective Lever Movement - In Ground Effect

In the IGE hover, with zero wind, the collective lever controls height above ground - a small increase in collective lever increases the height, after one or two oscillations. This assumes a steady position, both laterally or longitudinally. See Figure 14-5 for a graph of this.

In an OGE hover, when you change the power, the helicopter will continue to climb or descend*.

OGE, (or if there is a wind or groundspeed when IGE), the collective lever is a rate–of–climb controller. Increase the collective lever above the power required to maintain height, and a steady rate of climb happens. Again, this assumes the airspeed hasn't changed.

* Within reason of course. The power required to hover OGE does not change much within 500' of the starting point, unless you descend into ground effect.

Any power change causes an all–too–frequent problem when learning to hover, namely controlling heading. Any small changes in collective lever change height and introduce problems in heading control, etc. Instructors should encourage students to be very smooth about changing power when hovering close to the ground. Any variation in airspeed changes the power required to maintain height, making things worse...

Pedals

In the hover and low speed, pedals have one basic function - to keep the nose pointed where desired. In a zero wind hover, the pedals control yaw rate.

When there is a side wind in the low airspeed region, the pedals are still used to control heading of the fuselage, but have some complex effects. Hovering with a relative 225° wind in most helicopter will cause problems* which you'll see as a lot of dancing on the pedals. This is covered in more detail in Chapter 34,"Further Peculiarities of The Helicopter".

In terms of exercises to develop budding helicopter pilot's talents, different relative winds always present a challenge. An exercise that helps to build confidence and experience in anticipation is changing height while maintaining heading with winds on each of the 4 cardinal† points. Figure 14-6 shows these four points.

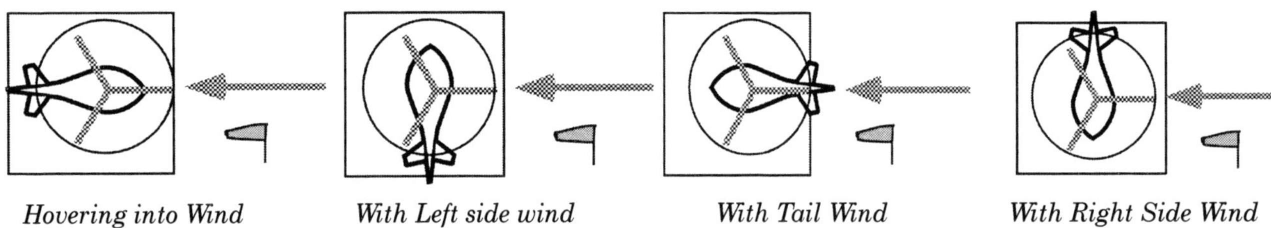

Figure 14-6 Hovering with Different Relative Winds

N_R Control

This next section assumes the pilot is able to maintain the N_R constant - simple, if you are in turbine–engined helicopter or a governed piston engine. If you are fortunate enough to be learning in a piston–engined helicopter without a governor, then this is just one of those things you have to learn to do as second nature. The best advice I can pass on is to learn to listen to the sound of the piston engine and rotor, anticipate what is going to happen when power is changed and also how to glance at the N_R gauge and take its reading so you don't have to spend too much time staring at it. Rather than large movements of the throttle, the previous discussion about pressures also applies.

If you think it's difficult to use a Western-style throttle, consider what the Russian pilots have to do - their throttle works the other way‡ from ours. In other words, to increase throttle in the West, move the throttle in the direction the fingers point. As the collective lever was raised in an Eastern–bloc built helicopter, it is necessary to roll the hand in the other direction (that is, back towards the pilot or away from the direction the fingers point) to our convention.

Hovering With A Purpose

It is difficult to teach hovering, there is no doubt about that. It is also very frustrating to learn. At first, it appears nearly impossible to understand what is happening, and well beyond the capability of mere mortals.

Here's two methods to make it easier. (Before we get into the details, it must be said that it's really quite pointless to try to learn to hover in a large field, safe as it may seem. There is nothing to look at to give you feedback about progress. Get into an area where there are some tangible objects, like fence posts, signs or small trees and shrubs to look at.)

* Other–direction–of–rotation rotor systems will have a problem with relative 135° wind.
† I suppose one could say this exercise should be practiced religiously
‡ Can't say it's the wrong way, because it works

Partial Control Technique

Give the student only one control to work at a time, with some specific exercises. For example, if you've given the student the cyclic stick to fly, then exercises for movement from one clearly identified place to another will teach some of the basics. If the collective lever is given, then the exercise should be to change height, again with clearly identified targets. For the pedals, turns to point the helicopter at specific objects (do it in both directions) should give an appreciation for the effects of these controls.

Lots of Things to Do

The next set of exercises is slightly different from the previous. This involves placing the student in the hover close to an object, and then giving directions to move to another close-by location. For example, "From this sign to that sign, and we want to be 5 feet behind the other sign, facing in the direction of the road".

When the student has stabilized briefly at the new location, give another location to move to-making sure to move sideways, backwards, turn, etc.

With either or both of these methods, eventually the student will learn about hovering.

Specific Exercises for Learning Hovering

Taxing Along a Line

Hover taxing along a line with different wind directions relative to the nose of the helicopter should help to show you the way the cyclic stick controls groundspeed and lateral drift. I've found a taxiway, or road to be a good training aid. Start by taxing slowly along the road with the nose pointing down the road. Maintain a distinct object, such as a centerline or edge of the road passing directly between the pedals. When this has been mastered, then start moving to one side of the road or the other, maintaining heading and stabilizing just long enough to know you have stabilized.

If the wind is from one side, the learning point will become obvious - the lateral cyclic stick controls lateral drift, while the longitudinal cyclic stick controls groundspeed. Pedals are controlling heading. Become more precise with practice.

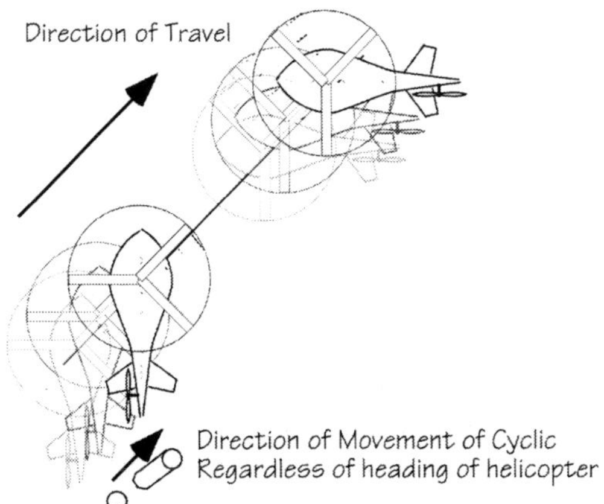

Figure 14-7 Taxing along a Line

When this has been mastered, then turn the helicopter so it is pointing away from the direction of travel. 30° from the direction of travel is about as large as you want to point away from where you are going. Repeat the exercise above. This will teach several skills at once in a very indirect manner. Some of these skills are anticipation of wind effects, realization that cyclic stick controls groundspeed and drift, and pedals control heading.

Changing Height While Hovering

The next exercise involves pointing at a specific object, such as a building and getting the student to change height while staying pointing at the building. Obviously, the helicopter should be kept over the same spot on the ground while all this is going on.

Have the student climb to 10 feet above the ground, pause and then descend to 3 or 4 feet or even lower. Repeat this until the coordination becomes second nature.

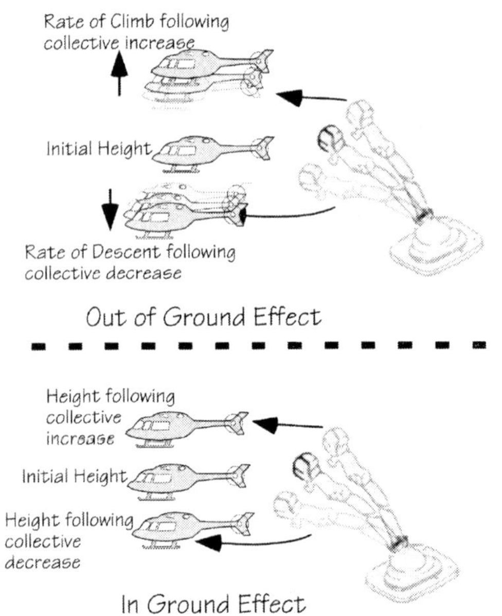

Figure 14-8 Changing Height in the Hover

The student is showing good technique when the power changes are smooth and coordinated with pedal to maintain heading.

Figure 14-8 shows the effect of making a collective change in two different situations - out of ground effect is shown on the top, and in ground effect on the bottom. Out of ground effect (OGE) the collective controls rate of climb and descent - from a steady hover increasing or decreasing collective will generate a rate of climb or descent respectively, and to re-establish a hover, it will be necessary to go back to the original collective position and torque. In ground effect (IGE) the collective can be thought of as a height position controller a small change in collective position will result in a change in height after oscillations damp out.-

Changing Heading

Next have the student maintain height and position over the ground while changing heading. Use prominent objects spaced around the horizon, and tell the student to turn to point at different objects. Turn in both directions.

The student is showing good technique when the heading changes are started and stopped smoothly, pointing at the desired object, and with minimum height or position change.

Practice this in winds up to the limit of the helicopter if possible, in order to show the effects of side and rear winds.

Moving Around

This is where it all starts to come together. Pick out an area where there are lots of natural cues and have the student move from one area to another, using different relative headings. Don't always have the helicopter pointing at the object being moved at, nor have it always pointing into wind.

Be careful backing up!

Hovering with Different References

Given the wide variety of places helicopters are used, it's reasonable to expect that sooner or later, you'll run into a situation where the references available for hovering will be less than perfect, and certainly won't always be out the front window. Have the student practice hovering close to a sign or clump of grass out the side window, very close to the skid. This will show how sometimes these references aren't the best in the world, but that they can be used, as long as the tendency to overcontrol is, well, controlled.

Back to Flying

The first thing that happens as the helicopter accelerates is the height of the flight path above the ground will be difficult to control, if collective lever were to be used. Fortunately for us, we don't change the collective lever position, and can easily control the height with the cyclic stick.

This situation arises because the power required for level flight (that is, to maintain height) reduces dramatically in the first few knots of airspeed from the hover*. See Figure 3–5. A large change in collective lever position would be needed if height is to be kept constant at say 20 knots of airspeed. More likely, the longitudinal cyclic stick is used to control the acceleration and height above ground and the excess power is used to accelerate the helicopter.

* Be it a zero groundspeed or zero airspeed hover

A second problem is directional characteristics start to be felt as air passes the vertical stabilizer and the torque balance changes due to inflow effects. In real terms, this means a bit of dancing on the pedals will be needed to keep the helicopter pointed in the desired direction. You will note I did not say ball in the middle or skids straight in the direction of the flight path - this will be discussed shortly.

The third problem is inflow roll may cause the helicopter to translate sideways, or perhaps even roll slightly, as speed increases. This is discussed in Chapter 23,"Advanced Helicopter Aerodynamics".

The pilot must consider how to avoid putting the helicopter in a position from which it would be difficult to make a touchdown if the engine stopped. This will be discussed in more detail later, but for now, don't worry too much about it - as a student your instructor should take care of this until you get the basics under control.

Turns in the Hover

No Wind

The pedals are meant to control the yaw rate of the helicopter, and if there is zero wind, that is exactly what they do. Pressures on the pedals will change the rate of yaw, and it may be necessary to apply pressure to the opposite pedal to stop a turn.

When there is a wind, however, the pedals control yaw rate and also work with the lateral cyclic stick to overcome some other effects.

With Winds

With any sort of wind, the rotor disk must be kept at an angle into the wind to hold the helicopter in position over the ground, regardless of the wind's direction relative to the fuselage. This causes some problems when the fuselage is turned to different relative directions to the wind.

For example, when turning from into wind to a left side wind, the helicopter undergoes a dramatic change in relative airspeed direction. In airspeed terms, the fuselage is changing from 15 knots of forward airspeed to 15 knots of left airspeed, but the rotor doesn't 'see' any change of direction of airspeed. The tilt of the thrust vector relative to the airframe must be changed from the '15 knot forward airspeed tilt' to the '15 knots of sidewind from the left'. As far as someone who is looking only at the rotor disk is concerned, the tilt of the disk should be nearly motionless, as the rotor disk doesn't care which way the fuselage is pointing.*

What does the pilot have to do? He must position the cyclic stick so as to maintain position over the ground, regardless of where the fuselage is pointing. In carrying out a full 360° turn in the hover with wind, it is normal to see the cyclic stick describe a circle with respect to the cockpit (or fuselage) opposite to the direction of turn.

Another way of looking at this is that as a helicopter turns about a spot on the ground, the cyclic stick position with respect to the wind doesn't change, but cyclic stick position with respect to the fuselage does.

Put another way, the rotor disk has to keep nearly the same tilt relative to the ground to maintain the airframe in position, but the cockpit controls must be moved to change the rotor position relative to the airframe. The easy way to consider this is that the cyclic stick must stay in the same place with respect to the wind as the airframe rotates, and the pedals are used to control the yaw rate. In the hover with the wind on the left side, for example the pedals must also balance out the new conditions of side force as the wind is trying to turn the helicopter.

A later chapter on engines and governors raises the matter of height changes caused by pedal movements. These are normally minor when slow changes in heading are made, but can complicate things if yawing rapidly.

* This, of course, isn't quite true - but it illustrates the point.

For the pilot, the main thing is to anticipate effects as the helicopter is yawed, and to keep visual references in mind. I have found it most worthwhile to stress looking in the direction of the turn and determine what you wish to be lined up with when the turn is finished, and remember to maintain position over the ground.

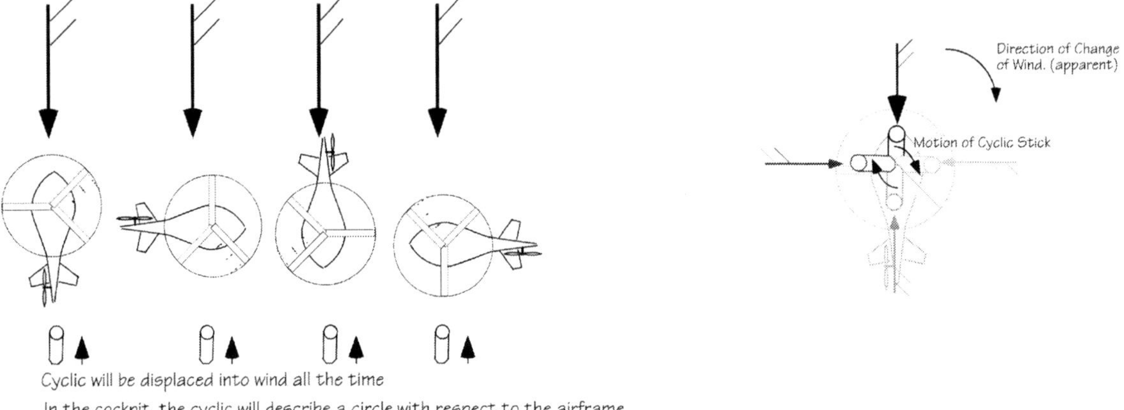

Figure 14-9 Hovering Turns with Winds

In the Low Speed Environment

Somewhere, sometime, in your helicopter flying it will be necessary to change position and stay more or less in the hovering environment. Normally, it is worth pointing the fuselage in the direction of movement, not just to be boring, but to keep the skids aligned with the direction of movement. While the cyclic stick controls the position and rate of travel, the pedals keep the nose pointed as desired. The reason for keeping the skids aligned with the direction of travel is so that in the event of an engine failure, there is one less thing to take care of.

Useful Training Exercises

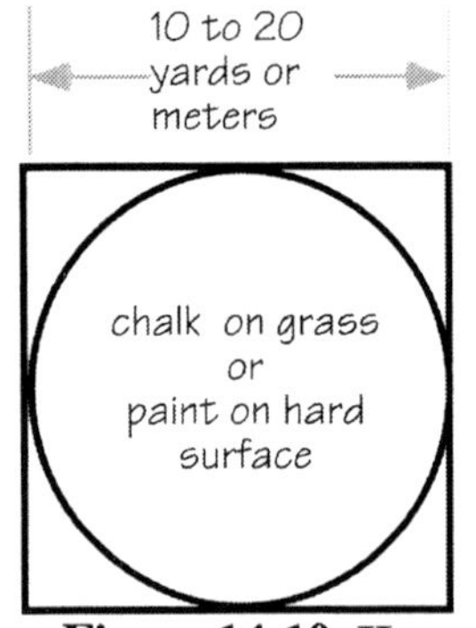

Figure 14-10 Hover Training Circuit

There are several exercises useful for confidence building as much as for coordination. So many different things are taught indirectly from these exercises it would be difficult to list them all. To mention a few, the student learns instinctive use of controls, judgment of the space of the aircraft, becomes able to automatically monitor the engine instruments and effect of the wind. The exercises require a square and circle to be marked out on the ground - about an hour's work, but it pays huge dividends. Figure 14-10 shows such a pattern.

General Handling in the Hover

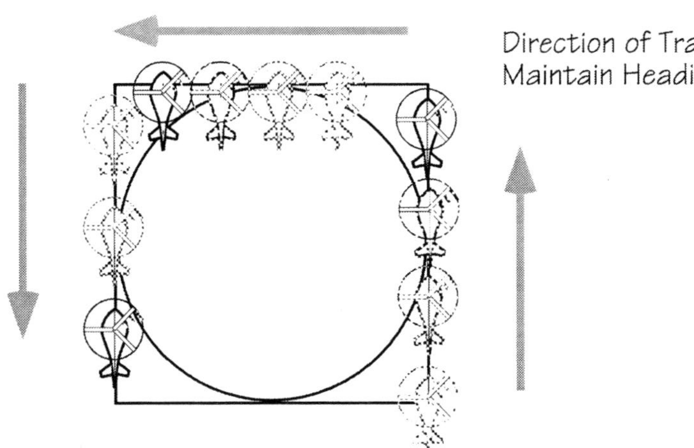

Figure 14-11 Hovering Around the Square

The first exercise is the constant heading square. Place the helicopter on the ground at one corner of the square, and then lift-off and proceed around the square, maintaining the same heading and the pilot's seat over the line. At the end, the helicopter touches down on the same heading. Carry out this square, first facing into wind, and then repeat for the other three cardinal wind directions. Really vicious instructors might get the student to fly this with a 45° angle to the wind, especially if that puts the relative wind in a position of difficulty (see See "Loss of Tail Rotor Effectiveness" on page 383. for some cautions). Figure 14-11 demonstrates the general conduct of the exercise.

The next exercise does not, as far as I know, have a proper name. I call it turning about the nose. The helicopter is placed facing into the center of the circle, and then proceeds to move around the circle, while pointing the nose of the helicopter into the middle. Again, flight instructors with a vicious streak will first demonstrate this by going to the left, and then make their students do it going the other way. (It's generally easier to go in one direction in most light helicopters!) Figure 14-12 shows this exercise.

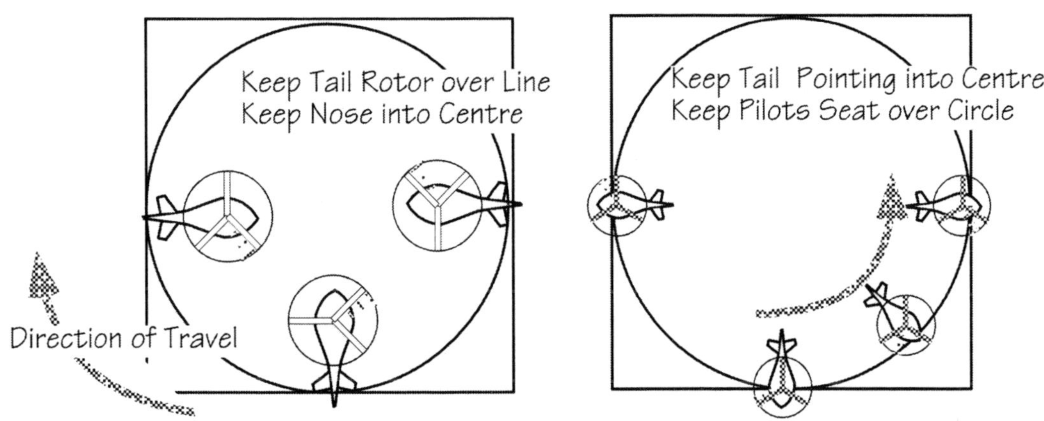

Figure 14-12 a) Nose Pointing Into the Center of the Circle b) Tail Pointing into the Center of the Circle

The final exercise in our general handling trio is nearly the same as the last, except the nose is pointing out, and the tail pointing into the middle of the circle. Figure 14-12 b) gives an idea of the flight path. The pilot's seat should be over the circle on the ground and the aim is to have steady progress around the circle.

Taxing to the Side or Rear

Remember, when you move across the ground the changes in wind speed (airspeed, if you like) relative to the airframe are quite large in percentage terms. For this reason, it is necessary to understand some performance effects, and for this I will refer the student back to Chapter 3.

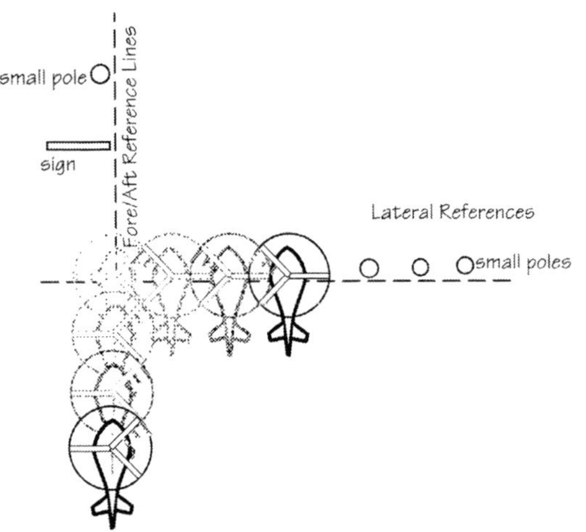

Figure 14-13 Lateral and Fore-Aft References

One of the main concepts about moving to the side or rear is to have two separate references to make sure the ground track is the desired one. (If you are lucky enough to have a line, that counts as two ground references.) The pilot must choose where these references are with respect to the helicopter, and keep the helicopter moving along the line given by those two references. Remember the cyclic stick controls both groundspeed and relative position with respect to the line. collective lever controls height above ground and pedals control the way the fuselage is pointing.

When moving backward, things are made more difficult by a lack of good rear–view mirrors in most helicopters (well, that's the way to back up a car or tractor–trailer unit, isn't it?) and a concern about hitting the tail rotor. ~~If~~ When you do a turn make sure the way behind is clear, how do you know how far it is safe to back up - make a note of a good lateral reference to use as a stopping point.

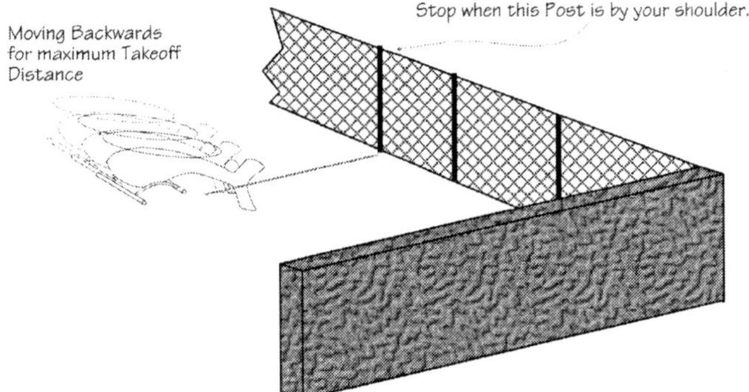

Figure 14-14 Backing up References and Stopping Point

For this reason, most helicopter pilots forced to hover backwards use a little more than normal height above the ground, and also have a good set of references to the front and side.

Ground Taxing Skid Helicopters

Who would ever want to ground taxi a skid–equipped helicopter? Surprisingly, I've had to do it once*, after I had parked and other equipment that came that couldn't be moved or disturbed. The principles are pretty nearly the same as hovering, except the lines between which control does what become slightly more blurred. For example, the total size of the forward tilt of the thrust vector will control the ground speed. This can be changed by changing either the tilt or the magnitude of the thrust vector, or both. Some texts state categorically the collective lever controls speed of taxing, but in my experience, it is the combination of collective lever and cyclic stick.

Summary of Chapter 14

This chapter has shown some of the subtle ways to enjoy the true home of the helicopter- hovering. Hovering is the most fascinating part of helicopters, and the one that gives most of us the greatest pleasure. Getting to and from the hover is next, as we can't stay in one place motionless all the time.

* Since its happened to me, I assume its also happened to others, and will happen again.

'Twixt Heaven and Earth,

(or - Getting To and From the Hover)

Introduction

The previous chapter covered hover, and the one prior to that forward flight. This chapter will take you between those two states, as well as through some of the (slightly) more advanced maneuvers that might be expected for someone with a private pilot license.

First we have to deal with several terms which can cause trouble.

Transition

A transition means a change from one condition to another. In our case, it can mean going from the hover to forward flight or from forward flight back to the hover.

Slipping and Crabbing

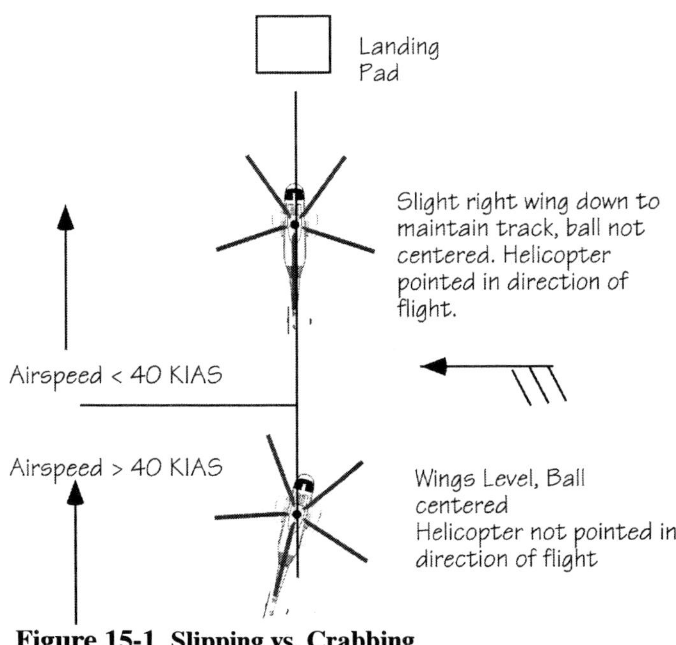

Figure 15-1 Slipping vs. Crabbing

These two terms are introduced here as they have an important part to play in the transitions between forward flight and hovering. *Slipping* is the act of moving across the ground with the ball out of balance and the fuselage pointing in the correct direction, while *crabbing* is the act of flying with the slip ball in the middle and the fuselage pointing somewhere other than directly in front of the helicopter. See Figure 15-1 below for the difference. At different times during the transitions to and from the hover, you'll use these techniques to keep a straight flight path. Note the change between slipping and crabbing happens just about the same airspeed as we define the break between forward flight and low airspeed.

Transition to Forward Flight

There comes a time when hovering has to stop (fun though it is) and forward flight must be made. This is a time of many rapid changes that are difficult to describe and difficult to repeat exactly, and which require the pilot to compensate instinctively.

What is meant by forward flight? Remember, we drew the line where the pitot systems start to work with any accuracy - 40 KIAS. Forward flight adds a directional stability aspect, and changes the way the flight controls work slightly. They become more similar to a fixed–wing airplane's controls.

Clearing Turns

Although this is probably more a 'safety point' than a 'control the helicopter' point, it is appropriate to mention it here. Prior to deciding to charge off into forward flight, it's good to check the coast is clear behind you. A clearing turn of at least 90° to check behind, beside and above is always worthwhile*.

'Normal' Transition

It must be stressed there is no such thing as a 'normal' transition. It would be impossible to define such a maneuver for all helicopters and situations. You will know an 'abnormal' transition when you see / perform one.

Height Control

During the transition to forward flight, the airspeed is always increasing, all with the power kept constant. While no power is 'gained', the excess power over that needed to hover is used to accelerate the helicopter. As mentioned earlier, in the Chapter 6,"Basic Helicopter Performance" the power required to maintain height reduces as the airspeed increases, but the pilot doesn't want just to maintain height, but to accelerate as well. In this maneuver, the height above ground can be controlled by longitudinal cyclic, and the aim is to increase airspeed and height simultaneously. The profile chosen should keep the helicopter clear of the height velocity curve (discussed in more detail in Chapter 18,"Engine Failures for Beginners" and Chapter 30,"Advanced Engine Failures").

Ground Track

The difference in techniques used for track control between low airspeed and forward flight is often referred to as the difference between *slipping* (ground track maintained by lateral cyclic, but the slip ball out of the middle) and *crabbing* (maintain track by keeping wings† level, ball centered and an appropriate heading to keep the drift to zero). This was discussed earlier.

During the first part of the acceleration and climb, the important thing to watch is the ground track. If accelerating with a cross wind, maintaining ground track is only slightly more difficult.

Maintaining the skids in the direction of travel during this early part of the transition is important for engine failure considerations. The helicopter touches down much better when the skids are aligned with the direction of travel, so always keeping the skids pointed in the that direction makes one less thing for the pilot to worry about should the engine quit. The best way to do this is to initially point the helicopter in the desired direction with the pedals, and then use lateral cyclic to maintain the track. Pedals will be used to maintain heading. At some point (probably about 40 to 50 KIAS) a change is made from ground reference to airmass reference or 'forward flight' - then the slip ball or slip string is put in the middle.

Translational Lift

At some point in your helicopter career, someone will talk about '*translational lift*' during the transition to forward flight. If the similarity of the two terms doesn't confuse you, the explanation of what happens might. The normal explanation is that somewhere around 15 knots of airspeed, the rotor magically becomes more effective and the helicopter wants to leap into the air.

The explanation will be partly correct. If the rotor disk can be thought of as a wing of the same span, then such a wing would start to show lift at the same sort of speed. The rotor is really being influenced by the change in inflow, which increases the lift it produces.

Whenever the induced flow or inflow is not vertical with respect to the disk, translational lift is occurring. It will improve the efficiency of the rotor disk as a device which is pumping air, but the effect is first noticeable at between 10 and 15 knots of airspeed, and becomes more noticeable as speed increases. Both the main and tail rotor are affected by translational lift. See "Collective Angle vs. Airspeed" on page 243.

* Silly as it sounds, I have heard of one rescue crew who got so enmeshed in the rescue, that they didn't see the overhead wires directly above them, and climbed straight up into them, with electrifying results. As far as I know it did not make the newspapers under 'Current Events'.

† OK, probably should say fuselage...

Other Transitions to Forward Flight

The Chinese have a saying about there being "a thousand paths to the top of the mountain". Since helicopters are all about flexibility, it stands to reason that there is more than one way to get from the hover to forward flight.

Cushion Creep*

This technique is also called the 'fixed collective' transition. The cushion creep technique is used when there is enough power to hover in ground effect, but no higher. Even then, the height above ground might be very low. The technique requires that the power be maintained constant, (obviously, or you'd descend and hit the ground) and a very slow acceleration into forward flight be started. The reason for the slow acceleration is that a fast acceleration will tilt the thrust vector too much, and the loss of even a slight amount of the vertical component will be enough to cause the helicopter to descend. As the airspeed increases, the helicopter will suddenly develop more lift and literally leap into the air. The only problem is that sometimes, the helicopter will start to over-run the downwash, and may descend just before getting more lift. Not a pleasant place to be if the ground is not smooth, but you might be able to squeeze just a fraction more power out of the engine to get you past this condition. A worthwhile technique for developing co-ordination, it may also mean you should look at your performance charts if you have to do this on a regular basis.

Steep Climbout

This is a transition which has the helicopter climbing vertically more than accelerating horizontally to increase airspeed. It may be used to avoid obstacles, or some other reason, but climbing steeply should be used only with the full knowledge of the possible consequences, as it can put the helicopter into the Height Velocity curve. If you're stuck having to use this technique, better to know how to do it safely.

Some folks call this an *altitude over airspeed* technique, as you're increasing altitude before you increase airspeed.

Start with a slight amount of forward speed and apply power to the limitation that is applicable (for example, takeoff power). Maintain the climb at takeoff power while slowly increasing the airspeed and keeping the ground track under control as well. When safely clear of obstacles, change the rate of climb for forward speed and reduce power to the next appropriate limit.

The important points here are to be aware of being in or near the avoid part of the HV curve. Be prepared for the engine to fail and know exactly what you are going to do if it does fail†. The only useful clue for forward progress will be indications of groundspeed, as the airspeed indicator probably won't work well until you have a lot of height.

Running Takeoff

This is one of the few times when you'll see the words 'takeoff' in this book‡. It's used here as it covers a maneuver that incorporates both lifting off and transitioning to forward flight at the same time.

Why Running Takeoffs?

Why should we bother with a fixed wing type takeoff when helicopters are all about hovering? There are several reasons-

- The first and most important is that it is an excellent coordination exercise. It develops knowledge and understanding of lift and control of the thrust vector,
- Secondly and much less important, there may be times when you don't have enough power to hover out of ground effect (or maybe hover in ground effect either) for starters.

Don't learn the wrong lesson!

* No relation to a 'lounge lizard' I hope.
† Reasons are covered in more detail in Chapter 18,"Engine Failures for Beginners".
‡ As promised

How It Works

The running takeoff takes advantage of the power required vs. airspeed curve (Figure 6-4 on page 57). From the hover OGE to V_Y, the power required to maintain a constant height above ground decreases quite markedly. So if you can just make it into the hover, but can't hover at the desired height, you might still be able to get into forward flight if you have a large smooth, open area in front of you.

How to Carry Out a Running Takeoff

The running takeoff is only slightly different from the normal lift-off, the main difference being having forward speed before leaving the ground. Be warned- you need quite a smooth surface and a open area with lots of room facing into wind.

Face into the wind. Lift into the hover (3-5' AGL) and note the power required. At some power slightly below that required to hover at (try 5 - 10% less), the helicopter will be light on the skids. A bit of forward cyclic will start the helicopter moving forward, and more forward cyclic pressure may be needed to keep moving forward. Keep the skids straight with pedals as this will reduce the ground friction. If there is any wind, at about the point where translational lift happens, the helicopter will suddenly rise off the ground. Keep the groundspeed increasing, and the position of the collective lever constant. Just like snow skiing, keep the tips of the skids up. This technique is better shown on hard surfaces than grass, and certainly easier with wheels or skis than skids.

Cautions on the Running Takeoff

Aside from the training environment, if you can't get into the hover at all *don't try a running takeoff*. You're way beyond the performance capabilities of the machine.

Caution *Just because you know how to do a running takeoff with less power than it takes to hover, doesn't mean that you can actually use this to lift more payload. If you can't hover at 3' above the ground in most helicopters, you're well overweight for the conditions.*

If you are practicing this, and things start to go wrong, merely add power to lift clear of the ground. Better to have some slight embarrassment than to make a mess of a perfectly serviceable helicopter. In real life, you won't have any excess power available, if you can't hover...

When trying to accelerate into forward flight, attempt to maintain less than 10 feet AGL, and accept that the rate of acceleration will be slower than normal. You will see that too large a nose low attitude will tilt the disk too much and you will descend again, and if you happen to stub your skids on a small tuft of grass, it can have a large (and mostly negative) effect.

That having been said, the running takeoff is an excellent coordination exercise!

"Maximum Performance Climbout"

Many books and some flight manuals talk about a '*Maximum Performance Takeoffs*', and go on to discuss a takeoff out a confined area where it is not possible to hover above the obstacles (that is, out of ground effect). The Maximum Performance Climbout is not something for the faint of heart, and not to be encouraged for beginners.

The reason for discouraging the maximum performance takeoff is that in a really tight situation, the pilot simply does not have enough information to know if he can safely carry out the maneuver. "Best Angle of Climb Airspeed" on page 255 explains about best angle of climb and the problems associated with it.

How can I convince you that it's not a good idea to try this without some very careful deliberation and lots of experience?

An Example of Getting Caught

There you are, having just picked up your passenger in the middle of the football stadium. He's a lot bigger in real life than in pictures - in fact, he's huge. Way heavier* than the standard you're used to, thought of or perhaps planned on. It's hot, and the wind has died down to almost nothing. You can just stagger into a five foot hover, but can coax the machine no higher. No problem, you say, the maximum performance takeoff I was shown in Weird Willies Flinging Wings flight school will save the day.

* I was going to say 'weigh heavier', but that's stretching puns too far...

Since it's the middle of the summer, the goal posts are down and you have the whole field to use for the takeoff run. Since it's a football field, you have a good idea of the distance you have available, and maybe you know the height of the seats at the end you have to pass over (but then again maybe you don't...)

How can you find out if you can clear the seats? You won't find the answer in any flight manual.

What airspeed would you accelerate to prior to starting to climb? You won't find that in the flight manual either, and even if it were there, the pitot system may not work accurately at that speed.

What airspeed will you maintain in the climb until clear of the end of the stadium? Still another bit of information missing from any flight manual.

One Flight Manual says something to the effect of:

- "The angle of climb depends on the density altitude, wind and weight. The more critical the conditions (i.e. higher density altitude, weight and low wind), the more shallow the climb angle *possible*. Caution must be used in making a steep climb as if the airspeed gets too low, the climb performance may reduce to zero or even negative values.
- The climb angle required will depend on the height of the obstacles and the clear area in front of the obstacles. Operation in the Height Velocity curve will probably happen during this maneuver."

Holy smokes! How can this be accepted as an every–day maneuver? The answer is simple- we practice it, and take chances*, and get away with it often enough to think it's OK.

Back to our example...

So you decide to risk it. You want to make best use of the space you have, and taxi back to the edge of the field and accelerate at 5 feet above the ground until you judge that if you start to climb now, you'll clear the end zone seats. You start to climb. Things appear to be going well, until a whisper of wind comes over the top of the stadium and hits you as a downdraft. You know this because litter from the seats above you starts to swirl down toward you. Your rate of climb slows- OK, you say, I'll trade a bit of airspeed for climb... and you bring the nose up just a bit and watch your rate of climb drop to zero and then you start to descend into the end zone seats... Get the picture?

Don't rely on the maximum performance takeoff to get you out of a tight spot!

Some helicopters have performance charts for takeoff distance over a 50' obstacle. Good. The problem is that you often won't know the distance on the ground, or whether the obstacle is 50' high or more. These charts also assume a climb speed of V_Y, when you're probably more interested in maximum angle of climb...

Downwind Transition

Sounds like a contradiction doesn't it? If you start off with a tailwind when hovering, and have to transition to forward flight, be careful. First of all, you might not have enough power to hover at zero airspeed (see the chapters on performance to understand why), and secondly, the distance it takes to get forward airspeed can be a very long way indeed.

Assuming you have enough power to carry out this transition, and have completed one successfully, try one with limited power, a quasi-running takeoff if you like. Do this only with an instructor, and be prepared to add sufficient power to get out of the ensuing mess. You were warned.

Turns After Transition

It may sound a bit over-cautious, but don't try to turn until your airspeed is at least 1.5 times the windspeed. For most of the flying you'll do in training, this shouldn't be a problem, but it's worth remembering for later in life.

* Some might say this is a calculated risk, but that implies you've thought about things...

Approach and Touchdowns

The details of this maneuver are covered in the following paragraphs; but it is worth mentioning that prior to starting the approach, pre-nominate the place you're going to stop. This develops the discipline of judging your approach profile and closure rates. Just like hovering in big open fields is a poor way to learn to hover, aiming in a general sense to approach somewhere in a big open field without any idea of where you want to stop is not a good idea - it's sloppy. While anywhere may be satisfactory, it won't build self–discipline or teach judgment of rates of closure, rate of descent and so on. These are particularly important when learning to fly helicopters.

The first part of this section will deal with transitions back to the hover facing into wind. Downwind comes later...

Transition Back to the Hover

Most flights should terminate in a controlled touch down. Helicopters normally stop first, then touch down. Getting the helicopter from forward flight to the hover requires some judgment and training.

First of all, in training, starting all approaches to the hover from the same initial conditions of airspeed, altitude and position is a typical fixed–wing method of flying. Helicopters are all about flexibility, and flexibility requires judgement, which requires experience. A variety of experience in how to judge the variables should be stressed when learning. Figure 15-2 shows the various stages from forward flight back to a hover.

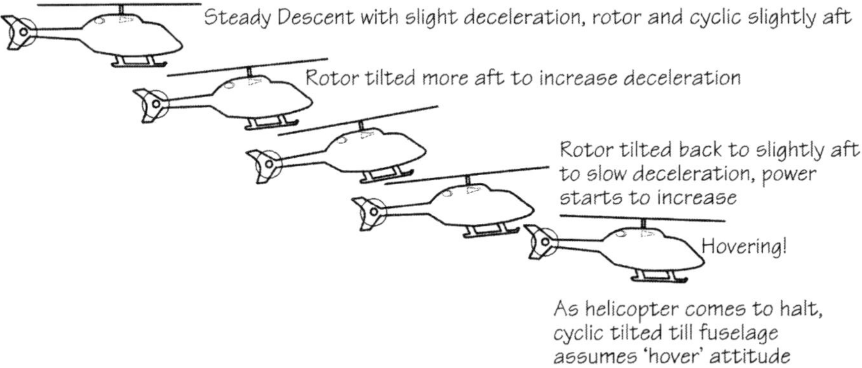

Figure 15-2 Transition Back to the Hover

During any approach, an important concept is to reduce the power first and start decelerating before descending*. When shooting boring, plain–vanilla traffic patterns, reduce the power prior to turning on base leg and start the deceleration in the turn. The helicopter should be lined up on final with the speed decreasing. If the power has not been reduced, the airspeed will build up on final and it will be necessary to flare quite a bit to get rid of it. With the power decreased early and on the correct airspeed, the pilot can concentrate on rate of closure and glide path angle. It is much easier to add power than to try to get rid of speed. With more advanced situations, such as a turning, decelerating approach, the aim is to coordinate the controls so as to arrive at the desired spot in a smooth manner.

With the spot chosen for the final hover, the rest is a matter of judgment of rate of change of groundspeed and rate of descent, rate of closure with the spot and so on. By changing the entry conditions (altitude, airspeed, position with respect to the desired spot and so on) the pilot will learn to judge these things instinctively, and develop flexibility for the conditions that will be met during any flying career.

From a technical point of view, the approach involves the helicopter going back along the power required curve, into the (more–power–for–less–airspeed) back side of the power curve. Since the approach probably started from a low power setting anyway (power for level flight at *VY* minus some to start the descent) and must terminate with the power close to the maximum required (i.e. power to hover), a large power change must be anticipated.

* If you don't believe me, try doing an approach where the power is not reduced early.

Learning to Judge...

One of the problems of learning to fly helicopters, particularly true during approaches to the hover, is learning how to judge perspective and rates of closure. Perspective is the relative position of objects, and how they change. Rate of closure is the relative rate of getting to a spot. These two items are used all the time in driving a car (whether you know it or not). Adding the third dimension of altitude merely extends what you already know.

...Perspective

"...the effect of distance upon the appearance of objects, by means of which the eye judges spatial relations."

Judging perspective in helicopter flying is often taught as putting a spot on the ground (the spot where the approach should terminate) in a certain place on the windshield, and keeping it there until the very final stages of the approach. In my view, this is incorrect. The pitch attitude of the helicopter in a descent changes with airspeed, and wind conditions change the flight path. 20 knots of wind will require a different pitch attitude and hence a different spot on the windshield than a no-wind approach*.

A more precise method of teaching perspective is to use two different spots on the ground, and note the change in position between them. (This is somewhat similar to the vertical cues discussed earlier in "Vertical References" on page 127.) If the relative position and angles between the two spots on the ground remains nearly constant, then the approach is on a constant path. For example, a bunch of grass behind a small sign will be a certain position above the sign, and if it stays in the same place relative to the sign, then you will stay on the same glidepath. If the grass moves further below the sign, the glide path is becoming more steep and you are *overshooting* or will arrive after the desired point. If the grass moves above the sign, the glidepath is becoming more shallow and you're going to *undershoot* or arrive before the desired point. Figure 15-3 shows this in simple form for changes in shapes.

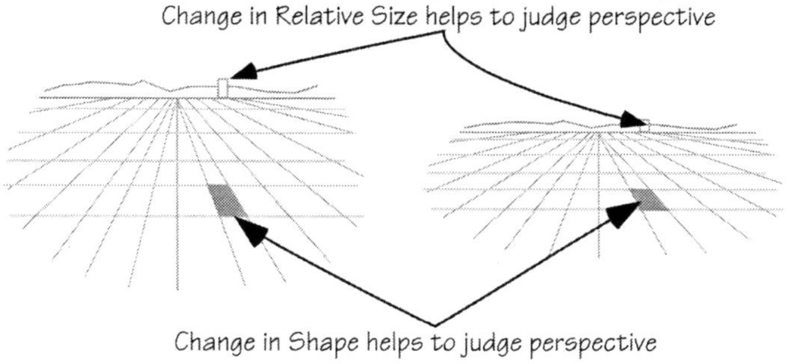

Figure 15-3 Judging Perspective

If you're lucky enough to be learning near an airport with a *Visual Approach Slope Indicating System* (*VASIS*) or *Precision Approach Path Indicator* (*PAPI*), you might use these lights to see about the effects of perspective.

The point is that the references are not taken with respect to a spot in the windshield, they are taken with respect to the ground.

* If this is how you were taught, you probably aren't using that technique and have learned from experience. Learning in spite of the teacher...

It's not necessary to use two objects lined up one behind the other for obtaining perspective - the two sides of a runway can be used - if they start to change angle relative to one another, then the glidepath angle is changing as well, as shown in Figure 15-4.

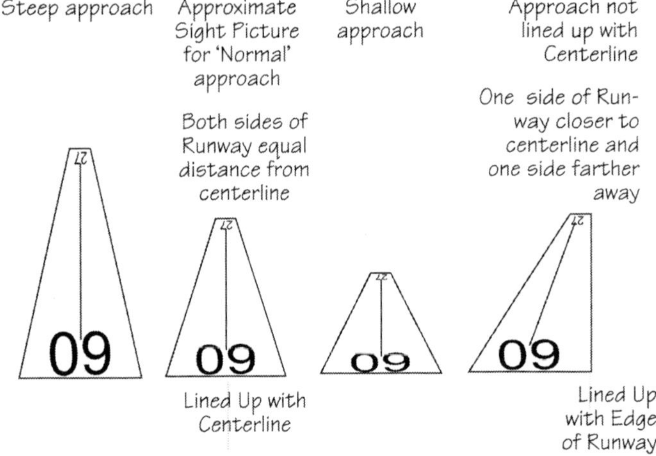

Figure 15-4 Changing Shape of Runway

Whether you know it or not, you're using perspective to judge many things.

...Rates of Closure

Learning to judge rate of closure is another one of the tricks a helicopter pilot needs in the bag of tricks and experience, and here I can only say that lots of experience is the key to learning how to judge rates of closure.

From a cruising flight condition, it is necessary to transfer from an airspeed reference to a rate–of–change–of–groundspeed reference. You must learn to judge the rate of change of speed. I guess it's like asking exactly how do you judge how much brake to apply to come to a smooth halt at a stop sign? Only experience...

The concept in the helicopter is to maintain a rate of progress across the ground. The primary control for this will be the longitudinal cyclic. Initially, it will be necessary to use the airspeed indicator for cross reference, but with experience, visual references should be sufficient.

'Normal' Approach

There is no such thing as an absolute, textbook perfect method to conduct approach to the hover. Can't be. There are so many variations of glidepath, deceleration rate, wind, and so on that each approach will be different. The term 'normal approach' should be reserved for an approach which is neither too shallow or too steep, not too fast or not too slow.

The keys to the approach are four-fold, and were given before, namely:

- sight picture
- into wind
- rate of closure
- use of perspective

If you can keep all of these in mind, as well as the other items such as terrain, obstacles and so on, and the approach doesn't resemble either a Boeing 747 on final (a shallow approach), or a dive bombing attack (a steep approach) then I would think it might qualify for a 'normal' type approach.

Suitable Rate of Descent

During the approach, glance at the vertical speed indicator (VSI) from time to time. The rate of descent should be reasonable steady, and well outside the conditions where vortex ring state can develop. (Vortex ring state is discussed in Chapter 19,"Peculiarities of the Helicopter") Typically, it should be less than 300-500 feet per minute when you're below 100 feet above ground. If it's too high, consider going around.

Adding Power

During the approach, the pilot has to judge when to add power to stop the rate of descent while at the same time maintaining the rate of travel across the ground. This requires practice, and one of the things which adds to the difficulty is the very large effect of adding power on forward speed. Typically, when the helicopter is decelerating and the rate of descent is too high, the pilot will add power and come to a halt at a height above ground that is far higher than wanted, and in a position well short of the desired hover point.

Sometimes you'll hear the term 'loading the disk'. This means that you have some collective pitch and power applied to the rotor disk, as opposed to nearly flat pitch and no power.

The thrust vector is tilted slightly aft (to decelerate) and is small (to descend). Increasing the size of the thrust vector will add more of a decelerative force, and as the thrust vector is tilted aft, will slow the forward speed of the helicopter.

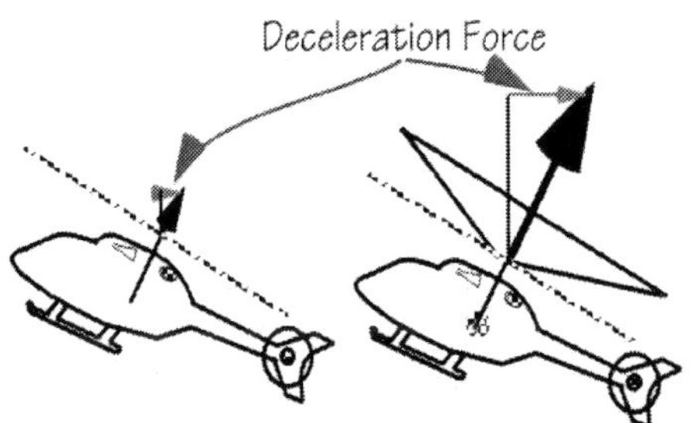

Figure 15-5 How Adding Power Stops Forward Motion

Simply stated- when the nose is up to decelerate, adding power will stop you more quickly. You probably don't want to stop this quickly when you add power, so get used to adding forward cyclic whenever collective lever is increased, in order to maintain the rate of closure to the landing spot. Figure 15-5 shows the problem.

Helpful Hint

Fast Approaches

You'll probably get to see a fast approach sometime in your training. I can say this with some certainty simply because of the nature of learning to fly helicopters. We all eventually see the extremes, whether by good luck or poor management...

The fast approach is one where you have a lot of groundspeed (and airspeed) close to the ground and close to your landing spot. You realize this too late to make a small change in pitch attitude to correct it, so, in order to save the approach, you decide to make a large pitch attitude change. The problem is that, due to the low height above the ground, you stand a chance of burying the tail rotor, or using it as plow. If that wasn't bad enough, then you may well forget to add the necessary power to stop the helicopter descending into the ground. Things will happen pretty fast during the last stages of this approach, and if you're not anticipating what can happen, you may get burned!

Slow down early - it's easy to add power or more forward cyclic, but it's difficult to look good with a huge flare at the end of the approach. It's also difficult to think about the other things you should be considering at this time in the flight, like landing surface, the winds, and so on.

Steep Approach

The steep approach must be conducted with care, as it is easy to develop too high a sink rate that is difficult to stop. What you can get away with in a light weight, low density altitude condition may not be safe in a heavy weight, high density altitude. It's too late to realize you don't have enough power to stop the rate of descent when the engine is at it's maximum power and the N_R is drooping...

The first item with the steep approach is to make sure the helicopter is pointing into wind. A downwind approach is bad enough, but a steep approach downwind is really asking for trouble.

The next thing is to make sure that power is applied early in the approach. This is for two reasons- one to make sure the rate of descent doesn't get away from you, and secondly, to make sure you will know if the engine is going to reach a limit. You should know if you're going to reach a limit early enough in the approach to be able to overshoot and try a different method.

Obviously, if it's a steep approach, the groundspeed should also be low. You're more interested in loosing height than killing groundspeed, so don't start off with both things stacked against you. Groundspeed control should entail very small corrections in longitudinal cyclic, and a flare should be superfluous. Power may need to be gradually increased during the approach to prevent the rate of descent from increasing, as well as thinking about the previous point of having power applied early.

Be aware of the possibility of vortex ring state ("Vortex Ring State" on page 176)

If you can, judge your approach so that any final power application will take you into an in-ground effect hover, or at worst make your touchdown not too abrupt.

The No-Hover Touch Down

Sometimes it is necessary to make an approach and touch down without stopping to hover. Loose snow, dust, limited power and a small landing area are all be good reasons for needing to make a no hover landing*. The real trick is to be able to do this so that the rate of descent and the forward speed come to zero at the desired spot on the ground all at the same (and proper time).

One of the problems with this type of approach / landing is that the ground cushion takes more time to develop than you may have available by the time you want to land, so you have to retain some power in reserve to stop the last little bit of rate of descent.

I can only advise lots of practice for this. Learn to judge rates of closure and rates of descent, and anticipate the loss of performance just prior to touchdown.

Downwind Approach to the Hover

It should be part of every helicopter pilot's training to have experienced approaches to a downwind hover, under very tightly controlled conditions. The reasons for experiencing this are many, but the best one is to learn to recognize the signs when you don't have any other way to determine the wind direction. These signs should be sufficient warning to the pilot to avoid this direction of approach normally unless very well prepared and fully aware of the problems and consequences.

An approach that is 'normal' in all other aspects but downwind should be a good starting point.

Don't do this with more than about 10 knots of tailwind.

Everything will appear 'normal' until the last part, where the airspeed indicator drops to a meaningless figure while there is still appreciable groundspeed, and then when the tailwind starts to take effect and make the directional control a bit more challenging, as well as height control as the bottom suddenly seems to drop out.

If the student did that approach without too much difficulty, or was too cavalier and thought everything was just fine, then try the same exercise with a limited power situation. That should convince anyone that it's good to try to avoid downwind approaches unless you really know what you're setting yourself up for.

Not only do you have to contend with the change in performance as you go through zero airspeed and to the tailwind, but there are all the handling issues with directional control and longitudinal cyclic. If you can avoid a downwind approach by choosing a different approach path, seriously consider it.

Approaches with Turns

Try doing the approach with a continuous turn so that you roll out on your final heading just about the time you come to the hover. There isn't much different, except that the sight picture involves some judgement of rate of closure in a turn.

* I hope these happen one at a time. Getting them all at the same time would be a real test of character...But Afghanistan comes to mind

Line-Up

I can't let this section go by without harping on a pet peeve of mine- – looking outside to ensure you are lined up with the desired direction.

When carrying out approaches to a runway or a spot which has some natural lead-in lines, keep your eyes outside to make sure you don't turn too little or too much and go off the straight-in line.

Helpful Hint

While this may seem strange for helicopter pilots to worry about, there are many instances in later flying where this discipline is needed, and it may as well be learned early in the game. If you want to know why this is important spend some time underneath the final approach to a light fixed wing training airplane runway and watch the pilots who don't look outside. You can tell them because they overshoot or undershoot the turn from base leg to final approach course (runway alignment if you like) all the time. Judgement of the turn is needed throughout the turn, as rate of turn can be changed by any number of things such as wind, etc.

Turning into a Downwind Approach

Do this into wind until the student gets the hang of things, and then- in a very controlled manner, you might also try doing an approach with a turn that takes you into a downwind situation for hovering.

VIP Approaches - Mastery of the Machine

A way to develop mastery of the helicopter is to try to carry out a very smooth lift-off to the hover, accelerate to forward flight, cruise for a short period, and approach and make a zero–speed (no hover) touch down very lightly. Practice as if there were a person on board you were trying to convince to hire you on the basis of your ability to make helicopter flying as calm as a ride in a chauffeur–driven limousine. This person wants to be flown somewhere so effortlessly that they didn't notice either lift-off or touchdown. Try to make the whole flight so smooth it wouldn't spill their gin and tonic*, and the touch down so delicate that you will have to announce your return to terra firma. If you can do this, then you have mastery over the machine.

Running Landing†

Smooth touchdowns are much easier to achieve in running landings than touch downs from the hover. (The reasons were discussed earlier.) As far as techniques are concerned, use about 10% less power than needed to hover as the target power setting. Bring the helicopter to a level attitude at a slow airspeed (20 KIAS or less) about 1 - 1.5 feet off the ground and then slowly decelerate with a very slight nose up attitude. The skids must be aligned in the direction of travel. Again, this technique takes advantage of the power required curve - as the airspeed decreases, the power required to maintain level flight increases. Since we are restricting the amount of power available, the helicopter will settle to the ground with some forward speed.

Wait until the motion stops before lowering collective

Helpful Hint

Depending on the helicopter and the surface, the deceleration should be fairly gentle, but be careful when lowering the collective while the helicopter is still moving across the ground. If the collective is lowered too quickly at a high ground speed, the transfer of weight from the rotor to the skids may result in a very rapid deceleration at best and at worst, a forward nose-over.

The other task, aside from controlling ground speed and deceleration. is keeping the heading under control, and very small corrections in the pedals is all that should be needed. If there is a strong side wind and you are on a very smooth surface (a paved runway or hard-packed snow), then some lateral cyclic corrections may be needed as well.

* Or whatever their libation of choice happens to be...
† Just like 'takeoffs', the phrase 'landing' is used deliberately here

Traffic Patterns or Circuits

Depends on which part of the world you grew up in, whether you call this sequence of events a *traffic pattern* (USA) or a *circuit* (rest of the world). What we're talking about here is the lift-off, transition to forward flight, climbing, turning, cruising, descending and approach to a hover at the same spot you started from, as. Aside from a good training maneuver, it doesn't have much use - or does it?

Remember that earlier I said that one of the things about helicopters was their inherent flexibility*?

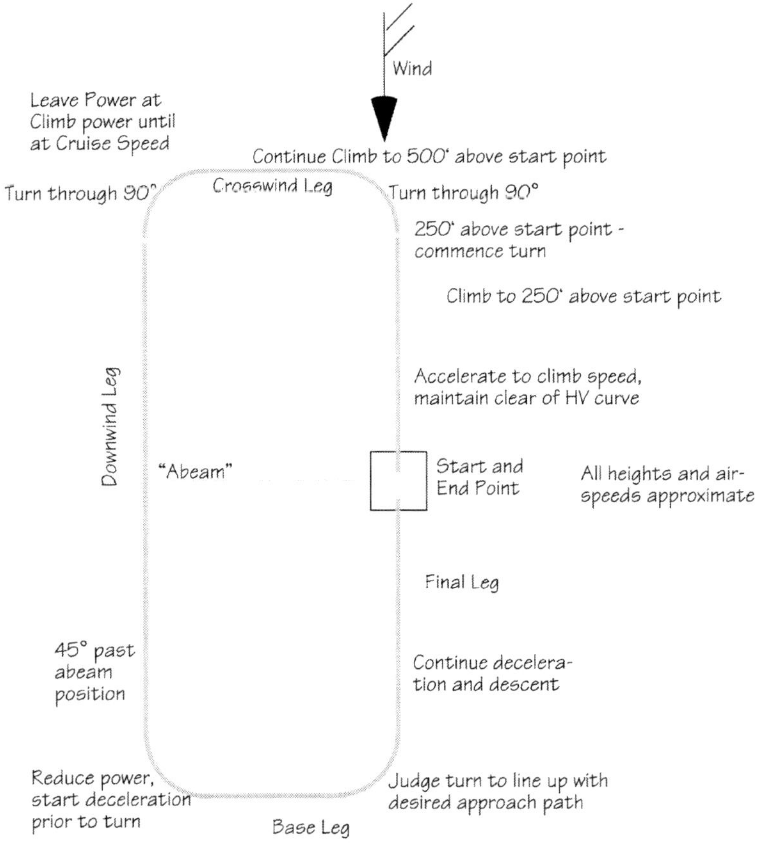

Figure 15-6 Typical Traffic Pattern / Circuit

Traffic patterns arose from a need to regulate a large number of aircraft in a training environment, (in 1914 there were no radios) and also to standardize the way airplanes entered and left an airfield. We continue to use them for the same reasons- they help to make sure everyone knows where the other traffic <u>should</u> be, and where they are going. A typical traffic pattern (or circuit) is shown in Figure 15-6.

We should be less than complete slaves to traffic patterns / circuits. If helicopters are about flexibility, then helicopter pilots need to understand how to use the traffic pattern to develop the skills necessary to operate their machines. This may involve changing some of the things in the traffic pattern.

Hopefully wherever you are learning to fly, you are not stuck in a pattern which requires you to always turn from crosswind to downwind at Farmer Brown's barn, downwind to final over the small duck pond, and be on final over the burger joint on the corner. If so, then get your instructor to take you somewhere else to do some variations on traffic patterns.

Do traffic patterns / circuits at different altitudes, different distances and different airspeeds on downwind, to learn how to judge perspective and closure rates. Try approaches to a spot that is quickly pointed out to you.

What do Traffic Patterns Teach / Show

Having slammed the traffic pattern if used mindlessly, it must be said that it does have some redeeming qualities. A well flown traffic pattern will show a lot about a pilot. It is only necessary to think about the many different maneuvers which have to be strung together in a smooth coordinated manner. A well flown traffic pattern shows, among other things, judgement of rate of descent and rate of closure, the ability to take in the big picture of wind, terrain, performance and a whole host of other indefinable

* If I didn't say it earlier, I'm saying it now- OK?

things has been developed. Turns while climbing or descending and changing airspeed, acceleration and flight path control during the departure - the list goes on. If there is other traffic, then the ability to adapt to those conditions also is developed.

Confined Areas

One of the advantages of the helicopter is the ability to land in small places. Very small places, in fact. We don't need no stinking runways...

Confined areas are the culmination of learning a whole host of skills, and mostly are about applying judgement. Already learned handling skills need to be applied in a new way.

There are a host of ways to learn how to get into a confined area. Rather than give detailed advice, the student must learn how to weigh up the factors and decide on which is the least harmful (or most beneficial, depending on how you look at it) way of putting the helicopter into an area that is less than wide open.

Some of the things to consider are:

- *Size* (is it big enough?)
- *Shape* (is there a particular way I have to go into the area?)
- *Slope* (does the area have a pronounced slope I'll have to deal with when I get there? This could determine the path I have to take, see above.)
- *Surface* (is there something unique in the surface, like blowing snow I have to hover above until it clears?)
- *Sun* (is the sun going to be hiding something due to shadows that I won't see until I'm nearly there?)
- *Surrounds* (are there wires that may be hidden, or trees?)
- *Shear* (is there likely to be wind shear, especially on deep confined areas on a windy day?)
- *Obstacles* that may determine the approach path or departure path
- *Departure (path)* - before I go in, how am I going to get out?
- *Arrival(path)* What am I going to use to navigate (what identifies the approach and departure paths from readily identifiable objects I can see here)
- *Wind* (is the wind strong enough to dictate that only one approach and departure path are possible?)

Performance must also be considered. By its very nature a confined area will probably require a hover out of ground effect to clear obstacles (or it wouldn't be a confined area). Will you have enough power to take off? I've had to drop passengers off more than once because I didn't have enough power...

It is interesting to note that in training, students are seldom given the opportunity to approach a confined area which is clearly unsuitable. What a shame that they don't get a chance to develop that most highly prized of judgements- learning when to say no.

One examiner I know chooses a spot (tree, rock, etc.) that is deep in the bush and inaccessible, and then asks students to land there. The student is expected to choose a good site close to the spot and not get suckered into something too small. The students have to learn that customers have legs...

Summary of Chapter 15

This chapter and the previous two have covered a lot of the early maneuvers which will be used in learning how to fly helicopters. Some of the techniques may be unorthodox, but have proven useful for me. The next chapter makes a complete break from this train of thought, and revisits lift vectors, but with a view to understanding how they work in autorotation. This is in preparation for the chapter that follows it, which covers the actions in the events of an engine failure - an exciting time for all concerned.

16 Lift-off and Touchdown

Introduction

Before you can do anything worthwhile in the helicopter, before you can hover, before you can attain forward flight, you have to remove the helicopter from the clutches of Mother Earth. That may appear simple, but is actually a complex action which deserves attention.

I cannot stress enough how important it is to make every lift-off slowly and deliberately, so the transition from ground to air is under control. The reasons for this concern will become clear later.

'Controlled manner' means the change in power from 'just–before–clearing–the–ground' to 'hovering' is small, under control and can be stopped at any time. This can be accomplished in the following way - apply collective lever until the helicopter is light on the skids, that is, a large part of the weight is being supported by the main rotor. If the cyclic stick and pedals are moved slightly, they have a noticeable effect on moving the fuselage. Pause here while you put the N_R in the correct range for hovering (or the governor settles down). When everything is under control, smoothly and slowly add enough collective lever to lift-off. The aim is to lift-off to a low hover, maintaining position over the ground and pointing in the same direction.

Caution

If anything is not normal, like lots of lateral stick needed to hold the wings level, or a roll rate you didn't expect, STOP!

One of the things you should be doing constantly as you raise the collective lever is mentally noting the cyclic stick position. If the cyclic stick needs to be moved to some extreme position to keep the helicopter level, something is not correct! But what's the 'correct' control position?

The problem is you have no way to know what the control positions will be in the hover, and here you are sitting on the ground. Don't worry- it's actually easy to sort out.

The following discussion assumes you're starting with the helicopter facing into the wind.

Flat Pitch to Light on the Skids

You've completed all the pre-takeoff checks, the area is clear, and now you're ready to lift-off. We're going to split this maneuver into several small steps. The first part, from flat pitch to light on the skids will appear to you as if nothing is happening, and by most measures, that's true. You need to remember you're putting a lot of power into the drive system, and moving weight from the skids to the rotor system. Up to the point where *'light on the skids'* occurs, (when the skids stop supporting most of the weight) it doesn't feel like anything is happening.

How Do you Know 'Light on the Skids'?

That depends on the helicopter, and there is no definite answer for all types. Most of the sensation will comes when you sense the cyclic stick and pedals start to move the machine.

In some helicopters with oleos, the helicopter appears to be 'flying' long before the 'light on the skids' stage. In this case, the lift off is nearly always much more precise and controlled, as the pilot knows what is happening long before the ground is left behind.

Centering the Controls

You obviously wouldn't start out with the controls stuffed into one corner of the cockpit prior to lift-off. But 'center' is a relative thing, and will change according to the wind and a host of other variables. How can you find out where the 'center' of controls is for every lift-off?

Let's start with the pedals.

Ideally, we would start this exercise out on a frozen surface, with nothing to stop the helicopter from turning in yaw. Since that's difficult to arrange for everyone in reasonable climates, and hard to organize in Canada for at least 6 months of the year, we'll have to start on a smooth, paved surface.

Caution

Be very careful with this exercise! Don't try it on grass!

When the collective lever is partway up to the 'light on the skids' position, add a bit of pedal. Either direction will do. Raise the collective slowly. Notice how the helicopter takes a while before it starts to yaw? Add pedal in the opposite direction until the helicopter starts to yaw in that direction. Somewhere between those two positions will be the ideal 'central' pedal position.

Now add a bit more collective lever, and repeat the exercise. Note it now takes a lot less pedal movement to get the helicopter to respond. Again, the ideal position is between the two places that will yaw the helicopter. If you're really observant, you'll notice as the power is increased, the 'central' position is moving more towards a left pedal slightly forward of pedals neutral (or lined up with each other).

Hopefully, you'll progress quickly past this stage and learn to add just a bit of pedal at a time and see what happens. The aim is to lift-off with no yawing, but for beginners, a bit of yaw with appropriate corrections is OK*.

The cyclic stick is not much different from the pedals in determining where 'neutral' is. From the same collective lever position, slowly move the cyclic stick back and forth until you see the helicopter rocking just a little bit. Between the two positions is the 'neutral' you're looking for. Add a bit more collective lever, and you'll note a little less movement is needed to produce the same rocking (remember you now have a bigger thrust vector to tilt, so to produce the same moment, less tilt is needed to move the machine).

Unless the cyclic stick is in the correct position fore/aft, the helicopter will move. The other way to look at this is that if the nose of the helicopter starts to move up or down as you increase collective lever, the cyclic stick isn't in the correct position. All you need to do is smoothly move the cyclic stick in the correct direction, just enough to stop the movement.

From 'Light on the Skids' to the Hover

When you're light on the skids, don't mess around with the cyclic stick unnecessarily. Wallowing around in this condition is asking to stub a skid against something that will fight back.

Several things will transpire here as you lift-off. First of all, don't expect to just leave the cyclic stick where it is and to have a perfect hover. Won't happen. The helicopter will need to be placed in the hover, and that means adjustments to the controls.

For example, a change in longitudinal CG from one trip to the next will require a different cyclic stick position to balance all the moments. You won't be thinking of this while you do the maneuver, but that's what's happening. The pitch attitude in the hover most probably won't the same as the sitting on the ground attitude. Don't sweat it for now, just accept it.

Some helicopters will roll a significant amount when lifting to the hover- especially if the instructor and student aren't the same weight.

Real proficiency at (or a good feel for) lift-off is indicated by being able to stop with the toes or heels of the skids just touching the ground.

The advantage of the slow, smooth lift-off is if things don't feel OK, or things go wrong, things can be corrected or the lift-off stopped. A rapid lift-off often leaves little room for error.

Airborne!

Once airborne, check engine temperatures and pressures are normal, the controls 'feel' correct for the weight and CG, and the power required to hover is normal for the conditions. (Obviously, this presupposes you have a chart of the power required to hover.) Power is also important in most other phases of flight, so it's worth noting how much you're using here.

I make it a habit on every takeoff to note out loud the engine parameters, the controls and the CG.

* OK. I'll admit it. Lift-off with a bit of yaw will happen in just about every helicopter, even with experienced pilots.

Rapid Lift-off

I know of only three times there is need for a rapid lift-off. The first is from the deck of a ship that is pitching / rolling / heaving*, and you need to be clear of it quickly. The second is if there is a need to lift-off with the minimum of downwash. In both cases, it is necessary to smoothly and quickly apply power and the entire sequence must be tightly controlled. cyclic stick should be nearly in the middle (slightly into the known wind) prior to raising the collective lever. The lift-off–without–downwash was shown to me in a helicopter notorious for lots of downwash, and since we were light, resulted going up like an elevator resulted in hardly more downwash than we had at flat pitch - amazing!

The third reason for a rapid lift-off is if ground resonance is encountered. Since this is an emergency situation and it happens awfully quickly, I'm not sure what advice could be given - ground resonance is covered in Chapter 34,"Further Peculiarities of The Helicopter".

One of my reviewers noted he once did a rapid lift-off immediately after unloading his passengers, because his fuel was low and he had a hot date. He forgot momentarily about the full load of baggage in the aft hold. He was promptly reminded of its presence when he lurched into the air and had to stuff the cyclic stick full forward.

Lift-off out of Wind

If you're unlucky enough to have to lift-off with the wind coming from behind or from the side, don't despair. The techniques are not much different from into wind. If you already know where the wind is coming from, then you can bias the cyclic stick into it, and adjust the pedals accordingly. Follow the directions above for adjusting the 'neutral' position of the controls, and the lift-off won't be much different from into wind. Pedals will need more attention than lifting off into wind.

Touching Down From The Hover

Flat Surfaces

It should be straightforward to touch down from the hover. Well, it is and it isn't. I have seen helicopters that are impossible to look good in when touching down, due to tail wheel bounce, or a skidding motion of the wheels when they touch down, regardless of how smoothly the pilot tries to control things. There are others it is impossible to mess up. There are touchdowns, and there are arrivals† and we're trying to prevent arrivals.

You shouldn't be looking down to judge height - perhaps a bit obvious a statement, but you should be getting all the cues you need from objects in front of you. You'll be getting cues from lots of places, and you'll need to be glancing around a lot. Quick eye movements, as opposed to head movements are all that are needed.

Some folks say when the ground appears to be about level with your ears you should be just about touching down, but that's a bit too broad a statement for me‡. Since you'll eventually learn to fly a lot of different helicopters, here's a technique that has worked well for me.

A smooth touch down can be made if the pilot anticipates when the skids are going to hit - every time. The last foot or less should be at a low rate of descent with the pilot telling himself "the skids ought to be touching down..... 3,2,1, now". Obviously, the place of touchdown should also be pre-determined for the sake of pride, if nothing else.

If you were measuring, you'd notice the amount of collective lever movement is non-linear as you get closer to the ground, but that's of academic interest only.

When close to touching down, there should be very little rearward movement, and certainly no sideways movement. The reasons for this will be dealt with in Chapter 19, but for now, keep away from these two unwanted motions - the visualization is for a straight vertical touchdown.

* The pilot may also be heaving if prone to sea sickness

† We won't talk about 'arrivals' - you'll know them when you see them, and you'll have plenty of practice at them as well.

‡ someone noted that you'd be neck deep in dirt by that time too...

Previously, vertical cues were mentioned. Another reason for using close-in cues and vertical cues is to consider how objects far away, near the horizon make small angles, (subtend is the more correct technical term) and how these angles change very little with changes in height. A large building a long way away makes a small angle with the eye, and changing height by one foot is an insignificant amount of angular change with respect to that building. A close–in cue subtends a larger angle and has a larger change when position changes, especially vertically. Figure 16-1 shows this angular effect. Use cues suitable for the task.

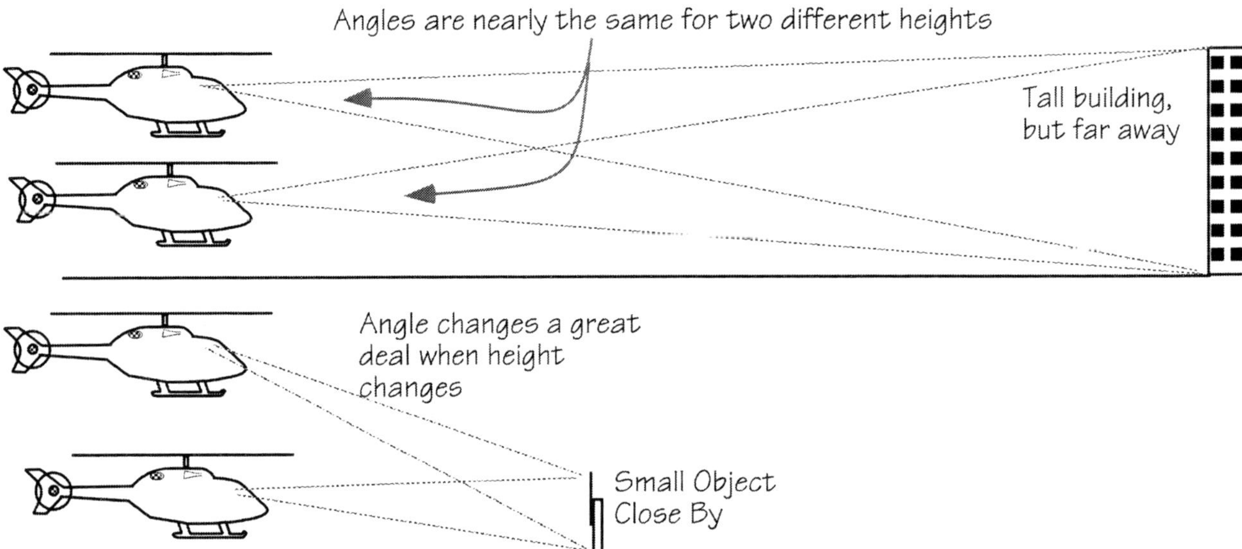

Figure 16-1 Subtending Angles

Developing Coordination

Just as hovering with winds from the 4 cardinal directions (relative to the helicopter) helps to develop many skills, so does lift-off and touchdown with those same wind directions. Lift-off and touchdown in these conditions is not easy, and often not pretty, but it does teach anticipation and coordination of control inputs. Every chance you get to practice this (within the limits of the machine and your own personal limits of course), make the effort.

Don't Overcontrol

It's easy to start to overcontrol near the ground. There are lots of cues and it's pretty hard to ignore the thing you're trying to land on... For the beginner, consider even the very best pilots will admit the perfect landing is rare.

A Neat Trick for Smooth Touch Downs

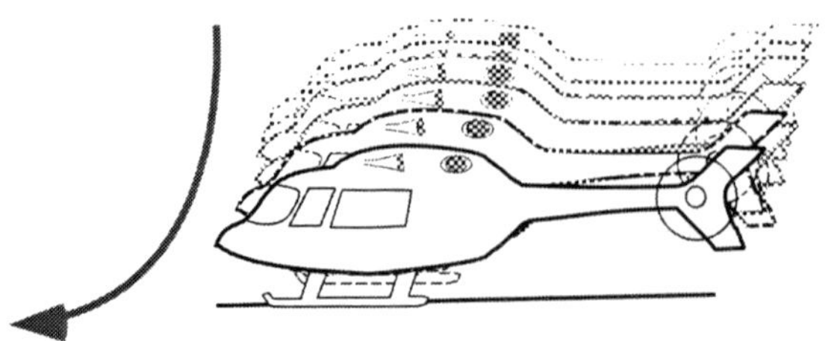

Figure 16-2 Smooth Touchdowns from the Hover

A neat trick to make your touch downs smoother is to have just the slightest amount of forward speed - a slight 'J' effect as shown in Figure 16-2. There is no aerodynamic reason for this, but a perceptual one - we humans* have eyes in the front of our heads, and get most of our depth perception from moving forward. Unless we look directly down, and have good cues to give us some idea of rate of closure, we don't have much depth perception in that last few inches prior to touchdown. If you look straight ahead at the cues when moving vertically without a good vertical reference, you would not see much worthwhile. Now you know why...

* Any extra-terrestrials reading this - sort it out for yourselves. You're probably way ahead of us anyway.

Once you've got the skids in contact with terra firma, pause briefly, but try not to move anything for a short instant. If the ground is firm and level underneath you, then smoothly lower the collective lever all the way down, but be prepared! Don't forget the pedals as you lower collective.

Not all ground is firm or level or of even consistency. I've seen people bend skids by having a hole below one part of the skids, or nearly roll over. Accident statistics are made up of too many landings on ground that, sadly, wasn't really suitable.

Sloping Surfaces

Not all the world is flat and lots of places where helicopters operate could not be called 'prepared surfaces'. It is useful therefore to consider how to smoothly and safely touch down on a slope. First of all, it is necessary to know the limitations of the slopes the helicopter can handle. The reason there are limits will be explained later. Having determined the maximum slope allowed from the limitations section of the FM, it is a question of finding a slope less than this limit to practice on.

The landing area may be arranged so the helicopter can be (or perhaps must be) landed parallel to the slope, nose up the slope or nose down the slope. Each direction has it's own technique.

So how do we touch down smoothly and safely on ground which has a slope? Let's consider a cross slope first. Across slope touch downs are really about controlling roll rate, once the uphill skid is on the ground. We control roll rate by controlling the lateral component of main rotor thrust. (We'll ignore the lateral thrust from the tail rotor for the moment.)

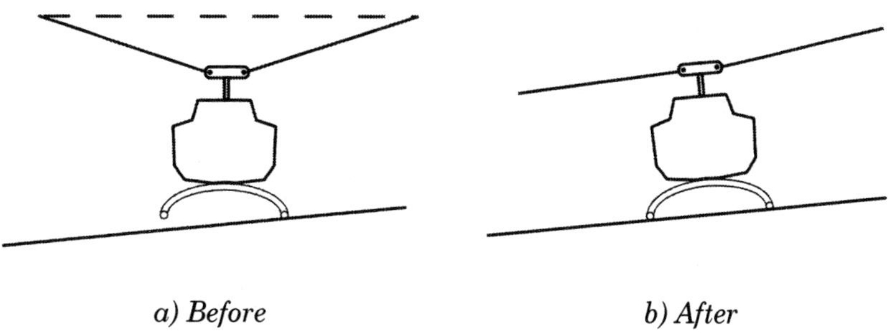

Figure 16-3 Sloping Ground Simplified

There are two separate (and extreme) ways to get onto a slope with skids parallel to the slope (a cross slope if you prefer). If we examine them both, and then pick a middle way, it might be easier to understand. You won't see the either extreme method used in training helicopters, but it helps to show the overall picture.

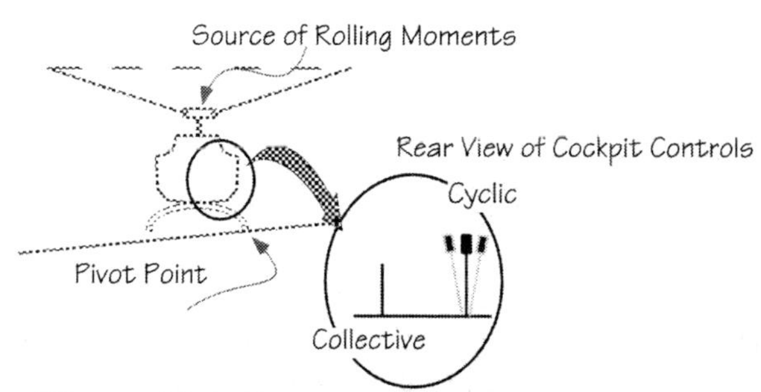

Figure 16-4 Controlling the Rolling Moment

First of all, we can do all the controlling of the roll rate by using only a small amount of collective lever and large amounts of lateral cyclic stick. Alternatively, we can control the roll rate by using mostly the collective lever* and very little lateral cyclic stick. Both are changing the lateral component of thrust to control the roll rate.

If using the mostly-lateral-cyclic stick method, slowly tilting the thrust vector downhill (i.e. lateral cyclic downhill) causes the helicopter to roll in the desired direction. This has the disadvantage

* It might be worth considering that for helicopters with hingeless rotor heads, such as the Lynx and MBB BO-105, collective lever–only method is preferred due to bending moments in the rotor head

that the vertical component of the thrust vector is still quite large, and supporting most of the weight of the helicopter. There is little force to stop the helicopter from sliding downhill as there is very little friction force between the ground and the skids.

Using the mostly-collective lever-method reduces the amount of thrust and the helicopter will pivot around the uphill skid. Unfortunately pivoting around the uphill skid also tilts the disk with respect to the hill, so at one point both the reduction of thrust and the tilt with respect to the hill may cause a larger–than–desired roll rate.

Those are the two extreme methods. Somewhere in the middle lies the best technique for most helicopters. This is a combination of lowering collective lever and applying lateral cyclic stick into the slope to keep the thrust vector nearly vertical with respect to the earth. A vertical thrust vector will mean a very low (probably zero), roll rate.

The end result is the same, the roll rate is controlled by a combination of tilt and amount of thrust vector. Lowering the collective lever is necessary, so is tilting the thrust vector with respect to the airframe. The rolling moment can be controlled by keeping the thrust vector parallel to the horizon. A combination of the two controls, for tilt and amount of thrust vector should keep the roll rate firmly in check.

So how do we do this in the cockpit? Start by being just above the slope, skids parallel to the slope. Gently descend until the uphill skid is just touching down (the previously developed discipline of saying when the skid will touch will be useful). Pause here, and lower the collective lever just a smidgen* with perhaps a touch of cyclic stick into the hill. This will ensure the uphill skid is firmly in contact with the ground, and will prevent the helicopter from pivoting around the toe or heel of the skid. This pivoting is likely to happen as you change power during the rest of the touchdown. If you don't get the skid firmly onto the slope at this point, perhaps it's because the skids aren't exactly parallel to slope. Make a small adjustment with the pedals if necessary to line up the skids with the slope.

Now lower the collective lever another smidgen or two. Note the helicopter will roll slightly downhill as the total thrust vector is reduced. You can control the roll rate by adding some cyclic stick into the hill, as you lower the collective lever. Another way to look at this is to keep the rotor disk parallel with the horizon all the time, regardless of the fuselage attitude.

(If you don't keep the cyclic stick moving with respect to the horizon, but let it stay where it is with respect to the fuselage, the rolling of the helicopter around the uphill skid will tilt the rotor downhill, which is not what you want.)

Continue lowering the collective lever until you are on the slope with both skids (again your peripheral vision and sense of the space of the helicopter ought to tell you the downhill skid position with respect to the ground pretty closely). If you run out of lateral cyclic stick and still aren't down, don't go any farther - the slope is steeper than it looks.

What if the slope is too steep? Since there is no way to measure the slope prior to attempting to touch down on it, we might have a problem.

First of all, maintain some margin of control. If you are running out of lateral cyclic stick, and still have lots of power on, and the roll rate is not under positive control - don't go any further. Similarly, if you sense the roll rate is not what you'd like, *stop trying to land!*

Tail Rotor Side Thrust

Earlier, it was mentioned the tail rotor side thrust would be ignored for early discussion. Now it is time to put it into the equation.

Tail rotor side thrust has a large effect on the ease or difficulty of touching down on a slope, as it confuses the control of the rolling moment. Remember whenever the collective lever is moved, the tail rotor thrust must be adjusted to maintain heading. When combined with the lateral cyclic stick movement needed to control the lateral thrust and rolling moment, it is easy to see how the two can work together or in opposition. The best advice is to make very small changes in pedal and anticipate the effect of lowering the collective lever.

Some folks think that having the tail rotor pushing you into the slope will help to keep your there and makes that direction easier (for our light training helicopter it would be right skid upslope).

* A small precise unit of measurement equal to the thickness of feather.

While You're On the Sloping Ground

You may wish to keep the cyclic stick into the hill for the whole time you're there, or once you get the helicopter solidly seated, you may wish to re-center the cyclic stick (with respect to the fuselage). Either way, if you're going to unload passengers or stay there for a while with the engine running, think of what can happen to the lateral CG.

For example, if you're in a machine like the Bell 47 with twin fuel tanks that are high up on either side of the fuselage, the uphill tank may well drain into the downhill tank, which could put you outside lateral CG limits.

Wind Across the Slope

Wind can either help you or hinder you on a slope landing. If the wind is from uphill to downhill, then you've already had to add some lateral cyclic stick into the hill before you ever start the touchdown process. You may not have as much lateral cyclic stick to handle the slope as you thought. If the wind is from downhill to uphill, it should help the situation.

Lift-off from the Slope

Now you're on the slope, it's necessary to lift-off again*. The lift-off is best made slowly, and starts by putting the thrust vector perpendicular to the horizon, or slightly on the uphill side of perpendicular. Most pilots tilt the thrust vector into the hill a considerable amount and take out the excess tilt as the collective lever is increased. Regardless of the technique you end up using, the aim is to co-ordinate the control of cyclic stick and collective lever so that as the size of the thrust vector increases, it pulls the helicopter underneath it and you lift-off the downhill skid first. If the cyclic stick were to remain in the middle with respect to the fuselage, then the thrust vector would try to pull the helicopter off the ground with some lateral component of thrust, generating a roll rate - this is discussed in more detail in See "Dynamic Rollover" on page 180.

As the collective lever is raised, the weight is transferred to the disk and the helicopter pivots about the uphill skid until it is in equilibrium. Depending on the slope and the power, it may be difficult to stop the uphill skid from sliding downhill as there is very little friction to hold it in place. The main point here is to take things slowly, - don't worry about small changes in bank angle - the visualization is to lift-off smoothly to a hover directly above the position where you were sitting a moment ago.

Nose Upslope / Downslope

Just as the cross–slope technique is all about controlling roll rate, the up (or down) –slope technique is all about controlling pitch rate.

If the helicopter is going to be nose up or down the slope, then it's time to think about clearances for tail rotors or tail booms. If the helicopter is already hovering 7° nose up, then a 10° nose–up slope will require quite a lot of forward cyclic stick as the collective lever is lowered.

If the nose must go down the slope for the same helicopter, then the tail guard will probably hit first. Think about how you are going to recover if the slope is too steep before you start, and what the criteria will be for abandoning the attempt.

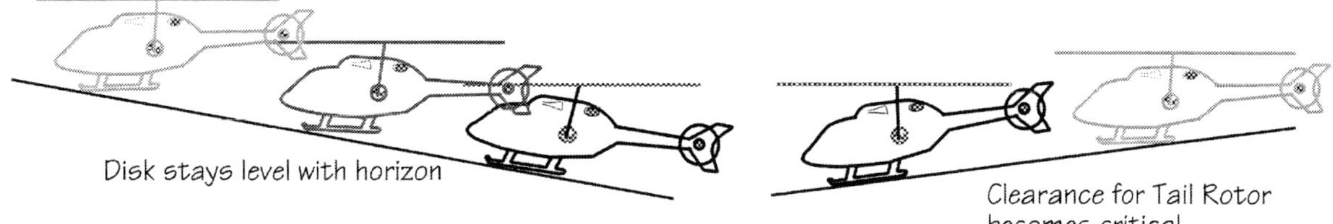

Figure 16-5 Nose Upslope and Downslope

* Unless you necessarily want to shut down there and be towed away...

ONE LAST WORD ABOUT SLOPING GROUND

Never turn your tail toward the hill, unless you've absitively, posilutely* certain you have plenty of height between the tail rotor and the slope. If you're in doubt, turning the tail away from the slope is generally the best insurance.

Summary of Chapter 16

This chapter has covered the basics of getting from the ground to the hover and back again. While a lot of this may seem pretty simple, it is actually one of the keys to being a polished and professional pilot.

I can remember one student of mine who was pretty reasonable in every other way, except he wasn't self-critical enough in takeoffs. He was content to let the helicopter wander in yaw and position during the lift-off. To his credit, when this was pointed out to him, he improved dramatically. I'm still wondering why no-one in his previous 1,500 hours had made him be smooth and precise.

* More creative spelling...

17 Introducing Emergencies

Emergencies - General

In general, there are two types of emergencies in helicopters - those that require immediate, undivided attention (such as engine failures), and those to which a more leisurely approach can be taken*. In all cases, there are some golden words to be remembered:

- Aviate
- Navigate
- Communicate

in that order of priority.

- "*Aviate*" means 'do what you have to do' to keep the helicopter under control.
- "*Navigate*" means to avoid obstacles and other things hazardous to your continued aviation, as well as knowing where you are.
- "*Communicate*" is the last priority - tell someone you have a problem and where you are with the problem.

Oh, yes. - Don't Panic!

Training will (or should) teach you how to deal with emergencies. There are enough surprises in life without making more for yourself.

Typical emergencies center around failures of systems on the aircraft such as engines, electrical systems and so on. Other emergencies, such as blades coming off, are extremely rare.

Critical Emergencies

These are emergencies which require immediate action and memorized responses without reference to the checklist. Previous comments (Chapter 11,"Dear Student")about which emergencies are critical, and which are non-critical, apply.

After "Aviate", one thing that needs stressing in dealing with critical emergencies, is

Never be in a hurry to shut anything off

There are a few things that might need to be shut off in a hurry, such as the fuel supply in a fire, but these emergencies are relatively few. By all means know which things need to be shut off, and how to shut them off quickly, but make sure it's the correct thing to shut off. More than one non-emergency has turned into a real emergency because someone got too fast with switches.

Good advice on emergencies is always available after the fact, but some good sayings that have stood the test of time:

It's sometimes better to do nothing than the wrong thing

Once the really critical actions had been completed, it's time to reach out and wind the clock (but ths doesn't cover digital clocks...).

Dual Concurrence (or Double Checking)

In a single–pilot helicopter always put your hand on the switch, and then confirm out loud it's the correct switch before moving it. If it needed shutting off, the extra few seconds to make sure it's the right thing is time well spent.

In a dual–crew helicopter, get the other pilot to confirm it's the correct switch before it gets moved.

* There are fortunately very few where you can do nothing at all.

Carpenters have a good saying about this sort of thing-

Measure Twice - Cut Once

For Pilots it might be:

Look Twice, Switch Once

What Emergencies Can Happen

I remember reading of a military study on emergency procedures several years ago which had some very interesting conclusions. It was discovered that more than half the actual emergencies encountered were not covered by the existing manuals or procedures being taught in training. It was also rather surprising to find that many of the procedures listed in the manuals had never happened. Quite a lot of time and effort was being spent in training for these procedures. Gives one pause for thought...

Unanticipated Emergencies

A more sobering conclusion to the same study was over half the emergencies that did occur were not in the manuals. The crews were thus unprepared for whatever happened to them.

I was asked to comment on a military accident for which a definite cause had not been determined. There appeared to be nothing wrong with the machine following an extensive technical investigation. After reading through the board of inquiry, it appeared obvious the cause was an encounter with vortex ring state from a 200' hover. The crux of the matter was to determine if the pilot in command was to blame for causing the accident, and I was able to convince the powers that be the pilots had not been adequately trained for this emergency. The final proof was the problem was so poorly understood within that particular military that the board of inquiry, made up of experienced senior pilots, had not considered vortex ring state as a cause. If they didn't consider it, how could the pilot even know about it?

As a Student

You'll be expected to memorize all the emergency procedures. This is a good thing. Memory may replace reason when things get a bit unusual, and the discipline of memorizing is always useful.

The logic is also pretty good for requiring memorizing- you may be flying by yourself and won't have time (or enough hands) to get out the book to check the procedure.

You'll be helped to learn the emergencies by your instructors. They'll give you plenty of emergency procedures to practice, and part of the reason for the practice is so that you don't get so bogged down dealing with the emergency that you forget to fly the helicopter.

Another reason for the practice is to develop the sense of perspective on how the emergency will affect the part of flight you are in. For example, an engine chip light on short final, less than 100 feet above the ground should be dealt with after you're on the ground, while a simulated fire in the cruise might require the student to set up for a maximum rate descent as a first step to getting to a safe place (since many single engine helicopters don't have a fire extinguishing system...)

Too much stress can detract from the situation, so don't panic, in any emergency.

Chip Detectors

The technical details of chip detectors are dealt with in Chapter 9,"Instruments and Warning Systems".

If you're a helicopter pilot, you're going to have an encounter with a chip detector sooner or later. Like all emergencies, it's normally no big deal, and there is no reason to panic if all you have is a chip detector light*.

Know what to do when this happens, and land the helicopter at the nearest suitable place to find out what the problem is. Also know the maintenance history of the machine - some manufacturers permit only one chip every so many hours, and if your machine is making metal more frequently than that, perhaps you don't want to be flying it until it gets fixed.

Also know what you as the pilot are permitted to do in terms of checking the chip detector plugs, and whether a ground run is needed after you clean the plug off and find little or nothing worthy of note.

* If it's accompanied by other indications, like grinding noises, sudden changes in power, etc., then maybe a mild, small amount of panic might be tolerated.

Realistic Emergencies

There is a tendency in flight instruction to load up the student with several emergencies at once, particularly if the student is able to handle the situation. This may be good as a learning exercise, but can become counterproductive if the scenarios can become too artificial.

It reminds me of hearing of the military flight school where the emphasis was on being tough, and the final checkride supposedly had the poor student:

- at night, total electrical failure, with an underslung load, one engine inoperative, downwind, approaching a pinnacle, with the hydraulics failed, and the right pedal locked forward of neutral.

If the student was able to handle all those things, the instructors were supposed to take out the survival knife and reach over and stab the student in the leg to really simulate stress and pressure.

In general terms, there is no point in setting up artificial situations (such as described above) with a series of unrelated emergencies.

On the other hand, if the hydraulic pump is powered by the engine (and not the transmission), then when practicing engine failures, the hydraulic pump should be failed as well.

Where to Handle Emergencies

While at first glance, this might sound silly- the obvious answer would appear to be 'where they happen', but that's not always the case. Remember to fly the helicopter first. Make sure you're in a safe flight condition to do the next steps of the procedure. This should either be safely airborne, or on the ground or with a good idea of what is going to happen when you move that switch.*

Some Typical Emergencies

As a student or private pilot you may be faced with an emergency for real. I'd love to be able to tell you which ones you'll see, but if I had that power, I'd be rich. Have a read of the occurrence/ incident reports that your RA will publish, and think about those. Read accident reports, not for any ghoulishness, but to understand what the symptoms / signs in the cockpit were, and analyze what the crew did, and then what you would do.

People go to a lot of trouble to write the emergencies section of the FM, and it's not because they are trying to make life difficult for students. These are real problems, and you need to be aware of how to handle them.

Summary of Chapter 17

This chapter has covered some of the basics of emergency procedures. You'll get lots of practice in training in handling the helicopter in these sorts of situations, (all simulated, I hope!). There is a natural tendency to want to do things quickly in training, when sometimes a bit of a pause in thought might be appropriate.

* The one whose position and function you know from your blindfold cockpit checks...

18 Engine Failures for Beginners

General

Engines, being of earthly construction, are bound to fail from time to time. Since the helicopter depends upon this device for support, losing it can be critical. It need not, necessarily, be the end of the world. It is very prudent to know what are the symptoms of an engine failure, what must be done about this inconvenience thrust* upon you, and your options.

Interestingly, statistics show since helicopters stop first and then land, the chances of surviving an engine failure are much better than surviving an engine failure in a fixed wing airplane.

This chapter covers the very basics of engine failures and autorotations in single–engine helicopters - it should be sufficient for the beginner. For example, no turns are considered in this chapter. More advanced techniques are in Chapter 30,"Advanced Engine Failures".

The 'normal' sequence of events that should occur when practicing autorotations will vary from helicopter type to type; but the principles remain the same. It must be stressed autorotations are not a 'by the numbers' procedure.

Some normal disclaimers are also needed - first, all the techniques here are generic, and may not always work on a particular type of helicopter. Secondly, the aim of teaching autorotations must be firmly remembered - there is no point bending the helicopter to split hairs about esoteric points of technique - if the helicopter can be maneuvered safely to a low height above ground and low groundspeed, to survive the landing, the aim has been achieved.

Simulated vs. 'Real' Engine Failures

There is an important difference between 'practice' and 'real' engine failures. With the practice failures, the student may have greater warning of the failure than the 'real' thing.

The first reason is that the mere fact the training or check flight includes autorotations prompts the student to expect engine failures. Additionally, the instructor may announce the failure prior to closing the throttle, or the student may sense the instructor getting ready (telegraphing his move by a change in posture, etc.), or more commonly, the student feels the throttle move. In any case, the effect is the student is ready and waiting for the engine failure. Modern engines are quite reliable, which is fortunate for safety and peace of mind, but unfortunate in another sense, as it lulls us into a false sense of security. Engines don't give the same warning as instructors, and a real engine failure will be a surprise. The aim of practice is to educate the student to what should be done in real life, and make the necessary reactions as instinctive as possible†. A 'real' engine failure may well be different in terms of engine deceleration time, warnings and so on, but this depends upon the type of engine‡.

Warming-up for Autorotations

Athletes warm up for their events, and helicopter pilots should be the same. Since autorotative landings are not normally practiced by most helicopter pilots on a daily basis, and there is a great consequence for error, it is prudent to re-align the various senses and motor reactions of the pilot, to re-acquaint oneself with the maneuver. I know of several autorotation training–related accidents that could be traced to a lack of warm up.

I am also aware there are those who say 'real' engine failures don't give much warning, and don't permit the luxury of warming up. That is true, but since a large number of helicopter accidents happen in practicing autorotations, it stands to reason any thing that can prevent problems is worth doing. Since helicopter pilots need lots of practice in autorotations in order to develop their skills and judgment, they need to warm up.

---

* Another inadvertent pun, I'm afraid, but this one was found by one of the editors.
† Instructors should also be cautious about being too aggressive in simulating surprise engine failures.
‡ Having had a 'real' one, I can attest to the element of surprise. Fortunately training did overcome surprise.

The warm–up should be a gradual buildup, starting with vertical landings from the hover to re-educate the seat of the pants with where the ground is, followed by engine failures in the hover, running landings and hover–taxi engine failures, quick stops and then power recovery autorotations and finally engine off landings from traffic pattern altitude. All of these are relatively straightforward and easy to understand, but the quickstop deserves special attention.

Vertical Landings

The first part of the warm up is nothing more than a slow rate vertical landing from a hover - the only difference is the pilot should say out loud when the undercarriage is expected to hit. Do this two or three times until it is judged perfectly: the skids/wheels etc. touch down when expected.

This maneuver re-sets the seat–of–the–pants senses (proprioceptive cues for you techies) with where the ground is.

Also, it is worthwhile to point out where the horizon crosses the windshield when the helicopter is hovering*. This is one of the cues to tell the pilot the attitude where the thrust vector is vertical. It helps to have the student physically point this out. One light helicopter on low skids has the possibility of rocking back onto the tail rotor guard or 'stinger' to show the incorrect attitude for the flare close to the ground or touching down - a useful exercise.

The next part of the warm up is to conduct some running landings at slow forward speed - again, the aim is to judge exactly when the undercarriage is going to touchdown. The reason is the same as the vertical landing.

Engine Failures in the Hover†

Next, try some engine failures in the hover to re-acquaint the senses with the rate of collective lever application, judging how to control the yaw and drift to touch down with a degree of skill.

It is wise to review what happens to the hovering helicopter when the engine fails. First the helicopter yaws, as the requirement to counteract the power to the main rotor has disappeared. How much it yaws depends on the power being used, relative wind speed and direction, and so on. The amount of yaw is of less importance than the visualization of 'stop the yaw' - don't try to keep the original heading, as if the engine failure is real, there will be some considerable yaw before the failure is recognized. As one of my friends noted - the amount of pedal movement needed is huge‡.

Next, as both main and tail rotors are slowing down rapidly, the effectiveness of the tail rotor is going to reduce. This has no real effect on its ability to stop the yaw, as the main rotor reaction is likewise reducing, but it has a marked effect on the translating tendency. Typically the helicopter drifts to the side slightly immediately following the engine failure. The aim of the pilot is to stop the lateral drift. There may be some longitudinal drift (depending on the wind), which is OK as long as it is a forward drift. Stop any lateral drift, as it can tip you over.

Having stopped the drift, the next aim is (using the collective lever as necessary) to touch down at an acceptable rate.

Judging Collective Lever Application

Some students have difficulty judging collective lever application. Like many other things, they need experience of how to use the rotational energy, when to use it and how rapidly to use it. Before we get into the nuts and bolts of how to use rotational energy, we need to discuss what it is.

Rotational energy is the energy stored in the rotor due to its whirling around. Like kinetic energy, it depends on a square function - the energy of a rotor turning at 100 RPM is four times the energy of a rotor spinning at 50 RPM. Since we can extract this energy and turn it into lift, and the amount of lift produced will also vary as the square of the rotor speed, it doesn't take much mathematics to show the lift available at the high end of rotor RPM is much greater than at slower RPM. If you're trying to stop the helicopter descending, it will take a lot more collective lever movement to generate the lift if you start at a low rotor RPM than at high rotor RPM.

---

* I used to say on the ground, but then I found a helicopter that hovered nose up quite a bit and would scoot away from the flare if put in the 'on the ground attitude'. Hence the emphasis.

† I've been told in New Zealand or Australia, if you refer to an engine failure in the hover as a hovering autorotation, you get your wrist slapped - they say the rotor is not being driven by the air so, it's not in autorotation... Transport Canada are evidently pretty touchy about the term too.

‡ A technical term again. Opposite of 'smidgen'

All this complicated explanation is to show it's difficult to figure out how to use this energy!

Here's a method to help show this. Holding the helicopter at a low height (less than one foot above the ground) and maintaining it there with increasing collective lever after the engine is 'failed', until there is no more lift will help show how to apply the correct amount of collective. At some point, as the collective lever is being increased and angle of attack is increasing towards the stall, the rotor will stop producing lift. When the rotor stops 'flying', the helicopter plummets the short distance without harm. This teaches a lot about controlling collective lever inputs!

Once the helicopter is close to the ground, the collective should only move up. If you've pulled too hard, don't push down - wait. Helpful Hint

In summary of the engine failure in the hover – the aim is to stop the drift and yaw, maintain position over the ground (within reason), and cushion the touchdown.

High Hover Engine Failures

Not all hovering takes place at 3-5 feet above the ground. So how do you handle an engine failure if you're 15' above the ground and the engine goes for a powder*?

This calls for a different technique than the low hover method. A lot of things are going to happen – simultuously.† You won't be able to let the helicopter descend slowly while raising the collective, or even holding the collective lever in the same place.

It will be necessary to provide a sharp downward movement of the collective lever to persuade the helicopter to start down. How much down collective lever and how rapidly it needs to be added can only come from experience. The aim is to use this precious rotational energy and thus, lift of the rotor, in the wisest possible way.

As the helicopter nears the ground, a rapid up-application of collective lever will be needed to stop the rate of descent. How much and how rapid will depend on the situation. Just remember any energy in the rotor doesn't do you any good if the touchdown is going to be threatening to your physical body.

Self-Initiated Engine Failures Hover

Typically, many students, asked to do a self–initiated engine failure in the hover, spend quite a while 'getting ready', and are slightly afraid to close the throttle on themselves. It may help if the instructor closes the throttle without much warning to show the student they really were ready for the failure at any time.

While the student is getting ready to roll the throttle off, roll it off without warning. Tell the student they were ready all along, they just didn't realize it. Helpful Hint

Practice the engine failure in the hover until the actions become instinctive and the student is able to discuss the sequence of events, and self criticize his performance.

Quick Stops

Quick stops are practiced for several reasons, firstly they duplicate most of the flare part of the autorotation quite well and secondly, they are an excellent coordination exercise for beginning pilots‡. See Figure 14-3 for the sequence of events in the quick stop.

To fully understand the reason for practicing the quick stop, consider the main purpose of the flare in the autorotation - to stop the rate of descent. A secondary reason is to decrease ground speed but the main purpose is to stop the rate of descent. A beneficial side effect is to increase N_R.

The first quick stop should use a slow airspeed and gentle flare. Increase both the airspeed used and rapidity of flare on the next quick stops until the collective lever is nearly full–down in the flare. In all of them, practice maintaining a constant height above ground during a quick stop.

* I've been advised that this would only apply to female engines, and that would be sexist. Sorry.
† More creative spelling, I'm afraid.
‡ OOPS - almost said 'young pilots' there- that would be age-ist!

Concentrate on maintaining altitude with the cyclic stick until the cyclic stick is ineffective in holding the helicopter at a constant height, that is, bringing the nose up won't keep the helicopter at the desired height above the ground.

The next control input is one of the secrets for a successful autorotation - the helicopter must make the change from a nose up, decelerating attitude to a disk level attitude for touchdown. How this is accomplished has a great bearing on the quality of the touchdown. In many helicopters the cyclic stick is not the best control to level the helicopter!

Try doing a quickstop the 'wrong' way to show this important point. Use the following control sequence - at the end of the flare, as the ground speed comes to zero and the helicopter starts to sink, level first with the cyclic stick, and then add collective lever to stop the descent*. The results will be less than satisfactory†, particularly compared to the 'proper' sequence of collective lever first as a check, and only then if this check does not bring the helicopter to the level position, then make a small adjustment with the cyclic stick.

The reasons for not using the cyclic stick to level the helicopter are many:

- the cyclic stick is not very effective, as it is only changing the direction of the very small thrust vector. It takes quite a lot of cyclic stick to level, if only the cyclic stick is used.
- forward cyclic stick introduces forward speed again. One of the purposes of the flare is to reduce ground speed, and using forward cyclic stick undoes this work.
- forward cyclic stick introduces a nose down pitch rate. This pitch rate continues past the 'level' attitude, and must be stopped prior to touchdown, particularly on soft ground, in order to prevent the nose from digging in. The only way to stop this pitch rate is with aft cyclic stick, leading to a lot of cyclic stick activity at an already busy time.
- forward cyclic stick bleeds N_R unnecessarily. When the helicopter is flared and the cyclic stick pulled aft, the N_R increases - the opposite happens when the cyclic stick is pushed forward - the N_R decreases.
- finally; it is not needed: using the collective lever to check the descent rate accomplishes the change to a level attitude with none of the disadvantages.

Finally, a note of caution- don't try too rapid a flare downwind, as it is possible to get into vortex ring state in this condition, especially if a rapid collective lever check is used at the end. Since this maneuver is also a key to many other things, again see Figure 14-3 on page 130 shows the sequence of events from the start of the quick stop to the hover.

The Flare

The purpose of the flare is to stop the rate of descent, and it has at least two other useful effects - it slows the forward speed to make the landing less dramatic, and it increases the N_R. The main purpose, is to stop the rate of descent. Remember this and autorotations are much easier to learn and fly.

There is no text book, by–the–numbers procedure for how much to flare, where to flare, or when to stop the flare. This is a visual maneuver (but see "Autorotations at Night, in Clouds, etc." on page 409 on night and instrument autorotations), and requires some judgment. Judgment implies experience, and hopefully a variety of experiences.

Some flight manuals (most military ones, it seems) have some very precise wording the pilot is expected to be able to remember at an infrequent moment of extreme stress; for example:

At 100 feet above ground, flare the helicopter to 10-12° nose up, using approximately 2" of aft cyclic stick. At 25 feet above ground, level the helicopter and apply collective lever to control the touchdown.

How absurd. In an attempt to reduce everything to an absolute minimum level, the adaptability and judgment of the human pilot has been sacrificed‡.

Typically, the part of the maneuver that gives the most grief is the flare - either too much or too little, too soon or too late. Too much flare is caused by too much aft cyclic stick for the airspeed that results in the helicopter climbing instead of not descending. At this point, don't continue to pull back on the cyclic

* Don't carry this to extremes - the point is to show the effect, not crash.

† Even non–pilots who watch this demonstration from the cockpit comment "This doesn't look or feel correct".

‡ I'll stop this particular train of thought here, it deserves a whole chapter or book on its own.

stick - the helicopter will stop climbing and eventually start to descend again. Now is the time to re-stop the rate of descent and judge what to do to salvage the situation. Too soon starting the flare will end up with too low an airspeed close to the ground, making the flare effective. Too late starting the flare may result in too rapid a flare and climbing.

Remember, in a real engine failure, there is no opportunity to apply power and go around! The student must learn to correct his mistakes.

So What Should You Do?

Note the reaction of the helicopter in the flare: is the helicopter climbing, descending, or maintaining a constant height? If the flare is judged and carried out correctly, the helicopter maintains a constant height above ground as it decelerates - the height maintained depends upon the helicopter, the terrain and so on - the important part is that height is maintained as the helicopter slows (or perhaps a more exact term is the height above ground is under control). In terms of visualization - the ideal picture is for the helicopter to describe a flat flight path.

The obvious question is how much flare is needed? The answer is just enough to stop the rate of descent. Only experience will show the amount, and even then, the best that can be said is small errors will be made in every autorotation.

In the flare, the N_R increases as the rate of air flowing through the disk increases - it should be permitted to increase, unless it gets too high. In a real engine failure, you might be excused if you oversped the rotor while saving the helicopter. Being trained professionals we like to keep the N_R in the green.For every helicopter, there is an airspeed, normally slower than 40 to 45 KIAS, when the flare is ineffective in stopping the rate of descent. Bringing the nose up only succeeds in the helicopter falling through and hitting the ground tail first. Be aware of it, and judge when you have to accept landing with the forward speed and use the collective lever only to stop the descent.

Don't get too slow prior to starting the flare. Helpful Hint

There is a tendency to think because the ground is rushing up, we should start slowing down. You need to overcome this*.

Flare Effectiveness

The purpose of the cyclic flare is to stop the rate of descent, but only if the helicopter has forward speed across to the ground. If the helicopter were descending at zero–airspeed on a calm day, would a cyclic flare make any difference to the rate of descent? Obviously not. If the helicopter were descending at 60 KIAS into a 60 knot wind (descending vertically with respect to the ground again) would a flare be necessary? Again, obviously not. (some would say you'd need to add forward cyclic stick as the collective lever was added...)

On a calm day, when descending at 60 KIAS, a flare is needed to stop the rate of descent, so somewhere between the extremes, the flare becomes ineffective. What to do?

First of all, make sure the ground speed and airspeed is high enough to make the flare effective. My experience has been for airspeeds below about 40 to 45 KIAS, the cyclic flare is really ineffective in stopping the rate of descent, regardless of the helicopter type. This is one reason for the 'recommended airspeed' for autorotation found in the FM - you don't want to get too slow.

("Another Type of Autorotation" on page 339 will deal with an animal of a different nature, the constant attitude autorotation.)

Secondly, if you weren't able to keep the airspeed/groundspeed up, then get the skids level, aligned in the direction of flight, and use the collective lever at the opportune moment. Don't use all the collective lever at 100' AGL in a panic- the fall will hurt. Wait, with ice in your veins instead of blood, and pull when it's appropriate.

In my limited experience, judging when a flare would be ineffective has been easy, and students sort this out satisfactorily with little prompting. They still need to see the technique however.

* I nearly said 'groundless fear' here, but thought better of it.

Collective Check - Why It Works

Assuming you had enough airspeed to flare, and the helicopter is at the end of the flare, with very little forward speed relative to the ground, and is in a nose high attitude – now it's time to get the fuselage level and land. As previously mentioned, the best way to go from the end of the flare to the touchdown is via the collective lever check. The only helicopters I have seen where the collective lever check did not work were tandem rotors - but for nearly every single–rotor helicopter, it is the best method to get the helicopter level.

Why is this? The cyclic stick is only used for tilting the thrust vector generated by the main rotor - and when the helicopter is in autorotation, the thrust is equal to the weight, and is relatively small. A large amount of forward cyclic stick is needed to generate the pitching moment needed to level the helicopter, compared to that needed in 'powered' flight.

At the end of the flare, the collective lever should be nearly fully down. The helicopter is in a nose up attitude, and the ground speed is low. A small but positive check up in collective lever increases the main rotor blade pitch, and hence the thrust, at the expense of some N_R. The effect of the increase in thrust with the nose up attitude creates a couple about the center of gravity - since the CG is normally forward of the rotor mast*, the natural effect is for the thrust vector and the weight to try to align themselves, bringing the nose to a nearly level attitude, without any movement of the cyclic stick. This leveling of the nose is self–correcting - normally it stops the helicopter at the disk level attitude. As the disk approaches the level position, the couple becomes weaker, and when the nose is nearly level, the couple has diminished. This is shown in Figure 18-1.

Coupling of Forces in Leveling Helicopter

I had occasion to convince an unbelieving student that the collective lever would do all that was needed. At the end of the flare, I took my hand off the cyclic stick and leveled the helicopter and completed the touchdown without using the cyclic stick. I do not recommend this as a normal method, (the conditions were ideal) but it certainly got the message across!

If the CG is a long way aft of the rotor mast (not common in single rotor helicopters), then the check could have the opposite effect to that desired. If the CG is very close to the rotor mast, then the collective lever check may also not be as effective. If you are well practiced, then a combination of collective lever check and cyclic stick will obviously be the best solution, but remember raising the collective lever will increase the size of the thrust vector the cyclic stick is tilting.

See Figure 18-1 for the way the coupling of forces works when a 'collective lever check' is used.

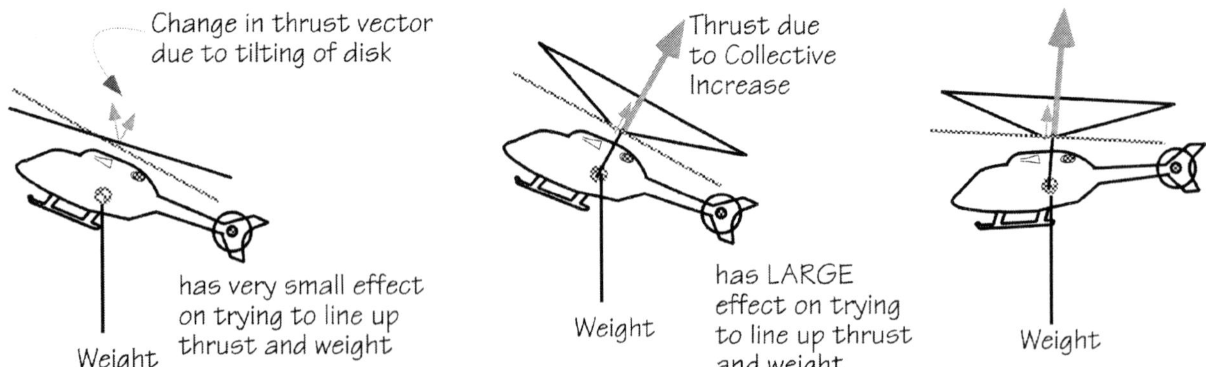

Figure 18-1 The Collective Lever Check

Well, so far, we haven't even gone more than 100 feet above the ground, and we've learned a lot. Now we go slightly higher.

* ...but not all helicopters have the CG forward of the mast- so beware.

Power Recovery Autorotations

The next step in this warm-up is the power recovery autorotations. It has this name as the maneuver terminates with the power on and the helicopter hovering. The main teaching points in the power recovery are the judgment in the entry, descent and flare.

Set up the helicopter in a position where it is going to be possible to 'make' the desired landing area. For the sake of argument, the flight manual says the optimum airspeed for autorotation is 60 KIAS. At about 500' above the ground and aligned with the landing area wind direction, lower the collective lever (fully down in most helicopters), put the slip ball in the middle, maintain the desired airspeed and reduce the throttle to idle.

At this point, it is worth stating that, a properly maintained (i.e correctly rigged main rotor pitch links) helicopter will have the N_R adjusted so it is within the limits set by the manufacturer. See "N_R in Autorotation Descent" on page 78 for more details about autorotation N_R.

During the descent, maintain the 'normal' airspeed, and note how the wind affects the glide path - is the helicopter going to be short of the landing area or overshoot it? Make a note so the entry point can be changed for the next attempt.

One of the things to note in the descent is that at 500' AGL, there are very few, if any, cues to the relatively rapid descent towards the ground. Secondly, the airspeed remains constant if the pitch attitude is kept the same. Note the airspeed, but don't stare at it. This checking should be a momentary glance inside to make sure the airspeed hasn't changed.

Note to instructors - one of the kindest things you can do for students in autorotations is cover up the airspeed indicator - make the student fly by attitude and looking outside.

Helpful Hint

If the N_R is slightly high, then a small amount of collective lever can be applied to bring it into the proper range. A little experience will tell if you pull up too much, and there are several ways you know if the N_R is too low. First, you should be able to hear it - the sounds of the blades and transmission are different than 'normal', and you should be aware of that - hearing is an excellent sense. Get proficient at using noise to judge whether the N_R is too low or too high - then it is not necessary to look at the N_R gauge - and more time can be spent looking outside. The other way the pilot knows if the N_R is too low are the various warnings (either audio or visual) - get used to them, and don't worry too much if the warning light or horn comes on*.

At the start of the flare, apply throttle to bring the engine back into the picture of flying the helicopter. The throttle should be fully open before the collective lever is raised. In many helicopters, the engine coming on–line causes more handling problems for students than landings without the engine. It becomes necessary to coordinate the pedals as well - the engine introduces yaw effects absent in the real autorotation. In the Gazelle, it is necessary to use nearly full travel in the pedals (from full left to full right†) at the end of a power recovery autorotation.

In many helicopters, you'll end up in a stationary hover beyond the point where you were aiming (or would have got to in a 'real' engine failure). Accept this and you'll prevent overtorquing the helicopter in trying to make your intended spot.

Helpful Hint

The power recovery autorotation exercises many skills, while eliminating the risks of the final part of the autorotation. If the whole exercise ends in a power–on hover instead of a no–power landing, then in 'real' engine failures, the touchdown is relatively easy. Having maneuvered the helicopter to a zero groundspeed, low height condition (almost all the energy has been used) with a good amount of N_R to cushion the landing, the amount of damage to the airframe and occupants should be minimal.

* Hopefully your helicopter has a low rotor N_R warning.

† On the Gazelle, the rotor turns the 'other' way to our generic machine.

Power recovery autorotations to the hover have 95% of the skills necessary and less than 1% of the risk involved with actual touchdown autorotations.

Getting Back to the Hover

Once the throttle is open and the engine is on line, the power recovery autorotation is the same as the quick-stop. Taking the helicopter from the decelerating, nose up attitude to the hover is carried out in the same manner - a check on the collective lever first, followed by a small correction with the cyclic stick to get to level, some coordination with the pedals to keep straight, and the helicopter should be in a level hover.

Student Debriefing of Autorotations

Having the student debrief each autorotation immediately after it happens develops skills at observing and correcting mistakes, as well as helping them to relax. If possible, have the student talk throughout the maneuver about what is going on* – this helps when the debriefing comes. One instructor insisted the student recite nursery rhymes to improve relaxation. Video recording the autorotation from inside the cockpit helps a lot...

'Real' Autorotations

Obviously, having successfully completed the warm up, the next step is the landing where the engine is out of the picture. There should be few, if any surprises in this maneuver using the 'standard' speed - the only difference is the flare and touchdown, and even the touchdown has been practiced in engine failures in the hover.

Eyes Out of the Cockpit!

On a philosophical note, if the engine really fails, there is almost nothing inside the cockpit worth looking at to help the pilot land the helicopter successfully†. First of all, none of the engine instruments are worth looking at - the engine has failed. Secondly, none of the other instruments help the pilot to judge when, where and how much to move the controls to make the landing. Altitude from a pressure altimeter is of no use - it's just a number, and may be useful only if it is height above ground‡. Most light helicopters don't have radar altimeters, and there is no magic formulae to tell what height to be at what distance - there is no way to measure the distance anyway. Airspeed only tells you how fast you are traveling through the air, (as opposed to how fast you need to go to make it to the clearing), and so on. It is far better to concentrate on looking outside.

About the only instrument you might want to look at is the slip ball.

The first source of trouble is spending too much time looking inside the cockpit. Watch what the student is looking at, out of the corner of your eye (looking straight at the student may be unnerving for the student**...)

I make it a habit to get students to look outside by covering up favorite instruments such as airspeed, or by putting my arm across the top of the instrument panel to make sure they don't look inside - the results are always better autorotations.

* This isn't going to be easy to do the first few times, but it pays huge dividends.

† Certainly there a few instruments that will help a bit, but they can also be replaced by other senses if operating in visual conditions.

‡ Advocates of the use of QFE (a British way of using barometric pressure) are no better off. If the ground is a different elevation from the airfield, you still know nothing of any value.

**Depending on the student, it could be unnerving for the instructor too.

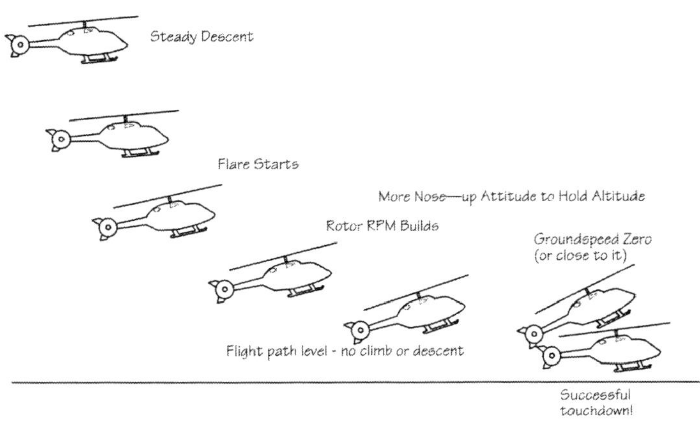

Figure 18-2 Autorotative Sequence

As the helicopter gets close to the ground several things happen - first of all, the ground starts to rush up. This phenomenon (called ground rush for some strange reason) is to be noted, but not worried about. It helps to judge rate of closure with the desired landing area. At this point, it also becomes evident that the rate of descent should be stopped. Don't start to reduce speed early just because the ground is rushing up at you.

A more typical error is not completely arresting the rate of descent - the nose is raised, but the descent continues at a lower rate, and the helicopter is danger of hitting the ground with forward speed, a rate of descent and not level. Concentrate on making the flight path parallel to the ground, and this error is cured. The whole sequence will look something like Figure 18-2. If you were to compare this to a normal landing sequence in a fixed wing airplane, it would look somewhat the same, only the descent is much steeper and the change in pitch attitude much larger.

Autorotative Performance

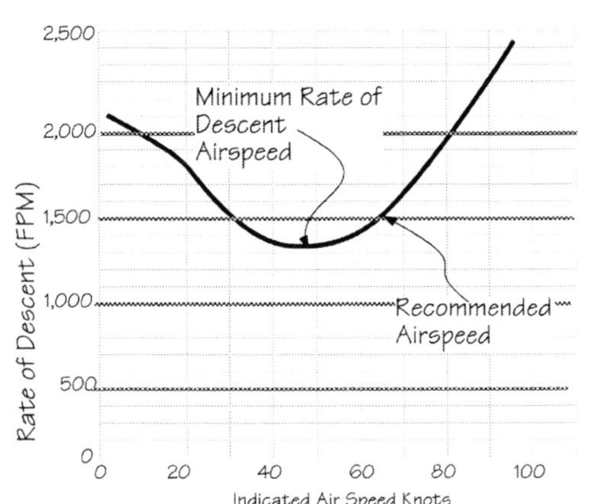

Figure 18-3 Rate of Descent vs. Airspeed.

It is worth spending some time looking at the Rate of Descent vs. Airspeed chart shown in Figure 18-3 below. Note the 'normal' airspeed for autorotations, the maximum range airspeed and the maximum permitted speed (V_{NE}) in autorotation. The use of these and other airspeeds for autorotations will be covered in Chapter 30,"Advanced Engine Failures".

Some Final words

The aims of teaching autorotations are several:

- increase confidence that helicopter flying is safe,
- develop the skills necessary for flying helicopters and most of all,
- learn how survive if the engine fails.

It was mentioned at the start of the chapter that helicopters accidents are generally more survivable than those in fixed wing airplanes because we can stop first and then land.

Think about a helicopter descending in autorotation at about 2,000 feet per minute and 60 KIAS of airspeed. The vertical speed is about 20 knots and the forward speed is 60. Which can hurt more? The forward speed, obviously.

Reviewing this information, it might seem contradictory to my often repeated advice about the purpose of the flare being to stop the rate of descent, and reducing speed was a secondary purpose. The two are really working to the same aim. The aim in learning autorotations is to develop quite a few unique skills, and the flare is the most important part of that.

In a real situation, you probably won't be able to get rid of all the forward speed or the vertical speed. You need to chose which is most important and act accordingly, and the only way you'll learn which is best is by practice.

Some Words on The Height-Velocity Curve

More details of the *Height Velocity curve* are contained in "Height Velocity (HV) Curves" on page 336. The student will undoubtedly be told highly inflammatory tales of the HV curve. At this stage, the best advice is to respect the curve, and when operating on your own, stay away from the areas shown as AVOID.

Summary of Chapter 18

This chapter has covered the very basics of autorotations and should be sufficient to get the student pilot past the first hurdle of this unique type of maneuver. More details on autorotations and their variations are in Chapter 30,"Advanced Engine Failures".

It should be obvious autorotations need a lot more attention than they receive in most training establishments. A consistent build-up in technique and some common sense thinking about what each phase is for will help with the understanding of this maneuver. The main teaching point is the development of judgment and experience.

Power recovery autorotations have 95% of the teaching points and 1% of the risk of full, engine–off touchdown autorotations.

It must be stressed in the view of many experienced helicopter pilots, practice engine failures ensure the pilot can cope with the situation, but the odds of it happening are slim. The exercise does significantly improve the ability of the pilot to control the machine in variable conditions.

19 Peculiarities of the Helicopter

Introduction

The helicopter is a machine that can operate with a freedom unmatched by any other aerial vehicle. This inherent flexibility also has its pitfalls - there are a great number of peculiarities the pilot is likely to encounter that are not well described, perhaps rarely occur, and have very unusual characteristics should they happen. This chapter will deal with a few of the more common ones. Several other less common phenomena are covered in Chapter 34,"Further Peculiarities of The Helicopter".

Loss of Translational Lift

This commonly–used expression is a bit misleading, and causes some confusion. Before we explain what it means, perhaps it is best to explain what *translational lift* is.

Simple stated, thanks to the additional air flowing into the rotor at even low airspeeds, the rotor system produces significantly more lift at the same collective lever pitch setting than at zero airspeed. Strictly speaking, the rotor has not become more efficient, it just has more air being pumped through it, resulting in more lift. This phenomenon becomes evident starting about 15 knots airspeed, so it can happen in a zero–groundspeed hover with 15 knots of wind. As a side effect, the change in inflow also results in less drag on the rotor, which the engine sees as a reduction in torque

What is Translational Lift?

Translational lift happens whenever there is a relative wind across the rotor disk. Whenever the induced flow is not completely vertical to the rotor disk, there is translational lift. At very low wind speeds, the effect is often masked, and by 10-15 knots (depending on the helicopter) the effect is noticeable.

Having described what translation lift is, how do we lose it? The answer is complex, and has a great deal to do with knowledge of the wind and other conditions. Assume for a moment that we are on an approach into a landing site, and we are uncertain of the wind, and also do not have a large margin of power available over power required to hover in ground effect. We are hoping to make the approach to a low height, in–ground–effect hover, so we know we must be cautious with power.

Somewhere on short final, we have the groundspeed reducing at a controlled manner, and the rate of descent likewise well tamed. Airspeed agrees closely with what we think it should be at this stage of the approach. As we continue to reduce speed and the airspeed indicator is reading below 20 knots, the rate of descent suddenly starts to increase (or if you like, the helicopter starts to settle more quickly than you might like), without apparent warning. What has happened, and what should we do about it? The answer is, that unless we were silly enough to do the approach downwind that the extra lift provided by the air moving through the rotor disk has gone away. We have lost translational lift.

Look again at Figure 6-4 on page 57, (Power Required in Low Airspeed). Perhaps it may help if we draw this same curve the opposite–to–normal way, in order to show what is happening with both airspeed and time as the helicopter slows. This is shown in Figure 19-1. Note how the power required to maintain level flight increases dramatically as airspeed decreases as the helicopter decelerates towards the hover.

It's worth stating something unusual here - helicopters require more power to fly more slowly. Not many other mechanical devices are like that. Cars are certainly not like that. Most of the airspeeds fixed wing airplanes operate at are not like that. Only helicopters regularly exploit this part of the flight envelope, and so it's worth emphasizing. It takes more power to fly more slowly.

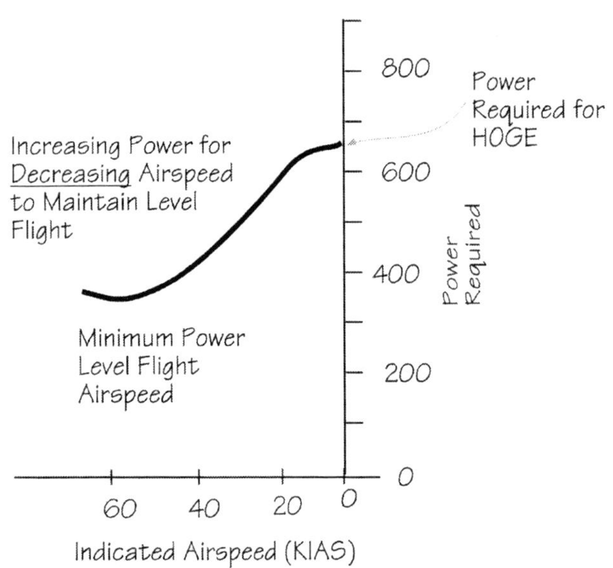

Figure 19-1 Reversed Power Required vs. Airspeed (and Time)

Unless the pilot is aware of this performance–related aspect and is ready to apply power prior to the increase in power required (or as some want to call it, loss of translational lift) a surprise may be in store.

The reason for the surprise is that the helicopter is now slowing down (and so would require more power to maintain level flight), and descending (so it will need extra power to stop the rate of descent). If power is not added to maintain the level flight, then the helicopter will descend at an even faster rate, and even more power will be needed to stop the faster rate of descent.

The cure? Don't be too hasty on approach. If the descent and deceleration are too quick, the change in power at the end will have to be more rapid, and unless you are practiced at it, may be even more surprising. A good rule of thumb is to make sure the rate of descent is less than 300 feet per minute as you pass 100' AGL, and that the rotor disk is more or less parallel to the ground, as a way of making sure things are under control. Ground speed will be the best clue, as airspeed will probably not be reading anything meaningful. Be aware of the requirements of power and don't be taken by surprise! If you are terminating the approach to a hover OGE, then be even more aware of the potential for trouble.

If you're making a 'normal' power-on approach, ensure you have the disk 'loaded', that is, taking power from the engine and with some collective lever pitch applied early in the approach, certainly prior to the last hundred feet of altitude. The reason for this will become clear in the next section...

VORTEX RING STATE

*Vortex ring state** is a phenomenon unique to helicopters. It is very similar to stalling and spinning in fixed–wing aircraft, that is: it is an aircraft in trouble.

Prior to reading the rest of this, - describe the symptoms of the beginning stages of vortex ring state. What conditions is it likely to happen in? Not the technical answers, - the "What I will see from the cockpit" answers. If you cannot answer these questions immediately, this section may be enlightening.

As in a fixed–wing aircraft, it is impossible to tell the symptoms of a stall without ever doing one, and so it should be with helicopters and vortex ring state. Learn what the symptoms are, and when you see them, get out of those flight conditions.

Vortex ring state is often mistakenly called "settling with power". To be very clear: - "settling with power" is a misnomer - it could happen if the power required exceeds the power available (or used) for that airspeed. The helicopter may settle or descend with power on, but probably not be in vortex ring state. Vortex ring state is a more clear, precise definition.

The technical reasons for vortex ring state are explained just a little later.

Impossible Descent Conditions

This may come as a surprise for those of us who thought we could do anything with the helicopter. There are descent conditions we just cannot handle. Figure 19-2 shows what is possible in a powered descent, and then in autorotation. Note that some of these will put the helicopter into a situation conducive to vortex ring state. Not healthy.

* The term settling with power is very misleading and won't be used. I'd ask you to remove it from your vocabulary.

Not Just in Descent

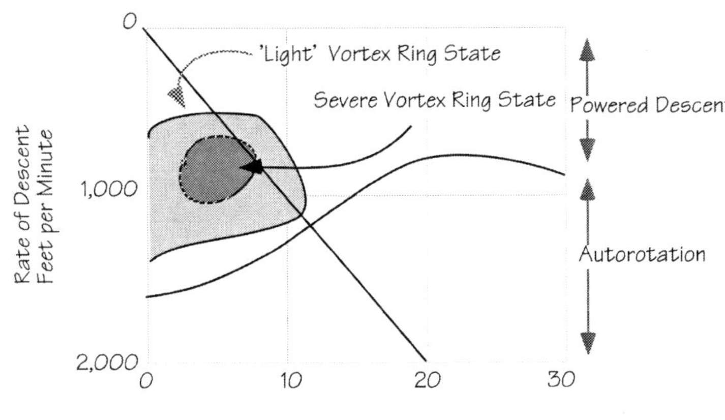

Figure 19-2 Descent Angles Possible

Vortex ring state can happen other places beside a vertical descent. Anytime the rate of descent is close to the induced velocity from the main rotor, vortex ring state is close by. A very rapid flare at a a low power setting, with a rapid collective lever application, can set up the conditions. Be warned!

Demonstrating Incipient Vortex Ring State

It is possible to demonstrate at least the initial stages of the phenomenon in the following manner*. I am advocating only seeing the initial stages for at least two reasons- the first is that taken too far, vortex ring state is like spinning in a fixed wing airplane- there is an unpredictable aspect to it, and we don't want to be unpleasantly surprised, and secondly, we can see everything we need to see from the initial stages.

At a safe altitude above the ground (at least 2,000 – 3,000 feet AGL), find out the wind direction- this can be determined by the direction cloud shadows are moving, if you are lucky enough to do it on a nice day. If it is a cloudless day, the wind direction at the surface is probably quite close to that at altitude. Turn so the helicopter is flying downwind.

Put the helicopter in level flight at minimum power airspeed (typically 40 to 60 KIAS) and note the power being used.

Reduce the power slightly - about 10% below the power for level flight in this condition. You now have a choice - decelerate or descend. We want to decelerate while maintaining altitude and heading.

As the helicopter slows below about 20 KIAS several things may happen - the first symptom may be a very low frequency airframe vibration unlike what is normally experienced in transitioning to the hover. This may also be described as a moderate buffet in the airframe. This is the first and foremost sign of impending vortex ring state, and should be treated the same way as a stall warning in a fixed–wing aircraft. These symptoms tell the pilot something is wrong and ought to be corrected.

Rate of descent will develop to about 500 to 1000 feet per minute in this case, and the airspeed will be reading zero or very low.

I know there are organizations that say this can't be demonstrated safely, but the intention here is not to get into fully developed vortex ring state- merely the incipient stages so you can see the symptoms.

Uncommanded Attitude Changes

The second symptom is uncommanded pitch, roll and yaw. In other words, if you don't move the controls, the helicopter will be changing pitch and roll attitude as well as heading. If possible, avoid the temptation to control the helicopter to maintain heading and pitch and roll attitude†. The airframe should be being tossed around slightly, and not by the pilot's actions. This is the second, unmistakable symptom of vortex ring state.

In a light helicopter, with no hydraulics, we may also see rapidly changing forces in the flight controls.

* The first time you try this, do it with an experienced helicopter instructor who has taught it before.

† Be reasonable- if the nose is wandering around a bit, then don't do anything- if it looks dangerous, then control the helicopter to get out of vortex ring state - see the recovery actions.

Making the Situation Worse

The third and final symptom is that an increase in collective lever only makes the situation worse. Try raising the collective lever slightly - there may or may not be a change in the rate of descent, or the buffeting, or the uncommanded pitch roll and yaw. On occasion, the bottom can literally drop out from under the helicopter, but normally a small collective lever increase may show a small increase in rate of descent. This symptom doesn't always show up.

Exploring what happens in fully–developed vortex ring state is why there are experimental test pilots- not something for the student pilot. Very high rates of descent and turbulence strong enough to roll the helicopter to extreme bank angles have been reported from flight test programs. This is in fully–developed conditions, and should not be a problem in the demonstration just described.

In real life, recover at the first sign of the symptoms of Vortex Ring
Better yet- learn to avoid it!

The learning point is to recognize the symptoms and recover at the first sign of the vortex ring state. It's like stalls in fixed–wing aircraft - once you have been taught how to recognize the symptoms, for the rest of your flying career, you are expected recover at the first symptoms. We should be the same in the rotary wing world.

Recovery

Recovery is simple: - lower the nose with a smooth cyclic stick input to about 20° to 30° nose down (if you are lucky enough to have an attitude indicator with pitch marks on it). In a qualitative sense, use much more nose down than you would normally use in transitioning to forward flight. Being timid is of no use at this point. A small amount of forward stick (such as used in a transition from the hover) would not be enough to get the rotor disk clear of the 'disturbed air'. The helicopter must get forward airspeed quickly to have 'good' air flowing through the disk. Use a reasonably large, positive but smooth application of forward cyclic. Better to be a bit bold than timid.

If desired, the collective lever can also be reduced when the nose is lowered. The amount of movement of both depends upon the height above ground in the real situation. The reason for the demonstration at a safe height is if you ever encounter the 'real thing', the recognition of the symptoms should be immediate, and the recovery action instinctive - lower the nose and get out of there.

Wrong Advice

One military manual on helicopter aerodynamics boldly states:

- "Recovery from vortex ring state may be initiated during the early stages of vortex ring state by putting on a large amount of excess power."

Wrong, and for several reasons-

- The early stages are often not identified - if you were smart enough to identify the early stages, you probably wouldn't be in the bad position in the first place.
- Secondly, there is no gauge in the cockpit to tell you if you are in the 'early', 'middle' or 'too-late' stages.
- At the wrong time, applying on excess power will only make the matter worse
- What if you don't have any excess power?

I am surprised they have any helicopters remaining with advice like that.

In simple terms - vortex ring state is most likely to be encountered whenever the helicopter is placed downwind at low speed out of ground effect. Watch out on approaches where the wind is changing, or you are not certain of the wind direction or speed! If you feel strange vibrations, have uncommanded pitch, roll or yaw, boldly put the nose down and get airspeed to stay away from the vortex ring state.

Vortex ring can happen in other times and places as well. A very aggressive flare in calm winds or with a tail wind can definitely set you up for a surprise.

The Why of Vortex Ring State

Having covered the from–the–cockpit symptoms and recovery actions, now it's time for the theory of how vortex ring state happens.

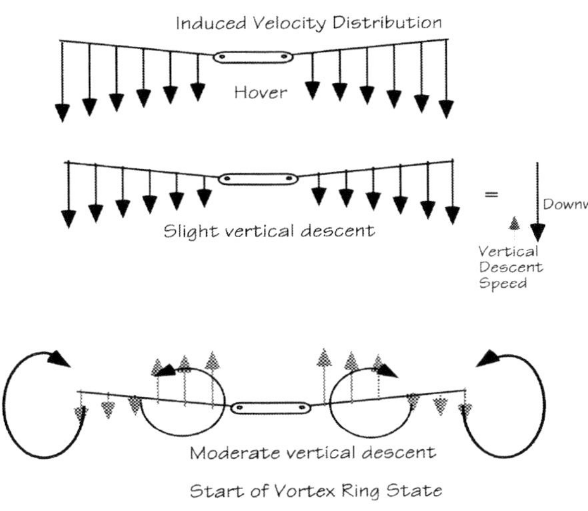

Figure 19-3 Vortex Ring State Conditions

Figure 19-3a shows the a very basic way of understanding how vortex ring state is likely to be formed. The vertical speed where things start to go wrong is about the same as the induced velocity of the rotor - this is another way of saying the conditions for vortex ring will be different for different weights, density altitudes and so on, as well as different for different helicopter models. Figure 19-3b expands on this situation.

Literally, vortex ring state is descending through the rotor downwash, and results in the helicopter trying to eat its own wake. Conditions when it may happen are not easily repeatable, and have often struck without warning.

Why The Symptoms?

Low frequency airframe vibrations are likely because the interactions between the downflowing induced velocity and the upflowing rate of descent are producing turbulence that is hitting the fuselage and causing things which normally have air flowing smoothly past them to resonate. Windows and other large panels are like sheets of tin and can make quite significant amounts of noise.

Uncommanded pitch roll and yaw is due to the sudden disappearance of either downwash or rate of descent in one part of the rotor disk, or large parts of the disk. If the rotor suddenly has a large change in the airflow, there will be a change in the drag that the engine may take some time to correct. The balance in yaw has been upset and the nose of the helicopter will move. The pitching can be due to air striking the horizontal stabilizer changing suddenly from hitting it on the top to hitting it on the bottom.

Preventing Vortex Ring State

The best prevention is to be aware of the conditions that can provoke the situation, and avoid those conditions. The most common condition is an approach with a tailwind. If you have been unsuccessful in avoiding the conditions, then control the rate of descent to stay out of the most likely cause. If you can't avoid using a rate of descent that could get you into trouble, then know what the symptoms are, and how to recover when the symptoms appear.

Rollover

Too many helicopters fall on their side and beat themselves (and sometimes the crew and passersby) to death. Why? There are at least two ways this can happen - statically or dynamically.

Static Rollover

Static rollover is necessary to consider when landing on slopes and discharging passengers or cargo. It occurs any time when a line drawn vertically (with respect to the earth) through the center of gravity of an object falls outside the base of the object. Basically, a line drawn down from center of gravity of the helicopter must lie within the width of the undercarriage. Otherwise the helicopter may roll over. Figure 19-4 shows this graphically.

Static rollover is relatively rare, but it is possible. I know of one helicopter type that used to be frequently landed on slopes well outside the published limits - the maneuver was accomplished by doing a coordinated flare to stop on the slope, either sideways or nose up the slope. Power (thrust) was always held at a high setting while on the ground. Taking off required accelerating off the slope - what the pilots didn't seem to realize was if they shut down on the slope, the helicopter would have fallen over.

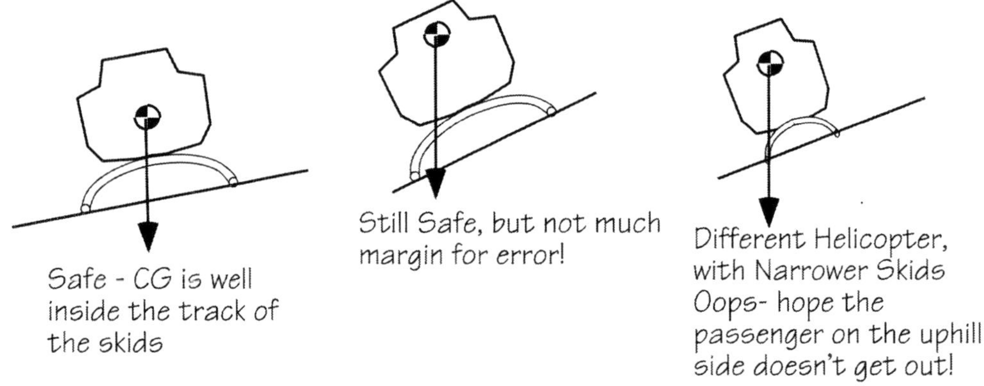

Figure 19-4 Static Rollover

The angle for static rollover for most helicopters is well outside the limits for landing off-level, but this introduction to rollover needed to start somewhere simple...

Dynamic Rollover

Dynamic rollover is more frequent than static rollover, and has the potential to affect nearly all helicopters. From the accident summaries, dynamic rollover appears to most affect teetering rotor designs. The explanation for this is that moving the cyclic stick laterally on articulated or hingeless rotor heads generates a rolling moment*, which can affect the fuselage and stop a roll rate. Moving the cyclic stick laterally on the teetering rotor helicopter tilts the disk and thrust vector, but nothing more†. The teetering rotor head must wait for the thrust vector to persuade the fuselage to move, and the fuselage is stuck to the ground.

Dynamic rollover is different from static rollover in that there is rolling motion involved, caused by the introduction of rotor thrust. While dynamic rollover appears to be most common when taking off or landing on slopes, it can also occur on flat ground. There are two basic ways to look at dynamic rollover - on landing and on takeoff (It can also happen on level ground on takeoff).

Dynamic Rollover on Landing

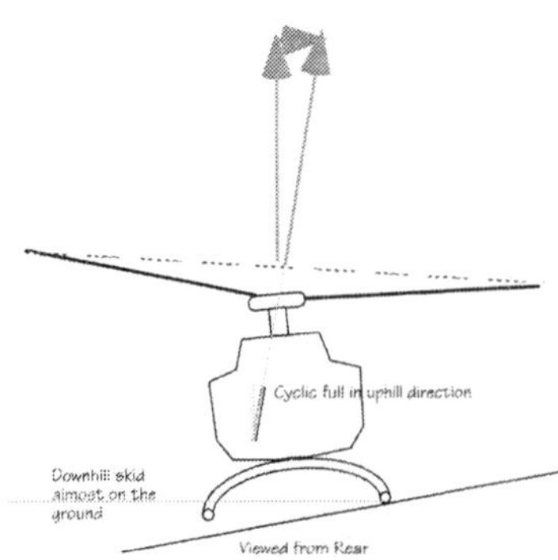

Figure 19-5 Dynamic Rollover

Dynamic rollover on landing can occur in the following situation. The helicopter has landed on a slope and has one skid on the ground, but there is not enough lateral cyclic stick travel to keep the rotor disk level with the horizon, nor to control the roll rate to put the other skid on the ground in a controlled manner. Figure 19-5 shows this situation.

When landing in this condition, if the roll rate is kept under control, there is little likelihood of rolling over. If however, there is not sufficient lateral cyclic stick to hold the skids level, then think twice about letting the skid settle onto the slope - you may not be able to stop the helicopter toppling over. If you can't stop the roll rate at a constant collective lever position, the helicopter will certainly roll when collective lever is lowered, and there is a smaller thrust vector to be tilted.

* See "Hinges" on page 229 for more details on how this works.
† This is explained in more detail in Chapter 23,"Advanced Helicopter Aerodynamics".

In our example helicopter, the effect of the tail rotor thrust on dynamic rollover must also be considered, since the helicopter hovers slightly left wing down. Lets say this is 2° left wing down in a neutral lateral CG condition. In this case, the tail rotor thrust acting to the right may help if landing with the right skid up the slope (as there is less change in roll attitude), and may make things worse if landing with the left skid up the slope (more change in roll attitude).

Of course, side and rear winds further complicate the matter, adding side force to the fuselage, changing the power required to hover, and so on. Lateral cyclic stick has to do more than just take care of the roll rate - it must also take care of tail rotor thrust when the helicopter is balanced on one skid.

Dynamic Rollover on Takeoff

While the most common cause of this all–too–frequent occurrence is mismanagement of the cyclic, it can be induced by the lateral CG being displaced, or even out of limits.

Taking off is much the same problem. If the thrust vector isn't vertical (or slightly into the hill), there is going to be a horizontal component of thrust that faces downhill and tends to rotate the helicopter towards the downhill side. Since a vertical line from the CG is probably close to passing through the downhill skid anyway, it is likely that as collective lever is increased to lift-off, and both components of thrust increase, the helicopter may roll about the downhill skid.

Basically, takeoff dynamic rollover is due to the thrust vector held away from vertical and outside the width of the landing gear. When the helicopter is holding only one skid in contact with the ground, and that the uphill skid, - all the moments start to react around that point, as opposed to the CG. If the CG of the helicopter is out of limits, it takes a lot of lateral cyclic stick and horizontal component of thrust to counteract that, while the skid is in contact with the ground. If there is a side wind, this must be taken into account, and it is now acting through the point of contact with the ground.

One Skid Stuck on the Ground

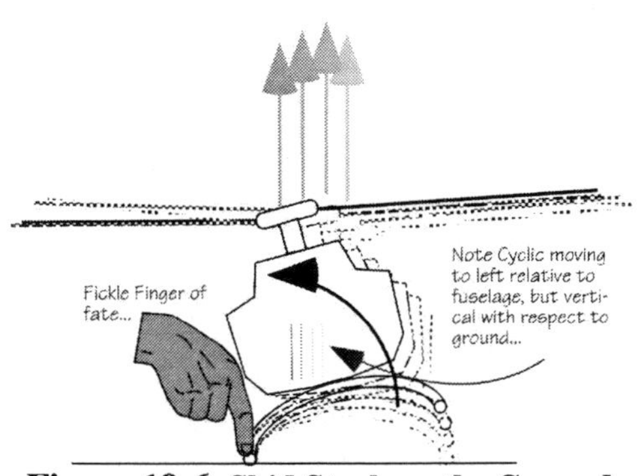

Figure 19-6 Skid Stuck on the Ground

An all–too–common problem is snagging of skids, either under a hard crust of snow, or with stray cables. A skid that has sunk into the mud, or even soft asphalt can want to stay there. The end result of a too–rapid lift-off in this case is nearly always a helicopter on its side, and possibly a pilot looking for a job. Why does it happen? Figure 19-6 shows one way of looking at it. In words, the problem is that the thrust vector is going to work around the point of contact on the ground, as opposed to the CG. Tilting the thrust vector won't help much as the thrust vector must still work around the pivot point (not the CG of the helicopter), and unless the pilot removes the thrust vector quickly, (i.e. lower the collective lever immediately) the result is a foregone conclusion.

Action in Event of Dynamic Rollover

If you are unfortunate enough to encounter dynamic rollover, it's too late to start thinking about what you are going to do. Plan for it for every lift-off and landing, on slopes or level ground. A collapse of the landing gear, or landing platform and so on, can all turn a normal landing place into a slope landing in an instant - know what to do before it happens, as it's far too late when the angle of bank gets too high!

In most cases, the only solution is to rapidly lower collective lever and get rid of the thrust vector. In this book it is impossible to cater for all possibilities, so the only advice, besides prudence, is to take things carefully.

Lift-off should always be a slow, deliberate maneuver - the sermon on this was issued earlier. A slow, deliberate lift-off is particularly useful if the ground is soft, or the helicopter is on skis in the snow, or the platform has any obstacles on it. Wires can get wrapped around the tail end of skids.

Pay close attention to lateral cyclic position and don't get close to the edge of control. If you can't move the cyclic laterally, you're on the control stops, and you have no more roll authority.

As a matter of interest, model helicopter pilots have an interesting way of learning their very difficult method of flying, and it is related to rollover. They tie two long, thin bamboo poles together in the form of a cross and attach these to the undercarriage of the model helicopter, sort of like training wheels on a bicycle. How we would do this in full size helicopters needs exploring...

Retreating Blade Stall

Retreating blade stall is encountered infrequently in modern helicopters, as flight envelopes and hydraulic systems keep most of the symptoms at bay. It is the most limiting aspect of high–speed helicopters. The reason is that the retreating half of the disk must produce the same amount of lift as the advancing side, but it is a losing battle. The higher the forward speed, the greater the angle of attack of the retreating blade sections must be, but this makes them operate closer to the stall angle of attack, and so on.

If you observe the limits of the FM, you will never get into retreating blade stall - or can you?

More than one light helicopter can encounter retreating blade stall, within the limitations of the FM. Let's review the causes.

The main cause of retreating blade stall is too high an angle of attack on the retreating blade (hence the name of the phenomenon). The blade stalls (lift ceases to increase and drag increases as the AoA increases) and very large nose down pitching moments are produced on the blade. For at least one helicopter, these forces can be strong enough to overpower the hydraulic system. Since we're in a light training helicopter without hydraulics on the flight controls, we'd feel strong feedback forces in the cyclic stick and collective lever.

In more technical terms, the causes can be any one (or all) of:

- too high airspeed,
- too high collective lever angle,
- too much forward tilt to the tip path plane (possibly due to the CG being too far aft, requiring the retreating blade to be at a more pronounced mechanical pitch angle and hence AoA than a forward CG would give), and
- N_R too low.

You will notice, if you are comparing this book to other books that I've not put in two commonly quoted causes such as high gross weight or high G maneuvering, as these are not really 'causes', but contributors. High gross weight by itself won't put you into retreating blade stall, but having too high an airspeed for the collective angle (which would result from trying to hold an airspeed too high for the weight) would. High G maneuvering is not itself a cause, as you can turn pretty steeply and generate a lot of G at a low airspeed and not get into trouble. High G loading is only a problem at high speeds, and again is a product of several things, such as too high an airspeed for the collective angle (you need collective angle to generate any G loadings).

The results in the cockpit are varied - the first hint of trouble might be a one per rev vertical bounce, (as each blade will stall at a slightly different angle or react in a different way) or a stiffening of the controls (notable especially in one helicopter without hydraulics - the collective lever wants to move down (probably a good thing), on another helicopter with low pressure hydraulics, the cyclic stick and collective lever get very stiff). At this first hint of trouble, reduce the severity of what ever it is you are doing (going too fast, pulling out from a dive, etc.) - if you don't stop now, the next events are going to be slightly worse.

When fully developed retreating blade stall occurs, the retreating blade is not producing as much lift as it was just before the stall - but the advancing blade is still working - and the result is a roll toward the retreating side, which is accompanied by a pitch-up of the nose, since everything happens 90° later. The two can be quite violent, and means the pilot no longer has control of the flight path of the helicopter - a less than ideal situation.

Recovery at the first signs of retreating blade stall is straightforward - lower the collective, stop pulling back on the cyclic* (and for helicopters without governors, increase the N_R).

I had occasion, as part of a larger set of trials, to look at the onset of retreating blade stall in a helicopter particularly prone to the problem. The symptoms at V_{NE} started with only slightly more than 1G (with a moderate pullout at high density altitude), and as density altitude reduced, we could go to higher G levels at the same TAS before the symptoms appeared. Finally, we were able to get reasonable G levels before we ran into the symptoms - at the higher density altitudes, we could get retreating blade stall at some quite low airspeeds.

Others have reported some quite mild symptoms - increased forces on the collective lever prior to increased cyclic stick forces. Some helicopters develop large enough forces on the collective lever that the pilot can't maintain collective lever position and the situation self-corrects.

Symptoms

The symptoms of retreating blade stall are, in order of occurrence: vibrations, possibly a 'bounce' in the airframe, possibly a roughness in the cockpit controls as the blade pitching moments from the retreating blade feed through the flight control system, ineffectiveness or stiffening of the controls, pitching up of the nose and rolling in the direction of the stalling side. Not all of these will occur in all helicopters - underslung (or teetering) rotor systems, for example, are self-correcting in this area - if retreating blade stall occurs, the blades even themselves out.

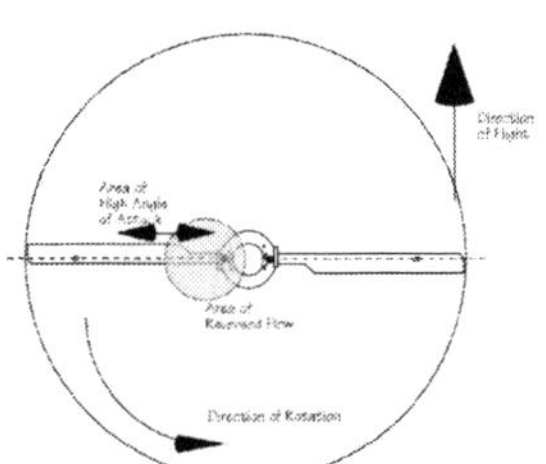

Figure 19-7 Retreating Blade Stall

Obviously too high a forward speed will cause the problem. The retreating blade cannot produce enough lift.

I have heard of one instructor who would regularly exceed V_{NE} to show students the effect of retreating blade stall on his light helicopter. Words fail to express the degree of stupidity he demonstrated or the effect of his message (limits don't really mean anything) to the students.

Blade Sailing

Watch the stopped main rotor blades of a helicopter sitting in the wind to understand how much they react to low airspeeds, producing lift even in a light breeze. This can cause problems when starting and shutting down.

During every start and shutdown, there is a time when the blades of the helicopter are literally out of control. There is not enough centrifugal force to make them stay horizontal, and the rotor controls of cyclic stick and collective lever are ineffective due to the low speed, or perhaps lack of hydraulic pressure. During this time, the blades can be influenced by winds and do rather unexpected things. They will flap up if they encounter a wind acting on the leading edge, and at slow enough rotational speeds, may also flex alarmingly. This flapping and flexing can lead to the blades hitting tail booms, and so on. Even fitting droop and flap restrainers ("Droop Stops / Flap Restrainers" on page 226) may not prevent the blades flexing too much.

Despite the best intentions of many people, it has proven impossible to provide fool-proof advice on how to prevent this problem for all helicopters. Some larger machines with rotor brakes can start engines against the rotor brake, and pre-load with enough power so that when the rotor brake is released, the blades spin up so quickly that excess flapping is avoided. Of course, a rotor brake will assist in preventing blade flapping during the shutdown.

I had occasion during some trials to see how effective the wind was at turning rotors when on the ground. We had to shut down a Chinook with the tail into wind, which was about 20 knots. After the engines had stopped, the rotors kept on turning, slowly, but still turning at about 20 RPM due to the wind hitting the front rotor, which had a very pronounced forward tilt to it. We gave up after 10 minutes and used the rotor brake to stop it.

* Except for tandem rotor machines, see Chapter 35,"Other Helicopter Types"

The relative direction of the wind when you land can be important, depending on your helicopter type. If you have a two bladed rotor system, you may be better off landing with the wind to one side, as opposed to directly on the nose. The logic for this is dictated by the chance of the blade flexing down and hitting the tail boom.

If the wind is on the nose, then as the rotor blade slows down, the relative airspeed can cause the lift to change quite dramatically. If a gust suddenly causes the advancing blade to see an increase in speed, it will flap up and be at it's highest at the front of the helicopter. Unfortunately, this will also mean the lowest part will be at the back, just where some inconsiderate designer put the tailboom. Some manufacturers give specific advice in this matter, but not all do. Those which do speak on the subject seem to recommend putting the wind at 7 to 8 o'clock.

Summary of Chapter 19

This chapter has covered quite a few of the peculiar things that occur because of the freedom of action of the helicopter, and because of the nature of rotary wing aerodynamics.

The next chapter covers the flight manual and its mysteries.

Flight Manuals, Rules and Regulations

Why?

I'm writing about the Flight Manual because there are lot of people who are flying who don't understand the implications of the flight manual, and if you learn some of the subtle points early, you may avoid embarrassment.

*The Civilian Flight Manual**

In a legal sense, most countries require the pilot to be responsible for knowing all the necessary information to safely complete each flight. This includes knowing the limitations as well as the normal and emergency operating procedures for the helicopter. This information is typically found in the Flight Manual (FM) and may be supplemented by ground school or factory training supplements. The FM is the legal document for information relating to the helicopter and in most countries is required to be carried in the helicopter.

The FM will not teach the pilot how to fly in general, nor specific piloting techniques for the machine, and is certainly no substitute for sound judgment. Even so, prior to your first flight in any helicopter, a thorough read of the FM is essential.

Sections of the FM

Each helicopter type has a slightly different FM layout, but in general, the FM should have the following arrangement:

Certification Authority 'Approved' Sections

These are sections the certification or regulatory authority (Federal Aviation Administration (FAA) in the USA, Transport Canada (TC) in Canada, Civil Aviation Authority (CAA) in the United Kingdom, etc.) approves. We'll call such authorities the *Regulatory Authority* (*RA*) This covers all the information required by the RA for operation†. The chapters in this section include:

Approved Pages

If you look at the bottom or top of most pages in the first section of the FM, you may see the words "RA Approved". This means the manufacturer is required to provide this information and RA has to ensure it is correct. This legend may not appear on every page, particularly in the performance section. It will not appear on pages in the 'Manufacturer's Data' sections.

Miscellaneous Administrative Pages

Title, Table of Contents, Amendment Log, List of Current Pages - all of these are designed to make sure the information is all there, and up to date.

Limitations

This section is definitely an 'Approved' section.

This section includes the limitations on operation, (such as crew or VFR only) plus engine, airframe, rotor, weight and CG and other system limitations. Normally the markings that should appear on the flight instruments is also included as well as the placards that will be in various places in the aircraft. For some large helicopters (certified under FAR 29), the Height Velocity (HV) curve is in the limitations section‡. Note the weight and balance limitations are shown here, but the method of calculating them may not be in this first, 'Approved' section.

---

* Military FMs are covered later - they are generally more complex and have much more information, particularly performance–related and systems descriptions.

† A subtle note- this is *all* the authority requires. It may not be all you would like or need to know, but it's all the authority requires.

‡ The reasons for this will be detailed in "Part 29 Helicopters and the HV Curve" on page 338.

Note the words at the beginning of the section say 'mandatory', 'required', etc.

•

Caution

Be aware that exceeding these limitations (such as overloading the helicopter) will invalidate the certificate of airworthiness, leaving the pilot somewhat alone from a liability point of view, since the insurance is invalid without a valid certificate of airworthiness!

Normal Procedures

This is an 'Approved' section.

This section will include the normal procedures for a flight. Typically, these will be checks required for pre-flight, engine start, systems, takeoff, cruise, approach, landing, shutdown and any miscellaneous operations. The contents of this section would form the basis of any checklists the pilot might wish to make up.

Emergency Or Abnormal Procedures / Malfunction Procedures

This is an 'Approved' section.

This section is self–explanatory - it details the emergency procedures to be followed should any of the situations described arise. Normally, it does not differentiate between what are critical emergencies and non-critical ones.

Emergency Definitions

A brief word here about some definitions.

Land Immediately

For many helicopters, a serious omission from the emergency section is the definition of 'Land Immediately'. Some manufacturers I've talked with have said even though they know there should be 'Land Immediately' emergencies, they are under pressure from their legal (and marketing) personnel to not put them in, as it gives the impression the helicopter is unsafe. Hogwash.

'Land Immediately' means to put the helicopter down, under control, prior to losing control or power to the rotor. Landing in trees if over unbroken forest, or ditching in the water, or on the least pointy bit of rock, but under control, are all preferable to pressing on and discovering the transmission really has broken up, or you really are out of fuel, or the fire won't go out...

You should consider any confirmed dual indication of transmission failure (such as loss of pressure on both gauge and warning light, plus unusual noises, possibly high transmission oil temperature etc.) as being serious enough you don't want to fall out of the sky with the blades stopped. The 'Land Immediately' emergencies, if not included in your flight manual, ought to be.

Land As Soon as Practical

This means land at the nearest suitable landing site, which may not be particularly convenient, but landing is more prudent than continuing.

Land as Soon as Possible

This means land at the nearest approved landing site. Continued flight is not a problem, but you don't want to prolong your exposure.

Notes, Cautions and Warnings

These are ways the manufacturer has of bringing your attention to some specific information that might otherwise slip your notice.

Notes

Notes are meant to draw attention to an operating procedure or condition it is essential to highlight

Cautions

Cautions are slightly stronger than notes. They are intended to show an operating procedure or practice which if not strictly observed could result in damage to or destruction of property. Not following the recommended procedure could be expensive.

Warnings

Warnings are the most serious. They point out areas where there exists the danger of damage to equipment, injury to personnel or possibly even death could occur if the procedures are not followed.

Procedural Words

In most manuals, the exact definitions that the manufacturer intended are for some words are laid out. Evidently some people can't read dictionaries or understand basic English.

- Shall -a mandatory word. You *must* do this.
- Should - a recommended word. It would be a good idea to do this
- May or Need Not - the procedure is optional
- Will - something that is going to happen in the future.

Having helped in a small way to make sure flight manuals and procedures clear, I can assure you that a great deal of care is taken in making sure the words are used correctly.

Performance Data

This section, may contain pages that are 'RA Approved' as well as non-approved pages. The information is normally only the bare minimum in civilian manuals, and starts with the power assurance or topping checks for turbine engines (to ensure it is operating at its minimum rated output). There is no easy way to check the power of the piston engine while it is installed in the aircraft. Further pages and charts deal with hover performance (normally ability to hover IGE and OGE) and takeoff and landing and climb performance, and possibly the HV curve. There should be a chart of airspeed corrections.

The performance data in the flight manual will be slightly conservative, or it should be. The manufacturers don't want to sell you a machine that will not meet the performance they are saying the machine will have, and the certification authorities will spot check this to make sure the data shown is conservative. As the labels on the car fuel economy stickers say- "your mileage may vary...", but at least you'll be varying on the safe side.

Don't believe those who say the manufacturers pad the data to make their machine look good. The Certification Police (oops, regulatory authorities) make sure it is capable of being met by a properly maintained machine. I've delayed approving charts because the helicopter originally wouldn't do what the manufacturer's chart said it would do.

No Altimeter Correction Charts

As an interesting aside, it is worth noting no Western helicopters have altimeter correction charts in the FM, simply because it's not required by regulations. The fixed wing manuals for later aircraft do require these charts that tell you how far off the altimeter is (notwithstanding the perennial ± 50' error permitted). Also noted without comment is the fact someone has blessed helicopter ILS approaches with a much lower than fixed-wing decision height of 200' (legally one must base this height above ground using the barometric altimeter...)

Flight Manual Supplements (FMS)

...are often a source of confusion. Supplements contain information relating to modifications* to that helicopter, and how they affect the basic FM. For example, if an air conditioning unit is installed, and it did not form the basis of the original certification, then it is optional equipment. If you have such optional equipment, then the appropriate FMS must be put in your FM. The supplement on this kit would have sections dealing with changes in the limitations, normal operating procedures, emergencies, performance and so on. Trolling through these supplements is often a time consuming and difficult process, but necessary.

* But not necessarily all the modifications that are possible.

A problem is that it is often impossible to co-relate the data if two or more optional equipments are installed. For example, particle separators and an air conditioning can both be installed, but what is the total effect on performance*?

Since there literally thousands of possible combinations of optional equipment, it would be pointless to try to cross check every combination would work. The RA's job would be impossible, but the way out is to put the responsibility for compatibility with equipment already installed on the shoulders of the installer. You'd better hope they know what they're doing...

The other problem with FMS's is they confuse the heck out of checklists printed in the Normal and Emergency sections of the basic FM. If you have more than one piece of additional equipment added, the results can be pretty hectic. Another good reason to make up your own checklist.

Weight and Balance Information

This includes the information necessary to calculate the weight and CG for each flight. It should include a date of the last basic weighing, and the equipment included in that weight. There may also be tables for ease of calculation. Having calculated the weight and balance, it's necessary to verify its within the limitations laid out in the 'Approved' section. Since every civil helicopter will be different, this section often has the data from the technical log weight and balance inserted here for convenience.

Manufacturer's Data

This section is the information the manufacturer considers important for safe operation, but is not important enough to worry the certification authority about. It includes additional information to help in operating the helicopter. Note the subtle difference - this is a section that is not 'approved' by the certification authority-it doesn't mean it's wrong, just the certification authority has no legal requirement for data in this section.

Systems Descriptions

These may be included to help in troubleshooting problems related to say, the electrical system or hydraulic system, and normally include detailed schematic drawings.

As an aside here, I am amazed the rest of the flight manual can go to amazing lengths to detail limitations, fuel and oil quantities and emergency procedures, most of which are already on the instruments or placards and then go a long way in the opposite direction (i.e. no information) for other installed equipment. The number of times I have been given a new helicopter to fly and couldn't find out how to operate the radios or intercom equipment is beyond a laughing matter. There is no requirement to put this information in the flight manual in any section - how can this be?

Handling Servicing and Maintenance Instructions

This is where the information on daily inspections, fuel and oil requirements, servicing points, etc., might be included, as well as dimensions of doors, overall sizes, etc.

Supplemental Performance Information

This is for any additional information the manufacturer may consider appropriate, such as basic range and endurance figures, and so on. Note this is not necessarily certificated data, and may not be appropriate to the particular modification state of the helicopter!

Individualized Copy of the FM

Each helicopter will have its own personalized copy of the FM. This is due to the requirement for individual weight and balance for each machine, as well as the different modifications and supplements that might be installed. Even within the same fleet, different modification standards will make small, but important changes to the weight and CG position, and so each machine will require its own copy. The main section that will be different is the weight and CG part. There's another good reason for the individualized copy of the FM - most countries require a copy of the FM be carried in the helicopter at all times.

* Sometimes its difficult to find this out - other times its impossible.

Some Philosophical Words about the Civilian FM

The first thing that must be understood about the flight manual for most civilian helicopters is it contains the minimum information needed to operate the helicopter. This is due to the requirements of the FAA (who have been the leaders in helicopter certification, at least in terms of number of types certified, as well as being the first to carry out helicopter certification). The FAA's mandate concerning legislation has an interesting rule, namely, they may only make the minimum regulations for safety. This has translated over the years to much useful information not required from an absolute safety point of view being omitted from of the FM.

An example is range information. How far will this helicopter go with a full load of fuel? If you have tried to find the information, it's probably not in the 'Approved' section - it wasn't required by the certification authority, who quite frankly, aren't worried about it. From a safety point of view, the RA* doesn't care what the range of the helicopter is - only if it can takeoff at a given weight. If you think this is unfair, and picks on helicopters, fixed–wing aircraft, including Boeing 747s do not have range information in the 'Approved' section of the flight manual (it may appear elsewhere in the FM). The RA is only interested in the ability to takeoff and land and to meet certain climb gradients.

Put another way, it's standard practice to crucify the pilot that runs out of fuel, or doesn't land with sufficient reserves, but is given no good way to obtain the information on how much fuel will be required.

There is a very good reason for not putting range information in the 'Approved' section FM. Any external change, such as adding pop-out floats with their additional drag, would make a nonsense of any basic airframe range information. Even a set of seemingly harmless external protuberances can adversely affect the range, and if it was in the 'Approved' section, it would have to be re-certified, and re-printed for every little bump, bulge and add-on. This is expensive, time consuming and counter-productive.

The other sad fact is that anything in the flight manual can be used in a lawsuit. Manufacturers are very wary of including any information that can be used against them, and is not required by law.

A suggestion to get around this problem - get a good fuel flow meter, hook it up to your GPS and think about the way to determine best range airspeed.

All those negative things having been said, the FM is still better than nothing, and provides a very good basic and often very concise indication of the limitations necessary to fly the helicopter.

Another point about the FM. It is required to be carried in the helicopter at all times, but why? For most light helicopters, it's not likely that the pilot would take it out to refer to it at all- not enough hands, and not enough time available. It's certainly no help in an emergency- if you have to look up the procedure in the FM (or even in your own home-grown checklist), then you're in a lot worse trouble than you thought.

More Philosophy...

What is required to obeyed in the flight manual? The words in the introduction to each section provide some clue. The Limitations section says that observing the limitations in this section is mandatory, required by law, etc., so that's pretty obvious. (As if other discussions in this book don't make it clear why obeying these limits is a good idea.) Performance data is pretty hard to make up yourself, so you should pay attention to what is there. The other sections (Normal and Emergency procedures) are noticeably silent in the saying whether it is mandatory to follow the procedures therein. It's a good idea to follow what's there, but, well, the best I can say is 'those who have ears, let them hear'.

* I don't want to pick on the FAA; all the other certification authorities have about the same attitude.

Certification Basis

A quick word hear about the certification basis for helicopters. Any aircraft is certified according to the requirements of some regulation, such as FAR 27 or 29. Older helicopters were certified to CAR 6 or 7. As of this writing, there is one other new certification basis being proposed in Europe, for very light (less than 450 kg.) helicopters, called Very Light Rotorcraft (VLR).

What is not commonly known, is that for the rest of the life of that helicopter model, it only has to meet the requirements* that existed when it was first certified. Thus, for the Bell 47, which was certified under CAR 6, it only has to ever meet those certification rules, to the amendment status in force at the date of application for certification.

So what? Well, the reason this is mentioned is that the different certification requirements will determine what information will be put in the flight manual. Early models only required hover in ground effect performance, for example.

Reasons for Rules

Having operated in three different military environments, and several different civilian organizations, I can state with some confidence that nearly every rule in every rule book is the result of an accident or problem. Being written by fallible humans, the rules attempt to cover every situation, and often fail miserably, resulting in a great deal of frustration and stress. Every rule was placed with good intentions, and whether you know the reason for the rules or not, do your level best to obey them.

Be prepared to justify your actions if you can't obey the rule, and most rational people will listen if you have a good reason for breaking the written word.

Besides, as a friend of mine said 'There must be order in the universe.'

Having said that, it is worth remembering that in an emergency, rules can be broken. Don't break a rule and then claim it was an emergency, but remember that rules don't apply when your life is in danger...

Two more Pet Peeves

Earlier in the book, the terms 'takeoff' and 'landing' were mentioned as being less than clearly defined. It would be nice to see someone somewhere come up with a precise definition of this for all the regulations that talk about takeoff and landing.

The other legal definitions that give me a problem are 'taxi', 'air taxi' and 'hover taxi'. Defined as two different items, it's hard for us pilots to keep them separate. Wish someone would straighten this out.

Reasons for Limitations

There are a whole host of reasons for many of the limitations in the flight manual and it would be impossible to cover them all here. The best thing that could be said is that there is normally a good reason for any limitation, else the manufacturer or certification agency wouldn't put it there. It is necessary to respect those limits, from a legal, if not practical viewpoint.

That is not to say there is no margin in most limitations - but how much of a margin is a matter the manufacturers and certification authorities are keeping to themselves. Don't you think the manufacturers would like you to have the most performance possible within the bounds of safety? The margins are there to protect against infrequent, inadvertent excursions beyond the red line. The manufacturers and certification authorities know we are human†.

There doesn't exist an experienced helicopter pilot who hasn't broken a rule, or inadvertently exceeded a limitation and got away with it. This often leads to a cavalier attitude to rules and limits. "Agust made me exceed Vne by 2 knots the other day, and nothing happened - does that mean Vne isn't really Vne? - how fast can I go?"

Don't go looking to deliberately break limitations - such an attitude must not be allowed to persist - because there is no-one who has broken a physical law and not paid the price. How far beyond the limitation are those unbreakable physical laws? Best not to find out...

* There are some retroactive regulations for things like seat belts.

† Aliens have probably already sorted out self–limiting helicopters

For example, the chief pilot of one manufacturer passed on the following story. Two pilots flew into the plant and after coffee, asked the chief pilot 'What's the real top speed of our helicopter?' The chief pilot responded with the FM limits.

'No, no, no', said the two men, with a conspiratorial wink, 'what's the real top speed?" Again the same response from the chief pilot.

'OK,' said the two men, 'perhaps we have a failure to communicate - how fast has it been tested to?'

'Not much faster than the FM limit, just enough for certification purposes,' said the chief pilot. 'There's a margin there for airspeed indicator calibration errors, and slight gusts, but it's not for everyday use. The V_{NE} is the V_{NE} published.'

'Perhaps you don't understand,' said the two men - 'We just cruised in here from the last fuel stop at 30 knots above the published V_{NE}, using takeoff power (more than allowed in cruise in this machine), and it was smooth as silk.' (For this helicopter, the V_{NE} was below what could be achieved with takeoff power). After the chief pilot stopped choking on his coffee, he tried to convince these two there was good reasons for the V_{NE} published in the FM, but he was sure they weren't listening.

Sadly, he related that the tail fell off that very helicopter some weeks later, but legally nothing could ever be proved that the higher than permitted speed was the cause. 'Nuff said? How would you like to take over the machine these two pilots had just flown?

Another Way of Thinking About Limitations

I don't wish to encourage the wrong attitude towards regulations or limitations. My experience, as well as that of nearly every other pilot is that we have all:

- broken rules (when no one was watching or could tell we were breaking rules, or perhaps we were ignorant of the rules to begin with...)
- busted limitations (inadvertently or perhaps with malice and forethought), but not generally by much or for a long time.

None of us has ever been able to break a physical law. Limitations, inevitably, come down to physical laws. Whether someone is watching or not, breaking limitations will eventually hurt. Metal doesn't forget, and one day, when you are least expecting it, abused metal will decide its had enough.

Stay within the limitations and try to obey rules.

Side Wind, Sideward Flight and All That

There is a lot of confusion about what the limits of the helicopter are when operating in the low airspeed environment. Terms such as sideward flight and rearward flight are used to the confusion of many. What do these terms mean?

There is one way to put things in perspective. Does the helicopter know it is moving with respect to the earth, or does it react with respect to the wind? The answer, obviously, is that the airframe only knows about the wind. The only part of the whole process that knows how things are going with respect to the earth is the pilot*.

A more correct term is side or rear wind. It should be obvious that this will take the combination of wind and helicopter movement with respect to the ground. For example, if the wind is 10 knots, and the helicopter is hovering over a spot on the ground with the left side to the wind, the relative wind will be 10 knots of left side wind. If the helicopter moves to the left at 10 knots of groundspeed in the same wind, then the relative wind will be 20 knots of left side wind.

Is it a Limit Because Its in the Limitations Section?

Mostly, the answer is yes. The numbers are pretty clear, the logic not hard to follow. There are some areas where the lines aren't so clear.

What does the phrase "The Hoverfly Helicopter has demonstrated hovering in winds of 17 knots from any direction" mean? Does the fact that this phrase is in the limitations section of the flight manual mean it's a limitation?

* Unless of course, there is some sensor measuring ground speed feeding the automatic flight control system.

The term "The helicopter has been demonstrated hovering in winds of 17 knots" has been derived from old certification requirements that only required this capability*. It did not mean that this figure of 17 knots was a limit, and it did not mean that the helicopter was capable of hovering with a great deal of control with a wind from the worst possible azimuth (whatever that direction was).

Modern certification criteria have addressed this problem with more detail, but still do not spell out what the limitations are exactly. For example, the limitation in the manual may or may not have some margin of tail rotor control remaining. Military requirements are slightly stiffer than civil requirements and have tail rotor control margins and rate of turn requirements in the maximum side and rear wind conditions.

What is meant by control margin? Simply, having some control travel remaining. In this case, the pedal should not be full against the stop in the worst side wind, as stated in the limitations section.

There are several helicopters that have handling problems within the area demonstrated for certification.

What advice can be given to the pilot about this? Pay attention to the wind, know where it is relative to the nose of the helicopter, learn how to judge its strength at any time, and know when to accept hovering with a side or rear wind. Know what you are going to do if the left pedal is full against the stop and the nose is still turning right!

Of course, on a more philosophical note, perhaps it's a good thing the limitations aren't well spelled out, because with the present airspeed indicating systems, the pilot would have no way of obeying them anyway!

Power Ratings and Limitations

What is meant by a power rating? What exactly does a 5 minute takeoff rating mean?

It means that when engaged in a takeoff (whatever that is), that power level may be used for up to 5 minutes. After 5 minutes, it is expected that the power level will be reduced to the next lower limitations (typically continuous power).

Does that mean that if you only climb 500' (and this takes 1 minute) that you can use the takeoff power rating for another 4 minutes to give you a higher cruise speed than you might have with continuous power? I wish I could give you a good answer, but all that can really be said is that if the manufacturer did not specify a maximum airspeed for the limitation, then by silence they are saying it's OK†.

Similarly, you can use 5 minute power for the necessary 5 minutes, and then reduce power for a brief period, and apply 5 minute power again...

This situation has been improved on some newer models of helicopters that incorporate cycle counters for different power levels. This will ensure that those who use the equipment will pay for it!

The Military Flight Manual

The military FM is completely different, and in most cases much more comprehensive than the civilian version. Typically, it has more detailed descriptions of the airframe, systems and so on, and much more performance information. One of the reasons for the greater performance information is that military fleets will have a great number of identically–equipped helicopters, and so it is relatively easy to make sure the data is there for each machine.

Another reason is that the FAA is only concerned with safety, and the military is concerned with safety, performance and military effectiveness.

Warnings, cautions and notes are typically more pronounced, and emergency procedures are separated into critical (often called bold-faced, which must be committed to memory) and non-critical emergencies.

That having been said, there is also a great tendency for the procedures for flying the helicopter to be detailed excessively. I used to jokingly say that one day we would see the following in the front of a military helicopter manual:

- "This manual covers the normal, emergency and wartime operation of the Neverfly helicopter. When read in conjunction with the related manuals and flying order books listed below (*a minimum of 10 should be listed*), it covers every conceivable situation that may be encoun-

* It actually was 20 m.p.h., which is 17 knots...

† I'll wait for the hollers of protest on this one, but if the manufacturers meant something else, they should say so, clearly.

tered. Only the procedures in this manual or the applicable references are to be used. In the unlikely event a situation is encountered which is not covered by this manual or the references, no action is to be taken without consulting higher authorities."

I stopped saying this some time ago, when I came across a military manual that said 'Procedures not listed in this manual are prohibited" - cold comfort for the crew who are doing what helicopters do best - being flexible.

Visual Flight Rules (VFR)

Most countries have a definition of VFR that is:

- A table of visibilities and distances from cloud that define the weather minima to be used for VFR.

So what? Well, what about when the visibility and clearance from cloud criteria have been met, but there is essentially nothing to look at to give the pilot references? I'm not talking about navigation references here- GPS and other navigation aids have solved the problem of how to find your way from A to B. I'm talking about things to look at to tell the pilot whether the helicopter is straight and level, turning, climbing, descending, etc.

Your on your way from Lower Rubber Boot to MiddleofNowhere, at night, when it is very clear, visibility greater than 50 miles, but high overcast clouds with no moon or stars visible. As if it's not bad enough to live in either the place you're flying from or to, it's worse in between, and there is not a single light on the ground. Do you have any references to tell whether you are straight and level or turning or even where you are?

What about if you are trying to fly in daylight over a snow covered lake, with legal visibility (but not great). Can you tell by looking outside if you're descending or climbing? Unfortunately history tells us more often than not, you don't have the necessary references.

VFR doesn't just mean having the visibility and cloud numbers- it means having something to orient the aircraft in pitch, roll and yaw, to determine if you're climbing or descending, turning and so on.

I'm not advocating the we need to file IFR for these conditions, as there are a lot of other problems associated with this (fuel reserves, need for an instrument approach at the other end etc.), but we do need to make sure we don't abuse the system and have the regulatory authorities step in to help us.

V Speeds

A lot of use has been made so far of a shorthand method of identifying some generic speeds. The following is a more complete list for helicopters

Shorthand	*Definition*
V_D	*Design Diving airspeed*
V_H	*Maximum speed in level flight with maximum continuous power*
V_{LE}	*Maximum speed with landing gear extended*
V_{LO}	*Maximum speed for operating landing gear*
V_{MINI}	*Minimum airspeed for instrument flight*
V_{NEI}	*Maximum speed for instrument flight*
V_{NE}	*Never Exceed Speed*
V_{TOSS}	*Takeoff Safety Speed for Category A Helicopter*
V_X	*Airspeed for best angle of climb*

Shorthand	*Definition*
V_Y	*Airspeed for maximum rate of climb*
V_{YI}	*Airspeed for climbing in IMC*

Summary of Chapter 20

This chapter has covered the FM, some rules and regulations that are common to most countries. The FM is important for not only basic understanding of how things work, but also from a legal point of view, covers the things the pilot must do to stay within the law. The rules and regulations touched on here are some of the ones that are often encountered and not well understood.

The next chapter will cover a wide range of subjects that don't conveniently fit anywhere else, and are of importance to the beginner helicopter pilot.

21 Miscellaneous

This chapter comes at the end of the 'Beginners Book'. Since there were a whole lot of things which didn't easily fit into the chapters, but needed to be said, they've ended up here.

Where the Pilot Sits

Helicopters are different from fixed wing airplanes in many ways. One of these is the normal location of the pilot in command's seat. In most fixed wing airplanes, it's on the left. In most helicopters, it's on the right. Why?

The real answer is probably lost in the mists of time which congregated around the birth of the helicopter, but normally reliable stories point to the first helicopter instructors having flown from the left seat, but with only one collective to be shared between the instructor and student, which the instructors had used with their right hand. The instructors had enough problems learning this new mode of flying, and didn't want to re-educate themselves at the same time as teaching new students. A decision was made to instruct from the left seat and equip the helicopter so it could be flown from the right seat. Later models incorporated a collective for the left seat, in the same relative location as for the right seat, that is, to the left of the seat. Just like the QWERTY keyboard, most of the world has stuck with it. There are several Western helicopters which can be flown from the left seat as pilot in command. All Russian helicopters have the pilot in command in the left seat.

Radios and Air Traffic Control

The radio in a helicopter works the same* as it does in a fixed–wing aircraft, but the inherent flexibility of the helicopter has somehow managed to befuddle the minds of quite a few Air Traffic Controllers. The number of strange (and sometimes impossible) things ATC has asked me to do because I was in a helicopter would fill several pages. Things such as hover at 1,000 feet above ground while I wait for a fixed–wing aircraft to takeoff below me when all I wanted was to cross the runway. Hovering IFR instead of doing a standard holding pattern, the list is pretty long. Most helicopter pilots of my acquaintance have had similar experiences, and as a result, we all tend to adopt a different way of dealing with Air Traffic Control than stiff–winged pilots.

This approach can best be summed up as 'positive communication'. It is better to tell Air Traffic what you want to do than ask them to decide for you. For example, if you want to cross the runway at an airfield with little other traffic and there are no set helicopter procedures, tell ATC you want to cross the runway at the mid–field. If you ask them for permission to cross the runway, then they make you go to one end or the other, and typically they will tell you this when you are very close to the runway, and you must make rapid turns (which may thrill your passengers, but is unlikely to win many friends).

A bit of experience will help with this, but ATC in general is equipped only to handle machines that takeoff and land on runways. Making helicopters follow these same rules is like making large trucks use railway tracks.

On a more pro-active approach, have a visit to the control tower and explain what you are trying to do. Eye-ball to eyeball contact over a cup of coffee works wonders. Something strange happens to communication when wires or radios get in the way.

Negative Radio

In busy training environments, the problem of Air Traffic Control has led to many helicopter traffic patterns† being conducted with 'negative radio calls'. In these situations only, it is not necessary to talk to ATC to lift-off, reposition, land and so on. Every pilot is expected to be responsible for separation and lookout, and it seems to work! It's especially enjoyable to do this when there is a mixed pattern of fixed–wing and rotary–wing, and the fixed–wing radio traffic is quite busy and full of frustration...

---

* and as well or as poorly, depending on your point of view

† circuits for some of you

Safety Statistics

Another interesting aspect of this problem with Air Traffic has to do with the relative number of movements that helicopters do. ATC involves quite a few statistics, and aircraft movements are one of these. In some countries, where it is necessary to pay for takeoffs and landings, not reporting these as movements may save the helicopter operator money, but it also means we don't get counted in the same way as fixed wing flights do.

Helicopters are viewed by most of the public as flimsy, unsafe machines. The truth is the opposite- we have slower speeds for operating close to the ground, with better view of what's going on in front and many more suitable landing areas than any fixed wing airplane. We can fly slowly when the visibility is poor, and in the event of things going wrong, normally can touchdown with very slow forward or vertical speed. On the minus side, helicopters operate in a much less prepared environment- landing on a highway at night, by the light of police cars to pick up accident victims is not something any fixed wing operator would routinely contemplate. With this flexibility comes a greater number of unknowns, and that's what causes most of the problems.

In terms of takeoffs and landings per flight hour, no other aircraft type can touch the helicopter. Since most accidents happen in takeoff or landing, that's why helicopters have such a high accident rate per flight hour. Accidents per takeoff/landing are actually quite a bit lower than fixed–wing - maybe because we do so many more of them...

Ground Handling Wheels

Nearly every light helicopter you are likely to fly in training uses skids for landing gear. This means some other way has to be found to get the helicopter moved around on the ground. The typical solution is ground handling wheels, which can be detached from the skids when the helicopter is flying, and attached only to move the machine in and out of hangars.*

Learn how to attach and detach these wheels the safe way - get it wrong and you may end up eating teeth!

Safety for Others

Your primary concern while flying the machine is for the safety of your passengers and yourself.

The helicopter is a dangerous machine, even when just sitting on the ground with the rotors turning. People get hurt walking into rotor blades and tail rotors with all too great a frequency. What is an easily visible object when still is an invisible meat grinder when turning. Various government agencies and industry associations have produced pamphlets and brochures to make sure passengers and other ground personnel get briefed properly. Rather than repeat their advice here, contact these agencies and see what they can offer - most are only too glad to help.

While you may wish to appear cool and casual about the briefings, there are very good reasons why you should prepared to spend the time and effort to ensure the passengers are well versed with the proceedings. The legal requirement will go away long before the pain of an accident to one of your passengers will slip from your mind or wallet.

Going Solo

If you haven't gone solo yet, reading this section first might help you. If you've already gone solo, it may help to recapture the magic.

The first time you go solo in any type of aircraft is a magical experience, and remembered for a lifetime. Going solo is a milestone to be treasured. Someone has trusted you enough to let you take this expensive and fragile piece of machinery out by yourself, and you can justifiably be proud of that. What awaits you?

In a light helicopter, aside from the magic, there is another aspect which makes for an interesting time.

* Interestingly, it also means that commercial helicopter pilots are much closer to their maintenance personnel than fixed wing types.

First of all, the helicopter will react differently. The weight will be less, so you'll require less power to hover, you'll accelerate more quickly, and descend more slowly. The pitch attitude in the hover will be more nose up, and the stick farther forward. The helicopter will seem to float a lot more when descending, and the view to the side the instructor normally sits on will be much better *. Those are the physical differences.

The mental differences shouldn't be that much different, but they are. There is no one in the other seat to keep an eye on you, to remind you to do things. There is also no-one there to block the view, or check that side is clear for turns!

Don't rush things, and don't do anything new and different. There will be time enough for new things later. More lecturing than this, your instructor has probably already given you. Congratulations!

Cross Country Flying

An essential part of your training and experience will be in cross country flying. This is not significantly more difficult than in a fixed wing airplane, except for the problem of how to handle maps and other material- prepare well in advance!

One point that is worth making- in a single engine helicopter, always, always, always have a place to land picked out. I hate flying single engine helicopters over forests- as one of my punish friends said- this is one area where the bark bites...

The cruise airspeeds of helicopters are relatively low, and with even a moderate wind can cause large drift angles to appear. Be prepared!

Another particular pet peeve of mine related to helicopters is the relative lack of suitable maps for our use. 1:500,000 scale maps (sectionals) are OK for cruising at several thousand feet above the ground at speeds over 100 Knots. They are not so great for trying to find Uncle Elmer's farm on Route 123. The Europeans have better maps at 1:250,000 scale. While these exist in North America, they do not have aeronautical information on them. Consider getting suitable maps for your local area if you do a lot of flying.

Single Seat and Ultralight helicopters

Helicopter flying is expensive, as anyone who has explored the subject in even the most brief manner will attest. In the last 5 years there has been an explosion in the number of ultra light helicopters on the market. Some take full advantage of the new materials and engines, and represent an interesting technology. It is easy to see the attraction of a light, inexpensive helicopter, and why these have grown in popularity and numbers. They certainly represent a more affordable way to achieve unrestricted aviation, but therein lies one of the problems. Some words of advice if you are contemplating buying/building/flying one.

Inexperienced Pilots Shouldn't Be Flying Them

The very people who want to own and fly ultra light helicopters, that is, the inexperienced, low time, hour–building pilots without much money, are the very ones who should not be flying them. This may sound unusually harsh. This is not because the pilots are stupid, mean or evil, nor that the machines are inherently unsafe or difficult to fly.

Given some of the laws of physics and materials, lightweight helicopters may have larger factors of safety in some parts than larger machines. The problem is that unless the helicopter has undergone a certification process (i.e. been tested and shown to conform to a recognized airworthiness standard), you don't know what you're buying. One light machine that has been popular sold as an kit-built helicopter suffered from control system failures - if the designer hadn't tested the control system to be able to stand up to the loads (plus a large factor of safety) that occur in operation, then how would you as the pilot know it was OK? Having the control system fail isn't something you want to experience, regardless of your flying time. A type certificate is your guarantee that it at least meets the minimum requirements shown by experience to be necessary for safe flight.

* At least, considering most of the helicopter instructors I had, but they were all male, and if I said anything more, it would be sexist...

The real problem with kit-built machines is that the inexperienced helicopter pilot can get into trouble very easily, and without an instructor to watch over you, situations can get out of hand with amazing rapidity. Take single seat helicopters as an example. There will be no-one there to take control if you mess up the first lift-off or run into trouble. No big deal, you say, people have been flying single seat, no-dual trainer fixed–wing airplanes for a long time. Yes, but before they did, they also had a license and experience in a wide variety of different types of aircraft before they went solo. It also appears that the early pioneers in aviation had a much deeper appreciation for things mechanical that many of us.

Get A Private Pilot's License First*

So it should be if you plan on going to fly a single seat helicopter. Some manufacturers require potential customers to have at least a private pilots license. This will prove that you can pilot a machine to a minimum standard, and understand some of your own limitations.

Go back for regular checks with an instructor. Light helicopters can be just as unforgiving as a larger one, and with no-one to watch over your shoulder, the ability to make mistakes increases incredibly. The ability to pick up bad habits increases even more. The light disk loading and power loading of this type of machine means that techniques cannot always be transferred to heavier helicopters.

The license is a good first step, but there is another step which also very important.

Get Experience in Several Different Types

I would suggest that you should have flown three or four different types of helicopters prior to going solo in your ultra-light or single-seat helicopter.

By the way, the advice about flying several different types is also relevant even if you weren't contemplating flying a single seat helicopter. Many things are learned when transitioning to another type, a synergy of experience, if you will.

Why the recommendation for flying different types? I wish I could put my finger on what happens when several types are added to the log book, because then it might be something that could be bottled and sold. As far as I can determine, it helps to develop a philosophy of flying, and rub away the mechanical reactions that are only appropriate to one type of machine.

For example, one popular type of very light helicopter has an overhead cyclic with direct control of swashplate tilt†, instead of a stick. This takes a little getting used to, and if it's your first different type of helicopter, that may be one thing too many to overcome.

After that advice, I would also add that you should be prepared to lift-off very slowly- those who fly mechanically using "I–need–to–pull–the–collective–up–to–about–here–and–wiggle–the–cyclic" type of lift-off will get into trouble pretty quickly. Those who use a slow, "raise–the–collective–a–bit, –see–where–it–wants–to–go–now" type of lift-off will be more successful.

General Words of Advice

Don't ever think you're the best (helicopter) pilot in the world. Be quick to correct anyone who tries to brand you as such. Being the best you can be should be sufficient for anyone.

Don't think accidents can't happen to you. I don't know of anyone who ever set out to deliberately have an accident...

Don't leave any helicopter alone with the rotors turning and engine running. Ever.

Don't ever start a two bladed helicopter with the rotors fore and aft. There are those of us who have, and those who will, start with the blades tied down...

Don't land on railway tracks...

Shutdown

This didn't fit comfortably in any other section, and it comes at the end of the flight, so it should come at the end of the first book as well...

* One of my reviewers said this should be made extra-double bold, glow in the dark lettering

† Well, almost direct. There was a mechanical linkage to make sure the cyclic worked in the instinctively correct manner.

Most engines need to be cooled down, whether they are piston or turbine. This is covered in Chapter 10,"The Piston Engine" and Chapter 29,"The Turbine Engine" respectively, and will be laid out in the FM.

When the engine is shut off, the rotor will coast to a stop. If you have a rotor brake, know when and how to use it. Some rotor brakes are best applied and held to the full on position till the blades have stopped completely to obtain even heating of the disk, others need to be modulated for a smooth shutdown. Know what your helicopter needs.

If you don't have a rotor brake, when should you get out? Some rules would have you stay inside at the controls until the rotor comes to a halt, others are less clear. Rather than provide definitive guidance, let me ask a question. What can you do to control the rotor blades once the rotor has slowed to less than 10–15% of their normal speed? Would you be better off outside making sure that someone doesn't walk into the blades? Are you more liable sitting in the helicopter or outside it?

It makes little sense to me to be sitting inside when the blades are agonizing through the last revolutions, bouncing up and down. If the helicopter is parked downwind, they make take quite a long time to stop (they are in autorotation sort of). Rotor brakes help to eliminate this problem, but think about these things as you wait for things to come to a halt.

When the blades are secured, then have a look at the helicopter. This is a good time to check for oil leaks, as the oil is warm and most likely to seep out. Some manufacturers require that fluid levels be checked within a certain time after shutting down to get an accurate reading – check your manuals.

Finally, do the paperwork, and then enjoy yourself! You've just had a successful flight.

Summary of Chapter 21 and the Beginner's Book

A lot of new ground has been covered in this book. It will stand you in good stead for the flying you will do as a student. After that, the fascinating world of unrestricted aviation opens its horizons, and there is a whole lot more things to learn there. The ride is just beginning...

For the Professional Helicopter Pilot / Instructor

For the Professional Helicopter Pilot

By this time, you've flown helicopters long enough to know how magical they can be, what useful tools they are and what sheer fun they are. You're earning your living doing something amazing. May I offer some words of advice?

Helicopter Pilots Are Different

Regardless of what Harry Reasoner said, helicopter pilots really are different. The main difference between us and fixed wing pilots is that, by and large, we use our machines to help others do their job, and so we have to know a bit about how others do their work.

Some of the differences are:

- we may work alone
- we may be the only representative of the company
- we work where the rules are less than crystal clear
- we work where there are fewer people watching
- we don't have an extensive support system of hangars, refueling trucks, runways, air traffic control, weather reporting systems and so on
- quality control of the operation is up to each individual pilot

That having been said, some people absolutely thrive on this independence, and others can't handle it at all. It's important to remember that too much independence can lead to some fixed ideas which may not have a basis in fact, so reality checks are also important.

Ever wonder why helicopter pilots don't have a union*? Someone tried it once, and couldn't get enough pilots in one place at the same time...

Legal Implications

By now, the technical aspects of flying helicopters ought to be second nature to you. You'll continue to learn, for sure, but the basics are pretty well ingrained.

The legal implications of being a professional pilot are pretty immense. The various rules and regulations that govern operating a commercial aircraft are not going to ever win a Nobel Prize for literature, but it is necessary to know, understand and obey them to keep yourself free of long-term trouble.

In the simplest possible terms, you are responsible for everything to do with the care and safety of your passengers and cargo, as well as those innocent bystanders on the ground who might be affected by your aircraft or flight path. Everything from noise to nuisance can come under those categories, so consider what you do carefully!

The legal implications of your job are contained on lots of pieces of paper called regulations. As a professional pilot, you should know more than just the words, but also what is behind those words, and what is the intention of the rules.

Maintenance

You will now have to become more intimately involved in the maintenance of your helicopter. In some jobs, you'll have to do a lot of the minor maintenance yourself. In other positions, you'll hardly be allowed to open a panel. But whatever your professional position, you'll need to know quite a bit about maintenance and the people who keep your machine airworthy.

You need to ensure that you know how write up maintenance problems, in clear and unambiguous terms. Perhaps more importantly than that, you need to know that you must write up maintenance problems. There are two reasons for this- if you don't write it up, it may not get fixed, and you have legal responsibility to ensure that the aircraft you are flying is maintained properly.

---

* Aside from some offshore companies who operate from a single base

Service Difficulty Reports (SDRs)

Most national regulatory authorities (FAA, Transport Canada, etc.) have a system of tracking problems on aircraft that will ensure that things which go wrong consistently on aircraft get noticed. This system is called the Service Difficulty Reporting (SDR) system, and relies on the maintenance personnel to report problems they encounter in maintenance to the authority. Pilots can also file these reports if they see something wrong, and should try to make sure the maintenance people do their part in this.

Don't worry about a lot of paperwork, just report the problem as best you can. You won't get scolded or blamed for a poor report- any thing is better than nothing.

Your Part in Safety

...is huge. You may be the only quality control check in the operation if you're by yourself. You may be responsible for filtering the fuel out of the drums of fuel, or for checking the weather or the conditions of the underslung load cables. You can't be sure in this business what you'll be responsible for, but you can bet that it's pretty wide reaching.

Experience

Experience is a pretty tough teacher. It gives the test first, and the lesson later.

You'll have a quite a few experiences in your flying career. Make sure you learn from them, and if you can pass them on to others, please do.

Care and Feeding of Passengers / Customers

It's not easy being a helicopter pilot and having to deal with a public that is often more than slightly ignorant of what you can and can't do safely. How do you handle someone who has asked you to do something which is illegal / impossible / unsafe (pick one)? How do you handle someone who says that the last pilot did it with no problem?

Remember you have a responsibility not only for any passengers, but also to the folks on the ground who might be innocent bystanders to all the aerial goings- on. If you're not happy doing something, then say so, and refuse to do it. You may lose your job over this, but at least you won't be responsible if something does go wrong (and often times they will eventually.)

You need to brief your passengers on the necessary safety items, ensure things are co-ordinated with any ground personnel (those who might be rigging underslung loads, for example - do they have radios on the right frequency?).

You also should be aware of the pretty awesome legal responsibilities you may have as the pilot in command. Check with your company operations manual, or ask for advice, if you're not sure.

Make a Decision

Often the first thing to do is to say 'No'. This means at least some decision has been made. In many accidents, no decision was made, no review of the situation that was developing took place and thing just deteriorated until the final link in the chain broke. It's also relatively easier to convert a 'No' into 'Yes' if things change than the other way 'round.

As an example of making a decision- consider aborted approaches. If you don't like what you see as you are coming in to land, go around and try again. It's far easier to tell someone why you went around, than it is for someone else to try to figure out why you continued to land when things were unsuitable.

There is very pertinent saying among the sailing fraternity:

Helpful Hint

It's far better to be on the shore, wishing you were out sailing, than to be out sailing, wishing you were on the shore.

Philosophy of Instruction

No one ever learns completely by watching someone else do something. If this were true, we'd all be champion figure skaters, or professional sports stars. Since learning requires activity on the part of the student, the instructor is not really there to teach, but to help the student to learn.

Remember your students are entering a world full of different words, concepts and ideas. Don't try to overload them too quickly, but at the same time, demand they use the correct terms and can explain the concepts to you. Give the student breaks in flying in order to prevent them from becoming too tense.

Don't make flying helicopters sound like it's so difficult that only the exceptional few can do it. You learned, so can others*.

Avoid sudden maneuvers and especially violent maneuvers (without good reason). Most people are apprehensive when first experiencing helicopters, even if they are experienced aviators.

If the student enjoys the trip, it will help to maintain a positive outlook for the training.

Instructors are not there to show how superior they are to students.

Procedures that seem complicated or appear to be rushed will become easier to understand and suffer less from 'time compression' as they become more familiar.

Test the student frequently, but fairly.

Ask questions that should be answerable, and use these to build to new material. Don't ask questions that can be answered 'yes' or 'no', as:

- it's easy to guess
- you may give the answer away by the way you ask the question.

Questions that are preceded by 'How' or 'Why" are good for getting explanatory answers.

Sarcasm, fear and ridicule have no place in the instructors repertoire, as easy as they are to use. They don't prove much, and if the student is sensitive at all, can really offend. Several hours of careful teaching can be undone in one minute.

As an instructor, you'll finally learn (hopefully) all the things you were supposed to pick up as a student.

Terms to Use

Make sure your students know the various terms you will be using, and what they mean. When I was instructing at the US Naval Test Pilot School at Patuxent River, Maryland, we always had a moment or two of confusion when first flying with a new student. Students came from all US and many foreign military services. When, as the instructor, I would ask the pilot to terminate the engine failure approach and try again. If I said 'go around' to a Navy pilot he'd ask 'Go around what?'. If I said 'Waveoff' to an Army pilot, he'd look at me as if I was nuts. If I said nearly anything to a foreign, non-English speaker, I would get blank looks. So I made it a point to define what I meant by these terms as one of the first parts of each briefing.

Measuring or Predicting Pilot Performance

First of all, there are no objective definitions or defined standards by which we can measure the performance of pilots. Since we can't agree on a standard, it is reasonable to expect we'd be unable to predict if someone could meet that standard. Trying to predict in training if a pilot will be good or bad has not been successful, as there is very little predictability of talents and abilities at this early stage. After all that discouragement, it seems that good pilots do all of the following:

More Philosophy

Get some books on teaching. The FAA Flight Instructors handbook is a jewel, and contains a lot of good general guidance. Read other books on teaching to get a flavor for what this calling is about.

If you've been an instructor for a while, go learn something new to see what it's like to be a student again.

An example of this might be to try (with a suitable safety pilot) from the left hand seat with your left hand on the cyclic and your right hand on the collective. You'll probably remember some of your student experiences again very quickly.

* Nearly every one, that is. There are those who will not ever make good pilots, and it is your duty to help point this out to them.

Preflight Briefing

The pre-flight briefing should cover what is going to happen on the flight, who is going to do what to whom and where, and what will be the aims of the flight. The first few lessons should also concentrate on the weather and how it's going to affect the flight.

If the student hasn't been flying a lot, or recently, then a review to make sure the previous lesson points are remembered is worthwhile. As little as two to three days can make a difference in what was remembered for beginners.

Preflight Inspection

Have the student prepare a weight and balance, as well as a performance planning card for each trip. Have the student determine the maximum altitude the helicopter can hover at for the weather conditions, and so on. While this may seem artificial, it will help to develop good habits later on.

Walkaround

Carry out the first walk-around in the hangar, away from other machines, noise, wind, etc. Without these distractions or the pressure of having to go flying, the teaching can be more thorough.

When doing a walk around, for example, show the student that the wind direction and velocity should be noted (air traffic may not always be there...). Point out obstacles that should be noted during start up or taxi, until you are able to have the student point out those relevant things to you.

Prior to the student going solo, or some appropriate point in the syllabus, go over the walkaround again in more detail, pointing out the things that have typically been found wrong*.

Concepts of Controls

Cyclic

While still on the ground, with the rotors turning, at ground idle and then again at full N_R†, have the student feel the sort of forces needed on the cyclic to change the tilt of the main rotor. The tip path plane should be visible and the student should be able to see the effect immediately. Small movements will show the effect, as well as stressing the need to keep hands (and feet) on the controls all the time.

Collective

The same procedure should be used with the collective, except the learning points are slightly different. The student should be able to see the tip path plane coning change without any tilting.

Throttle

Have the student make some changes in throttle to see the effects. Combine this with some collective movements (well below the amount needed to get airborne).

Pedals

Have the student move the pedals slightly and note the change in roll and pitch and possibly twist on the airframe even a small movement will have.

This is a good time to get the effect of N_R and manifold pressure sorted out.

Looking Outside

Stress the importance of looking out. When starting a turn, stress the necessity of looking in the direction of the turn, and saying 'clear right (or left).

There is a tendency for the student to spend too much time looking inside at the instruments. Teach a good balance between looking outside and occasionally glancing inside. If necessary, cover up the instruments and get the student to fly completely outside until it becomes second nature, and calling what the cockpit instruments should be saying. This will teach anticipation and the ability to glance at the instrument panel and read what it says (as opposed to what one thinks it ought to read...)

* ...with the machine that is, not the student.
† Some people call this 'flight idle', so now you'll now what they mean if you hear this term.

Limitations

There are a lot of limitations in a helicopter, surprisingly lots of limitations*. It would be impossible to expect a student to be able to obey all of them on the first flight. For the first little while, you may have to be limitations monitor, but you should be gently introducing the student to observing all the limits, and anticipating when these are going to be problems.

Make sure your student knows how to read the instruments and interpret and identify the necessary limitations without spending a lot of time staring at the dials. You may have to point out why the various red and yellow lines are on the instruments...

Following Through

As an instructor, you will do a lot of following–through when the student is flying, but this should

- be briefed to the student
- not be too obtrusive
- gradually disappear so the student gains confidence until

you can sit there with your arms crossed, or hands under your legs to demonstrate you have complete confidence in the student.

The FAA Instructors Handbook describes the 'Demonstration Performance' method very well, and should be a well thumbed reference.

Checklists

Have your student make up their own checklists- make sure it's correct and follows a logical flow. Then make the student memorize the important parts.

Questions and Tests

Questions are a way for the instructor to stimulate the student, to help get and keep interest in the subject, to guide thinking and finally to see if what you have been teaching has been learned.

If you're working with a large class of students, then you can only get to part of the students at a time. One on one, it's less of a problem, but you still need to ask the questions.

When the Students Ask Questions

If you can't answer them, say so. If you need to do some research, say so. Whatever you do, don't bluff. The students will certainly see, and you'll lose credibility. Perhaps the student should do some research if you think it might benefit everyone.

What are you Really Trying to Teach?

Among other things, the ability to learn for the rest of the student's flying career. Anyone who thinks they can stop learning as soon as they have their license shouldn't be given the piece of paper in the first place. Part of your job as an instructor is to make sure your student realizes every flight is a learning experience. Just make sure the correct lessons are learned.

Experience is a funny thing. I've seen pilots with 7,000 hours of time who turned out to have 7,000 repetitions of the same task, and who appeared to have learned nothing from it. I've seen other pilots with 1,000 hours who were wise beyond their years and hours. Aldous Huxley once said:

Experience is not what happens to a man, it is what a man does with what happens to him.

See the "What Good Pilots Do" on page 439, for some of the more subtle things your are trying to foster in students.

* No, I'll go even farther and say, way too many limitations

Even More Philosophy

Your students are undergoing a very difficult process in learning to fly helicopters. If you have been instructing for a long while, it is not easy to appreciate what it is like to learn. Maneuvers you have carried out repeatedly, and can see in very clear terms, are often going to be very rushed and confused for your students. Autorotations are a good example where students encounter time compression and you encounter time expansion, so both of you wonder if you were in the same world, let alone in the same helicopter at the same time.

If you doubt this, go and learn something new like sky diving or skiing, or a language such as German or Russian every once in a while to refresh yourself on what its like to be a student again.

A few basic hints that will pay dividends:

- Make sure the student is familiar with the cockpit.
- Use the same terms in the same way all the time.
- Don't suppose the student understands anything until he can explain it to you correctly.
- Have the student learn to debrief you on the good and bad points of each trip- this will develop self–discipline and self–criticism.
- Look at "Hovering More Easily" on page 127 for reasons why hovering isn't best taught in big open fields.

Specific Exercises

From time to time in this book, some specific exercises are used to show a point about how a helicopter works. If your student is understanding everything at a satisfactory pace, then you may be able to skip these exercises. (there is a school of thought that says it's worthwhile to show these exercises anyway, as they may be remembered later in a situation you've never thought of...) If you have a problem getting a point across, consider some of these, and probably make up some of your own.

Trusting the Student

At some point, it's necessary to let the student go completely. A difficult decision. You need to build up to this level of confidence, and the student needs to be aware you have developed that confidence. Moving your hands away from the controls as the student improves in skill and capability is one way. But be prepared...

Space Awareness

One of the difficult things for a student to learn about in helicopters is the space the aircraft takes up. In a fixed wing aircraft, this is typically only a problem on the ground, however with a helicopter, the problem is made worse near the ground and other obstacles. We have too many helicopter accidents I would classify as CFIT - Controlled Flight Into Things. How can we avoid this?

Truck drivers have rodeos to learn about the space their trucks take up. There are helicopter championships that have some events that could read across into good training exercises, but there are other ways to train the student about the space the helicopter takes up.

Start with the location of the front of the rotor disk. Ask the student to land so the front of the rotor disk is directly above a line on the ground. When the helicopter is shut down, see how close the guess was. Do the same thing for other parts of the helicopter. Mark out a very small square on the ground, just slightly larger than the skids, and have the student position the helicopter precisely in that square. To judge where the tail rotor is mark a spot on the ground, and ask the student to back up until the tail rotor is directly over the spot. Make sure there is plenty of space around the spot on the ground so you don't bump into something while training about 'personal space'.

What's the point of all this? It will teach the student to judge the location of things he can't immediately see, such as skids and tail rotors. It may help to learn to use more of his senses all the time.

Flying by the Seat of the Pants

In the early days, there were no 'Practical Test Standards' for students to consider as being all they ever had to know, or that instructors only taught to, so students would pass. Students were taught to survive the world they were going to operate in. Early helicopters were surprisingly sparse (the Bell 47 had no slip ball, for example), yet people seemed to fly the machines quite safely, or at least with the same problems or accidents we still see.

It appears (since I wasn't there) the emphasis was on having a feel for the machine.

Since then, we've had a lot of progress thrust upon us. It doesn't appear that progress has increased safety from any measurable perspective. Engines are more reliable, more power is available, mechanical systems have become more robust, but we still see the same ways to have accidents.

Is this a reflection on a lack of total airmanship? Are we trying to keep costs down for training while neglecting the safety aspects? Are we merely teaching to pass the 'demonstrated requirements' that may have little practical value?

Written Tests

Do multiple choice or even written tests adequately prepare pilots for the work they are to do for the rest of their life? An exam can cover a lot of unimportant stuff that's easy to ask questions about, while missing very important material.

The recent addition of FADEC engines has shown this aspect very clearly. I have spoken to several operators who have purchased a helicopter with a FADEC engine, and the successful ones were those who spent time trying to learn, really learn the system. They discovered the company school had not adequately prepared them to understand the machine, and needed to teach themselves what the system did and how it operated.

I know of several people who have handled what could have been very nasty crashes with skill and coolness because someone took the extra time to cover very important points that were left off the 'official' syllabus, instructors who made sure their students knew more than the minimum required. I suppose it's also a measure of the students that they showed they were interested and capable of understanding the additional information.

Pilots who fly mechanically, who will only do what the book says, might be at a disadvantage when an unusual emergency occurs. You should be encouraging a certain amount of flying by the seat of the pants.

Summary of Chapter 22

This chapter should serve to introduce the subtle changes in thinking that you must make to adjust to being a professional helicopter pilot. There are a lot of unseen pressures that you will have to live with, in addition to the physical stick and rudder aspects of flying. That's the main 'art' part of this half of the book. Some pretty advanced 'science' stuff comes next, but it will help to turn you into a real artist.

Advanced Helicopter Aerodynamics

REVIEW

Hover

As before, hover will be defined as either zero–airspeed or zero–groundspeed. The difference is important for performance and handling. As the pilot, you are probably most concerned about the zero-groundspeed hover.

This chapter is going to cover a lot of seemingly unrelated subjects, which all do come together by influencing the rotor and fuselage of the helicopter.

Review of Lift and Drag

The useful component of the reaction of the air passing an airfoil. The formula for lift is:

$$L = \frac{1}{2} \times \rho \times S \times C_L \times V^2 \qquad \text{(EQ 16.)}$$

Where

C_L = Coefficient of lift (from Figure 2-22 on page 21)

ρ = Greek symbol for rho (shorthand for air density) (in lbs. per cubic foot)

V = Velocity of the air at the section. We use RaF velocity. (feet/ second)

S = Surface area of the blade segment. (Square Feet)

The formula for the drag is the same, except C_D replaces C_L. Typical values of C_L and C_D for a symmetrical blade are found in Figure 2-22 on page 21 and Figure 2-24 on page 22.

AIRFOILS

Non-symmetrical Airfoils

The airfoils on most training and light piston engine helicopters are symmetrical, which have some advantages, but some limits in airspeed and C_L. The blade sections on most higher performance commercial-use helicopters are mostly non-symmetrical. This makes some significant differences.

Modern blade sections are developed by manufacturers or research centers to provide optimum characteristics of lift, drag and pitching moments. Figure 23-1 shows typical modern blade sections.

Figure 23-1 Modern Airfoil sections.

Lift and Drag

To determine the lift and drag for a whole blade, it is necessary to integrate the lift formula over the length of the blade, from the root to the tip, with the variables being RaF and AoA. To determine the lift of the whole rotor in the zero airspeed hover, it is assumed that the lift is the same in all the azimuth positions. The maths to calculate the lift in the hover are merely tedious, but not beyond most high school students. To determine the lift of a rotor disk in forward flight is another story. The maths become pretty fierce, as changes in relative airflow due to forward velocity must be considered and changes in AoA due to inflow angle must be known. We won't be that adventurous!

Lift to Drag Ratio

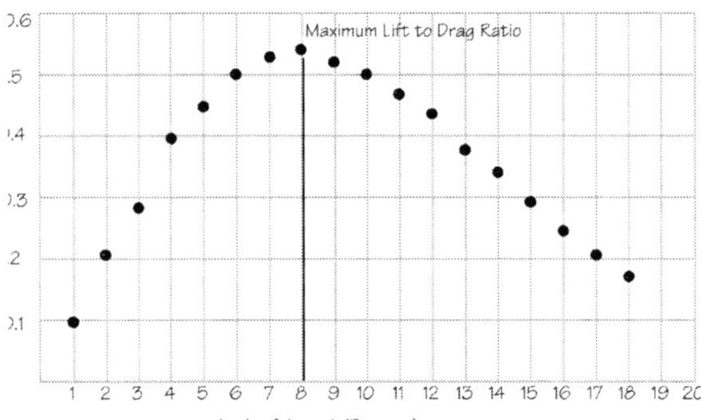

Figure 23-2 Lift Drag Ratio

We like lift, but must tolerate drag as an inescapable part of aerodynamic reality. We would like to minimize the effects of drag, and maximize the effects of lift. We can do this if we look at the ratio of lift to drag. An example of such a ratio, taken from the same curves we used earlier for our example blade, is shown in Figure 23-2 below.

One way to look at this curve is that we get nothing of value when the numbers are low, (not much lift and lots of drag) and we get more of value when the *lift/ drag ratio* is high. It should be obvious that AoA's in the region of 3-6° are optimum, and this is what we should be aiming for along the blade.

Changing N_R

An interesting part of this formula is that if everything else is kept constant, lift will increase as the square of the velocity of the air. Since the hovering (zero airspeed, that is) helicopter has only the rotational speed of the blades to produce the velocity of air. If the N_R is increased by 2% (and everything else is constant), the effect is not just a 2% increase in lift, but a 4% increase. Since the main and tail rotor are mechanically connected, the effects are also seen at the tail rotor.

Changing Density Altitude

If the air density is decreased (higher density altitude) and everything else kept constant, the lift produced by the airfoil at the same AoA would decrease. This effect is caused by ρ, the density term in the equation. Since it takes the same amount of lift* to hover a helicopter of the same weight, regardless of the air density, the effect has a rather roundabout way of appearing. If air density (ρ) decreases, the only way to produce the same amount of lift (at the same blade rotational velocity) will be to use a larger AoA. The only way to increase AoA in the hover is to increase the blade pitch using the collective.

If the AoA is increased both the lift and drag increase. The increase in drag is seen as an increase in power required to turn the blade. Hence it takes more power to hover at the same weight at higher density altitudes.

Another way to say this is:

- to produce the same amount of lift as density altitude increases, it is necessary to increase the AoA, and thus the power.
- when the induced velocity increases, this aft tilt of the lift vector increases, which increases the size of the resolved drag vector

This will increase the C_L, which is what is wanted, but unfortunately it also increases the C_D which is not what is wanted, and the drag required to turn the blades increases Much of this increase in drag is due to the increased aft tilt of the lift vector, due to higher induced velocity.

Compressibility Drag

Figure 2-24 shows the co-efficient of drag vs. AoA. This curve was measured at one airspeed, and you might think that since lift vs. AoA is good for a variety of airspeeds, drag was the same. Not so.

It turns out that for much of the airspeed range, the drag is the same at the same AoA, but remember that drag is a force that depends on the square of the velocity (airspeed). So, when the velocity doubles, the drag quadruples. When density decreases (higher altitude), the drag decreases for the same airspeed.

When the airspeed gets very high, the drag increases even more than the formulae predict. Careful measurements show that this increase in drag is proportional to the speed of sound (or Mach Number).

* Remember the example "Using a Crane to Lift Instead of an Engine" on page 55

Blade and Segment Aerodynamics

Blade CG location

Although the title of this section implies something to do with aerodynamics, a small matter of blade CG with respect to the feathering axis needs to discussed first.

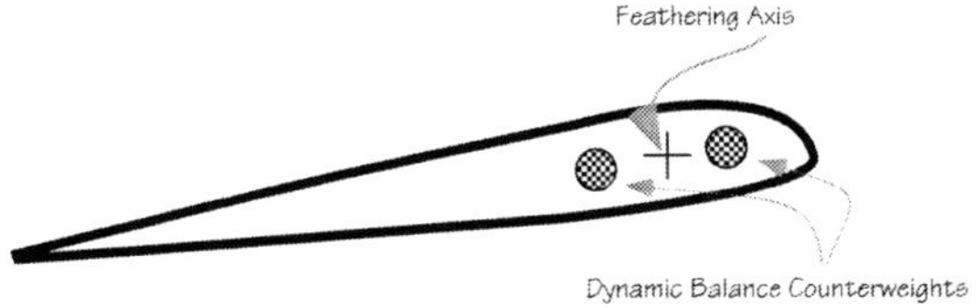

Figure 23-3 Blade CG Locations

The location of the center of gravity of the blade with respect to these axes and hinges is important. Most blade sections have the center of gravity on (or very close to) the feathering axis - pick up a section of blade if you have the chance: the weight in the nose is there for a reason. Aside from giving better inertia to the blade, it also moves the CG in line with the feathering axis, and can play an important roll in preventing blade flutter.

It is interesting to note that painting a blade will change the location of its CG quite significantly. There is a lot more blade area behind the CG than ahead of it, so the mass of paint behind the CG is more than that ahead, which has a large effect. Painting will upset the chordwise balance considerably - even if the blade is balanced laterally with an opposite blade. Fixed–wing airplanes often have a similar problem when their ailerons are painted.

AoA Changes due to Flapping

Consider the blade as a long thin wing, hinged at one end. Forget the blade is on a helicopter for a moment and assume the airspeed along the length of the wing is constant. The wing produces lift, and since it is hinged at one end, it flaps up to an equilibrium position. (weight of blade = lift produced by blade.) This is shown in Figure 23-4 below.

The height of this equilibrium position depends on the airspeed, the weight of the wing and so on. If the free end of the wing were lifted higher than this stable position, and let go, the wing would start to descend back towards its equilibrium position. (The lift vector is tilted more away from the vertical and the vertical component of the total lift force is smaller than in the equilibrium position.) The act of falling increases the angle of attack seen by the wing and that momentarily increases the lift. The slight increase in lift due to falling would not prevent the wing from falling, but would slow the rate of fall, and prevent the wing from going too far below the equilibrium position. A few oscillations and it would stop in the original place.

If the wing tip were pushed below the equilibrium position, the opposite effect would happen – i.e. the lift vector would be closer to vertical, and greater than the weight, so the blade would want to rise up. The rising up would reduce the angle of attack, which would slow the act of rising up, which would be self-correcting as well.

So what?

Well, a similar effect takes place on the rotor blade as it moves around the rotor disk.

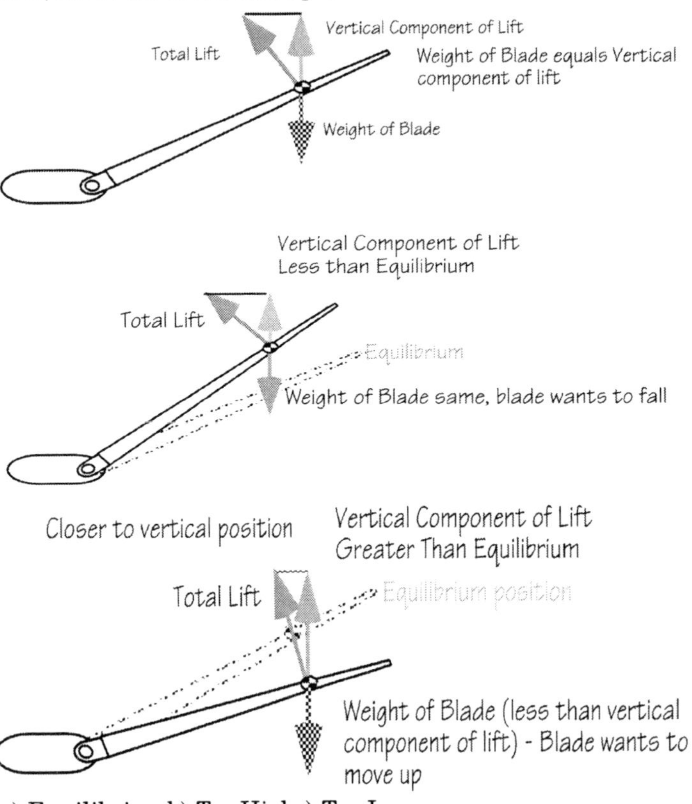

a) Equilibriumb) Too Highc) Too Low

Figure 23-4 Blade as a Wing

This AoA change due to rising and falling of the blade happens continuously as the blades go around, and contribute significantly to the difficulty in understanding (and calculating) the goings-on of the rotor disk.

AoA, Lift and Center of Pressure

Center of Pressure

Center of Pressure is a new concept, but in many ways equivalent to center of gravity. It is the point where all the pressure forces acting (along, above and below the airfoil) act. It is the place where all the lift force is balanced and has important implications for airfoils, and especially for helicopter airfoils.

Air passing over and under an airfoil produces lift. This lift acts at 90° to the RaF, through the center of pressure* of the airfoil, as shown in Figure 23-5. The small arrows in gray represent the pressure distribution on the wing.

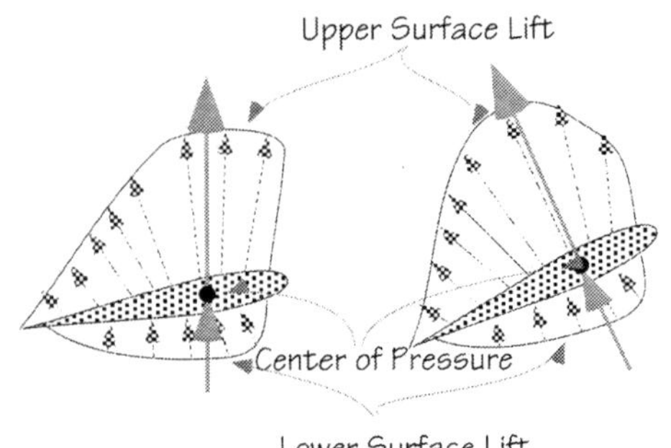

Figure 23-5 Lift and Center of Pressure for Symmetrical Airfoil

* Don't worry about how it's determined - accept that it is.

PITCHING MOMENTS

If we return to the earlier explanation of lift using spring balances ("Putting Together Some of the Basics" on page 7), we're going to clear up some earlier, simplifying assumptions. We used a single pivot and spring balance to measure lift, but an important aspect of producing lift and drag was not mentioned. The lift and drag are trying to twist the blade as well. If we add another spring balance to the front of the blade (or the back) we will be able to measure this force, in much the same as we measured lift. Since we know the distance from the pivot point, we can determine the pitching moment on the blade. First of all we'll look at the effects on a symmetric airfoil segment, and then on a non-symmetric segment.

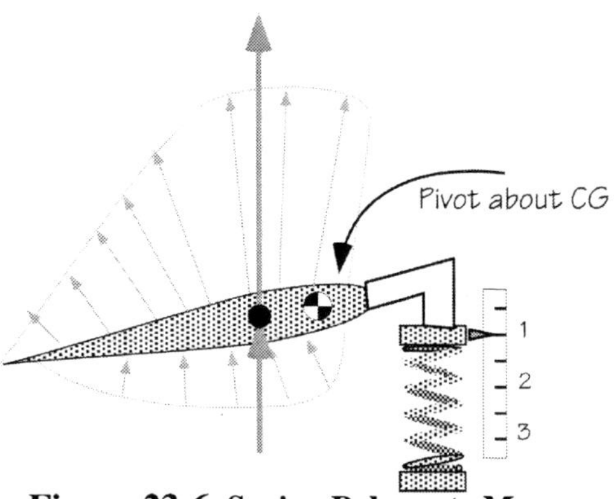

Figure 23-6 Spring Balance to Measure Pitching Moment

Symmetric Section

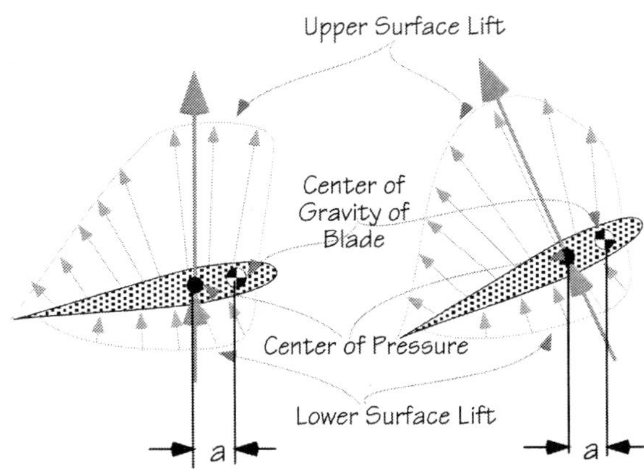

Figure 23-7 Pitching Moment on Symmetric Blade

The blade segment produces lift, which acts through the center of pressure of the blade, perpendicular to the RaF. Figure 23-6 shows this for a symmetric airfoil. Simple enough. As we change the AoA, the segment also shows nearly the same force on the spring balance measuring the twisting force, regardless of the angle of attack or speed. This is shown in Figure 23-7 below.

In a symmetric airfoil, the center of pressure does not move significantly with different angles of attack. In simple terms, the center of pressure is always in the same place, even if the lift and drag forces change size. The lift force multiplied by distance of the lift force to the pivot point makes a moment (force multiplied by distance) about the pivot point of the blade in that axis. If we manufacture the blade so the pivot point (or feathering bearing) is aligned with the center of pressure, there will be very little pitching moment produced. If the lift vector is on the pivot point, then there is very little pitching moment (large force times zero distance equals no moment).

The flight control system can be designed to handle a pitching moment that is small or doesn't change a great deal. So, even if we can't eliminate the pitching moment, but can keep it constant, we aren't in much trouble. In order to keep the pitching moment constant, the location of the lift vector should not change even if the size does. This is easily accomplished on a symmetrical airfoil, and that is one of the reasons why these airfoils are found on light, relatively slow helicopters.In this case, the pitching moments are shown at a distance from the pivot point, but in reality they are quite close.

The symmetrical blade section is not without its problems, and it is typically no longer found on helicopters weighing much more than 10,000 pounds, or with cruise speeds typically greater than 100 knots. If you want to go faster or higher, or squeeze more power out a given rotor diameter, a more advanced blade profile is required, and the non-symmetric section is needed. This has created a few problems.

Non-symmetric Section

In a non-symmetric blade, the center of pressure moves back and forth on the blade as the AoA changes. Since there are large variations in both velocity and AoA the size and location of the lift vector changes a great deal on a spinning rotor blade. The two varying parts of the moment, (the size of the lift vector and the distance to the pivot point (or feathering axis) of the blade) mean the moment about the feathering axis changes significantly.Some modern blades have reflexed trailed edges (i.e. angled down) to minimize the pitching moment.

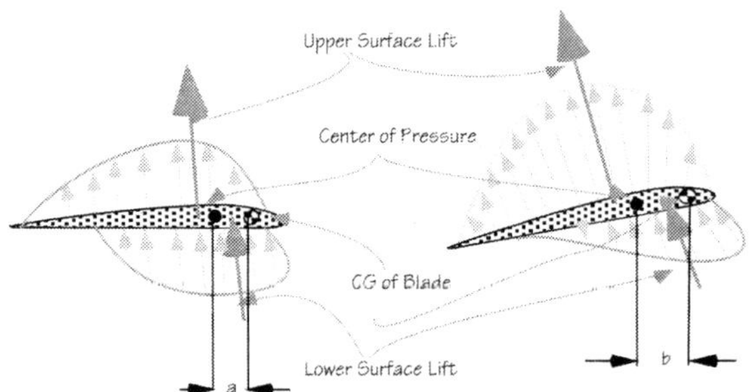

Figure 23-8 Pitching Moment on Non-symmetric Blade

The explanation for why pitching moment changes on a non–symmetric blade is the same as why a symmetric segment doesn't change - lift distribution. In a non-symmetric segment, the lift wanders* back and forth as the angle of attack changes. As it wanders the distance from the pivot point changes, varying the total moment created.

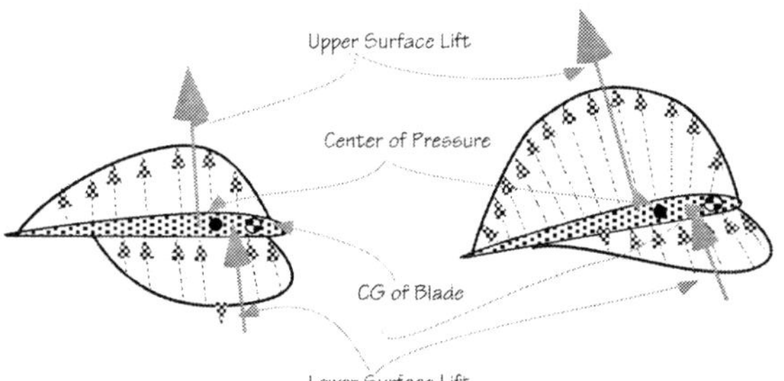

Figure 23-9 Lift Distribution on Non-symmetric Blade

Why the Fuss about Pitching Moments?

The simple reason is that *pitching moments* impact many areas of design - the hub, for example, must be stressed to take them, as well as the pitch change rods, the hydraulic system and so on. With a simple rotor blade with a symmetrical blade section, it may be possible to design the flight control system so no hydraulics are needed to overcome the pitching moments in flight. In fact, not many light helicopters would benefit from fitting a hydraulic system. With a non-symmetrical section in forward flight, the pitching moment and force change dramatically as the blade rotates. High and uneven forces make it impossible to move the cockpit controls without hydraulics.

As a practical example of the problem, the Bell 205 (or UH-1H) has symmetrical blades, and is controllable without hydraulics. When this model was upgraded to the Bell 212 / UH-1N with two engines, higher speeds and higher maximum weights, and a different rotor blade section, it was found to be impossible to raise the collective without hydraulics. A second hydraulic system was needed to ensure controllability following a single system failure.

BLADES

Blade Root Cutout

The part of the rotor blade closest to the hub is not particularly aerodynamic - that should be obvious to even the most casual observer. There is good reason for this: the blades, normally operating in very poor airflow, would not produce much lift even if they had a good shape, and the lift would be pushing down on the top of the fuselage anyway. The real-estate can be put to better use for drag dampers, and other paraphernalia associated with the hub and blade attachment. Typical values of blade root cutout are from 10-15% of the rotor radius.

* Wanders' isn't the correct word, as it implies the lift is free to do as it pleases, and it is always obeying the laws of physics, being a dutiful citizen.

Blade Tip Shapes

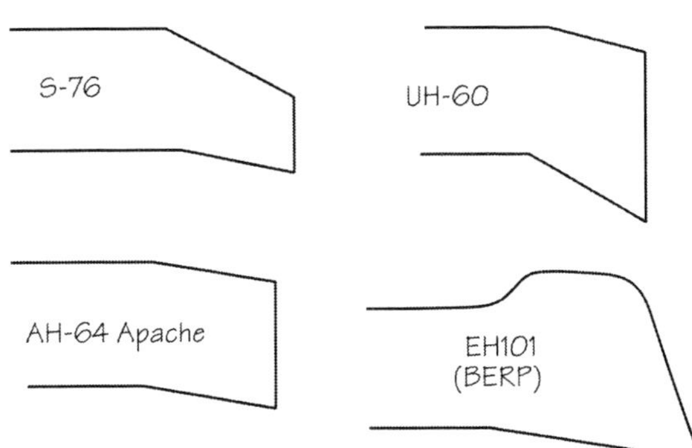

Figure 23-10 Different Blade Tip Shapes

Fixed–wing airplanes experience losses of performance due to wing tip vortices. Helicopters have the same problem. Various ways of reducing these losses associated with the tips of the rotor blades have been developed such as changes in tip shape that can also change the pitching moment of the blade Examples of these shapes are shown in Figure 23-10.

Twist

Blades are not always of constant airfoil section along their length and the pitch angle is not constant with respect to the root of the blade. Typically, the tip of the blade has a more nose–down pitch angle than the root, and the amount of *twist* can be between 8 - 10°. Some new designs have up to 18° of twist. This is shown in Figure 23-11.

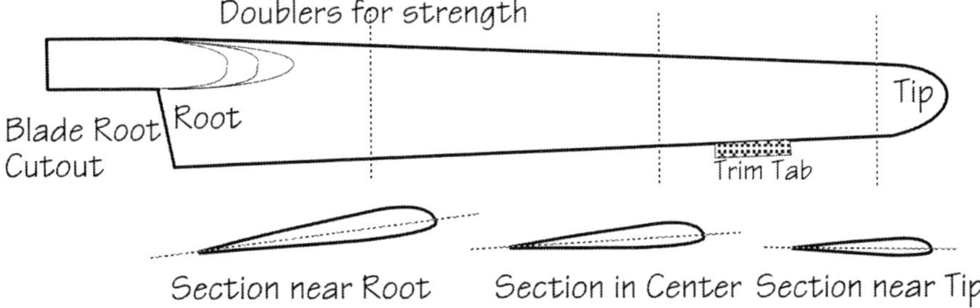

Figure 23-11 Twist and Taper of a Rotor Blade

Taper

Some helicopter blades *taper* both in width and thickness. The nearer to the tip, the smaller the width, as shown above in Figure 23-11. Taper is one way to more evenly distribute the lift generated by the blade.

Twist and Taper - Again

As previously mentioned, most blades have twist, and some have taper. Why is this?

Figure 23-12 shows the lift distribution on a blade with constant blade angle (i.e. no twist) in a hover*. Note that it is a parabolic (i.e. square function) shape, due to the lift formula - the lift generated is governed by the velocity squared, which is much higher near the tip than the root. (Losses associated with the tip have been ignored.) Note how little lift is produced near the root of the blade. This is not the ideal shape for the lift distribution.

* Wake up!!!- notice I didn't say which type of hover- it's actually a zero-airspeed hover.

More lift at the tip causes problems with too much bending of the blade a long way from the hub. This is very difficult to design for, and is another reason for incorporating twist in the blade angle.

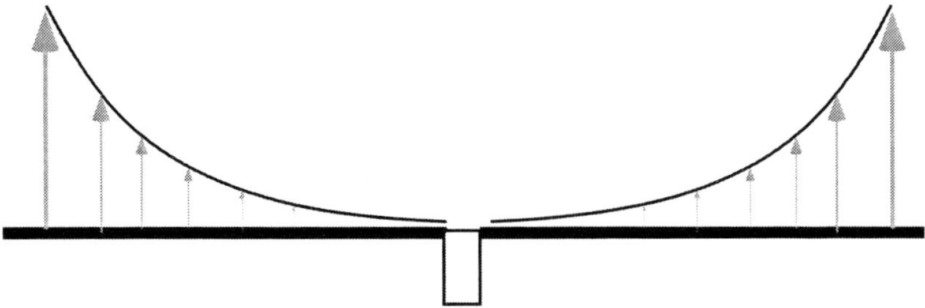

Figure 23-12 Lift Distribution with Constant Blade Angle in the Hover

To make the lift distribution more uniform along the length of the blade, something must be changed. If changing of blade sections to change the C_L is not possible, another option is to reduce the angle of attack on the high speed segments. Twisting the blade to reduce the segment's blade pitch angle, and thus the AoA, is an easy option. Figure 23-13 shows the lift distribution in the hover for a blade with ideal twist. Note how the lift near the root is greater with the ideally–twisted blade, but is less near the tip.

Another way to even out the lift along the blade is to taper the width, reducing its area (remember the 's' term in the lift formula?). Both twist and taper may be used to even up the lift along the blade. A triangular lift distribution is up to 5% more efficient than the parabolic shape with the untwisted blade.

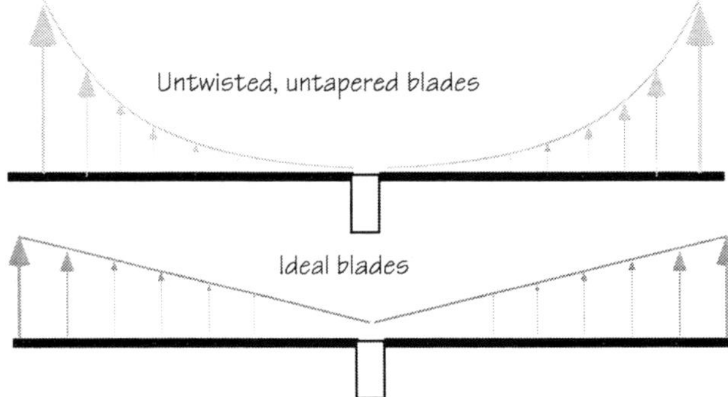

Figure 23-13 Lift Distribution with Ideal Twist

Lift to Drag Ratio Again

Another way to look at the reason for twist and taper is the Lift/Drag ratio. It's nice to have lots of lift, but bad to have lots of drag. Since we want efficiency, we look for the best ratio of lift to drag, and this can found by comparing the C_D and C_L to come up with a curve that is the most efficient - sort of the most lift for the least drag. Since engine power is required to overcome drag we want the most for our money... Figure 23-2 shows the L/D ratio for our sample airfoil.

Disk Aerodynamics

Solidity

The solidity of the disk is the amount of its area taken up by blades, as opposed to empty space. There is a compromise on *solidity* - more blades make for smoother overall flight, but vortices from preceding blades confuse the airflow around the advancing blade tips. A twin–bladed rotor has the least number of interference vortices (one–bladed machines have flown, but at least one had very uneven control forces). Solidity also makes the blades operate at an efficient AoA of between 5 and 8°. Figure 23-14 shows an example of low (left hand) and high (right hand side) solidity.

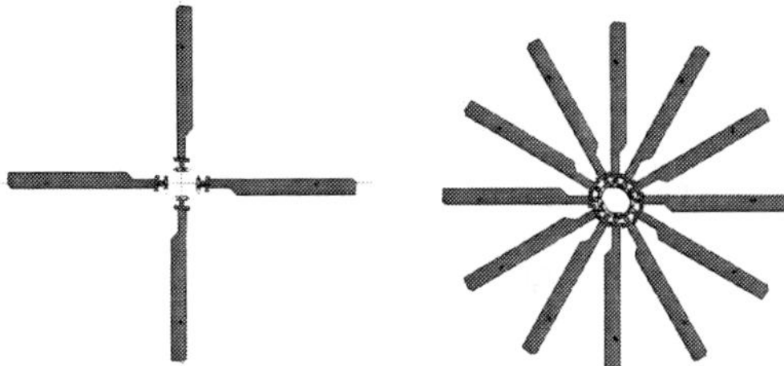

Figure 23-14 Solidity

Why 2 Blades May be More Efficient than 4

First of all, it's difficult to try to compare a two bladed helicopter to a 4 bladed one that at first glance appear to be the same. There are several that appear to be the same- the Bell 206L and the 407 come close, and the Bell 212 and the Bell 412 are also close. But not exactly the same. To begin with, the blade sections used on the rotors are different, secondly the powerplants are different and third, the maximum weights are different.

If we take each of these in turn, the answer will become clear. Different profile blades (or different airfoil sections) will be optimized for different things. The Bell 212, for example, was optimized for hovering, while the blades in the 412 were optimized for high speed cruise. Profiles that are not the same will mean that the amount of power used in each regime will be slightly different, and will produce different amounts of lift and drag.

Another reason why it's difficult, if not impossible to determine whether the same helicopter with two blades would be more or less efficient than the same one with four blades is that it is the total blade area that counts in hover performance. Why would you put two more blades of equal area on the machine and double the blade area? Good effects from changing the number of blades with the same total area will be outweighed by the bad effects.

For the same gross weight, blade area, tip shape, airfoil profile and tip speed, the two bladed rotor will have a lower aspect ratio (ratio of length to width) and higher tip losses. That is bad. But it will have a lower Reynolds number (a non-dimensionless number used in advanced aerodynamics) which will result in lower skin friction drag. That is good. The good and bad are probably about equal, so some other reason for changing the number of blades must be used- vibration, forward speed, etc.

AoA and the Disk

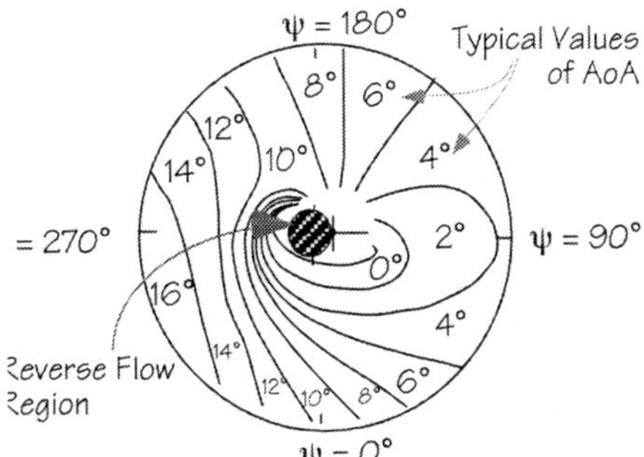

Figure 23-15 Typical Angle of Attack Distribution in Forward Flight.

Just as the relative airflow on a segment varies around the disk, so the AoA changes as well. Typical values of angle of attack for level flight at moderate airspeed are shown in Figure 23-15, which is looking down on the disk from above. The black circle in the center of the disk is the area with negative airflow - that is, the air is flowing from the trailing edge of the blade to the leading edge.

Advance Ratio

There is a shorthand notation for the relative speed of the advancing blade to the airframe airspeed. You may never come across it again, but if you ever read some of the more technical literature on helicopters, they use this notation quite a bit. This *advance ratio* (μ) is ratio of the tip speed to the forward airspeed.

Typically, the advance ratio limit for modern helicopters is around 0.4 - meaning the maximum forward airspeed is 40% of the tip speed. The accepted limit for retreating blade stall is an advance ratio of 0.5 - meaning the full length of retreating blade would be in reverse airspeed. Interestingly, the advance ratio will also determine the size of the reverse flow region on the retreating side - it will be a circle of diameter μ, with one edge touching the center of the rotor. If N_R is variable, then this will affect the advance ratio. Figure 19-7 on page 183 shows the advance ratio and retreating blade stall area.

V_{NE} and True Airspeed

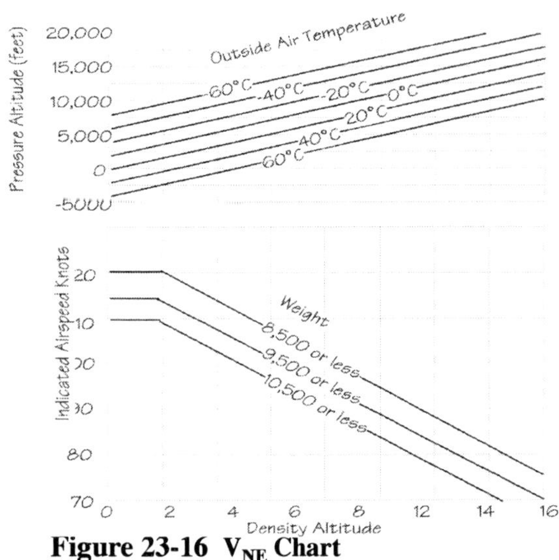

Figure 23-16 V_{NE} Chart

Figure 23-16a shows the V_{NE} as Knots, Indicated AirSpeed (KIAS) vs. density altitude for a typical helicopter. If you do the calculations from IAS to TAS for the atmospheric conditions, you'll note that V_{NE} as TAS doesn't change very much. Helicopter pilots aren't used to thinking in terms of TAS*, so charts like this are given in IAS.

Retreating Blade Stall Again

This is a good a place to discuss the retreating blade stall problem from an aerodynamic point of view. Since the rotor needs to produce equal amounts of lift on both sides, and the power required increases with density altitude, it stands to reason that if a limit is set for the V_{NE} at a low density altitude, this limiting airspeed will decrease as the density altitude increases. The other way to look at this is that the True Airspeed (TAS) for retreating blade stall will not change that significantly, but the Indicated Airspeed (IAS) will change due to density effects. This effect is seen in many helicopters as a decrease in V_{NE} with density altitude, an average of 3 knots per 1,000 feet above a certain height†.

Another interesting departure from our fixed wing brethern, who have a stall speed that is always the same IAS, but obviously different TAS. We have it at the same TAS and different IAS. But the type of stall is very different as well.

Retreating blade stall may be just one of the causes of variable V_{NE}.

Coning Angle Again

Coning angle may also be changed by changing the N_R, and hence the centrifugal force. I know of two helicopters that used much higher than standard N_R when lifting heavy loads, to reduce the stresses on the blades and hub (it also had a performance benefit and moved the rotor away from the stall).

The centrifugal force on the hub of a blade can be quite large - even a small piston–engine helicopter has over 7 tons of force at the hub.

Transverse Flow Effect or Inflow Roll

Somewhere during flying, the alert pilot will note the stick isn't behaving quite as it should. With a right side wind, for example, the stick will not just be to the right, but also displaced aft from in the zero–airspeed hover. In forward flight, the stick is moved not only fore and aft to effect a speed change and maintain level flight, but also left/right. Why is this? What is it called?

The second question is easier to answer - the effect is called *inflow roll* or *transverse flow effect*.

* Nor do we have Air Data Systems that give readings in TAS.

† But beware - some helicopters decrease V_{NE} more than 3 knots per thousand feet, and a few decrease less than 3 knots.

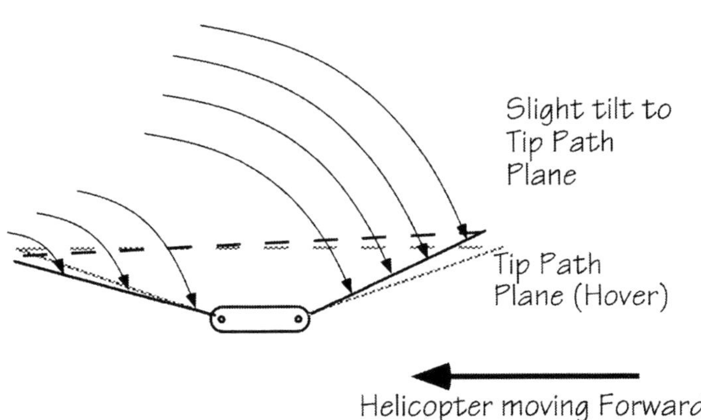

Figure 23-17 Coning Angle and Inflow Roll - Low Airspeed

The answer lies in the coning angle and the inflow of the air to the rotor. As the rotor disk is coned and tilted, the air entering the disk will be seen at each blade azimuth angle differently. This is shown in Figure 23-17. The tip path plane is tilted forward slightly in comparison to the hover, and the inflow is also coming from an angle just off the vertical. The combination is unique inflow angles at each blade azimuth, compared to the zero airspeed hover, where the inflow angle is identical (i.e. vertical) at all azimuths.

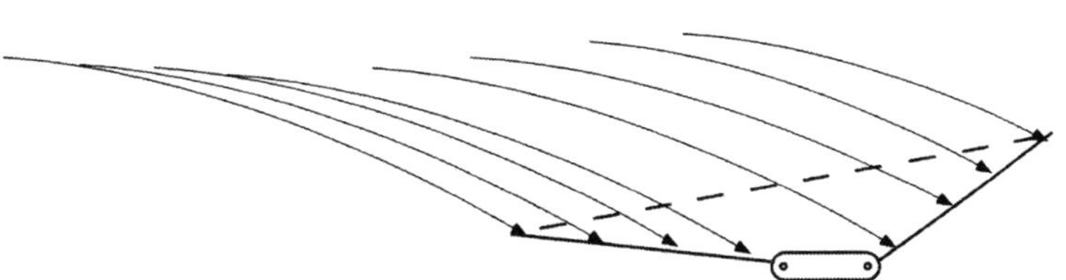

Figure 23-18 Inflow in High Speed Flight

The air at the back of the disk will have been accelerated for a longer time than the air at the front of the disk and has a higher downwash velocity, before it hits the rotor. See Figure 23-18 for the difference this will have on induced velocity at the front and rear of the rotor.

There are any number of places to start looking at this phenomenon, so we'll start at the blade at the rear of the disk (0° blade azimuth) and compare it to the blade at the front of the disk (180° blade azimuth). The blade at the rear has a steeper angle of inflow than the blade at the front, and reduced the angle of attack. This reduces the lift on the blade at this point, resulting in a lower than normal blade position on the right hand aide. The blade at the front experiences less of a reduction in angle of attack, and so produces greater lift, resulting in a higher blade position on the left hand side compared to the right. Higher blade position on the left than on the right will roll the helicopter to the right. To maintain a level fuselage attitude and straight flight path, the pilot must tilt the tip path plane back to level, using left lateral cyclic. So, as the helicopter accelerates forward, the pilot must correct with a small amount of lateral cyclic.

Applying the same principles to a zero groundspeed hover with a left side wind, the pilot has to hold not only left cyclic, but also quite a large amount of forward cyclic. The blade on the left side will see less reduction in AoA than the right hand blade, and so have increased lift, resulting in the tip path plane being highest at the rear. This tries to move the helicopter forward, and the pilot must compensate by adding rear cyclic.

In the cockpit the stick position will be moving not just strictly fore–aft as airspeed changes, but will require a bit of sidewards displacement as well. It is more apparent at high altitudes, when another effect due to air density comes into effect, but more about Lock number later. See "Lock Number" on page 370.

Stick Migration

Inflow roll and *stick migration* are present only in articulated rotor helicopters. Those with underslung (or teetering heads) don't appear to have this affect.

The inflow roll effect is not often seen by the pilot, because we don't normally pay close attention to where in the cockpit we put the stick. It is noticeable on some helicopters for the following reasons.

In many helicopters, the stick has no artificial feel system, or if there is one, only the force trim release (FTR) is used to take out control forces. Since we don't sense small forces well with our hands, if stick migration is present it often passes unnoticed.

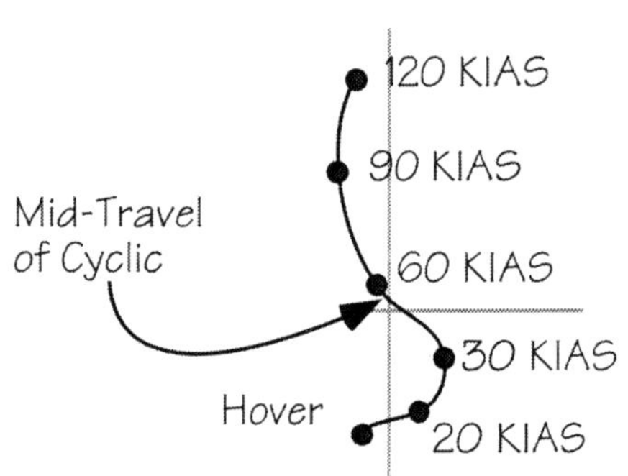

Figure 23-19 Stick Position vs. Airspeed, Overhead View

In the BO-105, BK-117 and MD 500 series helicopters, the cyclic stick does not have a FTR. All the control forces have to be trimmed out using a 4 way beeper trim, which can only be operated in one axis at a time. When a change is made to airspeed, it is noticeable that you must trim off not only a longitudinal force, but also a lateral one. It's no big problem, but if you are paying attention, it is noticeable. Figure 23-19 shows an overhead view of the stick position vs. airspeed.

Evidently, stick migration is due more to the height of the tail rotor from the CG than any particular hub type.

Tail Rotors

Location on Fuselage

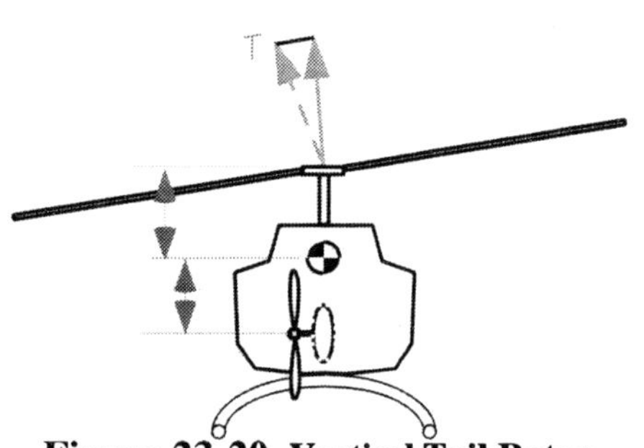

Figure 23-20 Vertical Tail Rotor Position with respect to CG and Main Rotor

Obviously, the tail rotor is located at the very back end of the fuselage, where it can have the largest moment arm to the CG. Why are some tail rotors located on vertical pylons and others not? First of all, the tail rotor is good at doing its job in the hover, and most of the low speed environment, but not in forward flight - there is a lot of drag and not much good associated with a propeller turning at 90° to the relative wind. To improve the directional stability of the helicopter in forward flight, the most common addition is a vertical fin (or numerous fins, depending upon the design). If a vertical fin is needed, why not place the tail rotor on top of it, for better clearance from the ground, less obstruction to the flow and so on? All of these are good reasons, but there is another less obvious one. The tail rotor pushes sideways to counteract the reaction of the main rotor. Like any other moment generating device, it acts through the CG - and in this case, the vertical CG position of most interest. Since this is relatively high in most helicopters, the tail rotor should be placed in line with the vertical CG when hovering to minimize the vertical distance between the two. If there is a great deal of vertical distance, then tail rotor thrust changes will be seen as a not just a yaw, but also as roll. Figure 23-20 shows the difference that the vertical position of the tail rotor makes.

The Sikorsky H-60 series canted tail rotor is even more interesting - because it is tilted off the vertical, whenever changes in tail rotor pitch are made, there is also a change in vertical and horizontal thrust components. The reason is partially to compensate for the unusually far aft CG position (behind the mast) at light weight.

Since the change in vertical thrust takes place a long way aft of the CG, it will affect the longitudinal pitching moment of the helicopter as well as the total lift. Because the tail rotor has a side component of thrust, it will also affect the rolling moment. To counteract this, there is mechanical mixing incorporated to change the longitudinal and lateral tilt of the main rotor when the tail rotor pitch is changed. Because this is accomplished mechanically, it is set for the design weight of the helicopter. At lower or higher weights than this design weight, the effect is either too much or too little, and the pilot must compensate in pitch and roll whenever the tail rotor pitch is changed.

Of course, putting the tail rotor on top of the tail boom means that a twisting effect has to be designed into the tail boom, but airframe designers do that sort of thing all the time.

Size, Direction of Rotation

The sizing of the tail rotor is a compromise like all other parts of these machines. It must be large enough to be able to start and stop yawing the helicopter in winds of certain speeds, and maintain heading in certain other side winds. The larger the tail rotor, the less power it takes to produce the same amount of thrust, but the more it weights Power to the tail rotor is power that can't be used for hovering.

The direction of rotation is important. Studies carried out many years ago showed that having the top blade turning rearward was the best direction for noise and tail rotor effectiveness. Several helicopters have gone through tail rotor direction and side of tail boom changes in their life, but now pretty well all are turning in the same direction, namely top turning aft.

It's also interesting to note that the pitch attitude at which the tail rotor will eat dirt is hardly ever given in any FM, civil or military. I know of at least one accident where the angle was measured and found to be quite small, and operational pilots were not aware of how close they regularly operated to this angle.

Aerodynamics of the Tail Rotor

The tail rotor often has to operate in very confused airflow. It is prone to the effects of all rotors, that is, its aerodynamics are affected by density altitude and N_R and angle of attack. Not only will relative winds affect it, but so will rates of rotation.

If you want an interesting exercise, plot the relative wind at the tail rotor for a helicopter in a zero groundspeed hover yawing at 30° second into a 30 knot wind. It is possible for the tail rotor to develop vortex ring state, and also possible to for it to not be able to produce the needed amount of thrust, even without stalling. See "Loss of Tail Rotor Effectiveness" on page 383 for more detail.

Summary of Chapter 23

This chapter has dealt with a lot of things. Among them were the more advanced aerodynamics of the rotor, hub designs and features, and a lot of miscellaneous helicopter aerodynamics. We have started to explain some of the more complex happenings of interest to the professional pilot or engineer. All of this should help understand the discussions in subsequent chapters.

Flight Controls and Rotor Heads

General

This chapter will cover a lot of the 'mechanical' things that come between your hands and the aerodynamics. Since you're a professional pilot, it behooves you to know as much about the machine you are flying as possible, and some of that knowledge should include basic theory of this vital part.

Tip Anhedral

Modern blades are starting to incorporate blade *anhedral*, or bending down the tips of the blade tips (as shown in Figure 24-1) to capture some of the lift that might be otherwise lost due to tip vortices. This provides a slight improvement in hover performance. There is an added benefit in that the tip vortices from one blade are forced down below the plane of the next blade as it comes by, improving vibration and performance as well. See "Vortices from Preceding Blades" on page 378.

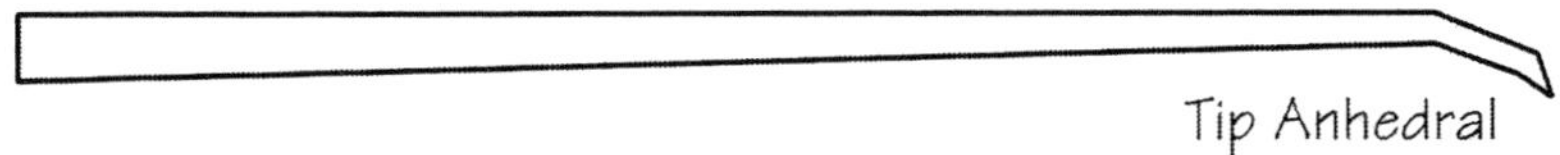

Figure 24-1 Blade Anhedral

Blade Inertia

Modern rotor blades have a compromise between rotor inertia for good engine failure characteristics and light blade weight. Rotor inertia is normally more critical on single–engine helicopters than on twin–engine machines, as there is a greater likelihood if the engine fails that the inertia will be worthwhile. Typical methods of increasing rotor inertia involves the use of high density weights (lead or brass are favorites) near the tip of the blade. Figure 24-2 shows the typical location of the weights

Figure 24-2 Typical Location of Blade Weights for Inertia

More Reasons for Lead–Lag Motion

"Reasons for Lead–Lag motion" on page 28 introduced two very powerful reasons for introducing a lead–lag freedom for the rotor blades, and hinted at a third. This third reason is called Hook's Joint effect. not easy to describe, but here goes anyway...

Hook's Joint Effect

The following discussion will assume a zero–airspeed hover for simplicity. The untilted rotor disk has the blades turning at an equal angular velocity at all azimuths. This is shown in Figure 24-3. When the disk is tilted, things change dramatically with regard to the speed of the individual blades, as far as the shaft is concerned. Confused? I'm not surprised.

The blades are still attached to the shaft, which continues to rotate at the same RPM. With respect to the new tip path plane, the rotor blades will still appear to be equally distributed - in a vacuum, this would be the case. The highest blade appears to have a shorter radius with regard to the shaft than the lowest blade. With respect to the rotor shaft, the two blades at the side would appear to have moved in the direction of the tilt. In other words, to be equally spaced with respect to the tip path plane, the blades would be unequally spaced with respect to the shaft, and vice-versa. Since the blades are attached to the hub and shaft, when they try to be spaced with respect to the tip path plane, it produces some stress and strain with the connection to the hub, which is attached to the shaft.

This apparent movement with respect to the shaft will introduce stresses in the blades as they try to lead and lag. This effect is known as *Hook's Joint effect*, and is yet another reason why lead–lag hinges are needed.

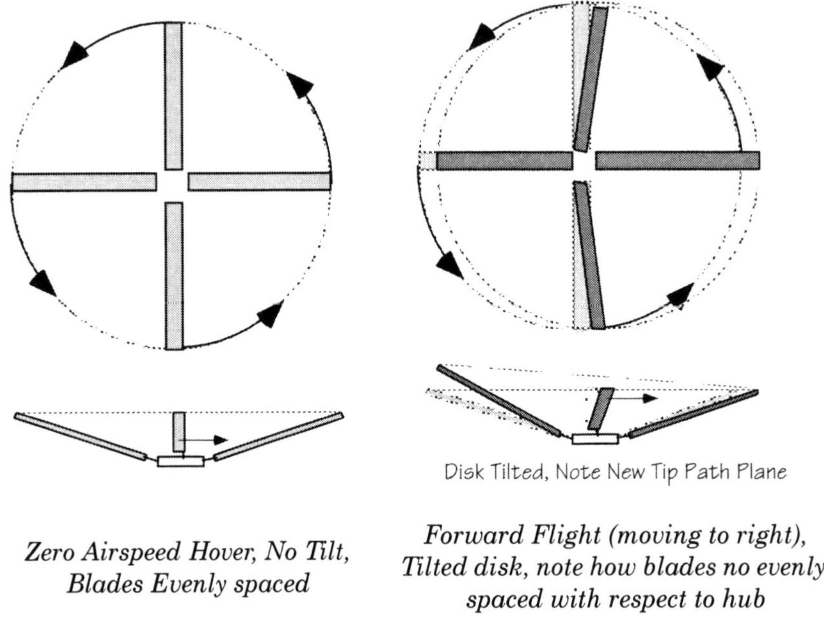

Figure 24-3 Hook's Joint Effect

Hook's Joint effect does not apply as much to the two–bladed underslung rotor, as the geometry of the hub permits only blade feathering. With no flapping hinge for each blade (Bell head only - the R-22 head is different) there is not a lot of change of coning angle with power. The effect still occurs, and the forces are taken out by a slight twisting of the shaft as the blades pass through the 090° - 270° azimuths.

So the rotor blade must be free to lead and lag, flap and change blade pitch in order to keep the stresses within it to a manageable minimum.

Articulated rotors use a lead–lag hinge to let the blade move and a lead–lag damper to control the amount and speed of movement. Most of the reason for the lead–lag damper is to do with ground resonance.

Two bladed rotors, by the way, would have severe ground resonance problems if they had lead–lag hinges.

Other Phase Angles

In Chapter 4,"More Basics of the Helicopter", it was mentioned that the pitch change rods should attach to the swashplate 90° in advance of the blade, due to gyroscopic effects. For two bladed rotors, this was easy, as the swashplate could then be made parallel to the desired tip path plane, but for other rotors it was more difficult to engineer.

A 90° phase angle may also result in large, sometimes heavy and flexible pitch change mechanisms, which given the high forces and stresses involved in modern rotor systems, can lead to other problems. One of the last things you want is the blade pitch changing due to flexing of the pitch change mechanism. Eurocopter, in their training manual for the Super Puma mentions a need to evenly space the hydraulic actuators around the swashplate to keep bending stresses in the swashplate to a minimum, and this required the phase angle to be changed and mechanical mixing to be added to the flight controls.

A pitch change mechanism could be made lighter and stiffer if it were shorter. This needs a different advance or phase angle, as shown in Figure 24-4. Previously we had used an arrangement where the swashplate was parallel (more or less) to the tip path plane. Now we can do something slightly different.

If the swashplate can be something other than parallel with the tip path plane, then some other phase angle can be used. For example, if the swashplate were to be tilted 45° out of phase to the tip path plane, so when the tip path plane was tilted directly forward, the swashplate was tilted down to the airframe 045° position, then the pitch change rod phase angle would be something other than 90°.

Some rotors even had the pitch change rod or link attached at the trailing edge of the blade. Negative phase angles will be necessary here, but you won't notice anything different in the cockpit. Some clever engineers have worked it all out for you.

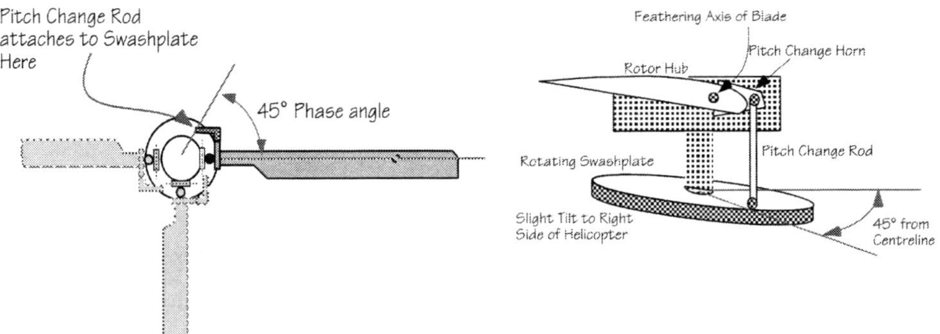

Figure 24-4 45° Swashplate Phasing Angle (a) Top View (b) Side View

Different phase angles are most often seen in three and more bladed rotors, where the swashplate may be tilted in an unusual manner. For example with the cyclic forward, the swashplate may not be tilted forward, but off to one side. The blade pitch on 090° azimuth is still minimum.

Rotor Heads

Lead–Lag Dampers

The lead–lag hinge permits the blades to move fore and aft relative to a nominal radial position. A problem can occur when the blades want to move too far, too fast.

The problem is that as the blade leads and lags from the optimum position, the blade CG moves with it. Since the CG of the blade is quite far out from the hub, this lead/lag movement could have undesired effects, like a lateral vibration or, at low RPM, possibly even ground resonance (see "Ground Resonance" on page 380). A way to prevent the movement from being too large or too fast is needed. Three different methods are in common use.

Types of Drag Dampers

Shock Absorber Type

The shock-absorber type of drag damper is the first type used and still the most common. It is simple, works fairly well, and requires little maintenance. It does let the blade wander quite a long way back and forth from the nominal position.

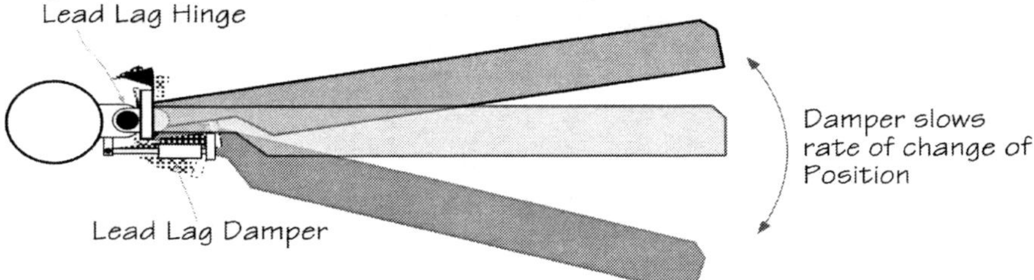

Figure 24-5 Typical Shock Absorber Lead-Lag or Drag Damper

It acts like the shock absorber in a car, to slow down the rate of change of velocity of the blade in the lead–lag axis. Problems can be encountered when the drag dampers are not well matched or don't work as advertised. Since this bad behavior may not always be present, it may only affect certain areas of flight. One flight test program had one airframe with different vibration characteristics than others. It only showed up in high power situations as a low frequency (about once per revolution) lateral oscillation, and was later found in ground testing to have one faulty drag damper. Modern tracking and balancing techniques will spot bad dampers quickly.

Elastomeric Type

The elastomeric type of drag damper uses a series of rubber and metal fingers to damp out blade lead–lag motion. This type has the benefit of returning the blade to a definite position, which helps to reduce ground resonance problems. The blades cannot wander far away from their proper geometric spacing, unlike the hydraulic type, which permit quite large excursions. The French call these type of dampers 'Frequency Adapters' as they modify the frequency of blade lead-lag.

Friction

The friction type of drag damper is found on older machines such as the Sikorsky H-19.

Cables

Another solution is to put cables between the blades - this is a fixed lead–lag damper: the blades are always in the correct position with respect to one another. Simple, cheap and effective.

Most rotors could do without the damper in flight, as they are only needed to prevent ground resonance. Newer bearingless rotors need the damper to prevent air resonance.

It should be noted that two-bladed rotors do not have lead-lag dampers. The blades still experience lead-lag forces, but these are absorbed into the main rotor shaft, which has some elasticity.

It should be noted that all of these lead-lag dampers can be affected by temperature.

Droop Stops / Flap Restrainers

General

Some limitation must be made on the amount of flapping movement the rotor blades have with respect to the hub. This is a problem peculiar to the articulated head. We've already seen why and how the blades need to be restrained in lead–lag. Having one end of the pitch change rod attached to the swashplate makes blade feathering self limiting. That leaves a problem of the blades flapping up or down. Flapping down can dent things like tail booms and fuselages, and flapping up can result in very large coning angles, as well as very high stresses in the hub. The solution are *droop* (down) and *flap* (up) *restrainers*.

Flapping and coning are normally only a problem when the rotor is at low N_R. Centrifugal force has not yet acted to keep the blade relatively straight out from the hub. Stopping and starting the rotor with winds from different relative directions can cause some pretty spectacular flapping - both up and down, and so droop and flap restrainers are often installed. (We may need to have higher flapping and lower drooping in-flight)

Droop and flap restrainers normally retract or extend under the influence of centrifugal force as the blades speed up or slow down respectively. An example of a head with both types is shown in Figure 24-6. The droop stops in the Bell 206 series is also shown, and they work by preventing the opposite side from going up.

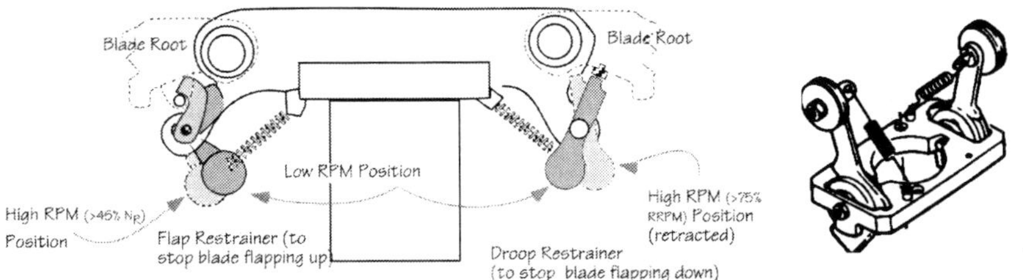

Figure 24-6 Droop and Flap Restrainers, Bell 206 Droop Stops

Droop Stop Pounding

Droop stop pounding can occur when ground taxing helicopters. The pilot moves the cyclic to change the rotor tilt and this may put some of the blades onto the droop stops. The problem can often by solved by raising the collective slightly.

Example of A Problem with Droop Stops

The UH-60A has a lot of forward tilt to the rotor disk with respect to the fuselage. Early versions of this machine sometimes experienced problems when starting with a tail wind. The blade on the left hand side (aft turning with respect to the fuselage, advancing with respect to the tailwind) had a lot of blade pitch. With a tail wind, this blade produced a significant amount of lift, (even at slow N_R). The blade would flap up and hit the flap restrainer, which was still extended due to the low N_R. Unfortunately, in the early days, the flap restrainer wasn't quite what it could have been, and when this blade flapping up happened, the flap restrainer would be hit hard enough to jam it in the extended (or low speed) position. This happened on two different occasions to me, and each time was felt in the form of two 'thumps' as the rotor started to turn, and then everything seemed to be normal. (The rotor had sped up enough for centrifugal force to flap the blade down again.) Hovering was no problem, but when transition to forward flight was attempted, the problem re-appeared. The jammed flap restrainer showed itself again at about 20 knots of airspeed with the stick moving forward, (and the retreating blade at a high blade pitch angle again, with a high flapping angle) when a very pronounced vertical vibration appeared, caused by the blade flapping up against the jammed flap restrainer. This put an end to aviating until the flap restrainer was changed.

Most helicopters that operate from ships (where relative winds can be quite high) need to have flap and droop restrainers, which must be in position before the rotor can be stopped. The restrainers are easy to spot when they are engaged, and are lit for night operations. This is also a reason for rotor brakes for shut down and start up.

On some helicopters, the droop stops are of such importance than ground crew have to observe the droop stops are correctly placed prior to shut down. What happens if the stops don't go into place? Two different helicopter types have had problems when droop stops broke as the machine was being shut down. It was necessary to keep the rotors turning for several hours while emergency cradles were built over the tail rotor pylon. This cradle had plywood covered in grease to let the blade with the damaged droop stop slide up and over the pylon without damage. Not an easy job to be a carpenter working under a turning rotor, maneuvering pieces of plywood. In both cases the effort paid off, as the affected blade sailed up the ramp and over the fuselage and was the only part damaged. If the cradles hadn't been built, the blades would have torn through the tailboom or fuselage resulting in very expensive damage.

In tandem rotor helicopters, failure of a droop stop would inevitably result in chopping the fuselage!

Lubrication

All these things whirling around to change pitch, lead and lag and flap need to work smoothly at great rates, and for many older rotor heads this means they must be lubricated* to ensure things are working properly. This involved oil lines or grease fittings. Naturally this combination of whirling things and oil/ grease results in leaks, look untidy (if not unsightly) and caused a mess. Newer rotor heads, with elastomeric bearings, have eliminated the need for lubrication. The latest generation of bearingless rotors have even eliminated elastomeric bearings.

Disk Axes

There has already been several hints that the rotor disk being more complex than it seems. There are several different ways of looking at the disk. Since there are several parts of the assembly, it might be natural to consider looking at the rotor with respect to each of them. The ways to look at the disk are with respect to:

- the shaft or hub (since these don't move with respect to each other)
- the swashplate
- the tip path plane

The hub is fixed to the rotor shaft, but the swashplate moves (tilts and lifts) with respect to it, so the rotor shaft can't be the only way to look at things. The swashplate is free to tilt and lift with regard to the rotor shaft, but we know that the blades move even more than the swashplate, so we can't use that as the reference.

Shaft Axis

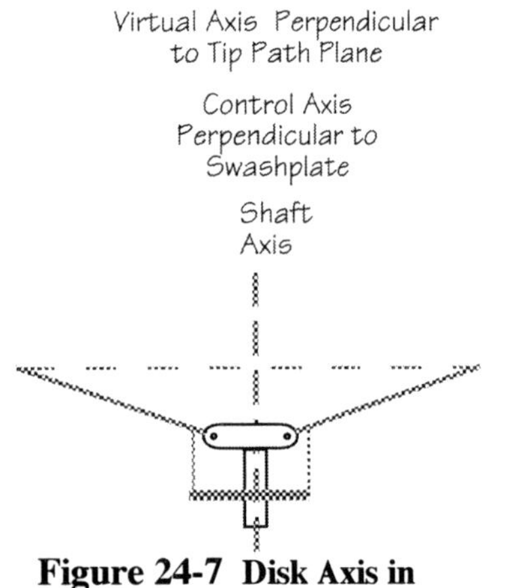

Figure 24-7 Disk Axis in Hover

The first way to look at the TPP is where it is with respect to the rotor shaft - this is called, obviously enough, the *shaft axis*, and runs through the shaft. (it could also be thought of as the mechanical axis) The TPP is more or less perpendicular to this axis in the zero airspeed hover†. The swashplate is also said to be more or less perpendicular to the shaft axis in this condition. This is shown in Figure 24-7.

Control Axis

In forward flight, the rotor shaft maintains its position with regard to the fuselage, but the swashplate and TPP do not. This brings in the next axis, called the *control axis*. The blades have a change in pitch when viewed from the shaft axis, but not when looked at from the control axis. The way to remember which axis is which, is that the pitch change rods are of fixed length, so the relative position of the root end of the blades to the swashplate is always the same. Another way to think of this axis is that is also the axis of no feathering- in other words, the blades all have the same pitch angle when viewed from this axis (sometimes it is called the plane or axis of no feathering). In the zero–airspeed hover, the control axis and shaft axis are the same as shown in Figure 24-7. Figure 24-8 shows the two axis separated in forward flight.

* No- we're not talking about old helicopter pilots needing drinks, although that is a good idea sometimes....
† Minor variations due to CG being ignored for the moment.

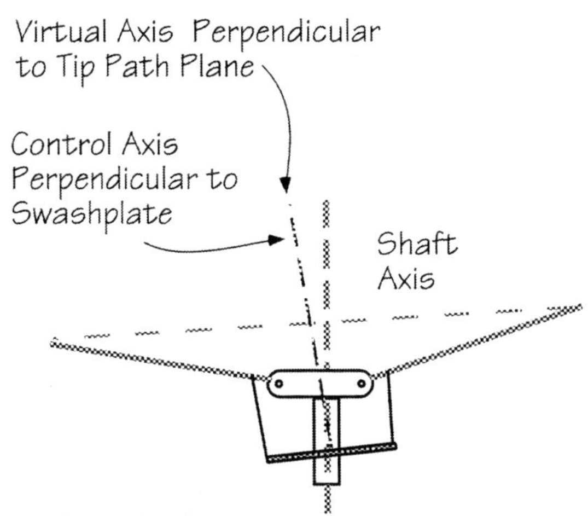

Figure 24-8 Disk Axis Convention

If that were all, things would be relatively simple, but it isn't. We'll visit the third axis next.

Yet Another Disk Axis

There is yet another axis. This one is very difficult to visualize, and is of academic interest only. The TPP is actually tilted away from the position the swashplate thinks the blades should be at, due to flapback. (The rotor blades react to airflow by flapping away from the relative wind (also called blowback), and the way it is created was shown earlier.)

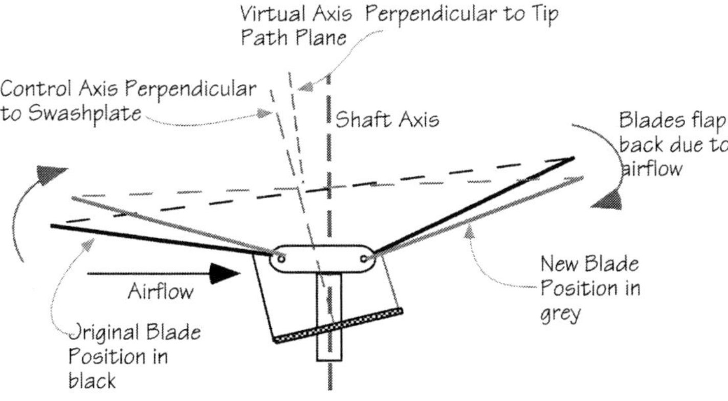

Figure 24-9 Virtual Axis

The axis of this tilted TPP is called the *virtual axis*. This is shown in Figure 24-9. Since in this axis, the blades are all flapped the same amount, it may also be thought of as the axis of no flapping. The reason for mentioning it is to bring home to the reader the fact that the blade tips may not be where the swashplate would indicate they might be. The angle between the shaft axis and the virtual axis is called the flapping angle. So what? What use is this information?

Well, to be honest, not a lot, except if you want to really understand the way the rotor appears to different parts of the system. For engineers and those who need to know, these axis are important, and you never know when you might come across them*.

HINGES

Articulated rotors have hinges to reduce the stresses that would otherwise reduce the hub to a useless piece of garbage. They permitted the first helicopters to be produced, but engineers have been laboring for years to get rid of them. Since they are still used in a number of machines, they need to be understood before we show how they've been eliminated.

Flapping Hinge Offset

The offset of the flapping hinge is an interesting point about the articulated head. One of the facts of a hinge is that no hinge will transmit moments across the itself, but it can transfer a force. When this hinge is offset from the center of the rotor hub, it can produce quite powerful moments, useful for controlling the helicopter. We have already seen in "How Lift Gets to the Hub" on page 26, the way the lift force is transferred to the hub, and now we'll see how the offset can produce rolling or pitching moments.

* ...either the engineers or the various axis - both can sneak up on you, although engineers tend to be more real than virtual.

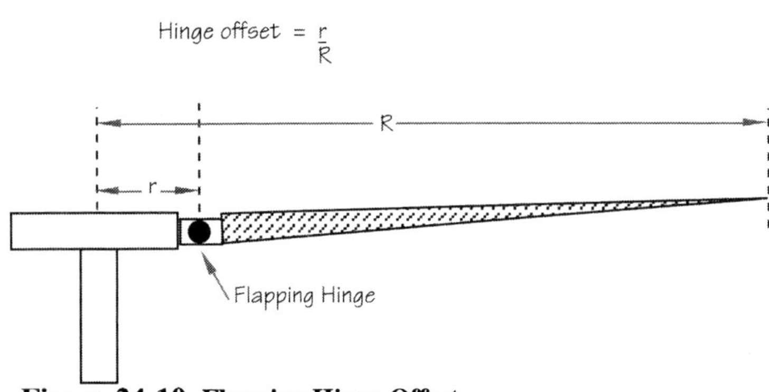

Figure 24-10 Flapping Hinge Offset

The distance of the hinge from the hub (the *offset*) multiplied by the force produced at the hinge produces a moment at the hub. Obviously the larger the offset, the greater the moment for the same force produced by the blade. No offset between the hinge and shaft gives no moment at the hub and this is the case with the 'teetering' head. Implications of this will be discussed in Chapter 33,"Stability and Control of the Helicopter".

The offset of the flapping hinge imparts a moment to the head when the blades are moved by the cyclic. This works as follows:

The rotor blade produces lift, acting at the blade CG. The combination of the lift vector and the centrifugal force make an angle at the flapping hinge.

The blade lift vector is tilted with respect to the horizontal, and has two vectors - one vertical and one horizontal. When the helicopter is in a steady condition, the horizontal force is balanced across the disk. When a cyclic control input is made, the blades must take up a new position with respect to the hub. This new position involves the CG blades moving vertically with regard to the hub, one up and the opposite one down. The horizontal component (i.e. centrifugal force) remains relatively constant on the two sides. With one force moving up, and one moving down, and these forces acting at the offset hinge, a fairly large moment is produced about the hub.

This moment only happens while the blades are moving up and down from the viewpoint of the hub, but while they do, they make the response of the helicopter crisp - something happens immediately when the controls are moved. When the pilot's input stops, (i.e. the helicopter is at the desired attitude) there is no longer any movement of the blades with respect to the hub, and this moment stops. This is shown in Figure 24-11.

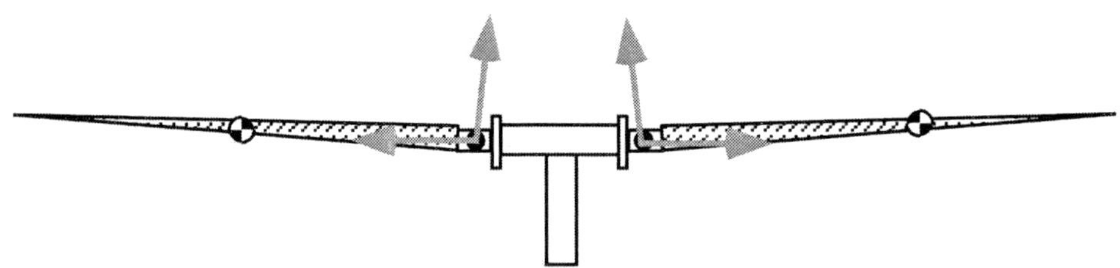

Figure 24-11 Forces Generated by Offset Hinge

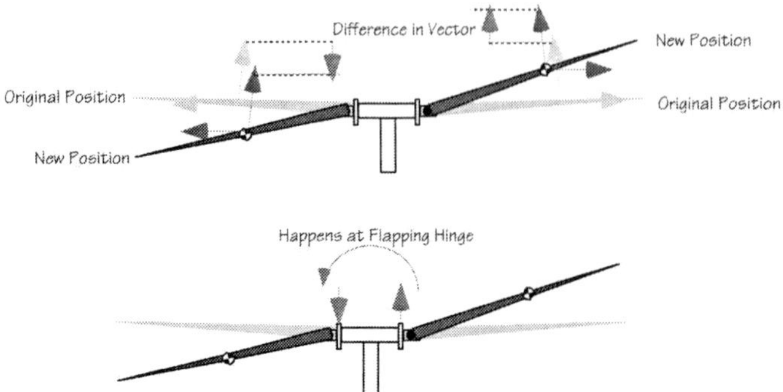

Figure 24-12 How Hinge Offset Generates Crisp Response

Of course, if you have difficulty visualizing this, then a simpler explanation is to use a piece of string pulled at both ends to represent the rotor blades. While this may sound slightly strange, remember the centrifugal force is quite a strong force, and that is what we are trying to represent.

If we suspend our helicopter from the string by just one point, representing a plain teetering rotor helicopter hub with no flapping hinge offset, then if we tilt the string, the helicopter doesn't tilt unless we translate the whole arrangement sideways. This sideways movement equates to the moment the hub makes with the CG.

On the other hand, if we make the rotor hub have two attachment points, then the when the string is tilted, the hub will tilt immediately. This is shown in Figure 24-13 below.

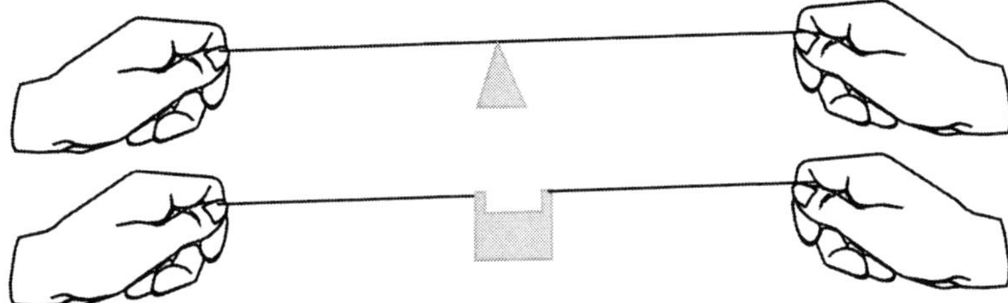

Figure 24-13 Strings and Attachment to Aircraft

Hinge Arrangements

There are many different ways the hinges in the articulated rotor head can be arranged. Some helicopters have the feathering hinge inboard, others put the flapping hinge closest to the hub. Obviously there is no perfect way to do this, or everyone would be the same.

Delta–Three Hinges

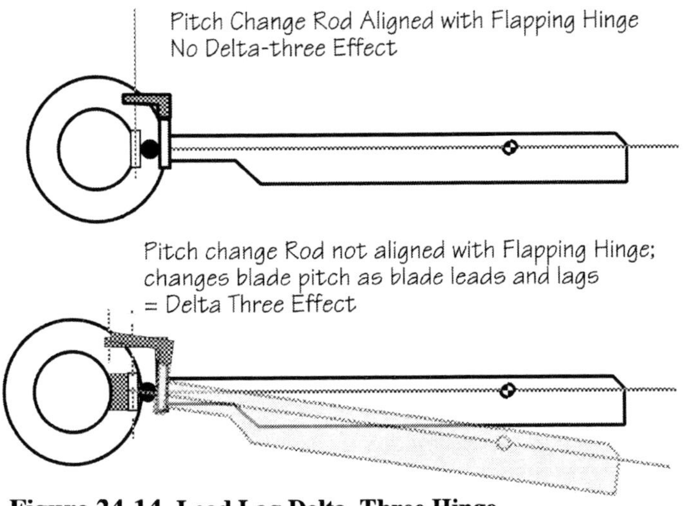

Figure 24-14 Lead Lag Delta–Three Hinge

Some hub–hinge arrangements have a coupling effect between either the flapping or lead–lag hinge and blade pitch, and is commonly known as a *delta–three hinge** - when the blade flaps up or leads–lags, the blade changes pitch. (These two effects are known technically as pitch-flap coupling and pitch–lag coupling respectively.) Delta–three hinges are often incorporated to improve ride quality in turbulence. Figure 24-14 shows a delta–three effect for a lead–lag hinge. Look closely at the head of the S-76, or A109, or CH-46 / 47 series. The Boeing 360 tandem rotor demonstrator had one head with a delta–three hinge, and one without.

In maneuvers delta–three hinges have unusual effects. When maneuvering briskly (for example, pulling up from a steep dive), the rotor speed and torque may change much more than expected, without the collective being moved. When the AoA increases in a turn, the drag changes as well, and the blades move back from their normal radial position. Moving back causes the pitch change rod to move with reference to the flapping hinge, and reduce the pitch on the blades, causing the torque to reduce or the N_R to increase (or both). The way to tell if there is a delta–three effect on the head is to look at the placement of the pitch change rod with respect to either the flapping or lead–lag hinge. If movement of the blade in either axis causes the blade pitch to change, then expect delta–three effects†. Now you know.

* This begs the question of what are delta–one or delta–two hinges - Ray Prouty explained in a long note to me, that Delta one and two hinges were hinges mounted at an angle, used in autogyros for flapping.

† I never understood this either, until I had to teach it. Looking at lots of different main rotor hubs was worthwhile.

Elastomeric Bearings

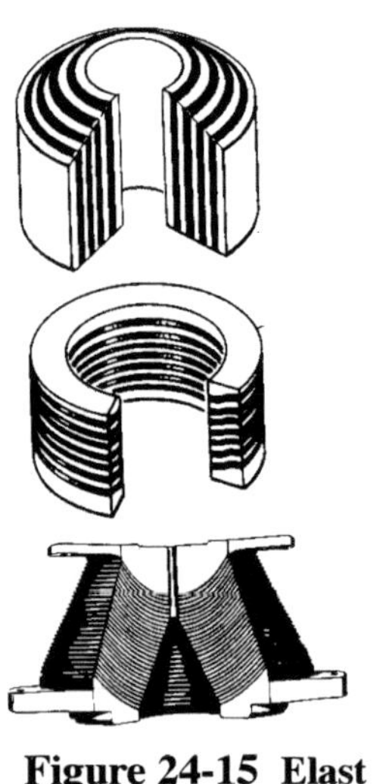

Figure 24-15 Elast omeric Bearing

The *elastomeric* head is really just a high-tech version of the fully articulated head, substituting rubber/metal sandwiches for the conventional hinges. These rubber/metal sandwiches are more streamlined and lighter than their metal predecessors and require very little maintenance. Figure 24-15 shows a typical elastomeric bearing. Being a mixture of metal and rubber, they may have odd properties in cold temperatures, but they don't drip oil or grease and hardly need any maintenance!

Figure 24-16 shows an articulated head that uses composite beams and elastomeric bearings.

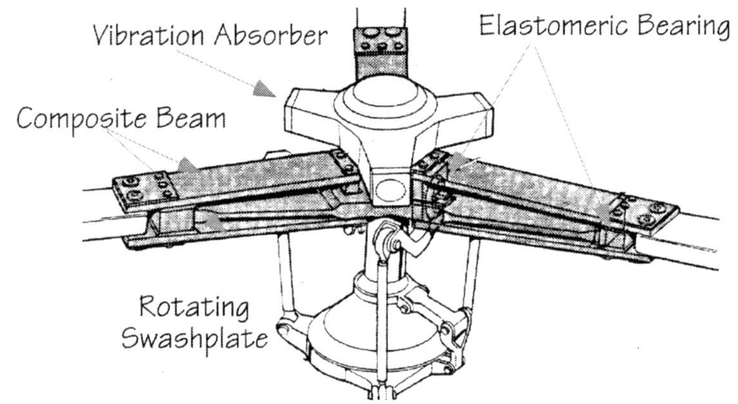

Figure 24-16 Composite Head with Elastomeric Bearings

Hingeless Rotor Heads

The *hingeless* rotor system is a more advanced version of the fully–articulated rotor hub. The various hinges are replaced with exotic metals or composites to absorb the stresses and strains imposed by the blades.

Instead of hinge offset, we speak in terms of 'effective hinge' offset - that is, where the flapping hinge would be if there were one. Typical values of effective hinge offset are at least twice that of articulated heads. This provides a very crisp control response, as not only is the horizontal component of the lift vector transmitted to the hub, but the vertical component can be used as well.

Just like the fully articulated rotor, there are different arrangements of the 'effective' hinges.

Hingeless rotor hubs are of two basic types - 'mature' designs using metal that still have a feathering hinge, and those using composites (Bell 430, MD 900/902 and Eurocopter EC-135) which have no feathering hinge. An examples of the 'mature' design head (i.e. Westland Lynx) is shown below in Figure 24-17.

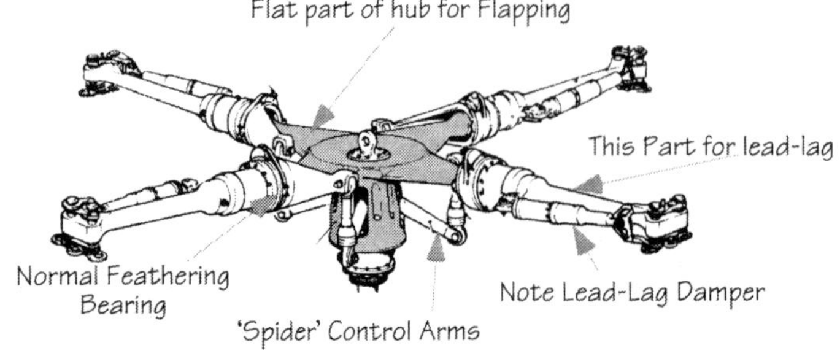

Figure 24-17 Lynx Head

New Rotor Heads

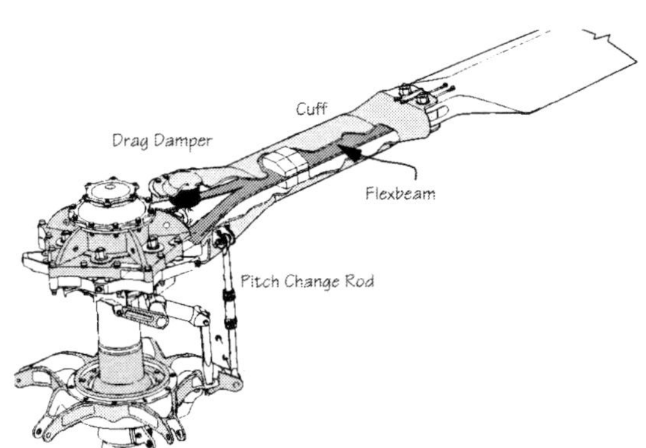

Figure 24-18 MD 900 Head

Advances in composites, as well as greater understanding of the aeroelastic effects of blades, have permitted the 'hingeless' rotor hub to be produced. Note it is not a rigid hub, as there is still movement of the blade. The hinges, (that you can't see physically) are still there. The composite head absorbs all the torques, shears and moments to permit the blades to be bolted to hub directly. The results have been impressive - reduced vibration levels, improved handling qualities and much reduced costs of construction and maintenance. A typical example of such a head (from the MD 900) is shown in Figure 24-18. Note there is still a drag damper (of sorts – it's closer to the elastomeric type than to the shock absorber type seen earlier). Modern hingeless hubs, made of plastics and metals, have removed part of the requirement for the lead lag for ground resonance, and the lead–lag hinge itself has disappeared (the plastic or metal is capable of absorbing the stresses). No-one seems to have be able to get away from the requirement for some sort of lead lag damper, but in the modern 'hingeless' head has them for air resonance as opposed to ground resonance.

The Teetering Rotor Head

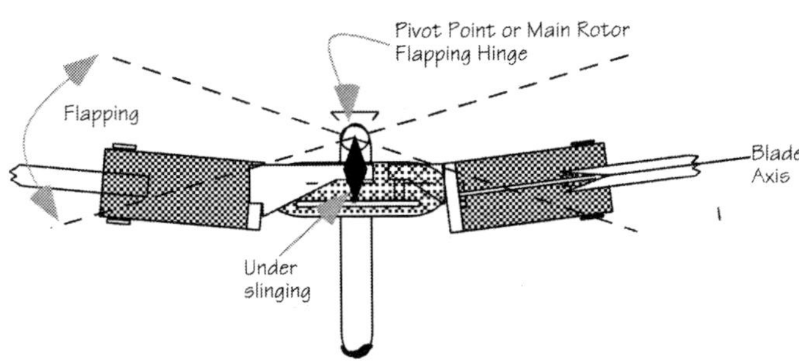

'igure 24-19 Bell Teetering Head

The simplest rotor head is the Bell teetering (or underslung, *semi-rigid*) design. It was the work of Arthur Young, who developed the concept to provide a stable rotor system from a mathematical basis*. That this hub type has endured for so many years is testimony to his work. Providing the center of rotation of the hub is below its pivot point on the mast, the hub will tend to self–center. It has advantages of less maintenance, lower space to park the helicopter and so on. Those who say the concept suffers from noise, vibration and handling at low G have not seen the improvements Bell has made in these areas. As to those who say it is old fashioned, nothing has yet replaced the wing and aileron on fixed–wing aircraft. Figure 24-19 shows the basic components of the Bell head.

The teetering head lets the various forces from the blades balance themselves. Earlier discussion developed the requirement for flapping and lead–lag hinges in articulated rotors. There are no such hinges in the Bell head, for the two blades are rigidly joined. When the lead–lag forces are present, the forces not absorbed by the hub are balanced between the two blades. Flapping differences between the blades and dissymmetry of lift are taken care of by letting the blades find their own balance. There is very little change in coning angle with power - the coning angle is pre-set in the hub†.

* He also wrote some fascinating philosophical books - one of the best is "The Reflexive Universe"

† The hub on the R-22 and R-44 has a flapping hinge; this may help to increase the control crispness, along with the higher rotational speeds.

Stabilizer Bars

Some teetering rotor heads have stabilizer bars between the cockpit controls and the rotor blades. How these work is relatively simple, and is shown in Figure 24-20.

The stabilizer bar is like a large gyroscope, and has some rigidity in space. It wants to keep spinning on the same axis, unless it is changed by a control input from the pilot. If there is no control input from the pilot and the helicopter moves underneath the stabilizer bar, (i.e. a gust moves it) the stabilizer bar makes a control input to the rotor in opposition to try to damp out the movement. This is shown in Figure 24-21 below. When the pilot moves the controls, the input is fed to the rotor and the stabilizer bar, so the blade moves and the stabilizer bar also takes up its new position in space. Typically there is a damper in the stabilizer bar mechanism to prevent it from reacting too rapidly. Without the damping action (seen as the time it takes a small pin in the system to move following a movement on the bar) the stabilizer bar would immediately try to take out the pilot–commanded input. A small problem is the bar works equally in both pitch and roll, where the requirements control response of the two axes may be slightly different.

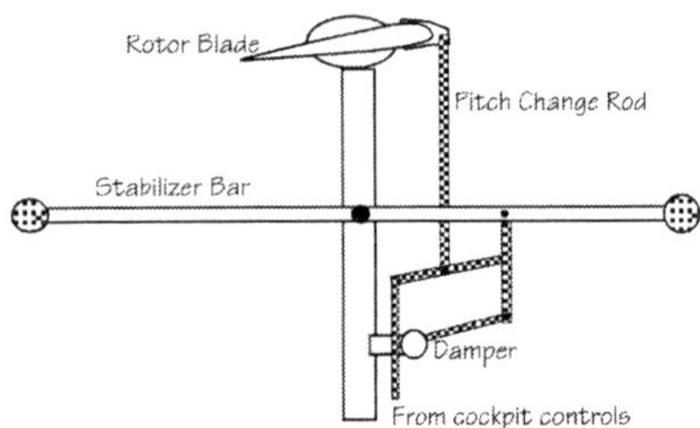

Figure 24-20 Stabilizer Bar

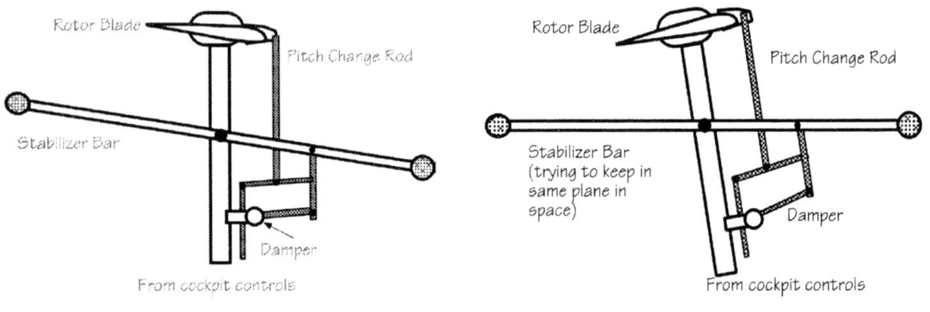

Pilot Input, Bar and Blade move

No Pilot input, only gust - bar tries to stay in one plane

Figure 24-21 Bell Stabilizer Bar in Action

The teetering head (with or without the stabilizer bar) has a reputation for docile handling and slow response to control inputs. The easiest way to understand this is to consider that the teetering head must persuade the fuselage to follow the thrust vector. In other words, the direction of the rotor thrust vector is changed, and the fuselage, hanging underneath* it, follows a short time later. There is no distance (or offset) between the flapping hinge (the teetering hinge in this case) and the rotor shaft, so regardless of the amount of the rotor flapping, no rolling or pitching moment can be applied to the shaft.

Obviously, if the helicopter is in a zero gravity situation, there is no tendency for the fuselage to follow the rotor disk. See "Mast Bumping" on page 393. for why 0G isn't a good idea.

* The previous edition said 'like a pendulum', but this was removed for a very good reason- see "Myths of the Helicopter" on page 435.

With a teetering rotor head, the helicopter responds only by virtue of the distance between the thrust vector and the center of gravity. In other words, the airframe is persuaded by gravity to follow the thrust vector. This is one reason for the height of the hub above the fuselage - it gives a larger moment arm to the CG of the helicopter.

A perceived shortcoming of the teetering head is its response to low (less than approximately +0.5G) or negative G situations. Such a situation can be encountered if the helicopter is 'pushed over' in forward flight*. In brief, the helicopter relies on some gravity to make the airframe line up under the rotor. With no gravity vector, there is no way to control the relative position of the rotor disk to the airframe. In forward flight, with all the aerodynamic forces acting on it, the fuselage wants to go in a different direction to the rotor, and the rotor can't prevent it. While this may be a valid technical criticism of the design, it is also expecting the machinery to do something it clearly was never designed to do. Sort of like expecting your lawnmower to trim hedges...

The real answer is to know the limitations and not exceed them. I am very surprised that the military services that operate these helicopter types do not have G meters installed to permit a limitation to be observed - it's like putting an airspeed limit on the helicopter and then taking out the airspeed indicator. End of sermon.

Flap or Hub Restraining Springs

The problem of slow response in general and poor response in negative G can be partly overcome by the use of flap or hub restraining springs, effectively a spring that passes a force proportional to the deflection of the hub from the neutral position to the mast. This force then moves the helicopter. The Bell 222 *hub restraining spring* have such a large force it is possible to do chin-ups on the free end of the blade and not produce significant amounts of flapping.

It is not possible to retrofit hub restraining springs to existing models for a whole variety of technical reasons. For beginners, the top casing of the transmission would now have to handle bending moments instead of just lifting loads. Some US Army UH-1's had hub springs for a short while, but they appear to have been removed due to high mast fatigue loads.

Hiller Control System

The control system used in Hiller helicopters is similar to the Bell system, but also unique. The collective and cyclic control systems are completely separate! The cyclic is used to control the paddles, which in turn tilts the rotor, while the collective system is used change the blade pitch. This is shown in Figure 24-22 below.

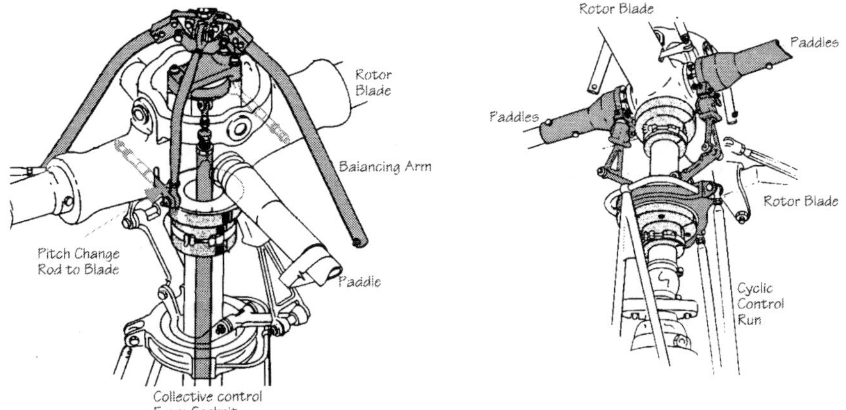

Figure 24-22 Hiller Control System

Note that there are adjustments on both control runs to reduce the effort needed to move and hold the controls.

* Not something you would normally do, or want to try!

Robinson R-22 and R-44 Hub.

The Robinson hub is a slight change in the philosophy of the Bell teetering head. As well as an underslung hub, it incorporates flapping hinges.

We have already discussed flapping hinges and how they generate a moment at the hub when the controls are moved. This, combined with the high N_R and tall mast make for a relatively crisp response to control inputs.

MD Series Rotor Head

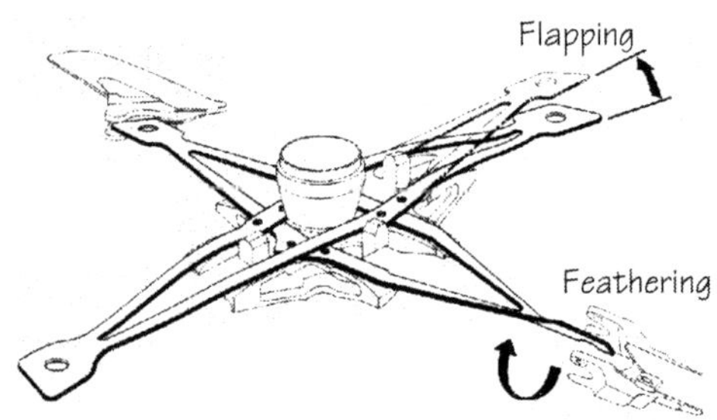

Figure 24-23 MD Helicopters Rotor Hub

The helicopter design that perhaps holds the record for the most name changes, currently known as MD Helicopters, but previously bearing Hughes, McDonnell Douglas and Boeing labels, has a different kind of rotor head / hinge arrangement. It is shown below in Figure 24-23. Note how the design incorporates the virtual hinges for flapping and lead lag.

Height of Hub Above the CG

An important feature of all teetering rotor hubs is that in order to have good handling, they must be mounted high above the CG. This is to provide a long moment arm above the CG, as it is only this moment that provides the control necessary. Conversely, nearly all other rotor systems can be mounted closer to the fuselage.

Blade Lag Angle

In both the hingeless and teetering rotor head helicopters, the problem of the drag equivalent of coning must be addressed. In a fully articulated head, there is generally no problem in letting the individual blades lag slightly behind the ideal radial position. In a zero–airspeed hover, they will all lag the same amount behind, and in forward flight, the lead-lag hinge takes care of things anyway.

In a teetering rotor helicopter, or a hingeless head, there is no easy mechanism to take out this constant drag force, except by angling the blades both slightly forward. Even one or two degrees of forward slant will help to keep the stresses in the root of the blade and hub low.

Negative Pitch

If a rotor disk can produce positive thrust, it stands to reason that it can also be used to produce a lot of negative thrust by use a lot of nose-down blade pitch. So what? Of what possible use is this? Ask anyone who has ever landed on a pitching, heaving ships deck and wanted to stay there. There is only one helicopter I've ever seen with the ability to use negative pitch, and that is the Westland Lynx family. Pushing down on the collective will produce about 1,000 pounds of downward force, enough to glue the helicopter to the deck in incredible seas*.

Summary of Chapter 24

This chapter has covered a lot of technical ground. Studying the control system of any helicopter is a useful exercise to see how the movements you command in the cockpit are transmitted to the rotating components.

If you want a real education on the subject, look at the flight control system of a model helicopter!

* Don't worry, when the helicopter shuts down, it is held on by a special harpoon arrangement.

25 Advanced Performance

GENERAL

There are some important differences between the performance of a light piston helicopter and a turbine powered helicopter.

For example, the turbine helicopter typically uses a torquemeter (although collective pitch may be used). Engine parameters such as TOT or N_1, can be used to some degree if these can be closely related to overall power required or available. The piston engine helicopter has only manifold pressure and engine RPM available, and these are difficult to use to measure performance directly.

FACTORS AFFECTING PERFORMANCE

Disk Loading

Disk loading is the amount of weight each square foot (or square meter) of the disk carries. It is of importance because it determines the power loading, or amount of weight each unit of power (i.e. kilowatt or horsepower) must carry. This is shown below. The formula for disk loading is quite straightforward, with the value changing with the weight of any one helicopter. Units are in pounds per square foot, or kilograms per square meter, and typical values range from 2 to $15\frac{\text{lb.}}{\text{ft}^2}$.

$$\text{Disk Loading} = \frac{\text{Weight}}{\text{Area of Disk}} \qquad \text{(EQ 17.)}$$

The disk loading is determined early in the design of the helicopter, and is one of many compromises made. There are advantages to both high and low disk loadings. The following advantages are presented in such a manner that you will have to think about the downsides (to find the disadvantage of low disk loading, read the advantages of high disk loading, and vice versa).

Disk loading changes very little in hover or level flight, as the coning angle of the blades will not make a significant change in area of the disk.

Disk loading also affects the N_R in autorotation, particularly when the loading on the helicopter is changed due to turning or flaring.

Low Disk Loading

A low disk loading means the downwash is low, and the helicopter will be friendly to work underneath. How do you think Igor Sikorsky could wear his hat without a chin strap in those early movies of the development of the helicopter? It had a low disk loading. Power loading will be low. Induced velocity will be low. N_R in autorotation will be slow to respond and the collective can be reduced to minimum in autorotation.

High Disk Loading

A high disk loading will mean the helicopter should be almost immune to gusts and turbulence. Rotor response in autorotation will be crisp. High forward speeds will typically be possible.

Power Loading

Power loading is the weight each horsepower (or kilowatt) must support in the hover. Because of rotor efficiency effects, the power loading and the disk loading are strongly tied to one another. This is shown in Figure 25-1, which shows two different efficiencies* for rotor systems.

There is an example on this diagram- the point labeled 'A' shows how two different rotor efficiencies will require different powers to hover the same weight of helicopter. Large differences in the efficiency can be due to twist, taper, airfoil geometry and tip shape. On a more practical day–to–day example, if the upper curve (more efficient rotor) is taken as a new, clean rotor blade, and the lower curve (less

* This efficiency is called Figure of Merit, and can never be greater than 1.0 (100%), but the practical limit seems to be 0.8 (80%)

efficient rotor) is a very old, dirty, pitted-leading edge blade, it can be seen how this is affecting performance. The less efficient blade can lift less weight per horsepower. Since the pilot is interested in the overall weight, with a dirty, less efficient blade, it will take more power to produce the same amount of lift.

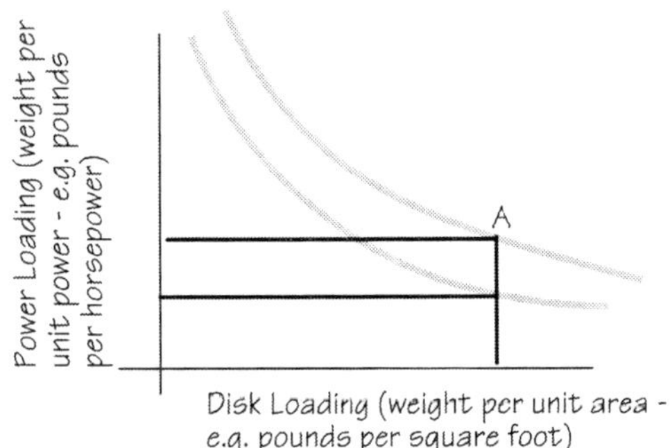

Figure 25-1 Power loading vs. Disk Loading

A lightly loaded disk can let the engine carry more weight per pound; but many other things like a design cruise airspeed, hangarability, empty weight and so on will determine the final rotor diameter and thus the disk loading.

By way of example, the EH-101 was designed with a very strict rotor diameter size. This determined the disk area, and mission equipment and fuel determined the weight of the machine. The result was a high disk loading, and demanded about 4,500 horsepower to hover the helicopter in the specified atmospheric conditions. There was also a requirement for a fly-away from an engine failure in the hover. A typical One Engine Inoperative (OEI) condition was calculated to require about 3,500 shaft horsepower (shp). The number of engines installed was dictated by lack of suitable 2,500 shp engines with contingency ratings of 3,000 to 3,500 shp. In the end, and for a number of other reasons, three 1,700 shp engines with contingency ratings to about 2,000 shp were used. It should come as no surprise that the helicopter now has excellent OEI capabilities.

Induced Velocity

In Chapter 2,"Introduction to Helicopter Aerodynamics", mention was made of *induced velocity*, and how it affects relative airflow (RaF). This section will expand on the earlier discussion. Without going into lots of theory, the rotor imparts a velocity to the stream of air flowing through it, and the speed of the downflowing air depends upon the weight of the helicopter, density of the air and area of the disk. The formula for induced velocity immediately under the rotor disk is given below. The higher the weight and the smaller the area, the higher the induced velocity. Helicopters with a high disk loading have a high induced velocity. High induced velocity gives a high downwash speed, which can create havoc with unprepared surfaces. There is a good reason why you should tie everything down if a CH-47 or CH-53 are in the area![*]

$$v_i = \sqrt{\frac{\text{Weight}}{2\rho\text{Area of Disk}}} \qquad \text{(EQ 18.)}$$

where:

v_i = induced velocity
ρ = air density
A = Area of the rotor disk

The velocity immediately below the disk is not the final velocity, as the air will actually speed up as it flows down. In much the same way as a stream of water will contract as it drops (seen with water poured from a pitcher), the downwash will speed up and contract slightly. The result is that the induced velocity is highest (in fact, doubled) and the rotor downwash area at its smallest (but most concentrated) about 1 to 1.5 rotor diameters below the helicopter. If you have to hover and minimize downwash effects, then it is best to hover above or below this height. On the other hand, if you wish to do the most damage...

As an aside, the downwash will also have a slight swirl to it, in the direction of rotor rotation. This swirl interacts with the relatively still air around it to form small vortices at the edge of the downwash, swirling out away from the helicopter. This may be visible if you are operating near water covered surfaces on a calm day, and can see these small vortices at the edge of the main rotor downwash.

* The KA-32 when loaded has an even higher induced velocity than these machines thanks to the co-axial rotor

Mach Number Effects

In cold weather, some helicopters experience a loss in performance due to the effects of high relative Mach numbers at the blade tips. This is even more pronounced at high forward airspeeds when the tip of the advancing blade has a very high True Airspeed (TAS). Without getting into detailed discussions of supersonic and subsonic flow, as blade tip speeds approach the speed of sound, there is a very large rise in drag. Most rotor blades tip speeds are designed to be well below this level, but some are not.

The FM of the Canadian Air Force Bell UH-1N talked about up to 5% loss of range in cold weather due to the effects of Mach number drag. The tip speed in cruise at sea level, -20°C,* was in the vicinity of 0.95 Mach (very close to the speed of sound). As the air temperature drops, the speed of sound decreases and the Mach number increases at the same True Air Speed (TAS). The tip of the rotor is always turning at the same TAS in the hover. Operational pilots used to reduce the N_R in the cruise in cold weather to minimize this effect. The performance charts showed a similar problem in the hover in very cold weather.

The cause here was a combination of high tip Mach number with high blade pitch angles and AoA. This caused a shock wave as the air tried to go over the top of the blade. Reducing the N_R considerably would regain some of the power being absorbed by the Mach drag. Unfortunately, the power turbine governor did not have this large a range, so a slight penalty in hover performance in cold weather had to be accepted.

Calculating tip Mach number is relatively easy, and the formulae below is for a tip speed in feet per second. For a helicopter with an advance ratio of 0.3, and a tip speed of 650 feet per second at 15°C, the tip Mach number is 0.75

$$\text{Tip Mach Number} = \frac{(1+\upsilon)\times\Omega R}{1,117} = \frac{(1+0.3)\times 650}{1,117} = 0.75 \quad \text{(EQ 19.)}$$

The value of 1,117 feet per second is only valid at 15°C. To know the tip Mach number at any other air temperature, you must divide the tip speed by the local Mach number. You can either look this up, or do the following simple calculation:

$$\text{Speed of Sound} = 49.02\sqrt{(460+T)} \quad \text{(EQ 20.)}$$

where:

- Speed of Sound is in feet per second
- T is in Degrees Farenheit

Hover Performance and Altitude

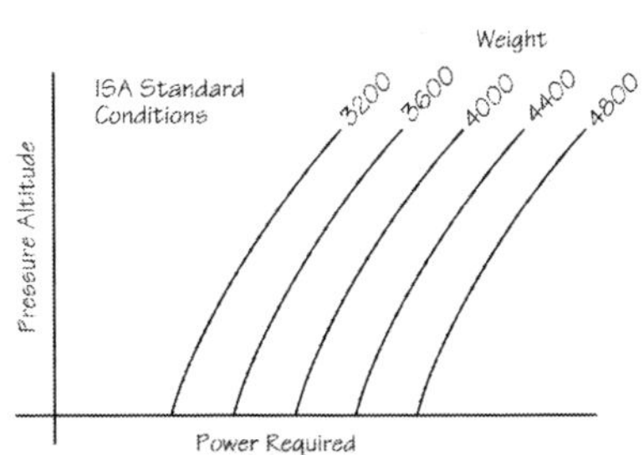

Figure 25-2 Power Required to Hover IGE vs. Pressure Altitude

It takes more power to hover the helicopter at a high density altitudes than at sea level using the same weight, height above ground and wind. The reason for this is that the air is thinner and the rotor blades must move more volume to effectively shift the same mass of air. The way to move more air is to use a larger blade pitch angle, and hence higher AoA. If you remember the C_L and C_D curves from Figure 1–16, at a higher AoA, the drag will be higher - hence the drag on the blades will increase, and the power needed to turn the blades (torque) will increase. The other part of drag on the blades, namely profile drag, decreases due to less friction, and partly offsets the increase in induced drag. The following chart shows the effect of not only increasing pressure altitude, but also the effect that changing the OAT from standard to ISA+25°C has at each weight. This effect is shown in Figure 25-2.

* Sea Level, ISA- 35°C since we went to so much trouble to discuss it before.

Surface Effect on Hover Performance

The type of terrain being hovered over IGE has an effect on the power required to hover. Obviously OGE, it doesn't matter, but remember the rotor doesn't know whether it's 10 feet above the grass or 10 feet above the trees - it's just pumping out air. Simplistically, some types of ground can soak up power quite easily. Long grass is an example. If the helicopter is hovered at low height over concrete on a calm day and then slowly taxied over an adjacent grass covered surface, without changing power, (either collective position or RPM), the helicopter will settle slightly when the greater part of the rotorwash is over the grass. Other good power 'sinks' are tall trees. OGE with respect to the forest floor may not be OGE with respect to the tops of the trees.

On some really high disk loading helicopters, like the CH-53E, hovering over water may actually make a small depression in the surface.

Sloping surfaces of course will spill lift out from under one side of the disk, and have a large effect on the power required to hover. All FM performance is given for flat surfaces.

Vertical Drag

The fuselage of the helicopter is subject to the downwash of the rotor, as are underslung loads, and this can also have an effect on the hover performance of the helicopter. The fuselage adds about 5 to 10% to the overall power required in the hover. In an extreme example, if you were to put a very large flat plate underneath the helicopter, at least equal to the rotor in diameter, the helicopter would not be able to lift-off, and the vertical drag would be excessively large.

Figure 25-3 Vertical Drag

I have heard of a deflated, streamed parachute underneath a helicopter soaking up lots of power. (It was to support a car being para-dropped after release from the cargo hook.) Even though the total weight to be lifted was well within the limits of the helicopter, it could not hover with the parachute collapsed and streaming vertically underneath.

Some helicopter FMs show this in an indirect way. Look at the supplement for fitting pop-out floats, for example, and in the Hover Performance chants you may see a statement to the effect of "Reduce weight by 50 pounds." This is a roundabout way of saying that the vertical drag of the pop-out floats is equivalent to adding 50 pounds to the weight of the helicopter (in addition to the actual weight of the floats) as far as the rotor is concerned.

Another Look at Hover Performance

The effect of density altitude on aerodynamic performance was discussed earlier. In Chapter 10,"The Piston Engine" and Chapter 29,"The Turbine Engine", the effect of pressure altitude and air temperature on engine performance (piston and turbine respectively) is shown. Unfortunately, combining the two performances (power available and power required) is only valid if you have these charts in your FM. There are two ways to do this, and both require knowledge of the power available and the power required. This is shown in Figure 25-4 below.

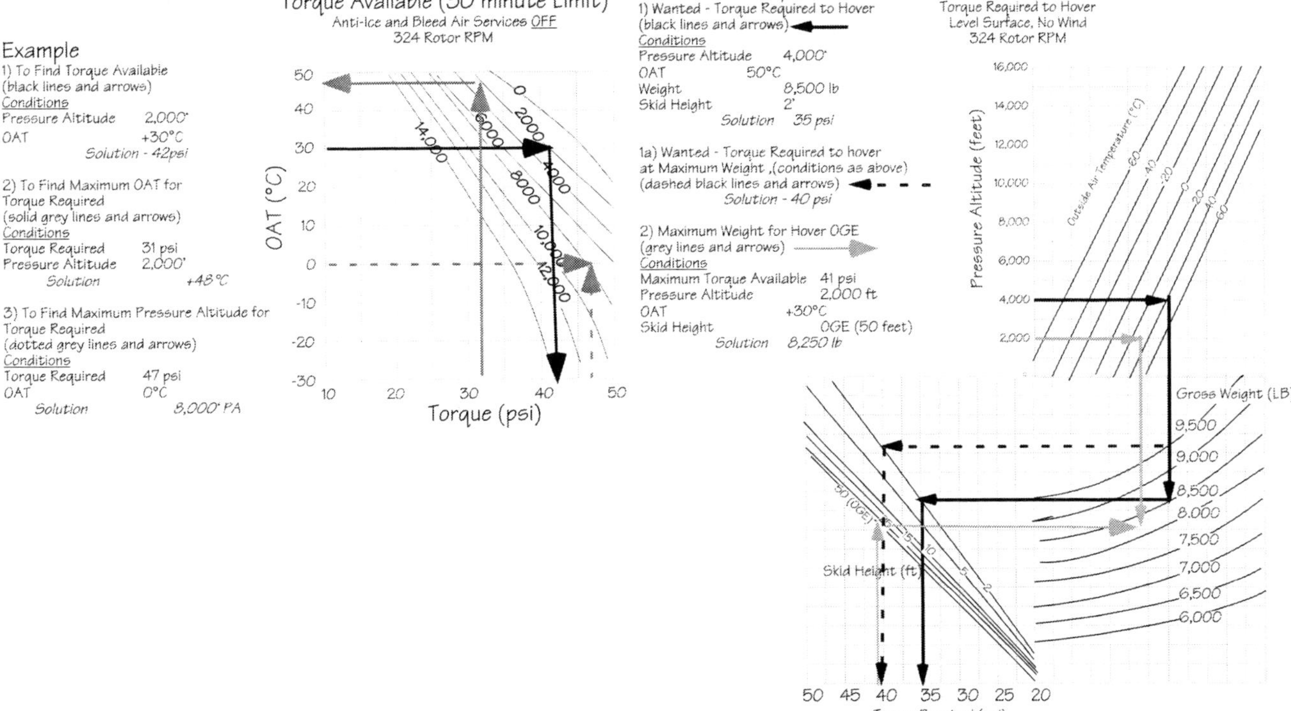

Figure 25-4 Military -Style Hover Performance Put Together

In all cases, the ambient conditions for Pressure Altitude (PA) and Outside Air Temperature are known. The examples in the right hand chart determine the power (torque) required to hover knowing the weight of the helicopter. After determining this, it is necessary to check if the engine will have this power (torque) available.

A second method relies on determining the power (torque) available from the engine, and then determining the weight that can be lifted in the given conditions. This is also shown in Figure 25-4 above.

A Neat Trick From the FM

There is another trick hidden in the power required to hover chart (the right hand one). If you know the pressure altitude and OAT, then you can determine the power required to hover at your maximum permitted weight (for this chart, it is only valid for no wind). Knowing the atmospheric parameters, you can determine how much power it should take you to hover at a given height at maximum weight. Obviously, if you take more power than that, you are overweight...

Typical Civil FM Performance Chart

Most civil FM performance charts aren't set up the same way as the military charts shown above. I don't know all the reasons for this, but among them might be a carry-over from piston engine helicopters and ease of interpretation by pilots. It certainly doesn't help to give the complete picture about performance. A typical civilian FM chart is shown in Figure 25-5 below*.

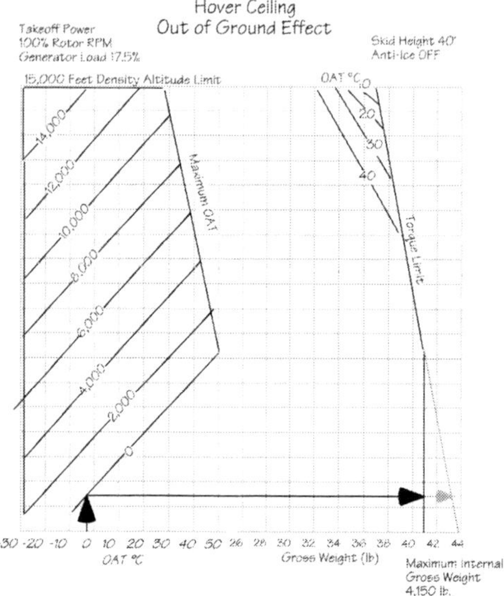

Figure 25-5 Civilian Hover Performance Chart

It is worth noting that this chart has a density altitude calculation on the left hand side, which is then corrected for temperature effects on the power available from the turbine engine by the additional lines on the right hand side. The information is all there, but has to be considered slightly differently. When the example is followed, it shows that the helicopter will be able to hover, but that it will be limited by maximum weight.

In fact, if the example of 0°C, sea level pressure altitude is used, it is obvious that this helicopter can hover OGE at maximum weight. But if you weren't really sure of your weight, and decided to use maximum torque as the measure of your performance, you would be deceiving yourself- the light grey lines are extrapolated to show that in this example, you would probably be at least 200 pounds over your maximum permitted weight. A military style power required to hover chart might prevent that mistake.

Level Flight Performance

In general terms, this section will take us from the influence of the ground on the performance to the influence of airspeed and a greater impact of the air mass. The arbitrary line distinguishing the two areas was previously defined at about 40 knots.

Indicated Airspeed and True Airspeed

For the altitudes and airspeeds that most helicopters fly at, there is not a lot of difference between indicated and true airspeed (IAS and TAS). Yet, if you go above 6,00 AMSL, the distinction starts to become significant and will certainly affect navigation calculations. Most navigation computers will handle this conversion nicely. Be aware that TAS is needed if you are going to try to figure out the wind speed and direction from your GPS receiver.

* If this looks the same as an earlier chart, it is.

Collective Angle vs. Airspeed

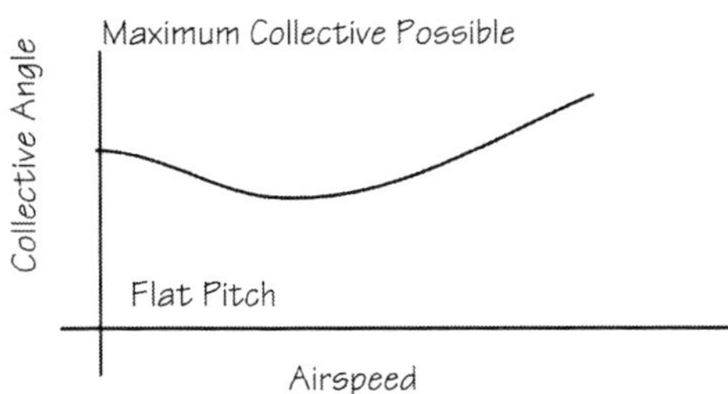

Figure 25-6 Collective Angle vs. Airspeed

The main rotor absorbs most of the power of the helicopter, so it would be reasonable to expect there to be a linear relation between collective angle and power. This simplistic approach ignores the effect of inflow on the induced drag of the rotor. Since many of the helicopters I have flown have been extensively instrumented, it has been instructive to look at collective position vs. airspeed and compare it to power vs. airspeed. A plot of collective position vs. airspeed is shown in Figure 25-6. Tail rotor power makes a difference, but does not account for all the power change seen.

With so little collective travel necessary during normal flight, why do we have such a large range of travel in this control? The answer is to permit autorotation, climbs and descents. There have actually been some helicopters proposed which did not have such a wide range of collective travel, and would have great difficulty in dealing with an autorotation. At least one was made - the Lockheed CL475 which used fixed pitch and variable RPM.

Power vs. Collective Angle

When transitioning from the hover to forward flight did you ever notice the torque used had reduced suddenly without the collective being lowered? Did you wonder if you had moved something and not known it? In all probability, you had just seen another interesting aspect of helicopter aerodynamics, called translational lift See also "Translational Lift" on page 140. Remember torque is the drag on the rotor blades.

The relationship between power and collective angle changes with airspeed. This is perhaps most vividly shown by setting the power for level flight at a moderate airspeed. If the V_{NE} of the helicopter is 120 KIAS, try 80 KIAS as the starting point. Note the torque, N_1 and TOT at this airspeed. Without changing the collective and from a safe height above ground, gently accelerate towards V_{NE}. (You will be descending, by the way...) Note what happens to the torque. (It should decrease slightly.)

Next, and still without changing the collective, decelerate to 40 KIAS and observe the torque. (You will be climbing...) The torque should increase slightly.

The changes in torque are due to the change in inflow of air to the rotor, changing the angle of attack on the rotor blades, which changes the induced drag. As the helicopter speeds up, the inflow through the disk is at a more shallow angle, and as the helicopter slows down, the inflow is at a steeper angle. The blade pitch angle (with respect to the airframe) does not change, but there is a large change in both AoA and induced drag.

There is no operational reason for this type of maneuver, except perhaps changing from cruise to climbing at the same power setting (for example, cruise power). If the collective position is not changed, chances are the torque will increase beyond the continuous limit as the airspeed decreases. The opposite occurs when the helicopter is accelerated from the hover - aside from any tail rotor power effects, the inflow through the disk reduces the induced drag at the same collective setting, and the torque reduces. But back to our example... When transitioning away from the hover - without changing collective position, the torque decreases. Remember, the engine is making up for drag, not producing lift.

Peculiarities of Low Airspeed IGE

At low airspeeds (around the zero–airspeed hover) airframe performance is often affected in very strange ways. At least one helicopter type has true zero–wind hover performance significantly better than shown in the manual because of this*.

* This raises an interesting question as to which manuals show the effect, and which do not. There is no simple answer, as depending upon the manufacturer and the date and place of certification, it may, or it may not. Sorry this isn't of more help.

Another Look at Power Required to Hover

or,

the Relationship between Power, Torque and N_R...

An interesting effect is the power required to hover is constant at the same conditions of height AGL, weight, density altitude, wind speed and so on. If the effects of rotor efficiency with N_R are ignored, the same amount of power is needed to hold the helicopter at the same height above the ground. This effect can be demonstrated quite easily.

In a stabilized hover, reduce the N_R to the minimum power–on RPM while maintaining a constant height. Slightly more collective is needed to hold the same height. The torque (or for a piston engine helicopter, the manifold pressure) will also be higher. (The reason is explained below.) If the N_R is increased to the maximum power–on RPM, the collective needed is slightly less than collective at normal RPM. The torque will be less at higher N_R.

Why? Remember torque is really a measure of drag, not lift, so you are measuring the change in drag, not the change in lift. As the power required (not the torque) is constant, since the helicopter is at the same height, if a higher N_R is used, then the blade pitch angle and AoA needed will be lower. If you refer to Figure 1-20 (CL and CD vs. AoA), at a lower AoA, there will be less drag. Less power to turn the rotor means the rotor is more efficient. There is normally a lower limit to this, usually the lower power–on N_R limit, but that may be set for different reasons than performance.

Before we explore further, it is worth looking at the relationship between power, torque and N_R.

$$\text{Power} = K \times Q \times N_R \qquad \text{(EQ 21.)}$$

where:

K = some mathematical constant, varying with each helicopter type

Q = Torque

N_R = Rotor RPM

For example, if the transmission puts out 935 horsepower at 100% torque and 100% N_R, then the K value would be 0.0935.

- 935 =.0935* 100 * 100

If the same helicopter were hovering at 78% torque and 99% N_R, it would using 729 horsepower.

- 0.0935x 78 x 99 = 729

For a given power setting, the N_R and torque can be traded one against the other. If power is fixed, and the collective raised, the torque reaction on the rotor blades will increase, driving up the torque. Since there is a fixed amount of power to turn the blades, the increased torque will mean the N_R will reduce. This is possible to demonstrate this in a turbine engine that has a manual control of fuel flow (i.e. a manual mode of governing).

When the power is fixed, (i.e. fuel flow is set constant in manual governor setting), and the collective is raised, the drag on the blades will increase, causing the torque to increase. Since there is no change in fuel flow, the engine cannot do anything except to let the rotor slow down slightly. The engine parameters of N_1 and TOT will remain constant, as the compressor is not being asked to change. The effect is usually very small and hardly measurable with cockpit instruments.

In some helicopters there is a slight improvement in rotor efficiency at lower than normal N_R. This is due to the decreased N_R increasing the angle of attack, but this is obviously only good up to a point. However, a more common problem is being torque limited. If you know about this formula, you can figure out how to get more power out of the helicopter in a legal way... I know of only one helicopter design that recognized this and had a power limiter, not just a torque limiter. It wasn't made in the West, either*.

The same effect could be seen if a fixed fuel flow (i.e. manual throttle) system could be employed.

Rotor Efficiency

The rotor will change efficiency as the N_R changes. This can be seen in the following manner. Earlier it was stated that the power required to hold the machine at the identical conditions of height above ground, weight and so on would be the same, regardless of the N_R. Changes to N_R would be reflected as opposite changes in torque at the same power. The engine will show the change in efficiency if the torque

* Of course, you're out of luck if all you have is a collective angle gauge and no torquemeter.

is ignored. The TOT and N_1 of a turbine engine can be considered to be independent of torque- if the engine has more or less work to do, it will show up in these two parameters. Note the change in these two items as you change N_R at the same height AGL - they may show a slight change in rotor efficiency. With the typical equipment fitted to existing helicopters, this may not be readily obvious, so don't waste too much time looking for it.

Ground Vortex Roll Up

The helicopter hovering IGE is producing a downwash pattern and a set of vortices that spread out around the helicopter. This is shown in Figure 25-7. In a zero–airspeed hover, these should be uniformly displaced about the airframe.

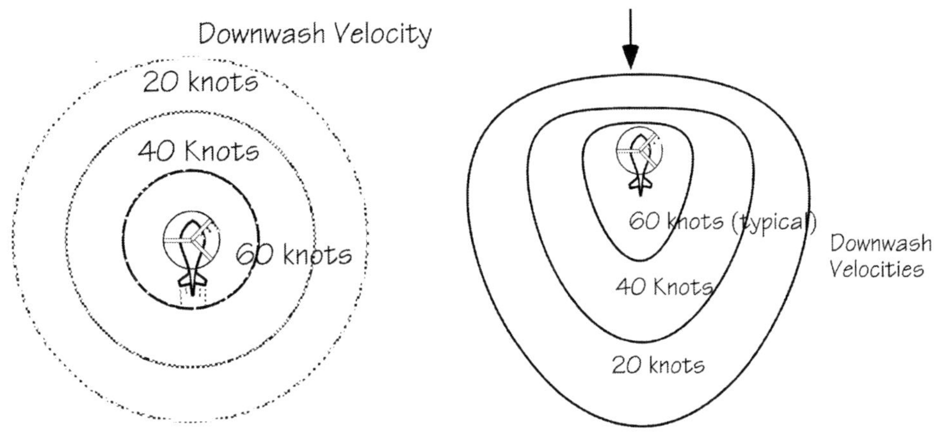

(a) Zero–Wind Downwash Pattern *b) 10 Knots Wind Downwash Pattern (typical)*

Figure 25-7 Downwash Pattern, Top View

Add a slight amount of wind on the nose and an egg-shaped pattern emerges, as shown in Figure 25-7b.

The helicopter of course doesn't 'know' if it is hovering with zero–groundspeed in 5 knots of wind or (in a no–wind situation) moving across the ground at 5 knots airspeed. With a 5 knot wind, the downwash pattern is pushed slightly closer to the front of the helicopter. (or if moving forward at 5 knots on a no-wind day, the helicopter moves closer to the edge of the downwash pattern). The edge of this vortex closest to the helicopter is rotating downward, as shown. At about 5 to 7 knots airspeed, this pattern of vortices is pushed back and starts to affect the front of the rotor. Since the air being pulled into the rotor now has a downflow component to it, the rotor is unable to impart as much induced velocity to it. The result is less of a push is given to the downflowing air by the rotor, and the total power given to the air is less. The helicopter settles slightly.

In practical terms, this effect is noticeable when transitioning forward over a lightly snow–covered or dusty field. The cloud of snow or dust thrown up is approached and just prior to penetration, the helicopter will settle slightly. In most conditions the amount of settling is slight, and the effect momentary, but if you happen to have to hover with respect to the ground in just that amount of wind, the overall effect is it will take more power than hovering with no wind. This effect is only noticeable at certain heights above the ground, so it will not always happen.

Figure 25-8 shows a sequence of events when the vortex will affect the helicopter as it accelerates through this region.

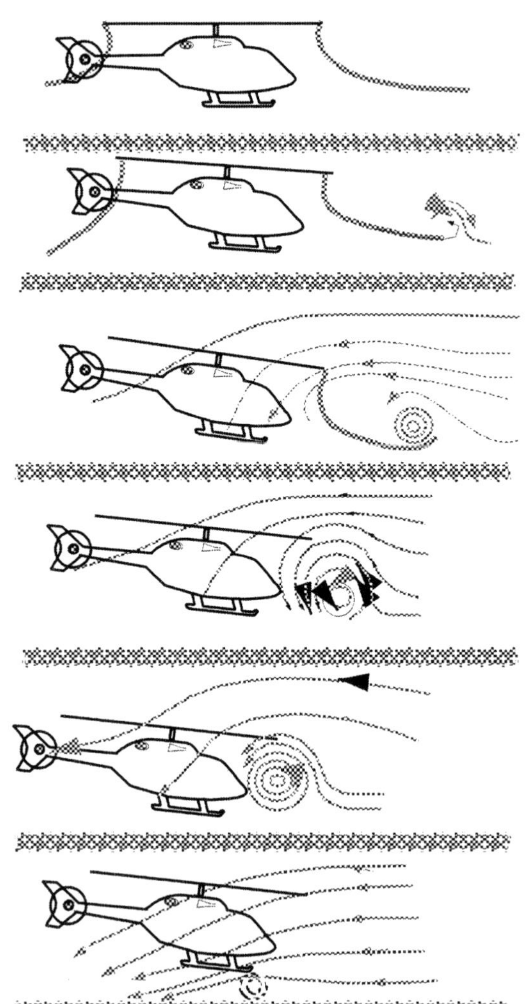

Helicopter in zero-airspeed hover with no wind

Helicopter starts to move forward, and vortex at front of helicopter starts to form and move towards the helicopter

Helicopter is moving forward with slightly higher groundspeed than panel above. The vortex formed by the actions of rotor downwash and wind is slightly larger and closer to the helicopter.

Slightly faster groundspeed and the vortex is directly underneath the front of the rotor disk. The re-circulating air is being drawn slightly into the rotor.

Slightly faster groundspeed puts the vortex solidly underneath the front of the rotor. More power is required to maintain height, as the vortex is giving a velocity to the induced flow it did not have before. Pilot must add collective pitch to maintain height.

Faster groundspeed than above, the vortex is now below and behind the helicopter, and the power required is less than above.

Figure 25-8 Sequence of Low Altitude Vortex

Low Airspeed Power Required - Again

Figure 3–5 showed the power required vs. airspeed for the low speed region. Figure 25-9 will amplify this earlier material slightly.

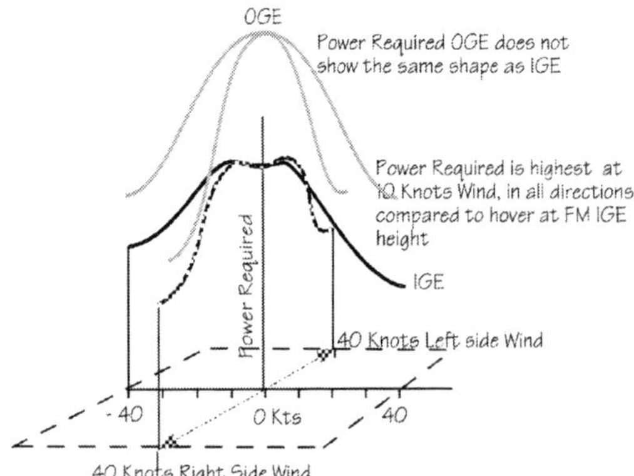

Figure 25-9 Power Required vs. Airspeed, <40 KIAS Side Wind and Rear Wind

Note how the power required in each of these two views shows that the maximum power does not occur at zero–airspeed if you start from an in-ground-effect hover. For the front and rear wind case, it takes account of the ground vortex roll up (only valid for some IGE conditions), and in the side wind, the extra power needed to drive the tail rotor. Starting from out-of-ground effect (OGE) the effect of the ground vortex is not present.

Range

There is simply no excuse anywhere for running out of fuel

Strictly speaking, range should not be included in this chapter as it is determined by engine fuel flow characteristics and not the airframe. However, since range and endurance are often considered as airframe performance, this is a good time to introduce the subject. The difference between power required vs. airspeed and fuel flow vs. airspeed is not difficult to understand.

Range in helicopters is not often given much attention, as most trips are short range - if the trip is that long, it's cheaper to go by fixed–wing. The only problem is this philosophy doesn't work for going to oil platforms, sinking ships, several short trips in one day, etc., so range calculations are important*.

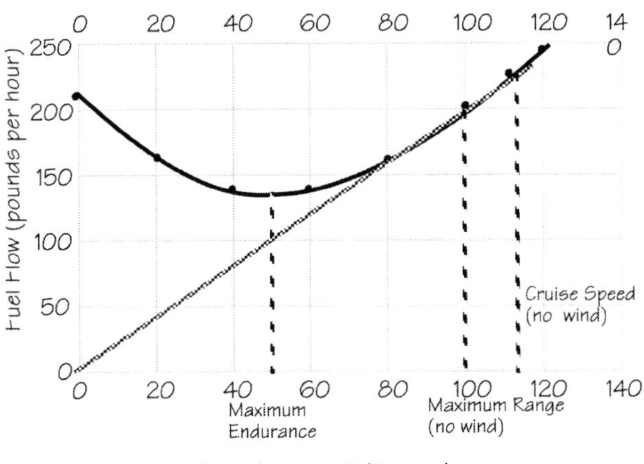

Figure 25-10 Fuel Flow vs. TAS

Range is a way of thinking about fuel - it's either distance or time in the air. To determine the best airspeed to fly for maximum range, a graph of fuel flow vs. airspeed (true airspeed (TAS) at that) is necessary. Such a chart is shown in Figure 25-10. Note this is valid only for one weight and set of atmospheric conditions.

Further calculations can derive a *specific air range* chart - this is distance per unit of fuel for the various airspeeds. Maximum range airspeed (or $V_{max\ range}$) in a no wind condition will occur when the specific range (distance per unit fuel) peaks, as shown in Figure 25-11. If you don't want to take the time to construct a specific range chart, $V_{max\ range}$ occurs where a tangent from the origin touches the fuel flow curve, as shown in the bottom half of Figure 25-10. Similar to the figure above, this is only valid for one configuration of weight and atmospheric conditions.

* Lots of FMs for helicopters certified in the early years have no information on range or fuel flow, anywhere. How you are supposed to figure this out without the charts is beyond me.

You may notice that the tangent is pretty close to the fuel flow vs. airspeed curve for quite a distance. This means that changing airspeed will not have a significant effect on the maximum range possible.

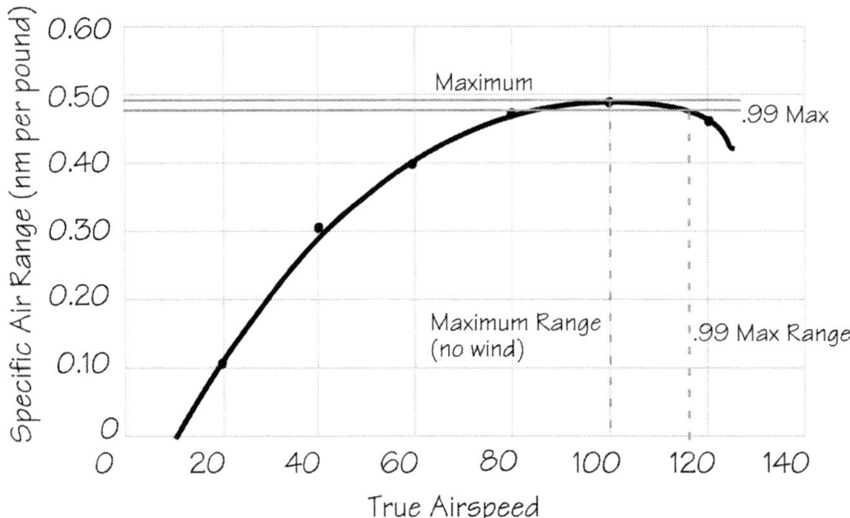

Figure 25-11 Specific Air Range (SAR) or Specific Range (SR) for one weight and altitude.

It may be difficult to fly accurately at the airspeed for absolute maximum range ($V_{max\ range}$), whichever way it is determined. Since there is a very small penalty for using a higher speed, the best range airspeed is often calculated as being the higher of the two speeds where 99% of best specific range occurs. This is easier to show on the diagram than to say in words. The logic is as follows– for a very small penalty in maximum specific air range (in this case 1%), why not pick the higher speed? A 1% penalty may reduce the time in the air, especially if there is a small headwind. In the example in Figure 25-11, the additional 1% penalty in fuel flow has resulted in a 9% improvement in time. In a headwind, the time improvement will result in a real range improvement. More about headwinds and tailwinds follows.

It is important to remember this best range airspeed is only valid for no wind, at the atmospheric conditions shown. If the airspeed is True Airspeed, it is necessary to calculate backwards to get the Indicated Airspeed (IAS) to fly, depending on pressure altitude and OAT.

Range Improvements with Altitude

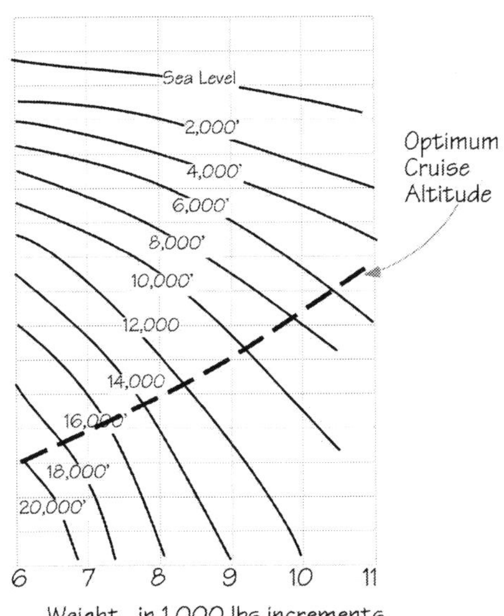

Figure 25-12 Range Improvements with Altitude

Turbine engines particularly have better fuel consumption as altitude increases, and there are some good gains to be made if the helicopter is flown at a higher altitude. The reason for the improvement is that the power required increases slightly with altitude, but the engine must 'work' harder to put out that power. Turbine engines operate more efficiently in terms of horsepower per unit fuel consumed (specific fuel consumption-pounds per horsepower per hour) at high power settings, and so operating at higher altitude will improve the fuel consumption. The reasons for this, from an engine point of view are covered in more detail in "Effect of Altitude on Fuel Consumption" on page 301, but the graphs showing it for airframe performance are included here.

You will also notice that there is emphasis on turbine engines here. Piston engines do not have the same characteristics as turbines when it comes to range variations with altitude.

Headwind and Tailwind Effects

Of course, there is always a wind to take into consideration. In most cases, it seems to be a headwind, regardless of the direction of travel. What to do? Very simply, if you have a plot of fuel flow vs. TAS, then draw a tangent to the fuel flow line from the wind speed. If there is a headwind of 30 knots, then draw the tangent from the 30 knot point. If there is a tailwind, draw the tangent from a line extended left of the origin, as shown in Figure 25-13.

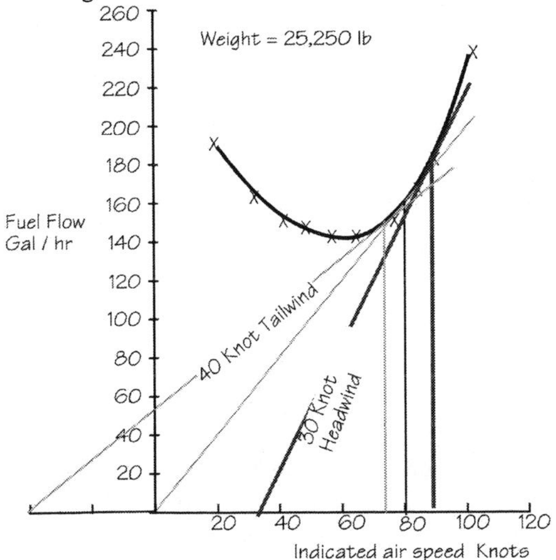

Figure 25-13 Headwind and Tailwind Example.

In the example above, the no–wind maximum range airspeed is 102 KTAS, with a 40 knot headwind, 114 KTAS, and with a 40 knot tailwind, 94 KTAS. The table below shows the effect of using these higher speeds. The distance to be flown is 100 nautical miles.

Condition	Groundspeed (Knots)	Time (minutes)	Fuel Flow (lb. / hour)	Fuel Used (pounds)	Remarks
No Wind	102	58	945	913	
40 Knot Headwind, using no-wind best range air-speed (102 KTAS)	62 (102-40)	96	945	1521	baseline
40 Knot Headwind, using optimum airspeed for head-wind (114 KTAS)	74 (114-40)	81	990	1335	12% saving in fuel, 16% saving in time.
40 Knot Tailwind, using no-wind best range airspeed (102 KTAS)	142 (102+40)	42	945	661	baseline for comparison below.
as above, but using opti-mum airspeed for tailwind (94 KTAS)	134 (94+40)	44	890	638	4% savings in fuel, very slight increase in time.

So there are some benefits to be gained by paying attention to your fuel flow. Another good reason to install a fuel flow gauge, and if you have an advanced navigation system, make sure the two are connected. You can learn a lot from the information, if you pay attention.

Point of No Return

If there was no wind, it would be easy to calculate the point of no return. It would be halfway between the start and finish. Wind makes life more difficult to calculate the point of no return. The point of no return, or the point of safe return as the more politically correct like to call it, is calculated by the following formulae:

$$\text{Point of No Return} = \frac{\text{Endurance at Cruise Fuel Flow (- Reserves)} \times \text{Return Groundspeed}}{\text{Groundspeed to Continue} + \text{Return Groundspeed}} \quad \text{(EQ 22.)}$$

If you want to ensure this formulae is mathematically correct for units, it is as follows:

$$\text{Hours} = \frac{\text{Hours} \times \left(\frac{\text{Nautical Miles}}{\text{Hour}}\right)}{\left(\frac{\text{Nautical Miles}}{\text{Hour}}\right) + \left(\frac{\text{Nautical Miles}}{\text{Hour}}\right)} \quad \text{(EQ 23.)}$$

Interesting how a Point is actually dependent on time, isn't it?

So we'll set up an example of going to an oil rig which is 240 nautical miles off shore. Our cruise airspeed is 120 KTAS, and at the altitude we'll be flying we burn 600 pounds per hour. We have 2200 pounds of fuel and want a 400 pound reserve. We've got a good breeze (40 knots) helping us on the outbound leg, but we're a bit worried about what this might do to the inbound leg if we have a problem. The weather at the rig isn't great, so we have to make a decision part way there.

That gives us 3 hours of total endurance at cruise consumption to play with. We're going outbound from the shore to the rig with a 40 knot tailwind, so our continued flight groundspeed is 160 knots, and our return groundspeed is 80 knots. Some important points about this formulae is that the endurance (time) is calculated at the fuel flow in the cruise speed you intend to use, not the endurance you would get if you used V_Y.

$$\text{Point of No Return} = \frac{3.0 \text{ Hrs (Endurance)} \times 80 \text{ Knots}}{160 \text{ Knots} + 80 \text{ Knots}} = 1 \text{ Hour} \qquad \text{(EQ 24.)}$$

Sounds pretty short, doesn't it? Until you consider that at 1 hour out using the tailwind, we're 160 nautical miles out, with 2 hours of gas left, and it's going to take us 2 hours to get back home.

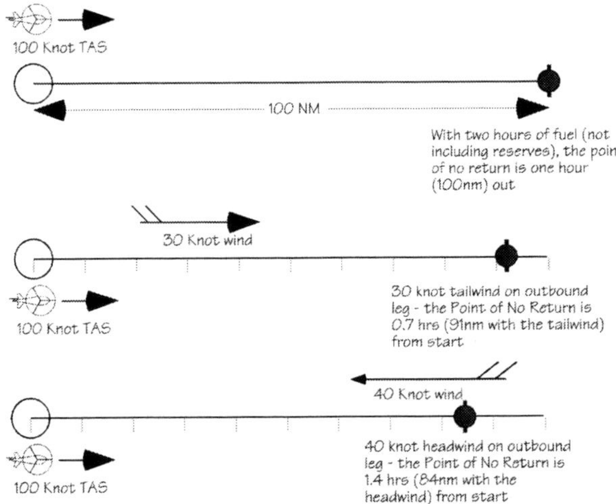

Figure 25-14 Point of No Return

Equal Time Point

The equal time point is the point (measured in distance, mind you) in the flight where it will take just as long to get back as it will to go on.

$$\text{Equal Time Point} = \frac{\text{Total Distance} \times \text{Return Groundspeed}}{\text{Continue Groundspeed} + \text{Return Groundspeed}} \qquad \text{(EQ 25.)}$$

If you want to check this formulae for units it is:

$$\text{Nautical Miles} = \frac{\text{Nautical Miles} \times \left(\frac{\text{Nautical Miles}}{\text{Hour}}\right)}{\left(\frac{\text{Nautical Miles}}{\text{Hour}}\right)} \qquad \text{(EQ 26.)}$$

The point of equal time for the same example flight would be:

$$\text{Equal Time Point} = \frac{240 \times 80}{160 + 80} = 80 \text{ Nautical Miles} \qquad \text{(EQ 27.)}$$

This sounds pretty close to shore, but this means that it's just as quick to go on to the rig from this point, as it is to go back.

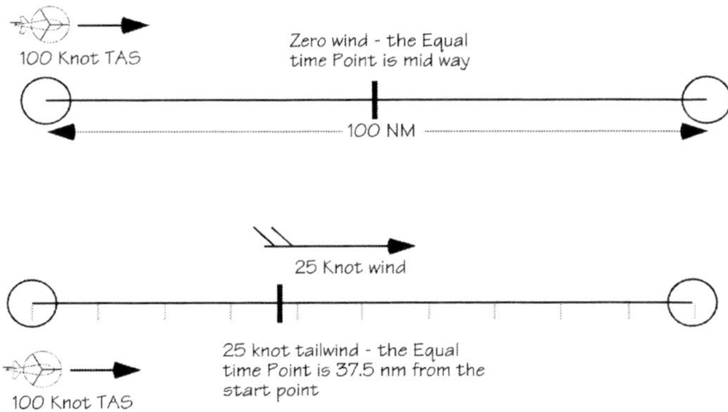

Figure 25-15 Equal Time Point

What If Something Goes Wrong?

Well, for single engine helicopter pilots the good news is that the navigation problems are simplified to the point of non-existence if the engine fails - you have other things to worry about. For those flying multi-engine machines, life is now more complicated.

Imagine you are regularly working between Godforsaken Oil Rig and Cold Beer airfield with your Star Streak helicopter, ferrying oil workers. You are always precise in your pre-flight planning because of the shortage of suitable alternates, and always calculate a point of no return. Since the homeward leg is always into a stiff wind, it makes things difficult.

So there you are on the outbound flight. The clock tells you the point of no return for the outbound leg (with a tailwind, naturally) will be coming up in 2 minutes, but you are past the point of equal time, so the quickest landing point would normally be your destination. Suddenly, one of the engines shows signs of distinct ill-health. Engine oil pressure drops rapidly, chip lights start to flash, oil temperature rises - and then the low rumbling noises start. The shutdown procedures in the FM are followed to perfection, and you turn towards home. After you collect your thoughts, you note your former dazzling cruise speed of 140 KIAS is now a measly 100 KIAS. Will you make it? Did you calculate a point of no return for single engine cruise speed? To refresh your memory, we have a 40 knot tailwind on the outbound leg, which is now a 40 knot headwind. Our endurance on one engine is slightly longer since the engine is operating at a higher power setting, and hence more efficiently- we'll say we get an extra 15 minutes from the fuel we've got on board. So our point of safe return (single engine) becomes:

$$\text{Point of No Return} = \frac{3.25\text{ hrs} \times 60}{140 + 60} = 0.975\text{ hrs (58.5 minutes)} \qquad \text{(EQ 28.)}$$

If you hadn't worked this out before hand, and decided to turn towards home, you wouldn't have made it without getting into your fuel reserves.

But other things can go wrong which affect the flying speed, even for single engine helicopters. What if the hydraulic system fails and you can't hold it at cruise airspeed for more than 10 minutes? Which way do you go?*

ENDURANCE

Endurance is another way of thinking about the fuel in the tank. Instead of distance, fuel can be converted into time in the air. Most helicopters have a fairly flat area near the minimum power speed (see Figure 25-10) - i.e. there is a wide range of airspeeds over which the power required (and hence fuel flow) does not change very much. For example, a low altitude search is best carried out at a slow–ish speed. Since ground speed is important to permit observers to search carefully, a slightly higher speed

* Sorry, this is a rhetorical question, and no answer is provided... .

can be used on legs into wind than downwind, with no appreciable effect on the endurance. In the example shown in Figure 25-10, the minimum power speed can be changed between 40 and 80 knots with only a 5% change in fuel flow per hour.

Radius of Action

Many helicopters are used in search and rescue operations off shore, and must have a good understanding of how long they can stay out on station. There are many ways this can be calculated, but the simplest one is as follows:

$$\text{Radius of Action per Hour of Fuel} = \frac{\text{Grdspd Outbound} \times \text{Grdspd Inbound}}{\text{Grdspd Outbound} + \text{Grdspd Inbound}} \quad \text{(EQ 29.)}$$

So, if we have a helicopter with a cruise speed of 120 KTAS, and enough fuel for 3 hours (2 hours at cruise speed and 1 hour searching on station, not counting reserves), and want to spend one hour searching as far out as possible. There is a 30 knot headwind for the outbound leg which, of course is a 30 knot tailwind for the return leg, so as far out as we should go to start the search looks something like this:

$$\text{Radius of Action} = \frac{90 \times 150}{90 + 150} \times 2\text{ hrs Fuel} = 56.25 \times 2 = 112.5\text{ nm} \quad \text{(EQ 30.)}$$

Note

This assumes that you won't go any farther away from base than the start of the search, and that the wind doesn't change

Not always valid assumptions

How to Trick A Navigation System

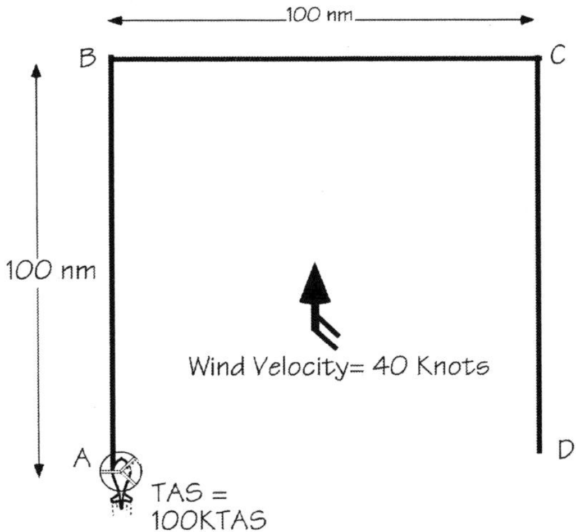

Figure 25-16 How to Trick a Navigation System

Beware of electronic gadgets that help you to figure out radius of action, or time–to–go to a way point! They *may* base all their calculations on existing ground speed and not factor in the wind correctly. An example of this is given below, using the conditions in Figure 25-16.

Let's say the helicopter is part way along the first leg, and is fortunate to have a tailwind. The pilot wants to know how long it will take him to get to the destination, or perhaps how long he can stay on-station searching. Depending on the complexity of the navigation system, it may tell him something other than the real truth. Try this yourself on your navigation system! It's relatively easy to set up such problems, and check them against a manually plotted example.

In this example, the helicopter is at point A, and has a ground speed from A to B of 140 knots. If the pilot asks the navigation system to tell how long to get to point D - he may not get the correct answer. If the computer bases the calculation on the existing groundspeed, it will tell you 2 hr., 09 minutes. (Some computers will assume you want to go directly to D - but that's another story). If there was no wind, the time to transit this route would be 3.0 hours. If the navigation system says something different - be cautious of its information!As you can see the correct answer is 3.45 hr., (3 hr. 27 minutes).

Leg	Distance	Groundspeed	Time
A to B	100	140	0.71 hr. (49 min)
B to C	100	92	1.08 hr. (65 min)
C to D	100	60	1.66 hr. (100 min)
Total	300	average 87	3.45 hr. (207 min)

Also remember if you're above 500' AGL, the calculation is probably wrong for the surface wind speed and direction. If you have a navigation system that is going to take you down to the hover at the surface based on wind calculations it makes from the cruise, you might be surprised....

Payload vs. Radius of Action

It is normal to see a chart of payload vs. radius of action in manufacturers pamphlets. They are quite straightforward in their interpretation, but the fine print needs to be examined to see if fuel reserves are included, or the pilots weight!

Rather than re-invent the wheel, I suggest the books by Simon Newman and Ray Prouty as having far more detailed information on how to calculate these figures.

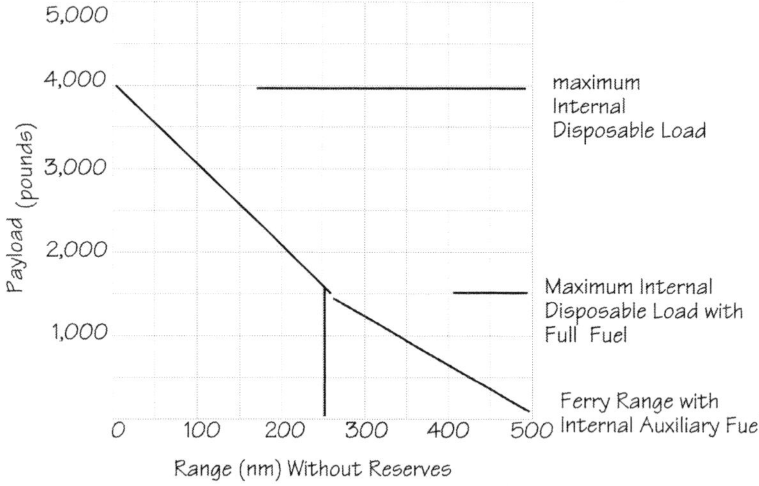

Figure 25-17 Typical Payload vs. Range Chart

Climb and Descent Performance

Aside from hover performance, why should we worry about climb performance? Fixed–wing aircraft worry about it for obstacle clearance when following Instrument Flight Rules (IFR). Climb performance is normally not as critical in a helicopter as the climb gradients are much steeper. In operations low to the ground, obstacle avoidance criteria are a minor problem. Sadly, most helicopter FMs do not have a lot of climb or descent data. Nevertheless, a few small surprises are to be found. Both climb and descent are normally shown in the extreme conditions - i.e., maximum power for the climb and minimum power (autorotation) for the descent. With one exception, anything else between these two extremes is controlled by power. A typical graph of rate of climb and descent vs. airspeed for maximum power climbs and autorotation is shown in Figure 25-18.

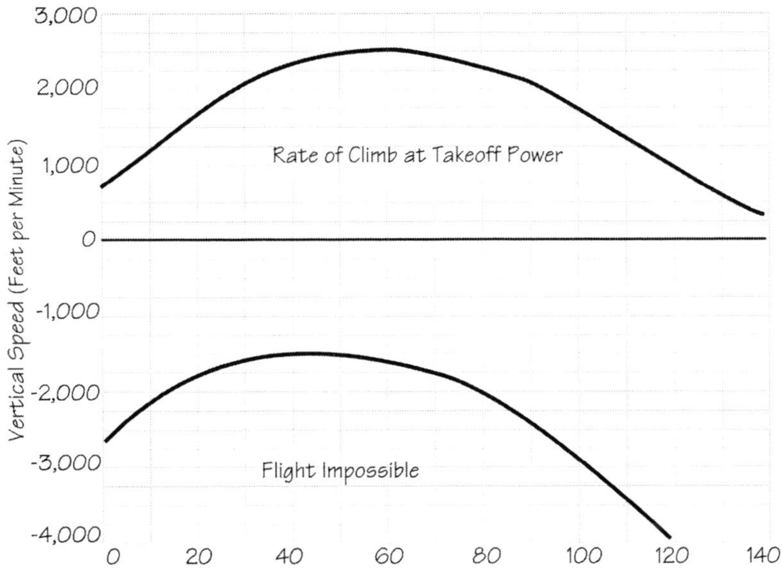

Figure 25-18 Climb and Descent Performance

Climbs

Vertical Climbs

Climbing vertically in the hover is a common way a helicopter is used. Long line operations, fire fighting etc., all require vertical climbs. What may be surprising is just like a propeller, the rotor system acquires slightly more efficiency when it climbs vertically. If the excess horsepower available over that required to hover OGE is known, and a rate of climb is calculated from this*, the rate of climb would actually be slightly higher than that calculated. Climbing vertically will almost certainly put the helicopter in the Height Velocity chart avoid curve however, and caution is advised, particularly with passengers on board.

Forward Flight Climbs for Best Rate of Climb

In forward flight, a chart of rate of climb vs. airspeed will have much the same shape as the power required vs. airspeed. The speed for best rate of climb may be slightly lower than the minimum power required airspeed (V_Y), but not significantly. For all intents and purposes, V_Y is close enough unless you are trying to set a time–to–climb record.

Rate of climb is the change in altitude vs. time - remember this subtle definition.

Be warned that winds will not make a difference on the *rate* of climb, but will have a large effect on the *angle* of climb.

Best Angle of Climb Airspeed

Climb performance of a different type is of interest if you are in a twin engine helicopter and have an engine failure immediately just as you are about to try to clear those trees immediately in front of you. The different type of performance is angle of climb, as opposed to rate of climb.

It's also of interest if you don't have enough power to hover OGE but have to climb over that interesting set of trees the boss planted at the corporate helipad...

What is the best angle of climb airspeed? How would you figure it out?

If you can climb vertically on one engine, then obviously the angle of climb is infinite. Unfortunately, most of us aren't that lucky. Angle of climb is shown in Figure 25-19 for a typical light helicopter with insufficient power to hover OGE.

* The mathematics of which are beyond the scope of this book

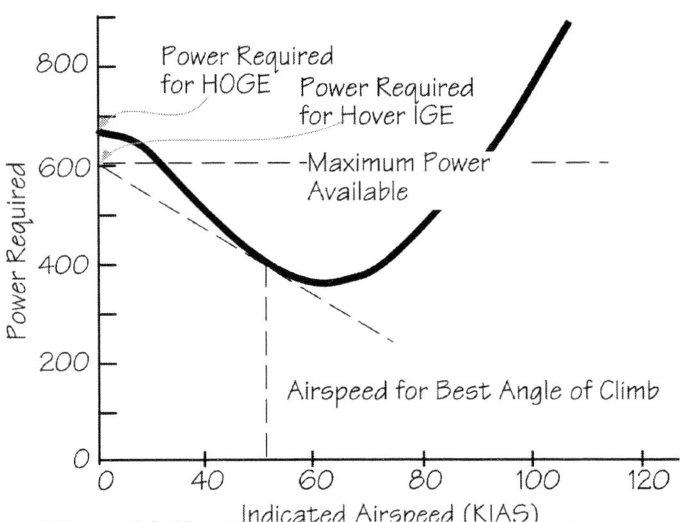

Figure 25-19 Maximum Angle of Climb Speed

It should be obvious that to figure this out for your helicopter will require an accurate airspeed system (both for the tests and to use the data you collect), and an accurate measurement of power. The data would have to be gathered for a wide range of weights and pressure altitudes and OAT's in order to be valid, but you may be able to get enough data to use this in very localized conditions, if you're lucky.

Obviously, it is prudent to only maintain this airspeed until clear of the obstacle, and then accelerate to V_Y.

Descent Performance

Descent performance is normally only of academic interest, but it is important to consider for several reasons. Firstly, it is important to realize it is not possible for the helicopter to descend under control in some profiles. There is an area between autorotation and powered flight where the rate of descent cannot be controlled. This is shown in Figure 19-2 on page 177.

The second point about descent performance is that if you wish to descend vertically at a rate of descent between zero (hovering) and autorotation at zero–airspeed, be prepared for a very nasty ride as you get into (and hopefully get out of) vortex ring state. This was discussed in more detail in "Vortex Ring State" on page 176. The point here is that there are some rates of descent that are not healthy in a helicopter, and many that are not possible in all airspeeds.

Figure 18-3 on page 173 showed the rate of descent in autorotation vs. airspeed. Please note it is possible to autorotate vertically in no wind - however, it is extremely difficult to transition directly from a hover OGE or a slow descent (100 to 300 fpm) to a zero–airspeed vertical autorotation (a small thing called vortex ring state must be passed through). To get these data points, it is necessary to start from a forward airspeed autorotation and decelerate to zero–airspeed.

Whizz Wheels

A pet peeve of mine is the lack of 'whiz wheel' calculators for performance planning for helicopters. What is the pilot to do when faced with different loads and weather conditions while operating in the field? Does he really have to get out the flight manual to tell him his performance capability, and if so, does it really help him very much? While he's flying?

What of the Search and Rescue crew who find they have to come to a hover somewhere high in the mountains - do they have to get out the flight manual to see if they need to dump fuel in order to safely hover? Is this satisfactory*? What can be done?

I have seen some interesting approaches to this problem - some very clever hand-held pocket calculators with the necessary data built in, some rules of thumb, and a simple whiz wheel, shown in Figure 25-20 which could be used to determine the power required to hover, and the power available under the same conditions. Simple, easy to use (even with one hand) and accurate enough to give the pilot an idea of what is going to happen†. Why don't they exist for all helicopters as a matter of routine?

* Hopefully you'll be saying - "No" - and maybe you'll come up with a solution...

† Sunlight readable, no batteries, no moving parts, NVG compatible (probably) etc., etc.

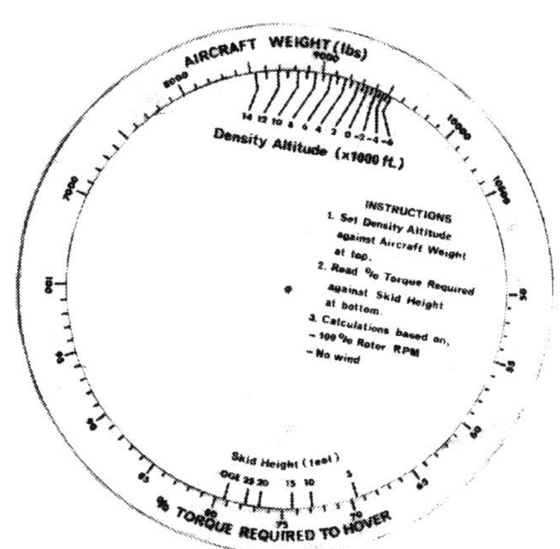

Figure 25-20 Performance Calculator

As long ago as 1980, there was an electronic, in-cockpit device for this but it didn't get much notice. We still don't have anything like it in regular use in the commercial world. The military are only just getting them as well. How much more conservative can we get*?

RULES OF THUMB

I'm sitting in my Wheezy-Breezy helicopter, in a clearing, with a rather heavy person in the other seat, and I'm not sure if I can make it over the trees ahead. Alternatively, I'm cruising through the Rockies in my Turbine Flinger and see a particularly attractive meadow to have a picnic in with my family of 4 - do I need to do a zero speed approach to the hover, or can I hover over the pinnacle next to it? How can I check the power available in either case?

I have heard of very few rules of thumb for checking power, but I will pass on two.

For the hover, in one popular piston engined helicopter, the rule required checking what boost was being used for a 3' foot hover, and comparing this to the placard for maximum boost for the ambient conditions. If there was more than 2" difference, you could do a vertical climb, 1" and you could do a combination forward flight climb at maximum climb angle airspeed (above translational lift)†, and if there was less than 0.5" difference, your passenger was either going to walk or go on a very fast diet.

For the turbine engine example in forward flight at minimum power airspeed, it was necessary to note the N_1 being used and then pull the power up to the takeoff power limit and note the N_1 available there. This resulted in the following table:

N_1 Margin	Approach Methods Possible
Less than 4%	Running Landing
4-6%	Low Hover in Ground Effect (IGE)
7%	Hover Out of Ground Effect (OGE)
More than 7%	Steep Approach to Hover Out of Ground Effect (OGE)

A similar table could be made using torque, but for this particular helicopter N_1 was more stable than the torque. Margins to determine the technique to be used to transition from the hover to forward flight can be found by determining the margin between the N_1 required to hover at 2' AGL and maximum N_1 were given in the following manner:

N_1 Margin	Options for Transition to Forward Flight
Less than 5%	Running Takeoff (but not recommended)
5-10%	Cushion Creep
10%	Hover Out of Ground Effect
More than 10%	Sustained Vertical Climb Capability

* Don't answer this question as I know there are some people out there who think closed in cockpits was a bad idea.

† But see Chapter 15,"'Twixt Heaven and Earth," for some cautions about this method

You should experiment a bit on your own machine and determine what suitable margins for different techniques would be. This table is just an example.

More Advanced V Speeds

There are, naturally, more 'V' speeds to be considered in the advanced performance. We have the following:

- V_Y airspeed for minimum power.
- $V_{Max\ Angle\ of\ Climb}$airspeed for maximum angle of climb.
- $V_{Max\ End}$ airspeed for maximum endurance

Summary of Chapter 25

This chapter has covered many aspects of airframe performance, starting from the hover and low airspeed and finishing up with forward flight climb and descent performance. They should make the pilot aware of the finer points of getting the most out of the machine.

Other Components

General

The commercial helicopter is not a simple machine. It is designed for reliable service, and some offshore twin engined machines have as many systems and redundant features as a jetliner. This chapter will cover, in broad detail, some of the concepts that may be found in most modern helicopters. As a professional pilot, you should know the systems in your machine in great detail.

Fuel Systems

A typical fuel system for a single engine helicopter is shown in Figure 26-1.

The fuel systems in most helicopters are quite simple - tanks to hold the fuel, and a way to get the fuel to the engine. There are two basic ways to get the fuel to the engine, either by pumping it, or by letting the engine pull it up. Of the two, letting the engine draw the fuel up appears to be the safest and most reliable, as it eliminates a possible source of failure (the airframe fuel pump) and will not pump fuel out if the fuel line should happen to break. Many engines have enough suction to operate without the fuel pump up to moderate altitudes. Pumps are often installed merely to move fuel between the various tanks for CG control.

Minor items in the fuel system will include fuel valves (to shut off fuel to the engine), fuel filters with bypasses in case they become clogged, warning indications of fuel clogging, and fuel quantity indicators. There should be a low fuel warning system, using separate sensors and power supplies. There may be separate jet pumps to circulate fuel and ensure the minimum usable fuel level is very small.

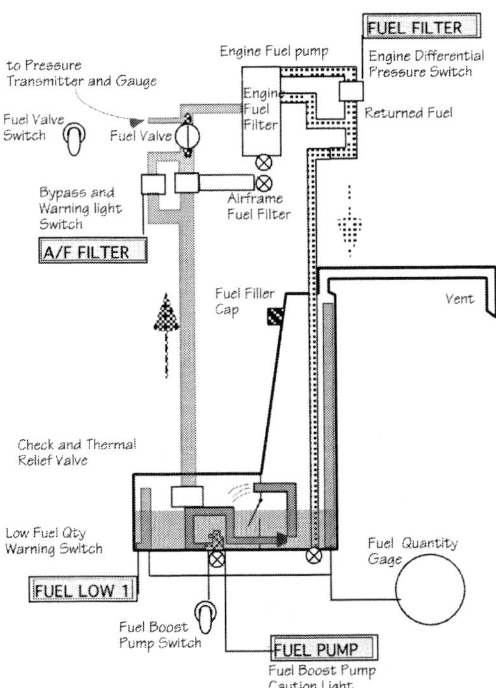

Figure 26-1 Typical Installation with Jet Pumps

Fuel Valves

A fuel valve is fitted to provide a way to stop fuel from getting to the engine in the event of a fire, or as a final, last ditch way to shut down the engine (if the throttle linkage broke, for example). Be aware that fuel between the fuel valve and the engine can be sufficient to keep the engine running for up to 30 seconds after the valve is closed.

Fuel Pumps

Most people think fuel pumps are installed to make sure the fuel gets from the tank to the engine. Partly true. Many helicopter engines are capable of running without the boost pumps up to pretty high altitudes. Fuel pumps are installed for this first purpose, to be sure, but there is another very good reason. Fuel in other tanks in the system need to get the fuel to the main tanks, and the most efficient way is with a device called the jet pump, which has no moving parts and required very little power. See Figure 26-1 for a diagram of a jet pump.

Low Fuel Warning Systems

Low fuel quantity warning systems are required on all recently built helicopters. They are installed for several reasons- to provide a positive indication to the pilot that has not been paying attention to the fuel quantity gauge; to provide a fall back in case the main fuel quantity system has failed in a manner that doesn't make itself apparent to the crew; and I'm sure you might be able to think of others. The point is that the systems are definitely there to tell the pilot to start to look for somewhere to land as soon as possible. I have read too many accident reports where the pilot continued to fly for 15 minutes after the 'low fuel' light came on and was surprised when the engine failed. The defence of 'the book says that up to 20 minutes of fuel are left' is pretty feeble, in fact no defence at all when most countries flight regulations require fuel to destination plus a comfortable margin.

A few minutes looking at the fuel system diagrams in the maintenance manual may show some interesting things. It should certainly convince you that a lot of thought went into its design and manufacture. The roll and pitch attitudes where fuel comes away from the intake should make you think twice about operating with low fuel states. It should also be noted that most helicopter fuel systems aren't particularly good at handling both low fuel conditions and rapid changes in fuselage attitude. When the fuel quantity is low, don't make rapid accelerations or decelerations - the fuel may slosh away from the intake to the engine, followed by an embarrassing silence from the power source.*

Most fuel tanks contain baffles to stop fuel sloshing around. Those that don't can mystify owners when the helicopter starts rocking in the cruise.

Other Parts of the Fuel System

For multi–engined helicopters, a cross–feed system is needed to make sure all the fuel is usable in the event of an engine failure. Why cross–feed systems? It is standard practice for each engine to have its own fuel tank in the event of contamination - one tank with bad fuel won't put both engines out of action.

When is the Fuel Gauge Reading Correctly?

You may be surprised to learn that the only time the fuel gauge in a civilian helicopter is *required* to read correctly (for certification purposes) is when the fuel tank is empty and the helicopter is in level flight. A recent change to the certification rules will mean that future helicopters will have a slightly more accurate system.

Some fuel quantity systems are of such poor quality that they only reliably indicate a gauge was installed in the cockpit - not the amount of fuel in the tanks. Fuel flow meters are not normally fitted, however they are useful for determining best range and endurance speeds, as previously discussed. When combined with a GPS, they can be invaluable.

Pounds or Gallons?

As an interesting aside, why are some fuel gauges marked in pounds or kilograms? The answer is that the engine doesn't really burn fuel in gallons per hour (particularly turbine engines), it burns weight of fuel, as it is mixing it with a weight of air. The density of fuel also changes with temperature, so most 'weight' based fuel measurement systems have a temperature correcting sensor included. Such systems also make it easier to calculate the weight of the helicopter.

A piece of brilliant design that came from France was the fuel quantity as a percentage, instead of pounds, gallons† or liters. The gauge is set in percent, and then the FM has a conversion table for whatever you want - pounds, gallons, etc.

Fuel Quality

Helicopters are used because a fixed wing can't do the job. This means that we get to see all sorts of strange, out of the way places‡. With this comes the problem of getting fuel into the helicopter. Fixed wing airplanes (aside from bush planes) typically don't have to worry about this too much, as most of their fuel comes from trucks or tanks with lots of filters and quality checks. When you have to roll the barrels to the helicopter by yourself, and possibly pump it by hand yourself, quality can be easily forgotten.

A short primer on refueling from barrels should be available from your fuel company, but perhaps more important than the advice is the reason for the steps to ensure there is nothing but fuel going into the tanks. Simply stated, there are often no filters between the tank and the engine that will stop water, and water can get into fuel, particularly jet fuel, easily. Several other hints:

- Tip the barrel slightly with the bung hole is uphill, so that any water will drain to the bottom.
- Don't use all the fuel in the barrel

* Also, don't use a lot of pedal which can slosh fuel to the side of the tank...
† Is that US Gallons or Imperial Gallons?
‡ Including some places we'd rather not see...

- Use a water tester
- Don't use a barrel that has been opened already.

Fuel Drains and Living in the Field

Which brings up the subject of fuel drains and living in the field. This, unfortunately, is a lesson all too typical in that people paid for it with their lives. I was asked to help investigate a helicopter crash in a foreign country. I will say that the country had recently come out from behind the Iron Curtain and was not associated (at least in my mind) with a long technical and engineering history. I was wrong.

Upon arrival, I had not expected to see the quality and quantity of reports the local authorities had prepared as a result of this accident. These officials had tried to discover the cause of the crash and had drawn a blank. All they could determine was that the engine had stopped prior to impact, but not why. I was at a loss to explain this until after the official investigation. The next-of-kin had provided me with a video of the helicopter taken from the ground during start-up and lift-off on the fateful flight. I had been surprised to see the helicopter had been kept outside, on a hill, and the refueling tank (on a cart) was not far away. A fuel sample had been taken from the helicopter on the morning of the crash, and it showed no water. It finally hit me* that perhaps the fuel sample may not have seen the worst case. The fuel tank drain in this particular helicopter was in the middle of the tank at the bottom. With the downslope towards the nose, it was possible that a considerable amount of water could be present and not be at the drain point. The fuel pipe to the engine for this helicopter was at the back of the tank, so as the helicopter lifted off to the hover (in a nose down attitude thanks to the 7 people on board), and accelerated and climbed and cruised (all in a nose down attitude) the water would stay at the front of the tank. When the sight-seeing flight was coming to an end, and the helicopter started to decelerate and descend (now in a nose up attitude) the water would flow to the back of the tank and get ingested into the engine. It was at about this point in the flight when the engine had quit. Was this the real cause? I never did find out, but it was the only one that made sense to all the people I spoke to. See Figure 26-2 for an explanation.

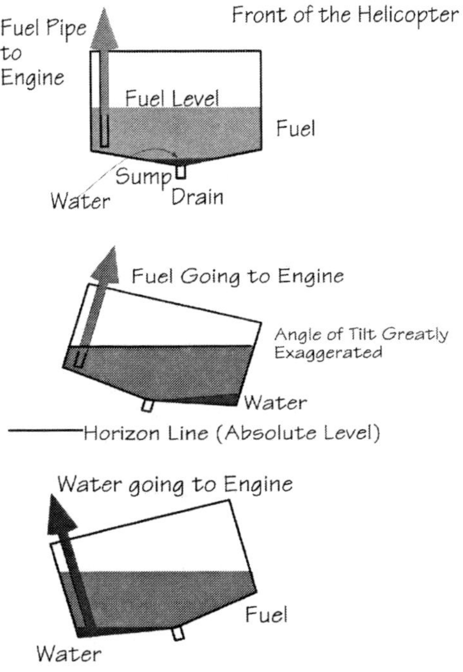

'Normal' situation. Helicopter sits on a level surface, sump is at lowest point. If any water is present, it sits at lowest point and is drained at sump.

Helicopter sits on nose-down slope. Sump is no longer at lowest point and water may not be found when sump is drained. Water remains in tank.

Helicopter hovers nose down, accelerates and climbs nose down, cruises nose down. Water does not get to intake to engine.

Later that same flight...

Helicopter nose is raised to start deceleration and descent. Water goes to back of tank and is pumped into engine. Engine flames out.

Figure 26-2 Crash Explanation

* After a request to Higher Sources for some assistance, I'm not ashamed to admit

The next of kin asked the obvious question - Why hadn't anyone noticed this problem before? Wasn't there some rule about doing fuel samples on a level surface?

The answer was that when the whole situation was known, it was obvious what the problem was. Helicopters get parked on off-level ground all the time, but no-one had thought about the consequences of always parking off-level.

Moral? If you're going to do a fuel sample, do it on a level surface, or know your fuel system well enough that you can be sure to see the dregs* lying in the bottom of the tank will come out in the fuel sample.

Fuel Jettison

More a feature on military helicopters, some civil machines feature these devices. They will dump fuel in order to reduce weight, using high rate pumps. Hopefully they automatically stop jettisoning prior to reaching a critically low fuel state.

Transmissions and Drive Shafts

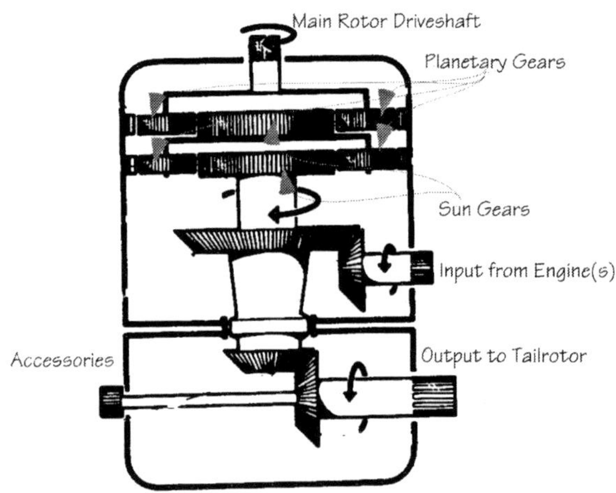

Figure 26-3 Typical Transmission

The transmissions of most helicopters are oft–neglected pieces of ironmongery. They serve to change the speed and direction of the engine output shafts and act as the means of transferring the loads from the rotor to the airframe. Additionally, they are convenient places to mount ancillary systems such as hydraulic pumps, anti-vibration systems and so on. They handle tremendous amounts of power with little complaint. There is not much else I can say about them, except - good work, design engineers. Since you may hear discussion about sun wheels and planetary gears, this is a good time to include a diagram of a transmission. See Figure 26-3.

While many military helicopters have been designed with transmissions that can run without oil for quite long periods of time, I've always felt most comfortable with civilian helicopters which have two oil pumps for the transmission. These typically have special piping and interlocks to ensure that in the event of a leak in a transmission oil line the standby pump will take over and pump the remaining oil only inside the transmission. See Figure 26-4 for an example of how such a system is set up.

* Dregs is normally associated with the sediment at the bottom of a bottle of wine. At least the cheap stuff I drink.

A point about oil pressure in transmissions. Too much can be almost as bad as too little. The pressure jets that spray the oil onto the gears are set to work at a range of pressures. If the pressure is too high, the spray pattern isn't correct!

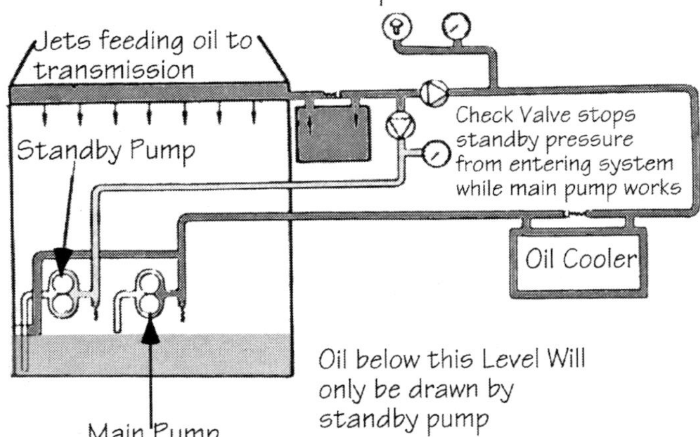

Figure 26-4 Duplicated Oil Pumps in Transmission

HUMS

HUMS is a tune we will all be, er, whistling shortly*. What is it? *Health and Usage Monitoring* (HUMS) is a way to continuously watch the various mechanical systems on the helicopter to see if they are working properly. This goes far beyond the normal chip detectors and fuel/oil filter bypass lights, and extends to monitoring vibration patterns on transmissions, rotor tracking and so on, throughout the flight. As of the time of writing this book, the initial results have been very encouraging. At least one helicopter has been stopped from taking off because HUMS said there was an unusual vibration pattern on the main transmission, which turned out to be a tooth of a gear *about* to fail. This is yet another example of safety being less expensive than an accident. The really big selling point is that the owner of the helicopter can track use (and abuse) very closely allowing maximum possible safe life of the engine and drive system.

I wanted to put in a diagram of a HUMS installation, but quickly realized it was way too complicated!

Electrical Systems

Electrical systems in most helicopters are fairly straightforward, and this section is only included because of some small effects these systems have had on my flying. Since they have probably happened to others, and will influence those going to fly helicopters, they are worth mentioning here. There are basically two types of electrical systems - Alternating Current (AC) –based and Direct Current (DC)–based†. A typical system incorporates buses to carry the electrical energy to the particular demand, circuit breakers, load meters and switches to check the functioning of the system. There is a requirement to use internally–generated power (AC or DC), battery power, and external power as well as to re-charge the battery in normal operations.

External Power

The main type of external power source used by most light helicopters is DC. However larger helicopters that are AC–based, may require an AC external power. What is not well understood is all these machines need to have the battery charged to let the external power into the helicopter. If the battery is flat, you can't normally hook up external power!

* Sorry about the bad jokes, I can't help it.

† I have seen only one helicopter type with a reasonable mixture of both types of generators, and it wasn't produced in the West.

Generators

Generators are also of two types - DC and AC. DC generators are typically also the engine starter in most helicopters, and hence are known as starter/generators. DC generators can be run at nearly any speed and still produce suitable voltage, but most have a specified minimum N_1 speed to put out the rated amperage. Some generators can produce such a load that they can literally drag a turbine engine down from a low N_1 speed to below a self–sustaining speed. More than one helicopter has a higher than normal N_1 speed for turning on the generator because of this.

Generator loads are also typically only given for continuous use. It always used to amuse me to see how often the controversy about 'leaving the first generator on during second engine start' would flare up in twin engine helicopters with electrical engine starting systems. Seems like someone who was new to the rather ancient type would watch the starting procedure for the second engine and note that if the generator for the first engine had been turned on to recharge the battery, that when the second engine was started, the loadmeter reading for the first engine would be pegged well above the normal limit for the generator. Sensing that something was obviously wrong and that everyone before them was too stupid to have noticed this blinding oversight, the new person would advocate that the engine start procedure for the second engine should have the first engine's generator turned off to prevent damage to the generator. What they didn't realize is that the generator manufacturer, the aircraft manufacturer and the certifying authority had already looked at this and found it was OK. The generator also acted as a starter and was able to absorb the excess electrical load for the short time needed during the start.

Batteries

The battery of choice for most helicopters is Nickel Cadmium (NiCad), which provides lots of power with minimal weight, recharges rapidly and requires minimum maintenance. In warm weather, some operators use a normal lead–acid battery; but these are heavier and can have a corrosion problem.

There are some maintenance penalties with NiCad batteries. They can take a 'memory' of how much they have been discharged, and over time, if not used to their full capacity, they may not provide as much power as when new. One way to prevent this is to exercise them regularly, and to recharge them fully after each start. In most civil and military applications, they work well if exercised frequently. Battery temperature warning devices provide good piece of mind - should a battery overheat, it must be shut off quickly. If left to overheat, NiCad batteries can explode.

It seems to be standard practice if you're shutting down a long way from home to check the battery is charged prior to turning off the engine - turn off the battery with the engine still running and the generator loadmeter shouldn't drop noticeably.

DC–Based Electrical Systems

There are still lots of aircraft equipment that must be powered by an AC source, and for a helicopter that is DC–based, this means that *inverters* must be installed to convert DC to AC. These are typically solid state devices, trouble free and normally quite reliable.

If the DC generator also doubles as the starter for the engine, then there will normally be a cooling time between start attempts - this is to permit the heat built up in the starter to dissipate. Normally after several start attempts, a long time is needed for cooling, or melting of the core will likely occur.

AC–Based Electrical Systems

AC generators are used when a large amount of power must be supplied - for example, de-icing rotor blades or for high–power military equipment such as search radars. They must run at a fixed speed to produce a stable alternating frequency, typically 400 Hz. Normally these generators are driven by the transmission rather that the engine, requiring the N_R be kept within 10% of a constant value. This means if the engines are set to IDLE, for long periods on the ground, the AC system will not be running at the correct speed, and will drop off line.

AC systems are used for complex helicopters, and on almost all helicopters over 10,000 lb. as they offer significant weight savings for the wiring. When the capacity of a DC system is pushed too high, it becomes difficult to reliably switch power in the buses in the event of failures. AC switching is much easier due to lower amperages for the same power.

The AC generator normally incorporates over– and under–frequency protection systems to ensure avionics are not affected by off-frequencies. In-flight this is not normally a problem, however if a large transient droop happens, an under-frequency system could drop off the electrics at an embarrassing time. To prevent this, a ground contact switch normally removes the under–frequency protection when airborne. On the ground, the ground contact logic switch will drop the AC electrics off when the rotor slows down. This has the disadvantage that the rotor cannot be slowed to an idle RPM while on the ground waiting for passengers. On the other hand, if you need to de-ice blades...

AC based helicopters still have some items that are DC–powered. Changing from AC to DC current is accomplished by the use of rectifiers.

AC based systems also have a problem with paralleling the AC systems - each generator must be in phase with the other. This can cause problems in transferring loads from one generator to another, or one AC bus to another - if the phase of the generators or buses is not the same, the transfer will not be smooth or may not happen at all. In one hair raising incident, a friend of mine said it was 8 seconds before the electrical system came back on line following a single generator failure. This was eight lifetimes, because it was at night, over the ocean, in a 40 foot hover with the autopilot maintaining the aircraft in position.

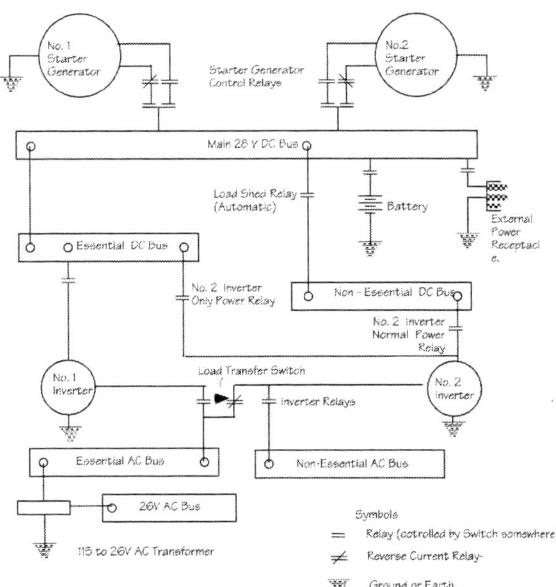

Figure 26-5 Typical Electrical System

Electrical Failures

It is useful to make up a list of the power that each electrical system in the helicopter draws. Why worry about it? If you are flying in a not–so–pleasant environment and lose the main source of electrical power and must rely on the battery, the unnecessary loads can be shed by turning off circuits and/or pulling circuit breakers.

It's also useful to look at which systems are powered from which buses. In one helicopter flown extensively at night, the radar altimeter was powered from the non-essential DC bus, so if a generator was lost, the radar altimeter was also lost. It was possible to switch the non-essential bus so it was always powered, and the checklist was changed for night flying.

In a more modern note, if you have a FADEC equipped helicopter, there is normally a backup for the FADEC computer in the event of a generator failure (because the battery will probably fail 30 minutes later), but what about all your caution and warning lights? They're going to go away when the battery fails. Just hope it's not at night.

Circuit Breakers

Most helicopters have a huge number of circuit breakers in the cockpit. Compare this to most fixed wing airplanes of equivalent weight and size, and you'll wonder why.

Sometime circuit breakers are used as switches, which is a round-about way for the manufacturer to say 'we're too cheap to change these to switches'. The argument that there are no switches with adequate circuit breaker protection in them hasn't been valid for many years.

If you have only circuit breakers in your aircraft and are regularly using them as switches, consider getting them changed.

Additionally, you might try pulling all the circuit breakers prior to a routine maintenance or servicing. More than one machine has been found to have CBs that were corroded in place, and which would never had popped. (there is normally no maintenance requirement to check circuit breakers...)

Circuit breakers may be used in emergency procedures, and if so, they should be prominently marked and easy to pull out. If you think you may have difficulty pulling the CB, then make sure you have an adequate puller with you.

It is interesting to note that Russian helicopters have only circuit breaker switches, and they are all turned on and off every flight, as this keeps the mechanism operational, and ensures the circuit breaker will work properly in the event of an excessive current.

When a Circuit Breaker 'Pops'

Circuit breakers exist to protect a device or part of the helicopter in case of an over-voltage or amperage in that line. When this is sensed, the circuit breaker will pop, and typically show a white line. It will be easy to feel, as it will stand proud of the rest of the breakers.

Caution

Do not reset a circuit breaker more than once!

Hydraulic Systems

Reasons For Hydraulics

The hydraulic system in most helicopters is there for reducing the effort the pilot has to make to move the flight controls. In some modern helicopters, the helicopter may not be controllable without such a system. If there are two hydraulic systems installed, you can bet it wasn't because the manufacturer wanted to promote sales of replacement hydraulic pumps and hoses*. Combat damage considerations would be a valid reason for two systems in military helicopters.

From a philosophical and safety point of view, if the helicopter is not controllable for even short periods of time without hydraulics, then two independent systems need to be installed for redundancy. One older helicopter with a single hydraulic system had very high control forces with hydraulics off. Ten minutes of holding the controls at cruise airspeed is enough to wear anyone out. How can the manufacturer ever expect anyone to fly it for half the possible range is beyond me. Why this long? If you are halfway home from the oil rig, over water, and the hydraulics have had enough, you have no option but to continue to fly (and probably at cruise speed)!

By the way, if there is no limitation in the limitation section of the FM on airspeed with hydraulics off, then it's not a limitation, merely a recommendation.

Different systems have different emergency philosophies. One helicopter manufacturer makes the hydraulic system switch so that it must have electrical power to turn the hydraulics off, and another makes a system with both an operating and a standby hydraulic system that switches automatically to the standby if the main one fails. One military insisted on a 'Total Hydraulics Off' switch on a helicopter that was unflyable without hydraulics, because they had such a switch in an earlier version of the helicopter that was slightly different in the blades! Learn the system, how it works and how to trouble shoot and correct problems in-flight. Learn to control the helicopter in spite of the forces on the controls!

* It's because the helicopter wasn't safely controllable with only one hydraulic system.

Typical Hydraulic System

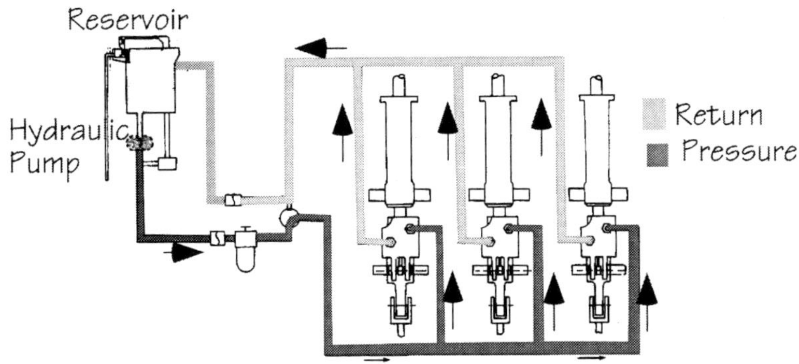

Figure 26-6 Typical Hydraulic System

A typical hydraulic system has a reservoir, a pump powered by the transmission, pipes and supplies power to actuators. The actuators take their signals from the flight control system. The pump is powered by the transmission so that hydraulics will continue to function during an autorotation*.

A typical flight control actuator is shown below in Figure 26-6. Note how the pressure moves the body of the actuator, until this movement causes the pilot valve (that remains stationary) to cover over the holes to the actuator.

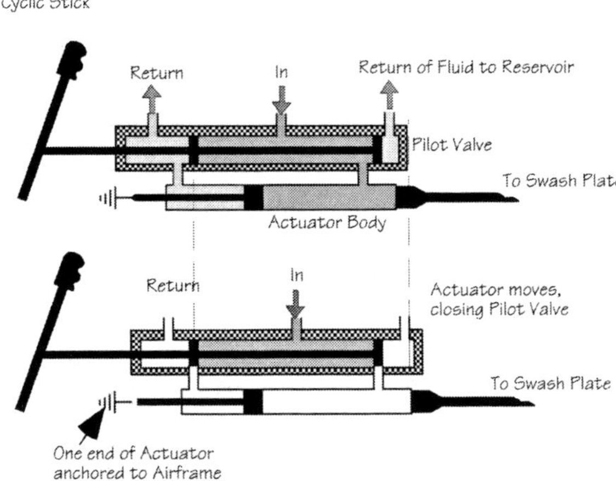

Figure 26-7 Typical Flight Control Actuator

Unpressurized Reservoirs

Many helicopter hydraulic systems do not have pressurized reservoirs. This keeps the costs and weight down, but has a potential problem. If the helicopter ever gets into an unusual attitude that is sensed as zero G by the fuselage, the hydraulic fluid will float away from the pump intakes, and the flight controls will 'freeze†' until the airframe gets back to a positive G situation. Sounds far fetched, but it has bitten more than one helicopter pilot.

Hydraulic Emergencies

Typically, a hydraulic failure should be a non-event. If only one system is fitted, then the helicopter must be controllable without the system, and it is worth learning how to fly the machine without it. The Saunders-Roe Scout (now retired from active service, fortunately) had its maximum airspeed restricted early in its career when it was discovered that above a certain airspeed, a sudden hydraulic failure would literally rip the cyclic out of the pilot's hands and flip the helicopter inverted. An accumulator of hydraulic pressure was installed to give a few

* One model of an early piston engine helicopter had it powered by the engine - when the engine failed, you had two emergencies - an autorotation without hydraulics!

† Not to mention that the pilot will probably go cold as well, for a short period of time

seconds to get the helicopter under control if the hydraulic pump failed. As well, a red warning light would flash when the pressure dropped. Scout pilots learned that if they saw a red light (and there were several others that hardly ever came on) they would automatically slow down before the hydraulic accumulator lost pressure.

It is also difficult to simulate hydraulic emergencies, as there are more types of failures than just loss of pressure. If the failure is a loss of fluid, be prepared for it to be different to what you may have practiced. Procedures used in training may not be representative of the real things. For example, flying with the hydraulics switched off but with fluid still in the servos is not the same as having one servo jammed. The procedures in the manual should cover all the failures.

De-Ice / Anti-Ice systems

Most commercial helicopters have electrically heated windshields to prevent ice and mist from obscuring the view, and heated pitot and static sources. Some have ice protection for the engine, but that's about all that is provided. This means that flight by helicopters in icing is not common, as, without the protection for the blades, nasty things can happen.

A system to permit helicopters to fly in icing conditions is not commonly fitted, for the simple reason that they are complicated, heavy and expensive. There are only two western commercial helicopters with these systems, namely the Super Puma and the EH-101. All large Russian helicopters have de-icing systems - why don't ours?

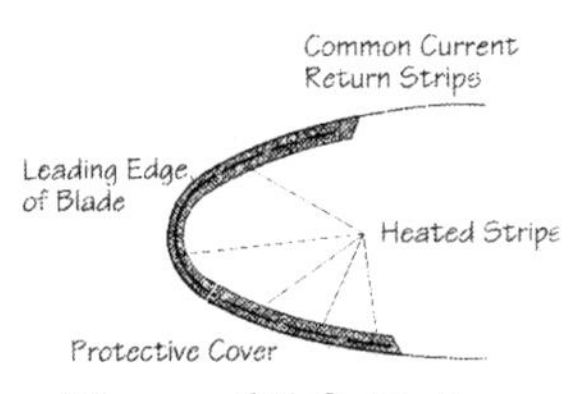

Figure 26-8 Rotor Blade Heating Elements

The main feature of this system is the blade heating arrangement. See Figure 26-8 for a view of the way the rotor blade is heated electrically. Note that the blades are not all heated at the same time.

Obviously, some way to control this system is needed, and the controller typically has several different ways to schedule heating of the blade elements, depending on the conditions. Nothing is ever as simple as you think it is, and de-iced rotor blades are no exception.

Finally, how does the massive electrical current get from the generators to the rotor blades? A very big set of slip rings is used, adding to the complexity. The tail rotor needs a set of slip rings as well...

De-Ice vs. Anti-Ice

The difference between de-ice and anti-ice systems is subtle, but important. A de-ice system will remove existing ice, while an anti-ice system will only prevent it from forming. Anti-ice systems need to be turned on prior to ice forming.

Landing Gear

General

Something needs to come between the fuselage and the ground besides sheet aluminum! Since helicopters operate in many extremely hostile environments, but don't need to land first, then stop; a type of landing gear different to that attached to fixed–wing aircraft is needed. Varieties include skids, wheels, skis, fixed floats and emergency floats. They all have their strengths and weaknesses. Interestingly, most of the load carried by the landing gear is very often at the back cross–tube or rear wheels in a tricycle arrangement.

A problem for all undercarriage is ground resonance, which is covered in more detail in "Ground Resonance" on page 380. Ground resonance is one of the reasons why not all skid equipped helicopters have a simple cross tube and skid arrangement. Some are set up with front and rear cross tubes, others with a rear half tube, others with single rear attachment point, and so on. Two–bladed rotors have a more simple arrangement of landing gear than others because of the reduced possibility of resonance on the ground.

Wheel equipped helicopters have a special problem with regard to ground resonance, as they not only have tires, but also shock absorbers. If either of these are out of tolerance they can help to set up the necessary oscillations for ground resonance.

When the Bell 212 / UH-1N was modified from a 2–bladed rotor to the Bell 412 4–bladed system, it was necessary to change the rear cross tube from a two–point mount to a single–point mount, because of the response to the new excitation frequencies produced by the 4 blades.

Skids

Problems with Wires, Cables and Other Hazards

A perennial problem with skids is snagging things, ranging from wires and cables on the ground to chain link fences, and stretching to sheep horns. Seems a sheep rancher used to use his helicopter to help persuade reluctant rams to move by hovering beside them and nudging them with the skids. This worked well until a ram decided to toss his head sideways at just the wrong moment and caught his full set of curled horns around the front of the skid. Helicopter and ram proceeded to fly in very small circles for several moments until a ranch hand wrestled the ram off. Needless to say, the helicopter was way out of every CG limit ever written, and the pilot and ram were very lucky to get away. History does not relate the ram's fate.

On a more serious note, skids can catch in cracks in platforms if the skids are small in diameter. Wires or cables can snag across a skid very easily. The point is that these things happen - beware! Look at the section on dynamic rollover in "Rollover" on page 179 to see why this is important.

It can happen to wheels and floats as well!

Wheeled Undercarriage

The wheeled undercarriage has found great favor on helicopters that operate from airport ramps or ships. Wheels have problems of their own - wheel brakes have to be fitted, a means to turn the helicopter while on the ground has to installed, not to mention a way to stop the helicopter turning when not wanted. Tires needs to be sized for the type of surfaces that will be landed on and space made in the fuselage to stow the wheels if they retract. If they don't retract, the drag penalty is higher than a skid undercarriage.

Two naval helicopters, the Westland Wasp and the Lynx, are fitted with wheels that are only there to permit them to pivot on the deck - the wheels are no use for taxing at any other times, as they are permanently angled with respect to the fuselage.

Operations with Wheels

Using a wheeled undercarriage is not difficult, but does require some thinking. The first point is that wheel chocks are necessary to prevent the helicopter from rolling when the brakes are off. Small point, perhaps, but who takes the chocks away when you are by yourself and it's a single pilot helicopter, and the brakes don't keep pressure overnight? (Don't laugh - it happens.)

Positive steering control requires some weight on the steerable wheel (either nose or tail).

At touchdown, it is important to minimize sideways drift to prevent side loads from dragging the tires. In the hover, the wheel on one side will typically be lower to the ground than the other, so remember this. In fact, the effects of translating tendency are more marked with wheels, as one wheel will always touch down first.

When ground taxing, speed is controlled by a combination of longitudinal cyclic and collective - usually very little collective is needed, speed is mostly controlled by the fore-aft cyclic. But beware that too little collective and too much cyclic can cause droop stop pounding on some helicopters. Know your machine!

When turning on the ground, remember the tail will swing out a long way behind where you think it may turn. If possible, have a ground guide! It is normally possible to pivot around one main wheel (if differential brakes are fitted) so turns can be very tight. In some helicopters, backing up is also possible.

Turning on the ground is normally controlled by the pedals, some types may be different. Prior to lift off or touchdown, it is normal to ensure the steerable wheel is locked - this is to prevent sudden darts in an unexpected direction, and possible shimmy. If the wheel does not self center, it may be necessary to run in a straight line for a short distance to lock it.

Shimmy can be encountered when fast taxing and a bump nudges the wheel. If it occurs, stop or lift off immediately. Most helicopters have a speed limit for ground taxing - some manuals will say ground speed, others imply it - if in doubt, ask the manufacturer.

Tires, shock absorbers and actuators need to be serviced.

For most light helicopters, skids are lighter, have less drag, and take far less maintenance.

Rolling Over When Taxing Rapidly

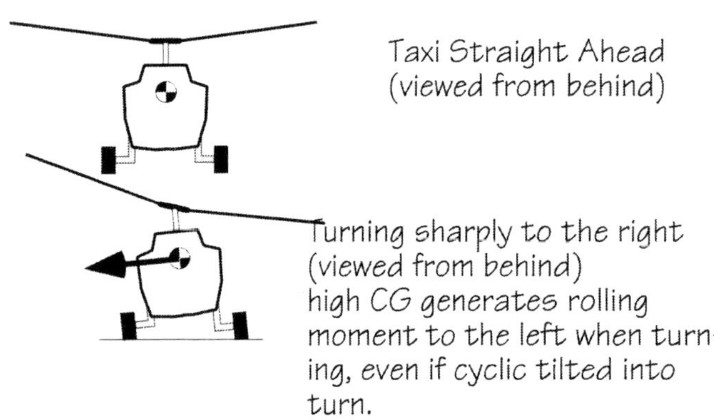

re 26-9 Rolling Over in a Turn while taxiing

A problem with some wheel equipped helicopters has to do with CG, tread width and turning. If the wheel tread is narrow and the vertical location of the CG is high (as it is with most empty helicopters – engines are not close to the ground), the helicopter may roll over out of the turn if attempting a turn while taxiing at too high a speed. Wind of course, may not help this. Don't taxi too fast or try turning too quickly!

Retractable Landing Gear

The retractable undercarriage is a way of improving looks as well as the cruise speed. But if you fit such a system, undercarriage retraction mechanisms and hydraulics need to be fitted, probably gear doors are needed, and a standby lowering system must be considered. As you can tell, I'm not a big fan of retractable wheels unless you really need them.

Lift-off (or Departure)

Remember to retract the gear! Hopefully you will remember prior to the maximum airspeed for gear extended. Normally there is no warning horn to remind you, so a mental note when above both V_Y and a certain height AGL and no longer able to land immediately is a good check. I used 200' AGL, 60 KIAS and no chance of making a suitable surface in 30 seconds for one helicopter I tested.

On the other hand, don't be too hasty. One friend was rather shocked to discover that if the landing gear lever was moved to retract and then immediately to extend, it took a long time (over 20 seconds) until safely locked down again. In the event of an immediate requirement to land right after gear retraction, one could be embarrassed. (He was able to get the post-takeoff checklist changed.)

Touchdowns

The first thing to remember is to put the wheels down (if they retract). Next thing is make sure the brakes are off (except for off-level or deck landings, see below). Some helicopters with retractable wheels have a low altitude warning if the wheels aren't down (and the ones without this system invariably have at least one wheels–up landing). A system to warn the pilot that he hasn't put the wheels down is needed*. Those that have an airspeed–based warning aren't thinking of touchdowns in very high winds. It is one of my habits to check the wheels down at 100' AGL, and again at 15' AGL as a last chance check.

Off-level Landings

Wheel–equipped helicopters landing on off-levels, or ships or other small platforms shouldn't move very much after ground contact. The pilot must set the wheel brakes prior to touchdown. The only problem with this is to remember to release them again after takeoff! Not many wheeled helicopters have a 'parking brake on' light that actually measures pressure at the wheels - they normally show the handle position.

A minor problem with nose wheel equipped helicopters is that trying to land nose up–slope is a futile exercise - nose wheels don't have brakes, and unless you are very lucky to have an ideal off-level where all wheels touch down at the same time, it is a very frustrating exercise.

* I don't care how good your pilots are, it will happen unless such a warning system is installed.

Wheel Brakes

There are wheel brakes on some helicopters that are so poor at stopping the machine you wonder why the manufacturer bothered. There are other systems that give the impression of being fitted to aircraft carrier style arresting gear. Typically those systems that use the feet to provide all the pressure don't do as good a job as those that use the toe brakes to control a larger reservoir. There is certainly no need to fit helicopters with anti-lock braking systems.

There are also two different ways to control wheel brakes- toe brakes and what I'll call a bicycle grip. The toe brakes provide differential braking capability, which is good for tight turns in cramped areas, but have the potential for one foot slipping off or making life complicated when both tail rotor control and toe braking are needed at the same time. The other type resembles a bicycle brake handle fitted to the cyclic stick, and is found on lots of Russian machines. While the first reaction is to consider this a throwback, it means that there is no problem doing a maneuver that needs both yaw pedal inputs and smooth application of both brakes, and that the feet don't need to do anything special for braking.

Skis

Skis are not just fitted for winter operations in snow, nor only to skid equipped helicopters. Many operators use them when touching down on (not in) soft ground is anticipated. There are two basic types of skis for skid machines - full length and bear paw type skis. Wheeled helicopters have skis similar to bear paw types.

Full Length Skis

Full length skis spread the load of the helicopter along the length of the skid, and typically have a small curl-up at the front to permit running landings. They have a small range penalty in cruise flight, and a small weight penalty. They will generally keep the whole length of the skid out of the snow, and let the helicopter do a running landing to keep ahead of blowing snow.

Bear Paw Skis

A compromise for skis is the bear paw, which is only fitted to the back of the skid. This arrangement works well, as most of the load is carried on the aft crosstube anyway. They often do not permit a running touchdown in loose snow.

Skis on Mud

As was previously mentioned, skis are not just used on snow. If the helicopter operates regularly off soft ground, then skis can be a big help. But beware. Skis can be stuck in the mud due to suction between the flat surface of the ski and the mud. Most skis now have lots of suction holes for this very effect, but if yours don't...

Dangers on Crusty Snow

This is covered in more detail in "Dynamic Rollover on Takeoff" on page 181, but can be summarized here as a problem with catching one edge of the ski or skid under the crust of snow.

Floats

There are two types of floats: fixed or utility (used when operating continuously from water); or emergency floats (used when the helicopter doesn't intend to land on water, but is forced to by an emergency situation).

Fixed Floats

Floats open up a whole new set of landing sites for helicopters, and are not restricted to water use. Swamp, ice and tundra are also suitable places to use floats. Floats also present some interesting problems. Because of their size and location under the helicopter, they have a pronounced effect on both performance and stability and control.

Fixed floats are little more than a series of pressurized rubber sacks attached to a frame. They are inflated to a low pressure, (about 1.5 psi) and normally have numerous individual chambers. The buoyancy factor is about 1.5 to 1.6 times the maximum weight of the helicopter. Since the float bags are filled with air, like a balloon, they are subject to the same type of physical laws.

Increasing altitude can cause the air in the floats to expand, and most FM's have a maximum differential altitude above the place of takeoff, to prevent the bags from bursting. Interestingly, touchdown in very cold water with warm floats can reduce their buoyancy quite a lot.

A good rule of thumb is every 1,000 feet in altitude or 5°C makes 0.3psi difference in air pressure in the floats.

Boating!

Fixed floats also introduce a whole new set of handling characteristics, and not just in-flight. When you are operating on the water, with the engine stopped, the helicopter is like a boat. It should have mooring fittings for the floats, mooring lines, paddles, life preservers and possibly an anchor if you want to fish in the middle of a lake.

While sitting on the water, the helicopter will also be subject to the wind and waves, and it is difficult to tell the helicopter is drifting unless two objects on shore are lined up for comparison.

Start-up / shutdown

The helicopter pilot who shuts down on the water will be faced with a handling problem*. Unless he is tied to a wharf, he is out of control for a short while. With no force to stop the helicopter from rotating (such as is provided by the grass when on land), there is some rotation of the airframe as the rotor coasts to a halt. Remember there is always a reaction of the fuselage to the main rotor's rotation. On land, or while the tail rotor is capable of producing thrust, this pirouette about the mast is prevented. On the water, when the main and tail rotor slow, the tail rotor cannot produce any thrust, and the fuselage will spin. The reverse will happen on start up - until the tail rotor reaches speed, the fuselage will be out of control. Remember this when operating near docks or other things that can bruise the helicopter - unless the helicopter is moored, it can spin out of control for the first few minutes. There will be a time at both start and shutdown when there is no control over heading!

Spray

Hovering over the water will cause spray - it's unavoidable. If the water happens to be salty or brackish, this can have significant corrosion implications. Washing the engine compressor after exposure to this type of water is essential.

Spray on the windshield makes it difficult to see things, and to judge distances accurately. If it dries, it also leaves watermarks!

Taxing on Water

Taxing on water takes some getting used to. The helicopter sits very low on the water, and there is a lot of float below the waterline. Watch out for snags and submerged objects. Turns are normally made with pedals and coordinated with cyclic. Normally, the maximum speed for water taxiing is when waves start to break over the top of the floats.

Liftoff and Touchdown from the Water

There are two basic fixed float shapes - streamlined and hot-dog shaped. The streamlined type have less drag and permit running takeoffs and touchdowns on water, whereas the hot-dog shaped ones normally need to make or break contact at zero–waterspeed. Touchdowns should be made into wind, and if possible into the direction of travel of the waves as well. Touchdown across the waves can cause pronounced rolling.

Following the Waves

There is a tendency to keep the helicopter level when waves cause it to bob up and down. This must be resisted, as it very easy to get out of phase, and your efforts to keep the rotor disk level with the horizon may disagree with the efforts of the waves. Small, unimportant items like tailbooms can get in the way of the blades.

If you start to see spray being thrown forward of the helicopter and wonder where it's coming from- it's probably the tail rotor trying to do its bit to dig a trench in the water. Not wise to attempt aviation after this!

Off-Level Touchdowns on Water

Yes, you read that correctly.

* With fixed floats obviously, or he'd have more than a handling problem if the water isn't solid.

Most water has a tendency to be flat on the top*. Yet every takeoff and touchdown to water is really a off-level touchdown exercise - how can this be?

On the water, the translating tendency is not restrained like it is on the ground. The helicopter will drift sideways when sitting, unless the main rotor is tilted to prevent it. A lot of tilt of the main rotor is needed, and as the power is increased to lift to the hover, this lateral cyclic must be moved towards the center. (More thrust means less tilt is needed to counteract the side thrust of the tail rotor.)

A certain amount of sideways acting thrust must be found to offset the tailrotor's effect. This can accomplished either by a lot of tilt of a small amount of thrust (at flat pitch) or a small tilt of a large amount of the thrust (at higher collective positions). Either way, it cancels out the sideways push of the tail rotor.

The way to see this translating tendency is to use shore references (but remember to use two or more that line up in front of you to assess the drift) or note the bubbles and eddies around the front of the floats if they are visible.

Lift-off and Touchdown from the Ground

With fixed floats fitted, all takeoffs and landings from the ground must be with zero–groundspeed, as it is very easy to scuff the bottom of the floats. While this is easy to do in normal conditions, it is also necessary to land with zero–groundspeed at the end of an autorotation - not so easy to do.

Landings on less than level ground is also more entertaining, as the floats will tend to roll under, permitting the helicopter to slide downhill slightly.

As an aside, just sitting in the helicopter on the ground, with the engine and rotors stopped can make people queasy. There are some very slow movements of the fuselage that the inner ear senses but are not seen by the eyes as the helicopter jiggles on top of the floats. Can make one feel quite unwell.

Other Effects of Fixed Floats

The main visible effect of the floats is caused by their drag - it takes more power to push this volume of air through the air, and this translates into a reduced maximum speed, and more fuel to travel the same still–air distance. Stability and control effects are covered under the heading "Fixed Floats Effect on Stability and Control" on page 366.

Emergency Floats

It is not prudent to carry large fixed floats if you don't intend to land on the water. It is also not prudent to fly over water without some way of landing on it in case the engine(s) stop. Even multi-engine helicopters have demonstrated the need for floats, as it isn't always engine failures that cause forced landings. If you don't think this is true, I suggest a long session in the dunker to teach you how to get out of a sinking helicopter†. The solution has been pop–out floats. These are normally housed strategically on the fuselage or skids and activated by pressurized air at the pilot's command. They provide a means to keep the fuselage afloat, at least until the passengers and crew can exit.

I would never view emergency floats as being the only thing needed to survive a water touchdown. Other items like life jackets and possibly a life raft would be useful while passing the time on the briny deep.

Use and Problems

There are not many problems with pop–out floats. Minor annoyances, such as no common way to test the float circuits prior to flight, or show the floats are armed are no worse than other differences between helicopters. The worst problem, to determine where in the emergency landing sequence to deploy the floats, is made worse by the lack of practice most helicopter pilots have. Simply stated, most never get to deploy the floats in training. The wisest solution to this I have seen uses the requirement for the floats to be deployed annually for maintenance

* At least any water that I have ever wanted to land a helicopter on.

† It should be mandatory for all helicopter pilots who fly over anything larger than mud puddles.

purposes. A pilot carries out the inflation under the conditions recommended by the manufacturer and thus gets experience of inflating the floats and a short bit of flying with them inflated. (Of course a water touchdown does not follow to see if they really work...)

Fire Detection and Suppression

I only mention this to show a difference between the 'Western' way of looking at things, and the 'Russian' way.

Most Western helicopters that have a fire detection system use a series of hollow wires with another wire inside. When a fire happens, the outer wire melts and the two wires touch, lighting up a warning light in the cockpit. In practice, the two wires often vibrate together, get moisture in them, are affected by hot gas leaks, and so on. Lots of false warnings occur.

The Russians, on the other hand developed a much more sophisticated system that has a variety of sensors placed around the compartment. This has different levels of logic for various conditions. To show the degree of their efforts, in the final level, the sensors will indicate a fire only when all of the following conditions exist:

- Air flow past the sensor must be more than 6 meters per second (about 12 knots) (The compartments are reasonably air-tight, so outside airflow would not normally be present.)
- The absolute temperature in the compartment must be more than 150°C (much hotter than normal)
- The rate of temperature change must be rising at more than 6°C per second.

These conditions will only exist, all together, if there is a fire.

The Russians are so confident in the system, and have so much experience with it (at least 25,000 helicopters have it, flown over 25 years, not to mention fixed–wing), that if a fire is detected, the extinguishing system is automatically fired.

Oh yes, they also put detectors and extinguishing ports in the transmission area...

Heating and Ventilation

While we are talking about the Russians, it's a good time to mention their philosophy on heating and ventilation systems. As one would expect, they pay attention to heating the inside of the helicopter. The only difference is they also integrate the design to include the source of hot air. Engine bleed air still provides the main source of heat, but the very large fan between the engine intakes on most of their machines also provide forced air for the ventilation system. The result is that there is always a large volume of air available for mixing with the heated air from the engine, and if you add an air conditioner, for the cooler air as well. It is not necessary to rely on the pressure of the engine bleed air alone.

This is also how they provide a degree of protection from nuclear and chemical weapons for their military crews and troops. Since there is a slight over-pressure in the cabin, a filter system added prior to pumping the air into the fuselage is very simple.

Seats

I can't write a book about helicopters and not say something about the seats. Unfortunately, I can't think of very much good to say about most of them. Many helicopter pilots have bad backs because of the seating, and I can't see a good reason why it should be like this. As a friend of mine said - "Why is it I can buy a car that is quiet, has a good heating and ventilation system and superb seats, all for about one percent of what even a light turbine helicopter costs? When I get into my very expensive helicopter, my back is sore after less than two hours, yet eight hours in the car is fine. I can't ever seem to get the temperature right in the helicopter, yet I can do it with one dial in the car. I have to wear ear protection in the helicopter, but I get great stereo in my car. Why?"

A small part of the reason for the bad backs is the way the controls work. To go faster in a helicopter, the stick is a long way forward, and if you are going to keep your hand on it, it is necessary to slump forward, rest your right hand on your leg to support your arm, and twist slightly to the left. The collective, in the left hand, is going to be pretty high up, and your left arm will be raised, further twisting the back around to the left. To top it all off, the pedals will not be neutral, so one leg will be stretched, and the other cramped. Add some vibration*. Ask any back specialist what this will do to your back over a long term.

To make matters worse, the seats in most light helicopters are not adjustable, and the flight controls (aside from the pedals) are likewise not adjustable. I remember seeing a contraption to adjust the cyclic position longitudinally. Great idea - why wasn't it put into the production version? Why isn't the seat adjustable?

Some seats are just plain uncomfortable, regardless of their ability to be adjusted. More than one seat has served, in a way, as a standby fuel quantity indicator. Just when you think your posterior (or sometimes back) can't stand it any more, it's time to refuel. Whoever says that a seat design is OK should be strapped into the seat in the airframe, and made to sit in it for twelve hours before they say it is really OK. Pilots with really long mission times (some US Army Special Force helicopters have eighteen hour missions) have obtained ideal seats, but these are the exception, unfortunately.

It seems the Royal Australian Air Force did a study of helicopter pilots and their backs. This study determined that more than 1,000 hours of helicopter flying was likely to produce some permanent damage to the spine. At the risk of launching a class–action suit - is it possible that bad seats have limited the earning potential of helicopter pilots?

Compasses

Most helicopter pilots come to know more about compasses than their fixed wing brethren, for the simple reason that a pilot is needed to carry out a compass swing in a helicopter and an A&P† can do it alone for an airplane.

That having been said, a few words about the standby compass in particular are in order. Be careful when using it. It is only required to be within 10° of correct to be considered serviceable. That's worse than your minimum skill level pilot is supposed to be able to navigate on a cross country flight.

Have you checked it against a known reference lately? Runway headings, etc. are good and easily found sources of magnetic information- the accurate heading should be in most airport offices.

It's worth your while knowing how the helicopter is set up for the compass swing, as many different, seemingly insignificant devices can have a large bearing‡ on how accurate the standby compass is reading. Is the compass swing conducted with the pitot heat on, or off? If the wires for the pitot heater run close by the standby compass, turning the pitot heat on or off will certainly show a transient effect, but what about the steady state. What about landing lights? And so on. Better to know or observe while you can

Windshield Wipers

Helicopters operate in some pretty lousy environments, and yet a lot of them don't have windshield wipers installed. On some machines, with very high curvatures on the windshields, it's easy to see why no-one bothered.

It's also easy to see why no-one bothers when the wipers are turned on with the plastic windshield being dry, and it gets scratched to the point of being unusable.

I've also seen big expensive helicopters where the windshield wipers doubled as a standby airspeed indicator. At 140 KIAS, the wipers were no longer able to stay in place and vibrated to the outside of the windshield. For this, someone paid over $20 million?

Summary of Chapter 26

This chapter has dealt with a whole mishmash of subjects. Hopefully it has covered ground new to the reader, or at least given a place to start looking for better answers.

* No, make it lots of vibration, and at low frequency to boot.

† Technician, AME, mechanic or whatever the maintenance people (nearly said chaps) who take care of aircraft are called

‡ The pun is deliberate...

Advanced Helicopter Flying

So How Do We Fly a Helicopter?

Previous chapters have concentrated on the mechanics of how a helicopter works. This chapter is going to show how we, as pilots, make it do what we want to do- a subtle but important difference.

Surprisingly, flying a helicopter is much like driving a car, riding a bicycle or any other activity where you have to control a machine. It is made more difficult by some particular aspects of both helicopters and the air, but the basics are the same.

Whoa! I hear helicopter pilots say - it ain't that easy! No - it isn't, but the fundamentals are the same, and understanding them will help make and keep better helicopter pilots.

Consider Figure 27-1 below - it is called the closed loop control diagram, and is the same for both driving a car and flying a helicopter. (This is a simplified version of the full diagram.)

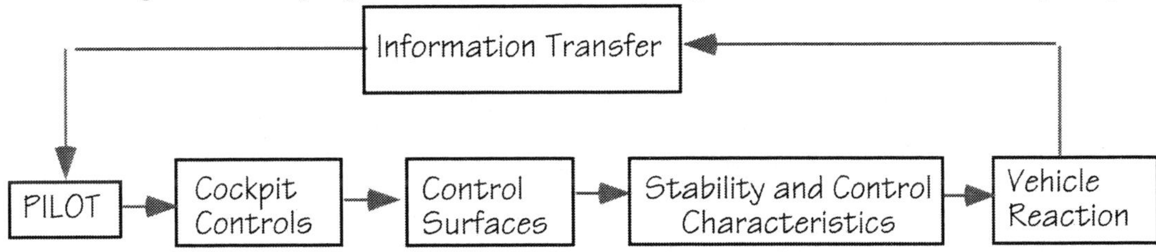

Figure 27-1 Closed Loop Diagram

Driving a Car Explained

The driver wants to be in the middle of the lane. Coming to a curve, an input is made with the steering wheel, which reacts through the steering mechanism to turn the tire and the car changes direction. This change in direction is 'fed back' to the driver visually as well as by a lateral acceleration and other cues, and another correction may have to be made so the car stays along the desired track.

How does the driver know how he is doing? Possibly by looking at the position of the car with respect to one edge of the road, or a whole host of other ways, such as the force it takes to turn the wheel, roll of the car, side acceleration and so on - all these are items of information 'fed back'. The important elements are the input the driver makes, and the information coming in about how the car is doing with respect to the curve. If the driver didn't look at the curve and how he was doing maintaining position, then he wasn't driving the car. The elements of this closed loop are the driver, the vehicle control system, its reaction, and the information pouring in on the driver.

Compensation*

How easy it is to drive the car depends a great deal upon the handling qualities of the car and the road conditions. If you have ever had a car with loose steering† or bad suspension you know whereof I speak. ('Herding down the road' was a better term than 'driving' for one old wreck I owned. I was compensating for the random steering all the time.) The same goes for flying a helicopter, only there are a few more variables. How easy or difficult it is depends upon the handling qualities of the helicopter, its stability and control characteristics and the environment. In my opinion, most light helicopters have only acceptable‡ handling qualities, but that's another story. The fact they are used effectively is a credit to man's adaptability.

Coming to a curve in the road, if the driver is looking at a particularly attractive member of the opposite sex on the sidewalk and not paying attention to the road edge, not only is the information inappropriate (and apt to earn a sharp word from the driver's significant other)

---

* not talking about monetary compensation, although we get too little of that in return for too much of the other kind.

† And we don't mean the nut behind the wheel either.

‡ As opposed to *ideal* characteristics. I know this is a subtle difference in words, but it makes a large difference in the workload of the pilot.

but it will be impossible to judge how much of an input to make to follow the curve. The information fed back is inappropriate. At high speed, looking at the road immediately beside the car likewise makes the information transfer inappropriate - the curve may not be seen until it is too late, or too many large corrections may be made for very small errors in lane position. Too much information is as bad as too little*.

Flying a Helicopter – Hovering

Flying a helicopter is almost the same as driving - lets look at hovering. The pilot wants to hover, that is maintain position, heading and height about the ground while someone hooks up an underslung load. To begin let's say the pilot can see the ground very clearly in front, and using a mirror, can also see the underslung load. Noticing the helicopter is slightly out of position, an appropriate adjustment is made on the controls by the pilot. This reacts through the flight control system and changes the tilt of the rotor disk slightly. This tilt changes the downwash a bit, causing the helicopter to move. The pilot assesses the movement and, seeing it is not quite enough, makes another, smaller input. This second correction, when it takes effect eventually, is judged to be sufficient. The pilot waits until an another error in position before making another control correction, and so on.

The key element is the information fed back to the pilot in respect of the helicopter position, rate of closure to the underslung load, etc. There are many other items of information coming in as well - peripheral vision for roll and yaw rates, proprioceptive (seat of the pants) feeling for vertical speed, etc.

Cruising Flight Example

Another example of the closed loop is straight and level flight at several thousand feet above the ground. For example, the pilot is trying to maintain the helicopter in a level cruise at constant airspeed with constant power. A gust makes the airspeed increase slightly. A small aft cyclic input is made to bring the nose up and let the airspeed drift back to the desired value. As the airspeed approaches the correct value, a second small correction is made to stabilize. If the new attitude is OK, no other changes will be needed, and the pilot can let the airspeed decrease back to the original value. If the correction is too little or too much, another input is made, and so on. If the airspeed indicator lags a great deal, the pilot may get out of phase - that is, the correction may be in the wrong direction at the wrong time.

So What?

Why go to the bother of writing all this? Of what use is it to the average helicopter pilot?

There are several very important concepts that need to be understood in the discussion of how we fly helicopters - one of these has been introduced as 'gain'. The next is to consider how the pilot fits into the loop.

To better understand this, return to the hovering example. It may be extremely difficult for the pilot trying to hover very accurately - over a small pad (a trailer, for example). Why is this? Does the helicopter respond differently over the pad than if it were 40 feet away from the pad? Does the helicopter 'know' something? Obviously not. The only part of the control loop that 'knows' anything is the pilot - the sole item that is aware of how accurately the landing gear must be placed, and must judge where the helicopter is with respect to the pad.

In this case, (hovering over a small pad), information is fed back at a very rapid rate. Literally fractions of a inch of movement are discernible. The pilot will probably be looking down through a chin window, trying to position the helicopter very precisely, but the response may not be what the pilot wants. Very small, rapid control movements will be the order of the day to try to get the helicopter into position.

Depending upon the situation, it is possible to get out of phase with the inputs. In trying to control things, the pilot only makes matters worse. This is used to be known as a pilot-induced oscillation (or PIO†), and the only way to get out of the situation is to stop the control inputs and try again.

* Please notice all that was said without a single sexist pronoun...

† This time-honored phrase (PIO) is a now a victim of political correctness. It has been decreed that it should be more correctly called Aircraft–Pilot Coupling (For us rotary wing types, it would be Helicopter–Pilot Coupling or HPC). Sorry, it's now OK to call it PIO again...

If the task requires this level of precise control (also known as a high gain task), then it may be necessary to use close references (it would be catastrophic to try to land on the pad while looking at something else...) and a different technique. The technique will vary depending upon the situation, but for the small platform a sliding lineup would be worth considering.

('Sliding lineup' involves hovering behind the place you want to land, lining up all the references ahead of you and maintaining those references in line while you move forward and descend at the same time to land on the spot without stopping over it, except very briefly at just a few inches above the spot.)

On the other hand, if the task does not require a high level of precision, using close references may lead to over-controlling. The helicopter is an inappropriate vehicle for humans to try to control to fractions of an inch for anything but very brief periods of time.

One of the most amazing feats of helicopter hovering I've heard of involved maintaining position over a laser beam projected from the surface onto a target mounted on the nose of the helicopter. The pilot was given a view of where the beam was within a very small window, and then was expected to climb vertically while maintaining the helicopter in position over the beam (other surveyors miles away would then sight on the helicopter). There were few pilots who could do this, and the only ones who could had to always keep the helicopter moving so they were continually correcting - there was no attempt to keep the beam perfectly in position- just somewhere inside the target. These highly skilled individuals could evidently keep this beam in position up to 5,000 feet above the ground on a good day. Glad it was them, and not me.

For most pilots, hovering at a low altitude with moderate precision requires the main area of regard for references to be about 20 to 30 feet in front of the helicopter. Looking closer (between the feet, for example) may lead to overcontrolling, and looking farther out (at the horizon) may lead to under-controlling and a poorly maintained hover. Previous advice about use of cyclic pressures instead of movements is worth remembering.

My experience of transitioning experienced pilots to new types of helicopters has shown repeatedly that where the pilot looks is one of the major determining factors in ease of hovering. The number of pilots I have corrected was something that really surprised me*.

If you learn nothing else from this book, I'll be happy...

Other Cue–Related Problems

Not all hovering tasks permit the pilot to see references easily. For example, hovering beside a ship underway† with an inconvenient wind direction may require the helicopter to face into the wind, but point in a direction from where the pilot can't see the ship. In this case he must get directions from another crewmember. This adds a large time delay in the control loop. The crewmember must compare where the helicopter is with where it should be with respect to the ship, translate that into verbal (and hopefully clear) directions to the pilot, who then must make the necessary inputs, which must take effect, which the crewman must decipher and so on. It's not difficult to see why mirrors and remote hover stations such as in the CH-54, Mi-26 and Mi-10 are such important aids for the pilot.

If you are having trouble with basic hovering, the first place to investigate is where the cues are coming from. If you are instructing, watch where the student is looking. Place your hand across the top of the instrument panel to force the student to look out farther if he is looking in too close, or try to give some specific exercises to move to a spot, and so on.

While on the subject of cues, it is useful to note that the cues must not be taken with reference to the airframe - as the airframe pitch attitude changes with different CG's. In other words, it's not a good idea to say when hovering that the horizon will always cross the windshield at the third screw head below the compass. While this reference line may be relatively OK, it will change with different CG's and weights. Most cues must be taken with regard to one another, outside the helicopter, and any cues that are relative to the airframe are for short term comparison only.

* I'm not sure who I learned this trick from, but - thanks!

† Another example of why the word hovering can be confusing- probably more correct to say maintaining position.

Why are Helicopters Difficult to Fly?

There is no doubt the first ten or so hours of helicopter flying are among the most humbling experiences one can go through. There are many parallels to learning to ride a bicycle* (or windsurf†)- somewhere, somehow, something clicks, and it becomes much easier.

Why is it difficult in the first place? Simply stated...

The helicopter is unstable, and takes a long time to respond to control inputs.

Ask any control systems engineer to put the two characteristics together - an unstable control loop and a long response time, and he will question your sanity on wanting to handle such a machine.

The instability of helicopters is a complex subject, and the books by Ray Prouty, Simon Newman and others do a very good job of explaining this in simple terms. Basically, if a helicopter were left to its own devices, it would oscillate in an ever–increasing manner, to the point where it would crash. Measuring the time a helicopter takes to start to diverge from a steady condition is a task for the engineering flight test team, and requires a lot of technical training to understand and test. For us, it is sufficient to know that a helicopter without an Automatic Flight Control System (AFCS) will diverge, particularly in pitch attitude, as various aerodynamic phenomena gang up on it.

The pilot's task is to stop these oscillations from developing. This is compensation for the shortcomings of the machine. Small, correctly timed inputs stop the helicopter from diverging from its hover attitude. If you look closely at how often control inputs must be made on a calm day in the hover in a typical light helicopter, it is about once every 5 to 8 seconds‡. Any other inputs are, strictly speaking, not necessary. Refer back to the rapid movements for the pilot trying to land on a small trailer and wonder if they are really necessary.

Note the word 'attitude' when referring to hovering in the paragraph above. In steady conditions, a constant attitude should hold the helicopter in the zero–groundspeed hover. Unfortunately, things are never steady, and any disturbance from the steady condition causes the helicopter to start its divergent tendencies. Again, it is the task of the pilot to stop those divergences from developing. More compensation.

Slow Response Explained

The other complicating factor is the slow response of the helicopter. This is due to a combination of an actual leisurely answering to the control inputs, and to the pillow-like nature of the air we operate in. First the slow response.

The hydraulic system introduces a small but measurable delay between the movement of the cockpit controls and the reaction of the actuators against the blades. Next, the blades themselves take some time to react and get to their new pitch position. These two items take about 0.1 seconds. The blades must move to their final new position, which takes at least one revolution to happen. At 360 N_R, one revolution is about 0.15 seconds.

Let's total that up.

$$0.1 + 0.15 = 0.25 = \frac{1}{4} \text{ second}$$

In control terms, this is a long time! The helicopter still has not moved from its original spot.

Since we're talking about our generic helicopter that has flapping hinges, when the controls are moved, a force is generated by the rotor hub, which will produce an acceleration in the cockpit and probably move the fuselage, giving some indication to the pilot that the control input he has made has some effect.

For a helicopter with no flapping hinge (i.e. a teetering head), the only thing that will have happened is that the tip path plane will have moved, but nothing else.

While there may be a change in attitude of the helicopter following the input, there will probably be no movement over the ground**. This discrepancy between change in attitude and no change in position is disconcerting and takes a while for students to get used to. For movement of the airframe to happen, the air has to be persuaded to react, which takes an additional, very perceivable period of time. A long

* Except the falling off part

† except drier...

‡ Not how often the controls are moved but how often the controls *must* be moved- many pilots waggle the controls needlessly, probably to make sure they're still connected.

**Even for those machines with fully articulated or hingeless heads - only an attitude change will happen immediately.

time has passed since the pilot realized he needed to make an input, with yet no movement of the helicopter. What would it be like to drive a car with this sort of delay between moving the wheel and changing position?

Consider our poor helicopter student - seeing an error makes a small correction, as instructed, but nothing happens immediately. What does the student do now? Yes - in goes a bigger input, just about the time the first one is taking effect, and things go rapidly downhill from there.

So there you have it, an unstable aircraft and a long time delay to control inputs - a potent recipe for disaster in any control loop, and part of the reason why helicopters are so difficult to learn to fly. We learn to fly helicopters slowly, and then after overcoming the inherent instability, we learn to anticipate and make corrections slowly.

We haven't even got into the cross coupling between the controls!

Cross Coupling

Nothing is ever simple in a helicopter - moving one control affects not only the desired axis, but also indirectly, all the other axes. For example, look what happens when a large change in pitch attitude is made to correct being out of position. If the helicopter has been hovering in a 10 knot wind, the power is set to maintain altitude for a 10 knot airspeed, the tail rotor has been set to balance the torque reaction and so on.

In the process of moving forward, let's say a ground speed of 3 knots is introduced. This means the airspeed seen by the rotor disk is now 13 knots. Unless the power is changed, the helicopter will climb (the power being used is correct for 10 knots, and is greater than the power required to maintain level flight at 13 knots), the torque reaction is now incorrect, as there is more dynamic pressure acting on the vertical stabilizer, and the lateral cyclic position is wrong as the inflow through the rotor disk has changed.

What can be corrected about this state of affairs? It would be an interesting experience to see if there is a cost and time saving to learn to fly, specifically hovering if the instability aspects of the helicopter were removed by the use of a simple AFCS. This should give students a more gentle learning curve. Once they had mastered the complexities of controlling a helicopter around the hover, introducing the instability aspects would be a small step.

The end result, of course, is the pilot has to make the helicopter hover. Compensation for the shortcomings of the machine must be made to close the control loop in hovering, level flight or wherever. How easy or difficult this is depends upon the helicopter, as well as the adaptability of the pilot. This is where the common belief that learning to fly in a difficult helicopter makes all other helicopters easy to fly, and make better pilots, has originated. It is difficult to argue with this theory.

Different Responses from the Pedals

If you ever stop to analyze what you must do with the pedals when making a turn in the hover, you'll discover a few surprising things. First of all, the pedals do not control rate of turn, especially in a no-wind situation. They are really yaw acceleration controllers. This means that if you want to start a turn, initially you will have to add some pedal, and then when the steady yaw rate is established, probably have to back off on the pedal input. This will only be true in a no-wind situation. It also means you will have to do some fancy footwork to get back to a steady, no turn hover.

It is also interesting to note that the pedals have different responses depending upon the direction of turn. The details of this phenomena vary from helicopter to helicopter in magnitude and direction, but in general terms, stopping a yaw turn in one direction may require only that the pedal input be relaxed, and in the other direction, it will require that opposite pedal be added to slow the rate of turn. Observe closely!

If you're instructing, don't try to burden your early students with this piece of trivia. It doesn't work in all wind conditions, and it's only an interesting observation. As far as I can see, it makes no difference in the larger scheme of things at all.

How to Hold the Controls

Cyclic

Strange that anyone should have to tell pilots how to hold the controls - doesn't it come naturally? In my experience, no*. Several things happen. Pilots become tense, as a result of how they learned to fly. They adapt and think it is natural to fly with a death grip on the controls. Secondly, they don't spend much time thinking about exactly how they are flying. Perhaps they know they are holding the stick too tightly, but they are too busy flying...

Most turbine-engined helicopters have hydraulically boosted flight controls. If no artificial feel system is fitted, very little effort is needed to move the controls. Pilots may be unaware of moving the stick. Fingers are good force sensors, but the hand and arm are very poor devices for determining small changes in relative position. For this reason, most pilots rest their right arm on the leg and use the wrist as the position sensor. Strangely, many pilots still have a death grip on the controls for no reason. Two fingers will do.

Overcontrolling

All the previous discussion about slow response and light forces on the controls helps to explain why some pilots overcontrol. Another reason might be that pilots end up stabbing the cyclic all over the place, and the law of averages determines that some of the control inputs end up being correct. The pilot soon develops bad habits that, believe me, are hard to break.

Some signs of the pilot not holding the controls properly are overcontrolling or 'stick stirring'. The cure for this, shown to me by an ancient instructor, consists of holding a pen or pencil so that the middle two fingers are held away from the stick. The only digits touching the cyclic stick are the thumb, forefinger and little finger. Its impossible to grip the cyclic stick tightly with this method, unless you like pain. The student will learn to relax (or else), and to help make small movements. Figure 27-2 shows this.

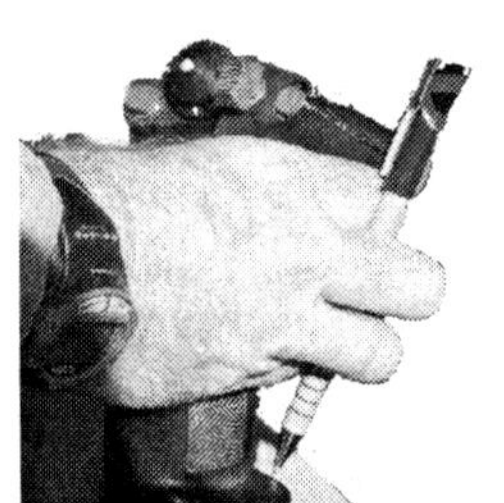

Figure 27-2 Two Fingers and the Pen.

In fact, a pilot stirring the stick can spill lift out from under the disk to the point where it makes a noticeable difference in performance. In some helicopters, stirring the stick in a circular motion at the necessary speed in the same direction as the rotor is turning can really reduce the overall lift.

Collective

Similarly, the left arm on the collective is used as a position-sensing device. It must make very small corrections without knowing exactly where it is with respect to the cockpit, or how much it should correct. In technical terms, this is an inappropriate device for a precision task. A solution I have found very useful is to extend the thumb of the left hand and let it touch the seat rail or other fixed part of the airframe. This technique provides a reference point for the hand, making it very easy to adjust the collective precisely. The hand only needs to slide up and down the collective a little bit as the angle changes. This is shown in Figure 27-3.

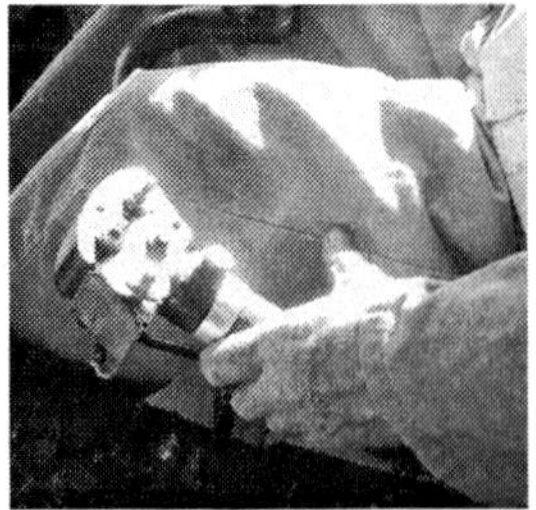

Figure 27-3 Sticking Out the Thumb

Pedals

Rest the feet on the pedals lightly. This is easy to say, but just wait until you have been flying for an hour or so, and then check to see if you are still resting your feet lightly. I'm surprised more pedals aren't bent by the great forces that are applied to both of them. Try to keep the legs loose and the forces on the pedals light, and you'll see what I mean.

* It wasn't natural for me, nor for lots of the experienced helicopter pilots I've taught.

This is as good a place as any to address a little–known fact - hinted at in previous sections - helicopter pilots are happy with less well–behaved aircraft than they should be*. What is meant by this?

Helicopter Pilots are Easy...†

In the flight test business, not only numbers are gathered or specifications compared. The way an aircraft handles from a qualitative point of view is very important. There is a scientific method of assessing handling qualities using the Cooper Harper rating scale, and it is based around the closed loop diagram shown in Figure 27-1. When teaching the use of this scale at test pilot schools‡ it has been noted that for the same task on the same aircraft, helicopter pilots would always rate the task as being easier than fixed–wing pilots. Since helicopters are unstable, with lots of compensation on the part of the pilot to fly it, the difference in ratings is understandable.

I remember teaching this qualitative evaluation exercise on a helicopter with various levels of automatic flight control stabilization. To give the students something to write about, we purposely left off the highest level of stabilization, and would ask them to hover. Hovering wasn't difficult, in fact slightly easier than an unstabilized helicopter, but it did require continuous attention and infrequent inputs to the cyclic to maintain position, even on a day with no wind. During the lesson, aside from asking them to describe what their control inputs were, and how accurately they were hovering, the question was posed: "Is the handling of this helicopter satisfactory without improvement for this task?"

Almost all the students said, "Yes, it's much better than the other light helicopter we fly".

After telling the student this was not a comparison exercise and that was not the question asked, the response was normally "Yes, this is satisfactory without improvement. It is good enough."

"Are you sure you wouldn't like this better?" I would ask, and then switch on the highest level of stabilization. This resulted in a rock–steady hover requiring almost no control inputs.

The pause before the student would reply "No, I like this" was never very long. After the student thought about this for a moment, I would say "In effect, what you said earlier was that you don't think this is necessary, so we'll have this level of stabilization removed and save the military a whole lot of money." The message was getting across. Perhaps the question should have been "Do you want to fly a helicopter like this for the rest of your life?"

I can't really blame the students - they had never seen anything better and had no way to compare what was good with what was really great.

Since we are used to compensating for the shortcomings of the way the helicopter handles, we are happy with less. Unless the helicopter community as a whole becomes more demanding, things will never get better. I noted sadly one particular program centering around re-engining a venerable and very popular machine (the UH-1H), where none of the competitors considered the addition of a small, simple AFCS to their bids. Such a system would have transformed the handling of the helicopter, but since none of the bidders had experience in the benefits, it did not appear to be considered. End of this particular sermon.

Artificial Control Feel or Trim Systems

Many light helicopters do not have an artificial feel or trim system, especially if fitted with hydraulically–boosted controls. Nevertheless, some do...

In a helicopter, it is sometimes necessary to make large changes in control positions, and hold the controls away from their original position for long periods. Maneuvers that would require such movements are transitions to forward flight, or quick stops. The control forces need to be quickly removed in more than one axis, and 4-way beeper trim systems are often not fast enough. This has led to a unique type of trim, referred to as the *force trim (FT)* system. Typically,

* Not only less well behaved aircraft, but often less money (sadly)...

† ...to please

‡ Empire Test Pilots' School, US Naval Test Pilot School, US Air Force Test Pilot School and École du Personnele Navigant D'Essais et de Reception (French Test Pilot School)

it operates by pressing a single button on the cyclic to remove force gradients in the cyclic and pedals. When the button is released, the force gradients are re-established with the new location as the zero force point. Helicopters with complex AFCSs and autopilots normally also have a 4–way trim switch (beeper trim). To avoid confusion, these systems will be called respectively, *force trim release* (*FTR*) and *beeper trim switch*. Typical locations are shown in Figure 27-4.

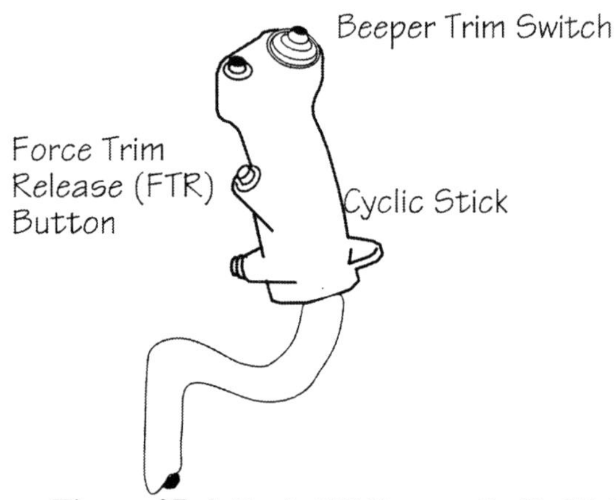

Figure 27-4 Typical Helicopter Cyclic Stick Control Grip -

Most of the time, the changes in controls position are quite small, and precise trimming of the forces is needed. This is where the beeper trim switch is used.

A hydraulic system removes the requirement for the pilot to provide the force to directly move the rotor blades (remember pitching moments?). It also removes the force the control surface will feed back to the cockpit controls, which can be an important cue to the pilot. In my opinion, some force should be necessary to move the cockpit controls away from the trim point. The reasons for this are:

- Non-existent force gradients mean the pilot cannot let go of the stick without applying friction. Friction, on the other hand, makes it difficult to move the stick a small amount smoothly and precisely. Many experienced pilots out there will probably disagree, but it really is the case.
- There is normally a lot of time when the pilot is not involved in actively controlling the helicopter, but is merely maintaining the helicopter in a steady condition. (The differences will be explained later.) In this case, it is nice to have a reference point for where the stick is going to go when it is released. Put another way, the pilot knows how far he is moving the stick by the force it presents to his hand (it needn't be a large force).
- The hand is a poor position-sensing device when it does not have a reference position - that is why many helicopter pilots fly with their right arms resting on the right leg - movement about the wrist provides the position cue. This posture often requires slumping in the seat, and aggravates bad backs.

In order to provide the pilot with adequate forces cues for stick movement and to permit an Automatic Flight Control System to function*, it is often necessary to add an artificial feel system. If long periods of steady flight conditions are needed (beside constant maneuvering, which requires continuous manipulation of the controls), some method to hold the controls in position is necessary.

* The reasons for this are discussed in Chapter 37,"Automatic Flight Control Systems".

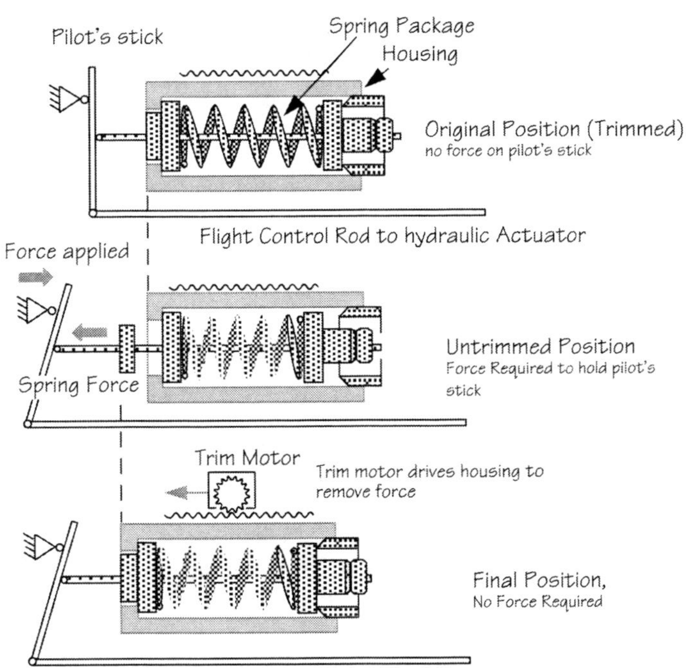

Figure 27-5 Typical Artificial Feel System

Artificial feel systems found in most helicopters are based on springs, clutches and trim motors. Figure 27-5 shows a typical artificial feel system, incorporating a trim motor.

From this force system, in our generic helicopter, a series of suitable mechanical linkages leads to the hydraulic actuators and the rotor head.

Control Forces

I have had the pleasure of flying a wide variety of helicopters and fixed–wing aircraft. Naturally, these had a wide variety of control forces, ranging from none (on most light helicopters), to truck–like. No helicopter has had the control harmony and feel of a well-designed, reversible control fixed–wing aircraft.

I understand the need for light control forces when conducting a precision task with small continuous control corrections, such as hovering with an underslung load. I cannot understand *no* control forces for this task. It's like driving a car with very light power steering.

It is also worth noting that control systems designers in fixed wing aircraft spend quite a bit of effort in getting rid of friction in order to make a better handling machine, and helicopter engineers are asked to put in a friction system to hold the controls in place. Have we lost sight of the big picture? Someone mentioned in passing that in many light helicopters, the pilot has to supply the mechanical characteristics to fly the machine, as well as fly the machine.

My operational military flying was on the Bell UH-1N, (Bell 212) a type that had no full-time control feel or AFCS, and on a mission involving a lot of hovering and underslung load work. The only time most pilots had the force trim turned on was during IFR. During the test pilots[*] course, all the helicopters,[†] even the unstabilized ones, had a trim feel system, which gave a force to the stick whenever it was moved from trim. I remember clearly my reaction when taking control of the UH-1N again (I had not flown for it for a year). The very first thing I missed when I tried hovering was the lack of control feel, and I asked for the force trim to be turned on.

To digress still more, I had the pleasure of flying the Polish W-3A. I had initially complained about the high control forces, however, after being able to place a very large load precisely on a very small trailer without much effort (and not being able to see the load: there were no mirrors), I was quite surprised at how much I came to like the control forces. Somewhere in the middle lies the optimum.

This still hasn't answered the question - why don't we have control systems with a good artificial feel? Perhaps it's because we have grown up without them, and can't be bothered to change. Helicopters, unlike fixed–wing aircraft, require large displacements of controls when changing flight conditions, for example from cruise through descent to a hover and landing. Large control displacements are needed to transition from one condition to another, but aren't always rapid displacements. The pilot has some time to reduce the forces to zero at the new stick position.

* In this case, a test pilot is an experimental or developmental test pilot, *not* someone who performs post maintenance or post production check flights.

† Gazelle, Sea King, Wessex, Scout and Lynx

Control forces have other uses besides providing a tactile cue to the pilot about where he is moving the stick. For example, on the ground, a force trim system would permit the pilot to let go of the stick with the knowledge that the stick wasn't going to wander off somewhere nasty. Those who have flown the BO-105 or BK-117 or MD500 series (which have only a beeper trim system) have had no great difficulty in adapting to these systems.

The AH-64 Apache was originally not fitted with a switch in the cockpit to turn off the force trim. The AFCS needed the trim system (see Chapter 37 to understand why) and it was not envisioned the trim should ever be turned off. US Army pilots had been used to a helicopter (AH-1) with a switch to turn the trim system off, and insisted such a switch be fitted to the Apache as well. Despite the protests of the manufacturer, one was fitted. Sure enough, someone decided they didn't like the control forces, and turned off the force trim system, and forgot about the stick while they got busy on the ground in the cockpit with the electronic magic. The result was a very interesting and expensive air-conditioning job when the stick vibrated forward and let the blades chop off parts the fuselage normally needed for flight.

In a more tragic note, an acquaintance was struck and killed by the blades when he exited a burning civilian helicopter. He was probably thinking of the military version of the same type he had been flying that had a trim system to hold the stick in place (the civil version didn't have a trim system at all). He shut the engine off, but not the battery and ran forward with the blades turning. In his haste, he had not frictioned down the cyclic. The cyclic vibrated forward and the blades came down as he ran. He had left the battery on, perhaps thinking there was a trim system to hold the stick in place.

My bet is if helicopters were given a force feel system with light breakout, a small gradient and a good force trim release system, (and no way to turn it off), after five hours of flying pilots would not part from it. Of course, if it were married to a good, intelligent AFCS, it would be one step closer to heaven...

Collective Release

Larger helicopters often feature a collective trim release, which holds the collective in place without the need for the pilot to keep his hand on it. Such a system should be seriously considered for many smaller machines as well. It does away with the need for an adjustable friction (that is never adjusted exactly for any two pilots) and stops the collective from wandering down or up. Having transitioned lots of pilots to different helicopters with this feature, it takes less than five minutes to make believers out of them.

On another pet hobbyhorse*, I wonder why those helicopters with a trim release system on the cyclic also use the same switch to release the force gradient in the pedals. The problem with this system is that if you want to re-adjust the pedal position it is probably due to a change in the power, not a change in the cyclic. Why no manufacturer has connected the collective trim release with the pedal release is still a mystery.

On a more humorous note, and certainly not wanting to poke fun at our Russian comrades, older Russian designs had a brave attempt at the same thing. One of their machines, the Mi-2, has a collective trim release, in the form of a large spring–loaded lever on the collective, When the pilot let his hand go, this would attempt to hold the collective in position. Unfortunately, the position was not continuously selectable - it was one of 15 or 17 notches in the collective travel. Murphy's Law dictates that none of these positions would exactly match the collective position desired, and so the pilot had to keep his hand on the throttle/collective all the time. If you let go, the collective slid into the nearest groove, which resulted in either a slow climb or a slow descent.

It should be noted that despite this system, and a throttle arrangement that works the other way to our convention, the Russians still manage to use this model to clean up at international helicopter flying competitions for many years.

Fuselage Attitudes†

A problem with helicopter flying lies in the attitude of the fuselage. It is possible (indeed, necessary) to climb with the nose pointing below the level flight attitude, and descend with the nose above the level flight attitude - flight path is not related to nose attitude. Fuselage attitude changes markedly with Center of Gravity as well - an aft CG will produce a more nose up position, and so on. This makes it difficult to use 'hard' numbers for talking about flare attitudes, etc. - the numbers will change with different CGs.

* At least one doesn't have to feed these pets

† Pitch attitudes as opposed to happy, sad, arrogant, etc.

Pedals Again

Feet and pedals are an interesting area. Pedal forces are too light in most helicopters - nice work by the flight control designers in getting the forces so small, but we need to re-think the whole problem. Feet are very poor force and position sensors. Control forces measured on the Gazelle showed less than one pound of force to start moving the pedal, and only two pounds of force to move the pedal one inch from the trim point. This helicopter's pedals aren't much different from most Western machines. For those of us who are past our prime, asking a part of your body (your foot) that regularly carries nearly 95 pounds (i.e. half my total weight) to sense only one pound and then sense the difference between one and two pounds or one inch of travel, is impossible*. (Most sensors used in aircraft have less than 1% accuracy –why should we humans be any better?) Anyone who has used fixed–wing, reversible–control–system rudder forces would agree - its easy to tell if you've moved the rudder - there is an increasing force with increasing displacement. These are more along the lines of the force needed to tell the pilot he is moving the pedals, and it should not be difficult to incorporate a way to remove these forces.

My experience has been that most helicopter pilots press very hard with both feet. They apply a lot of pressure with one foot and modulate the pressure and movement with the other one. For example, if the left pedal is to be moved forward, a large force is applied to the left pedal, and a force to modulate is applied by the right foot. No wonder our legs get sore after the first few hours of helicopter flying!

The Other Way 'Round

By the way, there is a lot of discussion and ~~old wives~~†' tales about how difficult it is to change from helicopters with one direction of rotation main rotors to the 'other' direction (not the 'wrong' direction, just the (politically correct) 'other' direction). Having switched many times, and trained pilots to fly both types, I can state quite confidently that the only pilots who ever had trouble where those who were mechanical, and didn't really visualize what they were doing. Even they got over the change quite quickly. The secret is to visualize keeping the nose pointed where you want it to be pointed, and disregard which foot you are pushing with.

I remember the flight evaluation for Rotor and Wing magazine on the Dragon Fly helicopter. I enjoyed the flight very much, but hadn't had much preparation before arriving in Italy. On my way home, I was reading the flight manual and realized that the main rotor turned the other way. I hadn't even noticed during the flight, and I think I turned several shades of red when I discovered this.

Tactical Takeoffs

Military helicopters, especially those engaged in shooting missiles from behind cover, often have to hover downwind to carry out their missions effectively. Hovering behind a treeline by itself is no big deal, but there is a potential trap waiting for those who are too cavalier in moving away from this situation.

If you are facing downwind and wish to turn to depart, there is a major performance consideration. At some point you will be moving through zero airspeed, and it would a good thing to remember that the power required to hover at zero airspeed out of ground effect is more than to hover downwind.

Secondly, if you are trying to look really sporting and use an angle of bank while turning into wind, remember that tilting the thrust vector will reduce the vertical component of lift. Just at the same time probably as you are going through zero airspeed...Wise old helicopter pilots tell me that you should use only yaw initially and wait until you are at least within 90° of being into wind before banking.

* Perhaps women, who are lighter and might have smaller feet, might be better at this than men, but that would be a sexist conclusion...

† Sorry- nearly made both a sexist and age-ist mistake.

Summary of Chapter 27

This chapter has also covered a lot of ground. It should have provided an insight into some of the ways we fly helicopters, and some of the problems we put up with daily. The next chapter will explore some of the instruments in the detail that professional pilots should find of interest.

More Instruments

Pitot Systems

The pitot system in most helicopters is one of the most misleading, misunderstood and least useful holdovers from seized wing aviation we have been forced to use. The airspeed indicator is simply not worth looking at in that part of the flight envelope that defines the raison d'être* of the helicopter.

The first reason for this contentious statement is that the pitot system on most helicopters shows airspeed only in the direction the airframe is pointing. Secondly, by its very nature, the typical pitot system does not indicate accurately at airspeeds below 40 knots†. The pitot system measures the difference between static and dynamic pressure, and at airspeeds less than 40 knots, there is not enough difference between the two to work properly. There is a good reason why the airspeed indicators on fixed–wing aircraft do not register below 40 knots. Airspeed is important to airplanes which can stall, and most fixed–wing aircraft stall at speeds greater than 40 knots, so they don't see a major problem.

Another reason for the unreliability of the pitot system at low speeds is due to the air not hitting the tube straight on - up to 12° from on-center can be accepted by most systems, but if the air is entering the pitot tube at an angle greater than this, large errors result. Figure 28-1 shows this angle. At low speeds, the helicopter is probably not pointing directly into the relative wind, and the slip ball is not a good indication of sideslip‡.

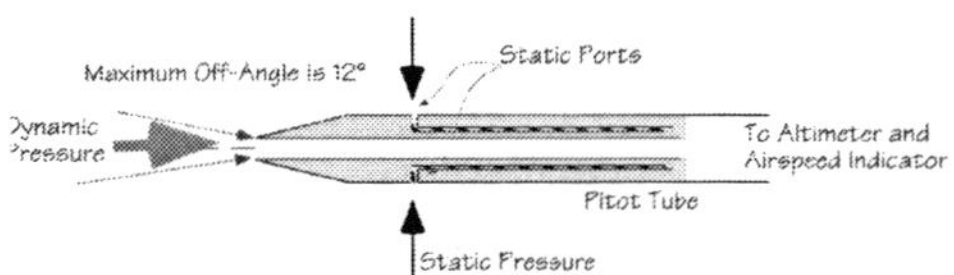

Figure 28-1 Relative Wind on the Pitot Tube

See Figure 28-2 for a diagram of the typical helicopter flight envelope and the area the airspeed indicator is not usable. Since large sideslip angles (i.e. greater than 12°) are permitted even at high speed, it stands to reason the airspeed indicator is not indicating correctly at these conditions. The situation is made worse when air is crammed down the static ports that are only supposed to sense static pressure. Then the difference between static and dynamic is really incorrect. There is a least one helicopter where any amount of yaw below 60 knots may drive the airspeed indicator to very low or zero values when there is still quite a lot of airspeed. Static ports are located on both sides of the pitot tube or fuselage, to hopefully eliminate any sideslip effects

.

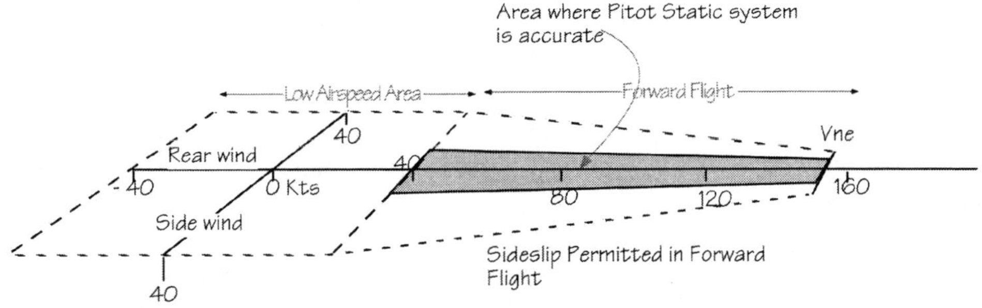

Figure 28-2 Airspeed vs. Sideslip showing area of Accurate Pitot -Statics

* That's French for the 'reason of being' - nothing to do with dried grapes.
† Regardless of what the flight manual says, or the markings on the airspeed indicator say.
‡ There is more detailed discussion about this later.

Side or rear winds affect these pitot static instruments as well - I have seen the airspeed indicator reading 40 KIAS with 20 knots of side wind, and 40 KIAS when hovering with a 30 knot tail wind. Why we as a community have accepted this state of affairs for so long is beyond me.

Altimeters

The same problems of accuracy in low airspeed can be applied to the altimeter - it is measuring static pressure, and as such must be assumed to operating in atmospheric, free stream air. This is often not the case, particularly when operating in ground effect. Typically an altimeter reading the correct altitude with the rotor stopped is slightly wrong when the rotor is at normal RPM on the ground, and more wrong as power is increased to hover IGE. This is due to the increased pressure of the air under the helicopter when hovering in ground effect. Hopefully, the altimeter is correct when hovering out of ground effect*.

Position errors affect these instruments as well. Only military flight manuals have an altimeter correction chart (all helicopter FMs should, but the civil ones don't require it) but they may only be valid for certain conditions. I know of at least two instances where adding other devices messed up a reasonable system. In one case, a wire strike protection system (WSPS) made a mess of the air around the combined pitot–static head and resulted in very large errors, but only with a laterally offset CG. With wings level, ball in the middle the offset lateral CG resulted in an unusually large sideslip that changed the pressure distribution around the static ports of the head. In another type, taking the front doors off resulted in the static ports (directly ahead of the door) being affected and the altimeter error in the opposite sense to that shown in the flight manual.

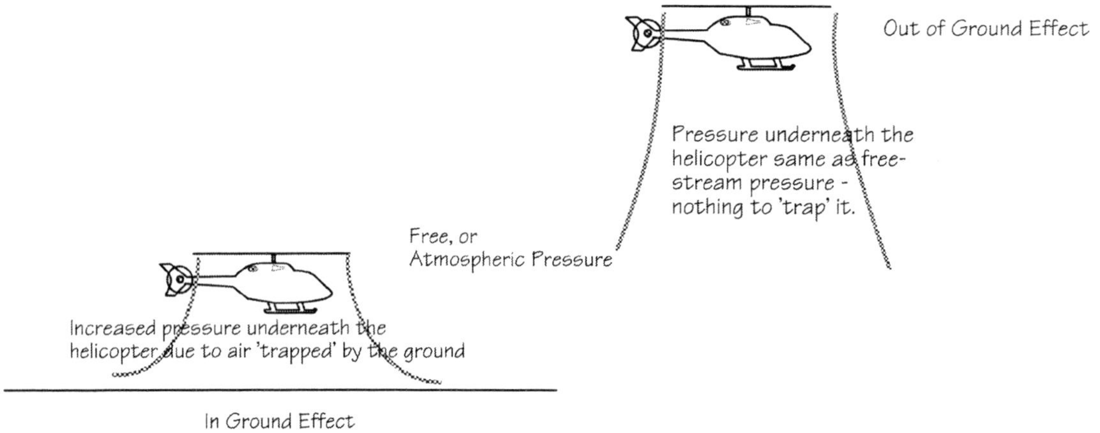

Figure 28-3 Ground Effects on the Pressure Altimeter.

Corrections to the Altimeter in Cold Weather

Most of you might be fortunate enough to fly where shirtsleeves are the order of the day, however, you never know, someone might be reading this book out of boredom on a cold Arctic night. If so, you should know about the effect that really cold weather can have on the pressure altimeter. This is particularly important if the flying is in Instrument Meteorological Conditions (IMC) and an instrument approach is needed.

Pressure altimeters are calibrated to indicate altitude above sea level in ISA conditions (covered in "International Standard Atmosphere" on page 43). Any time the atmospheric conditions deviate from ISA, there are errors in the pressure altimeter (as well as the airspeed indicator). When the temperatures are above ISA, the errors are on the 'safe' side, that is, the altimeter is indicating lower than you actually are. When the temperature is lower than ISA, the altimeter is lying the unsafe way

* Although you would probably never know, as this information is missing from most Rotorcraft Flight Manuals.

- that is you are closer to the ground than the altimeter says. In really cold weather, this can make a significant difference between the pressure altimeter reading and the actual altitude. In visual conditions, this is not normally a problem, as you can see the ground, and can hopefully avoid it.

If you are making an instrument approach it can be of real concern. The following table shows the amount that must be added to the indicated altimeter reading in order to be at the correct height above sea level. The altimeter source is the location where the altimeter setting is made (i.e the ground location - normally the airport).

OAT (°C)	Height above altimeter source (feet)								
	200	300	400	500	600	700	800	900	1,000
0	0	20	20	20	20	40	40	40	40
-10	20	20	40	40	40	60	80	80	80
-20	20	40	40	60	80	80	100	120	120
-30	40	40	60	80	100	120	140	140	160
-40	40	60	80	100	120	140	160	180	200
-50	40	80	100	120	140	180	200	220	240

For example, if you are on an ILS approach into Frozen Mukluk, Siberia, and the OAT on the ground is -30°C, and the following heights above the airfield apply to parts of the approach, you must add the following corrections:

Part of Approach	Altitude (MSL)	Height Above Airfield (Feet)	Correction to be Added	Altitude to Fly
Procedure Turn	4,500	1,000	160'	4,660
Final Approach Fix	4,400	900'	140	4,440
Missed Approach Point (DH)	3,700	200	40	3,740

Static Port Locations

The static ports on most helicopters are located on the side of the fuselage, and in an area where the airflow is supposedly undisturbed. This is to permit the air pressure there to reflect accurately the air pressure outside the rotor disk. Be aware of deforming the area around these static ports, and to think about them if you are considering flight in icing conditions if they are not heated.

There is no certification requirement for altimeter errors to be shown in the flight manual, and as a consequence, we have no way of knowing where the pressure altimeter is correct. Little comfort when you're flying a really tight instrument approach...

Even less comfort when you realize that helicopters are permitted to use a 100' DH on an ILS instead of the normal 200'...

So What?

The problem is that the primary pitot static instruments of altitude and airspeed are unsuitable for helicopter operations. This means that unless some other means of providing altitude (or height above ground) and airspeed (or ground speed) information to the pilot, the helicopter will never get away from fixed–wing–type approaches - airspeeds greater than 60 knots will be needed, and this will drive all the other approach criteria. Zero–Zero helicopter approaches will not happen until a better instrumentation system is devised. Until we have such systems as standard, we will continue to have problems with vortex ring state sneaking up on unsuspecting pilots.

For starters, we have some helicopters that have published speeds permitted on instruments that are lower than 40 KIAS. There is no indication how much margin there is between this speed and the airspeed where the ASI quivers and drops to a worthless reading.

What Can be Done About This?

The first thing we need to do is demand this problem be fixed. Ask for something better on your next helicopters. We have the technology to fix the problem, if only we ask for it (and are willing to pay for it).

There are several different low airspeed sensing devices on some advanced military or search and rescue helicopters. Here are two basic concepts -

LORAS (LOw aiRspeed System*)

A mechanically rotating pitot tube with sensors on both ends. This drives the pitot tube at a speed where there is enough dynamic pressure to measure the difference between an advancing and retreating side, and this must be the wind relative to the airframe. I have used such a system, and found it to be very accurate and useful in a whole variety of ways. The Russians have even gone one step further on their Mi-28 attack helicopter, and mounted pitot tubes on the end of each rotor blade. Their theory is that if the blades aren't turning, you're probably not interested in the wind in any case...

LASSIE†

A swiveling fixed pitot tube that uses the downwash from the rotor to obtain enough dynamic pressure to provide meaningful pitot information. The angle of the pitot tube with respect to the airframe is measured and the relative wind speed is determined. Found on the AH-1S on one side only, and on the Longbow Apache on both sides of the transmission fairing.

So, like a man with two watches not being sure of what time it is, do Longbow Apache pilots get confused about the airspeed really is??‡

RAH-66 Commanche System

The Commanche helicopter has added yet another wrinkle to the low-airspeed system. They evidently like the Russian pitot-tube-in-the-blade concept, but found that such a device protruding from the blade had a big radar signature. To maintain their stealth capability, they opted for a flat pressure sensor on the bottom of the blade, (like the B-2 bomber) and found this worked just fine.

General Comment on Low Airspeed Systems

Recently there have been a proliferation of helicopters that have been permitted to operate at pretty low airspeeds when on instruments. Some of these helicopters don't appear to have much margin between this low airspeed and the airspeed where the pitot static system stops working correctly. I'd suggest that the minimum airspeed on instruments ought to be at least 25% above where the airspeed indicator indicates within 5 knots of being correct under the following conditions- maximum lateral CG, ball up to 1 ball width to either side, at 500 feet per minute rate of descent (since you'll normally want this low speed during an instrument approach), and in a turn to 15° of bank. The '25% above' figure will give a slightly smaller margin as we now demand of fixed wing aircraft from the stall speed, and is not going to be add more than 15 knots of airspeed in any case. If we consider the airspeed at which the ASI stops reading correctly as being equivalent to the stall speed on a fixed wing aircraft, we should apply a 30% margin (same as fixed wing) above this speed. This will not be a great deal, only 12-15 knots, but it will be safe.

* OK, so it's not exactly right, but you get the idea
† No, not the dog.
‡ In fact, the information only goes to the fire control system.

Until we have the commercial pressure for zero–zero vertical or very steep approaches, we won't see these systems in widespread use. They are just what the doctor ordered for a great number of helicopter applications. Figure 28-4 shows the two different types of sensors.

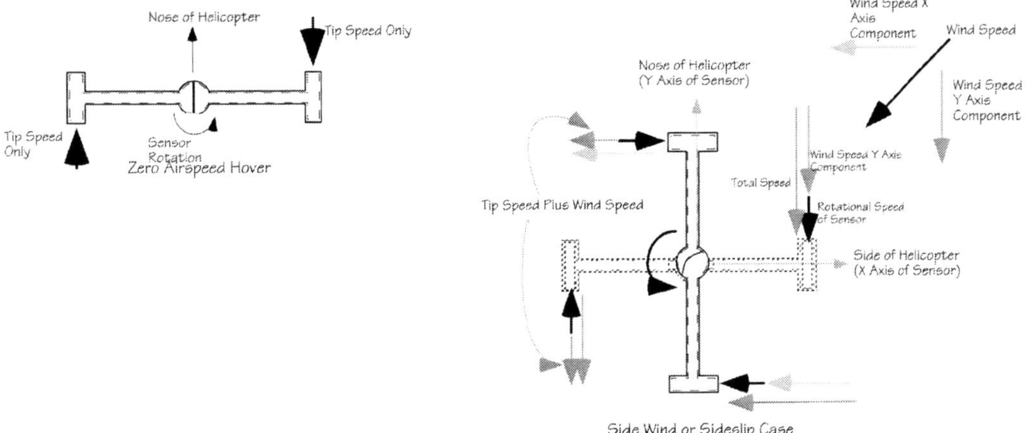

Figure 28-4 LORAS Operation

Obviously, such a system would need a different type of display than the standard Airspeed indicator. An example is shown in Figure 28-5. Note that the left hand side scale, vertical speed, is best taken from the radar altimeter or Doppler navigation system than a pressure source.

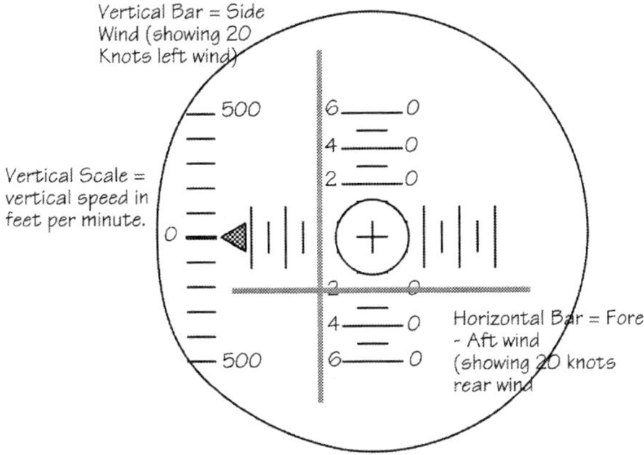

Figure 28-5 Low Airspeed Display

Another Reason for Low Airspeed Systems

Performance will always be related to airspeed, but instrument approaches will always be related to groundspeed and ground related events.

For example, if it is possible to carry out a zero-zero approach to a hover using a differential GPS*, then the problem will still remain of the possibility of having a slight tail wind on the approach.

At some point, it may be that the vertical speed and the wind react to be in one of the areas where vortex ring state happens. With a normal pitot static system, there will be no way to know if this is close or not.

* Something that will happen regularly during the lifespan of this book. It has already been demonstrated quite well.

Miscellaneous Instruments

Outside Air Temperature Gages

Next time you're in a hangar full of helicopters, see if you can find out what all the OAT gauges say, and what the real temperature is. You might be surprised at the spread of readings. Ask your mechanic if there is a requirement to ensure the OAT reads correctly in the maintenance manual for your helicopter.

In the flight test business, accurate temperature is necessary and the old meat thermometer types were not satisfactory. We replaced the standard gages with a system that was supposedly more accurate. but found that in direct sunlight, the black mass of the electronic box would affect the results, unless we put some insulation between the windshield and the black box.

Radar Altimeters

A device that is fitted to many larger commercial helicopters is the *radar altimeter*. It tell height above the terrain, sort of. What it really tells is the height above something that is reflecting a signal, which is a roundabout way of saying it doesn't always measure height above the ground.

Ice is a good example of where the radar altimeter will lie. Fresh water ice is transparent to the radar altimeter, as is snow. The radar altimeter may say 6' when you're on top of the snow covered lake. That means it's 6 feet to the water.

On the other hand, sea water ice (at least sea water ice that is less than about one year old) has enough salt and suspended material to reflect the signal. The real question is, how will you know which is which? Without tasting it, which sort of defeats the purpose of having the radar altimeter. I guess if you're that low to the ice that the thickness makes that much difference you need more help than a radar altimeter can give you.

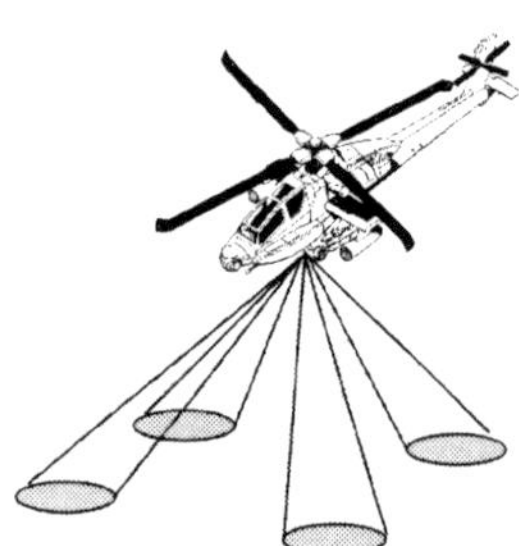

Figure 28-6 Radar altimeter patterns

In turns, the radar altimeter is not looking straight down, and so will misread. A brief description of the antennae is in order to understand this phenomena. See Figure 28-6, which shows the signal going out from the radar altimeter. In a turn of more than 30°, the beam is not going down vertically to the ground, and it will reflect off the ground some distance away.

It should also be obvious that radar altimeters can reflect off underslung loads...

Waves and Radar Altimeter

As most naval helicopter pilots have found, radar altimeters are very useful to keep you above the briny deep, but they have a nasty habit of following wave heights. If you are using a radar altimeter to hover, then either a smoothing circuit needs to be put in the radar altimeter to damp out the waves, or a vertical accelerometer is used in the height hold channel (discussed in Automatic Flight Control Systems, Chapter 37,"Automatic Flight Control Systems").

Vertical Gyroscopes and Attitude Indicators

This problem is actually quite old, and not confined to helicopters. It has to do with the principles of the attitude indicator gyroscope. These use vertical gyros to provide the signal to the attitude indicator. The gyro can operate in a continuously erecting mode or as a free gyro. At some angle of bank, which is different for each make and model of gyro, the gyro will go from being continuously powered into the vertically erect mode to being a free gyro. The problems start if the gyro is operated at an angle of bank just below that value or well above it for long periods of time. It's easier to describe a typical example.

Lets say the gyro is being continuously slaved to vertical if the bank angle is less than 6°, and above that value, it is acting as a free gyro. If you're flying straight and level most of the time, with the occasional bank to 15° to turn while IFR, then you'll never see the problem.

If you enter a very shallow turn, say 5° of bank, for example, the gyro will be trying to erect itself back to zero at some rate, say 2° per minute. So after 3 or 4 minutes of this very shallow turn, you might have an indication of level flight, when you know you're turning. You're not likely to do this, but if you're hovering with a side wind for a while...

The other example is a bit more insidious. If you're orbiting over the latest news story for several hours, doing a never ending 15° bank, you may notice your attitude indicator saying something stupid after a while. As if it weren't you weren't getting twisted around, now the instruments are joining the conspiracy. What's going on?

The answer is that the attitude gyro has gone into a free gyro condition, and has been running down for quite a while. The gyro will stop being spun up when it reaches 6° (in our example, yours may be different), and is now being subject to two different forces. The first is earth rate, (guaranteed 15° per hour by the Maker), and the second is random bearing drift. Earth rate drift is due to the gyro pointing to somewhere in space, and the earth is spinning underneath the gyro at the rate of 15° per hour (rate of rotation of the earth). Random bearing drift is the drift due to friction within the gyro. It can act in opposition to the earth rate or in combination with it, just to mess up your life.

So if your gyro starts to be something other than on the level about your bank angle, now you know why that might be happening.

Entering the Digital Era

Digital engine instruments and computer displays are slowly replacing analog mechanical instruments. We have an opportunity to take advantage of the technology, but as always, we are going to make some mistakes. The first point to discuss is strips vs. dial indications.

This argument goes way back (at least in aviation history terms) to the mid 1950s. There is no completely correct answer, but it seems that we are more analog animals than we know, at least for things that are rapidly changing. Personally, I prefer analog gauges, and I would like to see any computer display of engine parameters to be simple, with trend lines and the option of digital readouts for those parameters that need to be read with accuracy.

Too Much Accuracy

I've also seen where the capabilities of the measuring devices couldn't be well harmonized to the displays. For one particular helicopter, the sensors were capable of accuracy to the nearest 0.1%*, but the display would only show to the nearest whole digit (i.e. 91 or 92%). The display also changed color when the relevant number reached a limit. Here's what happened:

The system limits were set extremely accurately in the memory of the computer, lets say 92.6% was the continuous torque limitation. When the torque went above this value, the display changed from green to amber. So our pilot pulling up on the collective sets 92%. At least, that's what he sees. What he has really set is 92.4%. Then the torque creeps up just ever so slightly to display 93% (at 92.5% it will show the next highest value). No problem, the 93% is green. Suddenly, the 93% turns to amber. What's happened? The torque is now 92.6%, which is the takeoff limit, so the display turns amber. What's the point of all this advanced technology?

"Pilots need information, not data" **NOTE**

But Some Good News Too...

One of the things the digital age has given us is smarter instruments. They will beep, buzz, change color, flash and so on to let us know when things aren't right. It is also possible to combine the output of many sensors to give the pilot one display to show how close to limitations the helicopter is operating.

* Personally, I've never been able to tell time that close, and don't know anyone who can set power that accurately.

Figure 28-7 Eurocopter VEMD

If you think about it for a minute, a helicopter pilot is expected to monitor more variables than any fixed wing pilot ever has to, at the very moment when all attention should be directed outside (the hover, in case you couldn't guess). Finally, someone has recognized this and put all the data on one instrument- it automatically calculates which parameter is closest to the limits and converts that to a single gauge, so you as the pilot always can look in the same place to squeeze the last legal bit of performance from your machine. They made it nice and big too...

Summary of Chapter 28

This chapter has covered a hodgepodge of items that are related to the instruments fitted to more complex helicopters. The professional pilot should be aware of some of these problems in order to better understand how they can affect everyday flying.

The Turbine Engine

Introduction

Piston engines were covered earlier and first for the simple reason that they are used mostly in training helicopters. For those who fly piston engines professionally, or those who have superchargers or turbochargers, you may wish to look in specialized books for further information. This chapter will concentrate on the basic turbine engine, as fitted to our generic single engined advanced helicopter. Chapter 32 covers multi-engine installations.

In looking at the layout of this book, it was obvious that this was the largest chapter, but there are a lot of things about turbine engines which deserve the attention of the professional pilot, so I make no apologies!

It must be emphasized that turbine engines are very different from piston engines, in the way they operate, and their behavior and interface with the pilot. Be prepared to unlearn some things.

What is true for a piston engine is not always true for a turbine

Turbine engines are either free–turbine or fixed–shaft types. Since Free turbine engines are more numerous than fixed shaft engines, they will be covered first and in more detail. Fixed shaft engines are dealt with at the end of the chapter.

Turbine Engines Are Different!

Turbine engines are different from piston engines in many ways, some obvious, others not so obvious. Turbine engines are:

- smoother, with less noticeable vibration
- quieter (or at least different noise, and certainly less exhaust noise)
- lighter weight for the same horsepower (i.e. better power / weight ratio)
- more reliable (typically)
- verhauled at greater intervals (hours)
- easier to start in the cold
- require less maintenance between overhauls
- consume less engine oil

On the other hand, turbine engines also are:

- more expensive to purchase and overhaul
- thirstier (they consume more fuel)
- less tolerant of abuse
- more surprising when they fail (being quieter, they give less warning of failure)

Typical Free Turbine Engine

One of the first things that must be pointed out is that the turbine engine used in helicopters is related to, but not the same as, the jet engine found in most commercial airlines and military fighters. It is more closely related to the turboprop engine.

A typical turbine engine found in helicopters is shown in Figure 29-1. Note that there are numbers shown in the diagram. These relate to the various 'areas' in the engine, and are an international convention for numbering. For example, '0' relates to the atmospheric conditions before the air goes into the engine (and after it comes out). '1' is the front of the compressor, and so on. So, if we were to measure the temperature or pressure at the end of the compressor, it would be T_3 or P_3 respectively.

Our typical engine has a *compressor* section, where the air is compressed and air pressure and temperature are raised. There are two basic types of compressor- axial and centrifugal. The axial compressor has several stages or rows of fixed and rotating discs, and the centrifugal typically has a single rotating disc of complex shape. Some engines combine both types.

This air is passed to the *combustion chamber*, where fuel is added and burned. Note that not all the air is used in combustion, and at least half is used to cool the metal around the hot flame. The very hot, fast moving air passes through the *compressor turbine*, where energy is extracted to drive the compressor (so the whole process keeps going) and then through the *power turbine* (where the energy to turn the rotor system is extracted) and then out through the exhaust. Speeds of rotation are typically quite high (between 30,000 and 50,000 RPM on most small engines) and temperatures at the turbines are also quite high - around 700-900°C, especially in comparison to most pure jet or turbofan engines.

Some aspects of the turbine engine are that worth considering is that at idle, most of the power is used just to maintain the compressor turning. It stands to reason that at idle, the efficiency (fuel burned for useful work), is low. It is only when the engine is running at high power settings that the efficiency improves.

Turbines are natural engines for race cars. They are so good in fact that they are banned. An effective (but sly) way to ban them is to limit the size of the air intake. Over 75% of the air used is for cooling, which may come as a surprise. Consider that the flame of burning jet fuel (which has a temperature of over 1,400°C (2,500°F) must be cooled in a very short distance to something less than 700°C, to stop the metal from melting and it's easy to see why so much cooling air is needed.

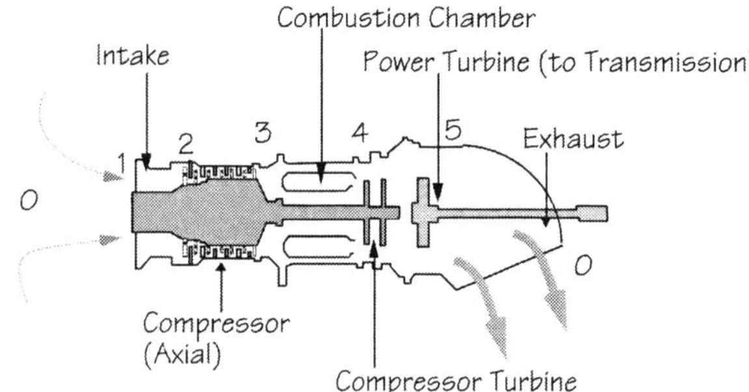

Figure 29-1 Typical Turbine Engine

A turbine engine typically does not have the ignition system on all the time. Some machines call for ignition on during approach and landing, in order to help keep the engine running in the event it flames out.

In the free turbine engine, there is no direct mechanical connection between the power turbine and the compressor turbine- that is, there is no set of gears connecting them, only a gas path. If you like, a piston engine is like a manual transmission in a car and a turbine engine like automatic transmission.

Terms Relating to Turbine Engines

Many of the terms used in turbine engines have no industry agreed standard, resulting in confusion, even with the international standards mentioned before. A typical example of this is TOT, TIT, ITT, T_4, T_5, even $T_{4.5}$ – all represent the exhaust gas temperature somewhere in the engine. The reason for the different names is the different places the temperature is measured. For consistency the abbreviations used in this book will be:

N_1 = Compressor speed
N_2 = Power turbine speed
TOT = Turbine outlet temperature
Q = Torque

Most engine and rotor speeds are expressed in percent (%) RPM to simplify the pilot's life. (Just think of the problem if the limits weren't in per cent- Compressor speed limits might be 25,675 RPM for continuous use and 27,450 for takeoff. With percentage figures, you only have to memorize three digits at the most.)

A small point here about the terms N_2 and N_R. They are often confused, especially when talking about governors. Since the two are mechanically connected, they normally are considered equivalent. It is only when the helicopter is in autorotation, or in a strange situation for twin engine helicopters that they are not mechanically connected (in these cases, the N_R will be higher than the N_2).

This is also a good point to mention that it's not possible to compare temperature or RPM limits between engines. The temperatures might be measured at different points in the engines.

Ratings and Limitations of Engines

Difference between Ratings and Limitations

A rating is the power the engine will develop when it is run at the limiting speed at ISA Standard Day conditions. Limitations are those proscribed limits put on the engine by the manufacturer to permit continued operation and longer life.

Occasionally, a torque limitation will appear that (coincidently) equals the rating of the engine. Most limitations are designed with normal use in mind, and err on the side of safety, with some provision made for in inadvertent excursions beyond this level. How much that margin is will remain a secret, so it is best not to exceed the normal limits, as you don't want to find out you were the one to go just beyond what the manufacturer had built in for careless pilots!

How Long is Each Limit Good For?

More than once I have heard that if there is a time limit on an engine rating, then if the rating has been used for that time, an equivalent time must be spent below the limit. For example, if there is 30 minute TOT limit, and the engine has been run to this TOT limit for 30 minutes, then, according to some, it is understood the engine must be kept out of that time limited rating for 30 minutes before it can be used again.

This is nonsense, for the following reasons - firstly, if that's what is meant, it certainly isn't spelled out in any manual, airframe or engine or certification guidance I've ever seen*. If that's what's implied, it should be spelled out. Second, and most importantly, I've checked with a few engine and airframe manufacturers and they all say that isn't the case.

Another false way of looking at this is to think that if something is damaged by overstressing, it can be made OK by under stressing it - this doesn't work.

Cycles

A problem of turbine engines is thermal stress and shock. It is not hard to understand that taking a piece of metal from a cool rest and suddenly heating it to 700°C while rotating it at high speeds is pretty hard on the metal. Do it enough times, the resulting damage accumulates and the metal fails. For this reason, most turbine engines count *cycles* - the number of times the engine has been started and used at takeoff power. Change the temperature and RPM quickly or a lot, and the cycles also add up. This is why most large jet engines have such long lives - cruising at high altitude for long times, they have few cycles, and lots of time at one power setting. Helicopter engines unfortunately have lots of changes in power, (read changes in RPM and temperature) and hence relatively short (but glorious) lives.

Cycle counters can range from dumb things which only count the number of times the start button has been pressed, to devices which monitor the number of times TOT exceeds certain values while the N_1 is above a certain RPM, or the number of times the collective has been raised while there is transmission oil pressure above a certain value. Pay attention to cycles if you have 'em. They will tell the story of abuse or tender loving care on the engine.

Measuring Temperature

It's not easy to accurately measure temperatures deep within the inferno of the engine, and as accurate as the cockpit indications are, they are really only approximate. The temperature indicated is really only a guess at what is happening to the metal, and it is for this reason that there are transient limits of temperature, particularly for starting. The real problem is that the

* And believe me, I've seen quite a few.

metal can't stand high temperatures for prolonged periods, and the short period allowed for a high temperature during starting (or sometimes during operation) means that this high temperature won't exist long enough to affect the turbine blades.

Density Altitude vs. Pressure Altitude and OAT

One of the major differences between piston and turbine engines is the effect of atmospheric conditions on power available. In simple terms:

- *the power available from a piston engine depends upon density altitude, whereas the power available from a turbine engine depends upon pressure altitude and temperature.*

Confused?

I can hear the questions from here - yes, - pressure altitude and air temperature do make a density altitude, but a density altitude can be made from a wide variety of pressure altitudes and temperatures.

An example is a 5,000' density altitude. It could be 9,000' pressure altitude at -40°C, or 1,800' pressure altitude at +40°C, or 5,000' pressure altitude at +5°C. However, 9,000' pressure altitude and -40°C will always be 5,000' density altitude. (at least close enough for the purposes of demonstration). Look at the density altitude chart (Figure 5-1 on page 45) to check this out.

The power available from a typical turbine engine is greatly different under these conditions, yet the density altitude is the same.

Perhaps the best way to demonstrate this is to look at the power available chart for a typical engine. Normally these are found only in military FMs; but the topping chart in most civil FMs can be used for the same purpose. Two typical engine topping charts are shown in Figure 29-2, with the power available for the three conditions just discussed. As can be seen, at the same density altitude (5,000' DA), the power available is quite different

The major reason turbine engines can develop more power with colder air is that many are 'temperature limited' at the turbine wheel. On a cold day, the air arrives at the combustion chamber cooler than on a hot day. Thus more fuel (energy and power) can be added to the air before the temperature limits are reached. More fuel in means more power out.

Atmospheric Condition			Power Available	
Press. Alt (Ft)	OAT (°C)	Density Altitude	Engine A	Engine B
1,800	+40	5,000	47%	63%
5,000	+5	5,000	59%	78%
9,000	-40	5,000	67%	95%

Simply stated:

- With only a density altitude, you cannot figure out the power available from a turbine engine

For very complex thermodynamic reasons, turbine engines are affected more by air temperature than by the density of the air, whereas a piston engine is more affected by the density of the air than the temperature. (Somewhere out there is a turbine engine designer who can explain this in one-syllable words, but one way to look at it is that only so much change in temperature can occur between the air at the inlet and the TOT limits of the turbine.)

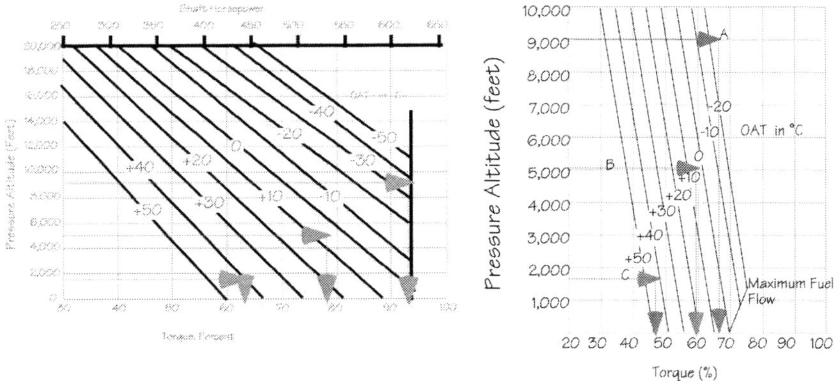

Figure 29-2 Power Available (Topping) Charts for Two Typical Turbine Engines

Most helicopter pilots operating from the same location see only the effect of the air temperature, as altimeter setting changes won't make much difference to pressure altitude (at least not as far as engine power is concerned). They know they have less power available on hotter days, or the TOT is higher on a hot day than on a cold day for the same torque used. The natural tendency is to blame the change on density altitude.

It is not correct to say power available for the turbine engine depends upon density altitude.

Less Power in Cold Temperatures

A problem not often encountered, but real nonetheless, is reduced power available in cold temperatures. It doesn't happen often because really cold temperatures mean very low (often negative) density altitudes. In these conditions, the power required to hover is also low. The reasons for this are complex, but can be summarized as a mass flow problem - the cold, more dense air simply cannot be stuffed into the engine fast enough, or perhaps the fuel flow is limiting. Look in your FM topping chart to check what the single engine power available would be in cold temperatures - say sea level, - 40°C. It might surprise you!

Effect of Humidity on Turbine Performance

Piston engines are affected by humidity, and high humidity situations can reduce the amount of power available, just at the time when the power required is increased*. Turbine engines are affected by high humidity only at very high temperatures and very high humidity levels.

Interestingly, Russian helicopter FMs show the effect of humidity at high temperatures.

Some helicopters take advantage of the effect of water in a different fashion. They actually inject water into the intake to cool the air and increase the mass flow through the engine at critical times. Pure water is needed in order to prevent scale building on the compressor blades. On the other hand, too much water can actually put the fire out if flying in heavy rain...

Effect of Altitude on Fuel Consumption

Turbine engines have another big advantage over piston engines - there is a big improvement in fuel consumption at high altitude. On a long trip, if the winds are favorable, great improvements in fuel consumed are possible. Of course if the winds are wrong, any benefit is lost, but it should be considered for trips longer than 50 NM. How it happens is quite simple, but why its not used is another of life's mysteries.

* You might be forgiven for thinking there is a plot against helicopter pilots at times like this.

We have already seen that the power required to hover increases with density altitude, and you can be assured that the same effect is seen on the power required for level flight - it increases as density altitude increases. Any engine will thus have to work harder to produce more power to maintain TAS as altitude increases. Since piston engines have reduced power available with increased density altitude, but most turbine engines have some power reserve, it's easy to see why piston engines don't try to go higher to save fuel.

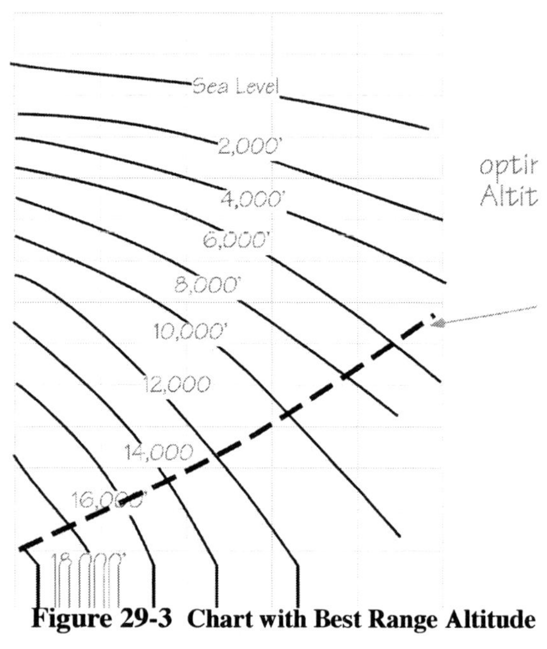

Figure 29-3 Chart with Best Range Altitude

The relative fuel efficiency of turbine engines is measured in a term called *specific fuel consumption* (SFC), which is the weight of fuel required to produce one shaft horsepower for one hour. At low power settings, over 60% of the effort produced by the engine goes to drive the compressor, and what is left over is useful power. When operating at high power (close to the design limits of the engine) the useful power compared to the power to drive the compressor is greatest, so proportionally less is used by the compressor. The SFC improves at these high power settings. So it makes sense to run the engine closer to the limits than at idle power. At high altitudes, this is the case, so the fuel efficiency improves considerably.

Combine the two factors- an increase in the power required by the airframe and the improved SFC of the engine to produce power and the effect is beneficial for fuel consumption.

In one helicopter's FM (reproduced as Figure 29-3) the optimum altitude for maximum range starts at 6,000' at maximum weight, and finishes at 14,000' when the helicopter is nearly empty*. I have seen up to 20% improvement in fuel consumption at 10,000' over the rate at sea level for the same TAS. Of course, if you're not interested in saving fuel...

There are even some who fly multi-engine helicopters who are willing to pull out all the stops for improved range, by shutting down one engine and using the remaining engine at the continuous OEI rating (where the SFC really improves...) Not recommended though for the faint of heart, and the other engine has to be shut down, not left at idle. (These brave crews cruise at 14,000' to make sure they have enough time to restart the other engine if the one they are using fails...)

Compressor Stalls

The turbine engine operates by stuffing large quantities of air down its throat and compressing this air to high pressures. The balances between the various stages of the compressor can be quite delicate, and if a sudden change in the pressure at the back of the compressor occurs, it can have quite upsetting effects on the air trying to be crammed in at the front. This can cause a *compressor stall*. Fortunately, compressor stalls are quite rare on most helicopter engines, but they can occur.

Typical events which accompany a compressor stall are inlet distortion, exhaust ingestion, snow, foreign objects and so on. Axial compressors appear to be more prone than centrifugal compressors.

Two Correct Answers Don't Make a Third...

A little knowledge can be a dangerous thing. Quite a bit of time was spent in my flying training learning about turbine engines. One of the things I remember about compressor stalls was, if one occurred and didn't go away, then you might help the situation if you could dump some of the pressure in the compressor prior to the stalled section. This could be carried out by bleed valves (often installed and automatically operated in the basic engine design) or by the use of bleed air services, such as heaters and de-ice/anti-ice valves, which also took away bleed pressure about half-way down the compressor. Much later in my career, I came across a helicopter (OH-58A) with a procedure in the FM for compressor stalls which stated,

* It also means that you can autorotate farther from that altitude.

- "In the event of compressor stalls, turn off the Heater and Engine De-Ice."

Certain this procedure was wrong, I asked where it came from. I started with Allison Gas Turbines, the engine manufacturer, who had never heard of the procedure. "Not something we've ever said," came their reply "First of all, you can't compressor stall that engine - we've tried, and secondly, even if it did, that procedure would be incorrect. It's not in our manual and we have no idea where it came from."

Next stop was Bell Helicopter, the airframe manufacturer - since the airframe was quite old, and out of production, I didn't get much help there. Eventually, I got hold of someone deep in the bowels of the US Army, who also weren't a lot of help, except for a jewel of a response. "If you have a compressor stall, one of the symptoms is the TOT is high." (Perfectly true.) "In normal operations if you turn on the heater or de-ice, it increases the TOT." (Again perfectly true.). "Therefore, if you have a compressor stall, you should turn off the heater / de-ice to reduce the TOT." Wrong - the problem is an airflow–through–the–compressor problem, not a TOT problem.

When I suggested to this gentleman that a book on basic turbine engines might be consulted before such conclusions were reached, I was not very popular. I succeeded in getting the procedure changed in the Canadian Air Force for that model of helicopter, but as far as I know, it's still in the procedures for other militaries who operate the machine, or even other models of that engine.

Interestingly, I rediscovered this problem several years later on other helicopters, and also discovered the procedures in FMs for engines which the engine manufacture had said could not be compressor stalled due to the single stage centrifugal compressor.

Turbine Engine Instruments

The main instruments for turbine engine helicopters are the N_1 (or compressor) speed, the temperature of the exhaust gases at some stage in the process, and the torquemeter. These are shown below in

Figure 29-4 Turbine Engine Instruments (L-R N_1, Torque, TOT)

Most instruments that show the state of the engine and related components do not require a lot of discussion, as most problems have a source elsewhere than the instruments. This is not so with the N_R and Power turbine (or N_2) needles fitted to most helicopters.

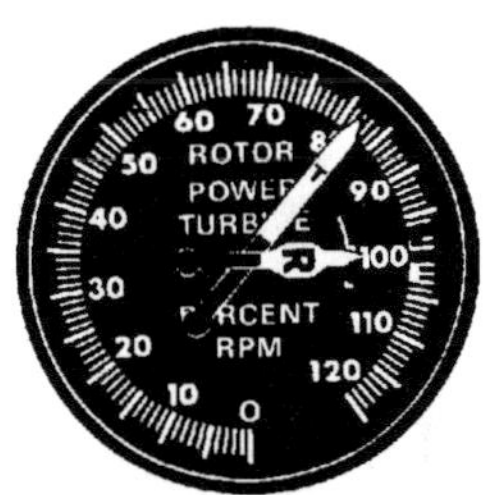

Figure 29-5 N_2 and N_R Needles

Back in the early days of helicopter flying, when piston engines were the norm, it was very important to know and understand about engine speed. It was more important than N_R, so the needle showing engine RPM was made the larger and more important of the two needles. This is shown in Figure 29-5.

Time has passed and progress has marched on. Turbine engines are much more reliable, and governors have been installed to keep the N_2 at a constant RPM. The N_R is now much more important, yet, it is still the smaller of the two needles. When are we going to get N_R needles larger than N_2 needles*? Or maybe there's a reason I don't understand...

* The latest models appear to have this fixed. The Bell 407 has a larger N_R needle than N_2. About time too. Ditto 427.

I can report in this edition that someone must have been listening. The Bell 407 and 427 have the N_R needle longer than the N_2 needle!

...And Sensor Failures

Any man-made part can fail. Sensors are man-made, and so will fail. Most of the time the failures are easy to determine and straightforward to deal with. Sometimes they are not so straightforward...

Nearly every turbine engine fuel control uses power turbine speed (N_2) as a signal. A particularly nasty situation is failure of the speed signal of this turbine. If this sensor fails, the fuel control thinks the power turbine speed is too low and adds fuel. Since there is no response from the power turbine signal, the governor continues to add fuel until either the fuel flow limit is reached, or the compressor can't produce any more air, or some other protection feature stops the process.

Even though the engine may have other protection features on it, why a second set of N_2 sensors is not fitted as standard has always been a puzzle*.

False Indications

More than one make of helicopter or engine type has a nasty single sensor failure case that has caused several incidents. Pilots did not understand the systems installed.

Image you are cruising along in your single turbine helicopter, fat, dumb and happy, lots of altitude, lovely day, and so on. Suddenly, your dreams are rudely interrupted - the engine failure audio starts yelling, the engine failure light starts flashing and life becomes more complex. What do you do? What has happened†?

The first prudent thing to do is lower the collective, and start looking for a place to land. Next, look inside to confirm the engine failure. The N_1 gauge is reading zero. Has the engine really failed?

Those of you answering 'yes' may be slightly premature, and also quite probably wrong. If the engine has failed (and not had a violent seizure) it takes at least 30 seconds for most free turbine engines to wind down to zero RPM. Were there any other symptoms of an engine failure such as a yaw or a sinking feeling? What is the N_R doing? What about the engine oil pressure?

In this case, the N_R and N_2 are closely matched, N_2 is greater than 90% and engine oil pressure is in the green... Confused?

The symptoms come from the failure of the N_1 tachometer–generator. The engine works perfectly well without the tach–gen, and has not failed. More than one person I know has carried out a forced landing because they thought the engine had failed, but didn't cross check to make sure it was a real failure‡. This system is not confined to one type of airframe or engine, so get out your books and study the systems.

Another Story About Sensors...

The Gazelle has a fixed shaft engine (the Turbomeca Astazou IIIN), with engine oil pressure being the 'medium' used for the fuel control unit. The engine is marvelous in many ways, but early versions had a major problem. To save weight and cockpit space, it was decided to fit only an engine oil pressure light (no gauge). If this light came on, it was time to expect an engine failure - or was it just a sensor failure? The recommended procedure was to set up for an autorotation and then shut down the engine prior to it actually failing. Since autorotative landings were slightly tricky in this machine, it wasn't long before someone cottoned on to the problem that a machine was probably going to be bent merely by a failed pressure sensing switch, and a second oil pressure switch was installed. Now you have to worry only if both lights come on.

Torquemeters

The torquemeter is a primary power instrument in the turbine engine helicopter. It is important to know where these torquemeters are located and what they really measure. Is it engine power output or is it mast power? Companies have varying philosophies and reasons for using different methods. Respect the limitations in the FM. The two main methods of operation are shown in the diagrams below.

---

* The Russians appear to have put two power turbine sensors on all their engines.

† In that order, please- don't try to diagnose before you take the first essential action.

‡ Why this hasn't been the subject of a change to the aircraft warning system or at least a note in the flight manual is beyond me. It's so obvious – someone should do something about it.

Oil Pressure Torquemeter

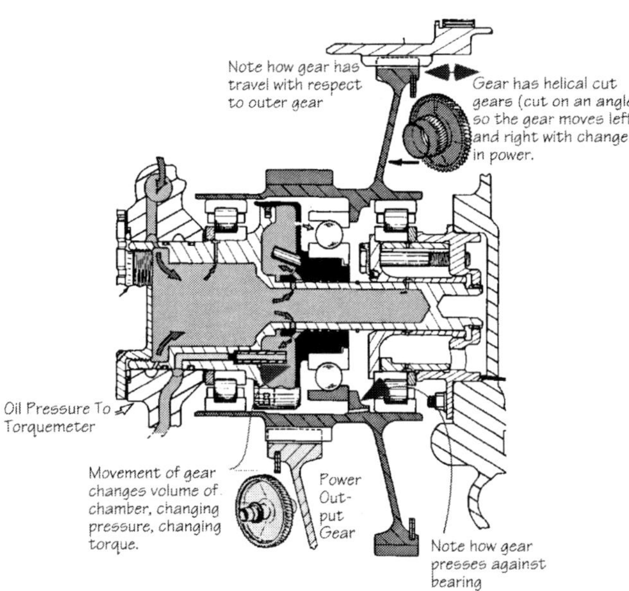

Figure 29-6 Oil Pressure Torquemeter

The oil pressure torquemeter is found in many light helicopters. It uses a series of gears in the engine accessory gearbox to move back and forth depending upon the power demanded from the engine. This gear moving back and forth changes the oil pressure in the chamber with the sensor. Engine oil is used as the medium. Examples is shown in Figure 29-6.

Dampers or accumulators in the system are added to take out the immediate effects of pressure fluctuations. One helicopter I flew had a modified engine installation with a torquemeter without any accumulators or dampers in the system. It was impossible to read the cockpit gauge. It fluctuated rapidly ±10% and the pilot had to guess as to the power he was using. In other helicopters, the same engine has an accumulator and a rock solid torquemeter reading. Obviously, the damper or accumulator means the readings do not respond as quickly as the power is really being applied, but it does take out fluctuations. The oil pressure torquemeter will also not read reliably until the engine oil temperature has reached a minimum value, so don't be in too big a rush to get airborne, if the oil temperature isn't within the normal operating range.

More Modern Torquemeters

Other types of torquemeters are also used. The two other most popular are the strain gage torquemeter and the optical sensor torquemeter. The strain gage is used to measure the amount of power being applied to a shaft. Since most helicopters have drive shafts between the engine and transmission, this is a convenient place to measure torque. At least one helicopter type measures torque applied to the main rotor mast in the same way. The other method is a variation and uses an optical sensor to measure the deflection of the shaft. See Figure 29-7 for examples.

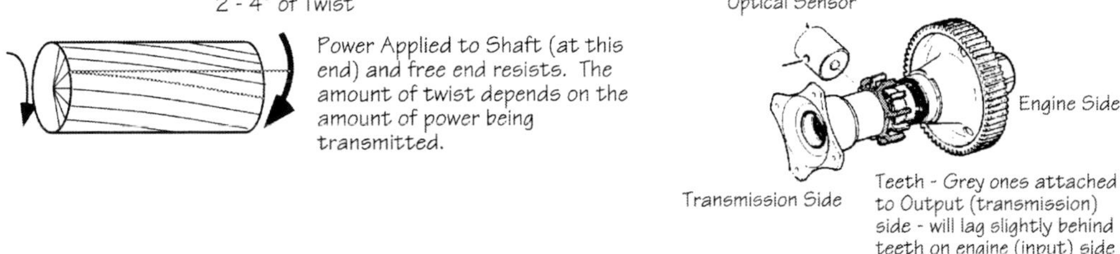

Figure 29-7 Strain Gauge Torquemeter

One helicopter manufacturer with these sort of indicators recognized the location of the sensors was causing a problem. In this case, one of the sensors was in the transmission - an engine torque limitation was used to protect the main rotor mast. The tail rotor required a lot of power, and repeated overtorques were reported when hovering. By changing the limitations to permit overtorques due to the tail rotor, the problem was solved, but it meant yet another item for pilots to observe and remember inside the cockpit, when they should have been looking outside.

Use of the Torquemeter

Of what use is the torquemeter in a modern helicopter? Certainly it displays the amount of power the engine is producing with a reasonable degree of accuracy but:

- is it really necessary, and
- can it be used for any other purpose?

The answer to the first question is that strictly speaking, the torquemeter is not needed - there are several helicopters flying which do not have torquemeters, or which have alternate procedures in the event the torquemeter fails. The torquemeter, in most cases, is used only to protect the engine or transmission from being abused.

A much better use of the torquemeter is as a weighing device. Unfortunately, using the torquemeter to 'weigh' the helicopter also requires that performance charts of a suitable type be available. The types in most civil helicopter manuals are not suitable for this particular exercise, but perhaps with a little effort we can change the order of things...

If the FM has a chart of Power Required to Hover, several things can happen. It should be possible to determine the power required to hover for a given weight, height above ground and wind condition, and check to see if the helicopter is using that much power at those conditions. If more power is being used to hover than required by the chart, then the weight is not correct. Used another way*, this is a good method of checking to see if you are over-weight. See "A Neat Trick From the FM" on page 241.

The Bell 212 I flew operationally was often used in very cold conditions, and often with underslung loads. We had no cargo hook weighing system, and as rough rule of thumb we would say if we could hover at 100% out of ground effect, then we were OK. I carried on in this mode in blissful ignorance for quite a while. It was only after I knew a bit more that I looked in the manual again, and did some rough calculations, and discovered we were often more than 10% over the maximum weight of the helicopter. Not surprisingly, the helicopters often suffered from structural problems where the cargo hooks were attached. If this little anecdote doesn't convince people to fit cargo hook weighing devices, then the one in "Knowing How Much it Weighs" on page 387, should...

GOVERNING SYSTEMS

The real differences between piston engines and turbine engines shows up in governors. Why are governors installed and what are they supposed to do? A typical helicopter turbine engine governing system is shown in below.

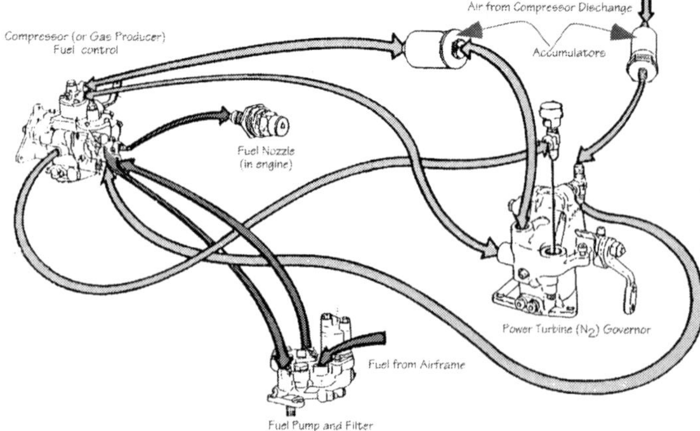

Figure 29-8 Typical Helicopter Engine Governor Installation

* No pun intended, believe me.

Any piston-engine helicopter pilot who has tried to control N_R at the same time as collective pitch knows how difficult it is*. (It is interesting to note Robinson Helicopters has installed governors on later models of the piston engined R-22 and the R-44) The governor in a turbine engine helicopter is supposed to keep the N_2 reasonably constant, and for most stages of flight, does a very good job. A few of its foibles need understanding.

Reasons for Installing Governors

There are many reasons for installing governors on turbine engines. Piston engines have a relatively fast response to throttle movements while turbine engines take a while to spool up and down. In the piston engine, power changes can be treated in a more cavalier manner than an ungoverned turbine engine. Early turbine engines also had a problem of compressor stalls (surging) or flameouts when rapid changes in the fuel flow were made. Governors have the benefit of working more quickly and smoothly than the pilot, and hardly ever make mistakes. A governor system was also the only way to handle multi-engine installations.

Another reason given for fitting governors is that the items displayed to the pilot are actually only a small part of the things that need to be controlled and monitored in a turbine engine. Imagine putting even more gauges in the cockpit and expecting the pilot to be able to monitor and control them!

The following discussion only deals with the single–engined helicopter with a free power–turbine engine - enlightenment for those with fixed–shaft engines or multi-engine installations will have to wait.

The governor in a turbine engine maintains the free (or power) turbine N_2 at a constant speed by varying the fuel flow and compressor speed. It may be possible to fine–tune this datum N_2 using a beeper trim. So far, quite simple. If the actual N_2 is different from this datum, the governor adjusts the fuel flow to change the compressor speed so the datum free turbine speed is regained.

In a turbine engine helicopter with a governor, the pilot does not directly control power *NOTE!*

The governor is controlling N_2 and the pilot is controlling blade pitch. The engine power is adjusted by the governor. Before further talk about governors a few more terms need to be defined.

Droop!

Two terms associated with helicopter engine governors – namely, *static droop* and *transient droop*, have caused a great deal of confusion over the years. More closely defining these words may make their meaning clear so they won't be misused. To begin, let's look at the engine before installation in the helicopter.

Droop Compensator

With a hydro-mechanical fuel control system, something needs to be added to make the engine governor maintain a constant rotor speed with different power conditions. That something is a *droop compensator*.

* Especially at a time when he is trying to do lots of other things, like hover.

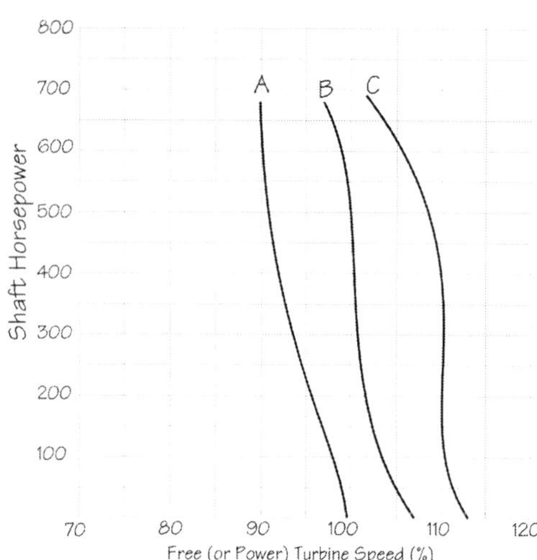

Figure 29-9 Power Turbine Speed on Test Stand

Figure 29-9 shows the power turbine output speed vs. power demanded in a steady situation. Note this is what the engine would produce when run on a test stand, not on the helicopter.

In this example, using the line B, the engine will start by running at 106% N_2 at no power output. Increase the power output to 600 shp and the engine is now running at 99%. We like things to be slightly tidier than this, so we install a droop compensator when the engines are fitted to the helicopter. This changes the characteristics of the governor so the engine produces 100% N_2/ N_R at all times. But each engine is slightly different, and the droop lines will still have different slopes.

The problem is that the droop compensator, being a mechanical device needs to be adjusted depending on the engine. Minor changes in air temperature, pressure altitude, etc., can cause the engine to adopt a different droop line - for this reason an N_2 beeper trim switch is installed. It permits the pilot to fine tune the datum N_2.

An engine with the characteristics shown in line A, could cause problems for the pilot if it were installed in the helicopter. Something needs to come between the engine and the pilot. On some helicopters it is visible as a cam in the collective linkage, shown in Figure 29-10. This device is a way to readjust the datum N_2 the governor maintains. Without this compensator, the N_2 would follow line A as the power levels are changed. Note this is only for steady, unchanging power conditions - the way of dealing with rapid power changes follows shortly. Stay tuned!

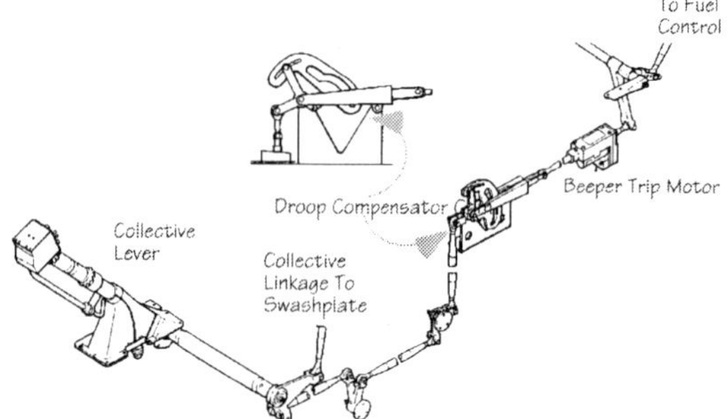

Figure 29-10 Droop Compensator Cam in Linkage

Static Droop

Static droop is the curve of N_2 vs. power in a steady condition. In other words, if the power were changed to x% torque, the N_2 would settle at and maintain y% N_2 until the engine ran out of fuel. This assumes the power demand does not change and the governor is good enough to maintain N_2 accurately. If it doesn't hold the RPM accurately at a constant power setting, the governor may be said to wander*.

* like the minds of small children...

Not all governors are designed to keep the N_2 constant at all power settings. Some are designed to change the N_2 over the power range. Figure 29-11 shows several different governor slopes - i.e. the change of the N_2 vs. static power. All of these governors exist on operational helicopters. An *Isochronous* governor has no long term change in N_2 with different power settings, and since this is the most common type of governor, it is used in the following discussion.

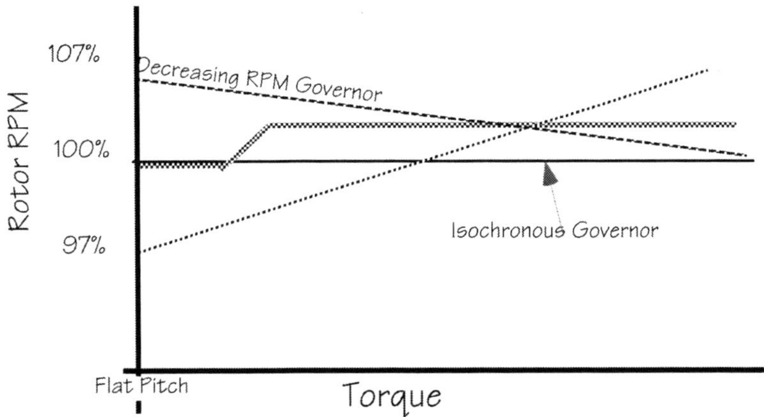

Figure 29-11 Typical Static Droop Curves of Some Existing Helicopters

Oscillating Governors* and Hysteresis

If the governor doesn't maintain the N_2 constant, it may be slowly oscillating, wandering or hunting.

It may also have hysteresis if, following a power change, it does not return to the same N_2 at the same power setting. An example of hysteresis would be if the N_2 were set at 100% at 50% power, and the power changed to 100% and then a short while later reduced to 50% again. After the transients have stopped, if the N_2 is 98%, then the governor has hysteresis. All of these shortcomings make the pilot's job more difficult. Even minor oscillations in the governor can make the pilot's task more difficult, and at least one light helicopter has such a sloppy governor that after a short while, pilots accept it doesn't hold N_2 within 2%.

Transient Droop

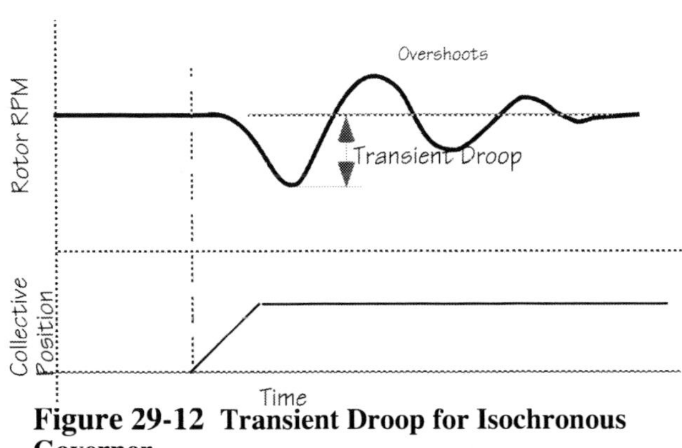

Figure 29-12 Transient Droop for Isochronous Governor

Transient droop is the change in rotor speed that happens briefly following a power change. It is completely different from static droop. This is the change in the N_2 immediately following a change in power. For an engine and rotor system, the amount of the transient droop depends upon the size and rate of the power change demanded. During development testing of the airframe the response of the governor will be adjusted so during a rapid power demand, (say from needles just joined in autorotation to 95% of continuous power in 3 - 4 seconds) the rotor will not have too much transient droop. It certainly should not cause the rotor or engine to slow to a point where electrical systems drop off line (if the aircraft uses AC power and needs to have a constant frequency†). As a special flight test, it tells a lot

* Of helicopter engines, not the head of a state who can't make up his mind.

† See the section "AC–Based Electrical Systems" on page 264.

about the governing system, but not the whole story. (Keep in mind this is a simplified explanation of a complex subject, and engine designers are requested to close their eyes for the duration of this section.) Aside from fast response, there should not be any overshoots or oscillations following the power change. A similar test would be carried out for rapid power reductions. Figure 29-12 shows a typical response for an *Isochronous* (constant speed) governor to a rapid power demand.

One of the more difficult tests for governors is the rejected landing. This simulates touching down lightly on the wheels or skids, lowering the collective fully as if to land, and, as the engine is spooling down, raising the collective briskly to lift-off again (simulates landing and discovering it *was* swamp you were landing on, etc.) This rejected landing is difficult for the governor to handle, because while the engine is decelerating, the governor is asking it to re-accelerate immediately. The variety of responses I have seen ranges from instant response with not the slightest hesitation, (which was quite comforting) to several seconds of hanging below the rotor accompanied by low N_R horns and panels full of lights, while the engine slowly sputtered back to normal speed (which was not so pleasant). Don't try this at home, folks!

Hydro–mechanical Governors

Since hydro-mechanical fuel control systems are most common in civil and military single engine helicopters at the time of writing, it is most useful to cover them first. Multi-engine systems are dealt with later.

The majority of fuel controls are hydro-mechanical - typically, they sense free turbine speed and attempt to maintain it at a constant value. They use air from the compressor as the way to sense changes from the compressor, and measure turbine speed mechanically. There may be 'stops', and possibly an overspeed system to prevent the turbines from running away and disintegrating. Mechanical linkages and bleed air lines are used for sensing and changing conditions in the engine. The typical hydro-mechanical fuel control is a complex arrangements of pipes and fittings and has many potential failure points. On one engine, a common failure is one of the fittings backing off, resulting in the engine running down to idle, mostly at very inopportune moments naturally. With minor differences, that is normally all you get with a hydro-mechanical (steam driven) fuel control. Normally it is necessary for maintenance personnel to make adjustments to idle speeds, range of N_2 beeper travel, and so on.

Because the fuel control does not respond unless there is an error in power turbine speed, the response to power changes is normally slow. Rapid power increases are not well handled as the engine must accelerate, yet avoid compressor stalling. Decelerating is even harder to do quickly without flaming out the engine. The slow response of most of these engines can be traced to the governing media (mostly compressed air). Accumulators are placed in the lines to reduce the effect of rapid changes in pressure, and these further slow the response.

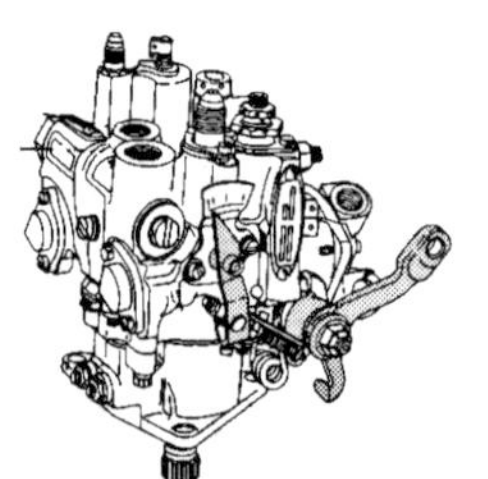

Figure 29-13 Typical Hydro-mechanical Fuel Control Unit

A typical hydro-mechanical governor is shown in Figure 29-13.

Why weren't these engines responding fast enough?

Consider the pilot applying a large collective–up application at the end of a quick stop, when the power is low and the rotor is nearly in autorotation. The compressor part of the engine is winding down in speed because it sees the power turbine is running too fast. With a hydro-mechanical fuel control, it is not possible to anticipate either the collective application, or the rotor speed being too high and falling.

Remember the fuel control won't think it should start increasing compressor speed until it sees the N_2 below the datum - by which time it is fighting not just to get back to the datum N_2, but also fighting an increasing power demand due to drag on the rotor blades. The engine really needs rate of collective change, not just collective position, to respond faster.

The response of a turbine engine to a rapid power demand is a compromise. Get the rates wrong and response can be too slow. Get it wrong the other way (too fast) and perhaps the engine may compressor–stall. Given the effects of a compressor stall are worse than slow-ish acceleration, the designers always err on the side of safety - the acceleration may be slow, but the engine won't cough at a bad time. Detailed reasons for slow acceleration are very complex and difficult to explain. The end result may be a slow response from the engine. Similarly, when the power is reduced rapidly, the engine can only decelerate so quickly because if the fuel were cut off too quickly, the engine would flame out.

Consider the Inputs!

For those who have spent some time trying to explore the plumbing of a hydro-mechanical fuel control unit, the number of pipes in and out, adjustments and so on is bad enough, but ask yourself - even if the designers wanted to - where would they put any more sensing inputs and outputs? The hydro-mechanical fuel control might end up being bigger than the engine it was controlling! How would you be able to put in N_R as well as N_2?

Electronic Fuel Controls

Electronic fuel controls are the next generation of fuel controls. They will supplant hydro-mechanical controls within a few years for reasons that should become clear in this section.

Before You Read Any Farther -

Helicopter pilots spend an enormous amount of their time monitoring engine and transmission parameters, matching torques, setting up engines, performing power checks and so on. Helicopter mechanics spend an disproportionate amount of their time setting up helicopter fuel controls (especially multi-engine installations with engines not matched in hours or characteristics), troubleshooting gripes about the engine response and so on. Think how this has affected your working lives!

There is another aspect - that of cost. "I think the overtorque was 5% for 7 seconds" says the pilot and upon checking, finds out that this means transmission overhaul. If it was 4% for 6 seconds it only means a visual inspection. Which would you rather have?

What if the pilot who flew the machine before you bought the machine had regularly overtorqued and used up 99% of the margin the manufacturer had built in?

Early Electronic Fuel Controls

Electronic controls for engines have been around since the early 1970s, but generally only in piecemeal fashion. Early models were analog in construction, and needed as much attention as the hydro-mechanical components they replaced. Failures were frequent and mystifying. Like many aspects of aviation, many things were learned and applied to the current generation of digital computers. Digital computers have increased in capability for memory, speed and hence computation, as well as reliability, resistance to electro-magnetic interference, and cost.

FADEC

FADEC means *Full Authority Digital Electronic Control*, "Full authority" because some early computer fuel controls worked only on a small part of the flow fuel to the engine - (conservative bunch, engine designers). To be completely correct, a FADEC will have the ability (full authority) to shut down the engine (and the necessary hardware and software to make sure it doesn't do it at the wrong time). The trend in modern helicopters towards lower main rotor inertia, and in turbine engines to increased engine inertia (heavier compressors, etc.) make it more difficult to maintain a constant N_2 in rapid power changes.

What Has All This Got to Do With FADECs?

Basically, some clever engineers asked "what could we use for controlling the engine, besides a hydro-mechanical governor?"

Instead of using bleed air as the governing medium, and a mechanical power turbine speed sensor, more accurate sensors could be used. For example, an optical sensor of rotor speed is much more accurate than the mechanical type, and sensitive TOT gauges, accurate to within 5°C can be used. More sensors could be used for redundancy as well for more complex decisions. There is now even more reason to use a digital computer to analyze these inputs and make intelligent decisions about the outputs.

In comparison to an electronic analog system, more accurate input data can be used, and the engine can have an acceleration and deceleration schedule of fuel flow vs. N_1 that is closer to the compressors capabilities.

Figure 29-14 shows the great variety of signals that can be processed by the FADEC computer, and how they all end up being used to control the fuel metering valve. There are a great many more signals than any hydro–mechanical system could handle, and more things can be calculated and compared with them. For example, if the N_R is high, and the engine has run the compressor speed down because the power is low, the system will be able to respond rapidly if the pilot raises the collective. Since there is logic involved, it can work as follows: the two signals (N_R and N_2) are compared, and if the N_R is higher than the N_2 and steady and the collective not moving, it keeps the N_2 speed at the datum. If the FADEC sees the N_R faster than normal and decaying, and the collective moving up, it concludes the pilot is going to apply power. To assist the engines response and reduce the amount of N_2 (and also N_R) decay, the computer runs up the N_2 to meet the N_R. The end result is a smooth application of power and reduced transient droop.

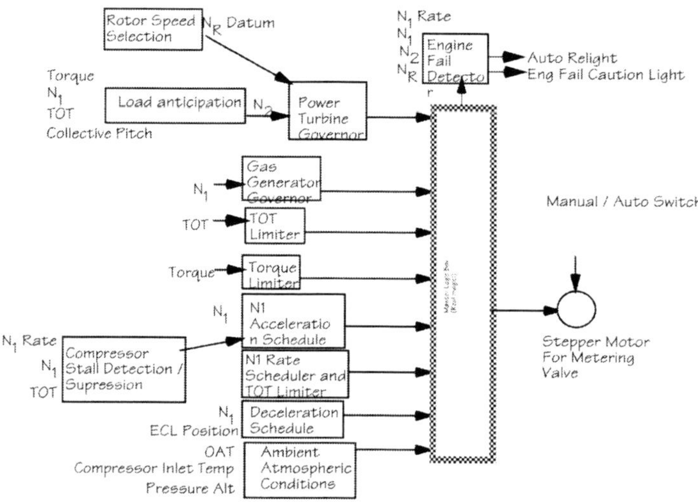

Figure 29-14 Rotor speed Logic

The list of benefits is just starting - no more engine setups - if the FADEC needs replacing, just plug it in and go. No idle adjustments, torque matching adjustments, acceleration time adjustments and so on. Several FADEC systems incorporate a built–in test (BIT) when electrical power is applied to the airframe, and test sensors and internal logic continually as they operate.

Most of the systems record data about overtemperatures and other sins against the limits and let the maintenance people take note of them. Some FADEC systems even are capable of continuous engine trend monitoring, so compressor washes can be scheduled more precisely, and even rapid degradation (power loss over an hour or so) can be detected.

Failures of Digital Fuel Controls

Ah, you ask, but what if the computer fails? First of all, since there are fewer connections and fittings, failures are less likely. Secondly, because of the internal logic checks, it will probably warn the pilot before it fails completely. During one set of tests, the design engineers warned of a remote possibility the computer could fail without warning the pilot first. Upon detailed questioning, it was revealed the maximum time before the pilot was warned of a failure was about 1/2 second, and then the worst the engine would do was run up to a moderate power setting (thanks to the default throttle position being about two-thirds of maximum power) in around three seconds. Thirdly, the types of failures are actually very small - the metering valve can freeze the fuel flow, run it up or run it down. This computer in this engine was designed to monitor the valve position, and make sure it didn't run up or down - if the computer saw a problem, its first reaction was to freeze the fuel flow. (not shut down the fuel flow, merely not change it). Unless you're superhuman, a one-half second is far too fast to be caught. All the engines with FADEC I am aware of have a manual reversion, and controlling the engine in this case is the same as a piston engine helicopter.

Since the first edition, more experience has been gained with FADEC engines, and in every situation I am aware of, the computer did exactly as it was supposed to- sometimes however, the pilots didn't know what the computer was supposed to do!

Practical Benefits of FADEC

So what are the practical benefits? As the pilot, you can literally ignore the engine parameters as the FADEC takes care of them. In one foreign helicopter with such a system, the Polish W-3, the advice to the pilot is "You know you are at takeoff power when the N_R and N_2 start to droop." But that's only because of the way this engine was designed.

During critical situations, such as practicing for single engine failures in a non–FADEC helicopter, the last thing the pilot wants to do is look inside to monitor a new set of limits he doesn't normally use, that are changing rapidly, and are probably slightly behind what is actually going on. Hardly good design practice!

Change of the Pilots Point of View

NOTE *Don't leap into a helicopter with FADEC and expect things to be the same.*

Engines may be started with the throttles at Idle or perhaps even at the Flight position. The Flight position may not be the maximum travel available, and advancing the throttle beyond this position may have no effect in the normal, automatic mode. Also, just because you're familiar with an engine type on one airframe, don't assume it will be the same on another. One engine installed on many multi-engine light helicopters has had at least two different configurations of throttles used by different manufacturers. Both installations had the throttle left in the mid-travel position between IDLE and MAX, however one airframer required a switch to be used to select the manual mode of the fuel control, and the other airframer merely required that the twist grips be moved away from the mid-position. The possibility for error is quite large.

Duplication of Sensors

It is interesting to note that FADECs often require some sensors to be duplicated, in order to preserve the integrity of the system. This also follows the advice given earlier about "measure twice, cut once...".

Some Improvements Possible?

Perhaps I am overly sensitive to protection features, having nearly been a smoking hole in the ground thanks to a transmission overtorque protection feature. I was not amused to suddenly be confronted with this when I least needed to be power–limited, so perhaps I have an axe to grind here (see "Torque Limiters" on page 436 for more sordid details). On the other hand, many of my friends have similar stories...

Of course, FADECs won't be perfect, and we need to think of ways they can be improved. One of my concerns is that we may end up protecting the engine and let the helicopter crash. Having nearly been a victim of this myself, perhaps I am overly sensitive.

Engines and transmissions are cheaper than airframes, lawsuits and people's lives, and it should be possible for the pilot to override the computer if he has to. Since all overtemps and overtorques will be recorded anyway, it would be better to have the pilot around to explain what happened than to try to decipher it from only a computer. I would like to see the logic work something like this:

- if the computer is limiting the engine output, the only thing that can happen if the pilot continues to pull up on the collective is that the N_2 and N_R will droop.
- If the collective is more than halfway up and moving up, and has been there for more than 2 seconds with the N_R decaying below the minimum power on limit, then the computer should drop all limitations and try to maintain the N_R.

No separate action (like pressing a button) should be necessary to override the computer, as in a moment of extreme stress, the pilot may forget he has to press this button. Let's face it, he won't need it very often, and may even forget it exists at the wrong moment.

For single engine helicopters, perhaps a training mode (similar to that on twin engine installations) might be available to show the effects of operating near limits, to simulate high altitude operations.

Manual Control of the Turbine Engine

Most turbine engines have some fall–back control in the event of failure of the normal fuel control. Typically this is manual or direct pilot control of fuel, and its use is approached with great caution in most machines. One military helicopter I know requires two pilots for this situation - the other pilot is there only to move the roof mounted throttles when manual control is needed. Why a switch on the collective and small motors to move the throttles was not installed doesn't appear to have entered into this military's way of thinking*.

Manual control is not a big problem - fuel flow roughly equates to power - the N_R depends on the collective position. If this is in a multi–engined helicopter, the second engine attempts to maintain N_2 to the best of its ability. The main item to control in this situation is the adrenaline level of the crew. Manual throttle is no big deal. Make all moves slowly, and think about them beforehand. For example, when coming in to land, if the power is too high for the condition, raise the collective to bring the N_R and N_2 to the desired speed. Then, with fixed collective, reduce the fuel flow (throttle) until the N_R and N_2 is at the bottom of the green arc, then reduce collective to bring N_R and N_2 to the maximum power–on N_R and N_2, and repeat the process. Most helicopters fly quite well with the N_R and N_2 below the green arc - the world won't end.

Question Time

You are in the hover in ground effect on a no wind day in our generic helicopter (remember, it has a turbine engine...). You are not operating close to the maximum engine power available, and you add a reasonable amount of left pedal. Assuming you don't move the collective, will the helicopter climb or descend? Why†?

(For those in French or Russian helicopters, add right pedal)

Tail Rotors, Governors and Free Drinks

Those of you who answered 'descend' can pay up the next time we meet. The answer is the helicopter will climb (if you haven't already tried it, it will!) The real question is why?

The answer involves the governor system. As the left pedal is applied, more power is demanded out of the entire drivetrain, so the N_R and N_2 droops slightly (transient droop). The governor tries to keep the N_2 (and also N_R) constant, so it adds some more fuel to the engine to bring the rotor back to normal speed of rotation.

The next part is slightly tricky, but I promise there are no cards up my sleeve. The frame of reference for the governor is the N_2 (and also N_R) with respect to the airframe. Think of this as how–many–times–per–minute–blades–pass–the–airframe–centerline. As the helicopter is now turning to the left, in the same direction as the main rotor direction of rotation, the governor thinks the rotor is still not back to its normal speed. Even a modest rate of turn of 30°/second is 5 RPM, which, for most light helicopters, is about 1% of the main rotor speed. Most hydro-mechanical governors can sense this error quite easily, and continue to add fuel to regain the datum N_2. Looking at the helicopter from outside, you would see the rotor speed up with respect to the earth. Recalling the lift formulae from as well, since lift is proportional to the N_R squared, the helicopter will climb.

The opposite is true if you add right pedal - the helicopter descends. Be cautious if you are going to look at this direction of turn. If there is any wind, it can bite!

Descending while turning right in the hover has a compounding effect if you are unlucky enough to encounter loss of tail rotor effectiveness ("Loss of Tail Rotor Effectiveness" on page 383). The very high rates of fuselage rotation encountered in this situation make the governor think the N_2 (and also N_R) is much higher than it actually is, and the governor reduces fuel in an attempt to regain the proper rotor speed. The rotor speed viewed from outside the helicopter is quite low, and since the tail rotor is connected to the main rotor, it is operating well below the normal RPM. Remember the thrust produced by the tail rotor is a function of N_R (squared as well - so a 5% reduction in N_R is a 10% reduction ($100^{\wedge 2}$ - $95^{\wedge 2}$) in thrust at the same AoA for the tail rotor).

* For those UK military Sea King pilots who read this - yes, it is 1960's technology in the fuel computers, but this is the 1990's and it should be possible to put switches on the collective to do this. The US Marines did for the VH–3! Then the co–pilot would be there for navigation and conversation.

† If you're wrong, I will gladly accept your offer of a beer or other beverage of your choice when we next meet.

Differences from Piston Engine

If either of these maneuvers are tried in a non-governed piston engine helicopter, and neither the throttle or collective are moved, the helicopter's response is the opposite for the simple reason the pilot is controlling power. Without a change in power, adding left pedal will cause the helicopter to descend, and adding right pedal will cause it to climb.

Transient Overtorques

The basics of the torquemeter were covered earlier in this chapter - this part covers the more immediate problems associated with the way they read.

Whenever a large change in power is made, either an increase or a decrease, there is a transient load applied to the components, or so it appears. This is particularly true when power is increased rapidly. The oil pressure torquemeter is most prone to this, as a hammer of oil pressure builds up which is read by the sensor as a torque spike or overtorque, when it may not be large.

Engine transmission monitoring is really inexpensive in the 1990s. Safety–critical parameters or expensive in terms of cost to repair should be automatically monitored to allow the Time Between Overhaul (TBO) to be extended to the maximum practical.

Mast Windup

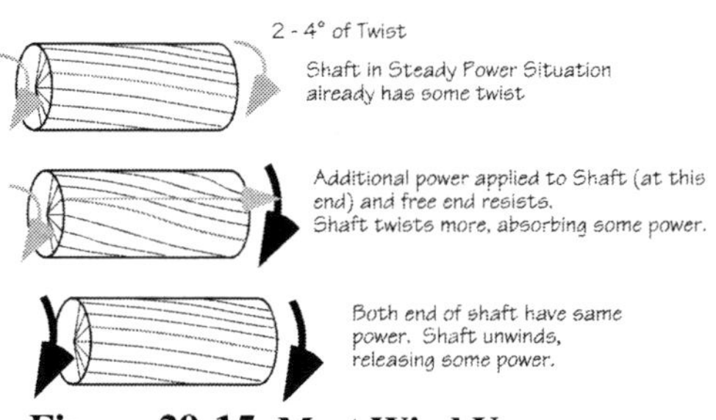

Figure 29-15 Mast Wind Up

A little–understood phenomenon occurs with nearly every torque–sensing system. If a specific collective and pedal position are set and a 'stop' in the controls installed so this collective position cannot be exceeded, and a rapid power demand is made, the static power level is exceeded for a brief time. One company investigated this in great detail and found the reason for the overshoot was that the various shafts in the drive system (between the engine and the transmission, and the transmission and the rotor head for example) were actually twisting slightly. It seems the shafts would absorb a small amount of energy while they twisted under the increased loads, and when things settled down to a steady condition, would 'unwind' to the proper power level. Figure 29-15 shows this in simple form. The *windup* or storing of energy in the shaft momentarily appears as a larger than normal power demand.

Interestingly, if the power is suddenly taken away, (as in an engine failure), the mast can also wind the other way. Since the control phasing is affected by the twist of the mast, in both cases, it can have an unwanted effect on the control of the helicopter.

Was That a Real Overtorque?

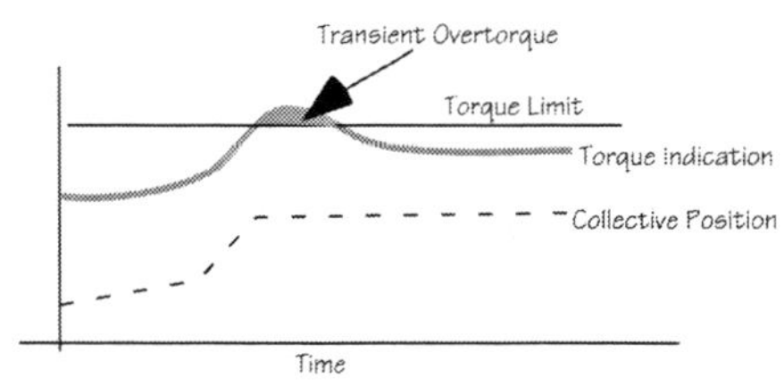

Figure 29-16 Transient Overtorque

These two problems raise the question that plagues helicopter pilots everywhere - was it a real overtorque, or a transient overtorque? The intelligent pilot should know what the system is showing and why it is showing it, and accept minor overtorques for very short (3-4 seconds) are probably not really overtorques at all, but fluctuations caused by the indicating systems. FADEC designers take note! See Figure 29-16 to help determine if it was a real overtorque or not.

Most FADEC systems can do this sort of calculation, and both prevent un–necessary maintenance while making sure what should be reported gets reported!

Turbine Engine Power Monitoring

The first question you might ask if you are buying a helicopter, whether new or used, is whether the engine is putting out the performance you're paying for. You're paying a lot for the engine, and you'd like to be sure you're getting your money's worth.

The next time you might be interested in the health of the engine is after you've had it some time. Is it still performing the way it should be? Does it need a tune up?

As turbine engines get older, components wear, compressors become dirty and in general the engine isn't as efficient at turning fuel into power. Performance in the FM is predicated on the engine being able to produce at least the minimum power guaranteed by the engine manufacturer. The question is how to check that the engine is up to that minimum level? As always, some confusing terms have been used for the different methods of checking this performance.

One method checks the engine when it is producing maximum power. For the purposes of our definitions this is called a *topping check*. This may be impractical for day–to–day use, for several reasons.

- If the power level needed to check the engine is outside the normal power required, it needs a special flight. For example, if the helicopter is transmission–power–limited, (a 650 shp engine in a 500 shp rated transmission) it is necessary to climb to an altitude and air temperature where the maximum power available from the engine is less than the transmission rating. This ensures the engine is capable of putting out its maximum power.
- The check may eat into the cycles of the engine.
- If the power needed for the check is in the One Engine Inoperative (OEI) limits in a multi-engine helicopter, this check may well eat into the contingency power life of the engine.
- With some digital fuel controls, it may not be possible to get to those power levels without an emergency situation.
- If on the ground, pulling the necessary power may produce a lot of downwash and noise.

Obviously, it's not an ideal day–to–day check, but we'll describe it first.

Topping Checks

Topping checks are performed on the engine to determine that it is putting out the necessary power. For those helicopters normally limited by transmission torque, it is necessary to climb to an altitude where engine limits are reached before the transmission limits. At the conditions specified in the FM, power is increased until the first engine limit is reached. The torque put out by the engine is compared to a chart (for example, the power available chart in Figure 29-2 on page 301) to determine if the engine is acceptable. Some engine manufacturers provide a chart to let this check be conducted at less–than–limiting conditions of N_1 or TOT. The aim is to determine if the engine is operating at the minimum level certified for the type. This check is not a regular day-to-day check, but performed prior to scheduled maintenance or if the power output of the engine is suspected to be low.

This leaves us with the problem of how to check on a more regular basis that the engine is operating properly. The solution is known as trend monitoring, and the difference between it and a topping power check are explained below.

Trend Monitoring Checks

Topping checks are time–consuming and hard on the engine. Why bother to cycle the engine to very high N_1 or TOT values when they are not normally used? *Trend monitoring* checks, on the other hand, are designed to be quick and easy to perform as well as using less–than–limiting conditions on the engine. They ensure the engine is operating as it should be. Immediately following a satisfactory topping check, on the ground power is pulled to a specified lower condition of N_1 or torque. The readings of TOT, N_1, Q, etc. are noted, and this forms the 'baseline' of the HIT check.

Normally a range of N_1 or Torque is used to ensure the engine bleed valve (if fitted) is either fully closed or fully open.

In normal day–to–day operations, the values for the *Health Integrity Trend* (HIT) check are taken from a chart. The numbers on this chart may appear strange, but they are nothing more than the original numbers converted to what the readings would be in a standard ISA condition. When HIT checks are a regular (daily) event, the results are compared to the baseline. As the engine ages, it deteriorates slightly - for example, as the compressor gets dirty, it has to work harder to compress the air at the same condition - this shows up as a higher TOT, or more N_1 than the baseline. When the deterioration reaches a certain stage, it is necessary to wash the compressor to restore its efficiency. If a large change is seen over time, another topping check should be made - the engine may be out of limits for power. Some newer FADEC installations also do this monitoring on a more or less continuous basis without the pilot having to do anything. Figure 29-17 shows a typical history of an engine undergoing a HIT check. Notice how the TOT reduces following the compressor wash.

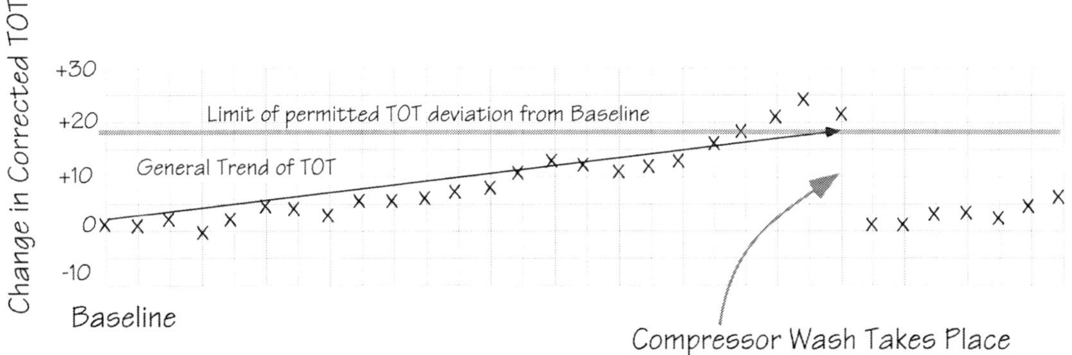

Figure 29-17 HIT Check History

Interestingly, trend monitoring checks are not mandatory for all civil helicopters. But, knowing if your engine can meet the specification power available in the FM is mandatory, according to some inspectors.

Russian helicopters have no torque meters, and their trend monitoring checks only worry about the relationship between the pressure at the back of the compressor compared to the front. This is similar to what airliners use on jet and fan engines.

On another note, many of the flight manuals do not have really clear instructions on how to check to see if the engine passed or failed the power check. There are no examples to follow on the chart.

Automatic Relight vs. Manual Air Starts

Many turbine engines incorporate an automatic relight system to reduce the effects of an engine failure due to rain ingestion or other minor problems. Good things, and I would applaud such systems being installed on all helicopter engines. There is one curious thing about these systems though and that has to do with why their manually controlled counterparts are not allowed on all helicopters.

The ~~Allison~~ (now Rolls-Royce) 250 series (non-FADEC versions) has a procedure shown in the manufacturers manual for an immediate restart in the event of an engine failure in flight. The procedure says basically to hit the starter button within 10 seconds of the failure, without moving the throttle away from the fully open position. I have no problem with that, and can relate that to many jet trainers with the same procedure.

Some airframe manufacturers have not incorporated that procedure in the airframe flight manual, but they will permit an automatic relight to be installed, which does the same thing. The excuse from the airframe manufacturers engineers is that the shock of re-starting the engine against the drive train is too severe and shouldn't be permitted. As if the shock of a crash landing wouldn't be worse... It is an emergency and not an every-day occurrence.

ENGINE–RELATED ITEMS

Intake Protection Systems

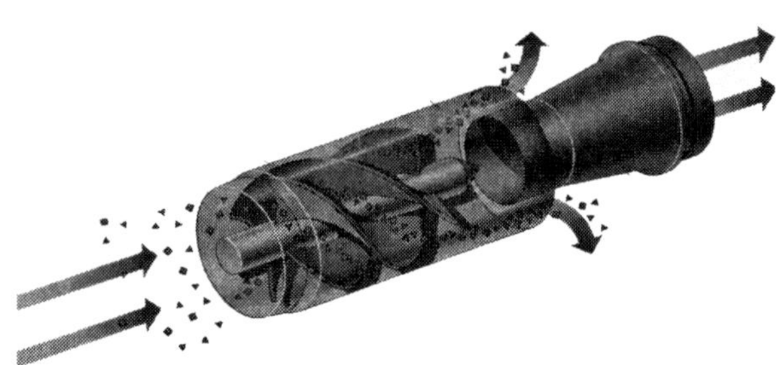

Figure 29-18 Swirl Tube Particle Separator

Turbine engines devour huge quantities of air, and as we know, not all of this air is clean. The effect of dirty air on a compressor can range from a minor annoyance and a small power reduction to literally grinding the blades to nothing (and the power to zero) in a matter of minutes. Normally some device is needed to separate the dirt from the clean air. This can range from specially shaped ducts to small swirl tubes. Normally these operate on the simple principle that dirt is heavier than the air, and if given a centrifugal effect, the dirt will continue on a path which doesn't take it to the engine. Simple and effective, but with one minor problem- what if the air is very cold and damp and prone to forming ice?

Anti-Icing vs. De-Icing

Many helicopter engines are not cleared for flight in icing, for the simple reason that the helicopter itself isn't cleared for these conditions. Thus they are not fitted with de-icing intakes. Many helicopter engines do have anti-ice intakes. The subtle difference in words is meant to say a de-ice intake will get rid of ice already formed, while an anti-ice intake will prevent it from forming. For operation in conditions where icing is likely to occur, it is wise to take precautions like reverse flow baffles or whatever the airframe manufacturer recommends.

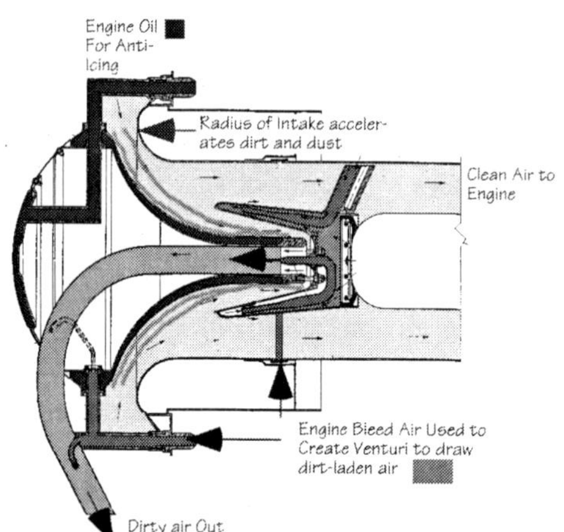

Figure 29-19 Side view of Polish Intake Protection System

The Russians have been operating helicopters in pretty severe conditions of snow and ice for years, and all their machines have ice protection systems on the rotor blades and windshields, and a very good engine de-ice system, shown below, which is a reasonable compromise between the particle separation problem and the ice problem. See Figure 29-19 below for a side view of such a system.

Bleed Air Systems

Bleed air services normally include bleed air valves, (used to regulate the engine), heaters, and anti-ice systems. Automatically operating engine compressor bleed valves are not normally under the control of the pilot, but other systems such as heaters, deicers and so on normally are operated by the pilot, and it is useful to know if they are working. Any bleed valve or system which is open will make a significant difference in performance, and its operations should be noted to the pilot.

Bleed air systems also indirectly affect the range of the helicopter, as the extra power the compressor requires to produce the bleed air has to be made up somewhere. Typical range penalties for operating a bleed air service such as the heater can be up 5% in some helicopters. Another good reason for installing a fuel flow meter.

Bleed valves

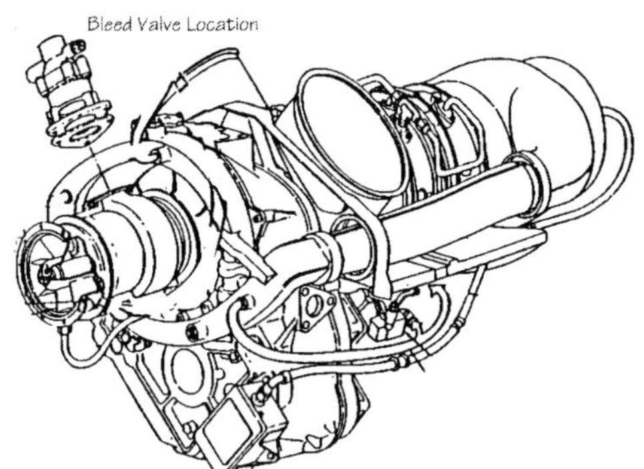

Figure 29-20 Bleed Valve Location

Bleed valves are installed in engines to ensure an orderly flow of air from the intake of the compressor to the combustion chamber. At various times in the operation of the engine, this flow is more delicate than others, and too much air can be produced by the compressor. A bleed valve is installed to vent this excess pressure and prevent the engine from hiccuping at the wrong time. Figure 29-20 shows where a bleed valve may be located on an engine. Figure 29-21 shows the N_1 conditions when the bleed valve should be open and conversely when it should be closed.

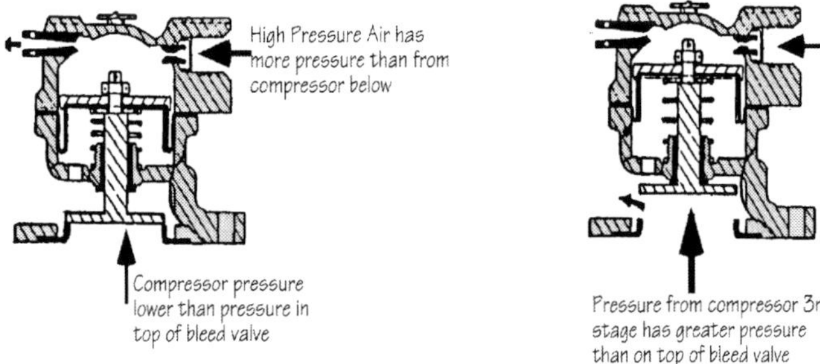

Bleed Valve Closed *Bleed Valve Open*

Figure 29-21 Bleed Valve in Operation

Heaters

Turbine engine compressors produce large quantities of high pressure, hot air. This is also a useful method to use to heat the interior of the helicopter, and so many aircraft use excess compressor air to heat. Since the engine has to work harder to produce the power needed with this air being taken from the compressor, it is normal to turn the heating off for takeoff and landing.

Air Conditioning

Air conditioners are just heat exchangers in another suit of clothes. The hot air provided by the compressor can be used to exchange heat and cool the interior of the cabin, in a manner not too different from a heater. The only problem is that the days when you want to use the air conditioner are the days you can least afford to have the extra power robbed from the compressor.

Performance Effects of Bleed Air Systems

Bleed air systems rob performance from the compressor, and make the rest of the compressor turbine section work harder to produce the air needed to turn the compressor. In cold weather the performance loss may be small, and hardly missed. In warm weather, it may have a significant effect on the power output of the engine. It is for this reason that most manufacturers insist on the bleed air services (at least those for creature comforts, such as heating and air conditioning) be turned off for takeoff and landing, when performance is critical.

(There may also be another reason for this- if the manufacturer wants these devices to be on for the hover, takeoff and landing, then performance charts must be developed for these conditions, with the services on. This is not cheap or easy to do, and the simple solution is to say- Off for takeoff and landing, and then the performance is unchanged from the basic helicopter.)

Being mechanical, there is a tendency for bleed valves to stick either open or closed. Post start checks normally ensure they are working, (and not stuck on) so make sure you carry out the required procedures. The check is more to ensure that the system isn't stuck on than that it can be turned on...

Some helicopters incorporate warning systems to tell if the bleed valve is open. Why don't they all have this?

Starting Against the Rotor Brake

It's a good thing for an author like me that there are so many different helicopter types with the same engine, because it shows up some things which are difficult to comprehend.

The response of one engine manufacturer to the question - "Starting engines against the rotor brake and effects on the turbine wheel? No effect that we know of, as long as the power and TOT are kept to a minimum."

One airframe manufacturer routinely starts the engines and holds the rotor still using the rotor brake to provide air conditioning prior to passengers arriving.

Another airframe manufacturer, using the same engines as above, wouldn't consider it, stating that the engine manufacturer wouldn't allow it.

Interesting how two different airframe manufacturers who use the same engine interpret things completely differently - one allows starts with the rotor brake on, and the other one doesn't (and then claims it's an engine problem...)

Turbine Engine Cool-Down

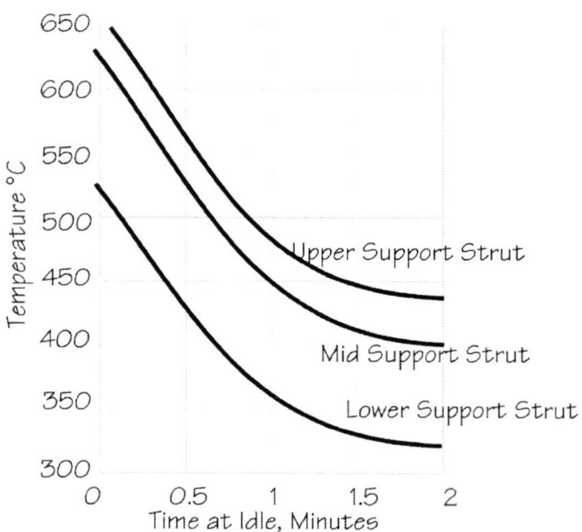

Figure 29-22 Temperature vs. Time Cooling

Most turbine engines require a cool–down period after they have been operating at high power settings. This is to reduce the temperature change between the high power condition and the 'off' condition. Even large fixed wing aircraft have this requirement, but we don't see it often, as they have to taxi to a parking spot after landing and this normally is sufficient for the cooldown. Helicopters are thus forced to sit at a low power setting or idle N_1 for a time to ensure all the necessary things stabilize. If you aren't convinced, Figure 29-22 shows a typical chart of temperature in a critical area vs. time spent cooling.

There are several things which must be mentioned about this practice:

- French designed engines, for some reason don't seem to need a long time for cooling down. What do they know that the rest of the world doesn't?
- Figure 29-22 above shows quite clearly that 95% of the effect has taken place in the first 1.5 minutes, so why is the final 30 seconds necessary? How much fuel does this take when multiplied over the millions of hours this engine has?
- There are some who say, if 2 minutes is good, 3 minutes is better. Nonsense, and in fact it can undo some of the good. If the manufacturer says 2 minutes in the published material, then use 2 minutes and badger the engine manufacturer (to reduce the cooldown time).

- The reason for the cooldown on one popular engine is due to oil being trapped in a particular bearing and getting overheated. Why doesn't someone invent an electric post–shutdown oil pump which runs for 5 minutes to pump oil around and save the fuel and engine running time*? Multiplied over the life of the engine it would pay for itself in fuel saved, and shouldn't be too heavy.

Emergency Systems

Some helicopters incorporate an emergency shutdown system which will sense a hard landing and shut off fuel, oil and electrics, as well as automatically blow the fire bottles. Nice work. Just don't have hard landings!

Fixed Shaft Turbine Engines

Some turbine engines are different from the standard 'free' turbine layout. These have a single shaft that drives both the compressor and the output. They are referred to as fixed shaft turbines because the turbine (there is only one) and compressor are fixed to the same shaft. There is no separate power turbine and compressor turbine- one does both jobs of driving the compressor and providing power to the rotor.

There is only one speed of operation in the engine - that is when the engine is running at normal speed, all parts of the engine are at that speed, both compressor and turbines.

The response to power changes in these engines is amazing - that is to say no droop except a small one in the most severe power demands. Governing uses oil pressure as the way to sense N_2 changes, resulting in very rapid response.

There are several penalties to the fixed shaft engine. All of these engines are noisy at close quarters, except when specially silenced. The fuel consumption is high in comparison to a free turbine, as the compressor must be optimized for only one condition of speed, whereas the free turbine compressor can change speed depending on the airflow requirements. There is a need for a heavy clutch assembly to permit the engine to be started without engaging the rotor. Engaging the rotor takes a long time compared to running a free turbine from idle to fly, and in-flight re-starts are typically difficult, as the engine has to be shut down to re-start it. It is also not possible to make a multi-fixed shaft engine helicopter.

On the other hand, they are incredibly reliable. Incredibly.

There are only a few helicopters which have a fixed shaft engine- the Alouette III and the Gazelle, as well as a small quantity of specially produced S-55 (or H-19) helicopters used for sight seeing.

Summary of Chapter 29

This chapter has covered the turbine engine in general terms and shown some of the ways it is different from the piston engine. A lot of things have been covered here- some of them may sound like heresy. Obey what's in the FM, and lobby like mad with the manufacturers to improve things.

* I only want a small percentage of the profits if it works. I'm not greedy.

Advanced Engine Failures

General

This chapter assumes the pilot has mastered the fundamentals of getting the helicopter from the point of engine failure to at least a survivable position near the ground, as discussed in Chapter 18,"Engine Failures for Beginners". More refined techniques are covered here.

This chapter deals only with the complete loss of power (or only engine, for single–engined machines) as well as the Height Velocity Curve. The more complex One Engine Inoperative (OEI) situation for multi-engine helicopters is covered in Chapter 32,"Multi-Engine Helicopters".

Autorotations

This section deals with the 'normal' sequence of events that should occur when forced to do an autorotation, or when teaching or refreshing autorotative landings. It should be very clear by the end of this chapter that autorotations are not 'by the numbers' procedures. I'm still learning something from every autorotation I do.

The same disclaimers given earlier need to be repeated here - namely, that the techniques described are generic, and may not always work on all types of helicopters.

Sensory Deprived, Multi-Variable Maneuver

In technical terms, autorotations are the most sensory–deprived, multi–variable maneuvers any aviator can be called upon to conduct. In simple terms, this means there isn't much worthwhile to look at to help you, and there are lots of changeable things. For example, no little magic moving light* appears on the windshield and says - "You will land here"; no flight director shows you how to coordinate the controls for a safe landing. The marvel isn't that some practice autorotations end incorrectly, but that so many real engine failures are handled reasonably well.

If we look again at the closed loop diagram in Figure 27-1 on page 277, this time with an eye to what the pilot is supposed to be accomplishing, we find there is really very little in the way of useful information being fed back at any time in the autorotation. This previous sentence may take a long time to make clear, so bear with me.

The pilot needs to know what exactly it is that should be attained. For a successful autorotation, it means arriving at the desired spot. Unfortunately, there is no instrument that will tell you that, so you have to rely on other information to determine your rate of progress, and what you must do to correct the situation. This chapter will help develop the skills necessary to use that information.

The Big Picture

Many organizations do not permit touchdown autorotations except in regular checkrides with an instructor. Another damper on this important skill is insurance coverage - most insurance companies do not like the added risk involved in practicing autorotations†, mostly due to a bad history of accidents during this part of training. However these problems do not reduce the requirement for training.

The end result is that many important skills in judgment are not exercised regularly. How this problem can be solved was discussed in "Power Recovery Autorotations" on page 171. The aim of autorotations is to arrive safely on the ground. Safely on the ground has one over-riding criteria - you can walk/hobble/crawl away from the aircraft. Even if it is not flyable you thank the good Lord‡ for your incredible luck, it's still a safe arrival.

---

* The fixed wing fighter community has these a lot in their Head-Up Displays. The lights are called velocity vectors or flight path markers, and they really are magic. Wish we had them.

† They don't have much choice about real autorotations, although I'm sure some people would try to prohibit them as well.

‡ or Deity of your choosing

Where to Practice Autorotative Landings

For most skid–equipped helicopters, hard surfaced runways are much better for doing autorotations than soft ground, especially grass. Surprised? So was I.

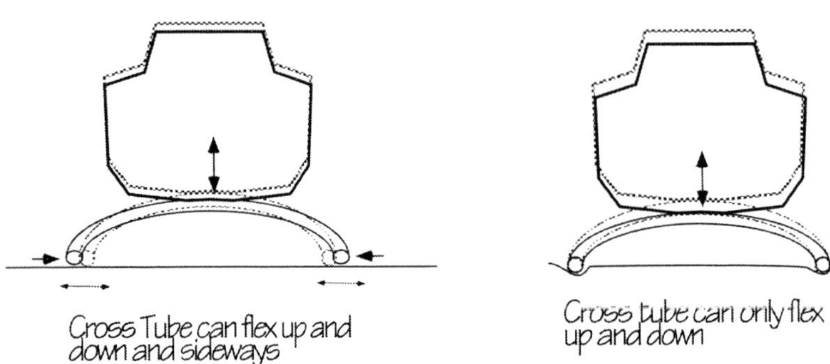

Figure 30-1 Cross Tube Flexing and Not Flexing

Soft ground may appear to give nicer touchdowns that feel better to the pilot, but may be harder on the airframe. In one model of helicopter, repeated autorotation landings in soft ground eventually bend, and sometimes break, the rear cross tubes. The rear cross tubes were meant to flex, and on soft ground, they cannot move in and out. The grooves the skids make in soft ground hold them in place and prevent them from moving laterally. Only the top part of the cross tubes flex. Figure 30-1 shows this.

An additional problem of landing on soft ground is that the friction of the grass on the landing gear is quite high, and tries to stop the helicopter quickly. This is made worse if the collective is lowered immediately on touchdown. Since the CG is relatively high in most helicopters, this can tend to stand the helicopter on its nose, and create problems with *'spike knock'* on those helicopters with a flexible transmission mount. Spike knock takes it name from the small spike on the bottom of the transmission hitting the restraining device. Figure 30-2 shows the effect of a sudden deceleration.

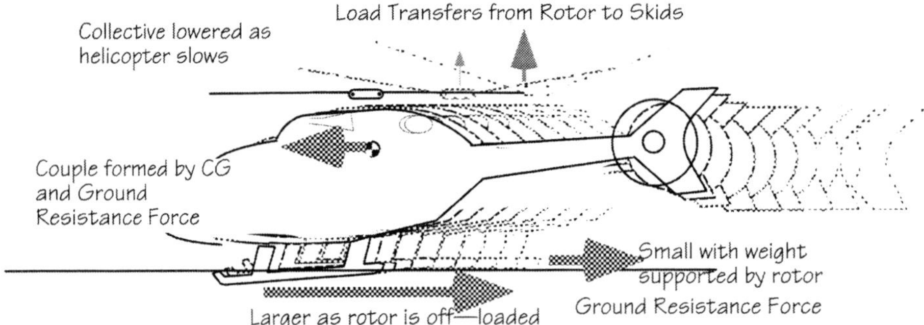

Figure 30-2 Sudden Deceleration.

The transfer of weight from the rotor to the undercarriage after touchdown needs to be carefully controlled - on soft ground, lowering the collective immediately on touchdown will almost certainly cause the skids to dig in, and the problem of nose-over is made worse. The only two times I have had problems with autorotative landings has been on soft ground, so there must be something to this!

Hard–surfaced runways and taxiways, even old, disused ones, are typically much smoother than grass areas. If you don't believe this, try driving over most grass autorotation touchdown areas in a car or truck at about 15 m.p.h. - about the highest speed you might touch down at.

Not all touchdowns have complete agreement between the heading of the helicopter and the direction of flight. On a hard surface, this is not a problem, as the skids don't dig into the surface and there is very little, if any, side force. On soft ground, when the skids dig in, there is a side force well below the CG. On soft ground, if the heading of the helicopter and the direction of movement of the airframe don't agree, there is a twisting of the airframe until things finally get straightened out*.

The only two downsides to using a hard surfaced landing area are that the noise is greater and the bottom of the skids wear out more quickly on hard surfaces - however, there are after-market add–on skid shoes that have a longer life than the original manufacturer's shoes†.

* Unlike most of my puns, this one is deliberate.

To re-iterate, landing on hard surfaces may appear to be rougher, but it there are a number of positive points -

- ground friction and deceleration rates for running landings are lower.
- there is very little chance of digging in, so spike knock is prevented.
- the cross tubes can flex as they were designed to.
- any misalignment between aircraft heading and direction of movement is easily taken care of.

In my opinion, there are many advantages to conducting autorotations to prepared hard surfaces, and the one major disadvantage is easily overcome. If you have a choice, always go for the hard surface.

Pre-Nominate the Landing Spot

When practicing autorotations, it is always useful to pre-nominate the spot for the eventual landing (or hover, for power–recovery autos). This will develop skills too numerous to mention, and force the pilot to look outside. It's sort of like learning to park a car - easy to do on a parking lot with no lines, slightly more difficult with other cars about.

Autorotations 'En–Route'

There are many reasons for giving student pilots practice or surprise autorotations at places and times other than the normal autorotation training areas - it teaches them to consider where they are flying (for example, flying over large areas of trees in single engine helicopters should always be avoided, unless you have at least partial knowledge of how events may transpire if the engine quits).

Instructors – be cautious of giving engine failures in these conditions - despite the desire to drive home the points to your pilots. More than one practice engine failure has turned into the real thing. You don't want to have to try to extricate yourself from a self-inflicted problem! *Caution*

CLOSER LOOK OF AUTOROTATIVE PERFORMANCE

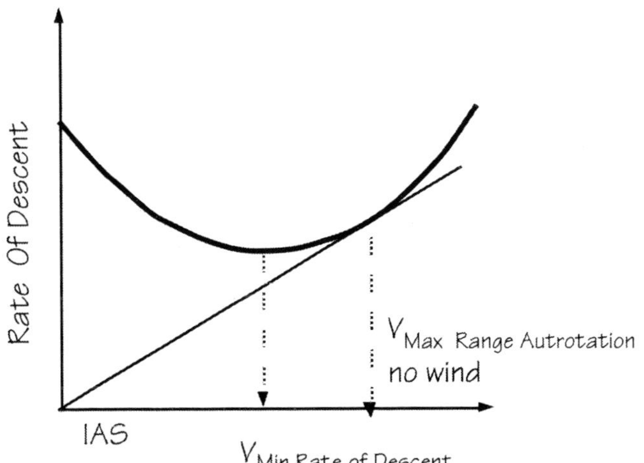

Figure 30-3 Rate of Descent vs. Airspeed.

It is worth spending some time looking at the Rate of Descent (ROD) vs. Airspeed chart repeated in Figure 30-3, with the addition of a line for the maximum range airspeed to use in a 20 knot headwind. Note that above 60 KIAS, the slope of the curve is roughly parallel to the tangent from the origin. This means that there is not a lot of penalty in using a higher–than–maximum range airspeed.

† No, I don't get a commission from them (yet), but would be willing to accept donations in small unmarked denominations.

Perhaps it is worthwhile to look at this curve in a different way - as distance descended and traveled over the ground for several airspeeds. Figure 30-4 below has the same information as shown in Figure 30-3, but in a different form. It shows the descent angles of various airspeeds, for a no-wind condition. As can be seen, there is not a lot of difference in the glidepath angle for any of the speeds. If you were only 500 feet above the ground (AGL), there might not appear to be much benefit from using anything other than the normal autorotation airspeed. This ignores kinetic energy, discussed later. From 1,000' AGL, the difference in distance covered between using minimum rate of descent airspeed and maximum range airspeed is about 20% (3,000' covered at the airspeed for minimum rate of descent vs. 3,600' covered at maximum range airspeed).

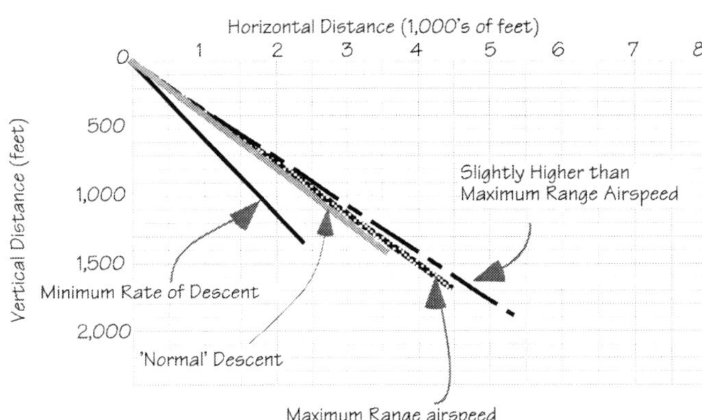

Figure 30-4 Descent Angles

Headwind Effect on Maximum Range in Autorotation

If we add a 20 knot headwind we get a slightly different result seen in Figure 30-5 below. The lines are shifted to the left slightly, but now it is possible to see the real benefit to using a higher airspeed. Now the horizontal distance covered from 1,000' AGL at V_Y is only 1,800', while that covered at slightly–higher–than–$V_{max\ range\ autorotation}$ airspeed is 2,800'. (We'll make up our own V speed here, to save space - $V_{max\ range\ autorotation}$ will become V_{mrauto}.)The reduction in horizontal distance covered using V_Y from no–wind to 20 knots of headwind is 40%, while the difference for the slightly–higher–than–V_{mrauto} airspeed is close to 25%. The reason in mathematical terms for the difference between the two is that a 20 knot wind is a smaller percentage of the higher–airspeed descent (20/80) than of the slower–airspeed descent (20/60).

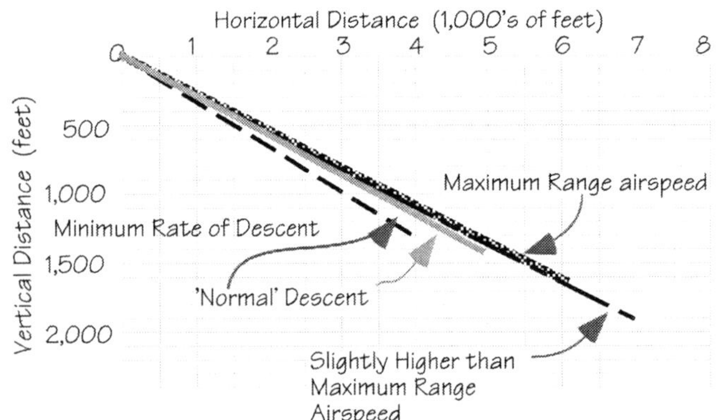

Figure 30-5 Descent Angle with Wind

Changing N_R

There is one more aspect to autorotative descent performance that needs to be addressed: the effect of reducing N_R. Figure 30-6 below shows the benefit in glidepath angle resulting from using the minimum power off N_R during the descent. The horizontal distance covered using 'normal' N_R (line A) is 2,800' while that using minimum power–off N_R (line B) is 3,800' if both are started from 1,000' above ground. 1,000 feet can be a long way when you have to get somewhere.

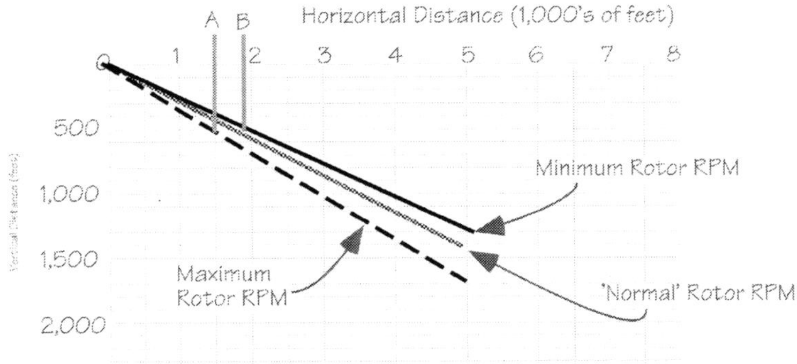

Figure 30-6 Effect of N_R on Glide Path Angle

So, if you are at 1,000' AGL with a 20 knot headwind and the engine fails, you can use your minimum rate of descent airspeed and normal N_R and travel a measly 1,800 feet, or you can use minimum N_R and higher than maximum range airspeed and travel 3,100 feet. If you had to cover at least 2,500 feet to get to the clearing, would you know how to do it?

Both of these previous sets of examples have been taken in isolation. In a real autorotation, the ride doesn't end with a constant airspeed landing - all that airspeed has to be converted into another type of energy, and this is where the real secrets of getting the most from autorotations lies.

Energy and Autorotations

The process of getting from the time/place of the engine failure to safely on the ground can be thought of as an exercise in energy management.

The helicopter in flight has three basic forms of energy - height with respect to the ground below it (potential energy), speed with respect to the ground (kinetic energy), and the turning blades (energy of rotation). From your high school physics, these energies cannot be created or destroyed, just transferred from one place to another*. The following table shows the way this transfer in an autorotation.

* At least in the sort of physics that helicopters are interested in.

Phase	Potential Energy $m \times g \times h$	Kinetic Energy $\frac{m \times v^2}{2}$	Rotational Energy $\frac{\Omega \times R^2}{2}$
Descent	Transferred to Kinetic and rotational Energy until it's nearly all gone (i.e. near the ground)	Maintained by conversion from Potential Energy	Maintained by conversion from Potential Energy
Flare	Not enough to worry about. Maintained by conversion from Kinetic energy	Used mainly to stop rate of descent and remainder transferred to maintaining/increasing rotational energy, until it's nearly all gone	Maintained and increased from Kinetic energy
Touch-down	None (hopefully)	None- small amount remaining is killed by use of rotational energy	Used to cushion touchdown

Cone of Possible Areas

These energies can be used in many ways (some positive, some not so good)- the point is that they can be used get the helicopter to a wide variety of places following an engine failure. The problem is how to describe this area. The best description that comes to mind is a cone extending down and around from the helicopter. Within reason, it should be possible to get to any suitable spot within this area. This cone is not valid for areas close to the ground, especially near the height velocity curve, but for a helicopter in a medium–altitude cruise, it is a useful concept. An example of such a cone is shown in Figure 30-7. If a wind is added, it only shifts the shape of the cone slightly, as shown in Figure 30-8.

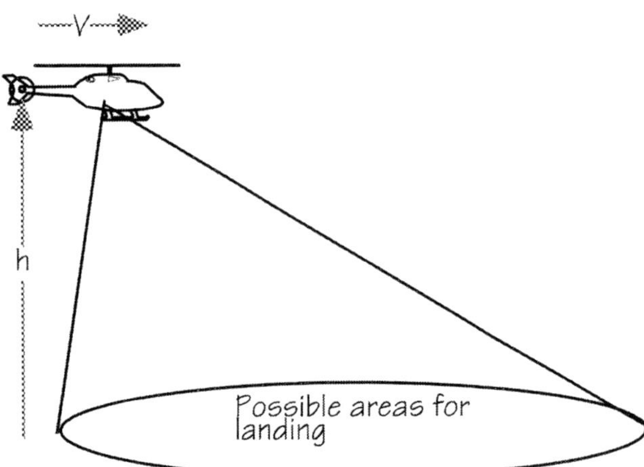

Figure 30-7 Cone of Possible Landing Areas

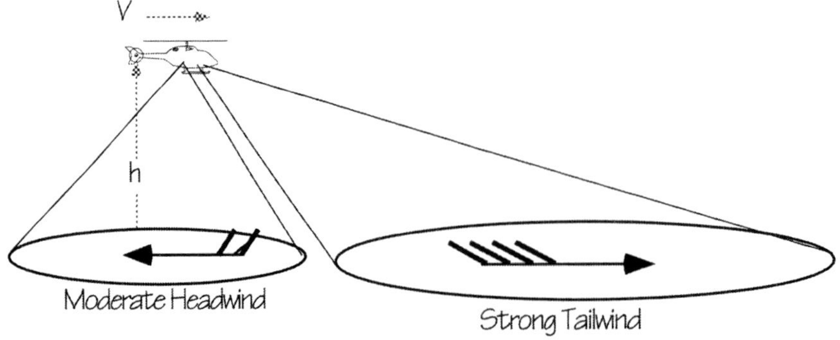

Figure 30-8 Cone of Possible Landing Areas, with Wind

Obviously, we can never predict when the engine will fail, and so we can't always be in the ideal position (as in training). The next section discusses the variations the successfully–trained pilot can handle to get to the necessary spot.

VARIATIONS ON THE THEME

Two variations quickly demonstrate the range of possible methods to arrive at a chosen spot. These are the zero–speed and the maximum range autorotation. Since maximum range will be flogged mercilessly later, a quick word now about the zero–speed autorotation is in order.

Zero–Airspeed Autorotations

The keen-eyed amongst you will have noticed by now that I have slipped from my normally boring preciseness about saying zero-airspeed or zero-groundspeed. There is a very good reason for this.

The first problem with this maneuver is that we can't measure zero airspeed ("Pitot Systems" on page 289 should have convinced you) The good news is that zero–groundspeed is close enough for the purposes of demonstration, and since we can't agree which one should be used, we'll just say 'speed'. A second equally important point is that this maneuver is not kept to zero speed all the way to the ground. The maneuver is actually a three part sequence -

- deceleration to zero groundspeed,
- descent at zero groundspeed, and then
- re-acceleration to 'normal' airspeed.

I couldn't think of a short, snappy name for a three part maneuver and 'zero airspeed' defines it well enough*.

This concept is best demonstrated by an entry from a higher–than–normal height AGL to give time and height to show the effect - I find 1,500' AGL overhead the entry point for a 'normal' (i.e. 500' AGL straight-in) autorotation to be suitable. Figure 30-9 shows the typical sequence of events.

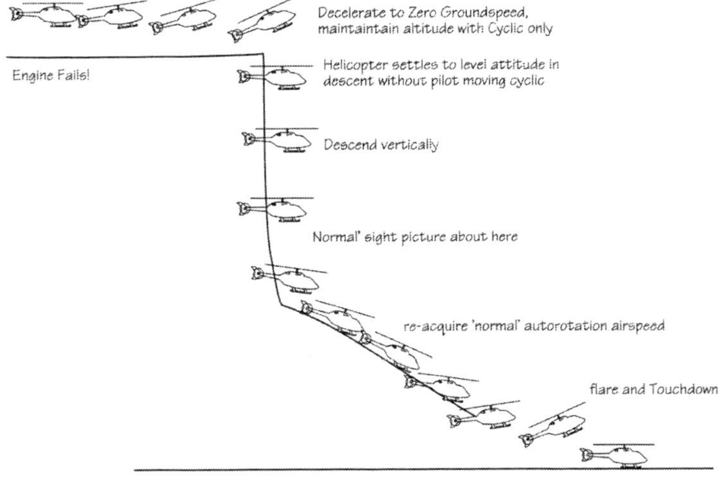

Figure 30-9 Typical Zero–Speed Autorotation

After the simulated engine failure, decelerate the helicopter, maintaining altitude until zero–groundspeed is reached, and maintain this attitude (not altitude), watching out the side window for drift. Note 'zero' groundspeed, not airspeed is used. Once the zero groundspeed has stabilized, don't mess with the pitch attitude for now. Descend in this leisurely fashion until the nominated landing spot appears to be approaching the 'normal' sight picture position. Then, briskly lower the nose to re-acquire a 'normal' autorotation airspeed. During this acceleration, the rotor is off–loaded and the N_R may decay. Don't worry - the helicopter is accelerating towards the flare point with a more–nose–down attitude than normal. The pitch attitude will be more nose-down than in a 'normal' autorotation. Don't worry! When the nose is raised to stop the rate

* Someone suggested 'stop, drop and plop'.

of descent (the flare), the N_R will recover, (and probably goes above normal N_R). This is due to the change in pitch attitude from the descent to the flare being greater than in a normal autorotation. In fact, if the flare is really abrupt, you might consider raising the collective slightly to reduce the radius of the pull out - the N_R will not increase as much, and somehow, it 'feels' OK.

It is important to accelerate to a reasonable airspeed in the re-conversion, at least the 'normal' airspeed used - don't worry if you get too high an airspeed, but do get at least the 'normal' airspeed. If you don't get enough airspeed, the flare is going to be very ineffective at stopping the rate of descent.

It *is* possible to descend vertically in autorotation, but don't try to take this all the way to the ground unless you are very practiced*. The only time I would consider this to be acceptable is the final part of an autorotation into a clearing in the trees. Without lots of vertical references, it is very difficult, if not impossible, to know when to raise the collective to stop the rate of descent. (I misjudged this once, and was very lucky...)

The zero–speed autorotation having been dealt with, it's back to the other variations.

Reverse Cone of Energy

Real life hasn't yet paved over, let along smoothed out the whole world. Suppose you are flying over a heavily–forested area, and there is only one suitable clearing you can land in. Wisely, you have placed yourself in a position where you think you can make it to the clearing. The concept of the 'cone' can still be applied, but in reverse. The pilot must be able to weigh the options to arrive at the landing site. Figure 30-10 shows this reversed cone of energy for a no-wind situation, and Figure 30-11 shows it with wind effects considered.

On a no-wind day, you could draw a cone centered on the landing site, defining the volume of the air within which it is possible to be, and make a safe landing in the clearing. (The cone is much larger than you might expect!)

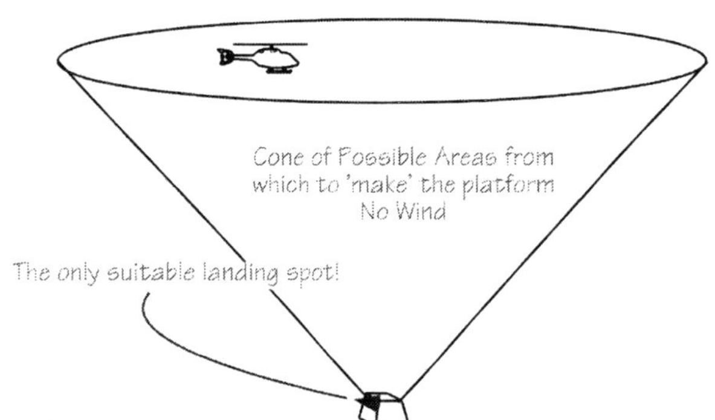

Figure 30-10 Reverse Cone of Energy Applied to Platform

Landing Site is Straight Ahead

Let's start with the clearing directly in front. You must coordinate the controls in a timely fashion to arrive in the clearing. How do you go about it?

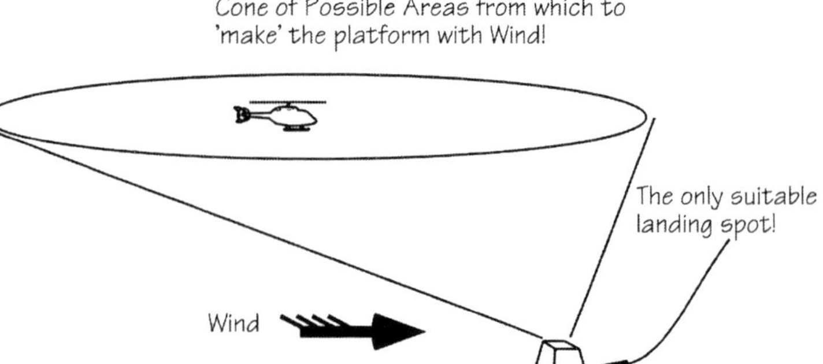

Figure 30-11 Reverse Cone of Energy Applied to Platform with Wind

Energy management starts to come into play now - you have the cruise airspeed (kinetic energy), the N_R (rotational energy) and the height above the clearing (potential energy) to play with. How should we use them?

At this stage, you are using up potential energy, and it can go into only two other forms of energy; N_R (rotational energy) or airspeed† (kinetic energy).

* or desperate!

† Some might argue decelerating to zero airspeed in this condition is also preserving potential energy, but only for a short while.

The first item is choice of the N_R and airspeed. N_R can be anywhere between the top to the bottom of the green arc, the airspeed can be anywhere from zero (yes, zero) to the $V_{NE\ Autorotation}$. Which combination are you going to choose and why?

That depends upon where you are when the engine fails. If you're a long way out from the landing spot, and it looks as if it is going to be a tight squeeze to make it, then you might be better using high airspeed at minimum N_R until your rate of progress becomes clear. If you are very close (looking at the clearing through your feet for example), then decreasing the airspeed to nearly zero and having the collective full down might be worth considering.

Three Basic Locations

Figure 30-12 Three Basic Locations

There are three basic locations you could be in respect to the clearing - ideally situated for the autorotations seen in training, too close to it, or too far away. Figure 30-12 shows these three locations. The ideal situation would require nothing more than lowering the collective and setting the airspeed to the one your instructor drilled into you and waiting for exact moment to flare. Seldom are we so lucky.

Too Close to the Landing Site!

An embarrassment! How could you possibly say to anyone, let alone another helicopter pilot (cough, cough, shuffle feet, look at ground)? "I couldn't make it into the clearing, it was too close."

In this case we must get rid of some of the energy, but in a way that will allow the maximum number of options - no sense throwing anything away. A 360° turn (or perhaps even less) could be carried out here. I don't like turns in autorotation as it becomes difficult to judge closure rates (especially if there is a wind), the N_R needs constant attention, and so on. Also, the wind changes with altitude, and makes life more difficult to judge things. At some point in the turn you have both turned your back on the landing site and are going away from it- not good things. Personally, I wouldn't turn.

My preferred option is to change airspeed - decelerate the helicopter to a slow speed while keeping the clearing in front, or at least off to the pilot's side. A zero speed descent with the clearing out the same side as the pilot is sitting means the sight picture doesn't change, and only a small, short–radius turn is needed to line up again. When the time is correct (and only judgment and experience show when this is), the nose is smartly lowered and the helicopter accelerates into a normal autorotation profile. This whole maneuver is just a variation on a zero speed autorotation.

Once in the flare, the rest of the maneuver is standard.

Landing Site Far Away

A more difficult predicament is the 'going for range' situation. The V_{NE} in autorotation would have been developed for a good reason* - go faster and the N_R decays. Between the normal airspeed for autorotation and this V_{NE}, there is quite a range of speeds to choose from. Consider Figure 30-3 (Rate of Descent vs. Airspeed) shown previously. The speed for minimum rate of descent is obviously where the rate of descent is lowest, and the V_{mrauto} is where a tangent from the origin touches the curve.

* I know of only one helicopter where there is not special V_{NE} for autorotation. It is quite incredible to come down at over 160 knots! Lawn Dart time.

At the moment of truth how to judge which airspeed to use? Since you have no way of knowing the wind between you and the landing spot, and time won't permit you to get out the graph of Rate of Descent vs. Airspeed anyway, and you can't measure either the height above ground or the distance to the landing spot, you are left with the Mk1 eyeball and trained judgment. There is no always–correct answer - but a good rule of thumb is

Helpful Hint

If you think you are undershooting, go faster.
If you think you are overshooting, go slower.

This may seem incorrect, but look at the situation this way. Going faster temporarily increases your rate of descent and steepens your descent angle, but that's not the whole story. On the other hand, you will have a much higher airspeed/groundspeed at the start of the flare.

Kinetic Energy in the Flare

To keep things simple, in the beginning of this discussion, we will deal only with the no wind situation, so it should be normal to consider using only the advertised 'maximum range' airspeed in autorotation. It should be normal, but this is not a normal book and we are interested in the whole picture. The published V_{mrauto} is the best airspeed for maximum range *only* if we were to ignore the energy available at the start of the flare. For this demonstration we want to use the maximum speed possible in autorotation, just as we used the minimum speed possible in demonstrating how to 'get rid of' range.

For sake of argument, let's say we have already decided to use the highest speed possible, with the N_R at the low end of the permitted power–off range.

Helpful Hint

Don't look inside for the N_R gauge, listen for the rotor, and possibly the low rotor horn. If the horn comes on, lower the collective slightly– just enough to make the horn go away.

Why go for the maximum speed? Isn't "V_{mrauto}" the airspeed to use? Not necessarily. The published V_{mrauto} assumes no wind, and a lot of altitude to descend through - a higher speed may mean the same or slightly steeper glidepath. The use of published V_{mrauto} also disregards the amount of energy available at the start of the flare. (Remember Figure 30-4 and Figure 30-5, where horizontal and vertical distance scales were used to show descent angle? There wasn't much difference in the glidepath angles.)

In a no–wind situation, using the V_{mrauto} results in a glidepath angle of x°, with a typical pitch attitude of 5° nose–low. With no wind, at the start of the flare, the airspeed and groundspeed* is 73 knots and the pitch attitude must be changed from 5° nose down, to 10° nose up†.

If we have a 10 knot headwind, the only changes from the no-wind situation are that the glidepath angle is slightly steeper, and the groundspeed is 63 knots at the start of the flare.

If we use 10 knots more airspeed (83 KIAS) than V_{mrauto} (73 KIAS) in the descent with this headwind, we have only a slightly steeper glide path angle than the V_{mrauto}, and the nose is slightly farther down (say 10° nose down). The groundspeed at the start of the flare is now 73 knots, and we must change the pitch attitude in the flare more, as the change in the flight path from the descent to the flare (zero rate of descent) is slightly larger.

Why all this emphasis on the higher speed? In summary -

- Published V_{mrauto} is the best range airspeed only for a no wind situation.

* Groundspeed is important because we have to get rid of energy with respect to the ground. Airspeed provides lift.

† All these figures are approximate- I never look inside to see what pitch attitude I'm flaring to, and I hope you don't either, except at night or on instruments, maybe.

Just like the way to determine best speed for range in the power–on cruising level flight in a wind, we draw a tangent from the wind speed, not the origin of the graph. See Figure 30-13.

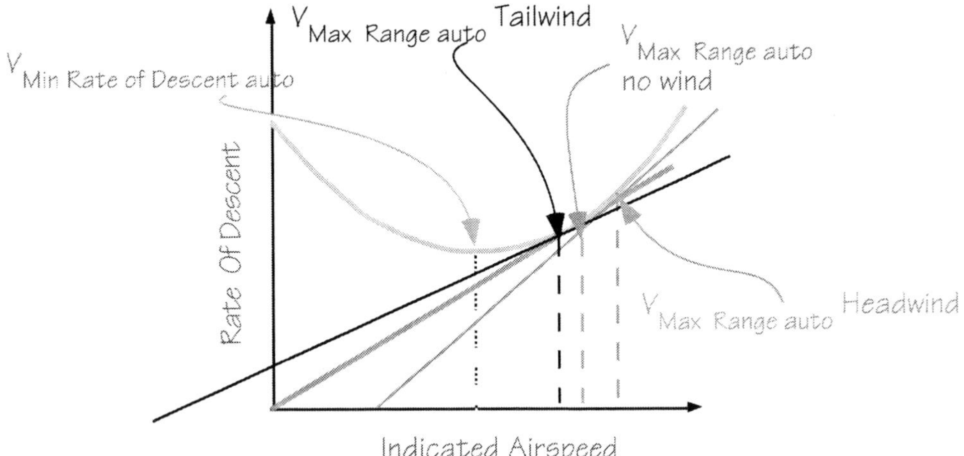

Figure 30-13 Rate of Descent in Autorotation vs. Airspeed, with wind

If you were autorotating from a great height, (for example 10,000' because you were crossing a wide stretch of water) then, maybe this new airspeed would be the one to get you to the far shore (assuming you had already passed the point where you could get back to the other shore) if there was a headwind. In our example, using maximum range speed factored for the wind gives nearly half a mile more distance from 10,000' into a 20 knot wind. On the other hand, most helicopters fly around at 1,000' AGL or less, so the difference in range possible due to wind won't be so marked. There is still one very convincing reason to use a higher than maximum range airspeed if you are uncertain if you will make the landing spot.

When the entire picture of getting to the landing spot is considered, using a higher airspeed/ groundspeed has one huge and often overlooked benefit. Remember the three types of energy - potential, kinetic and rotational. At the same height above the ground, (at the end of the descent) there is very little potential energy remaining, and it is the same regardless of the airspeed* used. The kinetic energy, the energy due to velocity, is definitely different between the two speeds. For those who don't remember high school physics, the formulae for kinetic energy is

$$:\text{Kinetic Energy} = \frac{m \times V^2}{2} \qquad \textbf{(EQ 31.)}$$

Note the squared (^{2}) term on the velocity.

Assuming nothing falls off the helicopter†, the difference between the two cases just discussed is quite large. The higher speed case has the mass (a constant) multiplied by 5239 (73 x 73), while the lower speed situation has the same constant multiplied by 3969 (63 x 63). This is a difference of 30% ($\frac{5239 - 3969}{3969} = \frac{1270}{3969} = 31.9\%$) more energy at the start of the flare! The effect is enormous. Even if the airspeed used was not the ideal one for the wind, and the glidepath was marginally steeper than it should have been, the increase in energy available for flaring more than overcomes this.

The relative amounts of kinetic energy at the start of the flare, for the different airspeeds ('normal', typical maximum range and our 'squeeze–everything–you–can–out–of–the–machine' autorotations) will determine the distance over the ground covered during the flare. The figures speak for themselves, but if don't believe them, try the different airspeeds yourself when you are next practicing autorotations.

* We will also keep the rotor RPM the same to avoid confusing the issues.
† And we don't run into a gravity hole

It is also interesting to compare the change of flight path from the descent to the flare. Look at Figure 30-5 to compare the descent angles. If the 'normal' autorotation airspeed were used, the flight path in the descent would have been much steeper, and there would be less energy available to change the direction of the flight path. So two benefits come from using higher airspeeds in a wind - more energy at the beginning of the flare, and less change in the flight path angle.

A larger change in pitch attitude results in a larger increase N_R in the flare, and the higher groundspeed means we have more kinetic energy to get rid of. Assuming things were really tight, and our flight path was going to take us short of the clearing, this extra energy could be most useful.

Obviously, nothing is free - it does take some extra height to get to this higher airspeed, but the payoff is worth it.

Why Try the Variations?

The two main variations in the airspeed, namely zero speed and higher-than-maximum-range airspeed, will show the two extremes of how to get to the clearing. It should start to develop your ability to judge the techniques to get you safely to the place you want to land.

All of these variations have been merely to get us to the end of the descent, and the next stage in the autorotation, namely the flare and landing are no different from what has been covered previously in Chapter 18,"Engine Failures for Beginners".

Applying the Energy Analogy to Slower Airspeeds

It is worth noting the reverse of the use of higher speed to give more energy in the start of the flare. The same logic can also be applied to slower speeds - energy available for the flare drops off rapidly as speed decreases. It takes energy to change the flight path, and when there isn't enough of it, the rate of descent can't be stopped by using kinetic energy (that is, by cyclic flaring). Taken to a ridiculous extreme, if you were descending in a zero–airspeed autorotation, flaring with cyclic wouldn't change the flight path at all. Surprisingly, at speeds below about 40 KIAS, flaring won't change the flight path either- there isn't enough kinetic energy. But we digress - back to the variations...

Other Situations with Respect to the Landing Spot

So far, we have assumed the suitable landing area is directly in front of us. What if it is just behind, or off to one side, or downwind? The only change this makes is that now we must turn to get into a good landing position - all other things remain the same.

The previous discussion started with the ideal set of circumstances, and considered three positions with regard to the clearing. This scenario follows the same sequence. Figure 30-14 show three other possible scenarios more graphically. In all but one of these situations, the helicopter is considered to be heading downwind.

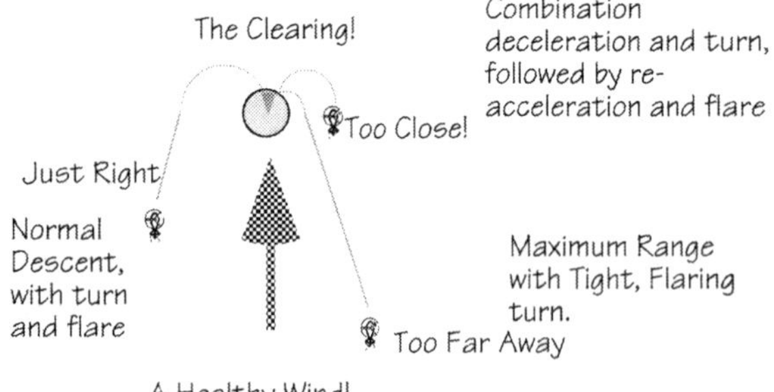

Figure 30-14 Other Possible positions with Respect to the Landing Site.

Ideal Situation - Alongside the Landing Site

If the clearing is directly alongside, then it is a matter of establishing the helicopter in autorotation, rolling in to a turn, and judging the turn to roll out nicely lined up and into wind. Two important things to consider here are firstly, the N_R increases during the turn and that it may be necessary to hold a small amount of up collective. The second point is to not lose sight of the landing area - keep looking at it, keep judging the closure rate, turn rate and so on. Nothing says the flare can't be made in the turn*. Since the turn took you into wind, things worked out really well. We should all be so lucky...

Alongside the Landing Site, Helicopter Heading Into Wind

The only slight difference between this case and the previous situation is that you may wish to make a 360° turn to land into wind. On the other hand, a series of s-turns may work as well. Other than having to turn harder and perhaps hold more collective to keep the N_R from overspeeding, it is no more difficult. How much altitude does it take to do this turn? Depends on how aggressively you turn, among other things. I've done a 360° turn from as little as 500'AGL†.

Landing Site is a Long Way Away Ahead

Life is seldom so simple as the last two examples - normally the clearing is off to one side, you are upwind of it, and why me Lord? Two things have to be accomplished - get to the clearing, and turn into wind. This is just a variation on the into–wind, long–range autorotation, and the flare can be made while turning if need be. Start to turn no later than abeam the landing point, and vary the angle of bank to arrive there. See Figure 30-15 for a diagrammatic explanation of where to start turning.

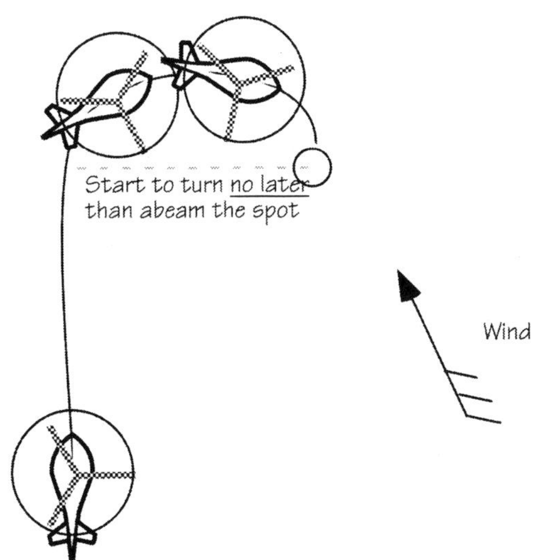

Figure 30-15 Where to Start Turning

The secret here is to focus on the landing spot, so, if you had laser beams instead of eyeballs, there would be two small holes where you want to land. A continuous "how-goes-it" is needed and no information suitable for making those decisions will be found in the cockpit. Only experience will develop the judgement for this decision.

Landing Site is a Long Way Behind, Helicopter Headed Downwind

First the good news - you don't need a long memory. From 500' AGL, anything passed behind more than 5 - 7 seconds ago is too far away. If you're within this short time frame, the first thing to do is turn - and turn hard. Roll on the bank angle, and pull the nose around while raising the collective slightly. Don't worry about raising the collective too much, the low rotor horn tells you very soon, and just lower the collective slightly to make the horrible noise go away. The greater the amount of G pulled in the turn, the more the N_R tends to increase, so judge collective application accordingly. Keep the airspeed up, and as you roll out of the turn, lower the collective and try for maximum airspeed and minimum N_R, for all the reasons discussed before.

It sounds very easy to write this, and hopefully to read it in the comfort and safety of a chair. If you are reading this while trying your first autorotation - put the book down now and look outside!

Of course, things won't be this cut and dried when you do it for real, but understanding the why and wherefore will help you concentrate on the flying outside.

* At least, I don't know of any such book- and if it did exist, it's wrong.

† Please don't write in saying you bent your helicopter trying to do it in less height that I did - it's not a competition.

Combinations!

Nearly any other situation with regard to a clearing is going to be a variation of one or more of the scenarios given above. If you can handle these variations on a theme about autorotations, you should be able to handle anything when the engine fails.

Intervention Delay Time

How much time does the pilot have between when the engine fails and when he must lower the collective? Obviously, in single engine helicopters, not a long time, and not all helicopters are the same.

In some helicopters, the rate of N_R decay following an engine failure is so rapid the pilot almost needs to have extrasensory perception (ESP) to know the engine is going to fail. In others, the pilot could almost step outside have a coffee and a smoke*, step back inside and still have lots of N_R. The intervention delay time is something measured in the development testing of the helicopter, and usually result in low rotor warning lights and horns, as well as determining the N_R they come on at.

Intervention delay time is not something the pilot *must* use - if the collective can be lowered at the very first sign of the failure, the pilot is in a better position than waiting until the low rotor horn begins to sound.

Run-Down Time of the Engine

By the way, the reaction of the helicopter to a sudden power loss (for example, due to a driveshaft failure or engine seizure) may be different than the way engine failures are commonly simulated in training.

The reaction of two similar helicopters (the Bell 206BIII and the 206LIII) to simulated engine failures is quite different - the BIII has a leisurely wind-down of its engine with 6 axial and one centrifugal compressor engine compared to the rapid wind-down of the single centrifugal compressor engine on the LIII. You can be assured that the certification flight testing will have been done both ways.

Height Velocity (HV) Curves

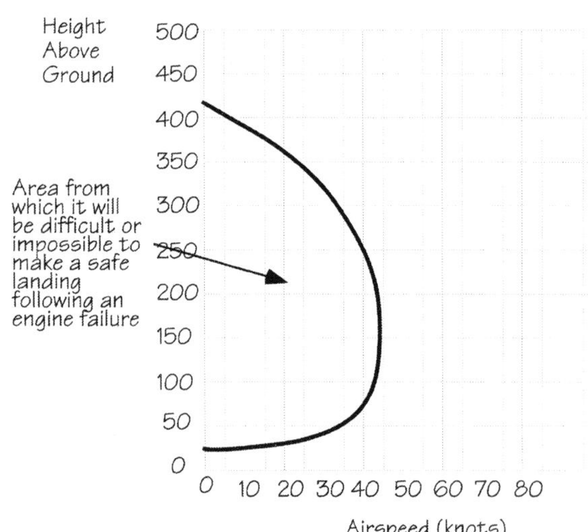

Figure 30-16 Typical HV Curve

No discussion about autorotations would be complete without something about the HV curve. This section deals only with single engine helicopters. Many–motored† helicopters comes in Chapter 32,"Multi-Engine Helicopters". A typical HV curve is shown in Figure 30-16.

The height velocity (HV) curve has been widely misunderstood and badly written about in many magazine articles and books‡. I have had the pleasure of teaching experienced helicopter pilots, as students at test pilots' schools, about this curve, and would like to pass on some observations.

A typical definition of the HV curve is

• "the area of heights and airspeeds within which it is difficult or impossible to safely land the helicopter following an engine failure".

The HV curve, like any other performance curve, needs to have the conditions relevant to it shown with the chart. Sadly, most FMs do not show these facts. What is often not mentioned in the definition is the constraints of weight, wind, density altitude, pilot intervention time, landing surface and so on that are relevant to it. The curve may not be exactly what you think it is, yet it is remarkably accurate and repeatable.

* ...back in the days when smoking was OK.
† New phrase alert needed!
‡ I hate to say this about other books, but it is unfortunately very true.

For certification purposes, the HV curve must be demonstrated at the maximum weight for the altitude being sought for certification. When you look in the manual, you can be pretty well* guaranteed the curve is for the maximum weight of the helicopter, at a high density altitude.

The overwhelming response of experienced helicopter pilots when they had finished a demonstration of the HV curve and how it is developed has been: "Why haven't I seen this before? Why has no-one bothered to show me what the characteristics of this helicopter were like from the hover at altitude?" Wish I knew, especially as it's a part of the flight envelope where the helicopter is most useful and does most of its unique work.

Most helicopter pilots undergoing training do not see a wide variety of autorotation entry conditions. Most are of the aligned–with–landing–direction, know–we–can–make–it, lower–the–collective–roll–off–the–throttle variety. Those entries also probably have the pilot very ready for the situation. The result is often an overly confident pilot about what happens to the helicopter from say, a 500' AGL hover when the engine goes on a long lunch break.

I know pilots who literally 'beat' the HV curve - they had an engine failure inside the avoid area on the chart. How is it possible they not only survived, but did no damage to the helicopter? When dissecting their incidents, it was apparent they were well trained in autorotative landings, knew the symptoms of an engine failure, were spring loaded to the engine failure reaction position, and had a suitable area in front of them. They reacted immediately and instinctively, knew where they were going to go and what they were going to do before the engine failed. They were also very lucky.

The HV curve is not a curve to be treated lightly.

Be prepared:

- Know what the reaction of the helicopter is to the engine failure in different airspeeds and flight conditions. The reaction of the airframe to an engine failure in a 1000' hover is very different from that at 60 KIAS.
- Know what you are going to do instinctively
- Know where you are going to attempt to land
- Be prepared for the engine to quit. (I know of one pilot who says he's always surprised at the end of a flight if the engine didn't quit!)

If you can react more quickly than the intervention time used in developing the curve, then you are that little bit better off.

If your helicopter flying regularly calls for you to operate in the HV area - such as slinging, military missions, photographic missions and so on, then ask yourself if you know what the symptoms of an engine failure really are at all the airspeeds you fly - including the high hover. You might be more than slightly surprised to notice how your helicopter reacts when you lower the collective from 10 or 15 knots of airspeed at 1,000' AGL.

The HV curve, by itself is not definitive in all respects of a safe landing, or of certain death if the engine fails. Be warned.

Ignoring A Part of Most HV Curves

Those of you who have compared the curve shown above in Figure 30-16 will notice that it is missing a portion shown on most flight manuals, namely the high speed, low altitude part. Why has it been left out?

The reason is that the way most curves are determined, namely using some intervention time, is, in my opinion, inappropriate for this part of the curve. I don't know of any helicopter pilots who would fly at this sort of height above ground at the speeds shown without being very actively involved in controlling the helicopter. Even if the engine fails, they are going to be extremely interested in keeping the helicopter from diving into terra firma, and might not even be aware immediately that the engine had failed. There is enough kinetic energy in the helicopter to control the machine, and assuming a suitable area, it should always be possible to make a safe landing.

* Certainly for any newer models of helicopter it will be at maximum weight and a minimum density altitude of 7,000'.

To be perfectly correct, if you were to wait one second before carrying out any actions following an engine failure in this flight regime, you would be first, have to have been asleep to not notice something wrong with the flight path, and secondly be deep in trouble. It is almost certain that any pilot would not be actively involved in flying the helicopter in these conditions and react instantly. If they weren't awake, they might deserve what happens to them.

So What's Missing about the HV Curve?

As previously mentioned, the first thing that is missing from the FM description of the HV curve are the performance conditions relevant to it.

Secondly, it is developed in very little, if any wind. A problem is that the wind at the high hover points is normally unknown. In my experience (and from what I have read), the presence or absence of wind at the high hover points has not made any difference to the resulting size of the curve. Some detailed engineering comparison tests shows the high hover point can be almost independent of weight, density altitude or even surface wind -others show a large effect of the same variables.

Thirdly, the curve involves a degree of delay between the engine 'failure' and the pilot taking any action. This delay is to simulate the typical pilot being caught unawares when the engine fails. Various parts of the curve have different delays, to take into account different levels of awareness of the pilot. For example, the high hover points (above the knee) have at least a one–second delay between the engine 'failure' and the pilot taking any action. Some military criteria call for two seconds - a very loooong time indeed.

The landing criteria is next on the list of unlisted items. Nothing says the touchdowns must be to zero–groundspeed. Most test points involve a running landing. Don't attempt to duplicate an HV test point and try for a zero–groundspeed touchdown. Most HV points in certification testing have quite long ground runs.

The final thing that's missing is training of pilots to know how to handle engine failures when operating close to, around or (shudder) inside the curve.

Development of the HV Curve

The way the HV curve is developed is beyond the scope of this book, but it should be mentioned that the whole process is approached with a sobering degree of caution and build up. There is a real potential to damage the helicopter as well as the crew. I do not wish to slam other textbooks, but more than one has got the development of the HV curve very wrong. Did you know there have been two helicopters* developed that had no HV curve? Do you think it likely they stayed airborne after the engine failed?

One book has claimed that the curves are deliberately made smaller for marketing purposes, however I have never seen any that were unrealistic for the conditions tested. I know of one civilian machine adopted for military use that had the high hover point raised by the military when they discovered that their supposedly superior military instructor pilots couldn't handle an engine failure at the civilian-developed high hover point. I don't know what that exercise proved, except it certainly didn't result in any great improvement in safety for the military, or degradation in safety for the civilians.

The test points are approached incrementally, and more than one test pilot is involved, just to make sure the results are repeatable. Having demonstrated how its HV curve is developed many times, I can say that for the Bell 206B, the curve in the civilian FM is very accurate. For example, an engine failure (simulated) in the zero–groundspeed hover at 420 feet above ground can be handled by someone who knows what they are doing. However, from a entry in hover at 350' AGL, even very experienced helicopter pilots abort the demonstration point, add power and go around. Similarly 45 knots in level flight at 200 feet is OK, if you knew what to do, but 40 knots at the same height is not - the helicopter literally falls out of the air.

Part 29 Helicopters and the HV Curve

The civil certification requirement for helicopters over 6,000 lbs weight and more than 9 passengers (FAR Part 29) requires the HV curve be placed in the limitations section of the manual. I used to not understand the reason for this, as fixed–wing aircraft don't have a gliding–distance–to–shore limitation

* The Dutch Kolibrie tip jet machine, and a specially modified Bell 206 with extra weights in the blade for greater inertia. Since you asked...

in the flight manuals. It's one of the subtle points about an aircraft that is certified for transport operations - you don't want to be hovering in an area where you can't safely land if the engine fails. But the rule changes with the number of seats that can be put in the helicopter.

When I worked at Transport Canada, we had an interesting experience with this from the 'interpretation of rules' point of view. An operator had been flying a smaller helicopter in the air ambulance configuration and then upgraded to a larger one. The smaller one could carry only 8 passengers in a 'normal' seating arrangement, and so, using the certification rules for this number of seats, the HV curve was in the Performance section of the FM. Their typical takeoff profile was a vertical climb to 100' AGL and then transition to forward flight. When they upgraded, the new machine had seating for 12 in the normal arrangement, so the HV curve was now in the Limitations section. They continued to use the vertical climb technique until it was pointed out to them it was illegal. The operator claimed the technique was safe, and used the example of an actual engine failure just after the top of the vertical climb. When we asked what would have happened if the engine had failed a few seconds earlier, say at 80' AGL, the operator replied that they would have hit the ground pretty hard, but that they were willing to take the risk. When we pointed out they would have been in violation of the certification rules, and hence have invalidated their insurance, they agreed to work with us to resolve the situation. Fortunately, we were able to get a Flight Manual Supplement for their air ambulance operation (when they obviously weren't going to be carrying more than 5 people), so they could once again operate within the rules.

The point here is that if you are operating a large transport-category helicopter, carrying passengers (capability for more than 9), then you'd best not be hovering in the avoid area, as you're breaking a limitation - even if you have the power to hover out of ground effect at 100' AGL.

Miscellaneous Points About the HV Curve

There has been some discussion recently about pilots being legally charged for flying within the HV curve and causing danger to persons on the ground. I would look at this the other way - just because there is an HV curve, doesn't mean the people on the ground would be endangered. What if there were no HV curve and the engine failed? Would the helicopter not land? What if the helicopter were outside the HV curve and the engine failed over the molten lava pits of a volcano? Would that be safe?

As another good reason to understand why you should be familiar with the HV curve is the lesson I have seen from nearly every pilot I have demonstrated this curve to. From a high hover, when the engine fails, the first reaction of the Bell 206B is to yaw and then sink vertically. Within a very few seconds, and without the pilot doing anything to the flight controls (except to lower the collective and stop the yaw), the nose will drop to about 30° nose down, and the airspeed will rapidly accelerate towards the normal airspeed in autorotation - 60 knots is reached in very short order. The point is that if the pilot pushed the stick forward right after the engine failure on this particular type of helicopter, he might get into serious trouble - the nose would be very, very far down indeed. This is not a fault of the machine, by the way, but of the system that doesn't show this to all helicopter pilots on this type.

The other thing to note about this, is that if you were hovering at 100' AGL when the engine failed in this model, you would have to work to keep the nose from pitching down, and if you did let the nose drop, you would not gain any airspeed at all to start to flare in that short distance.

One thing I can say about those who have seen the HV demo - they never try hovering at higher than normal skid heights without an extra-sensory awareness of the engine...

Another Type of Autorotation

There are undoubtedly many types of autorotations, but the only other common one I am aware of is the 'constant attitude' autorotation. This is particularly good if you are flying at night or in cloud in your single engine helicopter.

The technique is simplicity itself- turn into the wind, reduce airspeed to some low value (35 to 40 KIAS, plus about one-half the wind speed, and wait for the ground to rush up (this will require lights at night...). When the ground rush is quite apparent, raise the collective. There is not enough energy to flare, and the slight aft tilt of the rotor and fuselage will decelerate the aircraft quite a bit. The combined effect is a landing with a minimum of forward and vertical speed - hopefully survivable.

Summary of Chapter 30

It should be obvious that autorotations need a lot more attention than they receive in most training establishments. As previously stated, power recovery autorotations have 95% of the learning and 5% of the risk of full, engine–off touchdowns, especially when the judgment of airspeed and glidepath angle are the really important parts of autorotations. Nearly every variation in this chapter can be carried out quite effectively to a power recovery, with little risk and lots of teaching.

There is no such thing as the 'textbook' autorotation - mistakes will be made in every one. The main thing is to be able to understand the variables at your disposal, the ways you can use them and the overall aim - to walk away from the helicopter.

You should be able to identify and correct the inevitable errors quickly. One of my old flight instructor comrades summed up a pilot's progress at autorotations nicely: "He corrected for his own mistakes immediately."

It should also be obvious that the HV curve isn't what it always seems to be. Be prepared!

For those of you flying multi-engined helicopters, pay attention to the OEI procedures and think about how you're going to handle engine failures in those machines.

31 Advanced Emergencies

General

The emergencies the professional helicopter pilot may face are more varied in nature than those the student pilot expects to face. The helicopter is being used as a tool, and it is natural to expect different situations to be encountered. It is expected that since the helicopter is being used in a very regular basis as a way to earn a living that is exposed more often to unusual situations.

Tail Rotor Problems

The reason that Tail Rotor Problems are covered here, and not in Chapter 17,"Introducing Emergencies", is that in most piston engine helicopters it is possible to control N_R with the throttle. This makes it relatively easy to find a combination of collective and throttle that can handle the most difficult of tail rotor problems, namely a loss of control of the amount of thrust*. This is not so in most turbine helicopters, where it is difficult, if not impossible to control the engine in a timely manner to find that good combination of N_R and collective pitch to overcome the problem. Hence this section on tail rotor problems.

Tail rotor failures in the turbine engine helicopter are more difficult than in the piston engine machine because of the lack of direct control over N_R. In the piston engine machine, it is possible to directly control N_R and hence the overall torque reaction. In the turbine engined version, most do not permit the N_R to be varied outside of very small bounds, and in many, it is not possible to adjust the engine power with hands on the collective at all. Hence the problem of dealing with tail rotor control problems.

Reducing the Situations Possible

There are three basic problems that can occur with a tail rotor system- loss of drive, loss of pitch control at a high T/R pitch setting, or loss of pitch control at a low T/R pitch setting. Of the three, the loss of T/R thrust is the most common. Fortunately, it is also the one that is easiest to deal with.

Loss of Thrust

The tail rotor can fail to produce thrust for several reasons- driveshaft failure, gearbox failure, loss of blades due to striking something, and so on. The net result is that there is nothing to stop the fuselage from rotating in reaction to the main rotor torque.

The severity of the emergency will depend upon the amount of power applied to the main rotor at the time. High power demanded of the main rotor will normally mean that the tail rotor will also be producing high thrust. If the tail rotor drive fails in this condition, then expect the fuselage to rotate quickly.

For our generic helicopter, loss of tail rotor drive will mean the nose will rotate to the right, and at an alarming rate. Immediate action is required to salvage the situation. This brings up an interesting philosophy point.

Many helicopters do not have a hydraulic system for tail rotor control, and for those that do, it is very unlikely that the hydraulic system would give a hard-over to the tail rotor and even more unlikely that the hydraulic system would give a hardover to maximum left pedal pitch at a rate that could produce a rapid yaw to the left in the hover. You're already using most of the left pedal control range when hovering.

Thus if you are in the hover, and a rapid yaw rate develops, you don't have to think too hard to figure out which way the nose is rotating. It's probably going to go to the right.

* By the way, this whole discussion assumes that you've investigated obvious causes such as something blocking the pedals in the cockpit, or that if the pedals are hydraulically boosted, that switching off the hydraulics doesn't solve your problems.

Loss of Thrust in the Hover

The likely worst place for loss of tail rotor thrust to happen is in the hover, and the reaction is quite simple- get rid of the engine power and land the helicopter from a hovering engine failure condition. Easy to do in those machines that have throttle(s) on the collective. For those with a copilot, he should be briefed on shutting down both engines (at the same time) given the appropriate command. For those of you flying by yourself in a helicopter without throttles on the collective, especially multi-engine helicopters, figure out a way to shut the engine (or both engines) down, and then get back on the collective quickly.

Loss of Thrust in Forward Flight

Things are only slightly better if the tail rotor stops working with the helicopter moving forward. They are mostly better because the speed of the air flowing past the vertical stabilizer will help to keep the correct* end forward, but unless there is a long runway to land on, things still get difficult at the end.

Airspeed over the vertical stabilizer is necessary to counteract the main rotor torque, and unless a shallow fast approach can be made, it will be necessary to land without the engines producing any power.

The first problem is getting the helicopter under control. If you're in a fast cruise, and the tail rotor fails, you may not immediately be aware that it has stopped producing thrust. If you're in a slow–ish climb, with a lot of power, you may know it all too quickly. Your problem is get the helicopter under control to stop the yawing. For most helicopters, the best answer is airspeed, with minimum power, so a descent at high speed seems to be called for†.

So, having got the helicopter under control, the next step is to fly it to a suitable landing area. This may involve flying at some unusual fuselage attitudes, but once the helicopter is under control, you can become an experimental test pilot for a while.

A suitable landing area would be one that is long and quite smooth, however these are often scarce where helicopters operate, so consider how you're going to do a zero-groundspeed autorotative touchdown.

When you are in a position to make an engine-off landing, keep the airspeed up and enter a descent, close the throttle(s) and carry out a landing. Several manuals talk about a wind on the left being of some assistance (remember this is for the North American direction of main rotor rotation), this will depend on your particular type of helicopter.

I just wish the whole process were that simple, or that we had good simulators to practice this in!

Loss of Control of Tail Rotor Thrust

The length of the title of this problem gives some clue to the complexity. It's not that the tail rotor has stopped producing thrust, far from it. It's that you can no longer control it. Some people call it stuck pedals or fixed tail rotor pitch.

There are many different permutations and combinations of where the tail rotor thrust is when you loose control of it. They do fall into three major categories-

- just enough tail rotor thrust to hover, or pretty close to it,
- too much tail rotor thrust to hover, and
- not enough tail rotor thrust to hover.

The problem is how to tell which of these conditions you're in before you start to plan your approach and landing strategy. This is important, because for two of the three conditions, the consequences of getting it wrong aren't too bad, you can overshoot and try again. If on the other hand, it's the third condition you've misdiagnosed, then you can't overshoot easily and you could end up in a world of hurt.

Diagnosis of the Situation

Obviously the symptoms are going to be different for every different helicopter type, and to a limited extent will be different for changes in longitudinal and lateral CG, wind and weight.

The first and most common-sense thing to do is think what it is (or was) you are (or were) doing when the pedals stuck.

* I had originally said 'pointy' end forward till the other reader said that would be the tail...

† This is one area where I'm unable to give any positive advice, as there is precious little hard engineering experience or data.

If you were climbing at takeoff power, chances are pretty good the left pedal was forward, and you'd like to be able to use that much power when you try to land. If you happen to have been lifting an underslung load when the pedal stuck, you could be in for an interesting time, but we'll discuss that in a minute.

If you were descending and discovered that when you went to apply left pedal at the same time as adding collective and there was no response in yaw, then chances are pretty good, the tail rotor is stuck in a low-thrust situation, due to the right pedal being forward.

But sometimes, well, you just can't be sure whether you've got too much pedal, or too little for the hovering condition you'd like to be in just before landing*. Since getting it wrong can have unpleasant consequences, how do we figure out which way to plan our approach and landing?

Here's what works quite well for one popular turbine helicopter.

Set the airspeed for 70 KIAS, level flight and note where the slip ball is. It will typically be in one of three places, as shown below.

Your decision now depends on where the slip ball is.

Slip Ball Just Touching Right Side

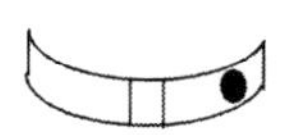

Figure 31-1 Ball Just Touchng Right Side

If the ball is just touching the right hand stop of the race, sort of bouncing off it every once in a while, then you probably have the correct amount of tail rotor thrust to hover into wind.

Slip Ball Fully Against Right Side

Figure 31-2 Ball Against Right Stop

If the ball is hard against the right hand stop, and trying to make dents in the right hand side, then you have too much T/R thrust to hover. Your actions are to reduce the N_R to the maximum extent possible with the N_2 trim, or if you can use a throttle, to the minimum power-on N_R. This will reduce the effect of T/R thrust (remember lift is proportional to N_R squared), so you may have slightly less overall T/R thrust to worry about when you get to the hover.

In this case, you can use a wind on the right side of the helicopter to help counteract excessive amount of tail rotor thrust being provided. It takes more tail rotor thrust (or left pedal, if you prefer) to keep the nose straight with a wind from the right hand side than on the nose, so use that to help keep you pointed where you want to go.While you are on the approach, the nose of the helicopter is not pointed where the helicopter is going. Don't worry about, remember to point the cyclic where you want the helicopter to go. Use a combination of collective and side wind to maintain the helicopter's rate of yaw. A little experimenting will show you the correct method.

Slip Ball Just to the Right of Center

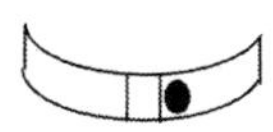

Figure 31-3 Ball Just right of Center

In this case, you have too little pedal (or tail rotor thrust, if you like) to hover. You need to do an approach with the aim of an engine off landing at the last possible moment. To do this, with some hope of possibly overshooting, a steep approach is needed, at about 50 KIAS, and 800-1000 feet per minute rate of descent. Maintain the throttle open until the 'flare', and then as the nose starts to rotate, roll off the throttle. Hopefully you have a throttle that is easy to use with your hand on the collective.

So What if You Don't Know What to Do for Your Type of Helicopter?

Obviously, the procedures described above won't work for every machine. You, being a conscientious pilot, want to know what the conditions are for your machine. What do you do?

* By the way, this whole discussion assumes that you've investigated obvious causes such as something blocking the pedals in the cockpit, or that if the pedals are hydraulically boosted, that switching off the hydraulics doesn't solve your problems.

I would suggest that it would be easy to figure out the symptoms if you start from a hover. Note the pedal position accurately (use a piece of masking tape stuck to the floor or fuselage close to the pedals and a bent paper clip to measure the position for repeatability). Set up a hover into wind, then a moderate rate of yaw to the left and to the right. Note the pedal position for each condition.

Now go into a moderate speed level flight condition, and apply those amounts of pedal and note the slip ball position. This will give be the start of a diagnosis procedure, should you ever be unfortunate enough to lose control of the T/R thrust.

If all else fails, remember you want to get the helicopter close to the ground, with low ground speed and low rate of rotation. Hitting the ground in these conditions is likely to be of minor significance compared to any other way.

For those of you with NOTAR, I guess you'll just have to use the loss of tail rotor thrust emergency for a fan failure...

Fires

Fortunately fires, particularly engine fires, are relatively rare events. This is good, because a great number of helicopters don't have a fire warning or extinguishing system. The other good thing, as least as far as safety is concerned, is that helicopters don't often fly at heights where it's going to take a long time to get to the ground if a fire should be detected one way or another.

There will be procedures in the FM for every helicopter to cover fires, but in general, the steps should be:

- Shut off the fuel to the engine, normally by using the throttle first, followed by a fuel valve.
- Shut off the electrics to the engine (this is probably mostly the fuel pumps)
- Activate the extinguisher (if fitted) into the engine or engine compartment.

Sounds pretty straightforward, but I'm still surprised we don't require fire detection systems to be fitted to every helicopter as routine.

Fires in the Cockpit

You would think that not much can burn in the cockpit of a helicopter. The seats are made of fire resistant material, there's not must to start the fire in the first place, and so on.

Yet, I've talked to people who've had radios start on fire and who were nearly unable to see within seconds. What would you do if this happened to you? What if somehow a short circuit in the wiring caused an electrical fire in the cockpit?

Can you jettison the doors of the helicopter, or open the windows enough to clear the smoke? Can you reach the fire extinguisher while you're still flying? Would you want to if you were by yourself?

Can you find the switches to shut off all the electrics in a hurry- without looking at them? Is the fire extinguisher in a place where you can get at it while in flight (its supposed to be...)

Not All Emergencies are in the Book

A quick troll through the summary of all accidents that happened to helicopters in one year (or at least those that got reported) shows some interesting things.

Not all the emergencies encountered were in the manuals. While this sounds strange, consider that at least 75% of the accidents were caused by the pilot, not by something mechanical going wrong. Who could write a procedure to stop pilots from doing things that were incorrect, or just plain dumb?

Be prepared! and use your head.

Some Emergencies have Other Implications

Some minor emergencies can have other implications which may be unexpected. For example, a fuel pump failure may not appear to have any effect if the FM says you can fly up to 6,000' with the pump failed. But look carefully - another section of the FM may say that the unusable fuel with a fuel pump failure could be significantly higher than the 'all systems operating' unusable fuel.

When to Inflate Pop-out Floats

The advice in many Supplements to FMs that deal with emergency floats is decidedly vague on when exactly you should activate the pop–out floats. Some say to wait until you're in the water, others suggest that just above the water. Which is the best place, and how will you know?

In the absence of specific advice from your FM or Supplement, consider where you might be, and what cues you might have to activate the floats.

If you're flying during the day, in good VMC, then it should be pretty obvious where and when you need to inflate the floats. On the other hand, if you fly a over the water at night (I won't even ask if you're in a single engine helicopter - the answer might scare me), then you should have a radar altimeter in order to know when you are low enough to inflate the floats- the airspeed indicator will tell you when you may be slow enough.

To Those Who Write Emergency Procedures

A plea...

Base the procedure on what the pilot can see and do in the cockpit, not on what has failed. The procedures have to be:

- easy to understand
- easy to do
- difficult to get wrong
- Not have confusing symptoms
- Never have the same symptoms for two different emergencies

Procedures should be written in a simple clear consistent format, identified by what the pilot will see in the cockpit (including, of course, caution and warning lights), and followed a list of simple actions to take. Some manufacturers will put in words about what emergencies are to be memorized, up to what point, and when they expect you to get out the checklist, but these are not common.

If you, as a pilot, see an emergency procedure that is not clear, may be incorrect, or find a situation which is not covered by the manual, write to the manufacturer. Send the letter registered mail, and keep a copy.

Emergencies Caused by Vibrations and Noise

Helicopters vibrate. A lot. But there are times when they vibrate way more than they should, and that's a good time to decide to put the helicopter on the ground. Lots of things can go wrong to cause the vibrations, and I can't give more specific advice about what is a sufficiently abnormal vibration to warrant stop flying. But if you feel something really unusual, best look at it on the ground.

Perhaps an example- Following major maintenance on a large helicopter (on wheels), while taxing out, one of the crewmen came on the intercom and said, in a very firm and authoritative voice to shut down, now. Being cautious, the pilots shut down and asked the crewman why he made the call. "I heard something funny overhead". This alone was unusual as this helicopter made a tremendous noise in the cabin, and how anyone could make out an unusual noise was a mystery. A thorough check revealed that a screwdriver had been left near one of the main driveshaft sections, and the noise the crewman heard was the sound of the screwdriver cutting its way through the shaft.

Summary of Chapter 31

This chapter has covered more emergencies that seem to happen to helicopters. It should have given the professional pilot pause for thought about needs to be considered for the comfort and safety of the passengers as well as those on the ground.

Multi–Engine Helicopters

General Introduction

This chapter will deal with helicopters with more than one engine. The basic differences between single and multi-engines will be dealt with first, with hydro-mechanical fuel controls being the lead item then FADEC controlled engines. This will be followed by the emergencies that might occur, then the more complex problems of how to make best use of the capabilities of such systems, namely Category A procedures.

There is a major philosophical question of whether a single is safer than a twin engined helicopter. First of all, there are twice as many engines to fail, plus some other additional items needed because there are two of nearly everything, so statistically, you're more likely to have an engine failure. On the other hand, if you have the right helicopter, you should have enough power from one engine to not get into too much trouble...

Terms

The terms used in this chapter for the two basic conditions of operation will be *All Engines Operating* (*AEO*) and *One Engine Inoperative* (*OEI*). These are commonly used in the helicopter community, so this is a good time to become familiar with them.

Background

To my knowledge, there are no existing multi-engine piston power helicopters still in service*. There are also no fixed shaft turbine multi-engine helicopters. The following comments thus apply only to free turbine engines. To be more specific, the first part of the chapter will deal only with free turbine engines with hydro-mechanical fuel controls. There are many important differences that are due to the introduction of computer control of the engine (*FADEC*), and these are highlighted separately.

Multi-engine installations are a compromise between installing enough power to keep the helicopter airborne when one engine fails and high fuel consumption. For example, it is possible to install two engines, each of which is big enough to hover the helicopter. The problem with this approach is each engine would normally be loafing at half power, and would have very high fuel consumption. Turbine engines are most efficient at high power settings, in terms of *specific fuel consumption* (SFC) or pounds of fuel burned per horsepower per hour. Operate the engine away from high power settings and the relative amount of effort the engine expends just keeping itself going is large in comparison to producing useful power. The ludicrous example would be to install a 3,500 shp engine on a 3,000 pound helicopter. At idle power setting the engine would provide enough to keep the helicopter airborne, but the fuel consumption would be enormous- most of the power would be used by the compressor, not the power turbine. This concept has been proven on several re-engining projects - installing new, more powerful engines without increasing the fuel capacity literally cut the legs (i.e. range) out from under the new model.

Typically, the OEI rating of engines fitted to Western helicopters is in the 75% of maximum twin–engine power. With the advent of super contingency ratings on FADEC–equipped engines, this ratio may change. For example, if a helicopter transmission is limited to 800 horsepower, then two 500 horsepower (continuous rating) engines, with contingency ratings to 650 horsepower might be reasonable.

* I understand the Russians are working on a twin Wankel engine model of a light helicopter.

Other Differences

A multi-engine helicopter needs to have other design features to take advantage of the safety of having two engines. For example, it would make little sense to have all the fuel for both engines come from one tank with only one fuel pump. Needless to say, this duplication adds complexity. See Figure 32-1below for the fuel system in a typical multi-engine helicopter.

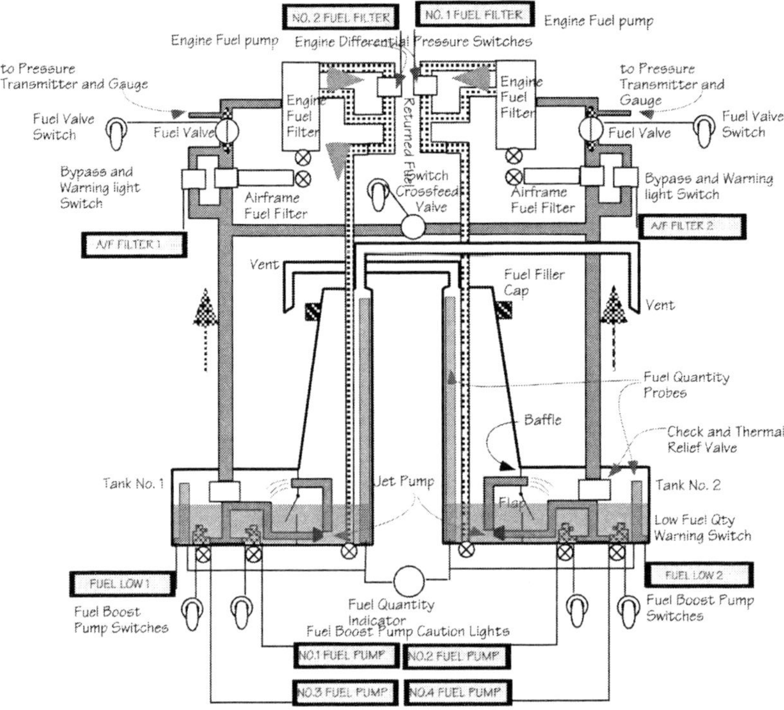

Figure 32-1 Multi-Engine Fuel System

Why are AEO and OEI Limits Different?

I'm surprised no one has cleared this up long time ago. If you have a twin–engine helicopter, there are probably different engine limitations permitted with AEO, and with OEI. For example, the continuous TOT limit (twin engine) might be 750°C, and the continuous TOT limit (OEI) is 800°C. Doesn't this strike you as a bit odd? How does one engine know if the other engine is operating or not? (This is for pre–FADEC engines only). Is this some dark plot to give the already too–burdened helicopter pilot something else to worry about? A fictitious example of such limitations is shown below.

Rating / Limitation	TOT	N_1	Torque
Twin Continuous	732	105	98.4
Twin Takeoff (5 minute)	785	105	110.6
OEI Continuous	785	106	110.6
OEI 2 Minute	843	108	126.0
OEI 30 Second	889	108	135.0

My questions were answered, eventually. The engine limitations are set by the engine manufacturer to be a good compromise between power and engine life. These limitations on the same model engine may be changed from type to type depending on the airframe manufacturer. One engine used in several different models has had markedly different results, depending upon what the airframe designers want. One experienced engine overhaul man said he could literally tell which model of helicopter an engine had come from by an examination of the internal workings.

The logic for different ratings works this way. If both engines are working, then the main concern is to maintain long operating life. The continuous limits are a good compromise, weighted towards the long life. If one engine fails, then the main concern is safety. For this reason there are various limited time conditions of operation - i.e. older engines have 30 minute and 2.5 minute limits, and newer engines have 30 second and 2 minute* 'super contingency' periods of operation to get the helicopter out of trouble. If there is need to operate continuously on one engine, it stands to reason this will only be for a maximum of the fuel load, and until a landing is possible. The OEI continuous limit is therefore set to be slightly higher than the twin engine continuous limit.

Power Matching - Non–FADEC Engines

When more than one engine is installed, a dilemma occurs - how can the power output of the engines be matched?

It is unlikely engines are perfectly matched in terms of power vs. N_2 or power vs. TOT. Other, practical considerations of wear and tear on the engines, imbalance of fuel consumption if the two engines are working at different levels, and so on make it worthwhile to match the output of the engines.

The first problem, namely engines not putting out the same amount of power vs. N_2 is solved by running the engines at the same output speed, but here, even small differences in the governed N_2 speeds can cause problems. Less than 0.1% difference in N_2 speeds can mean one engine is carrying all the load. With a hydro-mechanical fuel control system, it is often left to the pilot to match the torques.

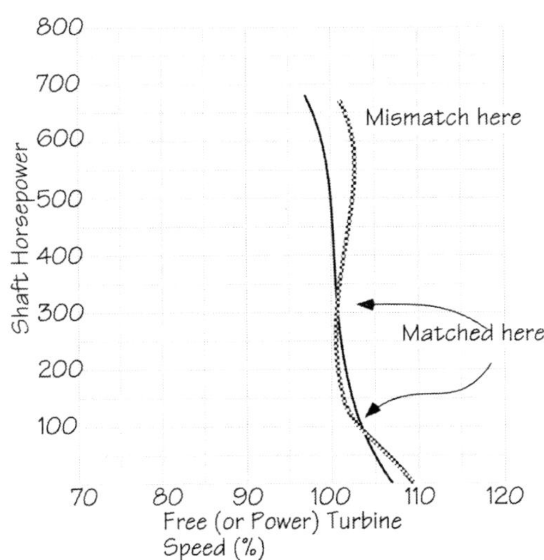

Figure 32-2 Different uninstalled droop curves for twin engine installation

Remember the different droop lines in the discussion about droop compensators ("Static Droop" on page 308)? What if two different engine had slightly different shapes to their curves - the results would be if the outputs were matched at one location, changing power would certainly make a difference to the power from each engine. This is shown in Figure 32-2 below.

Matching torques is one way to balance the output - the engines are at least putting out the same power and any difference between them shows in compressor speeds, TOT, fuel flow and so on. Matching torques can be automatic, or another task for the pilot.

When the two engines are matched at one power setting, effectively bringing their droop curves together, they may well not be matched at a different power setting. The pilot must then match up the power outputs if he changes the overall torque.

* I've put these two limitations this way around as if it were written the other way (2 minute and 30 second rating, someone might confuse it for the limitation on older helicopters that is a 2.5 minute rating.

Manual Torque Matching (non–FADEC)

When the pilot has matched torques there may be a mismatch in engines at a different power level. The engines may be matched (in terms of power vs. N_1) at the bottom end, but at the top end of the range, they may be different. The end result is the pilot constantly makes adjustments to match torques. Manual torque matching system does permit the pilot to get the maximum power available out of the engines at all times, but at the expense of pilot workload*.

There are several ways to let the pilot do this - either by collective mounted switches or speed select levers. With the collective mounted option, there are two additional possible methods. The most favored method has one 4-way switch - it controls the N_2 in one direction (fore/aft) and power from one engine in left/right. In this system, with the N_2 correct and one engine (the slave engine) lower than the master in torque, it is relatively easy to move the slave engine up. If the N_2 is too high it is necessary to adjust the N_2 down and then match torques.

Another method of collective–mounted switches has a separate increase/decrease N_2 switch for each engine. This system works on the theory that the pilot can determine if N_2 needs to be increased or decreased to match torques and set the N_2.

The most difficult to use, in my opinion, are roof–mounted speed select levers - one machine I flew (the British military Sea King models and other versions of the Sikorsky SH-3) needed a second set of hands to match torques when the pilot had his hand on the collective. In steady conditions, or with a good training, the pilot could adjusting the power for one engine. Perhaps an even worse system was the single lever with a knob on the end found on the Lynx. Adjusting torques here required the adjuster to pull down on the knob and rotate it to match the torques. Definitely a two crew task. Even after years of service, no-one had seen fit to replace these anachronisms with a simple, collective–controlled motorized system.

Automatic torque matching appears to be the answer, but is it really?

Automatic Torque Matching - Not Always a Good Thing

Most of the time, it's a good thing to have the power output of both engines automatically matched by a clever fuel control system. The pilot has one less thing to do, and is able to concentrate on flying the helicopter, knowing that the engines will be matched. But it's not always a good thing.

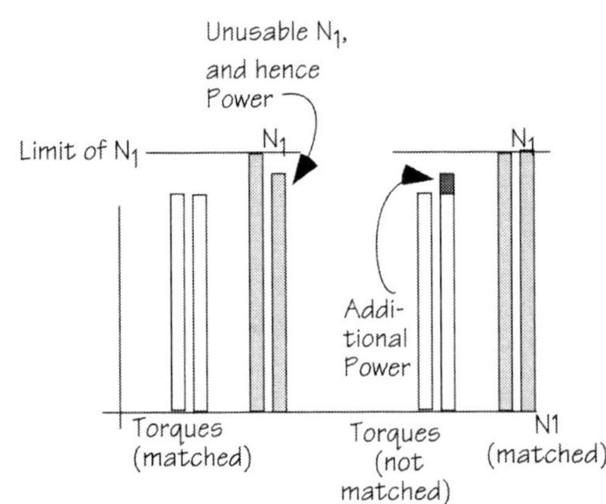

Figure 32-3 Maximum Power Not Available

Some of the power from one of the engine might be unavailable with some automatic torque matching systems. When two engines are matched in torque but not in other terms, such as TOT or N_1 speed, a problem arises. Let's say engine No. 1 is running hotter than engine No. 2. When the torques are matched automatically, the pilot is able to apply power until the first limit is reached. On a hot day, if the limit is not torque, but temperature, this means he is limited by engine No. 1, and the power of engine No. 2 cannot be fully exploited. See Figure 32-3 for a visual understanding of this problem.

What is perhaps more bothersome, at a critical moment, using maximum power, the pilot must put his head in the cockpit and determine which of a variety of parameters (typically, N_1, TOT or Q) which is the limiting one, and what must be done about it. If the torque has to matched manually, a decision of which engine to increase or decrease must be made. Having made the decision, he must change something, see if the change had the desired effect and repeat the process. Not ideal, and it's easy to see how a pilot could not use all the power available at a critical time.

* and I think we're already too busy...

Left Side vs. Right Side

So, for a twin engine helicopter is it safe to assume that both engines will be the same in terms of operating efficiency, performance and so on? Sometimes yes, sometimes no. For example, the A109C model has a slight, but noticeable difference in performance from the left to the right engine due to the inherent sideslip in forward flight affecting the intake on the right side more than on the left. I can't speak for all types, as I haven't studied them all, but be aware that one side may run hotter than the other for a number of reasons such as previously mentioned. Other issues such as age of the engine, state of the compressor and so on may mask or accentuate the differences. The differences may be small, but evident to the discerning pilot.

Multi-engine helicopters are slightly different than their multi-engine propeller driven seized wing brethren. Some twin piston-engine fixed wing airplanes have the engine on one side that is more critical than the other for failures. I don't mean one engine will fail more frequently, but rather that from a performance and handling point of view, the engine on one side may have more pronounced effects than the engine on the other.

While which engine fails doesn't really matter too much for most multi-engine helicopters, for some it is an issue. Despite the best efforts of airframe engineers and power-plant integration specialists, the engine on one side may perform differently than the engine on the other side. The reason is that the airflow around the helicopter is very complex and the engine intakes may not been optimized for the airflow differences between the two sides. (Marketing wouldn't like the left and right sides to look different...)

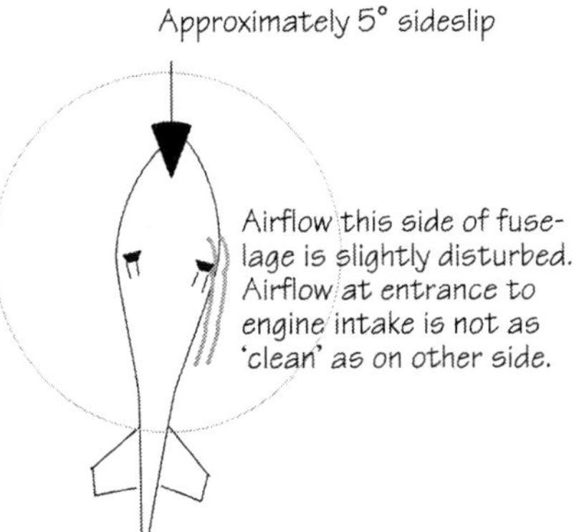

Figure 32-4 Left Side vs. Right Side Engines

The end result is that in some machines the left engine and the right engine may have slightly different characteristics of performance. This may show up as different power assurance figures or different procedures for the two engines. Of course, if you have three engines, and one of them lies across the airframe...

OEI PERFORMANCE

Level Flight

An interesting exercise can be made for multi-engined helicopters from a power required chart. Nearly every multi-engined helicopter has higher power available during single engine operations than when both motors are working. If the helicopter can't hover on one engine, what is the minimum airspeed that the pilot can maintain before he must descend in order to maintain a slower airspeed*? This is an interesting speed, because the pilot who is forced to land

* Yes, you read that right-

following an engine failure needs to not only maintain airspeed, but if he must also descend, he's got to stop the rate of descent as he gets close to the ground, and that takes power he may not have without bleeding off N_R. See Figure 32-5 below.

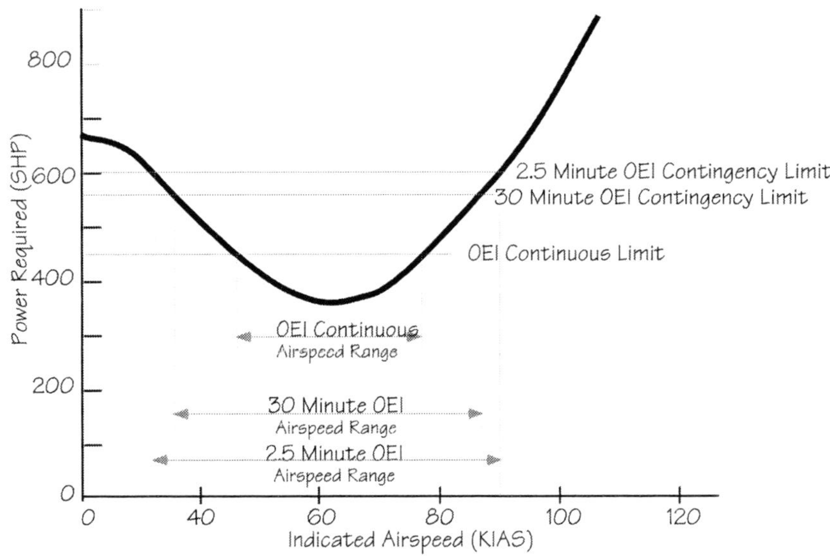

Figure 32-5 OEI Power vs. Airspeed chart

...and less than Level Flight Performance OEI

Descent performance is of interest if you are flying at high altitude in a twin engine helicopter and you lose one engine - you may have to go more slowly, but you also may not have enough power to maintain the desired altitude. What are your options? What can you do?

A drift–down rate of descent would be nice to know so you can tell air traffic (if you are IFR) or for any one of a variety of other reasons. (Will you miss the mountains ahead?) Again, you might be lucky enough to have these charts in your flight manual, and can refer to them when you've had the engine failure. (you weren't single pilot IFR when the engine failure happened were you??)

Best Angle of Climb Airspeed (Again)

As discussed in "Best Angle of Climb Airspeed" on page 255, there is an airspeed for maximum climb angle when the power available does not permit a vertical climb. This airspeed is the one to be used after the engine failure, until you are well clear of the ground and can go for the maximum rate of climb airspeed, or, if Category A, when the height for the second segment climb is reached. Power to be used for this maximum angle of climb portion should be the contingency rating for as long as it is permitted (i.e. may be 30 seconds, or 2 minutes).

Recovering Some of the Power

Most multi-engine helicopters have a requirement to turn off the bleed–air services following an engine failure. This is just the sort of thing a pilot is likely to forget at a busy time, and should be made automatic. There is a problem with this though, and it has to do with cold weather.

For example, you are flying between Frozen Mukluk and Frostbite in the middle of winter. It's -20°C, and no sun is visible thanks to low clouds and snow showers. You are crossing a large body of ice-floe covered water when one of the normally reliable engines in your Twin-Flinger helicopter decides to eat itself. You don't have to land immediately (in fact, couldn't if you wanted to...) and you have to press on to your destination. Immediately that the engine failed, the automatic bleed air dump worked and cut the heater off. But it is cold outside, and the windshield is starting to get pretty little frost patches on it. Even with the good engine putting out maximum permitted torque, the TOT is still miles away from a limit. But the automatic bleed air dump won't let you turn the heater on - what do you do???

In the winter, it is not normal for the engine to be operating near N_1 or TOT limits, even in an OEI condition. If the helicopter has had an engine failure and is required to fly home, it won't be able to use the heater or windshield defroster. Not a great piece of thinking. It should be possible to over-ride any automatic inhibitors of bleed valves, or permit the pilot to use the heater in cruise conditions.

OEI Airspeed Range

The easy part of multi-engine helicopter flying is determining the airspeed range (as restricted by power available) - easy, that is, in theory. In real life, the variables and charts are not always readily available. Remember the Power Required vs. Airspeed chart for OEI, Figure 32-5? It was for level flight only, not climbs or descents. What is the pilot to do who is forced to land on a spot in a no–wind situation following an engine failure with this combination of power required and available? The answer is that he had better be very precise in his application of power to stop the rate of descent, and not use all the power just to go slower.

Of course, there is one major supposition in this chart - namely the power available. Most multi-engine helicopters have different power levels available for emergency conditions. We will simplify the discussion and consider only two - a contingency OEI power rating, usable for a short period of time; and a continuous OEI rating. For level flight, obviously the continuous power rating would be used. The highest contingency rating is for short periods of time only. If the new 30–second limit can give a very large improvement in payload, and you need to be able to use it only to get to the safe climb speed, or to make a safer landing to a spot in no–wind then it's worth it any extra price you pay for it.

Engine Failures in Multi-Engine Helicopters

Just like fixed–wing multi-engine pilots have a more difficult life than fixed–wing single–engine pilots, multi-engine helicopter pilots with more than one engine have a more difficult life. Engine failures on departure and approach can cause large problems in both cases.

Engine–Related Emergencies

One of the main problems with multi-engine helicopters has to do with the various ways the engines can cause problems and how the pilot needs to be able to sort them out quickly.

Basically, the engines can fail in one of three ways- quitting, freezing in power output, or running away up. In each situation, the symptoms will be slightly different, and in the heat of the moment may be confusing. Consider that the pilot has only two main instruments, rotor / N_2 speed and torque, that he must consult before making a decision as to what has happened and what he must do about it.

Engine failures are pretty straightforward- the engine has stopped producing power. THis has been covered in detail elsewhere.

Having an engine 'freeze' in power output is one of those emergencies that shouldn't happen, but it has intruded on my flying twice. In both cases the engine 'froze' at a high power setting, and lowering the collective resulted in the rotor RPM going up. It was necessary in both cases to shut the engine down, and in one case only the fire handles would shut it down.

If engine failures and freezes were the only things that could happen, things would be relatively straightforward. In "...And Sensor Failures" on page 304 we discussed the possibility of a single sensor in most engines causing the engine to runaway up, but giving indications in the cockpit that were less than clear.

The situation related earlier is more severe in a multi-engine helicopter, as the other engine will be trying to the best of its ability to maintain the N_R (or N_2). To do this, the unaffected (good) engine will reduce power as much as it can.

To refresh your memory, this failure is the loss of the power turbine (N_2) speed signal to the governor. It will cause the bad engine to go to maximum power (the governor thinks the power turbine speed is too low and adds all the fuel it can to the engine) while showing cockpit indications of zero power turbine (or N_2) speed, high torque, TOT and N_1 on the affected (bad) engine. The other, perfectly functioning (good) engine has indications of low torque, TOT and N_1 (power turbine or N_2 speed on the good engine may or may not change to follow the bad one).

Typically, the result of the N_2 sensor failure is that engine producing all the power it possibly can, and going to that power level very rapidly. It is not uncommon for such a failure to run the engine to maximum power in less than 2 seconds. To complicate things, the signals given to the pilot are even more confusing - the engine at high power probably has the N_2 needle at zero in the cockpit. When you really look at what will happen in the cockpit, the situation becomes downright frightening- the engine with the failed N_2 sensor engine has gone to maximum power, the 'good' engine has gone to minimum power to try to keep the rotor RPM under control. The bad engine has high N_1, high TOT, high torque, but no N_2. If the bad engine has a mechanical overspeed protection system in the N_1 part of the fuel control, it may come into play just about the time the pilots recognize they have a problem - the bad engine, the one with the high values of everything, shuts off. The good engine, which has been trying desperately to keep things under control by going to as low a value of fuel flow as it can, is now suddenly asked to produce all the power. To make matters worse, the pilots have probably just pulled up on the collective to try to bring the high rotor RPM under control...

How can the pilot quickly and easily determine what has happened? Which engine is good and which is bad?

I wish I could claim credit for having invented this easy method, but someone in the US Coast Guard showed it to me. It is simple and only requires looking at one gauge:

- High N_R - High Engine Bad
- Low N_R - Low Engine Bad

Simple, easy to understand, and foolproof. I have tried to find fault with the logic and can't. So, if the N_R is higher than it should be, the engine with the high indications is the one that needs to be taken care of. If the N_R is low, then the engine with the low indications is the bad one. The rest of the emergency procedures are going to change from helicopter type to type, but are relatively easy to sort out in comparison to figuring out which engine is the one giving grief.

FADEC vs. Non-FADEC Engines

One of the major changes that has occurred in the last three years has been the advent of FADEC. See "FADEC" on page 311 for more details, but for the multi-engine helicopter, it has made a huge difference. In the old days, multi-engine turbine helicopters had engines with OEI ratings that were not significantly higher than twin engine operation. It really didn't seem to make a lot of difference to the performance, and some twin engine helicopters were pretty anemic in their OEI performance. Training for OEI was a pain, either because special training stops were fitted to the good engine, or the student pilot spent so much time looking inside worrying about the 'good' engine, that the benefit of training for OEI was often minor. You also had to worry about the good engine in an real OEI situation, as if you demanded too much power, the engine might well blast past limitations and literally kill itself trying to maintain 100% N_R.

Now FADECs have come along, and given huge improvements in OEI performance - in the order of 25 to 30% more power than continuous OEI for the important first 30 seconds. Payload now becomes believable and commercially viable again. Life has meaning. But there is a bit of a downside- you have to protect this 30" rating for when it's really needed. In fact, the regulations that govern helicopter certification (FAR 27 and 29) require that 30" power not be available to the pilot unless the other engine has failed or has had a precautionary shut down. I'll repeat that - with an engine with 30" power, that power must be protected so it is not, repeat *not* available unless the other engine has failed or has been shut down as a precautionary measure. So don't expect to be able to use the throttles to simulate engine failures and still get the same performance as you would in real life. The engine controls should have a logic that says something to the effect- "we know the other engine hasn't failed, it's only at idle, and so you will only get the 2 minute power level."

I had occasion to be checked out on the Polish W-3A, and part of the check out naturally included lots of engine failures at takeoff, and Category A procedures. I deliberately left one engine failure simulation until much later in the takeoff profile than I should have. The space we had set out for ourself was quite small, and after the safety pilot had 'chopped' the engine, I realized this could be quite a sporting event.

In any non-FADEC equipped helicopter, I am sure we would have burned out the good engine, and made a mess of the landing as we would have been more worried about the engine limits than in flying the helicopter. This machine had superb fuel controls, and I decided I wasn't going to look inside, just fly the machine and see what happened. I knew it was not possible to overtemp or overspeed these engines. The landing was comparatively smooth. We only drooped the N_R a few percent, and I was truly amazed. The future was here.

It also is extremely comforting to know that in an engine failure situation in a twin engine helicopter you aren't pulling the insides out of the good engine. With a FADEC, the pilot can concentrate on looking outside and let the computer monitor the limits.

Maximum Power Available all the Time

FADEC engine controls permit all the power from both engines to be used all the time. When one engine reaches its limit of TOT, its power is held and the other engine is then able to run up to its limit as well. Easier on the pilot, but only if the logic in the FADEC is set up this way.

Training Mode In FADEC Engines

One of the things that will certainly change is the way engine failures will be simulated - anyone who reaches up and grabs a throttle and yanks it back may be unpleasantly surprised. (One engine's 30 second OEI ratings conservatively cost about $2,000 per second.) From a flying point of view, expect smoother, more rapid response to power changes, rock solid N_2, and less worry about the limitations being exceeded.

Most helicopter airframe manufacturers and engines have installed special Training Mode switches on engines with FADECs. The purpose of this switch is to artificially lower the limits of the 'good' engine, so as to keep away from the expensive, super–contingency limits. When training, merely flip the switch to the Training position, and it runs down that engine, and limits the other one. There is also the added side effect of the computer automatically overriding the switch if it senses that the good engine has failed. Very comforting*!

Category A or Category B?

This subject causes a lot of confusion. For those who have only flown single engine helicopters, you can think of what you have done as Category B - that is, you are going to land (and quickly too) if the engine fails. A multi-engine helicopter can be either Category A or Category B, depending on the certification basis, weight and many other variables.

Category A is the way of "ensuring continued safe flight at all times in the event of the loss of an engine." It's the helicopter equivalent to the large fixed–wing transport category of aircraft, which can survive an engine failure at any time during the flight. Whether you knew it or not, every time you get into a commercial jetliner, you're in a transport-category airplane, and we're trying to do the same with big (and some not-so-big) helicopters.

In order to provide some benefit to having more than one engine in the helicopter, it is necessary to provide a way of surviving an engine failure at any time during the flight. The most critical time is usually in the hover or immediately after climbing out of the hover. To permit the helicopter to continue the flight (or to land) safely from this condition, the remaining engine(s) must provide quite a bit more power than normal. Most multi-engine installations provide about 75% of the power available at the AEO takeoff rating. The problem with this is the weight and fuel consumption of the engine suffers by operating at lower power than its design point in normal operations. The most common current engine limitations for OEI are 30 minute and 2.5 minute, but FADEC engines have 30" (super–contingency if you like) and 2' contingency ratings. The additional power is enough to get the helicopter out of trouble following an engine failure, and yet not over-design the engines.

* Especially for me, as one of the two real engine failures I've had was when we were OEI, and the good engine quit! Wish it had a switch like this!

Using this technique, it should always be possible to land safely immediately or fly away and land safely some other time, it stands to reason that there may be a penalty in maximum weight, and hence payload. Depending on the operating regulations and the ambient conditions, the departure or approach profile may have to be altered to take this into account, or the payload or weight restricted.

For this reason, a different series of performance charts has been produced. In certification terms, it is called a Category A procedure and calls for a lot more calculation on the part of the pilot, and determines payload (and revenue) for the existing conditions of wind, pressure altitude and temperature, dimensions of the clear area, height of obstacles, and so on.

There may be several of these charts, depending on the helicopter and the takeoff/ landing area to be used. In general terms the areas can be:

- Wide open areas with suitable landing areas in the takeoff direction (Long runways)
- Not so wide open areas, but still large enough to have some landing area (Short runway)
- Ground level (or very slightly above ground / water) heliports with only a small area available,
- Elevated heliports (such are rooftops, oil rigs, etc.) that have a drop-down area in the takeoff / overshoot flight path.

Each of these will have a different takeoff and landing procedure, with different weight limits, different flight profiles different things to consider. Each will be dealt with separately.

For one helicopter the Category A Flight Manual Supplement is nearly as thick as the main manual, and has tons more performance charts.

Common Points About Category A

There are several items which will crop up in each of these different scenarios. These are:

Takeoff Decision Point or *TDP*	Prior to TDP, if an engine failure occurs, the helicopter is landed back at the hover point or runway.
	At or after TDP, if an engine failure occurs, the helicopter continues on the OEI takeoff path
Landing Decision Point or *LDP*	Prior to LDP, if an engine failure occurs, the helicopter can do a balked landing, or may continue on its flight path to touchdown
	After LDP, if an engine failure occurs, the helicopter must be landed.
V_{TOSS} or *Takeoff Safety Speed*	The OEI speed used in the first segment climb (typically to 200' Above Takeoff Point)
Segment Climb	1st Segment- flown at V_{TOSS} to 200' Above Takeoff
	2nd Segment - flown at Vy to 1,000' AGL
Balked Landing	A landing which is rejected.

Figure 32-6 shows a typical Category A takeoff profile for a long runway.

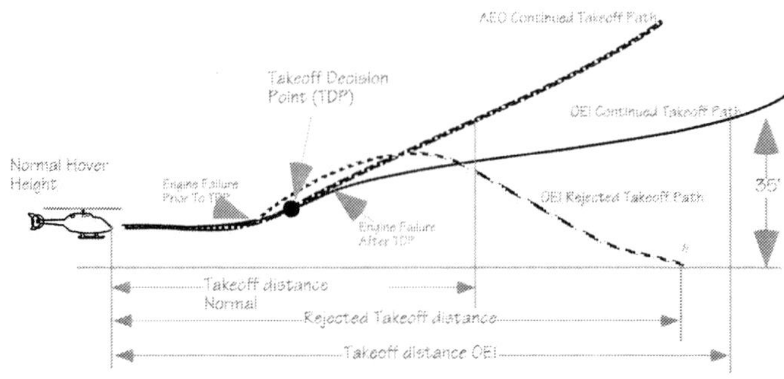

Figure 32-6 Typical Cat A Takeoff Profile - Long Runway

Using Everything You've Got

If you carefully analyze helicopter operations, an interesting difference emerges from fixed–wing flying. Helicopter pilots normally use only as much power as they need to get airborne, and fixed–wing pilots use maximum power to get airborne*. This has introduced an interesting twist to the multi-engined helicopter takeoff procedures.

A difference from the normal 'only–use–minimum–power' philosophy is that for some Category A procedures, notably the 'long runway', the power that *must* be used is takeoff power (or some specified increase above power required to hover). This is in order for the process to be repeatable for different pilots, and to ensure that the profiles and performance is attained.

Prior to TDP, if an engine fails, it is obvious that the maximum OEI contingency rating of the remaining engine(s) will be used to cushion the touchdown. If the engine fails at or after TDP, the contingency ratings will be used to get to V_{TOSS} (Takeoff Safety Speed), and then to V_Y. When the helicopter is at V_Y, the 30 minute OEI power will be used for climbing. (On newer FADEC engines, with the 30 second and 2 minute ratings, the procedures will be slightly different.)

Different Profiles

One of the things to bear in mind is that the performance will differ depending on the situation. Each of the situations below requires a different set of performance charts, and will give different payloads for the same atmospheric conditions. Helicopter pilots have nearly the same task as airline pilots in this regard†.

Short Runway Profile

Note the profile shown in Figure 32-6 -is for a long clear area ahead. The profile for a shorter runway is not significantly different. In both these cases, the same decision process is made.

Ground Level Helipad

One of the important points to consider here is that you need to have clear areas for the takeoff (and overshoot for landing) as you obviously cannot descend below the level of the helipad. A ground level helipad may not always be on the ground- it means there isn't any altitude that can be used safely to help with the OEI profile.

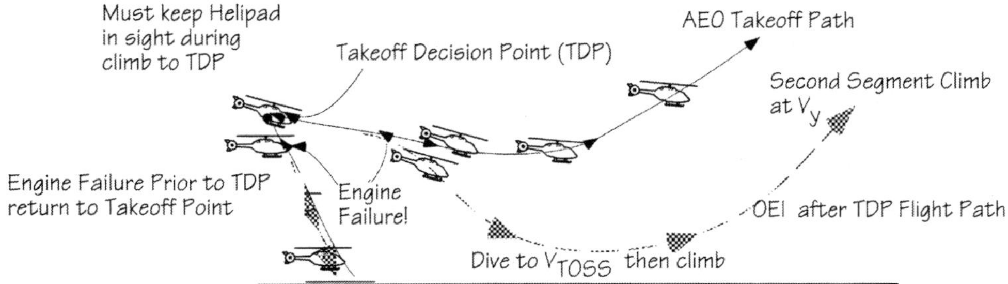

Figure 32-7 Ground Level Helipad Profile

Elevated Helipad

An elevated helipad permits the use of drop-down to assist in the OEI profile. Normally, a minimum clearance of 15' from the obstacles in the flight path are required. If you're doing this on the top of a skyscraper, then the 15' clearance is probably a moot point, but if it's from a 5 story parking lot in the middle of a built-up area, the obstacles in the flight path become

* There are exceptions in the FW world for noise abatement or increased engine life.

† Actually, more difficult. Most airline pilots don't do these calculations- their operations section does it for them.

important. Not a good idea to have to thread between smokestacks while trying to milk the last ounce of power from the engine... If the drop down height is restricted, then there should be specific instructions in the FMS about how to calculate the payload for the drop down available.

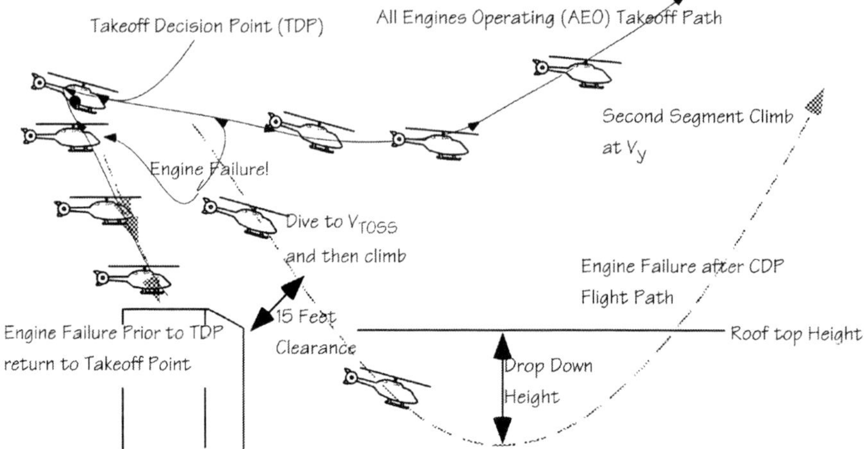

Figure 32-8 Elevated Helipad Profile

Approach and Landings

If the engine fails prior to landing, it should be no big deal. Not so fast! Things are still not simple, and a specific profile needs to be flown in order to ensure safety. Up to the Landing Decision Point (LDP), shown in Figure 32-9, if an engine fails, a go–around can be accomplished with a minimum safe clearance from the landing site. The powers used are the OEI contingency power ratings and the airspeed as published to get to V_Y. If an engine fails after the LDP, the profile is slightly different from normal, in that the OEI contingency power is used to cushion the touchdown.

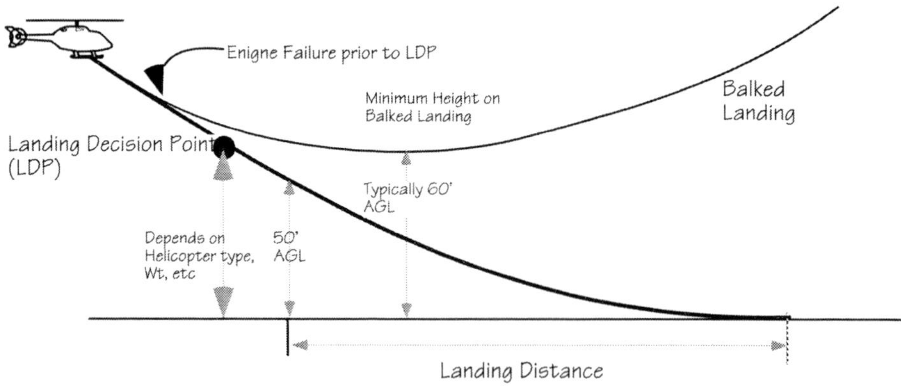

Figure 32-9 Landing Decision Point for OEI Condition

The Cat A procedures are not simple. The pilot has a lot to do - determining the takeoff distance available (particularly if operating from an unfamiliar site), knowing wind speed (if there is no air traffic agency to report it), height of obstacles and distance from the point of departure and arrival, air temperature at the arrival point and so on - in short, all the sort of things available at a major airport. As most helicopter pilots are aware, not all these things are known with the precision needed for accurate determination of performance, yet if anything happens, the pilot is likely going to be held responsible.

Use of Contingency Power

If you have an old-fashioned hydro-mechanically governed engine, with 2.5 minute and 30 minute OEI ratings, the answer is simple- there isn't any limit on the number of times you can go to 2.5 minute power. But the price you pay is a lot of pilot workload to monitor the engine, and not a lot of difference in power above the continuous limits of the engine. On the other hand let's assume you've had a single engine failure in your multi-engine ExecBus helicopter, with one of the latest FADEC engines with a 30–second OEI power rating, and you're operating it from the executive yacht. How many times in one flight could you need to use this contingency rating? Those who say only once, or even twice don't have the evil, twisted minds of those in the regulatory certification business*.

The worst case to consider is an engine failure at the TDP on departure from the executive yacht, and then a less–than–perfect approach, which requires a go-around for another approach, followed by a successful touchdown†. If the manufacturer has put a limitation on the number of times (lets call the number is 'n') this contingency rating could be used in the life of the engine, then to dispatch the helicopter on a mission, it must have n–3 cycles remaining - one for the first failure to get safely airborne, one for the missed approach, and one for the final touchdown. Each cycle is considered to be 30 seconds long. The price you pay for the greatly increased power is that when you use that rating, maintenance will be required.

General Criteria for Takeoff Techniques

Whichever type is used, it would be reasonable to expect that it was:

- simple
- safe
- repeatable by all pilots
- provide reasonable performance
- provide minimal risk and exposure time in high-risk areas

Heliport Takeoff Techniques

The techniques used in Category A procedures for heliports are different for each helicopter, and sometimes for different models from the same manufacturer. I'll call the three types:

- vertical–climb
- back-up
- 'sideways slide'

Each has its advantages and disadvantages, its proponents and opponents. Unfortunately, the FM for any one type of helicopter will typically only be based on one technique. Naturally, all the performance will be based on that type.

Vertical Climb

This maneuver has the helicopter climb vertically to a set height above the hover point and then transition to forward flight. It has the advantage of using takeoff power in its most efficient way (going straight up) and giving the pilot time to set takeoff power accurately. It also will probably provide good altitude data for deciding the Takeoff Decision Point (TDP) since the radar altimeter will be getting a good signal from the landing pad below. It gives the passengers a thrill to lift off like a rocket, as well.

The disadvantages of the technique are that should an engine fail before TDP, the pilot has an extremely poor view back down to the landing pad- which is straight below the helicopter. From 100 feet AGL or so, this may mean the heliport is not in sight without some other references. It also means the helicopter is descending vertically, which in a calm wind situation, can mean vortex ring state is a possibility, but shouldn't be likely as this technique has been tested and approved by the RA. The technique also means that a large vertical descent rate is developed which only the good engine can arrest, and this may not be sufficient to stop a high rate of descent that is misjudged. In general, these procedures aren't really great for night operations.

* I've had the therapy course since I left, so I'm cured!
† Followed by a large, stiff drink

Back-Up Technique

This technique has the helicopter backing up while climbing to the rear until it reaches a set barometric height above the heliport. This has the advantage that the heliport is always clearly in sight, and into wind (most Category A profiles have a limitation that requires the profile to be flown into wind). If the engine fails before TDP, it is a simple matter to drive back down the line to the helipad. Barometric height is used as the radar altimeter may not be giving good height information with respect to height above the helipad.

The disadvantages are not as many as for the vertical profile, however it does take some practice to get to know the sight picture for the back-up angle. It also requires considerable practice to use takeoff twin engine power while backing up, and the transition from backing up at takeoff power to transition to forward flight must be made briskly, which may not amuse Mr. Corporate passenger in the back. Takeoff power is used which will make the ride pretty brisk for the new passenger.

For the rearward profile, the helicopter uses takeoff power to climb backwards, and then once the TDP is passed, the nose is put to a specified pitch attitude to accelerate into forward flight. If the engine fails prior to TDP in this technique, the pilot has only to fly back to the hover point- down the same line he has just backed up

'Sideways Slide' Technique

This technique involves moving laterally away from the helipad, while climbing, and at some distance laterally from the edge of the pad, making the decision to continue, or to return.

This has the advantage of being not significantly different than 'normal' departure techniques, of not requiring a rush to set takeoff power settings, and of not pointing the helicopter at what may be the only obstacle around. At any time up the TDP, it is easy to slide back to the pad, and either land facing the same direction as the helicopter was facing, or turning into wind.

From a more technical standpoint, this procedure is easier than the others for the following reasons:

- the roll axis has a much lower moment of inertia than the pitch axis of the helicopter, so it is easier to change the roll attitude than the pitch attitude
- the roll axis has a much simpler response to control inputs than in pitch (there are few air-speed changes involved, but cyclic longitudinal pitch control activity in a backwards technique is very high). There are less long-term effects in roll than in pitch
- The field of view to the side and slightly down is pretty good in most helicopters, where the field of view over the nose in some machines can be pretty bad, and the field of view straight down is also not very good unless you have bubble side windows.
- The field of view to the side is less dependent on the pilot's eyes being set at the Design Eye Point (which isn't as well defined in helicopters as it is in fixed wing airplanes).

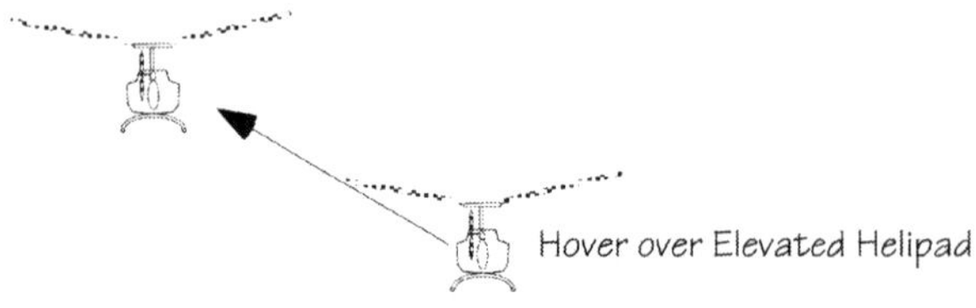

Figure 32-10 Sideways Slide

Where to Practice Single Engine Techniques

In simulators...

At an airfield where there is a long, into–wind runway or taxiway. Mark out an area that defines the helipad or heliport you are considering duplicating.

Reduce the weight of the helicopter to something you know you can safely handle on one engine.

With a FADEC installation with a training mode.

Summary of Chapter 32

This chapter has covered the complications and benefits that arise from a multi-engine helicopter. Like fixed wing Multi-engine aircraft, life only becomes more complicated when you add another engine. The overall level of safety goes up, and with new technology of FADEC engines, there is little loss in payload to operate out of very unusual areas. As these engines become more common on light twin-engined helicopters, and customers become aware of the benefits, we should see an increased demand for this type of equipment.

Stability and Control of the Helicopter

Don't be put off with the title of this chapter. We are not going to be exploring the mysteries of 4th order aero-elastic stability derivatives, just a brief outline of some of the ways the helicopter actually flies. Besides, "Life is too short to try to understand helicopter dynamics.*"

The first and most important part is to understand weight and balance in more detail than in Chapter 7,"Balance and Weight".

Weight and Balance

Weight and balance affect the helicopter in a much different manner than the fixed–wing aircraft. For example, the fixed–wing concepts of static margin (CG position with respect to mean aerodynamic center of the wing) are replaced by control margin (amount of rotor control remaining) and cross coupling effects. It is important to remember in a helicopter, the center of gravity has three distinct aspects - longitudinal, lateral and vertical. Other factors such as forces and moments generated by rotors and fuselage aerodynamics are often not symmetrical with respect to the CG. Before more detailed discussion about weight and CG, a few words about its calculation.

Weight and CG Calculations

A similar problem to in–flight performance calculations mentioned in Chapter 25 pops up with CG. Away from base, or in a rapidly changing situation, how does the pilot figure out his CG? Will it be within limits for the whole trip?

Most civil authorities require that CG be calculated for every trip, using the actual weight of passengers (instead of a standard weight like airlines use). Again, does our poor pilot, trying to earn an honest living:

- guess;
- get out the book and actually go through the motions of calculating the CG (unlikely, unless pressed);
- pre-calculate whether full fuel and how many passengers (or full passengers and how much fuel) will put the helicopter out of weight and CG limits (more likely the most common solution);
- or ignore the regulations and hope nothing happens?

Not calculating CG has led, in many cases, to not worrying about weight either.

Why not have a simple device like the one below? It was designed to be put onto 2 pieces of clear plastic, and, following the instructions, used to calculate the weight and CG - not only for a given condition, but also for every stage of the flight.

It works by first starting with the basic weight and CG, and then moving the scales over one another to add the passengers, fuel, etc. to see what the end result is.

In the example below, the fuel calculation has been shown twice - once in the normal calculations, and later on as a 'worst case' check. This second, worst case check is in light grey and is at the top left of the chart. It shows that as fuel burns off from the most forward CG condition, that the CG will always stay within limits. I know of no other way to check this easily.

* Ray Prouty

We discovered that one configuration of our military helicopters (UH-1N) with door guns and passengers would be outside CG before we got to minimum fuel - only by use of this device. If we had tried to do this manually, I'm sure we would still be in the office with the piece of paper and a pencil, and wouldn't have even thought about fuel burn.

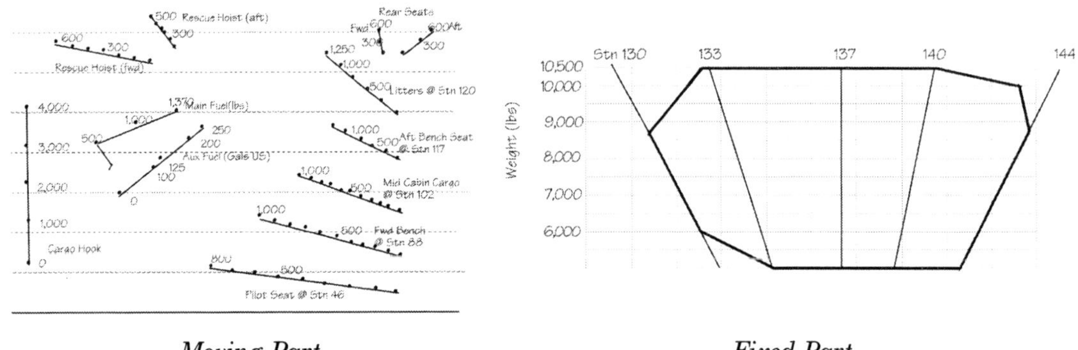

Moving Part *Fixed Part*

Figure 33-1 Weight/CG Calculator

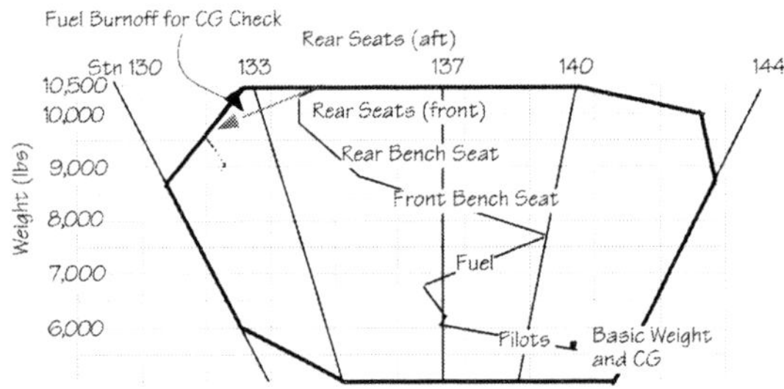

Figure 33-2 Final Result of Using Quick CG Calculator

Weight and Balance Effects

The effect of the position of the CG will be immediately obvious whenever the helicopter lifts to the hover. It will be reflected by the position of the flight controls. In a zero–airspeed hover, the rotor disk must be horizontal with respect to the earth's surface, and the fuselage will take up whatever attitude it needs. In forward flight, the main rotor needs to be tilted to an angle corresponding to the airspeed, regardless of the fuselage beneath it. For example, 120 KIAS of airspeed may require 200 pounds of forward thrust to counteract the drag. Of course it is not as simple as this, as the CG and fuselage aerodynamics and load on the horizontal stabilizer will all affect the fuselage attitude, which in turn affects the drag (more nose–down attitude equals more drag in most cases), but the point is made.

Lateral CG

Lateral CG is changeable in many helicopters, but is often ignored. Several flight manuals provide limits for the range of lateral CG, but provide no way of calculating it. Lateral CG affects the amount of lateral cyclic needed to maintain the fuselage level in the hover, and the amount of inherent sideslip occurring in ball-centered, wings level flight. See "Lateral CG" on page 66.

Vertical CG

The vertical position of the CG is perhaps more difficult to understand. It's never mentioned in any manuals, is never calculated, and doesn't appear to change very much.

Doesn't CG act vertically? - if so, isn't its vertical position immaterial?

When viewing the helicopter from the rear or side, the position of the tail rotor and fuselage area above and below the CG becomes apparent. How could the vertical CG could be changed? Put the gold from Fort Knox on the floor - or put lead lining over the belly pan for radiation protection - these would lower the CG considerably. Underslung loads also change the vertical CG dramatically.

INHERENT SIDESLIP

Inherent sideslip got its name because it is built-in, and part of the helicopter, and normally, there is nothing you can do about it. Figure 7-12 on page 71 shows the balance of forces in a top view in forward flight.

Inherent sideslip is another side* effect of the tail rotor, only it shows up in forward flight. The tail rotor is still pushing the helicopter sideways, and with the 'wings' level, the helicopters flight path has a sideways component to it. The amount of inherent sideslip depends upon the CG position (vertical, longitudinal and lateral), the weight, power setting and so on. Typical values are 3 - 4°. Obviously, if the helicopter is being pushed through the air sideways, there is a drag penalty to pay. This is one reason why some manufacturers put a slip string in the helicopter, so the cruise can be flown with minimum drag. Others advocate flying with the slip ball in the same position it was in the hover, and my experience with this school of thought is that is easy to do and makes for much less drag. Flying with the ball in some arbitrary non-centered position may not be the least-drag condition, and is best backed up by a slip-string.

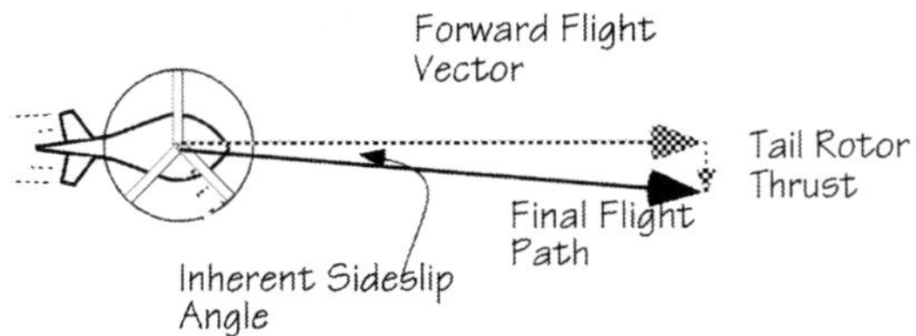

Inherent Sideslip

Some helicopters rig the attitude instruments and slip ball to automatically compensate for inherent sideslip - on level ground, the attitude indicator shows 2 or 3 degrees of tilt, and the slip ball is not centered. In flight, with the 'wings' level, and the slip ball in the middle, the helicopter actually is in a one–'wing'–down situation, but with minimum drag. Evidently when this was tried on one attack helicopter, the crews complained about feeling like they were flying with a tilt when the ball was centered (which, of course they were) - they could see this in the horizon being at an angle with respect to the canopy rails as well.

CROSS–COUPLING OF CG EFFECTS

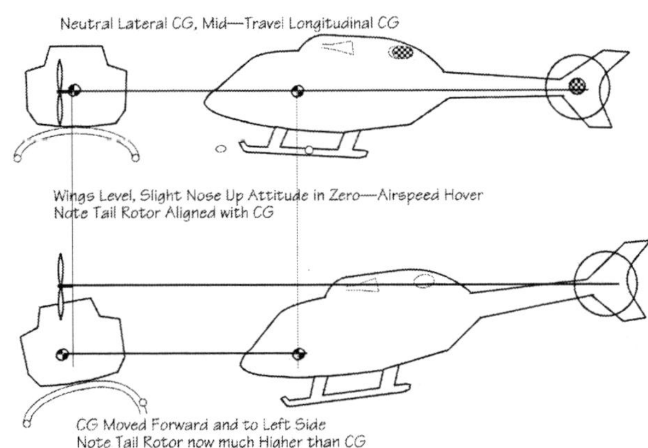

Figure 33-4 Cross –Coupling Effect of CG Movement

The position of the CG has a very large effect on the overall scheme of helicopter flying, and it is difficult to think of it in just one axis. For example, moving the CG to the left causes the fuselage to tilt to the left in the hover, and will thus change the vertical position of the CG, moving it slightly lower. Moving the CG to an extreme longitudinally also changes the pitch angle of the fuselage, which changes the vertical position of the CG with respect to the main rotor hub and the tail rotor hub. The coupling between these the CG and the sources

* Sorry about the pun

of moments acting at the CG is worth thinking about very carefully. Figure 33-4 shows how moving the CG in the longitudinal and lateral axis affects all the axes. In the second case, the tail rotor will now produce roll whenever its pitch is changed, which it would not in the original.

In another example, the AH-64 Apache can carry external fuel tanks, and if it is required to carry just one, (a non-symmetrical load) it must be carried on the right side. If the single tank is put on the left side, there is a significant penalty in tilt and drag in ball–centered flight. This is also one reason why the R-22 is flown solo from the right hand seat.

*Keel Area Ratio, or Weathercock Effect**

The concept of the area of the fuselage acted upon by a side wind was mentioned before, but needs to be explained in more detail. One term used to describe this is *keel area ratio* and comes from sailboats and nautical design. The wetted area ahead of the keel needs to be less than the area behind the keel or the boat will want to sail backwards. This was expressed as a keel area ratio. Some people call it *weathervane* or *weathercock* effect.

In helicopters, we need to worry about the ratio of the two keel areas ahead vs. behind the CG; as well as above and below the CG. Obviously as the CG moves, it affects both ratios. If we add fixed floats under the helicopter, we add a lot of area under the CG. The effect of this will be explored more fully later. Figure 33-5 shows the keel area effect.

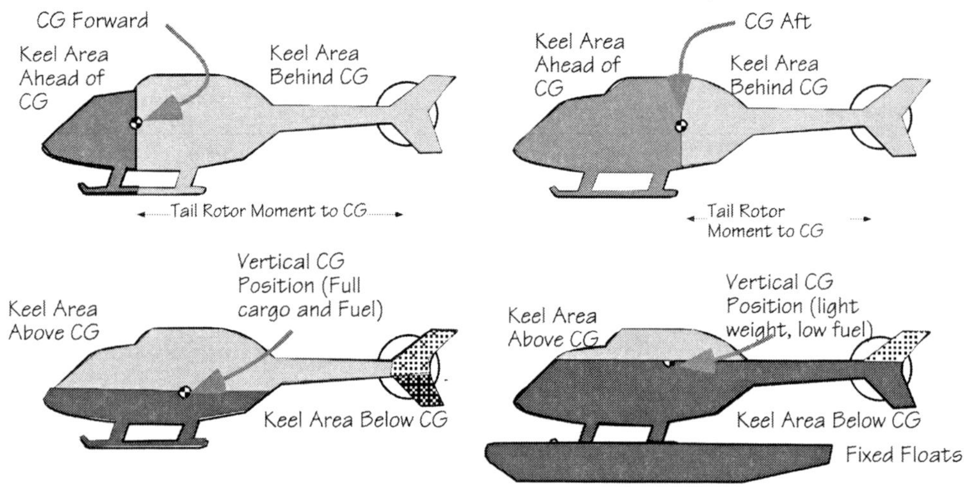

Figure 33-5 Keel Area Effects

Combining the keel area ratio effects with the balances of forces and it is easy to see why CG position is important. At a forward CG, there is less keel area in front of the CG than behind it, plus the tail rotor has a longer moment arm to the CG. With the CG aft, the keel area ahead of the CG is greater in proportion to the area behind (and so less stabilizing), and the tail rotor has a shorter moment arm. Since the distance the longitudinal CG can move is actually quite small, its effect on directional stability is relatively small, but when combined with the change of the moment arm to the tail rotor is significant.

Fixed Floats Effect on Stability and Control

The greatest effect of fixed floats is on how the helicopter handles with them fitted. In this case, the area below the CG has been increased dramatically. From a rear view of the balance of forces, any side wind (due to sideslip in forward flight or hovering with a crosswind) will have a pronounced effect. Hovering with side winds will be more or less predictable, except if you really look at the lateral cyclic position,

* It depends on which side of the Atlantic you live on as to which term you might want to use. If you have an agricultural or nautical background could also influence your choice of terms.

it may be opposite to what you expect - with a right wind, you may have left cyclic to maintain position. The effect with sideslip in forward flight is very interesting. See Figure 33-6 for a more graphical view.

Figure 33-6 Helicopter With Fixed Floats

If you enter an autorotation in a light helicopter with fixed floats, and try to be very precise keeping the slip ball in the middle, the result (at least in one type) is a circus of lateral cyclic and pedal movements. On the other hand, if only one pedal correction is made to keep the ball approximately in the middle, the result is no lateral cyclic activity. Why?

The reason has to do with the keel area below the CG. Figure 33-5 above shows the helicopter and its CG without floats, as well as the area added below the CG by the fixed floats. Since the floats do not weigh very much, the CG doesn't move down, but the keel area below it is increased.

When the collective is lowered, the helicopter yaws and a small amount of sideslip (side wind) is produced. Let's say that the sideslip comes from the right as the helicopter yaws. Since the floats are well below the CG the effect of this side wind is greater on the area below than on the area above the CG. This pushes the floats (which are well below the CG) to the left, which rolls the helicopter to the right. This is not the direction of roll normally expected (or wanted) with a right sideslip (technical term for this is negative dihedral). Left stick is needed to stop the roll, which in turn generates a left sideslip that generates left roll, and the circus starts. The clue here is to put the ball near where it's wanted and accept a slight out of balance condition.

If you wish the above description in more technical terms, the area below the CG increases the Dihedral effect and can lead to an unstable Dutch Roll. Fixed–wing aircraft on floats often have additional vertical fins to increase directional stability to cure the Dutch Roll problem - but I've never seen them on helicopters with floats.

Flight Controls

Having milked the CG position and balance of forces for all they're worth, it's now time to move on to how the helicopter is controlled.

Friction Systems on Cockpit Controls

Ah, friction systems - another hobbyhorse of mine. Friction systems are fitted to most light helicopters as a way of preventing the cyclic or collective from moving when they shouldn't. As such, they are acceptable, but are prone to wear, mishandling and over-tightening, and never seem to work really well. A friction setting that works for one pilot doesn't work for another, and with any friction applied making small, rapid, precise movements is difficult. About the only place they work acceptably is on collectives.

It's worth repeating the earlier statement that fixed wing airplane designers spend a lot of effort getting rid of friction in their control systems, and helicopter designers get asked to put it in.

Viscous Damping of Control Systems

Some times it is possible to move the cockpit controls faster than the helicopter can safely respond. A good example of this is the yaw axis. Early versions of the S-58 had a relatively under-engineered tail rotor and drive system. It was possible to add pedal so quickly that the tail rotor changed pitch more rapidly than induced velocity could follow. This gave an angle of attack at the blade that was above the stall AoA, and the tail rotor literally stalled. This large rise in drag was more than the drive system could handle and drive shafts were damaged. The solution was to reduce the speed of movement of the pedals. In another machine, the skin would literally be ripped off the tail rotors with large rapid pedal inputs. Strengthening the tail rotor blades only moved the problem to the join between the tail boom and the rest of the fuselage. It was necessary to introduce a way to stop the pilots moving the pedals so quickly, and a viscous damper was installed. It works much the same way as the shock absorber in a car. Figure 33-7 shows a damper* installation†.

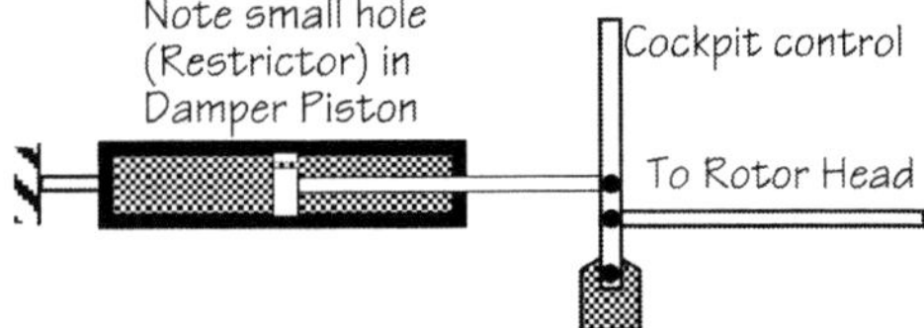

Figure 33-7 Typical Viscous Damper

Control Mixing

Some helicopters have very complex flight control systems, and have a lot of mixing built in to the mechanical controls. For example, mixing may change tail rotor automatically as the collective is raised. This sounds like such a good idea, one wonders why it isn't fitted to every helicopter. Unfortunately, aside from complexity, mechanical mixing can only ever be optimized for one weight and CG condition. If the weight and CG are different from this design point, the mixing will produce unwanted effects. Far better (and cheaper) to pay pilots to compensate.

Equations of Motion

There are not going to be any great explanations of equations of motion in this book. If you are interested, may I suggest the books by Ray Prouty, Simon Newman, Gareth Padfield*f* or Wayne Johnson listed in the Bibliography? Equations of motion are the way the helicopter reacts to inputs and gusts, and a large part of the whole story of how a helicopter flies. Equations of motion are difficult to understand without lots of studying, so we'll pass on, happy in the knowledge that those who need to know, know.

Control Margin / Limitations on Controls

The flight controls in the helicopter are not of unlimited travel, and have specific design points. In other words, characteristics of controls may determine some of the limitations of the helicopter and vice versa.

The extremes of weight and CG travel permitted in the FM may be due to the limitations of the controls. Obviously, one of the most important items in determining control margin is the type of rotor head - a teetering rotor head must generate all its moments by tilting the tip path plane relative to the fuselage, while a hingeless rotor can generate large moments by very small movements of the tip path plane relative to the fuselage.

Note *You should never be repeatedly hitting the control stops when flying any helicopter anywhere. If you are, look carefully at your CG.*

Head and Mast Bending Moments

In an articulated or hingeless rotor, there may be stresses transferred to the hub and mast that are large enough to warrant limitations. These stresses are due to blade forces being transmitted across the various hinges. For example, the lead–lag hinge can only permit movement and remove stress in the lead–lag plane, so it transmits forces due to flapping and feathering.

Both the BO-105 and BK-117, (hingeless–rotor helicopters) have a separate instrument in the cockpit to show mast bending moments. This gauge is used specifically for slope landings, but also shows stresses when maneuvers are carried out. The EC-135 has such a gauge, but it only shows up when it is needed. Clever.

* It's called a yaw damper in this installation. But be careful- in a fixed wing aircraft a yaw damper does something completely different.

† Other manufacturers just ask the pilot to be gentle....

Even teetering–rotor helicopters can be subject to this problem- the Bell 206B has an airspeed limitation for takeoff power (80 KIAS maximum if the power is above 75% torque) due to bending stresses that higher power settings impose upon the mast.

Longitudinal Cyclic

The fore/aft location of the CG has a large effect on the position of the longitudinal cyclic in all phases of flight. Figure 33-8 shows the position of this control for two different CGs when the helicopter is trimmed in level flight, climbs and descents. Note there is also a very large effect of collective or power on the control position. Depending on the type of rotor head, it is usual to design the cyclic to have some margin of control remaining at the maximum design speed and aft CG to counter gusts, etc. - there is a line drawn to show this. In this case, at the maximum forward speed there is 10% of forward cyclic remaining. In other helicopters, the minimum margin of control may be with a lateral CG and a side wind.

Other ways to interpret this diagram are that (for this helicopter) a CG change requires a large change in cyclic position, and that when the collective is moved from climb to descent, the pilot must make quite a large change in longitudinal cyclic position to maintain the same airspeed. Other helicopters, with different types of rotor heads might be very different.

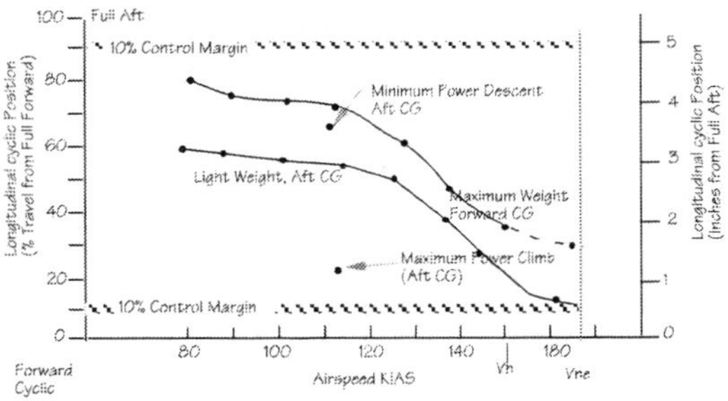

Figure 33-8 Longitudinal Cyclic Control Positions at Steady Airspeeds

Forward Cyclic

The two conditions when this is critical are typically maximum forward airspeed, and hovering with a wind from the right hand side, both with aft CG.

Aft Cyclic

Much like the forward cyclic, this is often at a minimum with an extreme CG, except that maximum rear wind is of concern with forward CG. Often the critical condition for this control is aft CG in a cross wind, due to the effects of transverse flow. Another design point is for a quick stop or autorotative flare, or an approach to the hover with a tail wind.

Lateral Cyclic

It should be obvious that lateral cyclic must be sufficient to generate a suitable rate of roll and to take care of the maximum design side wind at an offset lateral CG, but what about slope landings? One machine has a slope landing limit that is demonstrated in maximum side wind, worst case lateral CG.

Up Collective

Not normally a problem, as the transmission and engine should be the limiting factors in this area. I have found one helicopter where I needed to use all the collective to cushion the touchdown in an autorotation. There is another that needs nearly all (95%) the collective travel possible to hover, and yet another that runs out of collective in forward flight, before it reaches torque limits.

Down Collective

Full down collective is used on the ground (Flat Pitch) and in many helicopters in autorotation (but not all helicopters autorotate with the collective full down). Adjusting the minimum blade pitch angle, either by use of the pitch links or within the flight control runs, is used to set the rotor RPM in autorotation. The stabilized N_R in autorotation is checked against a chart of weight and density altitude to ensure the blades are adjusted correctly. See Figure 8-7 on page 79.

Tail Rotor

Just like the longitudinal cyclic, it is possible to plot the position of the tail rotor (or pedal position) with different wind directions and velocities, as shown in Figure 34-12 on page 382. The longer bars represent the activity the pilot was making to try to maintain the condition - the reasons for this activity will be explained later.

Left Pedal Remaining

This margin is often reached in right side winds, at maximum weight and aft CG. Two things related to CG gang up on the tail rotor. First of all, there is more side (or keel) area ahead of the CG. The wind acts on the whole side of the fuselage through the CG, and it wants to point the side with the greater area downwind (like an arrow). In more technical terms, the ratio of keel area ahead of the CG vs. behind the CG at its worst. Adding to the problem is the moment arm of the tail rotor to the CG is at its lowest, since the CG is closest to the tail rotor. The combination of a low moment arm, and worst keel area ratio means the tail rotor has to work its hardest here.

The design point for maximum tail rotor thrust is typically 30 knots of wind from the right side.

Right Pedal

The worst case for right pedal margin (or minimum thrust if you prefer*) is a turn in a high speed autorotation. There must be enough tail rotor to keep the ball in the middle in a 30° bank turn at $V_{NE\ Auto}$ This is one of the reasons for a separate $V_{NE\ Auto}$ in at least one helicopter.

Lesser Known Effects

Cross–Coupling

Cross–coupling is the term used when a control input in one axis shows up in another, undesired axis. For example, the pilot wishes to increase airspeed, so the stick is moved forward. The nose of the helicopter goes down, but it also rolls slightly. The pilot corrects for this subconsciously, but it is still an apparent effect. The reasons for the cross coupling are many and varied, ranging from control system characteristics, to aerodynamic and altitude effects. The professional helicopter pilot should be aware they exist.

Lock Number

This number (symbolized by γ) represents the ratio of the aerodynamic to inertial forces of the blades. It is one source of cross coupling. The formula is

$$\text{Lock Number} = \Upsilon = \frac{\rho \times \alpha \times c \times R^4}{I_b} \qquad \text{(EQ 32.)}$$

where

ρ = air density

α = lift curve slope for the blade

c = chord of the Blades

R = Radius of the blade

I_b = moment of inertia of the blade

The number itself isn't important. (If you look at the formula, all the items except air density are fixed at manufacture.) What is important to realize is that it is the difference between the aerodynamic forces acting on the blade, and the inertial forces. As the helicopter changes altitude, the aerodynamic forces on the blade change, and so does this ratio†. At high altitude, say 18,000', the density of the air is much

* Or perhaps you might like to know it as maximum thrust in the opposite direction to the left pedal.

† I hope the blades don't change radius or moment of inertia.)

less (50% of sea level), so the Lock number is half that at sea level. The blades will react much differently at altitude than at sea level, and for multi-bladed helicopters, the controls will not only feel more sluggish, they will produce very large off–axis responses. The two bladed rotor system just feels more sluggish, but since its phase angle is always 90°, it experiences very little difference in off–axis response.

Most helicopters are designed to operate at relatively low altitudes, and the controls are set up for those conditions. The phasing of the control arms is set for a Lock number that corresponds to those sort of altitudes.

If a multi-bladed helicopter such as the Gazelle is climbed to 18,000', moving the cyclic in pitch (back and forth) will also produce a response in roll - in fact, the ratio of roll to pitch can be quite high - I remember about 25% of the pitch response showing up in roll in this case.

I don't like to guess, but this may have been one of the contributing reasons the Soviets lost some Hinds in Afghanistan. There were reports of the Hind simply chopping off its own tail when turning hard. The logic works like this. The phasing and control system of the Mi-24 were set up for a variety of conditions, but one characteristic was that the flight controls had to be moved not just straight back and forth when airspeed changes were made, but also with quite a large amount of lateral re-trimming. (This helicopter isn't the only one with this - several Western ones have it too). When maneuvering hard - i.e. rolling rapidly the pilot thus had also to make some pitch corrections to maintain the airspeed. At high altitudes, this problem is made worse, and it may happen that rolling rapidly in one direction would add some nose up pitch the pilot didn't expect, increasing the G loading, and putting the helicopter into retreating blade stall, which could have caused the blades to flap back and chop off the tail... (OK so maybe it didn't work like this, but Lock number could have played a part.)

Lock number is one of the causes of cross–coupling, but the effect is only noticeable at very high altitudes, and is only apparent on articulated or hingeless head designs.

Rotor Head Type Effect on CG Range

Earlier ("Hingeless Rotor Heads" on page 232) mention was made of the hingeless rotor. It has a benefit of being able to transmit large forces when the stick is moved, which gives it very high agility. It also has another feature, namely the ability to handle very large changes of the center of gravity. More simply stated, an articulated rotor helicopter will need x% movement of the tip path plane to generate a moment due to CG, where a hingeless rotor helicopter will need perhaps one-tenth that movement (or 10%).

Solving Aerodynamic Problems

Aerodynamic problems abound on helicopters. There may be too much directional stability, too much power required on the tail rotor in the cruise and so on. Some very clever ways of dealing with this have been found. A good rule of thumb is that any aerodynamic device you see added to the back end of the helicopter is there to solve a problem. These can range from *Gurney flaps* (small pieces of metal bent at 90° to the airfoil at the trailing edge of vertical or horizontal stabilizers) to air dams and cambered fins. This section will explore some of those 'fixes'.

*"Anything that happens aft of the rotor mast is magic" - Ray Prouty**

Wings

Wings are seldom seen on helicopters, when it is quite obvious if the rotor didn't have to provide all the lift, it could be tilted forward more for higher cruise speeds, as well as improved fuel economy, possibly a better ride, and so on. Why aren't they used? The answer isn't simple.

Wings would need to be set on the fuselage at a specific angle to produce useful lift. As previously mentioned, the pitch attitude of the fuselage will depend on the flight condition and the CG. The range of CG movement possible in most helicopters means the fuselage angle may be different at the same airspeed, so a means of changing the wing angle for CG would be needed.

Secondly, wings create vertical drag in the hover, the very thing helicopters were built for. One experimental model of the Chinook had a set of wings that tilted to a vertical position in the hover to reduce the downwash load (or vertical drag).

* Who can't remember saying this in as many words, but it's the sort of thing that he would likely say.

Thirdly, the aerodynamic center of the wing must be placed at or close to the rotor mast to prevent adding any pitching moment as the lift changes*. This is normally somewhere near where the cabin is, so it is difficult to make the structural provisions. Of the helicopter manufacturers who have tried wings, none have put them into continued production - only one model (the Mi-10) has them, and if anyone would use something that worked, it's the Russians. The things you see for carrying missiles on most attack helicopters aren't airfoil shaped for good reason.

Another, slightly more bureaucratic reason was given to me for one model of the H-60 with rather large wings to carry fuel tanks. "Well, if they were wings, the Army said they'd have to have de-icing provisions on them, as the helicopter is cleared for flight in icing, so we made 'em blunt as we could. They are not wings."

Rudders

I often wondered why we didn't have rudders in helicopters when it was obvious that this was more efficient than trying to get the tail rotor or fenestron to do the same job in forward flight. Then along came the NOTAR concept, used in the MD520N, MD600 and MD900...

Now we have rudders, controlled by a combination of cockpit controls (do we now call them rudder pedals?) and an AFCS.

Horizontal Stabilizers

The horizontal stabilizer on most helicopters is there to keep the fuselage level in forward flight. Some are adjusted in position by collective and cyclic movement, more complex ones by an AFCS airspeed signal. The end result is the same - a downward–acting force of the inverted airfoil keeps the nose up. Unfortunately, this also causes problems in climbs and descents when the angle of attack is not small. For this reason, most fixed horizontal stabilizers have slots or spoilers to direct the airflow and keep the helicopter well behaved. The inverted airfoil shape and spoilers are used to induce a stall on the stabilizer in autorotation and make the upload as small as possible. This keeps the nose more or less level and reduces the amount of aft cyclic that is needed to maintain airspeed. For more information on horizontal stabilizers and their problems, see Ray Prouty's books.

Some helicopters incorporate elevator movement with the other flight controls, either by a mechanical interconnection or electronically from the AFCS. Mechanically interconnected elevators, (or synchronized elevators), move with the collective and longitudinal cyclic to help keep the balance of forces correct. Electronically controlled elevators are merely more sophisticated versions of the mechanical ones.

It is not unusual to see a different rigging angle between the two sides of the fuselage on any elevator - this is due to different airflow patterns from the main rotor.

Vertical Stabilizers

The vertical stabilizer, aside from being a good place to stick the tail rotor, provides directional stability to the airframe in forward flight. Think of it as the feathers on the arrow to keep the sharp end pointed forward. Some vertical fins have a camber, like an airfoil to off–load the tail rotor, others have a preset angle for the same thing. I have flown one helicopter with no aerodynamic fixes on the back end, a symmetrical vertical stabilizer and a very smoothly rounded fuselage. At aft CG, and high speed this helicopter was definitely squirrely†. The keel area ahead of the CG was trying to take over, and the airflow was breaking away unevenly. Again, for more discussion, see Ray Prouty's books.

End Plates

End plates are added to horizontal stabilizers to overcome a directional stability problem, in much the same way as the vertical stabilizer. There just wasn't enough room to put a big enough vertical stabilizer, and so various add-ons were made. End plates also benefit from operating in relatively clean air, away from the very confused airflow that exists behind the fuselage.

Gurney Flaps and Blunt Trailing Edges

If you look with a discerning eye at the back end of some helicopters, small details like Gurney flaps will come to view. A Gurney flap is merely a small piece of metal at the trailing edge of an airfoil, bent at 90° to the chord. While it looks odd, it works well, by providing a definite place on the airfoil surface

* If the wing were put in front of the mast, any lift would tend to move the nose up, and this is destabilizing.

† A highly specialized technical term used by experimental test pilots, difficult to translate into simple language.

for the flow to separate. The AS 350/355 series, which has gone through several iterations of single and twin engine versions, has a great variety of such shapes on the vertical stabilizer. The early models without the Gurney flaps are much more difficult to keep the ball in the middle than the ones that have them fitted.

Other helicopters noted for speed like the SA-365 Dauphin have a very blunt and decidedly unstreamlined trailing edge to the vertical stabilizer. The reason is similar to the Gurney flap- the flow needs to separate at a definite point on this airfoil, especially as any sideslip will make the vertical stabilizer produce yaw in an unwanted direction. The drag penalty is quite low, surprisingly. The designers are smarter than we realize.

Tail Boom Strakes

Some conventional helicopters have strakes fitted along the length of the tail boom in a seemingly strange place. The first example of this was the British military versions of the Sea King. This is another example of how complex helicopter aerodynamics can become, as these strakes stop the tail boom acting as a wing.

It seems that some tailboom shapes can generate quite a bit of lift in the wrong direction when subjected to a combination of main rotor downwash and winds from the side. A typical example is shown in Figure 33-9 below. With a wind from the right side, the main rotor downwash was hitting the tail boom with an angle of attack causing the boom to act like an airfoil and produce lift. Unfortunately, the lift was produced 90° to the relative wind, resulting in a large force acting to the left. Since the helicopter was already being pushed to the left by the right wind, this meant more tail rotor and more main rotor lateral tilt was needed than calculated. The pilot actually was running out of tail rotor authority long before he should have. A strake in the appropriate position on the tail boom, spoiled the lifting effect, while not adding any drag in forward flight.

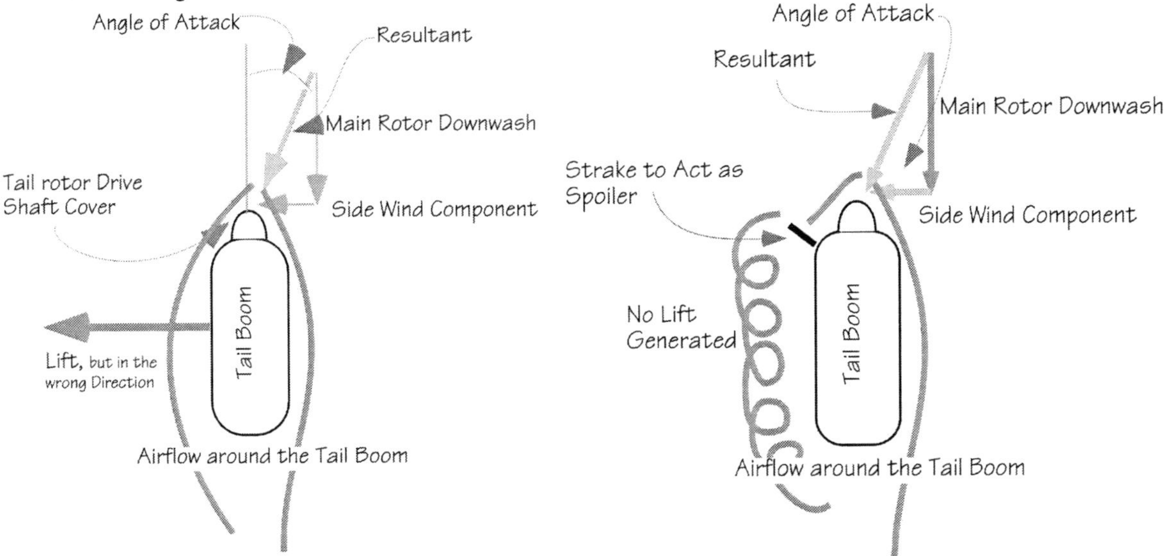

Side Wind Generating Lift (Bad thing)Strake or Spoiler Ruining the effect (Good thing)

Figure 33-9 Strake on Tail Boom

More Aerodynamic Fixes

Other aerodynamic fixes include the small vertical fins on the front pylon of the CH-47, and the air dam on the aft lower fuselage of the BO-105.

How We Control the Helicopter

It is difficult to know how much detail to go into in this section without a long and complex discussion of static and dynamic stability. There are two aspects to flying a helicopter - stability and control. Stability is what we want when we are in a static situation, such as hovering or cruising. Control is what we want when we wish to change things. The two are often mutually exclusive - too much stability, and you couldn't move things. Too much control, and you couldn't stay still. These subjects, while important, deserve their own book. Suffice to say that as pilots, we control the helicopter in three basic ways-

- Small, precise corrections, such as would be found in a hover or cruising flight. These are concerned mostly with assisting the stability of the helicopter.
- Medium–size movements of the controls when we want to change the situation, but not too rapidly. Such a movement would be transitioning from the hover to forward flight. We want a bit of stability and a bit of control.
- Large, rapid movements of the control, such as when you want to dodge a rapidly–approaching bird. In this case, the pilot wants to change things very quickly. This is more concerned with controlling the helicopter than the finer aspects of stability.

Summary of Chapter 33

This chapter has covered a lot of ground. Weight and balance and the hitherto invisible vertical CG position and the balance of forces in all three axis have been covered, as well as a look at inherent sideslip.

Keel area ratios, as well as flight control systems and rotor heads, and the determining factors for some of the limits of controls and flight envelopes have been discussed. A lot of detail has been presented here. Why?

Besides making the book thicker, and make you feel better about having spent the money to buy it, it's there to help explain how we really fly helicopters.

34 Further Peculiarities of The Helicopter

Wherein the author tries to point out some of the more unusual aspects of rotary wing aviation, and expound upon a few pet peeves.

Introduction

Chapter 19,"Peculiarities of the Helicopter" should have explained a few things to the reader. There are more to be uncovered here.

Helicopters are very different from fixed–wing airplanes in the manner in which they fly, the areas they operate in, the way they are used and how the aviation community sees them. Rotary–wing aircraft are truly unrestricted in their ability to move. Their inherent freedom and flexibility also carries some unusual aspects. Since there are quite a few of these unusual aspects, they have been arranged solely in order of likely interest.

Vibrations

Vibrations have been the bane of helicopters since early days. As forward flight speeds and load capability increased, the vibration problems have become worse. One old helicopter pilot, brought up in the days of Sikorsky R-4s remarked that he had only seen helicopters get noisier and rougher as time went on. These vibrations have had an effect on avionics, structures and so on, not to mention aircrew. Vibrations undoubtedly keep a lot of helicopter mechanics employed in keeping the machines at a low vibration level and fixing the results of too much vibration. This section presents a brief overview of the sources and solutions.

Types Of Vibrations

Vibrations in helicopters are typically divided into the way they are felt by the crew generally split into the source, the axis and the frequency. The largest sources of vibration are the main and tail rotors and thus split into low or medium (main rotor source) or high frequency (tail rotor source). Frequency of vibration is further split into 1 per revolution (rev) or n per rev, where n is the number of rotor blades. The axis of vibration really concerns only the main rotor, and is split into vertical and lateral.

It should be clearly understood that the vibration-reducing carried out as a part of normal maintenance of helicopters is only a very small part of the overall vibration spectrum. A quick look through the Journal of the American Helicopter Society will show lengthy discussions about types of vibrations we seldom ever hear about, but which are solved regularly by clever engineers. The phrase “fourth spanwise flapping frequency of a fully articulated blade” ought to give you some idea of the complexity. A physical example of the complexity can be gained by giving a sharp rap with the palm of your hand to a stationary rotor blade and watching the various ways it vibrates.

Determining The Type of Vibration

A rough method of determining which type of vibration is encountered is to hold the hand in such a way to show the axis. To determine if the vibration is vertical, for example, hold the hand with the palm down - if there is a vertical vibration, the hand may nod up and down. If the vibration is suspected to be lateral, hold the hand with the palm facing left or right. If the vibration is a high frequency, it may be felt best by touching the airframe lightly. High frequency vibrations can also put your feet to sleep.

Sources

Main Rotor

The main rotor blades are the largest source of vibration in the helicopter. The blades must produce exactly the same amount of lift and centrifugal force in every phase of rotation. A very tall order, even with the finest manufacturing - blades of different flight time are often mounted on the same rotor head, and even minute differences cause vibration problems. This is why most main rotor blades are provided with adjustments in the pitch change rod length, the trim tab, and balance* weights.

Rather than show the ways a blade can produce vibration, it is perhaps best to show when it will not produce vibrations. First of all, lateral vibrations are caused by inequalities between the totals of mass of each blade multiplied by the distance of the CG of that blade from the hub. Statically, this would show up on a teetering rotor head not being level in a no-wind situation (very rare, except in hangars). With the blades turning, this imbalance is amplified by the centrifugal force, and if there is a coning angle by the vertical position of the blade with respect to the hub. The static balance on a two-bladed rotor is shown in Figure 34-1.

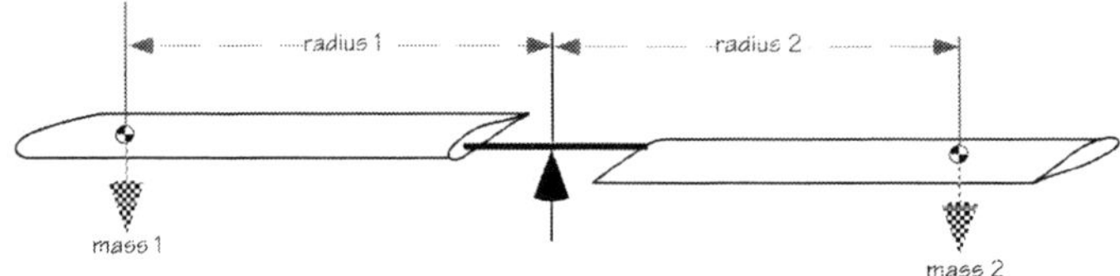

Figure 34-1 Lateral Balance

When the blades are in balance in this sense, then it is time to worry about them producing the same amount of lift at the same place on the disk. A simple explanation of a three bladed rotor with the blades producing different amounts of lift due to the blade pitch angle not being set correctly is shown in Figure 34-2 below.

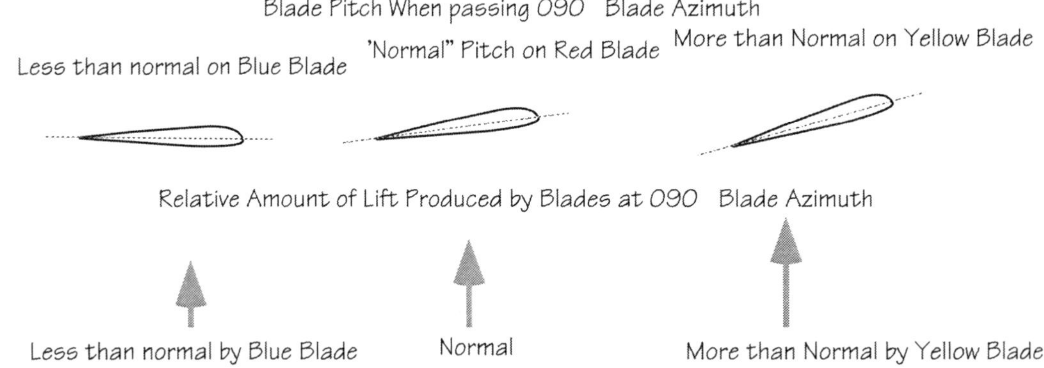

Figure 34-2 Blades producing Different Amounts of Lift

The solution to this is to make the blades produce the same lift at the same place. Methods to achieve this are to change the length of the pitch change rods or to adjust the small trim tabs set on the back of the blades. These are shown in Figure 34-3 below.

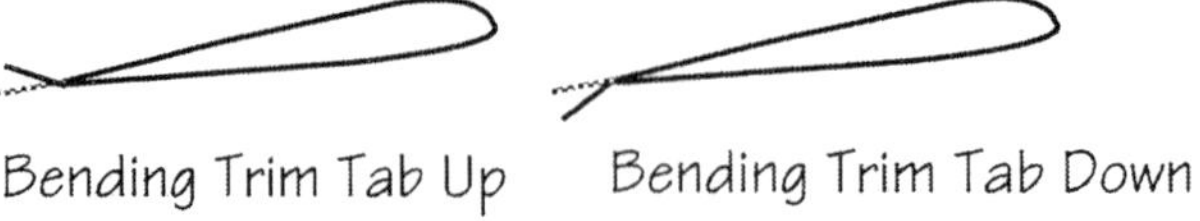

Figure 34-3 Trim Tabs and Adjustments

First, and most simply, vertical vibrations can be caused by the blades not producing the same amount of lift. It is not necessary that the blades be flying in the same place - it is necessary they produce the same amount of lift†. Different amounts of lift probably also means different amounts of drag, which can induce lateral vibrations.

At this point, it is necessary to start with the logic of how main rotor vibration is solved. In this case, let's start with the blades static. For two bladed rotors, the blades need to be mounted in the correct manner to ensure they have the same angle of sweep with respect to the hub. Articulated heads with

* The following notes are very general and may not apply to the specific instructions for all types of helicopters.
† Perfect track but a vibrating helicopter is for those with overly tidy minds.

hinges don't need to worry so much about blade sweep, as the blades will self-adjust. Those rotor heads with rigid attachments, such as hingeless designs, need to worry about this sweep adjustment.

The blades are statically balanced when the product of the weight and the moment arm to the center of gravity from the hub are the same. Note this does not mean the CGs and weights of all the blades are the same - just that the product is equal. Only when the blades are statically balanced* can the next step can be dealt with.

The next step is with the blades at less than full N_R at flat pitch, or Minimum Pitch on Ground (MPOG). The trim tabs on the blades must be set to a nominal value, if they are adjustable. The first method of getting the blades in track, so they are producing the same lift and 'flying' at the same position, is to adjust the pitch change rods.

When the blades are adjusted to all be in the same plane at this lower–than–normal N_R, then the pilot increases the N_R. Any change in the tip position between the blades is now due solely to differences in the aerodynamic properties of the blades. For this, adjustments to the trim tab can be made so all the blades are producing the same amount of lift at the same N_R.

The next stage is the hover. In this condition the lateral balance is now considered. There should be no difference in the lift produced by any of the blades. If the blade is out of balance, it shows up as a 1 per revolution (1 per rev) lateral imbalance, and is corrected by the use of weights in the root (and possibly the tip) of the blade. The lateral imbalance may change frequency and character when the N_R is changed from the minimum to maximum permitted. When the blades are all in balance in this condition, then forward flight is considered.

This is where things become slightly more complex. Any variations between the profiles of the blades may cause the blades to produce different amounts of lift around the disk, and with changing airspeeds. The general way to correct for this is to change the trim tabs on the blades. Note it is not necessary for the blades to be flying in the same plane to have a smooth helicopter. In a perfect world, yes they would all be in a straight line, but...

If there are drag dampers involved in the rotor head, then subjecting them to different loads on different blades exercises them differently, so this may introduce other types of vibrations. There is the possibility that drag dampers can be checked on the ground.

But things are never simple. Let's say we've adjusted the blades so they are all producing the same amount of lift, but have one blade flying at a different height than the others. This will produce a different tip vortex than the others, which will hit the following blade in a different span-wise location, causing yet another vibration source.

Rotor Head Induced Vibration

The main rotor head and rotating components may be the source of vibration. I have had occasion to run several different types of helicopters (Bell 412 and CH-47) without rotor blades†, and was surprised at the lateral vibration some showed. A closer look at the rotor head showed the chief culprit was the rotating scissors assembly, which did not have a counterweight opposite. This out of balance weight would be difficult to compensate for with the limited weight adjustments possible on the rotor head. Several designs include a compensating weight for the rotating scissors assembly, or put two scissors assemblies on opposite sides of the mast.

Tail Rotor As Source of Vibration

The tail rotor operates at a much higher RPM than the main rotor, and is one of the common sources of high–frequency vibrations. An out–of–balance condition here is generally felt through the pedals, or perhaps in the airframe itself. Tracking and balancing the tail rotor is not significantly different from the main rotor. In fact, as it is only conducted on the ground, it could be said to be simpler.

* There are many rotor heads where this is not possible, and it must be assumed that the blades supplied by the manufacturer are correctly statically balanced.

† Yes, without the blades, and yes, the engine governors worked just fine - they keep the N_R under control in a descent don't they - so they should work here as well, and they did.

Vortices from Preceding Blades

Fixed–wing airplanes produce tip vortices in their passage through the air, and helicopter blades are no different - the rotor blades, like wings, produce vortices, they are just a little harder to see in the general flow of air under the rotor. This is shown in Figure 34-4. These vortices do have an influence on vibrations, and in a rather unusual way.

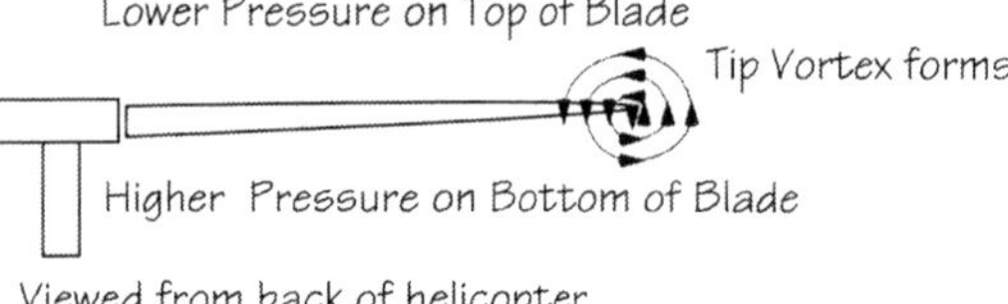

Figure 34-4 Side View of Tip Vortices

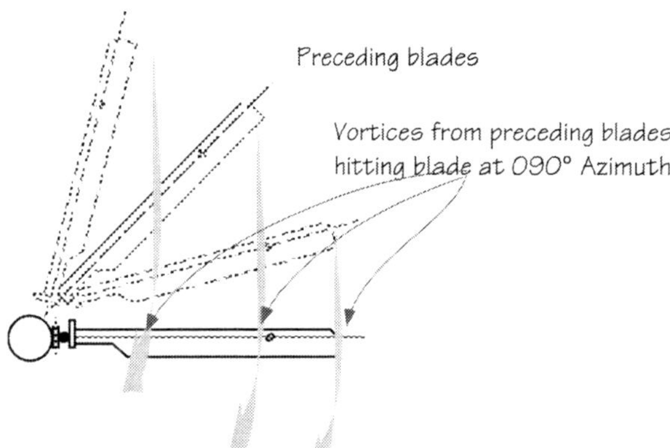

Figure 34-5 Top View, Tip Vortices

If we consider the blades from the 090° position (left hand side, or advancing) to the 180° blade azimuth (front of helicopter) only, we can see that they produce a tip vortex which is shed from the end of the blade. This tip vortex streams directly back* and hits the next blade to come around. In fact, each blade will be hit by a whole lot of vortices from the preceding blades. Up to the 6 previous blades have been found to have an effect. Figure 34-5 shows how these vortices hit the blade. These vortices will hit the blade at different locations along the radius, and may influence the vibration characteristics of the helicopter.

Airframe / Other Sources of Vibration

Often sources of vibrations are other than those caused by the rotor system. A loose set of skids produces a very strange type of vibration, for example. In one other case I know of, a long–term problem on one airframe was solved when an alert maintenance man read of an accident on a similar type where the loose drive shaft couplings were to blame. He found most of the vibrating aircraft's couplings severely damaged. Not only did he solve the problem, but also prevented an accident. This incident can have another lesson- report your problems to the regulatory authorities- you may save someone else's life!

Solutions to Vibrations

This previous discussions talked about solving vibrations from a maintenance point of view. There are other ways to control or eliminate vibrations. In general terms, they fall into three categories: passive, semi-active and active.

Passive Control

Passive control of vibration, aside from proper tracking and balancing of the rotor, is the main way of reducing vibration at present. There are many different techniques, and this is not an exhaustive coverage of them.

* In line with the inherent sideslip I might add.

Pendulum Dampers

Several helicopters have pendulum dampers near the root end of the blade, or attached to the hub itself. They are aimed at a specific vibration characteristic of the blade such as cancelling flapping of the blade that occurs at a higher frequency than once per revolution. Figure 34-6 shows a typical installation. The Kamov KA-32 has them only on the lower blades.

Figure 34-6 Pendulum Dampers

Bi-Filar Absorbers

Another way to reduce vibration is the *bi-filar* absorber. These work by employing heavy weights at the rotor hub. These weights are free to oscillate in a manner which will reduce the vibration from the blades. A typical installation is shown in Figure 34-7

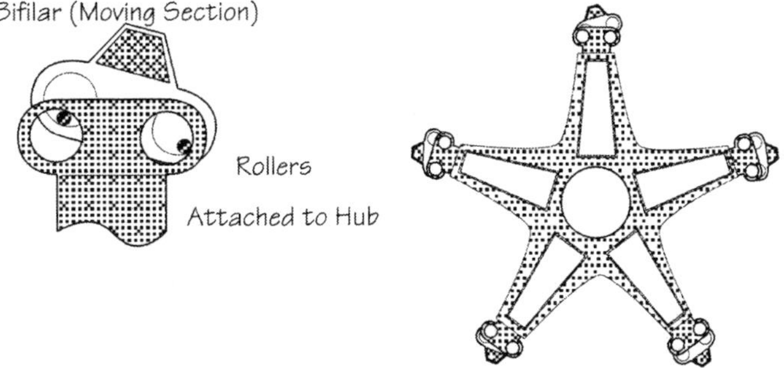

Figure 34-7 Bi-filar Absorbers

Other Vibration Eliminators

Other types of vibration eliminators have been developed, usually installed between the airframe and transmission. The first ones used a mercury–filled damper system which prevents frequencies which happen to be the worst frequencies for that rotor system from reaching the airframe. Mercury has been replaced by a more environmentally friendly liquid and other versions of this technology have been developed. The EH-101 uses a computer controlled mechanically driven system to produce a very smooth ride.

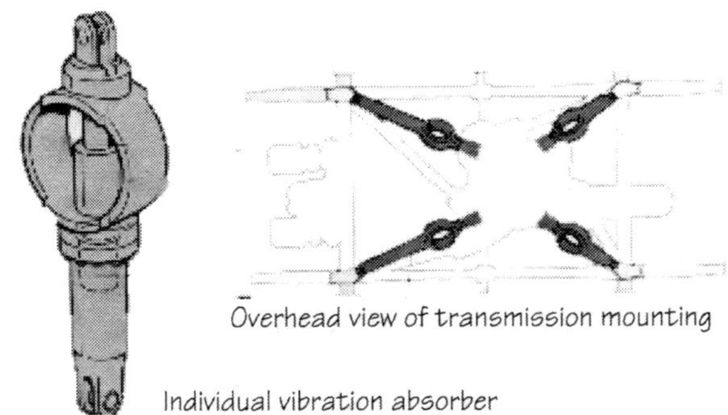

8 EH101 Vibration Absorber

Nodal Beam

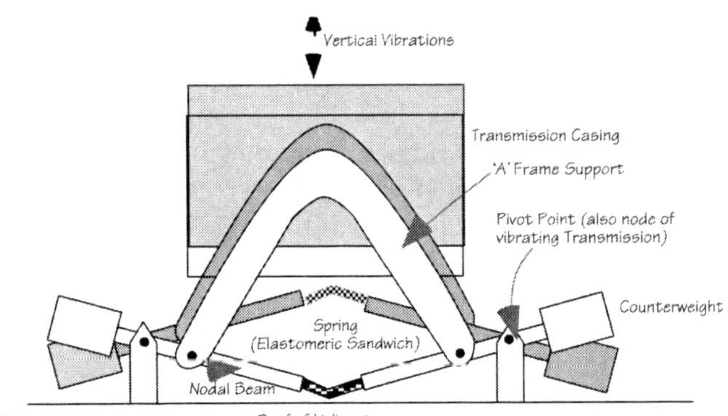

34-9 Nodal Beam Suspension

The nodal beam suspension system permits the transmission to oscillate while the mounts attaching it to the airframe are at the nodes (or non-moving points of the vibration) and see no movement. The fuselage gets a very smooth ride. Figure 34-9 shows a simple explanation of how this system works.

Semi-Active

At the time of writing of this book, semi–active vibration control is on only one helicopter - the EH-101. A sensor measures the vibrations being fed to the airframe, and a computer determines how much to move an actuator to cancel out the vibration. This actuator is part of the gearbox mounting structure. It is called semi-active because it is not acting directly on the blades.

Active Control

Active control of vibration of helicopter rotors has been successful in research, and involves a high speed hydraulic or electrical actuator acting on the rotor head to vibrate the rotor blades precisely out of phase to their normal vibration. The problems with the technology have been the size of actuator needed for the very high rates of movement. It may be a part of future machines. It is often known as Higher Harmonic Control (HHC).

Solving Track and Balance Problems

The old way to get rotor blades in track was to use a tracking flag and grease pencil marks on the blades. Surprisingly, it worked very well when conducted by skilled personnel. Unfortunately, not many people got a chance to get skilled at it, and many accidents happened. It also only worked on the ground.

The next step in the evolution was the strobe light and vibration sensor. This permitted the blades to be balanced in flight. The strobe light was not easy to use, and had the disadvantage that it wasn't as accurate in determining the blade track on the ground. (the tracking flag could show fractions of an inch difference, whereas the strobe light target was only readable to within one inch or so). Balancing a rotor took several flights, with only one adjustment per trip.

The current stage in the evolution is the tracking lens and vibration sensor. This combination permits all the calculations to be made in one flight and then all the corrections to be made at once. It is extremely accurate, and measures blade position to within one millimeter.

Ground Resonance

Ground resonance is a phenomenon of multi-bladed (i.e more than two blades) helicopters, and is due to the CG of the rotating blades getting off center. It happens typically during start-up, but it can happen on lift–off, or touchdown. The situation deteriorates rapidly, and if encountered, usually ends up with a pile of broken helicopter parts. The explanation which follows is a very simplistic one. Simon Newman's book has a particularly good section on this subject.

On Start-up

The problem with starting a multi-bladed fully articulated rotor helicopter is that the lead–lag hinges of the helicopter may position the blades at some strange combination of angles, resulting in the CG of blades not being on the center of the hub. See Figure 34-10 below for an example of evenly–spaced blades with their CG aligned with the rotor hub, and some blades with drag dampers which are not evenly spaced.

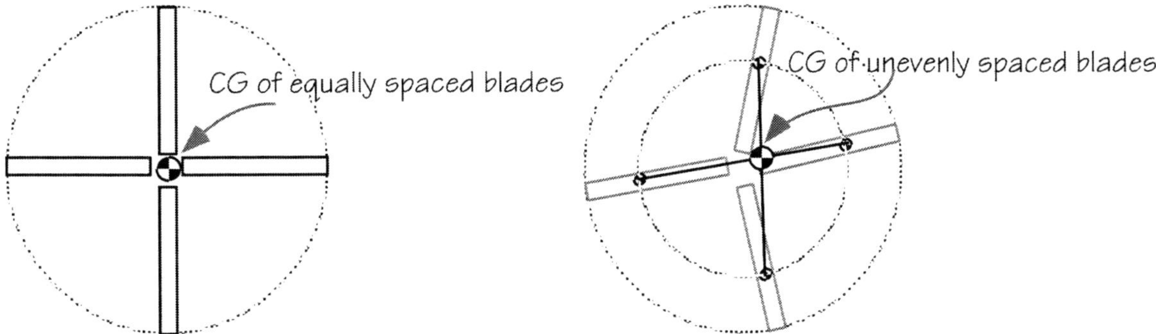

(a) equally spaced blades(b) unequally spaced blades on start-up

Figure 34-10 CG of Static Rotor Blades

When the blades start turning, the centrifugal force of rotation should quickly sort out the blade radial position, moving the CG towards the middle. The CG path then could be described as a decreasing spiral. This is shown in Figure 34-11a below. If something happens to move the CG outwards, such as a bad drag damper on a blade, or a landing gear leg that collapses or responds incorrectly then the situation deteriorates very quickly as the CG moves outward as shown in Figure 34-11b.

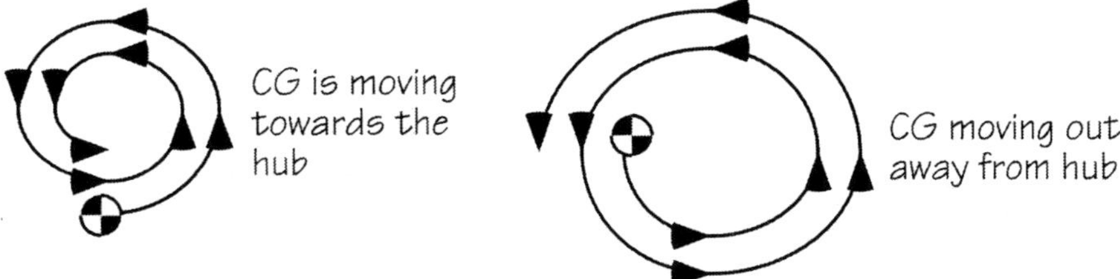

Convergent Blade CG - Good thing Divergent Blade CG - Bad Thing

Figure 34-11 Convergence and Divergence of CG for Ground Resonance

Symptoms of ground resonance on start–up are a divergent padding (i.e. slow wallowing from side to side or back and forth). The best advice that could be given is to either shut down immediately (and use the rotor brake regardless of the N_R - it's cheaper than replacing the whole helicopter) or, if possible, lift off.

It should be noted that as the rotor accelerates from zero to 100% N_R it goes through a vast range of frequencies that can, and probably will excite the fuselage. The chances of hitting a 'nasty' frequency if you landing gear is not set up properly is therefore pretty high. Another reason why helicopter designers are so highly paid (wishfully).

The reason for lifting off is to remove any interaction with the ground. Obviously, if the problem is more with the blades than the landing gear, lifting off won't solve the problem. Exactly how you should sort out the cause at a time when things are not going your way hasn't been determined...

One helicopter I flew, the Saunders-Roe Scout, (and I can use the past tense as they've all been retired, thankfully) used to have a procedure as part of the pre-flight which was there solely to prevent ground resonance. It was required to put on the rotor brake and walk or push each of the four fully articulated blades to the back of travel against their drag dampers. This ensured the blades were all evenly spaced and the total blade CG was in the middle of the hub. Evidently early in its life this machine had a problem with ground resonance on start–up and this was one way to solve it. I have tried this technique on several other multi-bladed machines which had some slight padding on start up, and it stopped this peculiarity in each of them as well.

In short, dampers on the rotor head and on landing gear are the two main ways of preventing ground resonance.

Resonance During Landings or Takeoff

In the in-between part of these maneuvers, when part of the weight is being taken by the rotor and part by the wheels, there is a time when the landing gear oleos are fully extended and not able to provide any damping. This is a time to be aware of the possibility of resonance, especially if there is a sharp lateral cyclic input.

Ground Resonance on Touchdown

The problem is similar to the start–up - the CG has moved away from the center of the hub and is diverging outwards. The causes are slightly different - possibly the pilot gets into a Pilot Induced Oscillation (PIO) laterally - one wheel or skid touches down and bounces up, the other one bounces at just the wrong time and so on. If there are shock absorbers in the landing gear, they could be out of adjustment, or tire pressures could be wrong, and so on. The result is that the combination of fuselage motion and rotor CG motion get out of phase. Again, if possible, lift off and don't move the lateral cyclic once in the air. This is, of course, the most general type of advice possible, and will not cover every situation, but knowing what causes the problem will go a long way to preventing it becoming disastrous.

When lifting off or touching down with the landing gear oleos fully extended, the helicopter is most prone to ground resonance. The landing gear struts cannot use any of their damping characteristics to help remove the unwanted motions that are set up.

A sharp bounce on one wheel can also upset the equilibrium of the rotor and set off ground resonance. Beware!

Tail Rotor Control

"Control Margin / Limitations on Controls" on page 368 discussed the control margins remaining, including the tail rotor and several other sections have talked about the piloting aspects of tail rotors. There are some parts of the relative wind envelope where tail rotor control is definitely not as crisp as it could be. Why is this? The answer lies in a rather detailed explanation.

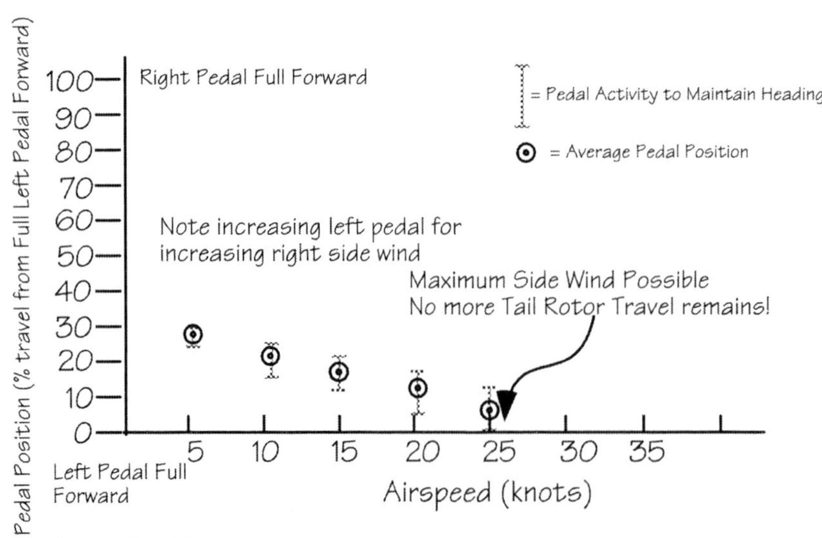

Figure 34-12 Tail Rotor Position vs. Wind, 090° Relative Wind

Figure 34-12 shows the tail rotor position vs. wind for a case where the handling could be called 'good'. That is, maintaining a specific heading with different wind speeds from the same relative direction is fairly easy. Note how there is an increase in left pedal required as the wind speed from the right hand side increases. As the increasing wind tries to turn the nose into wind, more pedal is needed to keep the nose pointing in a particular direction. The bars in the diagram indicate the pedal activity needed to maintain heading.

Before we talk about the 'bad' case, let's look again at the case shown above where tail rotor control is very predictable. Hovering with a wind from the right, let's say the pilot encounters a gust which increases the speed from 10 to 12 knots from the right. The nose of the helicopter wants to swing to the right, into the wind, and the pilot wants to retain the original heading. A small amount of left pedal is needed to stop the yaw rate, and as it takes more left pedal to hold the helicopter on heading with 12 knots than 10 knots of wind, with a few minor adjustments, the pilot is able to cope with gusts from this direction with little or no problem.

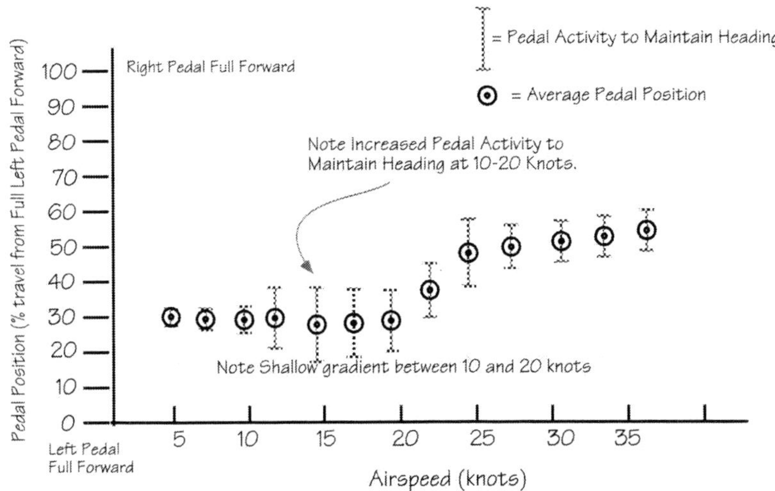

Figure 34-13 Tail rotor Control Positions, Relative 225°

Figure 34-13 shows the tail rotor position vs. wind velocity for a typical light helicopter which suffers from a problem* in holding heading. This is for wind from relative 225°, that is coming from the left rear of the helicopter.

Notice how the bars, indicating control activity are quite large at about the 10 knot position. Notice also how the 'trim' or steady state position for the speeds between 10 and 15 knots don't change? The two items are very related.

Imagine the pilot hovering, with everything stable, in 10 knots of wind from relative 225°. A gust up to 12 knots comes along from the same direction. This gust wants to turn the nose of the helicopter to the left, towards the increased wind. The pilot wants to retain the original heading, so some right pedal is added to bring the nose back. Unfortunately, because the pedal position for 12 knots of wind is just about exactly the same as for 10 knots of wind, the pedal added (i.e. enough pedal to stop the yaw rate) is too much, and the helicopter keeps turning right, past the desired heading. The pilot adds left pedal to stop the yaw rate and get back to the original heading. Unfortunately, the amount of left pedal is also too much, and so on - the pilot will end up dancing on the tail rotor for a very long time, and never get settled down.

So what does all this mean? It means that if you have a helicopter with a tail rotor and main rotor (as opposed to a NOTAR or tandem or other configuration), and you encounter an area of high workload on the pedals, it may not be just you having a bad day. This phenomenon is also applicable to helicopters with fenestrons or ducted tail rotors, and the reasons why it occurs at all, are well beyond the scope of this simple book.

If an Automatic Flight Control System (AFCS) is installed which has a yaw channel, this problem may be masked by the very swift action of the sensors and actuators in this system. It certainly can act more quickly than a human pilot.

Loss of Tail Rotor Effectiveness

Many conventional helicopters have suffered from what should be correctly called *loss of tail rotor effectiveness* (or LTE for short). At various times this phenomenon has been called tail rotor stall, (and I am sure many other misleading terms). The tail rotor simply is not able to produce enough thrust to stop the existing yaw rate. The tail rotor is not stalled, it is just inefficient.

* And most helicopters do suffer from this, French and Russian ones have it on the other side mostly.

Typically, this problem occurs when the helicopter is operating at low airspeed, out of ground effect with very little extra power available above the power required to hover. For the one helicopter where this has been studied in any scientific sense, (the Bell 206 series) the problem occurs most frequently when turning right from into wind to downwind*. The yaw rate builds suddenly and the tail rotor is unable to stop it.

The problems of the turbine engine N_2 governor, mentioned in Chapter 29, do not help the matter, and in fact contribute significantly to making the situation worse.

The governor senses the N_R with respect to the airframe is higher than the datum RPM it is trying to maintain, and reduces fuel flow significantly. For a helicopter spinning rapidly (120° per second is 30 RPM, or about 10% of a typical main N_R) the governor will reduce the main N_R with respect to the earth in an attempt to maintain the N_R with respect to the airframe. A 10% reduction in N_R will be a 10% reduction in tail rotor RPM as well, meaning the thrust from the tail rotor will be significantly reduced. Remember how lift is proportional to N_R squared?

The approved, proven solution is to add and hold full left pedal, apply forward cyclic, and hope there is nothing to run into while the airspeed builds up. The increased forward airspeed should put some moving air past the vertical stabilizer, which should generate enough force to help stop the rotation. It doesn't take much airspeed to influence the direction of flight of the helicopter. Once the yaw rate is reduced even slightly, the N_R with respect to the earth will return to the proper value, and the thrust from the tail rotor will begin to improve dramatically.

The other cause of the problem is that the pilots were looking out of the right–hand window and were unaware of the airspeed dropping to a low value. The turn was made with reference to the ground and pilots attempted to keep a constant groundspeed at the same time as turning downwind...

Of course, old timers used to say they stayed out of trouble by always turning to the left... This has the advantage that the airspeed indicator is indirectly in your field of view (you have to look across the cockpit anyway).

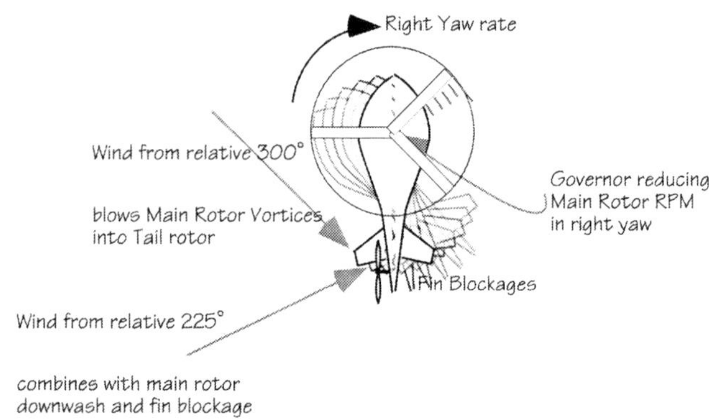

gure 34-14 LTE Causes

The technical causes of LTE are many, and can depend upon the relative wind direction at the start of the problem. Basically, they can be summed up as interference from the main rotor downwash with a wind from relative 330° or thereabouts, interference from the vertical stabilizer with winds from the sides, and a neutral gradient of pedal position vs. windspeed for winds from relative 225° (this was explained in the previous section). These causes are shown graphically in Figure 34-14.

Wingovers or Crop Duster Turns

Helicopters don't do aerobatics as a matter of course. You may see some pretty spectacular demonstrations from time to time, but that is best left to the experts in specially configured machines. About the closest helicopters come to aerobatics is in the wingover, and its been the source of enough trouble, thank you.

Wingovers, (also known as a 'return to target') are typically military maneuvers, although some civilian helicopter pilots have probably flown them without realizing what it is they are doing. This maneuver is mentioned here because, while it is exhilarating and good for developing confidence in handling helicopters, it has been the cause of far too many crashes. Figure 34-15 shows such a maneuver performed ideally.

* Interestingly, Bell Helicopter also found that: a) most of the time the accident helicopter didn't have enough power to hover IGE at the accident site, much less hover OGE and b) the tail rotors of most of the accident aircraft were not rigged correctly, so that even with full left pedal the tail rotor wasn't producing the power it should have been capable of.

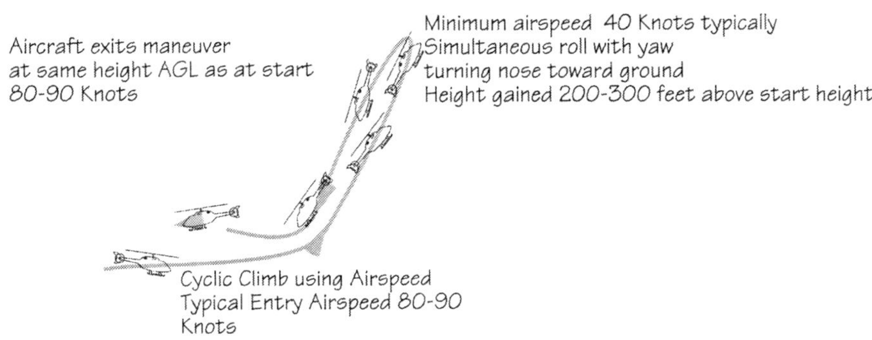

Figure 34-15 Typical Wingover

Before starting the discussion about this maneuver, I would stress that it is not possible to learn how to do this maneuver from a book. If you have a desire to see one, learn it from someone who has plenty of experience.

Wingovers are very dynamic. A typical one starts with a high–speed entry with a pull up to a fairly nose–high attitude. Collective is held more or less constant throughout. As the airspeed decreases, the helicopter is simultaneously rolled and yawed to reverse heading. This action puts the nose down to pick up airspeed to return on much the same line as the helicopter started, but heading the other way. For the sake of argument, let us assume the angle of bank is close to 90° at the top of the climb.

Because it is such a dynamic maneuver, it is often necessary to do it with reference to the ground for height and also speed. While the pilot is mostly interested in height, it is nearly impossible to ignore ground speed cues as well, and this can cause a problem. The problem comes when the maneuver is started with the helicopter facing into wind, ending up facing downwind.

In order to understand the rapidly changing sequence of events, let's look at the maneuver in zero wind. As the helicopter approaches the top of the climb with the slowest airspeed point, it passes through zero–ground speed, and the rotor is at 90° to the earth, producing thrust in a horizontal fashion. Since the airspeed is low (nearly zero), yawing is more or less normal and there is a smooth rate of turn. For our 'standard' direction of rotation main rotor, the natural tendency for the helicopter is to yaw to the right, and surprisingly little pedal or lateral cyclic will be needed. If the power is just right, the helicopter is momentarily hovering at 90° angle of bank. Gravity takes over and the helicopter starts to drop, but with the nose facing towards the earth and the airspeed increases smoothly in the proper direction (the direction the fuselage is pointing). Minor errors in judging the airspeed to start the turn at the top are not important, as there is very little change in control effectiveness in this low speed. With no wind, the transfer of energy (from kinetic to potential and back again) with respect to the earth is easy to understand.

Things get more complicated if we add wind. Again, the case where the helicopter is starting from downwind to end up facing into wind is slightly easier to understand, as in Figure 34-16. Everything is the same until the helicopter reaches the top of the climb, when it is in the zero–groundspeed condition (because the pilot is looking outside). As soon as the downward part starts, the helicopter has some airspeed, due to the wind. At no time in this maneuver with wind, is the helicopter in a zero–airspeed condition. From an energy standpoint, things get pretty complicated pretty quickly. As the helicopter climbs, it is trading kinetic energy into potential energy. Since the helicopter has more kinetic energy with respect to the earth (higher groundspeed), it can climb higher than in the no-wind situation. This greater potential energy can thus be traded for more kinetic energy as the helicopter starts to descend, but on the descent, the helicopter is already facing into wind, so it has a higher groundspeed for the same airspeed. Put in terms that pilot will be seeing, he has a lower airspeed for the same groundspeed, and since the helicopter will be at a high groundspeed at the bottom of the wingover, the helicopter will definitely be operating on the good side of the power required curve. The helicopter is in a much better position from a 'power required for the same groundspeed' than the no wind case.

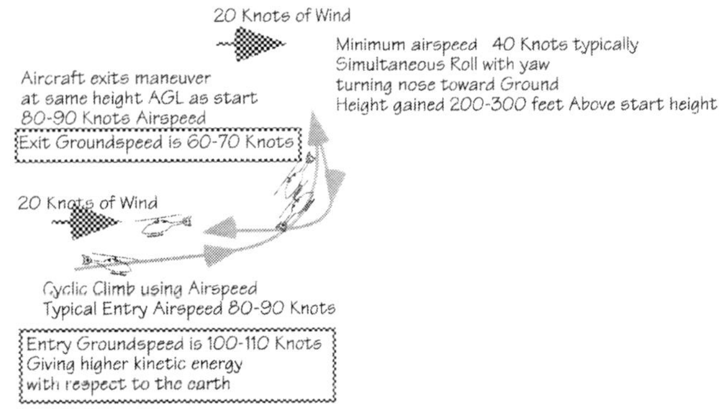

Figure 34-16 Wingover From Downwind to Into Wind

The into–wind entry with a downwind exit is the worst case, and is shown in Figure 34-17. The helicopter passes through not just zero–ground speed, but, shortly after, through the zero–airspeed condition. Since the rotor is producing lift with respect to airspeed, when the airspeed drops to zero, and the induced velocity drops away, the helicopter falls, quite rapidly. The helicopter must now accelerate to an airspeed again, but the pilot is watching things with respect to the ground and may not let the helicopter accelerate to the airspeed needed.

From an energy standpoint, in this case, the helicopter has a lower groundspeed than the no-wind condition, so it has lower kinetic energy with respect to the earth. Thus is can't climb as high, and will get less potential energy. With less potential energy, it can't pick up as much groundspeed. The lower groundspeed has a penalty with the tailwind- it means the airspeed that would be needed to get the groundspeed the pilot thinks is necessary will be quite low. If the groundspeed the pilot thinks is necessary on exiting the wingover is close to minimum power speed, the airspeed to attain this will probably be below minimum power speed, and hence any correction by the pilot using cyclic only may not be correct. It's not an easy situation to explain, and hopefully you will try to avoid it!

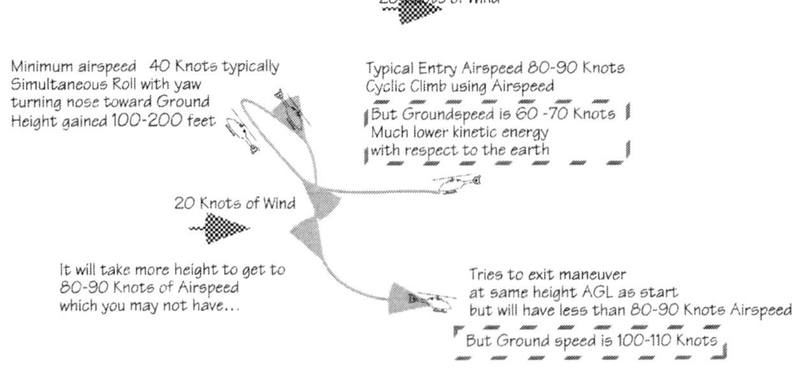

Figure 34-17 Wingover from into wind to downwind

Another common cause of problems related to wingovers is practicing the maneuver when lightly loaded, and then trying it again with a full load of troops to impress them with what fun helicopters are. The difference in weight makes a huge difference to the airspeeds and heights needed to successfully complete the maneuver. Don't try it at maximum weight unless you have built up to it with lots of height. In one instance I know of, the helicopter barely avoided a crash and ran along the ground for over 200 feet at about 80 knots before climbing away again - lots of damage to the airframe and landing gear, as well as the pilot's career.

Please, please, please, don't do wingovers from into wind to downwind without understanding how you can get into serious trouble, and leaving yourself plenty of altitude.

Who does wingovers? Crop sprayers, people showing off...

Fortunately, the very thing that could get crop dusters into a lot of trouble keeps them from flying- most crop dusters stop when the winds are over 5 knots. The winds badly affect the spray patterns and drift the stuff where they don't want it. Good thing too, as it stops them from seeing this nasty problem.

Rapid Rolling

When the helicopter is banked rapidly in forward flight (and it does not need to be to very high angles of bank), there will be a torque change. On some helicopters, this can be significant enough to cause a momentary overtorque, if the rate of rolling is aggressive. One reason which seems reasonable is that the change in angle of attack due to the roll rate will change the lift and thus induced drag on the blades, depending upon the direction of rolling. Rolling in one direction will change the AoA in a manner to increase the induced drag significantly, and rolling in the other direction will reduce the induced drag, reducing the torque, but only while the rolling is happening. The amount and direction of roll rate will determine the torque change - it's different for every helicopter, and is worth knowing about. Typically, a torque increase occurs when rolling in the direction of the advancing blade, and torque reduction happens when rolling in the direction of the retreating blade.

Underslung Loads

Helicopters are useful because of their ability to maintain position with respect to the ground*. This capability also makes them invaluable as mobile, aerial cranes. There are a few interesting items about carrying *underslung*† loads to be considered.

With underslung loads, every helicopter pilot becomes an experimental test pilot for a while. Each load is different, has different flying characteristics and affects the helicopter differently. Some can be carried at high speed with no problems, others try to fly the helicopter. Some are slow and docile, and other are always skittish. Some are deadweight, others lively.

Knowing How Much it Weighs

The first problem is determining the weight of the load. Too much puts you in trouble from a performance and legal point of view. Too little may not pay the bills in a timely manner. Every underslung load hook should have a weighing device fitted. Why?

The load being picked up may be up to 50% of the total weight being carried by the rotor and engine. This has a large influence on whether you can hover or not, and whether the airframe has been over-stressed. An earlier story in Chapter 25 outlined one problem - here is another story to help convince you.

The British Royal Air Force Puma was not fitted with a torquemeter, but had a collective pitch angle indicator - which seemed to work well enough. The problem was, the helicopter also did not have an underslung load weighing device, even though it was used for a lot of underslung loads. The pilots repeatedly used to ask for a cargo hook weighing system, and were told by some non–flying scientists that there wasn't a problem. The pilots were told they didn't really want a cargo hook weighing system, because:

- First of all, only mass is important, and the weighing system would tell them weight (a completely correct, but subtle distinction designed to confuse the issue; and useless as an argument).
- They didn't need to worry about weight, as the airframe was stressed for mass (not completely true).
- In forward flight, the drag of the load would be seen, and it was not really important... (tell that to the airframe that has to carry the load)
- Finally, the pilots were told, there was this marvelous book that had all the loads they were permitted to carry listed in it - these loads have all been checked, and the helicopters would never be overweight...

* Sorry if this is a bit pedantic, but a balloon can hover over a spot on the ground, if there is no wind...

† The term underslung will be used, instead of external loads, as a spray boom is an external load, and doesn't have nearly the interesting variation that something on the cargo hook does.

This whole argument was of course false, and especially ignored performance effects - weight really does matter as far as the engine and airframe is concerned. If it's a very light load with lots of surface area, then the rotor downwash will certainly have an effect. In forward flight, the drag may in fact cause structural problems after all - the cargo hook and airframe structure is only designed to carry so much.

But perhaps the worst part of this whole sorry problem was that the FM did not have any suitable performance graphs to help the pilots. The collective pitch angle limits said nothing about winds changing the amount of collective the pilot was permitted to use, and so as a result, the pilots would load up until they could just hover at the maximum permitted collective limit. If this happened to be in 30 knots of wind, then it was still within limits. When they went to hover with this load in an area where there was no wind, they were in trouble, because the collective pitch required exceeded the limits they were permitted. The 'standard loads' which had been advertised were also very often not standard at all - one time the crew struggled for quite a while to lift a Jeep and trailer - normally no problem, and after not budging it, landed to find out why they couldn't lift it. It turned out to be the bomb clearance Jeep, and had a sheet of half inch steel plate underneath... 'Nuff said? Get a cargo hook weighing device, and ask for better performance charts.

Why No Cargo Hook Weighing Devices?

There are some excuses for not having devices on the cargo hook to weigh how much is being lifted, but not many good reasons.To put things in perspective, every crane used on a construction site has to have a weighing device on the hook to make sure it doesn't get overloaded. How can we be less safe with a machine (i.e., the helicopter) which costs more and has the potential to do more damage?

We don't have cargo hooks because early helicopters could hardly get out of their own way, let alone lift much of an underslung load. They certainly couldn't lift enough of an underslung load to do any significant structural damage to the airframe or components, there just wasn't enough performance.

Times have changed. We now have helicopters which only require about 80% of available power to hover at the maximum weight permitted at sea level (even at the maximum external permitted weight). Most people are going to consider (mistakenly) that if they can hover using maximum power, they can't be overloading the machine (given the state of civilian performance charts which don't tell the power required to hover, this is no wonder).

Technically competent helicopter operators will fit underslung load weighing devices to their machines. Unfortunately, their less scrupulous counterparts won't, and will gain a significant commercial advantage. Maybe insurance companies will take note and require these devices, but that may be dreaming in technicolor.

Watching the Load

If there is no crewman to note what the load is doing, then mirrors are necessary. Watch the load as you transition from the hover - if it starts to fly in a way you don't like, slow down. If it still doesn't behave, then consider a turn to apply a load factor to get the load under the helicopter again. Otherwise, consider your options for getting rid of something that could rise up and hurt you. I've read too many accident reports of loads with a mind of their own.

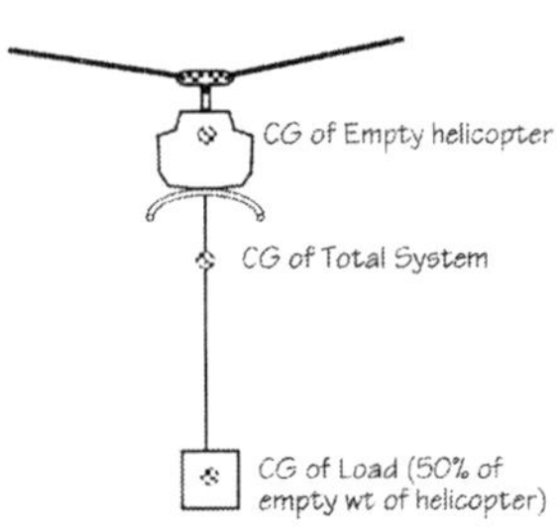

Figure 34-18 Helicopter with Underslung Load

Lets say the load is reasonably stable, but is swaying gently from side to side. The helicopter responds to this load movement and the pilot tries to correct, using lateral stick. Not much success in some cases, and the pilot ends up in a Pilot Induced Oscillation (PIO). Why the problem? Consider the vertical CG position of the helicopter/load combination. See Figure 34-18. It is shifted a long way below the normal empty vertical CG position. If the load is heavy, it now has a lot of effect on the helicopter. Even a modest load fraction of 25% is nothing to sneeze at. The source of all the controlling moments (namely the main and tail rotors) haven't changed, but have to affect a very different vehicle.

Adding to the problem is the way the cargo hook is attached to the helicopter. If it is a fixed hook, then every time the load swings to one side, it adds a side force to the helicopter at the cargo hook. As shown in Figure 34-19a, this produces an unwanted roll moment, and rolls the helicopter the wrong way. Typically, until the pilot gets used to it, corrections will be made out of phase.

If the hook is on a track and free to travel sideways, then it acts like a hinge, and does not transmit a sideways force to the helicopter, (unless of course, the hook reaches the end of travel). This is shown in Figure 34-19b. In either case, though, the load has an influence on the helicopter. The greater the fraction of the total weight is the load, the greater the influence.

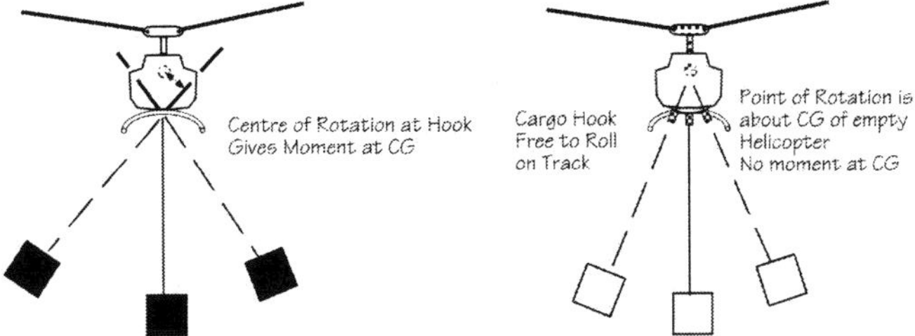

(a) 'Bad' Method of Installing Cargo Hook(b) 'Better' Method of Installing Cargo Hook

Figure 34-19 Underslung Loads

Problems

Problems with underslung loads are many. Probably the first one is downwash. The rotor downwash has its greatest velocity at about one-quarter rotor diameter below the rotor. If the load is light and has a large surface area, and is placed at about this distance below the helicopter, then the downwash may make it difficult to lift. The rotor is trying to lift both the weight and itself, and the harder it tries, the higher the downwash velocity - a vicious circle. One solution is to put the load either closer to or further below the helicopter to miss this maximum downwash velocity.

Downwash also effects the weight of the helicopter. A large surface–area load picks up some weight component, due to downwash. While the customer may not want to pay for it, it must be considered for performance effects. The helicopter doesn't know what is attached to the hook - whether downwash load or concrete.

CRAP Method of Load Obedience

The fact that some loads are prone to misbehavior, like small children, was mentioned before. But what can you do to keep them in line?

The CRAP method of solving underslung load oscillations in the hover and low speed is unusual, but it works in practice. The first time I ever heard of it was from some underslung load trials on a new type of helicopter in England when a piece of valuable military equipment was being carried. The customer would have been most upset if it had been jettisoned, and sure enough it started to give problems when transitioning to the hover. For some reason, the test pilots decided to use pedal to help stop this load oscillating from side to side, and it worked. They tried the same method with other troublesome loads, and it worked there also.

The technique worked as follows: when the slip ball is out to the left, be prepared to add right pedal when the ball starts to move to the right, but not before. Of course, the opposite is true if the ball is out to the right. Seems the acceleration to the side can be stopped by the change in side thrust resulting from the pedal being moved. Simple and straightforward. Oh yes, CRAP stands for Calibrated, Rapid Application of Pedal*.

* And I didn't just make these words up to be polite.

Weird Underslung Loads

I've read too many accident reports about strange loads, which on reflection were totally unsuitable for carriage underneath a helicopter. Fixed–wing aircraft can be carried, for example, but only if every possible method is used to stop the wing from producing lift. Even at 40 or 50 KIAS, a fixed–wing aircraft can still 'fly', and while you might like that from a performance point of view (less weight to carry), you wouldn't like it from a handling point of view - you would have no control over it.

Loads need to have directional stability if they are being carried at any sort of airspeed, and adding temporary tails or drogue parachutes might be worth considering.

One practice which has also caused a great number of accidents is leaving long line cables attached while in transit, in the belief that this will save time on the next load. These long line cables have a nasty habit of dragging back and up until the helicopter starts a descent at high speed, when the cable and tail rotor try to occupy the same airspace with less–than–happy results.

Flight Path Planning

Always remember that the load can come off - either because you want to get rid of it, or because something fails (the engine, the cargo hook, the straps holding the load together…). Several countries have rather strict legislation about this, and while restrictive on the use of helicopters in some ways, ensure public safety.

Emergencies With Underslung Loads

If you're slinging in a single–engine helicopter, you can be pretty sure the operation will put you in the avoid area of the HV curve, and you should be properly prepared. Jettisoning the load will make your autorotation slightly easier, but you need to be extra ready for the slightest hint of trouble.

Loads can get away from you, and here either a crewman (in larger helicopters) or very good mirrors will be necessary. If the load starts to bounce vertically, be prepared to lock your collective grip to prevent exciting the bounce. Sometimes a good sharp change in collective pitch can stop the bounce. Down collective seems to be a good direction in most of these problems, and the timing is everything - more specific advice I wouldn't want to give.

Training For Underslung Loads

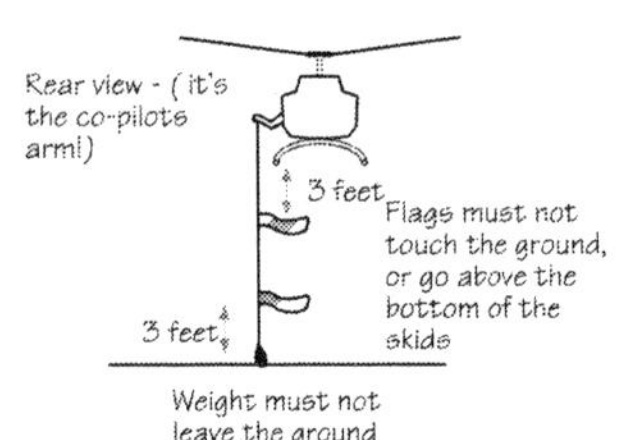

Figure 34-20 Rear View of Helicopter

For those operators who have to rely on a team operation to con the helicopter into position - (for example, with underslung loads, rescue winches, etc.), there are some easy-to-set-up exercises to improve teamwork. They also teach pilots about the 'personal space' of the helicopter, as well as anticipation. This sort of exercise is used in most helicopter championships as well, so you might be practicing to become a medal winner!.

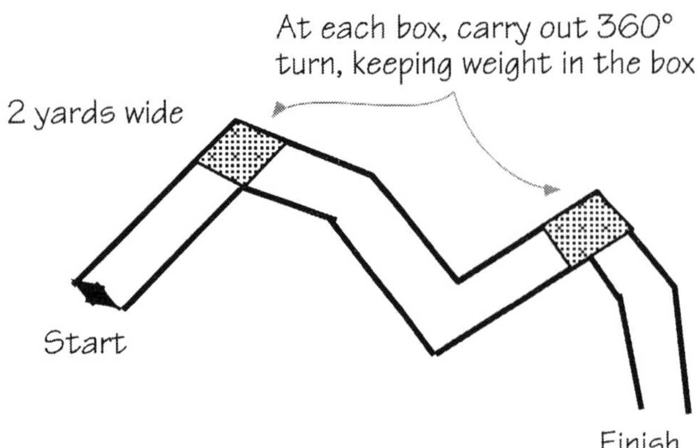

ıre 34-21 Helicopter Crew Underslung Training Course

There is no requirement to use a large, specially–rigged load - a rope with a weight is all that is needed. Have a crewman (not the pilot, please) dangle the rope out the door or hatch, and talk the pilot around a course on the ground - the task is to keep the weight on the ground with a minimum amount of rope in the crewman's hand. This exercise develops either very good teamwork, or a rapid falling out of friends - but the training value for junior helicopter pilots and crewmen is very large. Figure 34-21 shows the set up and course Obviously, if you are trying to train pilots to fly by themselves with underslung loads, the line should be attached to the cargo hook, and the upper flag is superfluous.

Automatic Flight Control Systems and Underslung Loads

Automatic Flight Control Systems (AFCSs) are covered in more detail in Chapter 37,"Automatic Flight Control Systems", but I would like to add a note here about how much an AFCS improves the handling of underslung loads. Even a basic rate damping system, which is relatively simple and weights very little, has a dramatic effect on taming a load. It seems that the ability of the AFCS to stop small rates from developing into larger ones stops unwanted excursions of the load from even starting. I had occasion to do some testing of the Gazelle with underslung loads, and the tests were carried out on the only Gazelle in British military service with both an AFCS and an underslung load hook. The tests were all with the AFCS off (to be representative of the in-service Army model), but occasionally I tried some flying with the AFCS on. The results were dramatic- like the helicopter was on rails, even loads which oscillated from side to side in turns in the 'bare' machine were tamed.

Uncommanded Jettison of Underslung Loads

I've read too many incident messages where an underslung load has fallen from a helicopter and the pilot swore he didn't touch the jettison button, yet the cargo hook was found to be fully serviceable afterwards. What happened?

Look at the typical cargo hook. It has a keeper to prevent the load from coming off the hook until released. Unfortunately, if the eye of the load strop which is attached to the hook is a bit too large, it can bounce around and drop away. See Figure 34-22 for a sequence of such an event.

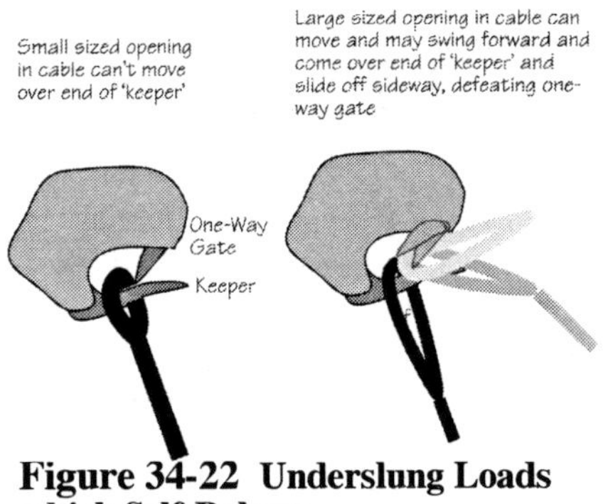

Figure 34-22 Underslung Loads which Self-Release

There is also good evidence that static electricity build up may short-circuit and trigger the cargo hook release relays

HIGH ALTITUDE FLYING

Flying at high altitudes in helicopters has its own rewards. First of all, you can often get airline captains to question their sanity when air traffic control tells them they are going underneath a helicopter. Secondly, the scenery can be better, especially in the mountains. But there are several things to consider:

- The engine power available will reduce, for reasons already discussed.
- The fuel consumption will reduce dramatically at high altitudes, resulting in longer range in still wind. Most notably on turbine engines, not pistons.
- The airframe power required will increase, again for reasons already flogged mercilessly.
- The reaction of the rotor to control inputs will be different (at least for rotor systems with more than two blades). The response will feel more sluggish.
- There may not be a great deal of thrust available from the tail rotor.
- In an autorotation, the collective will need to be kept fairly high to keep the N_R in the green.
- The maximum permitted airspeed will decrease due to retreating blade stall.
- You'll probably need oxygen.

The net result is that if you are going to really high altitudes, several things start to gang up - the reducing V_{NE} will eventually come down to close to the minimum power required speed, and at really high altitudes, they will be separated by less than 5 knots. If you're this high, the effect is not unlike balancing on the top of a broomstick.

ICING

About the best thing to say about icing is unless your helicopter is fully and completely equipped for it, stay out of it. For most helicopters- Don't even think about it.

There are all sorts of nasty things that can happen, not just to blades but to engines (do you have anti-ice or de-ice on the intakes*) and tail rotors.

If you get ice on the main rotor, autorotation characteristics will likely be much worse than a dogs breakfast, and since the engine may not be well protected from icing, autorotation might be something to be thought of. A lot.

Do you have a heated windshield to be able to see where you're going in really bad icing? That might be the determining step for not carrying on into really bad weather conditions.

Among the problems that can occur due to icing are a build up of ice on the main and tail rotor blades. Aside from an extremely large effect on rotor performance, which may not be immediately noticeable-(remember the engine instruments and torque meter will only tell you how much drag the blades are producing) which will reduce the lift producing capability of the blades, there is a danger that the ice could effect the control mechanisms for the rotor.

If you do get ice on the blades, it will produce some vibrations, which will help to shed the ice. Nice work, if you could guarantee the ice was going to shed evenly and not produce extremely large out–of–balance forces on the blades, and if you guarantee the ice wasn't go to be flung somewhere vital like the tail rotor...

What if you don't feel any vibrations due to ice, or notice any large change in power required- are you still OK? What about the possibility of ice build up on the fuselage - the tail boom is a lot longer than the fuselage and if it picks up a lot of ice, it might well put you outside the longitudinal CG limits...

Helicopters can be extremely prone to icing, as the main rotor blades have varying airspeeds and angle of attack along their length, which means one of those combinations will be just perfect for picking up ice. Skin temperature of the leading edge of the blade can provide some assistance in keeping ice away, but it varies along the length of the blade as well, and it's better not to have to depend on something which would only cause the ice to melt and refreeze farther back on the blade.

What if you have ice on the blades when you first venture up to your trusty steed? Aside from realizing too late that you should have put the blade covers on last night, what can you do? In most parts of the world where helicopters live their useful lives, there is a scarcity of de-icing trucks. I've seen blades scraped off with credit cards (a long process, and requiring a ladder); heard of them being destroyed by someone hitting them with a hammer to knock off really thick ice; and waited until the sun heated them sufficiently to melt the ice. I wouldn't try flying with even frost on the blades.

Why is Icing So Bad†?

Icing can mess up the very smooth flow over the rotor blades in no time flat. While this may be immediately noticeable sometimes, often it is not, and is only seen by a slight rise in torque at the same collective setting. Not many of us notice that sort of thing.

Ice also adds weight to the helicopter, and depending upon the size of the airframe, and the distribution of the components, can add weight where you don't want it. Too much weight in the tailboom can easily put the CG too far aft.

The main reason is that ice will disrupt the lift on the blades. On a single engine helicopter which must depend on the ability to autorotate, ice may eliminate that capability, without you knowing it until too late. Since that much ice would also affect your engine, it's double jeopardy.

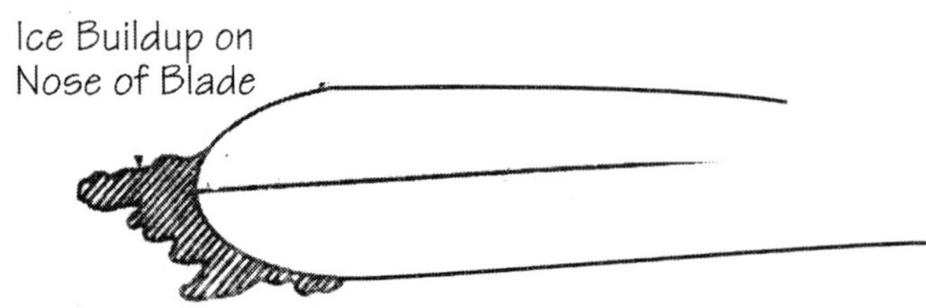

'igure 34-23 Icing on the Blades

* And do you know the difference between them?

† Besides the icing on cakes, do-nuts and cookies, which is full of calories, but that's a different story...

So What are 'Icing Conditions'?

The obvious answer is of course, any time you can see ice build up on the windshield, or windshield wipers or other parts of the airframe. Any time the visibility is below 1 mile with temperatures below +2°C, I would be very cautious. The reasons are that in these conditions, whatever is obstructing the visibility is bound to have water vapor in it, and that water vapor is quite close to freezing. How accurate is the OAT gauge on your helicopter? When was the last time you checked it against a known, accurate source?

What if it's at night? Do you have some way to light up the outside to see if you're getting close to the necessary conditions (as opposed to being in icing?)

What about those days when it's snowing pretty hard? Are you still safe? Do you have snow protection for the engine intake?

Snow

Snow can have all sorts of characteristics. The Inuit* have 30 different words to describe snow. The characteristic of most interest to us is the wet, sticky character that happens just around freezing, and the reason we are interested is that this sort of snow can cause all sorts of problems which have (and probably will continue to) catch out pilots.

Wet snow can block engine intakes very easily, it can build up on parts of the airframe and then let loose in a lump and head down the intake, and so on. Most turbine engines don't like snow mixing with the air - it tends to put out the fire. For this reason some machines operate with reverse flow baffles on the engine intakes. Snow can't make the sharp reversal of airflow needed to get into the engine, and so it scoots by.

Other helicopters get around the problem by burying the engine intakes completely inside the transmission area. Still others use deflector shields.

Flying in Your Own Dust

Helicopters move a lot of air to stay up, and if the air displaced happens to contact something loose, like dust or dirt or snow, it wants to share the joys of being airborne.

This of course poses problems for the person trying to maintain a semblance of order in the conduct of the flight (i.e. the pilot) - it is impossible to see the vital cues for hovering or touchdown, or any other maneuvers. There are lots of tricks for how to minimize the problem - some will be mentioned here.

First of all, know what the surface is likely to do when you are hovering and plan accordingly. If taking off, plan to lift-off vertically with enough power to quickly clear the area - the risk of engine failure if inside the HV curve may be less than hitting something you couldn't see.

If touching down, plan to maintain groundspeed and stay ahead of the dust/snow cloud if possible, or to terminate the approach in a high hover, and let the worst of the cloud dissipate prior to descending into it.

I cannot emphasize how much a Doppler radar low velocity indicator helps in this situation, especially if it has along and across velocities on the scale. I have flown zero horizontal visibility - zero ceiling touchdowns (simulated, of course) with this instrument and was glad to have it! The Russians have fitted all their large helicopters (Mi-8 and larger) with Doppler low velocity indicators - they have very good reason, called Siberian winters.

Mast Bumping

Mast bumping has reared its head again in the last few years, particularly for training machines. What mast bumping is, its the causes and effects are obviously an emotional subject since the results are generally catastrophic i.e. - people get killed.

---

* Eskimo to some of you, but they would really prefer to be called Inuit.

From the outset, it should be clear that the mast bumping to be discussed here is not the sort that may occur on the ground when conducting off-level touchdowns, although there may be some slight similarities. This section deals with mast bumping in forward flight due to mishandling the helicopter.

Causes for Mast Bumping

Mast bumping is a possibility in any teetering–rotor helicopter, with the exception of those with hub restraining springs - which eliminates only the Bell 222 / 230/ AH-1 2 bladed series, and they aren't used for basic training anyway.

In very simple terms, the teetering rotor head relies on having a thrust vector and a weight vector to keep the rotor disk and the fuselage in appropriate places. Just as the articulated rotor has flap restrainers and droop restrainers to prevent the blades from moving too far, so the teetering head has a limit to how far the head can pivot before it contacts the mast. In normal flight, this is no problem, as the thrust vector and the weight vector align.

Problems start to arise when the pilot 'pushes over'- i.e. tries to make the helicopter describe an outside arc. The main rotor total thrust vector gets very small i.e. close to zero-G and if there is enough airspeed to influence the fuselage, things start to go wrong. Since no–one has repealed the laws of gravity, the weight vector is virtually eliminated if the pilot commands such a flight path. The fuselage sees this as very low G - in other words a weightless feeling*. This zero–G situation can be accomplished by simultaneously lowering the collective and pushing forward on the cyclic, or by zooming and pushing over, but these are unusual maneuvers for a helicopter, particularly a civilian helicopter†.

What happens in the zero–G case is that the rotor is not producing thrust, but being a mass with some rotational speed, wants to continue on its flight path (remember the gyroscope?) in the same attitude. The fuselage is acted upon by aerodynamic forces such as relative airspeed, as well as tail rotor thrust. Remember tail rotor thrust? It caused problems in the hover by creating translating tendency, and in forward flight by producing inherent sideslip. It causes problems here as well, because it still pushes the fuselage sideways, when the rotor wants to keep going straight. The tail rotor is also probably not lined up with the CG and causes the helicopter to roll due to coupling. Result? The fuselage moves sideways and rolls. The pilot tries to stop the roll with lateral cyclic, but since the thrust is zero, gets no response, so a larger input is made. Meanwhile the rotor stays in place‡ until the mast and rotor head contacts.

The mast on most teetering rotor helicopters is quite long and the force of the rotor hitting it on the top may be sufficient to bend or break the mast. The rest is history.

But that is not the only possible cause of mast bumping.

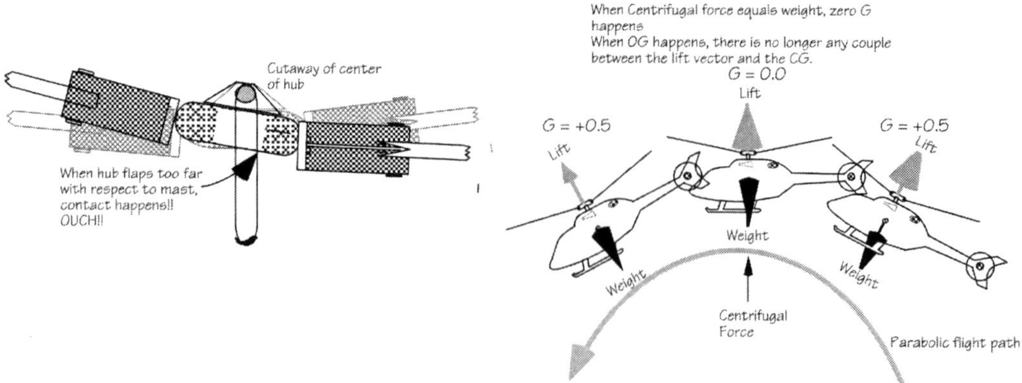

Figure 34-24 Mast Bumping

Too Much Sideslip

Remember that the rotor disk will flap away from the wind when it changes speed? This same thing happens when the wind changes direction - the rotor disk will attempt to flap away from the relative wind. In steady forward flight, the flapback is taken care of, and the controls rigged for it. If a large

* I have never seen a gust that can give anywhere close to zero G in a helicopter, and I've been in some pretty strong turbulence in lots of helicopters.
† For God's sake, please don't go out and try to do this yourself.
‡ or the other way around, depends on how you want to look at it.

amount of sideslip were suddenly introduced, the rotor would flap away from this new relative wind, and quite possibly tilt the disk to the point where the hub contacted the mast. How can this occur?

I can think of several ways this can happen - following a sudden failure which produced a lot of yaw, such as an engine failure or the loss of tail rotor drive, or the input of a very large amount of pedal on the part of a very inexperienced student who thought that pedals were how a helicopter was supposed to be turned in forward flight.

By the way, adding fixed floats to a helicopter with a teetering head only makes matters worse as far as the potential for mast bumping is concerned - in the event of a sideslip being encountered, the additional area under the fuselage will tend to roll the helicopter in opposition to the rotor flapping back. For example, if a sideslip is introduced from the left (due to an engine failure perhaps), the helicopter with fixed floats will tend to roll to the left while the rotor will try to flap back to the right, very quickly reducing the margin for mast bumping.

Other Causes of Mast Bumping

Other things can cause mast bumping. Rapidly reversing the controls, such as applying full left cyclic and then immediately applying full right cyclic as the helicopter starts to roll is bound to upset the system.

On the ground, trying to land on too steep a off-level can cause something similar to mast bumping, but hopefully the consequences won't be as severe as if the helicopter were in forward flight.

Too low a N_R can also cause a problem, but this is less likely in turbine engined machines, or those piston engine machines with rotor and engine governing systems. The reason the low N_R causes a problem is that the rotor blades will have less inertia and will flap away from any change in relative wind more easily.

High density altitudes and loading out–of–CG limitations can also reduce the margin for when mast bumping may occur.

What to Do In the Event of Mast Bumping

Like most of my advice, the best cure is prevention. Try to stay away from conditions that will get you into the situation. Don't bunt over ridge lines or power lines if you are in the military. Certainly don't try it in the civil world or you'll probably be in trouble with someone else.

If you do encounter a situation in-flight where you think mast bumping is likely, that is there is a lighter–than–normal weight in the seat of your pants, the pitch attitude looks funny, and the helicopter is starting to do strange things with regard to roll attitude - the best advice is 1) don't lower the collective (unless the engine has failed, of course), and in fact try to get positive thrust on the rotor 2) apply a slightly amount of aft cyclic 3) recover to a level flight condition.

Training to Prevent Mast Bumping

Like vortex ring state or autorotations, it is difficult to know the situation unless you have been shown it in training. There is an element of risk here.

I heard of one instructor who used to regularly demonstrate the low-G situation in a rather spirited manner. Tales would come back of maps floating in the cockpit and other stories. Note the past tense in the first sentence. One day his helicopter broke up in mid-air, and while no–one can prove it was due to mast bumping, the considered opinion is that he went too far.

There are several points to this story. If you are considering training to this condition, the first thing to do is put in a G meter, and I would recommend at +5/-2 range meter instead of the more common fixed wing +10/-5 model, as the former is more appropriate. The second thing to do is build up to this very slowly. Use a standard entry airspeed, say 90 KIAS and start with pushovers that only go to say 0.9 G, then on the next entry go to 0.8 G and so on. Stop at 0.5 G, for safety's sake - if not my sake. Maps floating in the cockpit, or shoulder harness straps that stand out straight is real zero–G stuff, and is *way* too close to the edge. Don't ever try this is turbulent air, and remember that the aim of the trip is to walk back into the office.

Design Eye Point

Most light helicopters do not have adjustable seats, at least fore-aft or vertical. Aside from making it difficult to accommodate different sized pilots, it makes it difficult for the pilot to adjust the seating position so his eyes are in a known position with respect to the airframe, known as the Design Eye Point. Another place where we have fallen behind our fixed wing brethren, as even in large helicopters, there is no guidance as to where to adjust the seat to ensure the pilot's field of view is optimum, nor that the references will be repeatable between pilots.

Summary of Chapter 34

This chapter has tackled some of the problems arising from the flexibility of the helicopter. Hopefully the previous chapters gave enough technical background to be able to understand some of the causes and solutions proposed.

I must re-emphasize the techniques mentioned here may not be suitable for all helicopters - if in doubt, ask the manufacturer for advice.

There are undoubtedly many other unique aspects to helicopter flying - they will have to wait for the next edition of the book. I welcome suggestions.

Other Helicopter Types

Brief History

When Arthur Young started work on developing what became the Bell 47, he found that there had been nearly 400 helicopter companies started in the USA in the previous 40 years*. Most of the designs have unfortunately been lost, but a wide variety have flown. It is worth looking over any strange types that are in museums to measure the progress that has been made, and to see the methods that were tried to achieve vertical, unrestricted flight.

The basics of all successful helicopters are the same - long, thin blades that rotate and produce lift. The only differences are in the type of rotor hub arrangement, and the way the rotors are used to produce both lift and control. The various hub types have been covered in previous chapters, and only different configurations of main rotors remain. Interestingly, one way to look at most of these other helicopter types is that they have one thing in common - none have tail rotors.

The following table summarizes the way various types of rotor configurations are used to produce control.

Rotor Configuration	Pitch	Roll	Yaw	Collective
Co-Axial	Side View	End View	Any View (differential Collective)	Any View
Tandem	Side View	End View	End View	Side View

TABLE 2. Other Rotor Configurations

Coaxial

The *coaxial* rotor system has two rotor heads stacked one above the other. The main advantage is in the improved hovering performance obtained by the lower rotor, due to the induced velocity from the upper rotor, and the lack of a tail rotor to offset the torque reaction. The tail rotor on a conventional helicopter typically takes about 5 - 10% of the total power, so using the power for lift helps to make the efficiency greater.

The coaxial rotor helicopter is usually stubby in appearance compared to conventional helicopters, but it can accept a large center of gravity range. The coaxial rotor system is relatively immune to winds. In terms of handling pitch and roll at the same as other helicopters, but since yaw control is affected by changing power between the two rotor systems, don't expect it to be either swift or precise. Since it has no long tail boom, most coaxial have large vertical stabilizers to generate directional stability in forward flight. Control of the blades is shown in Table 2. Figure 35-1 shows the cross section of the control system.

* And that was in 1942...

Maintaining directional control in autorotations is difficult, as the amount of differential lift between the two rotors is not high, and may in fact reverse. The rigging that produces a left pedal turn in powered flight may produce a different effect in an autorotation. In the KA-32, this has been fixed by use some clever linkages as shown in Figure 35-2, as well as a minimum airspeed in autorotation!

The Russians are the major producers of coaxial rotor systems at present, and the Kamov series seems to enjoy reasonable military and commercial success (at least technically, if not in sales in the West).

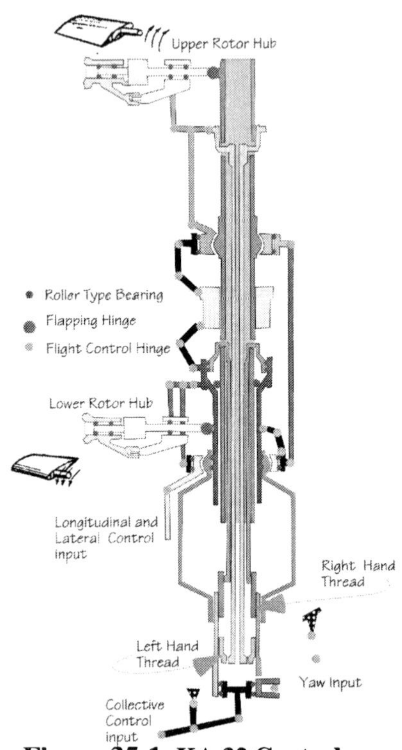

Figure 35-1 KA 32 Control System Cross Section

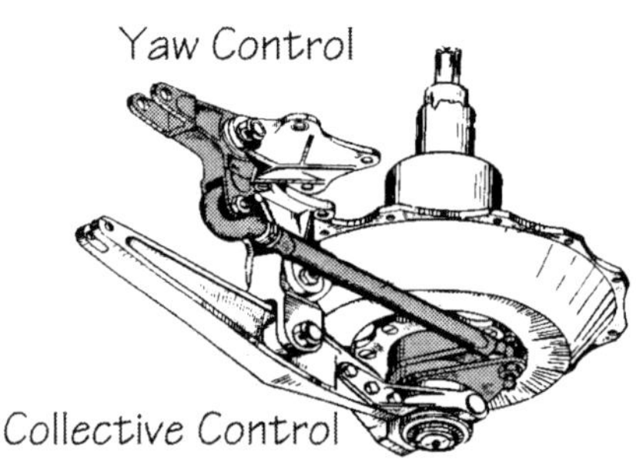

Figure 35-2 KA-32 Yaw Control Linkage

Tandem

The *tandem rotor* system has been tried by several companies, namely Bell (with the HSL), McCulloch (yes, the chain saw people) and a Russian company. The only ones in long production have been the Piasecki versions, starting with the HUP and H-21 and those made by its successor, the Boeing Vertol Company with the CH-46 and CH–47 series. These two have many features in common, among them highly overlapped rotors and a complex AFCS. Figure 35-3 shows the layout of a typical tandem rotor.

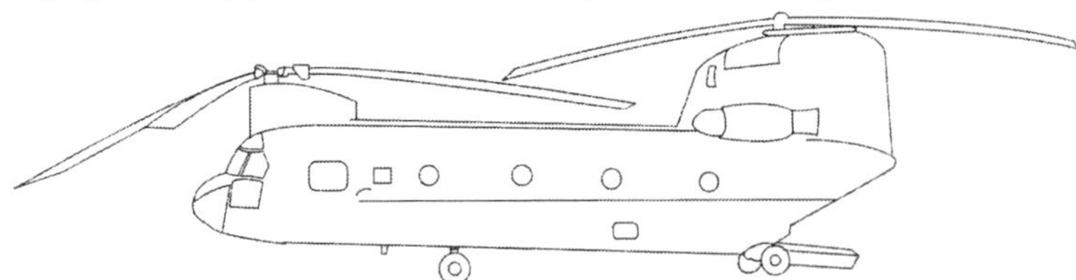

Figure 35-3 Layout of Typical Tandem Rotor

The tandem has the advantage of accepting a large load internally, with large variations on the CG position allowed. The lift is not split evenly between front and back - the rear rotor carries 55 - 65% of the weight.

The mechanics of the flight control system can only be described as a series of suitable mechanical linkages, and has to be seen to be believed. I am in awe of the men who designed the systems for both machines.

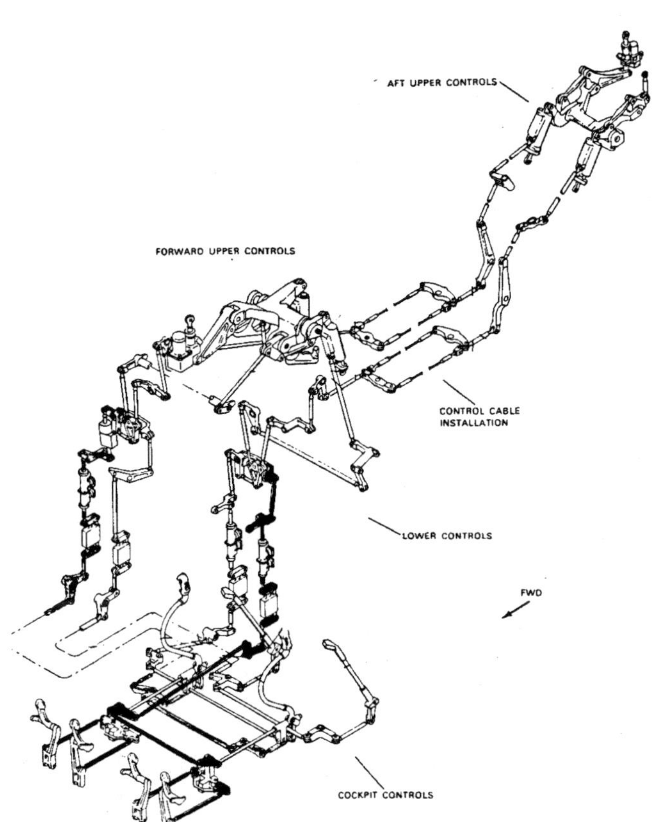

Figure 35-4 Tandem Rotor Controls

Roll control is straightforward, but longitudinal control is by means of differential collective between front and rear rotor. See Figure 35-4 for a typical arrangement of the rotor heads, noting that there are only two actuators to tilt the swashplate in roll and collective. What is not shown are the Longitudinal Cyclic Trims that tilt the swashplate to provide a more or less level fuselage attitude in forward flight, and are driven by the AFCS. This book isn't big enough to cover tandem rotor flight controls in the detail they deserve.

Longitudinal control will be less effective in an autorotation than in powered flight, as it depends upon some difference in pitch between front and rear rotors. With both rotors at minimum pitch, it means only one can increase, effectively reducing the pitching moment possible. In fact, more than one tandem pilot has discovered that the first action needed to level the helicopter at the end of a sporting quickstop is to add a lot of collective first (just like other helicopters, funny about that...).

Yaw control is by means of differential tilt of the rotor systems, so is not as positive as a conventional tail rotor.

Retreating Blade Stall in Tandem Rotor Helicopters

It may come as a surprise to know that the recovery action used in normal helicopters if retreating blade stall is encountered will get you into worse trouble in a tandem rotor helicopter. For those with short memories, the 'normal' recovery is to push forward on the cyclic, and then secondly lower the collective. In a tandem rotor helicopter, the rear rotor is carrying most of the load. Remember that cyclic control is mainly by differential collective. When a tandem rotor helicopter encounters retreating blade stall, if you push forward on the cyclic, the front rotor will decrease collective pitch, and the rear rotor will increase pitch, which is going to make the retreating blade stall worse. So, in a tandem, the first thing to do is not push forward, but perhaps lower the collective slightly!

Synchrocopter or Intermeshing Rotors

First developed by the Germans just before World War II, and actually the world's first production helicopter, the *synchrocopter* concept has not enjoyed the popularity it deserves. Simpler in many ways than other helicopters, it shares the advantages of the coaxial rotor in best utilizing the power from the engines and avoiding the use of the tail rotor. It is slightly lower in overall height compared to the coaxial design, and blade clearance is maintained by synchronization and axis tilting instead of vertical stacking of the disks. The only company still producing them is Kaman, who had a successful model in the HH-43 Huskie and more recently, appears to have found a ready market in the K-MAX for logging and vertical crane work.

Control is similar to the normal helicopter for pitch and roll, but yaw control uses differential lateral cyclic pitch. In forward flight, the large vertical stabilizers are used, however they don't work too well in the hover. To yaw the helicopter to the left in the hover, lateral cyclic is added to left side and taken away from the right side. A mixing unit makes this all transparent to the pilot.

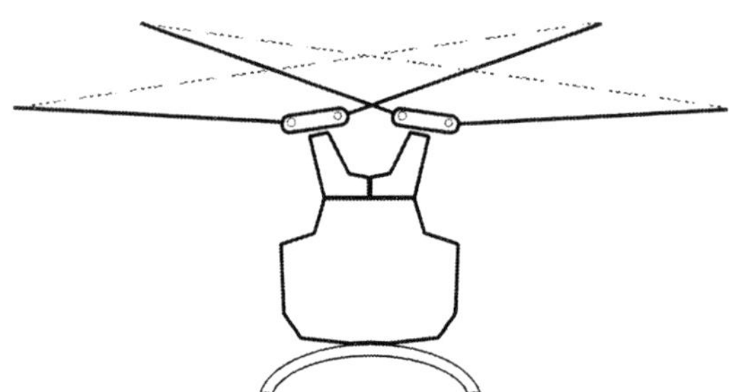

Figure 35-5 Synchrocopter Helicopter

It is interesting to note that the only current production intermeshing rotor helicopter, the Kaman K-Max, also uses the servo flap arrangement to control the rotor blades themselves.

COANDA EFFECT

There have been several attempts in recent years to harness the effect of blowing air across a surface to generate lift. This effect was discovered by Mr. *Coanda* many years ago, and only recently applied to rotary wing aircraft. There are two areas where this concept can be applied, namely improving the main rotor lift to remove the retreating blade stall problem and replacing the tail rotor. Of course, the military jet community can claim to have used this effect for years. Many fighters in the 1960's had 'blown' flaps and slats to bring their landing speeds down to merely unbelievable.

Main Blades

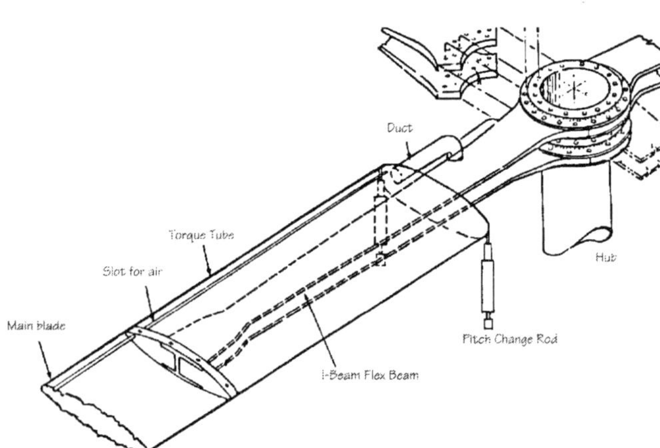

Figure 35-6 Coanda Effect used on Main Rotor Blade

Using the Coanda effect on the main rotor has not progressed beyond the experimental stage. Air is blown through the blades from the hub, and exits through special slots. The flow of air helps to pull air along with it, reducing drag and improving lift. Most of the air is introduced when the blade is on the retreating side, as this is the area of most concern. A more ambitious plan, shelved by NASA in the late 1980's, was to have the whole blade's lift and thrust controlled by blown air; the complexities of scheduling the air being slightly beyond the cutting edge of technology for that time*.

Tail Boom

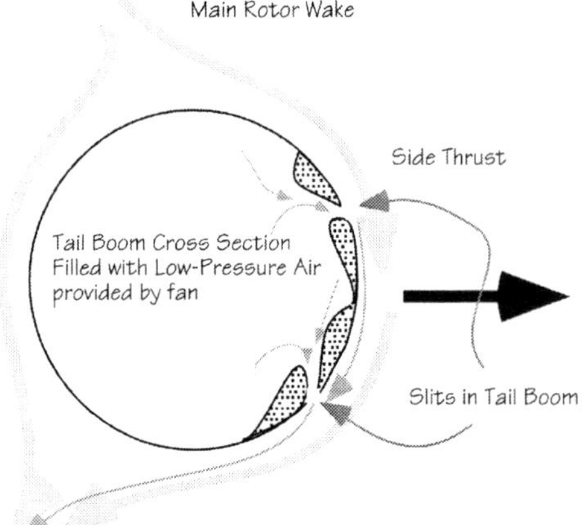

Figure 35-7 Coanda Effect On Tail Boom

The only current application of the Coanda effect for helicopters is on the tail boom of the NOTAR concept machines.

TIP JETS

Another way to eliminate the tail rotor is to have no part of the main rotor driven by anything connected with the fuselage. It is the reaction of the main rotor against the fuselage that requires a tail rotor to stop both rotating opposite one another. If the force can only be applied at the rotor, then there is no need for a tail rotor. One way to do this is to mount the device that propels the rotor actually on the rotor itself, and to date the only system that has worked at all is the tip jet.

* ~~I understand the test pilots on this program were particularly glad when the project was canceled- there were just too many things to go wrong with the air scheduling.~~In fact, one of the test pilots said they were really looking forward to the project.

There have been several relatively successful tip jet helicopters. One used jet engines at the tip, another used blown air exiting through the blade tips. I understand that the only one which achieved production standard, the Aerospatiale Djinn (pronounced 'gin') is still flying nearly 30 years later, cropdusting in Israel.

In all cases, special design was needed for the rotor blades, as they not only had to do their normal duty of providing lift and control, but also had to house fuel lines, control linkages for the engines, and structural support for the engines. An unanticipated benefit of fitting the engines on the end of the rotor blades is high rotor inertia - one light helicopter produced with tip jet engines had such high rotational energy that there was no Height–Velocity curve for engine failures.

The other way of developing power is to put hot exhaust gases out the tips of the blades to make them turn. This approach typically involves an engine mounted in the fuselage with complex ducting running to the swashplate and then out through the rotor blades, exiting at the tips. While not as complex as the tip jet, it suffers from friction losses in the ducting and requires specialized materials in the rotor blades to handle the high temperatures. When these projects were tried in the early 50's and 60's, materials that could handle the temperatures and stresses at the same time were just not practical. Perhaps, now that more sophisticated materials are available, these devices might be tried again.

Previous tip jets were both noisy and very fuel inefficient. Arguments for keeping trying with them was that people would get used to the noise (really!) and that fuel would be cheap. How times have changed.

A problem of tip jet helicopters is that it is difficult to control yawing - with no need for a tail rotor, it is difficult to control the direction the fuselage points, particularly in the hover. One hot–air jet design used a small rudder working in the exhaust of the main engine, but this was only marginally effective.

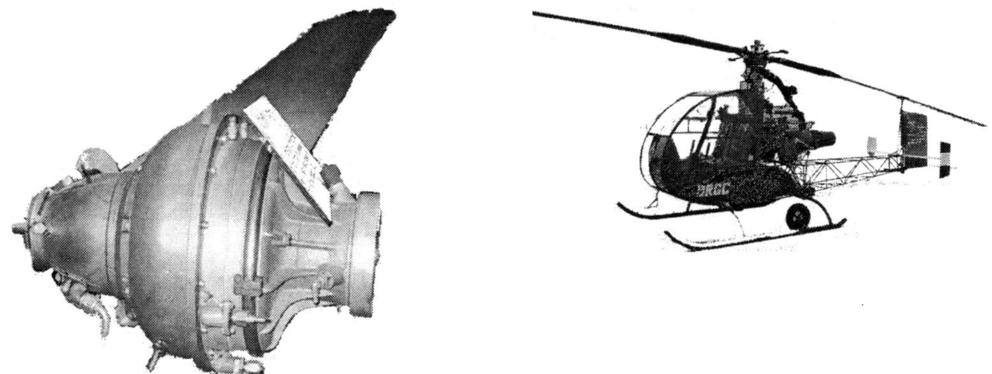

Figure 35-8 Tip Jet on Rotor blade, and pressure driven tip jet helicopter (Djinn)

Kaman Servo–Flap Controls

A unique way of controlling helicopter rotor blades is the Kaman servo-flap method. It is mentioned here, although it is used on a conventional type of rotor system because it's so different. The rotor blades on these helicopters are still free to feather like other helicopters. Basically, the *servo-flap* mechanism employs a small aileron–type device on the trailing edge of the rotor blade to change the pitch of the blades. Mechanical linkages from the rotor head run through the blade to this small flap, and the blade changes pitch in much the same manner as other blades. Pitch, flap and lag hinges are still present.

On the Kaman machines, the servo-flap controls are routed up the centre of the hollow main rotor mast. The 'swash plate' is actually below the transmission. What makes the servo-flap different is that it does not require any hydraulics between the pilot and the pitch change mechanism- the moment arm of the servo–flap to the blade is quite large, and given suitable mechanisms can be made so the effort required by the pilot is very low. The servo–flaps can also be tailored specifically for the blade loads encountered, and even have the possibility of automatic real–time tracking of individual blades for minimum vibration.

In more technical terms, the servo–flap also provides the whole helicopter with more stability with regard to angle of attack than other rotor control systems. It is easier to give wider margins for rotor blade flutter (something blade designers spend a lot of time making sure we are kept well away from) and reduces the requirement for an AFCS to give good IFR handling characteristics, especially in gusts. Finally it is lighter than other systems (since it needs no hydraulics) yet gives very high rotational inertia, which is good for autorotational characteristics.

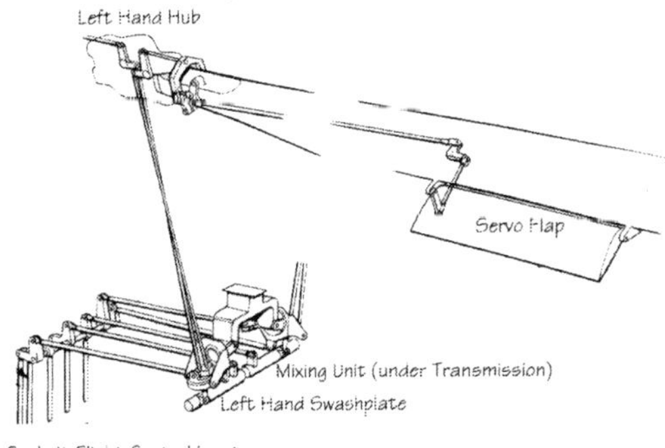

Figure 35-9 Kaman Servo Flap Details

The servo–flap is extremely simple in concept and execution, yet very effective and why it hasn't been more widely used is another of the mysteries of modern life.

Replacing the Tail Rotor

The tail rotor is a problem in many ways - it requires a lot of power to operate, it sticks out where it can be used as a brush clearing tool or people chopper*/slicer, it creates drag in forward flight, takes extra power that could usefully be used to provide lift, and so on. Some of the options in replacing it in total have been discussed in the previous sections, but there are also ways to retain its good points while eliminating the bad. The two main options are the use of a ducted fan or fenestron or the use of the Coanda effect on the tail boom.

Fenestron/Ducted Tail Rotor

Reasons

The *fenestron*†, or ducted tail rotor, is a tail rotor with a difference. There are some aerodynamic advantages to ducted fans (literally, fans with a shroud around the outside) and these seek to take advantage of it. Like all things, the first ones weren't as good as the more modern ones in terms of efficiency, and many lessons were learned along the way. Perhaps the biggest improvement of all is not blocking the airflow from the tail rotor (which most vertical stabilizers do very well) - the fenestron has no blockage. Figure 35-10 shows the fenestron.

Early fenestrons also had a very pronounced siren-like whine at one particular frequency, and often with a very wide range of angles. You knew when one was in the neighborhood.

* Sorry, another pun.
† Literally "Little window' in French

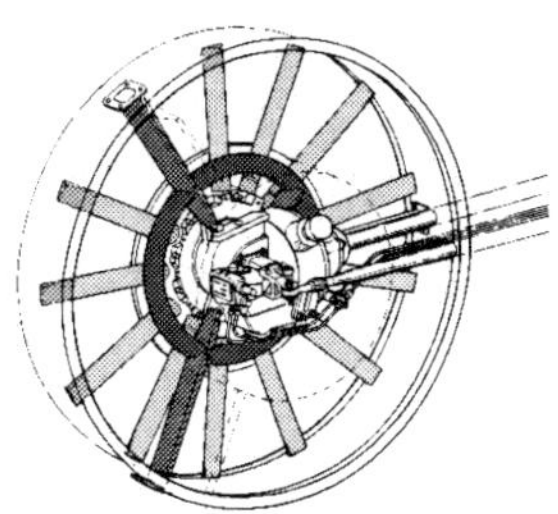

Figure 35-10 Section of Fenestron

Aside from the aerodynamic improvements as a tail rotor there are important safety aspects associated with this technology. It is extremely difficult to walk into a fenestron - a serious suicide wish is necessary.

More recently, the Eurocopter EC-135 and EC-120 have sported fenestrons which also have unevenly spaced blades and slanted stator vanes in order to reduce the noise generated by the fan.

Other manufacturers have experimented with imitations of the fenestron by modifying the vertical stabilizer and putting it around the tail rotor with good results, but none of these have appeared in production.

NOTAR

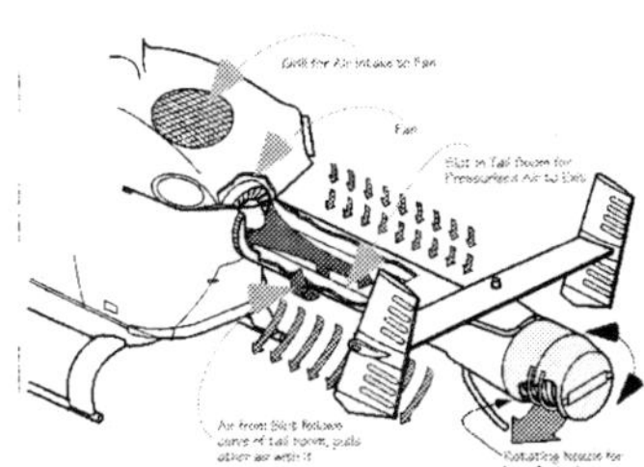

Figure 35-11 NOTAR Concept

The *NOTAR* (NO Tail Rotor) concept replaces the tail rotor with a circular cross–section boom with special slots and air ducts to provide the necessary anti-torque force. This has reached production as a retrofit in the McDonnell Douglas MD-520N, and as a new from beginning idea in the MD-900 Explorer. Thrust is provided by a fan driven from the transmission pushing a large quantity of low pressure air down the tail boom and out through the slits on the tail boom. A larger vent at the tip of the duct can be used to provide air to replace the controlling aspect of the tail rotor. There is also considerable advantage in that the lack of a tail rotor means no problems with people walking into the blades or backing the tail rotor into an obstacle.

Both of these other ways of controlling torque beside the tail rotor (NOTAR and fenestron) take slightly more power than the tail rotor in the hover, but have other advantages like noise and cruise efficiency.

Other Types

There are obviously other ways to achieve vertical flight with rotor blades. One of the more interesting ones I've seen was a multi-engine coaxial design which had two engines. So far, nothing seems too unusual, but this one has no change in blade pitch. Yes, you read that correctly- no change in blade pitch. Control is achieved in the vertical axis by changing engine RPM and N_R - with fixed blade pitch there is no other option, really. Changing the tilt of the thrust vector is achieved by tilting the whole of the rotating assembly in the appropriate direction. Since there is no collective pitch change, autorotation is not possible, but since there are two engines, this should be a rare occurrence. A further unique feature is that one engine is run at full power all the time, and the second engine is varied to control power. Whether this concept is successful, or joins the list that Arthur Young started in 1940 remains to be seen. Yet another example of this was the Rhyme copter developed in Japan. It was similar to the one described above, but had 4 small engines and was so light in weight, it was called a 'strap-on' helicopter.

There is also what I could call the 'flights of fancy' types of machines. These include machines with multiple ducted fans and individual engines in each fan; large delta wings apparitions with a large hole in the wing to hold a rotor which is closed in with louvers in forward flight; jet-borne devices that will hover and go Mach 2 with a windshield that has less substance and support than the one on your car and so on. The problem with these machines is that they ignore the realities of control of the machine, or the power required to hover, or the possibilities of engine failures, and so on. None of these machines bear up to serious technical scrutiny, and if you're ever asked to fly one, or fly in one, ask to see the certificate of airworthiness!

Summary of Chapter 35

This chapter has covered a lot of other ways of achieving vertical flight. Some have been commercially successful, others less so. Undoubtedly more ways will be found in the future.

36 Night and Instrument Flying

Introduction

Helicopters are more frequently called upon to fly under instrument and night conditions. For the military, this is nothing new, but for a lot of civilian helicopter pilots, it is a departure from their previous practice of "VFR at all costs". There is nothing inherently unsafe about either condition, but like helicopter flying by itself, it does need some thinking about.

Night Flying

The first thing to remember about night flying is only the pilot knows it's dark out there. The helicopter doesn't know whether the air is clear or foggy, day or night. Only the pilot...

There is also no truth to the rumor that dark air has no lift...

There are many problems with piloting a helicopter at night, and they mostly relate to not being able to see things. This means it is more difficult to judge rates of closure, see the wind from things like trees, grass and so on.

Hovering at night is made more difficult because of the poverty of cues - shining a searchlight on the ground below the helicopter can help, but shadows changing due to tilting of the fuselage can cause confusion as well.

Night flying is also not just going to be done around cities and airports with good lights and long, well lit runways. Hospital helipads, road accident sites, oil rigs, and so on are not normally well lit places. When you think about how much information is needed by the pilot to make the approach to a landing - things like rate of closure, rate of descent and so on, the need for some sort of lighting becomes apparent.

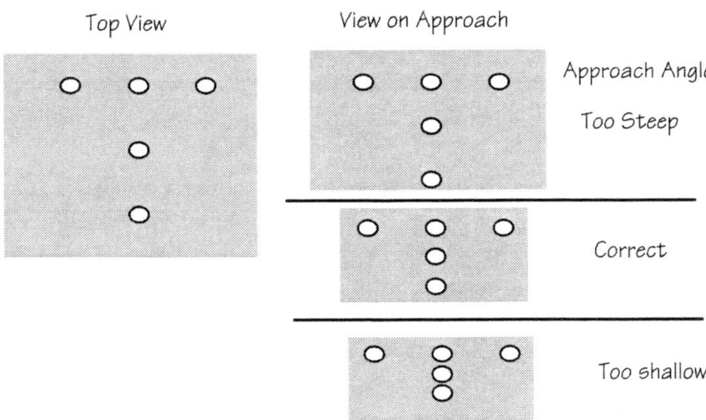

Figure 36-1 Night Landing T

Approaches need to be carried out to a set of references - i.e. more than one light. Until the advent of night vision goggles, it was standard practice in most militaries to use a T arrangement of lights and, if possible, to have a glide path indicator as well. The long part of the T gave line up, and the relationship of the top helped to determine glide path. Even so, it was necessary to pay attention to airspeed and altitude during the approach. (Landing lights were frowned on - it would give the enemy something to shoot at). A typical T is shown in Figure 36-1.

Landing a helicopter a long way from any other visual references, relying on only the relative size and shape of the lights at the landing site is another of our collective insanities. Fixed wing pilots long ago required that Visual Approach Slope (VASIS) lights be installed at major airports in order to stop problems with judging landings. Whey are we less demanding?

I hear some say that the reason is that helicopters can approach from nearly any direction, so it would need a lot of different approach directions. Not any more.

A recent development is the use of a portable night approach light system that has not only variable angles, but the capability to be switched on from the air. With suitable additional equipment, it can be motorized to point in different landing directions. (Others that can be switched on from the aircraft are fixed in azimuth and elevation.) The glidepath angle is sharply defined and the system also has flashing low– or high–on–glidepath indications. It can even be made to turn on the lights in the swimming pool as you're on final approach to impress your guests...

On another hobby horse, I've always found it disconcerting to make the final part of the approach with the airspeed indicator pegged at 0 knots (as the helicopter was well below the airspeed where the pitot static system accurately indicated anything except its installation). This exercise always proved to me that we humans really do get vertical cues from forward motion (and that we need a low airspeed system).

If you want to use a helipad at night, you need to consider that unless you are in an urban area with lots of lighting, that as soon as you fly away from the helipad, that you'll be in a black hole- be prepared to fly on instruments.

Engine Failures at Night

For the single–engine helicopter, an item of serious consideration must be engine failures at night. At least one country insists that any single–engined helicopter without a steerable searchlight must carry long–burning flares when night flying. The theory is that in the event of an engine failure, the flares will be fired, illuminating the area below, and last long enough for the pilot to make an autorotative approach and landing. How the pilot was to survive the ensuing grass fire, or the wrath of the local inhabitants whose houses were just burnt, was not of concern to the civil regulatory authorities. On a more serious note, the authorities had correctly realized that a non-adjustable landing light was of no use when carrying out an autorotation at night - when the helicopter flared*, all the visual cues disappeared as the light pointed skywards. Something to think about.

It is well beyond the scope of this book to address all the problems associated with night vision goggles, Forward Looking Infra-Red, thermal imaging systems and so on. Literally, many of these devices have turned the helicopter into an around–the–clock military or police machine. Advances in electro-optics will reduce the cost and weight and improve the performance of these devices so they will become as commonplace as personal computers, and no-one will consider flying naked–eyeballs–only at night ever again.

Night Vision Goggles (NVG)

NVGs have been around for quite a long time, but are just now finding their way into civil use. This is due to military pilots advocating them for some missions, but also due to the relatively low costs of the goggles themselves.

NVGs literally turn night into day, when the conditions are right. They won't work all the time, and have some definite limitations. For one thing, most cockpits need to be modified so that warning and caution lights won't overwhelm the light intensifying elements of the goggles, but must also still remain readable and usable during the day. Modifying the cockpit, and verifying that it works correctly at night with or without NVG, and during the day also is not easy or cheap.

It's also very unlikely that NVGs will be used for anything other than some specialized missions like crop spraying (surprised? - there's very little wind at night) or air ambulance where the risk is outweighed by the possibility of saving life.

The Myth of Night VFR

Unless you are flying over a brightly lit city, night flying is really not flying visually.

"But wait, " you say "the rules in my country allow night VFR if the visibility and cloud criteria are met."

True enough. What if you are over an area with no lights, and a high cloud cover? How can you tell the visibility in any case? How would you know if the visibility has decreased to below the required distance, or the cloud criteria have eroded?

But there is more to VFR flying than just visibility. Somewhere in most definitions of VFR are words like 'ability to orient the aircraft position and attitude by means of visual references'. If you have no visual references (i.e. you are over the dark ocean with no stars), how can you determine your attitude much less your position.

So, unless you are over a brightly lit city, treat night like it was IMC.

Most European countries treat night flying as instrument flying, for very good reason.

* This pun was not deliberate.

Instrument Flying

Before beginning this section, a distinction must be made between *Instrument Flight Rules* (*IFR*) and *Instrument Meteorological Conditions* (*IMC*). IFR means following the rules of instrument flight - this can be in very good weather, clear of cloud, using radio navigation aids, Air Traffic Control and so on. IMC means flying with sole reference to the instruments - namely no visible horizon, no ground references, no way to determine the helicopters pitch, roll and heading except from cockpit instruments. A subtle difference, but very important, as will be shown shortly. IMC can be simulated using an instrument hood, and it need not be in the airways structure*.

As far as the airways' (i.e. IFR) procedures are concerned, instrument flying in helicopters is very little different from that in an equivalent speed fixed–wing aircraft. Fixed–wing flying is a much cheaper way to learn instrument air sense, then it is only necessary to learn to fly a helicopter on instruments. This is a large enough step in itself - why is it so difficult?

IFR Flight Envelope

The first thing to understand about instrument flying in a helicopter is, aside from helicopters fitted with very complex autopilots and special instruments, only half the flight envelope is usable for instrument flying. Most light helicopters that are instrument flight equipped have a minimum airspeed when IFR† in the flight manual. For the sake of argument, lets say this airspeed is about 60 knots. Why is this speed there at all?

There are many good reasons for setting a minimum speed in IMC.

- Unless a low-airspeed sensing system has been fitted (discussed later), the airspeed system is pretty well useless below 40 KIAS. A 20 knot margin between minimum IFR speed and the speed where the ASI stops making sense isn't too large, and might be acceptable, if it weren't for several other problems, namely:
- The shape of the power required vs. airspeed curve around 60 KIAS is relatively flat, but, as speed decreases below this airspeed, starts to go negative - that is, more power is required to maintain level flight at a slower airspeed. If you haven't tried maintaining 40 KIAS in level flight, under simulated IMC, it's an interesting exercise. I wouldn't recommend it in real IMC.
- The helicopter has very little directional stability at these low speeds - very small amounts of out–of–trim can cause large yaw rates, and that makes it difficult to maintain heading accurately. The slip ball is very insensitive at these airspeeds, and a small amount of out–of–trim condition can cause large heading changes. Slip strings, of course, are not fitted to the inside of the helicopter, so it makes the instrument scan or cross check slightly awkward.
- There is very little, if any, static stability in the longitudinal axis below 60 KIAS. I'll avoid a very complex discussion, and say that even when trimmed for a particular airspeed, if a gust changes the airspeed, the helicopter is happy to stay at the new airspeed and not return towards the original speed. Another way to say this is any small change in longitudinal stick position will affect a very large change in airspeed in this region. In simple terms, it is difficult to hold an airspeed around 60 KIAS in anything other than ideal, flat calm conditions.

Why is Helicopter IFR Difficult?

All of this is merely to discuss why only half the flight envelope is usable, but doesn't tell us why it's difficult to fly helicopters on instruments in the first place. Unlike fixed–wing aircraft, which are more or less stable in both the longitudinal and lateral-directional axes, the helicopter is dynamically unstable in the longitudinal axis, and neutrally stable in the lateral directional axis. Big words - what do they mean?

* A safety pilot is needed however and someone to look–out on the same side as the pilot 'under the bag' is very worthwhile.

† See the confusion? Don't they mean when IMC?

There was some discussion earlier about instability in the hover. You may remember some discussion about the increasing oscillations and the requirement for small continuous control inputs or corrections to stop this from developing – they are equally valid here. Left to its own devices, in forward flight a helicopter will develop larger and larger pitch oscillations. The pilot must prevent these from starting, and in VMC, with good visual references, this is relatively easy. In IMC, only the instruments to tell the pilot what is happening. In turbulence, the attitude indicator, which is the primary reference for attitude, has enough 'noise' to be difficult to interpret the exact attitude with any precision and decide what to do at an early stage. Just like the hover, in calm conditions, the pilot must make corrections to stop the oscillation from diverging about every 5 - 8 seconds.

I remember many hours of flying on instruments in the UH-1N (without a stabilization system) when it was not uncommon for the altitude to change suddenly by 100 feet, or the airspeed to suddenly be 10 KIAS different with no perceived (i.e. seat of the pants) change.

Add to this the effects on the yaw axis when vertical gusts change the torque balance on the main rotor, and the picture becomes very confusing. Most helicopters without an AFCS and that fly in IMC/IFR (and they are almost all military) end up with the two pilots trading flying every 30 minutes or so - it's too tiring to keep it up for much longer than this at one time. Is it any wonder nearly every civil IFR helicopter has an autopilot in it?

Why aren't more civil helicopters flown IFR? The simple reason is that most civil helicopters are single–engined, and what happens when the engine fails*? Unless you have lots of clear air under the clouds so you have enough time to find a suitable place to land, it's not a good idea to be up there. In most European countries, it is not permitted to carry paying passengers in single–engine helicopters IFR. For the few given dispensation, there must be no cloud below 1,500 AGL in order to carry out a safe engine off landing.

Disorientation

One of the main problems of instrument flying in helicopters is that in real IMC, it is very easy to get disoriented (some people call it vertigo). Unless you are lucky enough to fly a big helicopter, the large amount of glass area provided to give you a good view of the world when hovering can easily provide powerful cues that will distract you from the instruments. I've seen people get disoriented several times, and had it happen to me. For this reason, nearly every helicopter that operates at night or in an area where there aren't really good visual cues for determining pitch and roll attitude, or height above the ground should have an attitude indicator, and the pilot should have an instrument rating.

Interestingly, it is only the operating rules that require an attitude indicator for night flying - the basic certification rules don't require it. Just another of the strange things in this world.

Hopefully when you get your instrument rating, you will be put in unusual attitudes and other situations where you will learn to trust your instruments, and also how to survive disorientation.

Useful Instrument Flying Exercises

The following are useful exercises to develop instrument flying skills. It is noticeable that they concentrate on IMC skills, as opposed to procedural IFR skills. These should all be practiced with an instructor or competent helicopter pilot as safety pilot.

Slow Flight

The first exercise is slow flight. Slow down to 60 KIAS and practice turns, climbs and descents and then combine turns with climbs or descents. While the maximum angle of bank you might expect to see for a standard rate turn is quite low (about 13°), you should try turns to 30°, just for the practice.

When changing power for climbs and descents, notice how difficult it is to keep the ball in the middle. When you get tired of doing this with all the instruments working, try partial panel with the attitude indicator failed, and if you have a turn and slip indicator, using the turn and slip to do a standard rate (rate 1) turn. Time turns through 60°, 90° and 180° of heading, on partial panel (i.e. no attitude indicator).

* Unfortunately, the engine failure rate on turbine single engine helicopters is still too high to permit carrying passengers IFR.

Once you get the hang of that, try slowing down to 40 KIAS and turning, climbing and descending. Be careful of letting the airspeed get too low, and also be prepared for very small angles of bank to generate large heading changes.

Changing Airspeed

Change the airspeed while maintaining altitude, from 40 KIAS to V_H and back.

Putting It All Together

The best training exercise for learning to fly on instruments is the coordinated climbing turn or descent. Basically, starting at a convenient airspeed and on a cardinal heading (East or South, for example) and at an easy–to–remember altitude (2,500' AMSL, for example), start a climb at 500 feet per minute and then start a standard rate (3° per second) turn. Every minute you should be 500 feet higher, and 180° different in heading. Work at it until you can be sure of the heading being 30° different every 10 seconds, and the altitude being 125' different every 15 seconds. Minor corrections to power, rate of turn and so on will be needed. This exercise will sharpen cross check skills immensely, and make following radials and ILS bars a piece of cake.

Inadvertent IMC

This is a touchy subject. There are numerous schools of thought on this, and lots of things to think about. Lots of helicopters which are very well equipped to fly in IMC crash while trying to stay in VMC conditions.

Consider your options before you set out on a trip. If you're in an area without many obstacles, and you're not likely to encounter icing conditions, and you're current in instrument flying, and not likely to mess up instrument approach procedures, then I would seriously think of climbing to a minimum safe altitude rather than trying to scud run.

I've had to do this three times in my relatively tame career. Each time, it was very straightforward. We had encountered deteriorating weather, and had the necessary conditions to be able to climb into IMC. We contacted the local controlling authority and were given permission to proceed IFR. (In one case we were a long way away, and climbed to the minimum enroute altitude for that area and tried to contact Air Traffic Control - we were so far away, it took us a while before we could get in touch with them, but we were well below any altitude they would have been using in that area anyway). Otherwise, no problems at all. ATC weren't upset at us, there was no grand inquisition to ask us why we did this, and everyone was happy.

I've done this in several countries, and no-one has complained about it. I was certainly happy to have this capability / ability!

In some organizations, IMC is the last resort, and pilots are led to believe that using the procedure just described is a career-ending move. Far from it!

Autorotations at Night, in Clouds, etc.

Just like we have no reliable long–term warning of when engines will fail, we have no guarantee they will not fail at night or other times of poor visibility. Even multi-engine helicopters can have occasion to use autorotations if they have fuel problems (a distinct lack of it, for example), or a tail rotor failure.

What to do if the need arises when you are not sure of the ground underneath, and have no choice about autorotation? The answer is in a little known technique called the 'constant attitude autorotation', invented (I think) in the UK. The name derives from the constant attitude maintained throughout the maneuver, although the name 'constant airspeed' might just as well be used - there is no flare at the bottom.

Typically, this autorotation uses a lower–than–normal airspeed, about 35 to 40 KIAS, plus half the windspeed, with the helicopter facing into the surface wind*. Maintain this airspeed all the way to the time of pulling collective pitch, and if any margins are to be given, err just slightly to a higher airspeed. Slowing below this slow airspeed quickly increases the rate of descent and makes it difficult to regain (or even hold) airspeed due to errors in the pitot static system.

* which means it's a good idea to keep a mental note of the surface wind direction and speed.

The effect for most of the descent is quite serene - there is little sensation of plummeting towards the earth. This changes dramatically at about 100' AGL, when the ground rush starts to become apparent in a real hurry. The philosophy of the constant attitude autorotation is that at night with the landing light on or in IMC (fog all the way down to low altitude), the ground would start to make its presence known at about this point.

A radar altimeter is really essential if you're going to fly in cloud for real, if only for this reason.

In daylight (the best place to practice this), wait until the ground rush is really quite pronounced (at about 50' AGL) before starting to feed in collective, slowly at first, and then as rapidly as needed. The amount of collective to apply is quite natural, but there is little room for error. Do not flare, accept the slight forward speed! It should be quite obvious to even the most casual observer that there is no point in flaring. From a technical point of view, there is not enough kinetic energy to change the flight path and it would only change the attitude on ground impact.

The logic for this maneuver is something like this: at night or in IMC, there are not enough cues for the pilot to judge height above ground for a flare to stop the rate of descent. The purpose of the flare is to stop the rate of descent and get rid of the kinetic energy of forward speed. A misjudged flare might mean hitting the ground with high forward speed as well as a vertical speed and is worse than hitting the ground with very little forward and relatively low vertical speed. So the constant attitude autorotation is a compromise.

For those of you who say this is silly - who would want to fly a single engine helicopter in cloud or at night - well, not only will people do it (it's normal in some militaries), but multi-engine helicopters can also have emergencies where an autorotation is the only way out. They fly at night and in cloud a lot!

Instrument Flying Rules (IFR)

I'm very disappointed that the Air Traffic system has not seen fit to recognize the special needs and capabilities of the helicopter. It is only within the last few years that we have seen helicopter-only instrument approaches which utilize a maximum speed on approach which is representative of the helicopter's capabilities.

While this is a big step forward, there is still much to be corrected. We need to have fuel reserves which recognize that helicopters can't carry as much fuel as fixed wing airplanes, so it is impossible to be able to carry alternate fields and fuel reserves and a meaningful payload. The chances of achieving a successful approach with the slower approach speeds the helicopter uses would also ensure that less fuel reserves would be needed. One of the other reasons fixed wing aircraft carry fuel reserves, runway closure, is also less of a hazard for helicopters, as we typically don't need runways for landing. All in all, we are being hampered by yet another hold-over from the fixed wing world.

With the advent of precision GPS approaches, perhaps it is time to revisit the fuel reserve requirement. As this book was going to print, I read that the FAA is relaxing these requirements - about time, too!

GPS and IFR

There is a great tendency to use a simple, hand-held GPS for a lot of helicopter flying. For VFR operations, this is a great idea (but see "Using GPS Intelligently" on page 434*). If you're planning to use GPS for IFR however, a hand-held machine can be lethal. One of the primary concerns of instrument navigation is reliability of radio navaid signals. For some of the radio navaids we use, (VOR, ILS) there are flags on the displays to tell when the signal is not correct or has been lost. For ADF, there is no flag to tell when the signal is lost, so it is necessary to listen to the audio signal during an ADF approach to tell if the signal suddenly goes away. GPS has an equivalent 'flag', and it's called RAIM, for Receiver Autonomous Integrity Monitoring. This is only found in IFR approved equipment, and its the GPS equivalent to the flags for VOR and ILS, or listening to the ADF. It tells the pilot that the required navigation accuracy for an IFR approach (0.3nm) is not available. For those of you who think this less-than-accurate state of affairs with GPS is never going to happen, I suggest you think again. I've read lots of reports from hand-held users where the GPS was found to be up to 80 nautical miles off, with no warning. Not the sort of thing to have happen on an IFR approach in the mountains, you'll agree. So, if you're going to go IFR, get an appropriately approved GPS installation. And learn how to use it.

*

Just to reinforce the point, you wouldn't think of routinely using your hand-held Nav-Com transmitter with VOR receiver to do a VOR approach would you? You do remember to monitor the ADF signal when you're using that for an approach don't you?

Helicopter Only Approaches

I've seen a few of these, and for the most part they help to utilize the unique capabilities of the helicopter. We need to learn from our fixed wing brethern though, as they have special tests that must be satisfied when an airplane is approved to for anything other than a 3° glideslope. We're slightly luckier in the helicopter world, in that most approach paths that are steeper than 3° don't cause a problem, but really steep ones (greater than 9°, for example) can be interesting to fly.

The other problem with helicopter only approaches is that they should only be carried out into wind. Again, our fixed wing brethern have a rule* that anything more than a 10 Knot tailwind must be specifically flight tested and approved. We seem to have ignored this, with the added peril that a tailwind on approach can lead to nasty things like vortex ring state. High crosswinds can also lead to some interesting crab angles at the final stages of the approach. A lot of work needs to be done before we get to the next stage, which is-

Zero-Zero Approaches

The zero/zero approach is one where the visibility is zero, and the ceiling is zero. In other words, some pretty intense fog. This is actually extremely rare, and there is generally some vertical and horizontal visibility.

We are a long way from achieving this in the helicopter world on an everyday basis. Previous comments on low airspeed sensing systems are very pertinent here, but more mundane things like how will we be able to transition from the approach to a go-around, or land safely in the event of an engine failure† at the very last part of the approach? What kind of lighting system will we need for the landing site? What kind of crosswind limits will be permitted?

Related to this subject is the need to consider what type of helicopters we are going to permit to do these type of approaches. If we stick to our major concern of engine failures (and this itself may not be the real problem in helicopter flying) then it is probable that only multi-engine helicopters will be permitted to conduct these approaches. Even if we then accept that Category A helicopters have good single engine capabilities, they aren't able to fly away from all conditions - the flight profiles are set up to make sure the helicopter can land safely from a failure on very short final, for example. So, if we have a zero-zero approach to the hover at some point the helicopter is going to be committed to land if an engine fails. So, being committed to land, it follows that we need guidance to touchdown (or some other low visibility) in case the visibility is really that bad. Given the capabilities of GPS and most especially Differential GPS (DGPS), this should be no problem.

I've seen some zero-zero approaches in helicopters that were absolutely spectacular, and if implemented would truly unlock the potential of the helicopter. A lot of work needs to be done to make this reality.

Single Pilot IFR

The helicopter, being a more expensive machine to operate, has more impetus to have only one pilot on board, in order to maximize the number of revenue seats on the machine. So what about single pilot IFR? I find it interesting to note that for IFR, we require two of nearly anything. (The US is the only country to permit IFR in single engine helicopters with passengers on board, although single engine fixed wing IFR with lots of restrictions is permitted in several countries.) We require two navigation aids, two altimeters, two radios, and so on. But the part that has been shown to fail most frequently, and in the most un-explained way, the part with the single information processor (brain) and single engine (heart), is permitted to operate without a

* Not well known or understood. It's buried in the airframe certification rules, and not spelled out in Flight Manuals.

† You will note that I'm not even considering single engine helicopters for zero/zero approaches.

backup. After I read of a pilot flying IFR by himself with passengers, at night, having a heart attack and landing the aircraft safely at a conveniently close-by airport, I really questioned this philosophy.

Summary of Chapter 36

We've covered a bit of night flying and instrument flying- two things which are often considered the same in the fixed wing world. For helicopters, they are two different scenarios, and both need special training.

Automatic Flight Control Systems

Introduction

Much of the success of the helicopter as a military and commercially successful vehicle is due to the AFCS. An unstable aircraft is transformed into a stable easy to handle machine, with features beyond the capabilities of the human pilot. Examples of these benefits are IFR certification, night hovering over the sea, and so on. Even the most skittish of helicopters can be turned into a docile, civilized machine with a simple AFCS.

This chapter is not a detailed coverage of helicopter AFCSs, but will show the principles of simple systems. These basics can be applied to more advanced systems.

Normally, helicopters fitted with an AFCS have hydraulically–boosted, irreversible flight controls*. Because of this, it is normal to have an artificial feel system installed. (Chapter 27,"Advanced Helicopter Flying" discussed the need for, and layout of, a typical artificial feel system.) Because the various systems in this chapter work in pitch, roll and yaw, the term control is used rather than stick, cyclic or pedals.

This chapter will attempt to de-mystify the AFCS. I have heard of one military helicopter where the combination of hydraulic system, stabilization system and autopilot were so complex that no-one understood it, and after some unsolved crashes, crews literally refused to fly the machine until someone could explain it to them in simple, everyday English.

Definitions

AFCS is defined as any augmentation of the mechanical flight controls assisting the pilot. The way terms are used will aid the understanding of any AFCS, and misuse will only obfusticate† the situation. The definitions used in this book may differ from those used by other organizations. At least one airframe manufacturer insists on calling any AFCS fitted to their helicopters a 'SCAS', whether it has control feed–forward or not. As with previous definitions, the main point is to make sure you ask questions if you aren't absolutely sure about the meaning of words used.

An example of confusion is in the term yaw damper, which, in fixed–wing aircraft, normally means an AFCS related to yaw, but there are helicopters that have mechanisms to prevent rapid movement of the pedals, also called yaw dampers.

Another term which will crop up repeatedly in this chapter is ***datum***. This means a specific attitude (or possibly other item such as airspeed) which the AFCS is attempting to hold. For example, if the datum attitude in pitch is 1° nose up, then the AFCS will be constantly comparing the existing attitude to this datum in order to determine if a correction is needed.

Why install an AFCS?

AFCSs are generally installed to:

- Overcome a stability and control deficiency, e.g., preventing a divergent oscillation or Dutch Roll‡.
- Improve the handling or ride qualities in general, or in some specific operating mode, e.g. holding altitude or airspeed, turning to and capturing a navigation track, hover augmentation etc.
- Carry out a maneuver the pilot is unable to perform either due to the accuracy required, or to the length of time over which it is necessary to carry out the task, or the lack of visual cues, etc. An example might be hovering over water at night.

The response of an AFCS is much more rapid than that of the human pilot.

---

* There are helicopters with reversible control systems with AFCS's.

† Look it up- it means 'confuse'

‡ No, not some exotic European pastry, but a combination of roll and yaw in forward flight which may happen and is difficult if not impossible for the pilot to suppress. Happens mostly to fixed wing aircraft, but can occur on some helicopters.

For example, typically a pilot can detect a change of pitch attitude of 1° (from the attitude indicator) 0.3 seconds after it occurs. This means an attitude change of at least 1° has occurred. There is a further delay of about 0.5 seconds while the amount of control correction needed is mentally calculated and then applied. In all probability, the attitude change is now much larger than 1°, and the pilot has to correct back to what is perceived as the correct pitch attitude. We can't read the attitude indicator very accurately, nor set the helicopter on it very precisely, so it will take several corrections to get things back to where they should be. On the other hand, an AFCS can detect a smaller disturbance (0.1°) more quickly (0.05 seconds) and apply an input to overcome the disturbance within 0.1 seconds. The combined effect is that with an AFCS, less disturbance gets to the airframe. Since in a helicopter everything is connected, when a small disturbance occurs on the airframe, it has other effects. For example, pitch attitude changes can affect other axis, so if they can be prevented, it will make the whole flight smoother. In short, an AFCS can detect smaller deviations more quickly and apply more precise corrections to a greater degree of accuracy than any pilot can.

Hierarchy of an AFCS

AFCSs can be extremely complex and difficult to understand. On the other hand, if we start with a simple arrangement, and build up from there, understanding is much easier. The first thing to be made clear is the way that parts of an AFCS fit together.

Figure 37-1 illustrates the various layers that can exist within an AFCS. For example, all AFCSs need rate damping, so that has been placed at the center of this diagram, as it is the foundation part. Not all AFCSs will include an operational autopilot, so it is placed at the outside.

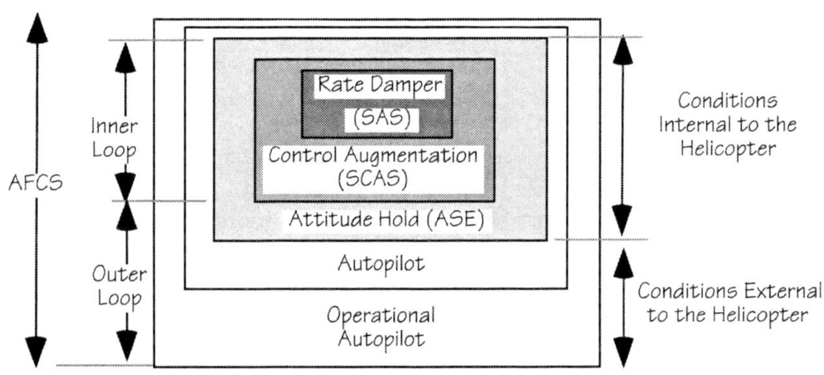

Figure 37-1 Hierarchy of AFCS

Please bear in mind the definitions used here, for example, internal and external conditions, rate dampers and so on, are for ease of understanding. The exact names these parts might be called in a specific AFCS may be different, but the principles remain the same.

AFCS and the Big Picture of Control

Earlier ("So How Do We Fly a Helicopter?" on page 277), we looked at how the pilot really flies the helicopter, and the closed loop diagram was introduced. If we add an AFCS to this diagram of control and feedback, it should be consistent. In Figure 37-2, the AFCS is now shown with two parts, the inner loop and the outer loop. Roughly speaking, these two loops correspond respectively to conditions internal of and external to the airframe.

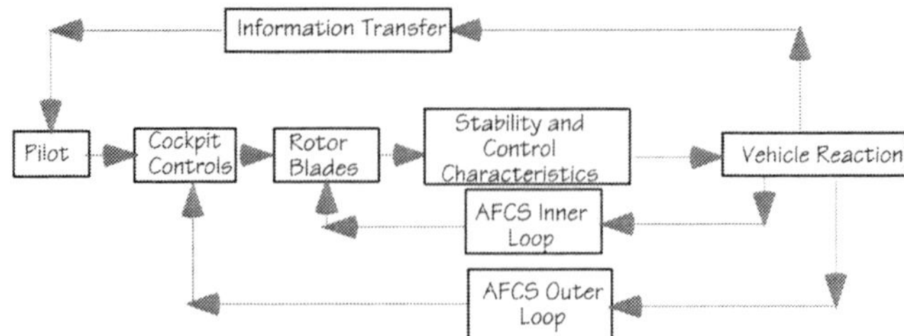

Figure 37-2 AFCS Added to the Control Loop

Internal vs. External Conditions

Internal conditions come from sensors related directly to the helicopter*, such as pitch, roll, and yaw attitudes, rates and accelerations. External relates to conditions outside the helicopter such as airspeed, altitude, track, and other navigational information. The inner loop of the AFCS typically handles internal conditions, i.e., items independent of outside events, while the outer loop may handle external conditions. Autopilots are typically outer loop devices.

Components of An AFCS

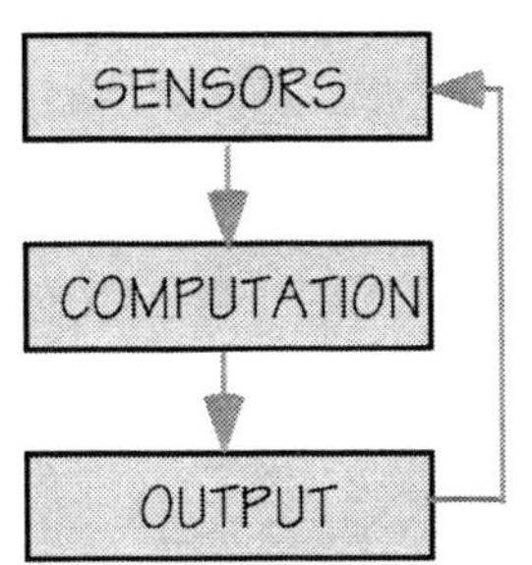

Figure 37-3 Main Components of an AFCS

The components of any AFCS can be divided into three sections, as shown in Figure 37-3.

Sensors

Sensors measure parameters and transmit information to the computer. Typical items sensed in AFCSs and the sensors used are given in the Table below.

TABLE 3. AFCS Sensors

Parameter		Normal Sensor	Alternate Sensor
Pitch Roll Yaw	Rate	Rate Gyroscope	Attitude Gyroscope (differentiated) Inertial Navigation System
Pitch Roll Yaw (heading)	Atti-tude	Attitude Gyroscope Compass	Rate Gyroscope (integrated) Attitude and Heading Reference System (AHRS)
Control / actuator position		Linear Variable Displacement Transducers	
Acceleration		Accelerometers	Differentiated Rate
Airspeed		Air Data System	
Altitude		Air Data System	Possibly GPS, Differential GPS
Height Above Ground		Radar Altimeter	Doppler, Terrain Comparison
Sideslip		Differential Pressure System	Low Airspeed System
Sideforce		Yaw Rate	
Groundspeed		Doppler	GPS
Navigation Data		Any navigation sensor	Flight Management System

* This is an academic definition, but is used to help understanding.

Computers

Convert sensor information and make decisions about the signals fed to the output devices. Digital electronic circuits are commonly used, but analog electrical, mechanical and fluidic AFCS computers also exist. Typical functions performed by an AFCS computer are given in the Table below.

Function	Example
Amplification	Increases signal level. Gearing in a mechanical system. Also called gain.
Integration	Derive information (i.e. rate integrated produces attitude). There are problems integrating small (i.e. near zero) signals
Differentiation	Differentiation is opposite to integration (i.e. attitude when differentiated produces rate). Cannot detect small changes in rate
Limiting	Parameter changes restricted to certain limits (e.g. may not permit rates greater than x°/second to be used).
Shaping	May be considered non-linear amplifiers (e.g. change sideslip signal with airspeed). Adapt the computer output to produce the desired handling characteristics or flight path of a helicopter.
Programming	Programs produce outputs that will allow a helicopter to fly predetermined maneuvers

TABLE 4. Computer Functions.

.More than one helicopter has had a self–induced problem resulting from an airframe vibration acting on the AFCS gyros and feeding this signal into the actuators. The actuators move very quickly in response to this signal, and produce more vibration. In this case, turning off the AFCS solved the problem, as far as the unwanted vibrations went, but left the pilot with a handful of helicopter to fly. Fitting a filter to remove normal rotor–induced vibration was a better long term solution.

Actuators or Output Devices

The output from the computer must be converted into a form that will result in movement of the rotor blades; typically, electro-mechanical or electro-hydraulic *actuators* are used. These actuators can be in different configurations, i.e., in series with the flight control, parallel to them, or a combination of both. Their function is to produce a movement of the rotor blades through the normal flight control system. The difference between series and parallel is explained shortly.

Actuator design is a compromise between:

- Authority (percentage of total possible control movement affected) versus rate of travel in a failure. For example, 10% authority in roll means the actuator can move the rotor disk 10% of the travel available in the cockpit in roll.
- Gain or rate of normal movement (% of travel per second).
- Size and accuracy of movement for stability and/or control.

Actuator Position Feedback Signals

The computer must know the position of the actuator to decide if it is possible to move the actuator* so it is necessary to feed a signal of actuator position back to the computer. This is simple, but there is a problem if this signal is lost (such as a broken wire), which may tell the computer the actuator has not moved, or is in the incorrect position. This can be solved by duplication of feedback signals. An additional use of the feedback signal is to provide an indication to the pilot of the status of the actuator, and possibly, permits a comparison of demanded and actual positions for troubleshooting.

Additionally, the response of the actuator in the event of a loss of signal, the occurrence of a larger than expected signal or loss of feedback signal must be considered. For example, if the actuator freezes in position, the effect of any failure may be minimal, but if the actuator suddenly moves to the extreme of travel, there will be a large effect.

* And more importantly, if it is reacting properly.

Actuator Position Signals to the Pilot

Figure 37-4 Typical API

The actuator position feedback signal is fed back to the computer, and possibly to an *Actuator Position Indicator* (API) in the cockpit; this is to indicate to both the computer and pilot that the actuator is operating correctly. If the actuator has moved to almost the end of its travel, the pilot is able to adjust the cockpit control to re-center it, and permit it to function in both directions. The API can also assist in trouble shooting operation of the AFCS*.

Series Actuator

A simple *series actuator* is shown in Figure 37-5, but this is not the only way to mechanize a series actuator. In this configuration, the actuator alters the length of the control run changing the pitch at the main rotor. When the actuator moves, the cockpit control is prevented from moving by the artificial feel system. Figure 37-6 shows a more detailed view of the interior of a typical series actuator. In the 'Big Picture' of control (Figure 37-2), series actuators correspond to the inner loop, acting quietly and unobtrusively to keep things from going off the rails.

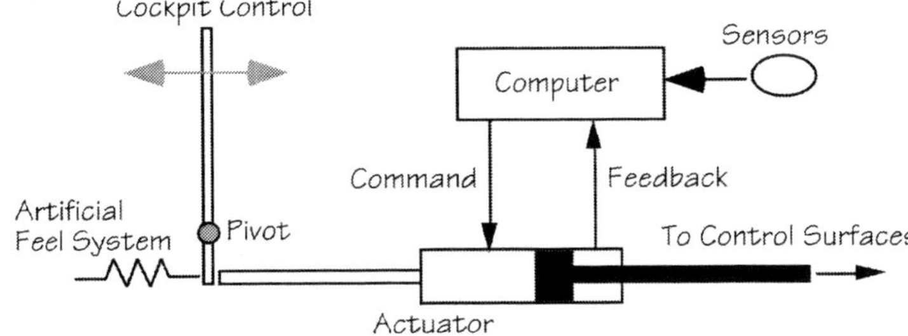

Figure 37-5 Typical Series Actuator Installation

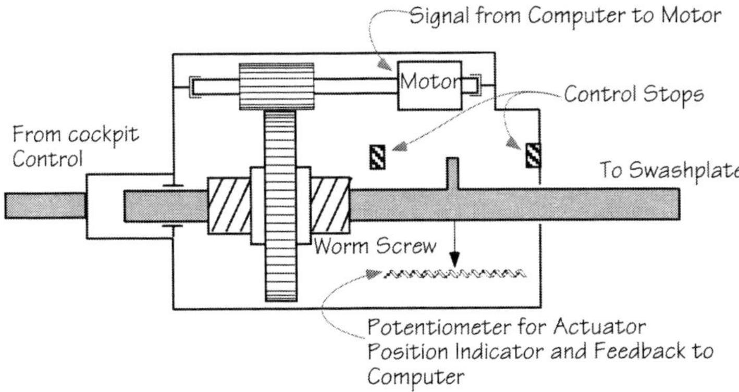

Figure 37-6 Interior Detail of a Series Actuator

The characteristics of a series actuator system can be summarized as follows:

- The actuator moves the rotor blades, but not the cockpit controls. If the artificial feel system is turned off, the actuator will move the cockpit control and not the rotor blades - obviously providing no stabilization. (A good reason to leave the force trim on.)
- The actuator operates at high speed to counter small disturbances quickly.
- The actuator authority must be limited (usually to approximately 10% of total control travel), so failures (hardovers or runaways) are not catastrophic. The remaining

* Most European designed / installed AFCS's incorporate this useful feature, and not many North American ones have it. European pilots seem to understand AFCS's very well. Is the actuator position indicator cause or effect?

travel of the cockpit control with the actuator fully extended or retracted is adequate to control the helicopter.

- A cockpit control position pick–off is not strictly required, but is often fitted with such a system.
- The actuator may become a rigid link when inoperative.

When the cockpit control is moved, the outer cylinder of the actuator moves while the inner output shaft remains stationary. This allows the pilot to re-center the actuator, permitting the system to continue functioning through its range. Due to its limited authority, such an actuator will probably not be suitable for autopilot functions, which require larger control movements.

Parallel Actuators

In order to function properly, the series actuator needs to be kept near the center of its travel. This normally requires the pilot to know the position of the actuator (another good reason for an API) and to move the cockpit controls in the appropriate direction to re-center. This is not a satisfactory state of affairs, except perhaps in a cheap and cheerful SAS system, as it requires the pilot to monitor the API, adding to his workload. AFCSs are supposed to reduce workload. In more complex systems, especially those incorporating an autopilot, the API is kept centered by a separate parallel actuator.

The *parallel actuator* is placed in the control run so the cockpit control will move when the parallel actuator moves. From a human factors standpoint, this keeps the pilot aware of what the autopilot is doing. This assumes the trim system is on. If the trim system is disconnected (normally by the force trim button or beeper trim), the actuator does not move the cockpit control, just the clutch mechanism. No AFCS functions will work with the trim off.

A typical parallel actuator is shown in Figure 37-7, and interior detail is shown in Figure 37-8. In the 'Big Picture' of control, (Figure 37-2) the parallel actuator corresponds to the outer loop of control, moving the cockpit controls, in order to keep the pilot informed of its actions. The characteristics of a parallel actuator system can be summarized as follows:

- The actuator moves the cockpit controls as well as the control surfaces.
- It can be given full control authority (i.e. be able to move the cockpit control through its full range of travel) as the actuator operates at a low rate, and a failure should easily be detected early.
- A control position pick–off is required. The reason for this will be explained shortly.

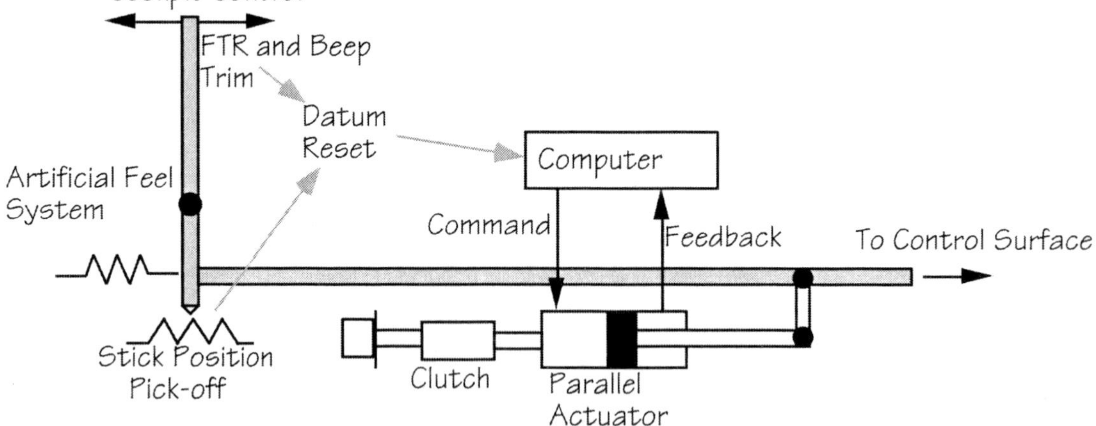

Figure 37-7 Typical Parallel Actuator Configuration

In order to save weight and avoid duplication, it is common to see parallel actuators with the artificial feel system installed. An example is shown in Figure 37-9.

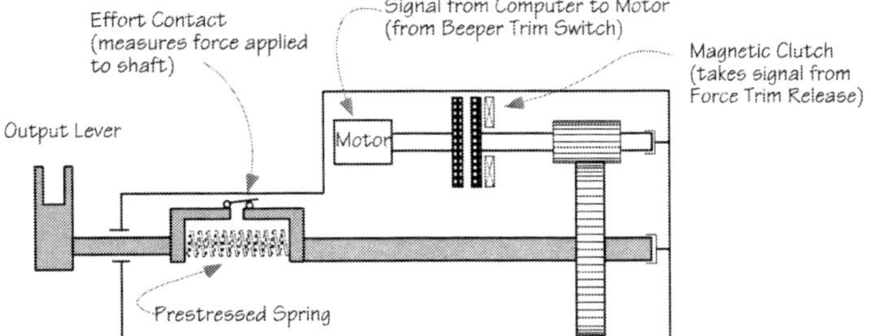

Figure 37-8 Detailed Interior Diagram of Parallel Actuator with Trim System

Combined Systems

A combination of series and parallel actuators can provide good short term stabilization, long term attitude retention and autopilot capabilities. Typically, when the series actuator reaches its limits of authority, the parallel actuator will move the cockpit controls to re–center the series actuator. A typical installation is shown in Figure 37-9.

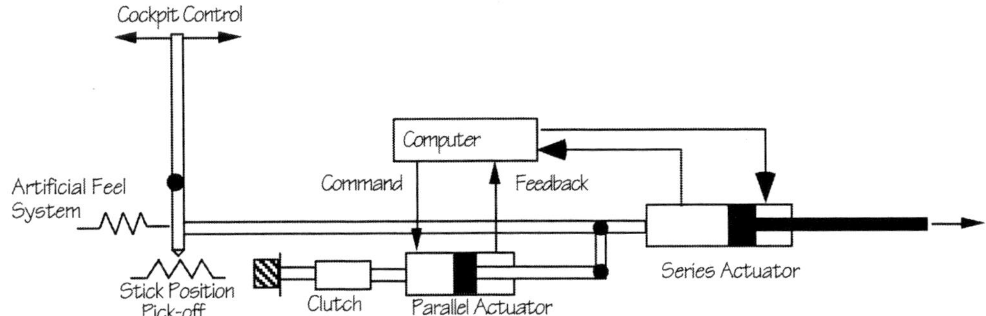

Figure 37-9 Typical Installation of Series and Parallel Actuators

TYPES OF AFCS

Rate Damping Systems

Rate damping is important for two reasons. First, it will stop unwanted rates of motion from developing and secondly, it may make rates commanded by the pilot more predictable. Rate damping systems are the building blocks of any AFCS, and are concerned mostly with stability.

It should be clearly understood that a system with only rate damping will not maintain a specific attitude. For example, while in cruise with the wings level*, a gust produces a roll rate of 2°/sec. to the right. The roll rate sensor will detect this shortly after it happens, and the computer will apply a correction. This correction will stop the roll rate, but the corrective action happens a short time after the initial motion. Since the gust will have had some time to act, and the correction happens after the event, the change in roll attitude (bank angle) must be corrected by the pilot. A rate damping system by itself will not return the aircraft to wings level.

A pure, very simple rate damping system may also cause problems†. For example they will have a tendency to allow the nose to drop during turns, when it would be normal to expect the system to help keep the nose up. In a turn, the nose is moving across the horizon, and the sensors, operating in the plane of the airframe, detect this motion as a pitch rate. The computer applies a nose down control input to stop the pitch rate. This causes the nose to drop, which is not desired.

* OK, so helicopters don't have wings - the phrase means no angle of bank.

† Which is why you won't see a pure, simple rate damping system installed - this paragraph is intended to show why you won't see them.

Stability Augmentation System (SAS)

Stability augmentation systems (SAS) were developed to overcome the problems associated with the simple rate stabilization discussed above. SASs vary in complexity. Some SASs will provide both rate damping and hold the helicopter loosely at a datum attitude. In this case the rate gyroscope is still the basic sensor, but its signals are integrated, using a "leaky integrator", to simulate an attitude signal that can be used as a datum.

A simple SAS may be understood from Figure 37-10. In the normal state, (i.e. straight and level flight, pilot not moving the control), the rate gyro sends a signal directly to both the computer and the leaky integrator (shown separated from the computer, for clarity). The leaky integrator produces a pseudo–attitude (that is, it is not using a real attitude, but has built up a pretend attitude) by integrating the rate signal over a period of time. This attitude is compared to that which existed 20 – 30 seconds previously, (hence the reason for the term leaky - the computer does not have long–term memory). If a gust disturbs the helicopter, the gyro sends a signal and the computer determines that a rate of movement has occurred, which needs to be stopped. The computer sends a signal to the actuator to move to stop the rate. The leaky integrator also receives a rate signal, which when integrated produces an attitude that is different (in error) from the attitude existing 20-30 seconds previously. The error is also sent to the computer, which sends a second correction to the actuator. The first signal stops the rate and the second signal returns the helicopter to the datum attitude.

For example - the helicopter has been in straight and wings level flight for some time, with the pitch attitude to maintain this condition of 2.5° nose up. The computer thinks this is the normal or datum attitude in pitch. A gust comes along which upsets the helicopter in pitch slightly, producing 1° per second pitch rate. The SAS computer has to stop the pitch rate, and as this will happen a slight time after the pitch rate has started (let's say one second for sake of argument), the pitch attitude will have changed as well, up to 3.5° nose up. The SAS just described will try to return the pitch attitude back to 2.5° nose up after it has stopped the pitch rate.

The leak in the integration means the pseudo–attitude will disappear after a short time and the system will regard the continually–updated new attitude as the datum. Simply stated, the system will try to maintain the datum, and it will attempt to return to this datum if it is disturbed.

Such a system can overcome the problem of the nose dropping during a turn by feeding a calculated bank angle signal to the pitch channel, and also by comparing the pitch attitude to the datum pitch attitude.

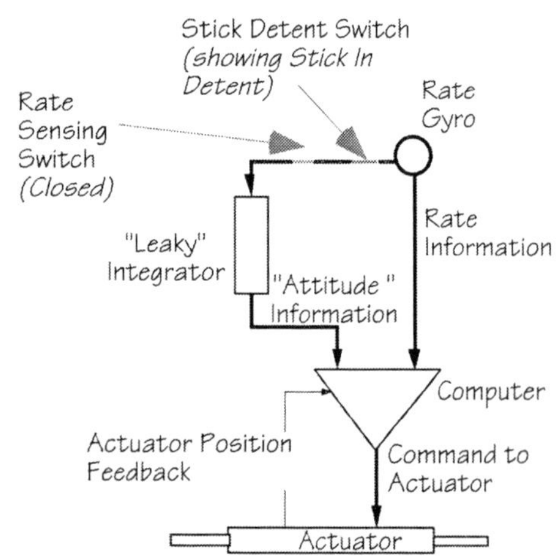

Figure 37-10 Diagram of a Simple SAS - Steady Conditions

Due to the errors in integrating very small signals from the rate gyro, such as in a steady condition with no gusts, the system will eventually drift off. Such systems can only be regarded as providing a limited duration attitude hold. But they work very well!

Pilot Commanded Inputs

The SAS and rate damping systems described so far would interpret any movement of the helicopter as a disturbance, whether commanded by the pilot or not. Unless we wish to turn off the AFCS to change heading or pitch attitude, then some way to permit the pilot to maneuver must be provided. Typically, the cockpit controls are fitted with a control position pick-off sensor, or Linear Variable Displacement Transducer (LVDT). This pick-off is quite simple, and normally in the artificial feel unit. When the control is moved away from the zero–force point, the switch sends a signal to the computer (literally - "the control has been moved - something should happen now"). In Figure 37-11, the cockpit controls of the previous example SAS have been moved to command a new flight condition. As soon as the control is moved, two things happen:

- the control position pick-off (LVDT or control canceller) disconnects the signal from the rate gyro to the leaky integrator and stops the pseudo attitude signal.

- a rate–sensing switch, in series with the control position pick-off, opens, also preventing the rate signal from going to the leaky integrator. It will remain open until the control is in the datum (zero–force or trimmed position) and the rate falls below a present value, which is normally around 2°/second.

There is a good reason for the 2°/second 'gate' or rate–sensing switch. Without it, the computer would try to stop the maneuver as soon as it sensed the control was back in the trimmed position. If a 5°/second roll rate had just been commanded and the control returned to the zero–force position, the computer would try to stop the rate immediately - the jolt would be quite abrupt. If the computer waited until the roll rate was less than 2°/second, and then applied the correction to stop the roll rate, there would be no noticeable jerk*.

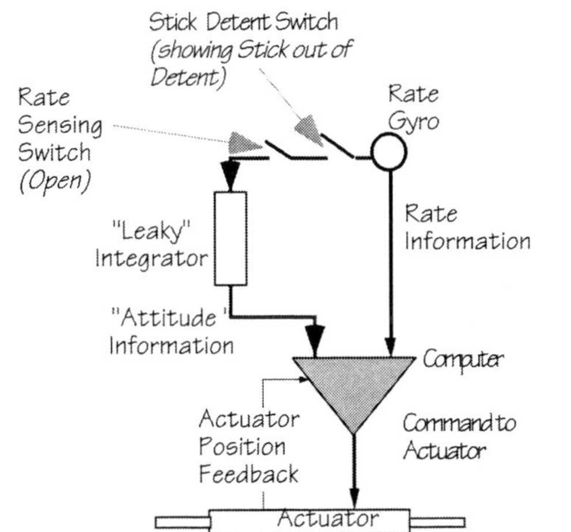

Figure 37-11 Diagram of a Simple SAS - Maneuver Commanded

It should be noted that even when the pilot has moved the control to a new position, rate damping is taking place (the rate gyro signal is going directly to the computer), but there will be no attempt to return to the datum existing at the beginning of the maneuver. The system only tries to maintain an attitude when the helicopter is in a trimmed flight i.e., maneuvers are not being commanded. This rate–sensing switch opens only after the control has been moved. If the control is in the trimmed position, and the rate sensing switch has closed, it will remain closed until the control is next moved out of the detent.

Retrimming

With the SAS just described, the computer will attempt to hold attitude to the datum existing when the control is in the detent i.e. no maneuvering is commanded. The helicopter will return to the datum attitude if disturbed by a gust or if the pilot moves the cockpit control and returns it to the same position. If the pilot uses the force trim button or beeper trim switch to re-position the control, a new datum attitude is established when the Force Trim Release (FTR) is let up.

Stability and Control Augmentation Systems (SCAS).

These are similar to the SAS. Instead of a control position pick-off canceling the attitude hold or rate damping signal when the control is moved, it feeds forward the control input to provide a larger initial response. Without this feed forward, the stick movement would be over-ruled by the rate damping sensing the movement of the helicopter.

* there's a joke about pilots lurking somewhere here, but it hasn't been found.

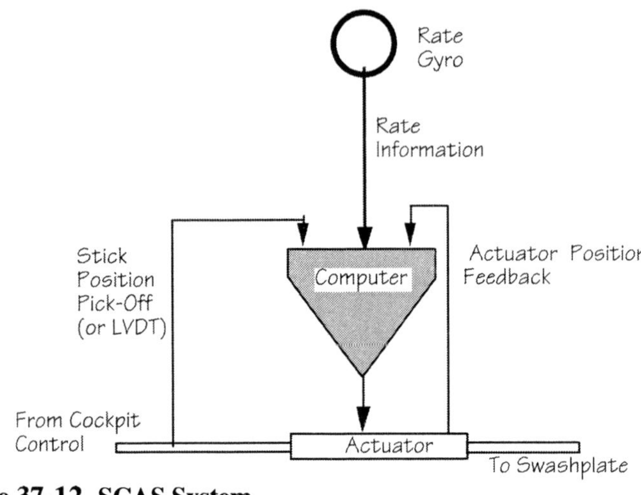

e 37-12 SCAS System

For example, if the control is moved, and the helicopter responds, the SAS would sense a disturbance and try to correct it; this would make the response of the helicopter appear sluggish to the pilot. The "*control augmentation*" part of the SCAS senses the control movement and feeds it to the actuator to produce an input. This causes the helicopter to move, which is, in turn, picked up by the sensors, and is damped. The pilot senses a crisp response. Figure 37-12 shows an SCAS system.

An example of the feed forward aspect is shown in the following time history of an SCAS. The first diagram shows no feed forward.

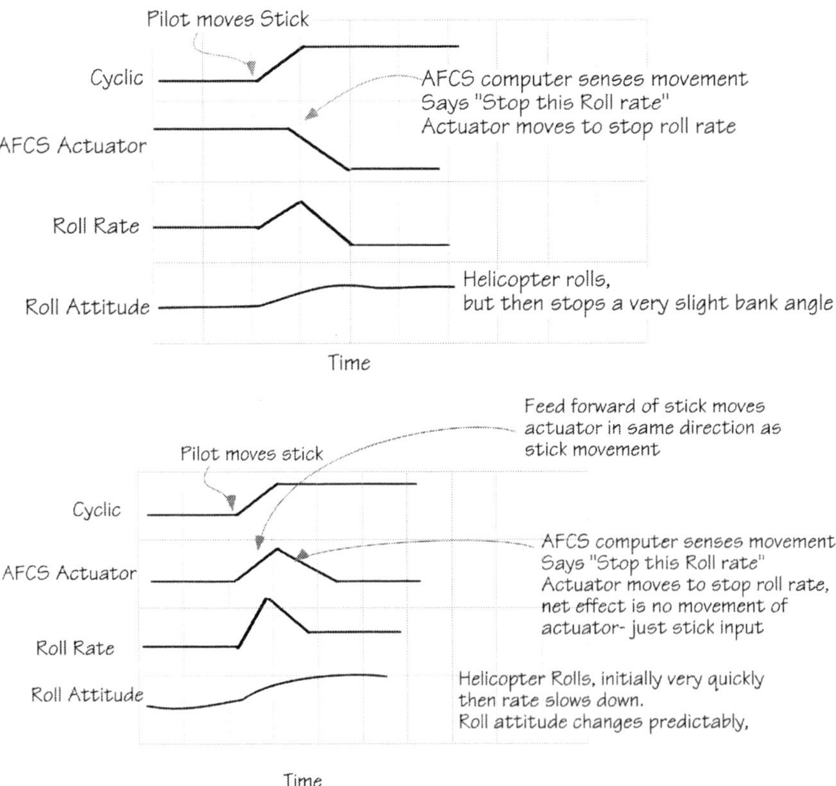

Figure 37-13 Feed Forward of SCAS Signal

Attitude Based Stabilization Systems

These are also called *Attitude* (or *Automatic*) *Stabilization Equipment* (ASE) systems. They are a refinement of the SAS system previously discussed. The differences are in the use of attitude gyros and parallel actuators. They form the basis for most AFCS, particularly those with autopilots. Such systems still require a means of rapid damping (provided by a series actuator) and SAS–type circuits, even if they are not immediately obvious. The pitch channel of a typical attitude–hold stabilization system is shown schematically in Figure 37-14. The attitude gyroscopes used in such systems are, typically, much larger than those used in SAS systems, and have better accuracy.

The use of a vertical gyro implies a stable, very accurate attitude signal is available. This means commanded attitudes will be held with great accuracy for a long time, e.g. 1° nose up will always be 1° nose up, and not 1° difference from the signal that existed 30 seconds previously.

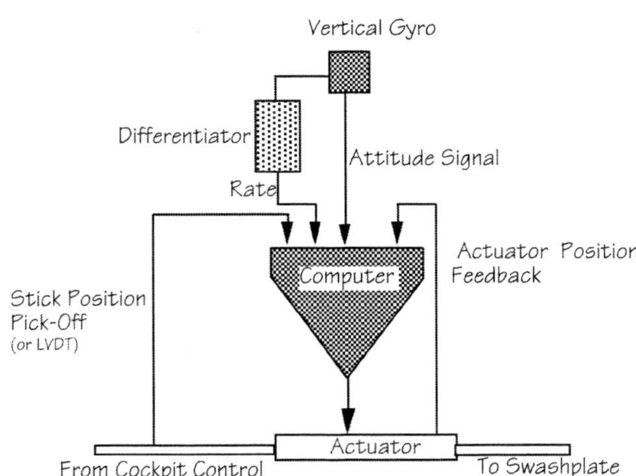

Figure 37-14 Schematic Diagram of a Typical Attitude Hold System

The requirement for the pilot to be able to maneuver still exists, and requires a control position pick-off, or LVDT sensor. When the control is moved out of the zero–force (or datum or detent position), this sensor temporarily disconnects the attitude signal from the vertical gyro. In the same manner as the SAS, it will also open a rate–sensing switch.

Hybrid Systems

One of the most interesting systems I have had the pleasure to fly was a hybrid AFCS. It incorporated a standard attitude–hold system, with options for airspeed hold, altitude hold, heading hold and so on when in the cruise. No big surprises there, except when the airspeed hold mode was engaged, a display in the middle of the Air Speed Indicator lit up with the commanded airspeed signal the AFCS was trying to hold. Re-adjusting this was as simple as holding the special beep trimmer in the correct direction until the desired airspeed was showing. That was neat, but the real surprise was in the tactical mode, which was meant for low–flying tactical missions. This incorporated an SAS with automatic trimming.

Automatic Trim Systems

There are some AFCSs that have an automatic trimming feature, which senses the movement of the stick and moves the artificial feel system zero–force position with the stick. These systems also permit the AFCS to retain all the augmentation features, while reducing the forces the pilot has to fly through. They work in the following manner:

- The pilot moves the stick aft, at the beginning of a quick stop or flare. When the nose is in the desired position, he will stop moving the stick, and the auto–trim system, which has been following up, will shortly have a zero–force condition at the new stick position. Since the attitude hold or rate–damping term has not been removed (the stick is continually re-adjusting the commanded attitude, due to the zero–force position), the nose–up attitude is maintained without the pilot moving the stick.
- When the pilot wants to re-adjust the nose position, he moves the stick again, and the automatic trim system follows up.

Obviously, it may be possible to trick such systems by rapid pumping of the stick, but, by and large, they work well - there is no requirement for a trim release switch, and the pilot is given carefree handling of the aircraft, with both fast response when he wants to maneuver and good stability for those times he wants stability

The two European helicopters that had this feature (AS 355 Panther and the A129 Mangusta) both were pure delights to fly - after I had trained myself to take my thumb away from the trim release and let the systems work. The results were both quite remarkable, and was as close to perfection as I could ask in helicopter handling. Why don't we have this in all our helicopters operating in the low–level tactical environment?

AFCS 'Upper*' Modes

The upper modes of the AFCS are those related to holding external events to the helicopter - events such as airspeed, altitude or height AGL, navigation course, and so on. They are normally part of the autopilot.

An item often not addressed when an airspeed hold is featured is that the pilot will want to know what airspeed he is commanding. If this feature is lacking, the pilot must fly manually to a new airspeed, and then re-engage the airspeed hold. Altitude and height holds are not quite so bad, as the helicopter can be commanded to a rate of descent and the new altitude or height captured at the appropriate time. Airspeed is a different story, and the best solution is to provide an indication of the commanded airspeed to the pilot. Changing is then merely a matter of holding the appropriate button until the new airspeed is in the window, and accepting that the AFCS will eventually get you there.

One helicopter I flew (the UH-60A) was 'advertised' to have an airspeed hold mode. It did, after a fashion. Many times we tried to change airspeed using the beeper trim system, but were never able to make it work. According to the manual, so many seconds of beeper trim would make so much change in airspeed, but this was not possible in flight. More detailed discussion revealed that when the beeper trim switch was pressed, the AFCS dropped the airspeed signal it was using, and went into an attitude hold mode for a variable period of 12 to 17 seconds, and then re-acquired whatever airspeed happened to exist at the end of the 12 to 17 seconds. The end result? The airspeed acquire function was not predictable, and the airspeed hold only worked when we had already set the airspeed. No-one ever used the beeper trim switch, we all manually flew the machine to the new airspeed and used the trim release. I will leave the reader to decide if this was progress.

Definition Problems

The effect on the helicopter once the control has been returned to the zero–force (*detent* or *datum*) position will depend upon the detailed nature of the AFCS. For example, if the system is designed to hold the attitude existing when the control was in the detent, it will try to return to that condition. If 3° nose–up pitch attitude was the pitch datum, and the pilot desired to make a small, temporary correction, when the control was returned to the zero–force (detent or datum) position, and the pitch rate had fallen below the rate threshold (e.g. 2°/second), the helicopter would return to, and maintain, 3° nose–up. Such a system is considered to be of the wing–leveler type of automatic stabilization equipment (in a pure definition).

Some systems will attempt to hold the attitude that exists when the control is returned to the zero–force (detent or datum) position and the rate switch has fallen below its threshold. For example, if the commanded (or datum) attitude was 2° nose down, and the pilot maneuvered and returned the control to the original zero–force (detent or datum) condition, the system would hold the attitude that existed when the rate dropped below the threshold (e.g. 1.5°/second). The strictly–correct definition for such a systems is *Rate Command, Attitude Hold* (*RCAH*).

Detailed discussion of the differences between AFCS types is beyond the scope of this book, but always beware of definitions!

Attitude Datum Re-Adjustment

One way to reset the datum attitude is to press down the FTR, fly the helicopter to the new condition, then release the FTR. This re-establishes both the control force and attitude datums. This method is often inconvenient, especially as the FTR removes attitude hold functions in all (pitch, roll and yaw) axes. If the pilot wishes to change the pitch attitude only very slightly, and leave the roll attitude and side force (i.e. slip ball position) as they were, then he has to work hard to not move the other controls (lateral cyclic and rudder pedals). Using the FTR causes the attitude hold in all three axes to be lost, requiring the pilot to hold the controls motionless in roll and yaw while only adjusting in pitch†.

It is also possible to use only the beeper trim switch, which may directly re-datum the system in the axis where the switch is moved, and move the stick as well. Some AFCSs carry this to an extreme by not moving the stick when the beeper trim is operated.

* I've not seen any AFCS 'Downer' modes, thankfully

† A difficult thing to do in turbulence, especially while trying to juggle maps, radios and cranky passengers!

The problem is compounded by the use of different control laws in each axis. For example, the pitch channel is often a rate–command, attitude–hold (RCAH) system, while the roll channel may be an attitude–command, attitude–hold (ACAH) system. In practical terms, to maintain a bank angle, it is necessary to hold the cyclic into the turn. Such systems have found favor in those helicopters operating at low altitude over the water. In IMC and night conditions, in a turn, if the pilot becomes disoriented, he has only to release the cyclic and the helicopter will roll to wings level attitude. In this case, the lateral cyclic is used to command a roll attitude (normally it commands a roll rate) hence the definition of attitude–command attitude–hold system.

Heading Hold and Coordinated Turns

Previous discussions have mostly been about the pitch and roll axis, however, yaw is also an important part of the overall control of the helicopter. Methods of changing from low speed, ground referenced operation to forward flight, airspeed referenced operation need consideration.

A note of caution: At least one helicopter model has adapted a fixed wing autopilot system, and doesn't work as described in the following paragraphs. Get to know your system!

Hover and Low Speed

In the hover and low speed regimes (below 40 knots of airspeed), one of the main tasks of the pilot is to maintain heading with the yaw pedals. In a pure (zero–airspeed) hover, the helicopter has no stability in yaw - it will stay pointing in any direction, and small changes of power will cause difficulties for the pilot to maintain heading. With a wind (from any direction or at any speed), the aerodynamics, particularly around the tail rotor, become extremely complex, and in some cases, neutral to negative gradients of tail rotor (yaw pedal) position vs. lateral airspeed are found. These make accurate manual control of heading nearly impossible. (This was discussed in Chapter 34,"Further Peculiarities of The Helicopter".) An AFCS yaw channel improves this situation tremendously, even if it only damps out rates of yaw. By preventing yaw rates from developing, the pilot's workload to maintain heading is reduced.

The differences between the yaw axis and the other axes are the sensors used and the means of disengaging the AFCS to permit maneuvering. The sensors used in the yaw channel will typically include a flux detector to sense magnetic heading, as well as rate gyros or attitude gyros. To sense the pilots demands, various devices can be used. The least obtrusive to the pilot is a force or motion sensor that senses when the pedals have been moved, or when a force greater than a preset threshold has been applied. More common is a micro switch on the face of the pedal, which is closed when the pilot places his foot on the pedal, indicating heading hold is not wanted. Unfortunately, this latter system means that to engage the heading hold, the pilot must take his feet off the pedals, which few helicopter pilots like to do. Other systems use the FTR to temporarily remove the pedal position signal from the AFCS circuit.

Forward Flight

In forward flight, the helicopter has some inherent sideslip. This prevents the use of a simple sideslip sensor for the yaw channel, and requires the use of a yaw rate sensor. In forward flight, the yaw channel is used in much the same way as in fixed–wing airplane, namely to maintain slip indicator ball position.

Various turning modes may be incorporated, ranging from a simple system providing artificial directional stability via sideforce or yaw rate sensors, to complex automatic turn facilities geared to specific operational tasks. Perhaps the most interesting area of the yaw axis is in the cross-over from the low airspeed regime to forward flight and vice versa. To blend the two functions as the helicopter accelerates or decelerates between these regimes requires the introduction of an airspeed sensor into the yaw axis. Below 40 KIAS, most flying is referenced to ground speed and alignment with the ground, and above that speed, flying is referenced to airspeed.

In-between Airspeeds

There is a gray area between the low–airspeed control strategy and the forward flight strategy, and problems occur when the helicopter transitions between the two in anything other than straight–ahead flight. Pilots have no problem with what to do, as they are adaptable, but some AFCSs get very confused.

For example, in yaw, one helicopter type has heading hold below 40 KIAS and turn coordination above that speed. If the pilot is doing a decelerating turn with feet off the pedals*, then as the helicopter slows below 40 KIAS, strange things start to happen. Instead of a ball-in-middle, more–or–less normal curving approach, a progressively increasing sideslip starts as the yaw channel tries to hold the heading it had at 40 KIAS. Unless the pilot does something, the helicopter will end up pointing in close to the same direction as it was when the airspeed dropped below 40 KIAS which is when the AFCS switched to 'hold–heading–through–the–yaw–channel' mode. If the pilot becomes alarmed at this unusual turn of events†, puts his feet on the pedals, a rapid yaw occurs as the yaw channel reverts to the normal way of doing business - very unsettling.

Autopilots

Autopilots hold the helicopter to an external condition, such as airspeed, altitude, track, etc. This is a simple academic distinction, and the definitions get very blurred in distinguishing between autopilots and attitude hold systems, particularly in the eyes of some manufacturers. For example, if an airspeed hold is an integral part of the AFCS and there is no way to switch this mode off, the manufacturer may say it's not an autopilot feature. Here, we are working on more academic definitions.

The function of the autopilot is to provide control of the helicopter, as opposed to assisting with stability. With the autopilot engaged, the pilot no longer directly controls the helicopter, but selects the flight conditions the autopilot is to maintain, and then monitors the functioning of the autopilot.

As the autopilot is a device that controls the helicopter, it still depends, like the pilot, on the helicopter possessing adequate stability. If the helicopter is deficient in stability, the autopilot, as the pilot, will find it difficult to fly to the desired accuracy. Stability augmentation is still needed to provide the necessary short–term damping.

Stability augmentation may be physically incorporated with the autopilot, but as it performs a separate function, it should always be recognizable as a distinct sub-system. Normally provision is made to allow stability augmentation functions to be used separately, even if fully automatic control is not required, or not available due to an autopilot malfunction.

Basic Autopilot.

A basic autopilot holds an external condition, such as airspeed, altitude, track, etc. This differs from the ASE holding a helicopter attitude such as pitch, roll and yaw. This is an academic definition used to differentiate parts of the system, e.g. some AFCSs feature airspeed hold without the option of attitude hold.

Operational Autopilot.

These systems perform a maneuver or series of maneuvers, such as an automatic ILS approach, flare and landing in low visibility conditions, or an automatic transition to the hover.

Facilities Available Through an Autopilot

The facilities that can be provided by an autopilot are limited only by the sensors, computing capabilities, control authority and complexity of installation, the imagination of developers and the paycheck of the purchaser. Below are the more commonly–available facilities and their principle characteristics.

Altitude or Height Hold

Altitude holds use signals from a barometric capsule; and height holds use a radar altimeter. Both may operate through the longitudinal cyclic. On light helicopters with simple autopilots, this is the only way they are installed. The cyclic channel actuation is a simple system, but only usable above V_Y and it

* Yes I know I said that this wasn't a good idea, but if it's the way the system will let the pilot fly, then some pilots will do things this way.

† You will have to believe me, this pun just dropped out as I typed it.

cannot be used simultaneously with an airspeed hold. A simplified description of operation would be if the current altitude is below the demanded or datum altitude, the cyclic will be commanded aft to raise the nose and climb to the datum altitude.

The reason that the longitudinal cyclic implementation is usable only above V_Y is that if the airspeed reduces below this value, the power required to maintain level flight increases. If the helicopter is operating above V_Y, raising the nose will decrease the airspeed and the helicopter will climb as the power required for level flight is lower at the new, reduced airspeed. When it reaches the correct altitude, the nose will be lowered and the speed will increase again. If the helicopter is below V_Y, raising the nose will further decrease the speed, but the power required to maintain level flight at the slower speed will be greater than before, resulting in a rate of descent. The nose will be raised further to stop the descent and attempt to regain the altitude, making the situation worse. This may continue until the airspeed decreases to zero.

The strange thing to me is that although some (but not all) helicopter AFCS using this method of altitude hold have warnings in the flight manual about a minimum airspeed for operation of the feature; none that I have seen put in an airspeed signal to cut out the feature below the V_Y airspeed. If you want to have an interesting adventure in such a helicopter, engage height hold and slow below V_Y.

For those helicopters that require height hold below V_Y, or need to combine altitude and airspeed hold, a collective–based system is the only suitable method. Previous chapters have shown the relationship between power and airspeed and longitudinal cyclic and airspeed. Below V_Y, the power required for a lower airspeed increases. At a constant power setting, the cyclic can control either airspeed or rate of climb, but not both. If both rate of climb (i.e. zero rate of climb is altitude hold) and airspeed are to be maintained, it is necessary to bring the collective channel in to change the power. This will permit the helicopter to hold height in the hover, or any other airspeed, as well as to maintain the airspeed (including zero–airspeed or zero–groundspeed).

Radio/Radar Altitude Hold

A vertical accelerometer may be used to smooth and shape the vertical response of the height–hold channel. A means of averaging the radar altitude signal has also been used to provide a mean sea/ground level reference. This is particularly needed when operating over waves, to prevent the radar altimeter from following the waves or getting out of sequence with them.

Speed Hold in the Low Airspeed Region

Airspeed hold is provided through the longitudinal cyclic in forward flight. Groundspeed hold and airspeed hold in the low airspeed region will require longitudinal and lateral cyclic control, and a multi-axis airspeed or groundspeed sensor. Because of rapid and large changes in sensed signals in this area, it is not uncommon to blend in acceleration signals as well.

Programmed Maneuver

An example of a programmed maneuver is the transition from a level forward flight cruise to the hover. This maneuver requires many signals, from a variety of sensors such as ground speed (along and across) using a Doppler radar or other source, combined with height (both barometric and radio/radar altimeter), vertical speed (radar altimeter, barometric, acceleration sensed or Doppler based), airspeed, engine and airframe data. These signals must be blended in such a way as to take the helicopter from an initial forward flight condition to the desired hover condition at a predetermined height above ground or water, on a predetermined heading.

As an example, with the helicopter in a cruise at 90 KIAS at 300' AWL (above water level) and abeam the specified hover point, it is decided to transition to a hover. When the pilot engages the transition down, the AFCS must determine from the speed sensors (groundspeed and airspeed) the relative wind. This is so it can next determine the navigation path to be taken to put the helicopter into wind during the final approach and hover. This calculated, the AFCS then maneuvers the helicopter along this path until the point where the deceleration and descent must begin. So far, this is not much different than an ordinary autopilot.

Once the deceleration/descent phase begins, things start to become more complicated. The helicopter must transition through the V_Y so that it is now operating in the region of increasing power for decreasing airspeed, and the AFCS must anticipate the power changes needed. The helicopter will also need to transition from airspeed based reference to flying (i.e. ball in the middle, wings level) to ground based reference (i.e. along and across track velocities, heading in the direction of travel, into wind, etc.). While doing this, the AFCS must also keep track of minor details like rate of descent vs. height above the surface (don't want to break the 1 minute to live rule*), bank angle, etc.

Complex Helicopter AFCS

An AFCS is fitted to reduce the pilot workload, or perform tasks the pilot would find difficult or impossible. The system reduces workload in normal operations by maintaining airspeed or other functions, and another part of the system is designed to hover the helicopter at night over the ocean when the lack of visual references would prevent the pilot from doing this manually.

Obviously the number of complex inputs to the system will be larger, and the controller and logic requirements are of greater complexity, but the outputs to the actuators are as previously discussed. The trim actuators are also parallel actuators.

The control panel of the AFCS (see Figure 37-15) has a number of modes to let the pilot use features appropriate to the flight condition. Attitude hold is always on, and only modes which are selectable are shown on this panel. Several modes are mutually exclusive because they use the same control run. For example, the airspeed hold mode (A/S) uses the longitudinal cyclic channel, so it is not possible to also engage the altitude hold (ALT) or vertical speed (V/S) mode at the same time as both these use the same piece of hardware (longitudinal cyclic). If the pilot is using a constant collective (or power) setting in turbulent air, he must choose between altitude hold with variable airspeed or airspeed hold with variable altitude.

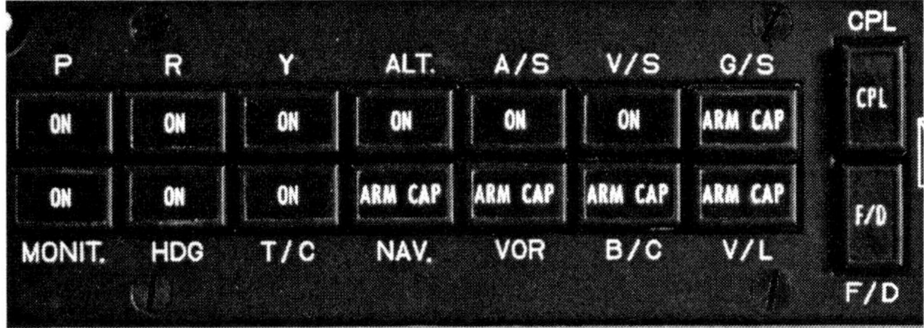

Figure 37-15 Control Panel for Typical Helicopter Autopilot.

When the A/S (Airspeed Hold) mode is engaged, a display in the airspeed indicator (ASI) shows the commanded airspeed. The pilot is able to adjust it to the desired speed by way of a separate beep trim switch, and the computer corrects the attitude to attain this speed.

In ALT mode (altitude hold), the AFCS, using the longitudinal cyclic, maintains the altitude at the time of engagement. To change altitude, ALT mode must be disabled, either by selecting another mode, such as A/S or V/S (vertical speed hold), and re-selecting ALT at the new altitude, or by turning off the ALT mode. A major limitation on ALT mode is operation through the longitudinal cyclic. It is only usable above V_Y as previously discussed.

* This unwritten rule states that you shouldn't have a rate of descent that would put you in the water/ground from your present height in less than 1 minute. For example at 500' AGL, the maximum rate of descent should be less than 500 ft. per minute.

Automatic Transition to the Hover

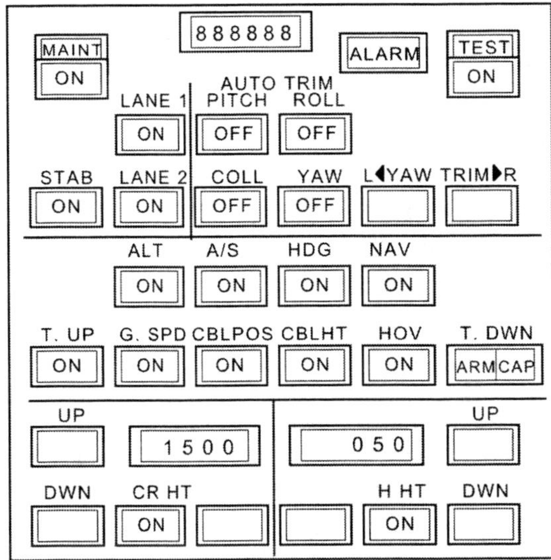

Figure 37-16 Complex AFCS Control Panel

There are numerous times when the helicopter must hover over water in conditions of poor visibility and weather. Even in daylight, such hovering is not ideal, as the combination of wind, wave motion and rotor downwash often mask the movement of the helicopter with respect to the water. The pitot static system also stops working well below 40 knots, removing the two most commonly used items of the pilots situational awareness. These items are absent at a critical time, while hovering, and during transition to the hover and back to forward flight. This information can be replaced with equally useful knowledge, such as height above water and groundspeed. Wind velocity can often be obtained from the navigation system computer. A Doppler sensor can provide the groundspeed, and a radar altimeter can provide the height above the surface, but it is extremely difficult for the pilot to integrate this information to arrive repeatedly in a safe hover in less than ideal conditions. It is far safer to program the AFCS to complete this task.

Why would anyone want to use this sort of maneuver? A suitably equipped helicopter (i.e. Doppler radar, dual radar altimeters for a minimum) with good handling characteristics should be capable of being flown by most pilots from the cruise to a zero–groundspeed hover at night over the water. Note that most, but not all pilots could do it. The other way to look at it is that even a good pilot will not always be able to do it, but a properly set up AFCS could always do it. It is a simple matter of economics then, because if a bad pilot can't do it, or a good pilot has a bad day and messes up, either the sonar dome doesn't get put in the water, or the person wishing to be rescued doesn't get saved, or in a worse case, the helicopter hits the water. The autopilot, monitored by a human will screw up much less frequently...

Some of the systems that are capable of these maneuvers have been very interesting to watch - they range from so mild and cautious in making changes that you might well be in the next county (and certainly be much older) before the hover stabilized, to so aggressive that the maneuver would make you apprehensive in daylight over land with good visual references, and at night over the ocean could definitely contribute to your grey hair count.

Transition from Cruise to Hover

At an appropriate location* prior to the desired hover point, the pilot selects the transition–down mode (labeled T.DWN on Figure 37-16). This engages all the channels of the AFCS to perform a pre-programmed maneuver. Decelerating and descending, the helicopter is following a profile to arrive at the height AGL the pilot previously selected on the Hover Height controller. At a certain pre-set airspeed, the yaw channel changes from balanced flight to heading hold mode, and the roll and pitch channels change from bank angle hold and airspeed hold (respectively) to previously set across and along ground speeds. The helicopter continues to descend and slow down until it reaches the commanded hover height, and the along and across groundspeed velocities are zero.

As the helicopter is now operating below V_Y, it is not possible to control altitude with the cyclic alone. The collective channel must now be used to maintain height above the ground or water, while the cyclic is used for lateral or longitudinal groundspeed.

* Unless the navigation system is extremely capable, this point must be decided by the pilot.

Information on the height, speed and rate of descent, as well as power, engine parameters, and position with respect to the start and end points, are all fed into the computer, and the AFCS completes the transition automatically.

If the pilot wishes, he can place the helicopter in the hover manually and engage the Hover mode when stable. Regardless of whether the transition was carried out automatically or manually, the pilot can modify the along and across velocity by use of the beeper trim switch on the cyclic.

At night over water, the transition from the hover to forward flight is also a very complex task in an area with little (if any) visual or suitable instrument flying information, the task is often performed by the AFCS. On the controller in Figure 37-16, for example pressing the T.UP button will make the AFCS fly a pre-determined profile to the previously selected cruising height, and airspeed. Both power (collective) and longitudinal cyclic airspeed profiles will be maintained.

Radio Coupled Operations

Many civil helicopters do not have as complex a system as previously described, but still have quite capable autopilots. The principles of operation of such systems are no different from those of a fixed–wing aircraft, namely, the sensor detects a signal, compares it with a reference, decides what action is to be taken to correct any errors, and commands the actuator to move in the appropriate direction.

ADVANCED CONCEPTS

Side Arm Controllers

Side arm controllers are nothing more than another way to mechanize control of the helicopter. They offer the advantage of moving the cyclic away from the center of the instrument panel, freeing up valuable display space. Different options for control are also possible, with the ultimate (?) being all 4 axes on one controller. These different options are shown in Figure 37-17 below.

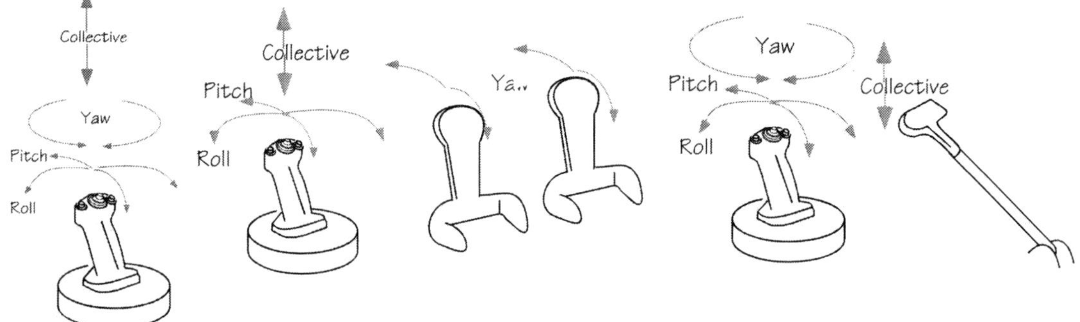

Figure 37-17 Sidearm Controller Options

Most side arm controllers are force sensing types - that is, they do not rely on movement to tell the flight controls the pilot wants something to happen. These sort of controllers have both advantages and disadvantages. On the plus side, they are inherently simpler, with fewer parts in the control system, and have high reliability, and do not require a separate force feel system. On the down side, they are susceptible to sharp (perhaps accidental*) inputs, don't tell the pilot where the control system is, make transfer of control difficult (you can't follow through), trimming can be hard (but these sort of systems should automatically trim - shouldn't they?) and finally, the buttons on the controllers need to have very low forces to operate, or the stick may sense the keying of the radio button as a control input.

It is interesting to note that several detailed studies of helicopter handling qualities have shown that there is no particular advantage to be gained by using a side arm controller over a center mounted cyclic stick - the decision must be based on other considerations such as space, redundancy, etc. As much benefit can be gained by a good AFCS as from a side-arm controller.

On the other hand, if you don't have to design the seat for an upright center cyclic, perhaps we can finally get seats that are comfortable for long flights. My back can't wait.

* I, for example, have never nudged the cyclic accidentally, or at least not more than 5 or 6 times...

Failures of the AFCS

Like any other part on the helicopter, the AFCS can fail. How badly the failure will affect you will depend on the complexity of the system and the flight conditions. If the helicopter really needs an AFCS to stay right side up, then the first failure shouldn't seriously affect the way the machines flies. If it's only one small component in one axis (roll, for example), then it may only affect that axis, and you might be able to identify and isolate the faulty lane.

Some helicopters with complex, duplicated AFCSs have a *VNE* restriction when one system has failed, but if both AFCS have failed, the *VNE* restriction goes away. What gives? The answer is that the characteristics of a runaway of the remaining AFCS are pretty severe- with both systems working, one AFCS is able to reduce the severity of the runaway effect, and if no AFCS is on, then the runaway can't happen, so go back to your original *VNE*.

If the AFCS fails, but the flight director (FD) is still working, then you might be able to hand-fly the helicopter using only the flight director. Be careful, and make sure you practice this in good conditions before you need to do it in the goo. The helicopter may not be the same as when the autopilot is on.

Minimum Height for Engaged AFCS

Most helicopters with an AFCS have a minimum height above ground specified for use of the AFCS. Why is this so? How does the AFCS know whether it is 500' or 10' AGL?

The answer has to do with hardovers or other failures of the AFCS. The pilot has to have some time to recognize the failure and take appropriate action. Certification testing will show what the height loss is if, for example, the AFCS failure is a nose-down hardover or runaway. It is obviously not wise to sit back, fold your hands and enjoy the flight and ignore the possibility that the AFCS can fail when you get close to the ground.

On the other hand if the weather is really bad, and you're short of fuel and this is your only chance to get down the ground and the AFCS does a better job of shooting the approach than you do, take your own advice.

AFCS Disconnect Switches

Most helicopters with an AFCS incorporate a disconnect on the flight controls. The logic is pretty hard to fault. If there is a problem caused by the AFCS, the pilot should be able to disengage the system without taking hands from the flying controls.

I've had to argue for this in some pretty complex helicopters and was told that the degree of complexity of the system and the various safeguards made it unnecessary. In fact, such a switch would introduce a single point failure in the system and actually reduce the safety level.

I took quiet satisfaction (but not much else) in reading about an incident in one of these helicopters where the AFCS failed into an oscillatory mode which generated such a high level of vibration and motion that it was impossible for the non-flying pilot to get his hands on the necessary AFCS switches on the center console for several heart-stopping minutes.

Summary of Chapter 37

This chapter has dealt with the complexities of the AFCS. By now, it should be clear that there are many problems that could be solved by the use of a simple AFCS, but that it is necessary to know how the systems work in order to fully utilize them.

Miscellaneous Musings

Type Ratings

I've had the privilege of working with several militaries as a pilot, and holding civil pilot licences from several countries. Obviously none of them are perfect, or everyone would be following that example. I've tried to take the best ideas and examples from each of them, and incorporate them. There have been others which make me wonder though...

I've often wondered at the wisdom of the lack of a type rating system for light helicopters within at least one authority (that will remain nameless). Of the regulatory agencies in the world, they appear to be alone in not requiring type ratings*. In theory, in that country, it is possible to obtain a private pilot's licence on an R-22, and then the next day, fly an S-76 or Bell 412, without having to demonstrate any knowledge or understanding of hydraulic systems, turbine engines, multi-engine concepts and so on. It is certainly possible to do a biennial flight review on one type of helicopter and have that be considered valid for all helicopter types. Only when the weight of the helicopter is greater than 12,500 pounds is a type rating required. The only saving grace appears to be insurance companies and (hopefully) common sense.

How long can this go on, particularly with the advent of complex equipment such as FADEC engines, GPS navigation and complex autopilots with approach capability and the like? Nearly every other country in the world requires a type rating for each helicopter type, normally as the result of accidents and incidents.

How To Survive

What can you do about it? Treat every new helicopter as if it required a type rating. Get appropriate training, hopefully from the company school, but failing that from an instructor who is deeply experienced in type. Going cheap on the check out can be expensive later on. Check to see what sort of break your insurance company will give you for attending the training course.

Get your professional association (you do belong to one don't you?†) to lobby for tighter rules on type ratings. It's in everyone's long term interests.

Technical Examinations

On the other hand, European countries seem to go too far. When I went to get my civil licence in one European country, I had to write examination papers on AC and DC electrical theory. No-one I've spoken to, before or since, could justify the detailed knowledge that was demanded on the test except for the lame excuse that I might be called upon to parallel the generators of an aircraft one day in the middle of nowhere without adequate maintenance support. Not only have I never had to do this in my career, no-one I've ever spoken to has ever had to do it, and furthermore would not be allowed to do it by their own regulations! Yet pilots continue to have to write the exams...

I also remain to be convinced that this requirement to regurgitate minutiae has significantly reduced the number of accidents. The statistics simply don't support this argument.

Minimum Equipment Lists (MEL)

MELs are a way of life in the commercial fixed wing world, yet don't seem to have found much favor at present in the rotary wing business. They have an interesting reason for being. Legally, without an MEL, everything on board must be serviceable and in good working order prior to dispatch.

This somewhat surprising statement is derived from the statement on most certificates of airworthiness which state that the certificate is valid only when "the aircraft is operated and maintained in accordance with the type design, and is a fit state for flight". Unfortunately, this a subtle statement, the importance of which is lost on most folks. It infers (i.e. says without

* I say nearly alone, as I'm not familiar with all the agencies around the world...

† Just as we got this into print, the Professional Helicopter Pilots Association (PHPA) has been formed. About time too. I hope this organization can give the same clout to helicopter aviation as the Airline Pilots Association (ALPA) has brought to the airline industry.

directly saying so) that if the type design called for it, it needs to be there. I wish it were clearly stated so that people wouldn't think it was OK to fly with something unserviceable or inappropriately modified.

The MEL is merely a way of saying that certain items can be unserviceable prior to departure, with certain restrictions. For example, on one helicopter type if the fuel quantity gauge is not working, and you have a way to determine the contents prior to departure (i.e fill the tanks), and the low fuel quantity warning system is working (or optionally you have installed a fuel flow meter), then it may be OK to dispatch for a short number of days until the necessary parts are obtained to fix the problem.

MELs are borne from a Master Minimum Equipment List (MMEL), which is for a particular type of helicopter (Bell 430 for example). This is drawn up between the manufacturer and the RA, and from it, an MEL can be drawn up by each company (and approved by their RA operations inspector) which operates one of those models. The MEL can't be more generous than the MMEL (obviously).

There is another way to get around the requirement for everything to be working prior to dispatch, and that is the acceptable dispatch failures items, or its equivalent. This is typically agreed between individual operators and their over-seeing authorities.

Why have an MEL? The reasons are not so obvious, but in general it is to prevent pilots from being pressured to accept an aircraft which is less than fully serviceable. When you're waiting for an important customer, or being pushed by the boss to take the aircraft that has a broken gauge, just this once, this flight is important, and we'll fix it immediately on your return (and you know this has been broken for several days...), the MEL can save your bacon gracefully. On the other hand, you can also accept an aircraft which has just had a failure if it is covered under the MEL without having to worry about whether you have made the correct decision.

Since the MEL is developed by people who are familiar with the aircraft, and have the opportunity to develop it in a very calm and reasoned atmosphere, they are able to consider all the implications, especially the next failure that can happen. Just because you have two of something on the helicopter, you don't want to take off with one broken, only to have the remaining one break inflight when you need it...

Using GPS Intelligently

There is no doubt that GPS has completely changed the face of navigation, and that it will continue to make huge changes for years to come. Yet for most of the time, it is only an aid to navigation, and we have become its slaves. Stories already abound of students who don't know how to navigate, or running into high ground while on a straight line flight in bad weather between two places.

As if these two points weren't bad enough, how many of us have put in the wrong information to the system, and then blindly trusted the steering advice the box provided? Garbage in gives garbage out.

There are also too many of us who would be completely lost if the power failed to the GPS if we weren't following along with a trusty map.

If you're using a GPS receiver for your professional flying, consider a checklist to set up the equipment for an instrument approach, (if approved for instrument approaches).

How Best to Use the Magic

So how best to use this magic? One or two ideas you may wish to consider are:

Don't ever plan to go fly directly to an airport or navaid, or other popular spot. Pick a point one-half or so miles away*, to the side of the direct line, or if you're going to an airport, outside the normal traffic pattern. This will keep you away from those who are wearing a groove in the sky between the two popular points, and it won't add significantly to the distance travelled.

Don't use the GPS as the only means of navigation. Program waypoints along the route to check your navigation on a map, and then only use it to verify you are on the correct track. Navigate by map, verify by GPS.

The largest source of error in most computers lies at the extreme end of your hand. The disease of digititis is all to common.

So use the GPS as an aid to navigation, not the sole source.

* You do know how to do this, don't you?

The real potential of the helicopter is waiting to be unlocked when we have widespread coverage of differential GPS signals, which will give accuracies of less than 0.5m (18"), and permit precision approaches to very low heights above the ground, possibly even to a zero-zero hover.

As this book is being written, several of these have been demonstrated successfully to a hover, including with a slight downwind component and quite steep glidepath angles.

Myths of the Helicopter

'Tail Rotor Stall'

I've read lots of accident reports where the pilot decided, for a variety of reasons, that the tail rotor had stalled. The reaction was to try to unstall it, by neutralizing the pedals. Since these stories appear mostly in accident reports, it's obvious this didn't work (or it wouldn't have been an accident, would it?).

Where this myth sprang up from will probably never be figured out, but it's wrong. I've never heard of a tail rotor stalling completely and, even it if did, that neutralizing the pedals would make any difference. The only company that has investigated this fully (Bell Helicopter) found that the best action was to apply full anti-torque pedal (left pedal for our generic helicopter) and try to get forward airspeed.

See the section on "Loss of Tail Rotor Effectiveness" on page 383 for a more complete explanation.

'Pendulum Effect'

Many helicopter books talk about the 'pendulum' effect, as if the helicopter had some magically properties to it that were caused by (or could be explained as if) being suspended from a mythical point well above the helicopter.

This explanation attempts to show why the helicopter appears to have a mind of its own in the hover, particularly for students. What it has accomplished is a greatly muddified picture - the helicopter is not suspended from a point above the rotor. The analogy might give the impression that, being suspended from a point, the helicopter would oscillate gently without correction, and perhaps even die down. This is not true.

What the pilot is seeing is the beginning of an oscillation which will increase in size with time, and requires the pilot to recover from quite quickly. The cause is the neutral static stability and negative dynamic stability that all helicopters without an AFCS have. The causes are complex and well beyond the scope of this book, but suffice to say, there is no pendulum effect.

There is also a myth that pendular action is responsible for 2 bladed rotor systems being immune to retreating blade stall...

'Stick Reversal'

There is one helicopter that has a very misleading and potentially confusing term in its flight manual. The problem it is supposed to discuss relates to static stability; but the term is incorrectly used. The term is stick reversal, which conjures up black and white early 1950's movies about test flying. In the movie, the intrepid test pilot, facing a very dangerous situation where the nose of the aircraft keeps dropping and the speed is increasing to life-threatening levels, Pulling back on the stick not only doesn't stop the nose from dropping- it makes it worse! Our hero saves the day, not by pulling back harder, but by pushing forward on the stick. On the ground he calmly announces that he had encountered 'stick reversal'.

Reversal implies the stick works in reverse to the normal sense - somehow pushing forward will bring the nose up, (and perhaps pushing left will cause a right roll). Sure that this was not the case in this helicopter, I investigated the problem, and discovered that at no time did the stick work in a backwards sense after all, yet the term is still in the flight manual. The explanation is relatively simple and relates to *static stability*.

Static stability is one measure of the tendency of the helicopter to return to the trim conditions - in other words, in straight and level flight, to increase and stabilize at a higher speed, the final position of the stick at the higher speed should be farther forward than the original. This means if the helicopter is hit by a gust (which, say, tends to slow down the helicopter), and the pilot hasn't moved the stick, the initial tendency will be for the speed to return towards the speed at which the controls were set prior to the gust.

Note the phrase *final position of the stick*, as the stick must still move forward initially to get the helicopter to accelerate to the higher speed.

Seems the problem for this particular helicopter and the very particular configuration is that the final position for the stick for a speed higher than the initial speed was slightly aft of the initial stick position. Now some people might think this means you have to hold the stick back to go faster. - Wrong - it means the stick must still move forward to start the process of going faster, but to maintain a higher speed, the stick position will be farther aft than the original. To go faster or slower from that new, higher speed, the stick will still work in the correct sense - forward to accelerate and backward to decelerate. The technically–correct term here is negative static stability gradient, not stick reversal. And for the most part, it's not dangerous.

I just hope no-one has got themselves into an unusual situation in this configuration and remembered what the flight manual said, and pushed the stick forward to slow down instead of pulling it back...

Torque Limiters

Since I've nearly been a smoking hole because of one of these, and it has to do with power output, this is an appropriate time to decry these devices. To paraphrase the words of one British aerodynamicist talking about afterburners:

Torque limiters are the work of the devil

The torque limiter in one helicopter (brand and model will not be mentioned) is particularly insidious. It doesn't just limit torque, it actively reduces torque by reducing fuel flow whenever it senses the torque is above the prescribed limit. This has bitten a few people quite hard, but only when they weren't prepared for it. The torque limiter on this machine is set for a level just above the takeoff torque limit, and is tested as a post-maintenance item. The check involves pulling in to that limit and seeing that the N_R droops slightly, and then reducing the power. That's all that's needed to check the system, and the pilots are left with the impression that the torque limiter was pretty straightforward. Little did they know.

These were pilots who were used to operating helicopters at the limit of engine performance, and knew how N_R would decay when the collective was raised operating at the torque limit.

After two pretty nasty incidents, where the pilots reported the N_R literally dropped like a stone, and some sleuthing through the engine maintenance manual a completely different story about how the torque limiter really worked surfaced. It appears that any time the torque was above the torque limiter value, the fuel control was commanded to reduce the fuel flow. Since the torque is measuring the rotor drag, when the torque limiter is first hit, it will reduce the fuel flow, which will reduce the N_R. This will reduce the lift, and the helicopter will descend, exactly the opposite of what the pilot is demanding or expecting.

The pilot, in all probability will raise the collective, further increasing the drag on the rotor blades and hence the torque. All the time the torque is above the limit, the fuel flow will continue to reduce- for example if the fuel flow when the torque limit was first reached was 750 pounds per hour (pph), one second after the limiter was reached, it would be reduced to say 725 pph, two seconds after it would be 700pph, and so on.

The poor pilot who is faced with an emergency where he needs to have the power will be pulling up on the collective to try to get the lift out of the rotor system and would be presented with a system which actively tried to reduce the power.

To add insult to injury, the value where the torque limiter was set was about 15% below the value where any maintenance action was required. If the torque limiter came on at 106%, for example, no maintenance action on the drive train was needed until 120%.

So, as you can probably guess, I'm not a fan of this type of torque limiter.

Health, etc.

Smoking

In these days of political correctness, there are probably fewer and fewer helicopter pilots who smoke. For those who still do, I hope you don't fly at night. The reasons for this are not obvious, but significant.

Night vision is very affected by oxygen content in the blood. Above 6 -7,000 feet AMSL, night vision drops off dramatically as the oxygen levels in the blood decrease. Smoking reduces the oxygen and increases the carbon monoxide concentration in your blood stream. A smoker at sea level may already have oxygen levels that are equivalent to what a normal person would have at 5,000', so if a smoker goes flying at night, they may not see much...

Fluids, Bodily

Just as the helicopter needs to have the relevant fluids kept at the necessary levels, so does the human body. If you are operating in high temperatures, take water with you. Evidently this keeps the kidneys functioning well. Remember that coffee and tea are diuretics and you will pass more liquid than you took in drinking them.

Having a drink of water every once in a while will of course necessitate 'comfort stops' every once in a while to prevent the bladder overpressure light from interfering with rational thought.

Stress

It is difficult to recognize stress in yourself. Hopefully someone else can see it before it becomes too much and destroys your sense of perspective and self-preservation. But remember you can't work long days doing a high stress job without burning out. No-one is immune from this. That is the reason for authorities dictating crew duty times.

Glasses

If you have to wear glasses when flying, make sure you have two pairs! I heard of a pilot flying by himself who had to stick his head close to the window to throw up (he had evidently got some bad food at an airport greasy spoon) and his glasses got pulled off by the wind blast. He was quite short-sighted and needed to have someone give him vectors to a landing site, as he couldn't see far enough outside to navigate!

Safety General

Safety takes effort and thought. It may make you look like a wimp, but at least you'll be there to be looked at. Safety is also cheaper than an accident - way cheaper.

Personal Equipment

If you fly outside of sight of home base, you should seriously think about survival equipment in your machine. Even a short spell of bad weather can be enough to put you on the ground overnight, and it doesn't take much cool weather to be pretty uncomfortable. Most countries dictate the minimum amount of survival equipment, but you are completely at liberty to supplement that. Be aware it might cut into your useful, revenue producing payload, but when you need it, you really need it.

A lot of words are about survival equipment could be included. I won't bore you with them, except to press home a few points. Where is the survival equipment you would need if you were to crash on your next flight and nobody could get to you for at least a day because the weather you were flying in was too lousy for sane people to come and look for you? Is it somewhere you could get at it easily? In an underbelly luggage pod which could get ripped off or trapped under the fuselage? Locked where it can't be pilfered, but you've just lost the keys in the sand? Can you open your survival equipment package if your hands are partly frozen, at night?

Helmets

It is strange that helmets are such an emotive subject when they have been shown to save lives. Aside from some newer, large helicopters, the windshields of most light helicopters won't stop birds much larger than a sparrow.

A large bird coming through the window not only will surprise the crew, but might also incapacitate them. In one accident where it took several months to find the helicopter, the investigators found the bones of an eagle mixed in with the bones of the pilot. It was surmised that the bird had hit the windshield and knocked the pilot (who was not wearing a helmet) unconscious. There have been other incidents where the pilot was wearing a helmet with the clear visor down when a bird struck and he was able to recover the helicopter.

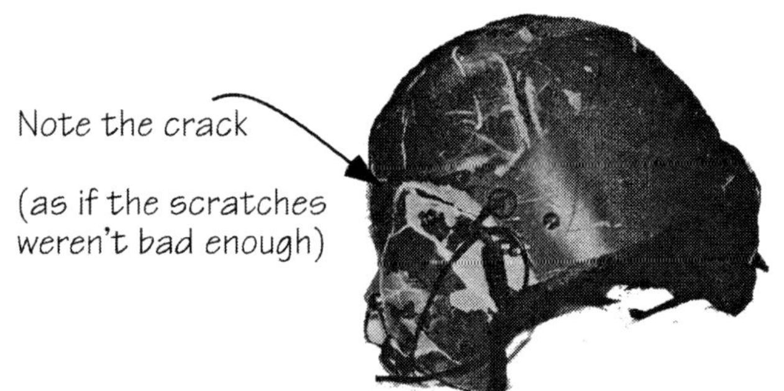

Figure 38-1 Helmet following an Encounter of the Very Hard Kind

That helmets save lives should not be questioned. What should be questioned is the mental health of anyone who says they won't wear one. I have had three bird strikes in my short flying career, fortunately all birds too small to be able to share the cockpit with me, but I feel naked without a helmet and clear visor when flying in a light helicopter with a plastic windshield.

Aside from the 'survive the bird strike' scenario, there is the other reasons to protect one's noggin should there be a crash. There are lots of hard things close to the pilot's head in the cockpit, and in the event of a crash, both seem to try to occupy the same volume at the same time. This is doubly true if you don't wear shoulder harness - a practice all too common in the long-line world. A helmet will prevent the small knock from becoming something more serious. In any helicopter, a helmet will protect your head from damage caused by trying to re-arrange the structure in a crash. That alone can mean the difference between life and death. A hard knock on the head can render the pilot out of action for a short while, just when he is needed most, or needs to look after his own survival most urgently. Being knocked unconscious for even a few seconds in a fire or underwater may be a few seconds too long.

So Why Doesn't Everyone Wear Helmets?

There are those who say that 'wearing a helmet will upset the passengers'. It might be interesting to see what would happen if insurance companies took an active role in saying that helmets must be worn by the pilot in command of helicopters which did not have a bird-proof windshield.

Those who complain that the pilot wearing a helmet may scare the passengers should reconsider their point of view. I would be slightly worried if I were a passenger in a light helicopter and found that the pilot wasn't wearing a helmet.

Birds!

There are a surprising number of bird strikes on helicopters. Given the frail construction of the front windshields of most light helicopters it is interesting to note that some of these end up with the birds, (or what remains of them), sharing the cockpit with properly appointed occupants. Having survived three minor birdstrikes, the following advice is given:

- •If possible, fly around with the landing light(s) on.
- •If possible, wear a helmet with a clear visor down at all times (more than half the migrating birds fly at night)
- •If you encounter a flock of birds, don't try to evade them. Most will go down and to the left, but you never know...
- •If you do have a bird strike, land and check it out. Shut down the rotor and look for damage on the rotor blades.

One other point about birds. They always takeoff and land into wind (without any navigation aids or windsocks to help them).

Immersion Suits

How long can you tread water*? How long will you last in water that is a lot colder than you would dream of taking a bath in? The answer to the last question is not very long. If you fly over any body of water larger than a mud-puddle then you should seriously consider an immersion suit.

The Helicopter is Not a Winch or Bulldozer

I've heard of too many accidents where someone, in the rush of the moment, tries to do something helpful with a helicopter, which ends up in a worthless pile of junk. Among these are:

- trying to push a partly submerged boat ashore with the skids
- trying to pull a stuck All Terrain Vehicle out of the mud
- trying to lift a log frozen into the ground

You may see helicopters do amazing things at airshows, such as lift traffic cones, or do pirouettes with the nose of one skid on the ground. Don't try these at home. And think carefully before you attempt to do anything out of the ordinary.

Good Examples vs. Bad Examples

We have a lot of emphasis on dissecting accidents to find out what went wrong, most often trying to figure out what the pilot did that was incorrect. While this is instructive, it's also pretty demoralizing. There are no new ways to crash a helicopter, no new ways to run out of gas, fly to low or hit obstacles. Aren't we emphasizing the wrong things?

Do we ever show an example of someone who prevented an accident by good judgement? Not often, yet these are the sort of examples we should be following. So what do good pilots do?

What Good Pilots Do

I'm indebted to an article by Captain Robert Besco, Ph.D. in Business and Commercial Aircraft magazine for sparking the following thoughts. The original words have been altered for helicopter pilots.

Good pilots:

Detect mistakes soon after they occur.

- These can be their own errors or errors caused of others (copilots, air traffic controllers, etc.). Note that good pilots still make mistakes, just that they catch them quickly.
- Mistakes will be considered to be errors (either those caused by the pilot or others, failures of equipment on board or related to the flight, anomalies (such as different readings from two related gauges or instruments, etc.)

Correct mistakes immediately

- They don't give mistakes the chance to pile up.

Cope with mistakes gracefully and uneventfully.

- We all make mistakes. I don't know of any perfect pilot, and I'm not sure I would want to fly with anyone who said they were perfect. How we handle mistakes (in fact, if we even admit we have made them) is a large sign of a good pilot.

Communicate their assessment of these errors without delay to other crew.

- Self explanatory, but perhaps some words of advice here. Don't be afraid to say this is an emergency. Tell Air Traffic Control, and use the words Mayday, Mayday. It will get their attention, and believe me, you won't have to fill out any unnecessary paperwork. It may sound corny, but it is worth thinking before the flight about what emergencies would prompt you to use the words Mayday, Mayday.

* with apologies to Bill Cosby and the Noah sketch.

Stay ahead of the helicopter and mission profile.

- "No surprises" is a cardinal rule of aviation.

Prevent the threat of existing or potential errors from increasing the possibility of errors.

- In other words, stay calm and don't panic. This will help to stop other mistakes from compounding the problem.

Develop and maintain an attitude of wariness to errors, failures, anomalies and diverging goals.

- Always look for inconsistencies in instrument readings, navigation equipment, performance indications and so on.

Have confidence that errors, failures and anomalies will be stabilized shortly after they occur.

- Know what to do when something goes wrong.

Say "NO" when they need to.

- Even if it means finding another job.

Apply superior wisdom, knowledge and judgement to avoid the situations which would require the application of superior skill.

- Prevention is better than a cure

Exert a stabilizing influence on others when thing start to go downhill.

- Keeping others calm and under control is a good way to insure that you will stay calm and get the best performance out of others.

Maintain an attitude of openness to suggestions and enquiries from other crew and outsiders.

- You never know when someone is going to give you a vital piece of information. A passenger in the back of the helicopter might be able to stop you from putting the tail rotor into a tree.

Adapt to long-term changes in the performance requirements and environmental conditions of the profession.

- Life is full of change. Learn to adapt to it.

SIMULATORS

Until recently, the only helicopter simulators were in the military or in large, corporate helicopter operations. The reason was that to carry out the calculations of blades forces and moments required very large amounts of computing power. Only large operations could justify the expense.

No longer. Microprocessors have evolved to the point of being able to carry out the most complex calculations at a speed that will permit excellent modeling of the rotor blades and provide a relatively low cost simulation tool.

Several helicopter simulators are now entering the market at prices less than US$~~1 million~~ (now $100,000 as we go to print). While this may still seem expensive, it is a huge breakthrough.

What is needed now is a recognition of the potential of these small simulators and an attempt by the basic training schools to use them to improve the quality of training while reducing the costs. Stay tuned!

Learning to Say No

One of things that is most difficult to learn to say as a helicopter pilot is NO. This is for two reasons - one is that we exist to use our aircraft to help others - that is why the helicopter is used commercially or in the military.

The second reason is that it is rare to be given experience in saying 'No' during training. Students are rarely, if ever, given the opportunity to make a decision about the suitability of weather. Looking at a number of accidents related to continued flying in bad weather revealed that instead of a conscious decision to press on, there was no decision either way.

I can remember quite clearly the first time I was put in a position to say 'No', and how this was a turning point in my flying career. I've since asked lots of helicopter pilots, both civil and military about when they learned to say 'No', and none of them could give an instance of being trained specifically on this essential matter.

During training, all the confined areas are either large enough or obviously too small, there was always enough power available, and we were never allowed to go flying when the weather was even close to questionable.

I remember listening to the head of the New York Police helicopter unit give a presentation on the first World Trade Center attack. He was not a helicopter pilot and was able to calmly analyze the situation and say 'No' to continued use of the helicopters to transporting firefighters to the top of the building.

I'm not sure there is a universal solution to this. Obviously, the training exercises for this must be pretty subtle. Reading and discussing accident and incident reports is a great starting point. Remember that none of these people set out to have a problem!

What do you do if you're given a job by your boss that is unsafe? Aside from telling him in the most delicate manner possible, which may cost you your job, (at least you'll be there to look for another one), consider sending a registered letter to the company, and possibly the aviation authority concerned.

Noise

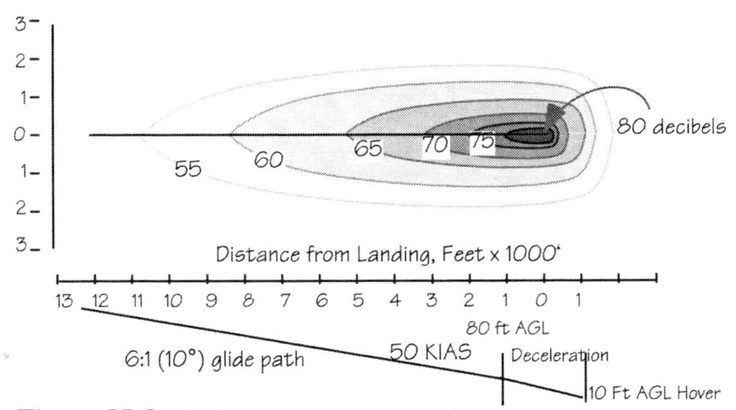

Figure 38-2 Typical noise on approach

Helicopters are not the most quiet machines. Because they normally operate close to the ground, there is a greater impact on those underneath than perhaps we as pilots appreciate. While many of the newer machines have been designed with noise reduction in mind, there are still a lot of older machines that need to be operated with some care and attention.Some manufacturers provide specific advice on how to reduce the noise a helicopter makes, both flying overhead and on approach. Figure 38-3 shows an example of this.

Summary of Chapter 38

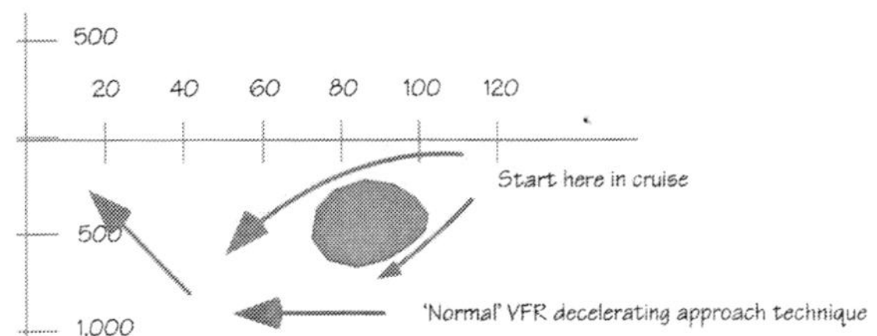

Figure 38-3 Reducing Noise on Approach

This chapter has covered a few of my pet peeves, and rounds out both books.

Thus ends my current attempt to contribute to the knowledge on matters rotary wing. Stay tuned!

You never know what you're going to learn when you set out to write a book. I thought I knew quite a bit about helicopters when I first started writing, but in an attempt to explain things which appeared perfectly clear in my mind, I discovered that perhaps I didn't understand them properly at all. I would recommend teaching or writing to anyone who really wants to understand a subject!

If you have any suggestions or comments* for future editions, please don't hesitate to get in touch with me. E-mail to - shawn.coyle@mojavebooks.com

I sincerely hope you have enjoyed what you've read, and that it has been of assistance in your work. Good luck, safe flying, and God bless.

* Corrections welcome also. Person with most corrections by end of Dec. 2003 wins a free copy of the next edition.

Bibliography

Foundations of Helicopter Flight, Simon Newman, Edward Arnold, 1994

Helicopter Performance, Stability and Control, Ray Prouty, Robert E. Kreiger, 1990

Advanced Pilots Flight Manual, William Kershner, Iowa State University Press,

Stick and Rudder, Wolfgang Langesweiche

Helicopter Theory, Wayne Johnson, Princeton University Press, 1980

Sikorsky Helicopter Flight Theory for Pilots and Mechanics, United Technologies, 1964.

Basic Helicopter Handbook, FAA Advisory Circular EA-AC-61-13B

Helicopter Pilot Manual, Jeppesen, 1996

The Ultimate Helicopter VFR Flight Training Handbook, Micheal Johnson, Johnson Aviation, 2001

Mike Beckers Helicopter Handbook, Mike Becker, Becker Helicopter Australia, 2000

Helicopter Principles of Flight, ancient manuscript from UK Central Flying School, RAF Tern Hill, UK Ministry of Defence (no date, so perhaps written just after paper was invented?)

Simple Rotorcraft, Sandy Mathieson, (unpublished manuscript)

Learning to Fly Helicopters, R. Randall Padfield, Tab Practical Flying Series

Rotary Wing Flight, US Army Field Manual FM-1-51

Fundamentals of Fixed and Rotary Wing Aerodynamics, Part I, H.E. Roland, Jr. and J.F. Detwiler, University of Southern California

Helicopter Aerodynamics Outline, Bell Helicopter Textron

Flying the Rotors, Bill Loftus, 1992

Principles of Helicopter Flight, W.J. Wagtendonk, ASA Press, 1996

Various Pilot Operating Handbooks, Flight Manuals, Maintenance, Overhaul and Training manuals and Canadian, US and foreign military Technical manuals, including: AS 350 series, AS 332, Bell 206, 407, 430, S-76, CH-135, OH-58A, CH-46, CH-47, PZL Swidnik W-3.

Training Material for a variety of helicopters from a variety of manufacturers.

UK CAA examination material for ATPL exams

FAA Advisory Circular 27-1 **Certification of Normal Category Rotorcraft**

FAA Advisory Circular 29-2 **Certification of Transport Category Rotorcraf**t

How to Fly Helicopters, 2nd Edition Larry Collier, revised by Kas Thomas, Tab Books, 1986

Numerous articles and papers from the **American Helicopter Society Journal and Forum Proceedings** (an organization worth joining just for the technical information in their journals)

Air to Air Heat Exchangers for Houses, William Shurcliff, Brick House Publishing Company, Andover, Mass, 1982. (source of the relative humidity charts, if you were wondering what a book like this had to do with helicopters)

Helicopter Pilot Manual, Jeppesen Sanderson, 1996

Helicopter Maintenance, Joe Schafer, Jeppesen Sanderson, 1980.

Weather Ways / Air Command Weather Manual (Canadian Forces Publications - no other data available)

Meteorology Self-Instruction Manual (available from Atmospheric Environmental Services, attn: AWTD, 4905 Dufferin Street, Downsview, Ontario, Canada.

Jane's Aerospace Dictionary, Bill Gunston, Jane's London, 1980

AP3456, British Ministry of Defence, no date given, but evidently used by Wilbur and Orville to study for their exams...

Definitions

Absolute Ceiling	The maximum altitude at which level flight can be maintained. The greatest height that can be achieved by that aircraft, except by zoom climbing.
Acceleration	the rate of change of velocity (both speed and direction). Can mean changing direction without change in velocity.
advancing blade	the blade which is moving forward into (or against) the oncoming airflow.
aerodynamic centre	point about which there is no change in moment with change in angle of attack.
air taxiing	movement of the helicopter by hovering at speeds less than 60 KIAS, at low height above the ground.
airfoil (or aerofoil)	a surface which is shaped to derive lift from air passing it. A body designed to move through the air and obtain a useful reaction other than drag.
airspeed	motion relative to the air
altitude	height measured against the datum of Mean Sea Level
angle of attack	the angle between the relative airflow and the chord of the airfoil
angle of incidence	an old–fashioned (and incorrect) term for angle of attack. More correctly, the angle of the wing on the fuselage of a fixed wing airplane, or the angle of the horizontal stabilizer on helicopter tailboom.
anticipator	a device for sending a signal forward.
approach	the flight path from cruise to hovering or landing.
articulated rotor	a rotor system with hinges for flapping, leading / lagging and feathering of the rotor blades
autogiro	an aircraft which has a rotor which operates in autorotation to produce lift and has a power source to produce thrust. May also be towed.
autorotation	the process of turning the rotor from air passing up from below also the maneuvers associated with flying and landing without power from an engine.
axis	an imaginary straight line passing through a point which is used to define motion or position
axis of rotation	a line about which a body rotates
azimuth	the angle taken from a reference
bank angle	the angle between the lateral axis and the horizon.
blade flapping	the movement of rotor blade about the flapping hinge, that is up and down with respect to the rotor hub
blade pitch angle	the angle between the chord of the blade and a reference line on the rotor hub
blow back	the movement of the rotor blades away from the relative wind without any control input. More commonly called flapback.
camber	the degree of curvature of the surface of an airfoil
ceiling	The maximum altitude that can be obtained. There are various types of ceiling, namely: Hover ceilings (in and out of ground effect), service ceiling and absolute ceiling

center of gravity	A point where the weight forces in the body may be considered to be concentrated.
center of pressure	the point on the chord line where the resultant of all the aerodynamic forces on the airfoil section may be considered to be concentrated.
centrifugal force	The force created by the tendency of a body to follow a straight line path against the force which causes it to move in a curve, resulting in a force which tends to pull away from the axis of rotation
chip detector	a device for detecting the presence of small pieces of metal in a lubrication system
chord	The straight line between the leading edge and trailing edge of an airfoil
co-efficient of drag	The non-dimensional value for the amount of drag produced by an airfoil section
co-efficient of lift	The non-dimensional value of the amount of lift produced by an airfoil section
co-relator	mechanical linkage between the cockpit throttle and engine throttle which is supposed to change the engine throttle due to collective position. Designed to reduce the cockpit throttle adjustments needed due to collective movement.
Coanda effect	The effect of a jet of air blowing out from an airfoil or other shape and reacting with the air passing
collective	The method of controlling the amount of blade pitch where all blades are varied in pitch an equal amount simultaneously
collective bounce	A phenomena whereby the collective is in resonance with the vertical motion of the helicopter, making the motion worse
confined area	A smaller than normal area for landing, or maneuvering a helicopter in. Requires special procedures.
coning angle	The angle the rotor blades make with the horizontal, due to the combined action of lift on the blades and centrifugal force due to rotation.
coriolis effect	the tendency of a mass to increase or decrease it's angular velocity when it's radius of rotation is changed. More correctly called conservation of angular momentum.
couple	two equal and opposite parallel forces tending to produce pure rotation.
cyclic	The control which changes the pitch of the rotor blades during each cycle of rotation. Used to control the tilt of the tip path plane.
damper	A device to slow the rate of motion. Can be used in hubs to slow the angular motion due to lead and lag, or in landing gear. A shock absorber on a car is a damper.
deadman's curve	A misnomer for the height velocity curve.
density altitude	The pressure altitude corrected for temperature and humidity.
departure	leaving an area, or in flight testing a loss of controlled flight
disk	the area swept by the tips of the rotor blades.
disk loading	the weight per unit area of the blade. Expressed in pounds per square foot, or kilograms per square meter.
dissymmetry of lift	The unequal lift across the rotor disk resulting from the difference in relative airspeed between the advancing and retreating blades.
downwash	The mass of air displaced by the rotor system.

drag	The force acting to retard an object as it passes through the air.
droop stops	The stops in the rotor hub which prevent the rotor blades from drooping when at low speed or static.
FAA	Federal Aviation Administration. The governing body for regulation and certification in the United States of America
feathering	The pitch change of the rotor blade which is due to collective or cyclic movement.
flap back	The act of the rotor disk flapping away from the relative wind.
flap restrainers	The restraining devices on the rotor hub which prevent the rotor blades from flapping to too high an angle when the blades are stopped or rotating slowly.
flapping	The act of the blade moving vertically about the flapping axis.
flare	The change in flight path from descent to level or a smaller rate of descent. Typically done close to the ground, and if done correctly results in zero rate of descent. Zero groundspeed is a secondary aim.
freewheel unit	A device placed in the drivetrain to permit the rotor to continue to turn after an engine failure, or to permit the rotor to turn faster than the driving part of the engine.
gravity	the force
ground effect	The effect of the ground on the downwash from the rotor. Normally acts to decrease the power required to hover.
ground resonance	A resonance in the helicopter made worse by contact with the ground.
gyroscopic precession	When a force is applied to a rotating mass, parallel to the axis of rotation, the rotating body will tilt in the direction of the applied force, but 90° farther around in the direction of rotation. Applies to all rotating bodies.
height	the distance above a datum, typically the ground.
height velocity curve	The curve defining the area within which it is difficult or impossible to make a safe landing following an engine failure.
helicopter	an aircraft which obtains it's lift by the powered rotation of rotor blades, and is capable of maintaining position with respect to the earth with no forward airspeed.
hingeless rotor	a rotor hub with no physical hinges in flapping or lead–lag. All motion relating to flapping, and lead–lag is taken by the structure of the hub. A feathering hinge may or not be present.
horizontal stabilator	A horizontal wing mounted in such a fashion as to assist in the stability of the pitch axis.
Hover Ceiling	The maximum altitude at which it is possible to hover using takeoff power. There should be a in-ground-effect and an out-of-ground effect hover ceiling
hover	Maintaining zero speed with respect to the ground (zero groundspeed hover) or the air, (zero airspeed hover)
hover taxiing	The act of moving across the ground at a slow speed. Typically a legal definition used by Air Traffic Control

IGE	In Ground Effect. Flight where the proximity of the earth has an effect on the performance or handling of the aircraft
induced drag	The drag due to producing lift
induced velocity	The air moving down caused by the rotor blades producing lift.
ISA	(International Standard Atmosphere) The standard agreed properties for the atmosphere, against which deviations are compared.
Knot	rate of speed meaning one nautical mile per hour
lead - lag	The back and forth motion of the rotor blades about the vertical hinge
lift	the useful force used to support the helicopter
manifold pressure	the pressure in the intake manifold of a piston engine, a measure of the power of the engine
mass	mean chord linethe line halfway between the upper and lower surfaces of an airfoil
moment	the product of a force and its perpendicular distance from its axis.
nautical mile	Measure of distance. One nautical mile is 1.15 statute miles, or 6,080 feet, or 1.85 kilometers. It is also equal to one minute of latitude at the earth's equator.
Nr	A shorthand for the rotational RPM of the rotor blades.
OGE	Out of Ground Effect. Flight where the proximity to the earth has no effect on the performance or handling of the aircraft.
parasite drag	the drag due to the fuselage passing through the air.
pitch angle	the mechanical angle between the chord line of the blade and the main rotor hub
pitch attitude	The angle between the longitudinal axis of the fuselage and horizon.
plane of rotation	The plane about which the body is rotating
pressure altitude	The altitude measured against a standard pressure setting (29.92" of mercury, or 1013 millibars)
profile drag	The drag caused by the shape of a body as it passes through the air.
rear wind	A wind coming from the aft part of the helicopter.
rearward flight	an term often misused. Strictly speaking it would be only be rear groundspeed. More correctly stated it would be the combination of rearward groundspeed and wind velocity and should be stated as the rear wind speed
reciprocating engine	An engine which uses a 2 or 4 cycle system, pistons and so on to produce power (as opposed to a turbine engine)
relative wind	the wind speed and direction relative to the nose of the helicopter
retreating blade	the blade which is going away from the direction of relative wind. Has the lowest tip airspeed on the disk
retreating blade stall	the stall of the retreating blade, due to high forward airspeed, angle of attack or G loading
roll or rolling	angular motion about the longitudinal axis of the helicopter
rotational energy	the energy possess by the rotor system due to rotation
rotational velocity	the rate of rotation of a body
rotor	a system of rotating airfoils
rotor disc	the area of the rotating blades.
RPM	Revolutions per minute.
RRPM	Rotor RPM. The rate of rotation of the rotor blades, either in RPM or percentage of a nominal value.
running landing	a landing with groundspeed at touchdown

running takeoff	a takeoff from the ground with groundspeed
seat of the pants	what you feel in your posterior parts as well as other bits, technically called proprioceptive cues
semi- rigid rotor system	a rotor system which has two rotor blades which are joined together. It has only feathering hinges for the blades, and blade flapping is with respect to the rotor mast as a single unit.
Service Ceiling	The maximum altitude at which a 100 foot per minute rate of climb can be obtained.
settling with power	an imprecise term for descending with slightly less power than needed to hover. More correct term is vortex ring state.
Side Force	A force acting to push the helicopter sideways
Side Slip	Lateral airspeed with respect to the longitudinal axis
sideward flight	an term often misused. Strictly speaking it would be only be side groundspeed. More correctly stated it would be the combination of sideways groundspeed and wind velocity and should be stated as the side wind speed. Needs to have a relative wind direction as well.
sidewind	the component of relative wind seen by the helicopter acting on the side of the fuselage. For example, hovering with a wind of 15 knots from the left provides a side wind of 15 knots. Moving across the ground to the left at 10 knots on a calm day provides a side wind of 10 knots.
skid	part of the landing gear also an improperly co-ordinated turn where the helicopter is drifting to the outside of the turn, with the slip ball to the inside of the turn.
slip	an improperly co-ordinated turn, where the helicopter is drifting to the inside of the turn, and the slip ball is to the outside of the turn.
slope	ground which is not level
stabilators	A combination horizontal stabilizer and elevator. Used to control the pitch attitude of the helicopter
stall	the loss of streamlined airflow on an airfoil. Caused by the angle of attack being high.
swashplate	the device used to transmit control inputs from the stationary fuselage to the rotating rotor
tail rotor	the rotor assembly used to overcome torque and control the yaw axis of the helicopter
takeoff	leaving the ground
taxiing	the act of moving slowly across the ground
teetering rotor	a common name for the semi-rigid rotor system. also known as see-saw.
throttle	the device for directly controlling the power output of the engine
thrust	the useful part of the lift developed by the rotor blade. The part of the total rotor force which is used to propel the helicopter in a horizontal manner
tip path plane	the plane described by the tips of the rotor blades
tip speed	the speed of the tip of the rotor blade

torque	the effect of a force acting at a distance from the point of rotation. The moment of a system of forces which causes pure rotation without translation or horizontal movement.
torque effect	the effect of the rotation of the main rotor on the fuselage
tracking	the art and science of balancing rotor blades to minimize the vibrations.
transition	the act of moving from one condition to another - i.e. transitioning to the hover or transitioning to forward flight.
translating tendency	the tendency of the helicopter to move sideways due to the side thrust of the tail rotor
translational lift	the change in lift which appears to take place at approximately 15 knots of airspeed
transverse flow effect	the effect caused by the flow through the disk which has a coning angle
V	shorthand for Airspeed
velocity	speed with respect to a frame of reference (air, ground, etc.)
vertical stabilizer	a airfoil oriented vertically to provide directional stability
VH	the maximum level (or horizontal) airspeed which can be maintained using the continuous power rating
virtual axis	the axis perpendicular to the tip path of the rotor blades
Vmin power	the airspeed where the minimum power is required to maintain level flight
Vne	Never Exceed Airspeed
Vne autorotation	the maximum speed permitted for use in power-off flight
Vno	Maximum Normal Operating Airspeed
Vtoss	Take Off Safety Speed
Vy	The airspeed for minimum power
yaw	Movement of the helicopter about the yaw axis- in the hover a change in heading, in forward flight a change in

INDEX

A

B